AUTOBIOGRAPHY
WITH LETTERS

WILLIAM LYON PHELPS

WILLIAM LYON PHELPS

AUTOBIOGRAPHY
WITH LETTERS

OXFORD UNIVERSITY PRESS
NEW YORK LONDON TORONTO
1939

Printed in the United States of America

TO MY WIFE

ANNABEL

ACKNOWLEDGEMENT

I EXPRESS my thanks to the Macmillan Company for permitting me to quote from some of my books published by them, especially *Teaching in School and College*, *The Twentieth Century Theatre*, *Essays on Modern Dramatists*, and *Essays on Things*: to E.P.Dutton and Company for permission to quote from my book *Appreciation*: to the Liveright Publishing Corporation for permission to quote from my book *The Excitement of Teaching*: and to the editors of the *Yale Review*, *Delineator* and *Cosmopolitan* for permission to reprint some of my articles with revisions: especially am I grateful to Charles Scribner's Sons, who have most generously allowed me to quote copiously from my monthly articles 'As I Like It' which I contributed to *Scribner's Magazine* during fourteen happy years.

PREFACE

ON *Friday* 20 *April* 1781 '*Somebody said the life of a mere literary man could not be very entertaining.* JOHNSON. *" But it certainly may. This is a remark which has been made, and repeated, without justice; why should the life of a literary man be less entertaining than the life of any other man? Are there not as interesting varieties in such a life? As* a literary life *it may be very entertaining."' Johnson had previously meditated on the same question, for in* The Idler *he had written, 'It is commonly supposed that the uniformity of a studious life affords no matter for narration; but the truth is, that of the most studious life a great part passes without study. . . . he is born and married like another man; he has hopes and fears, expectations and disappointments, griefs and joys, and friends and enemies.'* (*Powell-Hill edition of Boswell's* Life of Johnson, IV:98.)

Even if a literary life should not be entertaining to others, this particular one has been prodigiously entertaining to him who has lived it.

The lack of order, coherence, symmetry in this book is owing neither to accident nor to laziness; it is the way I chose to write it. Novels of particular communities or of particular lives often seem untrue because the novelist endeavours to form the events into a plot, with development and climax; whereas life itself has nothing but a time-line; and even that is reduced to a semblance of order only by the artificial divisions of clock and calendar. And the individual time-line is continually broken by memory and by anticipation. The pleasure of good conversation would be destroyed if conversations were 'organized' —forced to proceed in a definite direction, instead of being brittle, broken by interruptions. Dean Briggs used to say that Donne, as a poet, was like an unruly bird dog; ' he chases every wild thought that flies out of the thicket.' His poems are more interesting than an orderly epic on transcendentalism in twelve books, specifically condemned by another great poet.

Furthermore it is possible that readers who admire consistency may think I am either superficial or insincere in my admiration for writers of antagonistic and irreconcilable views. But intellectual curiosity annihilates consistency. How is it possible to be consistent in such a tragi-comedy as this world where God Himself seems so inconsistent? I love authors who give me stimulation and delight. Strong convictions should be accompanied by tolerance for other views and keen interest in them. Intellectual excitements like other excitements gain by variety. Some of my favourite modern authors are Browning and Schopenhauer, Barrie and Strindberg, Hardy and Chesterton, Housman and Francis Thompson, Dickens and Emily Brontë, Henry James and Dumas, Stevenson and George Moore, Swift and Emerson, Ibsen and Rostand, Goethe and Dr. Johnson, Mill and Carlyle, and in reading works of genius I am perhaps a little like Emerson's yellow-breeched philosopher, leaving the chaff and taking the wheat.

In reading the autobiography of a famous contemporary, I was mildly astonished to observe that he gave the names and addresses of all persons who had entertained him at week-ends and had shown him kindness in other ways. It troubles me that I cannot do this. If I should include the names of all my friends who have shown me hospitality and added to my happiness by their generosity and unselfishness, this book would be three times its present size and would in many places read more like a catalogue than a biography. Surely such specifications are unnecessary. My friends know that no matter how great or many may be my limitations, I am not lacking in appreciation.

To those who wonder ('Sir, you may wonder') why I print

so many letters, thus losing continuity and proportion, let me say this book would never have been written if it were not for the large number of letters from persons more important than the author. In this instance the Scripture text is reversed; the letter giveth life. Among the variety of things that have contributed to my happiness one of the most salient is my good fortune in having met so many distinguished writers. I am a hero-worshipper. Thus I am grateful for permission to print these epistles.

When I have finished reading the proofs, I hope that some persons may read the book. As for me,

> *I am afraid to think what I have done:*
> *Look on't again I dare not.*

W.L.P.

Branford College,
  Yale University,
    All Souls Day 1938.

CONTENTS

INTRODUCTION   xvii

1. EARLY CHILDHOOD   3

2. EARLY EDUCATION   12

3. BOYHOOD EXPERIENCES   23

4. INTERLUDE ON CATS   28

5. RUFUS H. PHELPS   38

6. THREE BLESSINGS   41

7. FIRST DIARY   48

8. REFLEXIONS ON ANIMALS   58

9. EARLY FRIENDSHIPS, MARK TWAIN, AND BILLIARDS   61

10. ASTRONOMY   73

11. MOODY AND SANKEY   80

12. CHINESE SCHOOLMATES   83

13. MY AUNT   87

14. EXPERIENCES AT GRAMMAR SCHOOL   91

15. THE HARTFORD PUBLIC HIGH SCHOOL   100

16. WALKING, WORKING, FROGS, LOVE 104

17. GOING TO THE THEATRE 111

18. CLYDE FITCH 122

19. LOOKING FORWARD TO COLLEGE 126

20. THE ROBBER 129

21. COLLEGE DAYS AT YALE 132

22. THE YOUNGER GENERATION 154

23. INTERLUDE: *HIC ET UBIQUE* 163

24. WILLIAM GRAHAM SUMNER 195

25. HENRY DRUMMOND AND SCHOPENHAUER 199

26. BROWNING 207

27. BEGINNING TEACHING 211

28. GRADUATE STUDIES AND SPORT 217

29. BICYCLING IN EUROPE 225

30. LIFE AT HARVARD 245

31. TEACHING AT YALE 279

32. MY FIRST BOOK 316

33. PROFESSORS 328

34. GEORGE SANTAYANA 332

35. THOMAS SERGEANT PERRY 350

CONTENTS   xiii

36. PLAYING GAMES   354

37. JOURNEY TO EUROPE   376

38. THOMAS HARDY   389

39. ROOSEVELT AND RILEY   405

40. EVENTS IN 1902   412

41. 1903   421

42. FIRST SABBATICAL YEAR   427

43. THE CITY OF MUNICH   439

44. LITERARY PILGRIMAGE IN ITALY   446

45. EVENTS IN THE THEATRE   460

46. WILLIAM DE MORGAN   468

47. QUEER SOUNDS AND SIGHTS   473

48. VARIOUS NOTES   477

49. FIRST JOURNEY TO CALIFORNIA   489

50. W.D.HOWELLS   502

51. MAHAFFY AND JAPAN   505

52. JOURNEY TO THE SOUTH   508

53. SECOND SABBATICAL   514

54. JOURNEY TO RUSSIA   522

55. GERHART HAUPTMANN   529

56. THE RIVIERA   534

57. THE FANO CLUB   542

58. HENRY JAMES   550

59. J.M.BARRIE   565

60. SINGING BIRDS   584

61. DOROTHY CANFIELD   588

62. CONVERSATIONS WITH PAUL HEYSE   595

63. FRANCE IN 1913   599

64. SOME EVENTS IN 1914   602

65. WILLIAM HOWARD TAFT   608

66. SOME EVENTS IN 1915–16   617

67. JOURNEY TO THE HAWAIIAN ISLANDS   624

68. VACHEL LINDSAY   629

69. AMERICA IN THE WAR   633

70. ALFRED NOYES AND OTHERS   649

71. MEA ORNAMENTA   657

72. JOHN GALSWORTHY   667

73. SECOND JOURNEY TO CALIFORNIA   685

74. SOME POETS AND NOVELISTS   688

75. A JOURNEY TO ANDOVER   699

76. EVENTS IN 1920 AND 1921 704

77. BRITISH DIALECT AND AMERICAN VOICES 711

78. ST. JOHN ERVINE 716

79. 'AS I LIKE IT' 737

80. A VISIBLE CHURCH IN AN INVISIBLE TOWN 742

81. MRS. WHARTON; CONRAD; BENAVENTE 751

82. AN AMERICAN IN ENGLAND 757

83. EDNA FERBER 771

84. THE CONVERSATION CLUB IN AUGUSTA 777

85. NOTES OF TRAVEL AND OTHER NOTES 783

86. GENE TUNNEY 792

87. JOURNEY TO EUROPE IN 1928 800

88. ANTHONY HOPE 813

89. GEORGE MOORE 818

90. Æ. 828

91. CAPTAIN LIDDELL HART & GENERAL J.G.HARBORD 836

92. EVENTS IN 1929–30 841

93. EDISON 846

94. NATHAN STRAUS, GRAND DUCHESS 849

95. HENRY FORD 857

96. JOURNEY TO ATHENS 862

97. THE POPE 881

98. MUNICH IN 1932 882

99. AN AMERICAN IN PARIS 886

100. PIRANDELLO, BERNSTEIN, DAUDET 891

101. HELEN WILLS MOODY 896

102. LITERARY AND CELESTIAL EVENTS 903

103. EMERITUS 908

104. OTHER EVENTS IN 1933 910

105. VARIOUS NOTES IN 1934–5 916

106. EMMA EAMES AND MUSIC 922

107. ENGLAND IN 1935 930

108. RADIO 939

109. CITY OR COUNTRY 941

110. INFORMALITY 947

111. REFLEXIONS IN THE NINETEEN-THIRTIES 954

INTRODUCTION

In looking back, I should have to change somewhat the famous words of Landor:

> I strove with none, for none was worth my strife.
> Nature I loved, and next to Nature Art:
> I warmed both hands before the fire of life:
> It sinks, and I am ready to depart.

Very fine, no doubt; although, written by Landor, the first four words have an oddity all their own. To fit my own case, I should have to say

> I strove with none. I always hated strife.
> Nature I loved, and God and Man and Art:
> I warmed both hands before the fire of life:
> It sinks, yet I'm not ready to depart.

The vast majority of persons are compelled to live without prodigious adventures and without the gratification of most of their transient desires; yet ordinary circumscribed existence can be exciting.

For although I have lived what is called a sheltered life, it has been anything but dull. Daily existence has often been thrilling. Apparently I have been and am much happier than most men and women. My happiness certainly has never come from resignation. It has been said that the happiest men and women in the world are those who have good health, a sufficient income, *and no ambition.* This would probably be true if we meant by happiness a quiet enjoyment of existence with the absence of worry or unsatisfied desire. I do not know whether I envy such people or not; I sometimes envy their calmness and self-control.

But I am not that kind of man at all; I have always been eaten up with ambition, I have had the longings described by Faust as he sat at his desk in the moonlight, and I worry about innumerable little things. I have never had a placid temperament. I have had two prolonged attacks of nervous prostration, one at the age of twenty-six and one at the age of fifty-nine, and my religious faith remains in possession of the field only after prolonged civil war with my naturally sceptical mind. Yet I have certainly lived a happy life.

Since I have lived without great adventures and yet with many mental alarms and excursions, why have I been so happy?

It is fortunate there are people of adventurous, pioneering, exploring blood, who love to go into deserts, trackless forests, appalling jungles, and mingle with savage or primitive races. They write, and we share their adventures without danger or inconvenience. I suppose there is no one who has less of the frontiersman in him than I. If I had all my expenses paid and a salary in addition, nothing would induce me to visit equatorial Africa or Mary Byrd Land. I have no desire to climb hitherto unclimbed mountains. Instead of being the first man up a mountain, I had rather be the last one; the mountain does not interest me particularly until it has had human associations. I agree with G.K.Chesterton who said, 'I will lift up mine eyes unto the hills but I will not lift up my carcass thither.' Fleet Street gives me a keener thrill than any lonely heights. Hot jungles and trackless snows may be beautiful, but to me they are not so beautiful as the Grand Central Station illuminated, or the North River by night, or Fifth Avenue by day or Fleet Street before sunset. I am a man of the city, and I like theatres, music, newspapers, and cultivated men and women. It may be that savages have admirable traits, but

I am sure they are not so agreeable or so trustworthy or so interesting as any number of men and women I know in New Haven, Connecticut.

Perhaps the chief source of my happiness lies in my gift of appreciation. I must have been born with it. When I was a child, everything unusual excited me; now that I am old, everything usual has about the same effect.

When I was six, and Christmas gifts were distributed in school, the present for me was placed on my desk. It is curious that I have forgotten what it was but have not forgotten my emotion. I was so overcome with awe and wonder and joy at receiving it that I looked at it in absolute silence, being unable to articulate. The foolish teacher said, 'Why, Willie, don't you like your present?'

After I had entered the Hartford High School at the age of thirteen, I was playing football with the huge crowd at recess, was knocked down, trampled on, and covered from head to foot with dirt and dust. No one paid any attention to me, except Clarence Wickham, the champion athlete of the school. He it was and no other, who picked me up, dusted me off, set me on my feet. I was not only 'lifted,' I was 'exalted.'

Montaigne said, 'Whatever are the benefits of fortune, they yet require a palate fit to relish and taste them.' Happiness is more dependent on the mental attitude than on external resources. This would be an absurdly obvious platitude, were it not for the fact that ninety-nine out of a hundred persons do not believe it.

I have always had a keen relish for agreeable sensations. Even as a little child, I responded gratefully—and usually with surprise—to any acts of kindness or to any courtesies from older people. And I well remember, when I was in the High School, calling upon Mr. Stiles T. Stanton of Stonington, a member of the legislature, to ask him to serve as a judge in the Prize Declamations. If he had looked at me contemptuously, and said 'I'm busy,' I should not have been surprised; he treated me, however, neither with contempt nor with condescension, but as if I were an equal. This may seem a small thing, but I have never forgotten it. He was a gentleman.

All kinds of outdoor games, winter and summer, were an inexpressible delight. And even as a little boy, I was intensely *conscious* of all this. In the midst of sliding downhill in the moonlight, or playing ball in summer, I would say to myself, 'Isn't this wonderful?' and in my adolescence, I remember saying to a girl, 'Isn't it great to be young?'

I mention these details, because the majority of persons do not so *consciously* enjoy their youth or any other thing while they have it. In a world filled with misfortunes, losses, drawbacks, and suffering, most persons seem to take good health, sanity, food and drink, wives and husbands, for granted; and appreciate them only too late. Not so with me. I seemed to have in the midst of enjoyment an inner knowledge of my enjoyment, an awareness of happiness; as often, in the midst of a public lecture, I make a remark that I never had thought of before; and while the audience is digesting it, I say to myself, 'How in the world did you ever think of that?'

When, at the age of six, I went to Barnum's circus, and 'the greatest show on earth' lasted from two o'clock till five, the three hours were undiluted bliss. I remember not only the gorgeous spectacle, but the joy with which I regarded it.

In his admirable *Life of Webster*, Dr. Fuess says there are two classes of men; those who get up in the morning rather heavy, sluggish, and perhaps depressed, gradually during the day become more alive, and finally in the evening are sparkling and vivacious—and the other kind, who are happiest and most lively at breakfast. Now I have always, from earliest childhood even until now, belonged to this latter class.

Like most boys and girls, I hated to go to bed in the evening, yet was forced to go at an early hour. Bedtime meant fun was over; no more excitement till the next day. Waking in the morning was full of promise. 'No dream's worth waking,' Browning said. I remember a picture in our house of a mother carrying a baby in her arms. The room was illumined only by a crepuscular light, and it was impossible to tell whether this twilight was of the dawn or of the coming night. I remember looking at that hundreds of times, and always hoping that it was the dawn. Then the child would have the day before it full of wonderful things, instead of nothing to look forward to. And indeed I have almost always felt a touch of sadness at nightfall; and almost always eagerness in the early morning. The best thing ever said about heaven in the Bible is that there is no night there. I have always wished—and now that I am old, I wish it with tenfold intensity—that sleep were not necessary. I have always begrudged the time we have to spend in sleeping or—too common an experience with me—vainly trying to sleep. If it were physically possible and my strength and above all, my eyes would permit, I should like to spend all the daylight in work and play, and read all night.

Bertrand Russell says it is a mistake to suppose that those who sleep well are spiritually inferior; perhaps this is true. There is perhaps no reason why we should consider our sufferings as a sign of superiority. Yet there is truth in what Goethe said:

> Who never ate his bread in sorrow,
>   Who never spent the darksome hours
> Weeping and watching for the morrow,
>   He knows ye not, ye Heavenly Powers!

That blessings brighten as they take their flight may be true with many persons; possibly they do not realize the happiness of health until they lose it, or the happiness of travel, sport, conversation, love, adventure, or what you will, until old age. But that has never been so with me. Waking in the morning, I always looked forward with joy to teaching my first class at college; waiting on the tennis court for my partners to appear, I was filled with active pleasure; and in the midst of innumerable experiences I have not only consciously, but self-consciously enjoyed them.

I am afraid if I continue in this vein, I shall become intolerable; but as this is an autobiography, it seems necessary to emphasize these emotions, as they are truly characteristic.

I have no doubt my ardent religious faith is largely responsible for the happiness that I have found in mere living; but it is not wholly responsible. G. K. Chesterton was profoundly religious and Arnold Bennett was certainly not. Yet it would be difficult to say which of these two men lived with more gusto. Arnold Bennett's attitude toward life was a chronic wonder, amazement, delight; the innumerable gadgets of modern existence pleased him prodigiously. And Mr. Chesterton used to say that he hoped he would never be too old to stare at everything; and that the most important emotion to preserve in maturity was *the enjoyment of enjoyment*.

The difference between my happiness as a child and my happiness as a man, is that in childhood I always wanted some excitement to take me out of the routine. The resumption of routine was often accompanied by a devastating if temporary sinking of the heart. With what ecstasy my brothers and I got through school on Friday afternoon and then went away to spend the week-end with my Aunt Libbie at Stratford! But how my heart sank as I had to go back to school on Monday morning!

Then Saturday was the golden day of the week. Now in a

certain sense every day is Saturday. Then I was always hoping for something different to happen. Now my hope is that nothing different will happen. I hope only I may be able to keep in sufficient health or vigour to go on with the routine. And I enjoy the hot bath in the tub as I used to enjoy the old swimming hole.

So, as I look back on childhood and youth, happy though I was, I have no regret that they are irrecoverable; I have no sentimental yearning for the past. I ran and skipped and leaped through those bright halls

Es glänzt der Saal, es schimmert das Gemach

and advanced into other rooms quite different but more interesting; because there was not only more to appreciate, but my powers of appreciation had developed.

My enjoyment of the best in music, art, and books does not detract from my enjoyment of more simple things; though I enjoy the best more than the second best. I am transported by the symphonies of Beethoven and by the operas of Wagner. Yet that does not lessen my enjoyment of Gilbert and Sullivan, of a drum and fife corps, of a brass band. As I grow older I find Shakespeare more thrilling, more enchanting; yet I relish a good detective story. I shall never forget my excitement in seeing Richard Mansfield as Richard III; yet I still love the circus and everything in it.

AUTOBIOGRAPHY
WITH LETTERS

AUTOBIOGRAPHY
With Letters

I

EARLY CHILDHOOD

I WAS born at the south-east corner of Elm and Church
Streets, in New Haven, Connecticut, on Monday the second of January 1865.

Both my parents were of Connecticut stock; my father
came in a direct line from William Phelps, who settled in
Windsor, Connecticut, in 1636; my mother's mother was
named Sophia Lyon; she was born in Stratford, Connecticut. On her side of the family I am remotely descended
from Sir John Lyon, of Scotland, who was married in 1376;
he was an ancestor of the Earl of Strathmore, and my
Aunt Libbie used to exhibit the Lyon family coat-of-arms
bearing the thistle. I am a lineal descendant of Theophilus
Eaton, the First Governor of the Colony of Connecticut in
1638. I mention these things, not because I am proud of my
Scottish and Connecticut descent, for why should I be
proud of something with which I had nothing whatever to
do?

The marriage of my father, the Rev. Sylvanus Dryden
Phelps (born in Suffield, Conn., 1816) and my mother, Sophia Emilia Lyon Linsley (born in Stratford, Conn., 1823)
took place in 1847. My father was a large, powerful man,
who developed strength and self-reliance as a boy. His
father, a farmer, died when the boy was only twelve. The
family were very poor and my father had to do a man's
work on the farm. He supported himself through school
and college, walking over a hundred miles from Suffield to
Providence, to enter Brown University. He had immense

vigour and never seemed to suffer from anything resem-
bling 'nerves.' When he was seventy-eight, he used to dive
and swim in water that was too cold for many younger
men.

My mother was highly-strung, and sometimes suffered
from acute nervous despondency. But most of the time she
was in high spirits and full of gaiety. She was insatiably
fond of playing games and was so amiable, so kind, so sympathetic, so warm-hearted, that she was intensely beloved
by innumerable individuals. She was an ideal pastor's wife,
visiting the sick and the poor, always conducting the adult
class in Sunday School, and for more than thirty years she
wrote two columns weekly for a religious journal. She was
one of the most lovable persons I ever knew and her death
in 1903 was the greatest sorrow of my life.

My parents had five children. The eldest, Sophia, was
born in 1848 and died at the age of twenty-two. A son
James I never saw. My oldest brother, the Rev. Dryden
William Phelps was born in 1854 and died in 1931. He was
never married. My brother Arthur, the Rev. Dr. Arthur
Stevens Phelps, two years older than I, was born in 1863 and
is living in California. Arthur and I were as close together
as two boys could possibly be; growing up together, sharing
everything. He was married to Miss Blanche Stroud,
and both their children are married; the Rev. Dr. Dryden
Linsley Phelps is a professor in West China and his sister
Céleste is married to William Fogg Osgood, Professor of
Mathematics at Harvard.

It took my parents six months after my birth to find for
me a name satisfactory to them and the family; for some
time I was called Frank Mansfield. Finally, as I learn from
my mother's letters to her sister, I was named William
Lyon, after my great-grandfather, a Colonel of the Governor's Footguards during the American Revolution, and one
of the founders in 1792 of the New Haven Bank. His por-

trait hangs today in the Directors Room. His son, my mother's uncle, was also named William Lyon.

My mother's father, the Reverend James H.Linsley, who died in 1843, was a very interesting person. He was a strictly orthodox evangelical clergyman and also an authority in natural history, especially in conchology. His immense collection of shells, arranged with their Latin names in his minute handwriting, attracted many scientific visitors to his home in Stratford; he also collected and mounted many birds. He had a passion for natural history, and for many branches of scientific research, as such matters were then understood. The other side of his mind was religious and theological, what we should now call Fundamentalist; and he was fanatical on the subject of temperance. He founded or helped to found the first Total Abstinence Society in Stratford; and I have seen the childish signatures of his two children, my mother and my aunt, affixed before they were six years old to a document in which they promised to abstain from intoxicating liquor. My aunt had a good singing voice and took lessons. One day Mr. Linsley found lying on the piano a song she had just learned; it was Jonson's 'Drink to me only with thine eyes.' He told her such a song was not fitting for a young lady to sing. He then erased the word *Drink* and wrote in the word *Eat*; henceforth she sang it 'Eat to me only with thine eyes.'

I have been informed that some psychiatrists today urge parents not to teach their children the familiar prayer 'Now I lay me down to sleep,' because it will suggest to the infant mind the thought of death and thus inspire fear at bedtime. The hard-boiled Puritan babies of New England got out of that prayer agreeable relaxation; they handed the responsibility over to God and went to sleep peacefully. I wonder what the psychiatrists would say to the verses my maternal grandmother, Mrs. Linsley, had for her mental furniture, for on the wall of a room in my house hangs a sampler, wrought by her little hands in 1790, when she was about five years old. It contains this cheerful poem:

> There is an hour when I must die,
> Nor do I know how soon 'twill come:
> A thousand children young as I,
> Are called by death to meet their doom.

The Puritans were determined not to let even children forget the certainty of death and the uncertainty of its hour. If they heard the laughter of children, they felt something ought to be done about it. And yet as carriers of gloom-germs, they were perhaps not so effective as our modern atheistical novelists. The Puritans felt that life was serious, but they had faith in the ultimate rightness of things; they believed this was God's world and that its darkness would be followed by eternal sunshine. Serious views of life seemed to them rational. But the modern pessimist, with no philosophy of life, and with no hope for humanity either here or hereafter, is as fully determined not to let us have any fun. The moment we try to enjoy ourselves we are called sternly to order. Now I cannot see that tears have any higher intellectual value than laughter; there may be as much cerebration in a comedy as in a tragedy. The Puritans believed that out of a dark soil bright flowers would spring; the modern pessimist offers us no flowers, but more dirt.

I am sorry my mother was brought up to regard drinking, smoking, card-playing, dancing, theatre-going, as wicked. I mean I am sorry for her. She would have loved cards and the theatre. She played many other indoor games and she went with delight to concerts and other entertainments. But neither my mother nor my father ever saw a play in the theatre or ever touched a playing-card.

One might naturally think that, brought up as I was in so intensely religious a household, where my father was the

Benavente in the Browning Chair, New Haven, 18 March 1923

Fortieth Wedding Day
Augusta, Georgia

My Father's House at 44 *High Street, New Haven,* 1868.
Mother and brother Arthur in lower window; sister (died 1871*)
in upper window; brother Dryden over the door; and Father at
fence with me*

Leaving Honolulu, July 1916
J.R.Galt (*Yale* 1889) *our host*

At the Henry Ford birthplace, 1931. Reading from left to right: Mrs. Phelps, Henry Ford, Mr. Phelps, Mrs. Ford, my brother-in-law, Frank Hubbard, and Mrs. Frank Hubbard

William Lyon Phelps, aged 8
Taken in New Haven

My Caddie at Augusta, Georgia

William Lyon Phelps at his desk in New Haven

pastor of the church and my mother the teacher of the adult Bible class, where we invariably attended two services and usually three on Sunday and the weekly prayer-meeting, and where no games and for a long time no secular reading were allowed on Sunday, my childhood would have been unhappy. On the contrary, my childhood and that of my brothers was very happy indeed. The intensity of my parents' religious convictions gave significance to their enjoyment of daily life. They abounded in good humour, and it seems to me now that the house was full of laughter. We frequently entertained guests; in those days a clergyman on his travels never went to an hotel, but always to some other clergyman's house. One of my earliest recollections is lying in bed and hearing from below the resounding laughter of my mother, as she talked with some visitor or caller.

It is always difficult to state with accuracy how far back in one's life one can remember; it is probable that many of our earliest reminiscences are in fact reminiscences of what we have been told. I feel sure of only one or two facts. I had a long illness that lasted for months, during which my fourth birthday occurred. My parents told me in later years that I was a sickly child, that they feared I would not live, and that finally in this long illness I was at the point of death more than once. Apparently this illness was a climax; for after I recovered, I grew into healthy boyhood and I suppose that during my life I have been more active than the average person.

I have a distinct recollection of my father coming into the room while I was in bed during this long illness, and bringing me a little tack-hammer as a present.

We had moved into a new house when I was three, and I remember a photograph's being taken of the house and of the entire family. I had on a white dress and was laughing as my father held me on top of the iron fence. My mother, sister, and brothers were in the windows. This house stands today, 44 High Street, New Haven; it is a square, brick house, with what was then called a French roof.

My sister Sophie died of typhoid fever when she was twenty-two; I was only six. I have missed her all my life. She was not beautiful, but she possessed extraordinary charm and the undergraduates at Yale were frequent visitors. As a 'kid brother' I must have been a nuisance; I came into the room interrupting agreeable conversation, and was sometimes bribed by the particular young man of the moment to go away and stay away. I have seen some of the letters Sophie wrote to her college friends and others; they reveal wit, intelligence, and charm. Although she was not formally engaged, I think she would have married the young man who called most frequently.

Men who love only once are among the rarest specimens of the human race; but there was another young man, who despite positive and repeated refusals from my sister, persisted in asking her to marry him. He had fought in the Civil War, had been wounded, and was a hero to my brother Arthur and me. A bullet had passed through his body, just above the hip. We were never tired of examining this scar, and putting our fingers into the hole in his side. We asked him endless questions about his battles. 'How did you feel when the bullet went through you?' He said he laughed.

When my sister was in the coffin on the morning of the funeral, and my mother and I were in the room, this young Lieutenant entered quietly and without noticing us, went to the dead girl and kissed her on the forehead. I asked my mother, 'Why did he kiss her? She's dead.' 'He kissed her because he loved her.' 'Well, was she going to marry him?' 'No.' 'How do you know that?' 'Because she told him she never would marry him.'

This man became a physician and lived to be over ninety.

He was never married and apparently never thought of any other woman. I used to see him at intervals of ten years or so; and he never talked about anything except my sister, and told me he was certain of being united with her in the next world. He said she was his Beatrice.

My sister, being so much older than my brother Arthur and I, had the unpleasant task of frequently taking care of us during the absence of our parents. We were a noisy, mischievous pair of small boys, and must have given her no end of trouble. Yet I never remember her saying a single disagreeable or angry word, though on one occasion she felt it her duty to whip us both. We were brought up on corporal punishment, a good thing for us. When I was either four or five years old, I strayed away and got lost somewhere down on Chapel Street, half a mile or so from home. Finally a policeman spoke to me, and eventually obtained the street and number of my home. I had disappeared about eleven o'clock in the morning and it was between three and four when the policeman brought me to the front door. I fully expected a whipping; my sister was the only person in the house. Perhaps the others were looking for me. Instead of whipping and scolding me, she greeted me with affection. Then she said, 'You must be very hungry,' and brought me some cold pudding. I recall my surprise at this unexpectedly agreeable reception and the ambrosial taste of that pudding.

My sister died on a winter morning just before dawn. I was wakened by a commotion in the house, and said to myself, 'Sophie must be dead.' Then my mother came into the room, almost insane with grief, crying out 'My God! My God!' I whispered to my father, 'What makes Mama swear so?' and my father told me, 'She is not swearing; she is praying.'

Two days later, when I was told that I was to be taken to the funeral, I leaped up and down and shouted and laughed in glee. I was not rebuked for this. My parents knew I had no real notion of the tragedy of my sister's death, and that the excitement of going somewhere in a carriage overcame every other sensation. It was the first time I had ever been in a hack, as we called it. I have no clear recollection of the interment; but I remember on the way back from the funeral, my brother Arthur, aged eight, burst into tears, and was comforted by my mother.

I miss my sister much more now than I did sixty years ago.

Here is a letter from my mother to 'Libbie,' written when I was nearly three years old.

NEW HAVEN, DEC. IOTH, 1867

MY DEAR DARLING SISTER,

Last night Willie was naughty and slapped me. I took him in my lap and tried to convince him how bad it was to strike his own Mamma. I said, 'Who takes all the care of little Willie?, makes and mends all his little clothes,' etc. He said 'There aint none body does.'

Arthur and Willie are now clearing the snow off the sidewalk. You ought to see them with their shovels at work.

At the age of four or possibly five, I came very near losing my life. Incredible as it may seem, a dose of arsenic had been laid on the library floor in a corner, to exterminate mice. My brother and I were crawling around on the carpet, while my father at his stand-up desk was preparing his sermon. We found the arsenic, thought it was sugar or something edible, and we stuffed a handful into our mouths. It tasted so unpleasant we began spitting it out and our father turned around to see what was the matter. He had us at the kitchen sink in a moment, and we expelled what was left and washed and gargled. Apparently we had swallowed nothing, for we never felt any internal unpleasantness. But I can taste it still—it was such a surprise.

I was reminded of this experience when I saw the play

Madame Bovary in New York in December 1937. When Constance Cummings stuffed her mouth full of arsenic, it looked exactly both in colour and in quantity like the arsenic I took so many years ago. I am glad the resemblance went no further.

When I was about six years old, playing with other boys on top of a lattice in the garden ten feet high, one of my playmates humorously pushed me off. Had I landed on my neck, I should have been killed. But I fell on my shoulder. I went into the library where my father was writing a sermon, and he found I could not lift the arm. He took me to our neighbour, the famous surgeon Dr. Francis Bacon, who examined the arm, said nothing was broken, but that I must wear a sling for a week. It is impossible to describe the rapture this gave me. To wear a sling! To go to school every day, with my arm in a sling, the envy of every boy. A hero decorated by a Commander-in-Chief for gallantry in action could not have felt more pride.

2

EARLY EDUCATION

I WAS sent to a private school on York Street, Monday, 4 October 1868; I was three years old; I am not sure whether it was then called a kindergarten; I have no recollection of hearing that word until many years later. The teacher, a Miss Morse, was kind. My father used to come for me at the end of the morning session. Once, as we walked home through a tremendous snowstorm, I was curiously interested in the spectacle of two men on the sidewalk, who were so drunk that they kept falling down. It seemed to me they were doing it for our entertainment, and I thought it was rather nice of them.

From the age of three to the age of five I attended Miss Morse's private school. When I was five I entered the regular public district Grammar School, called after the famous lexicographer, Webster School. I was the youngest and smallest boy in the establishment, and was in daily fear of the Irish lads, whom we called Micks. The boys and girls in this school represented every layer of society in New Haven; for on Crown Street dwelt many families of considerable affluence, while Oak Street and Morocco Street belonged to the slums.

The small boy is naturally a dirty little animal; I can say truthfully that although I have frequently been disgusted, I have never been shocked since I was nine years old. Dostoevski says the average schoolboy uses language that would make a drunken sailor blush, which describes accurately the daily talk I heard during recess and after hours in this school. The most blasphemous and obscene expressions came trippingly on the tongue and were used apparently with no sense of bravado, but as the common staple of conversation. Many of our modern novelists instead of being 'frank' or 'realistic' seem to me rather juvenile. They remind me of the small talk of small boys at the Webster School.

When I was five years old, I was invited to a children's party which became tempestuous. I was chasing a girl running from room to room, dodging in and out among the other children. She made a dash into the hall running straight toward the closed door that led into the street. Just as it seemed as if she must crash into it, she leaped to one side and I went headlong into this portal. I had raised my right arm to seize her, and this arm plunged through the large glass pane in the door. So far as I can remember, I felt no hurt, but an astonishing stream of blood spirted from my wrist. I had cut two arteries. The ladies screamed and dragged me hysterically to a wash basin, and turned the faucet on my arm; but the blood covered them and the basin and it seemed as if it would cover the room. I never saw so much flowing blood, bright arterial red, and as I remember, it seemed to come in tremendous jets (I had been running violently), that spouted several feet. Unquestionably I should have died in not many minutes; but my mother, who was in another part of the house, hastened into the room, drew me into a chair and closed her hand on my wrist above the cut and hung on with desperation. She called out 'You must get a doctor immediately!' In those days there was no telephone, no speedy means of transportation. Some-one had to find a carriage and drive a long distance; it was nearly an hour before Dr. Pierpont came. I cannot remember saying anything. My mother had checked the flow of blood—why no bandage or tourniquet was used I shall never understand. The Doctor sewed up my wrist with wire, then bandaged it heavily, and said that if anything happened in the night, he must be sent for. The huge scar on my wrist is there now; and I always smile when any physician attempts to feel my pulse; for he tries the right arm first and cannot understand why no pulse is discernible.

One night about this time—it may have been shortly after this accident—I dreamed that Jesus Christ was sitting on a white cloud whilst I and others were standing below gazing at him. Suddenly he called in a loud voice, 'Willie Phelps, come here!' When I told my parents at breakfast of this dream, which I thought rather charming, they looked very grave.

I have no recollection of learning to read; when I entered this school at the age of five, I could read aloud with ease, and it was only a five-syllabled word like 'particularly' that gave me any difficulty. I had a naturally good ocular memory for words and three times in the 'spelling down' matches I was the last survivor. Pride goeth before a fall; for on the fourth contest, I was one of the first to go down. The teacher pronounced the word *gem*, which I had never heard and had no recollection of having seen. I spelled it *jem*.

In later years my heart ached for those women teachers. The filth and dirt the boys brought into the schoolroom, the insolent manner in which they answered the teacher's questions, the ribald laughter that resounded on occasions skilfully prepared to produce it! No boy ever rose to recite without finding crooked pins, or tacks (and I remember one file) put in his chair to greet his down-sitting—then came the exaggerated howl of pain and rage, the backhanded blow, the teacher's vain remonstrance. Spitballs flew around the room, falling on the just and on the unjust.

One of the bigger and tougher boys ceased to be a problem at school, for he was arrested for rape, and sent to jail. His crime and his fate were for many months a subject of conversation.

I have often wondered whether I was really a physical coward at school or whether, because of my tender years and tiny size, my awareness of incapacity made me timid. However that may be, one of the innumerable advantages of growing up is getting rid of chronic fear. Because I was easily terrified, my heroes were naturally the tough boys and they never suspected my worship. At Christmas we all exchanged gifts anonymously, and then at a certain moment, every boy and girl opened the package on his desk. I had made my gift to the roughest and most dare-devil lad in the room. His desk was not far from mine; and when we both opened our parcels, he sneered at me and mine, insisting that he had got a much better present than the one that fell to me. I did not dare tell him I was his benefactor.

He was secretly my hero, because when most of the boys were whipped by the teacher, they cried, and he always laughed out loud. The harder she struck him, the more he laughed. I have never got over my admiration and wonder at this spectacle. When we were whipped, we had to hold out a hand, and the teacher hit it with a rattan stick. He would hold out his hand, and when she was through, he would offer the other one, laughing with delight. There were nine or ten whippings every day.

An excellent illustration of the mystery of personality was in daily evidence. There were twelve rooms. Every room had a female teacher and these twelve disciples in turn were ruled by a male principal. Every teacher and every boy and girl in the building were in mortal terror of this man; he was legendary. He dwelt apart in some throne room aloft; and it was quite possible to spend a year at the school and never set eyes on him. But his invisible presence was a terrific actuality. The teachers seldom appealed to the Supreme Court. Thus, I shall never forget my amazement one day while my tough hero was getting an unusually prolonged whipping from the teacher and treating it with more than usual risibility, she suddenly lost patience and said, 'I will send you up to Mr. Lewis.' My hero collapsed; his mirth changed to pleading terror. 'Oh, don't send me to Mr. Lewis! I'll do anything you say, only don't please send me to Mr. Lewis!'

What Mr. Lewis did to these lads no one ever knew, but strange tales came from these mysterious interviews. Perhaps he never laid hands on them; just looked at them until they were petrified with fear. He was the one salvation of the women teachers, and for over forty years he presided over that whirlwind of childish savagery, disorder, corruption, and sin, and somehow made citizens out of that unpromising material. One day, coming out after school was over, he spoke to me kindly, with a smile. I was in such terror I could say nothing; but as soon as I got around the corner I ran for my life.

Once in a while he would walk through our schoolroom, without looking at anybody or speaking a word. The most absolute silence marked his advent. He seemed to me of colossal size. Years afterwards, when I returned to New Haven, I marvelled at his tiny frame and puny appearance. Was this grey-haired little man the ogre of my childhood? For the strange thing is, that even in the vile language used at recess, no boy even then took his name in vain. John Lewis was a genius of discipline.

My father had been pastor of the First Baptist Church in New Haven for nearly thirty years; and in 1874, when I was nine, he accepted a call to the Jefferson Street Baptist Church in Providence, Rhode Island. Here we lived first at 34 Carroll Street and later at 5 Francis Street. At first I attended a district or grade school, very similar to the Webster School at New Haven; and here, at the

age of ten, I fell in love with a schoolmate, Ella Henries
—I wonder where she is now? She knew I loved her,
though in her presence I was tongue-tied, 'such was my
faint heart's sweet distress.' I call it love, because I had
the symptoms described in the mediaeval romance writers,
and they were good diagnosticians. I kissed her once only
and that was in the game post-office, and it was a miserable
effort. I shakingly aimed at her mouth and side-swiped
her on the cheekbone.

During the year and a half we lived in Providence, I was
'converted.' There were revival meetings at our church,
and one evening, when the Reverend Doctor Bixby had
been preaching, I stood up when they called for the un-
converted. It was not an explosive experience, but I did
feel very happy. My brother and I were baptized by im-
mersion by my father in March 1876; thus I have been a
member of the Baptist denomination in 'good and regular
standing' for over sixty years. One of the reasons I have
never deserted the fold is that the Baptists have no creed,
no ritual, no church organization; there is indeed no Baptist Church, only a collection of Baptist churches. No
organization has any control over any Baptist unit, any
more than the New York University Club has over the
Chicago University Club. Now while I admire the beauty
of a ritual and often attend Mass in a Catholic Church, I
am such an individualist that I feel more at home among
Baptists, Congregationalists, and Quakers.

Here for a few months in Providence I had my first intellectual awakening. I made progress with a rapidity that
in retrospect is inexplicable. There was an excellent private
school at the top of the hill opposite Brown University,
called the University Grammar School, kept by the brothers Merrick and Emory Lyon. It was an expensive school,
but in some way my father managed to enter my brother
Arthur and me (my oldest brother Dryden, after a year

at Yale, had accompanied the family to Providence and was an undergraduate at Brown) at a reduced rate. We entered this school in the Autumn of 1875, when I was ten, and left it in the Spring of 1876, when the family moved to Hartford.

I have often wondered what my mental development would have been had we remained in Providence. I should have been prepared for college at the age of fifteen, possibly fourteen, and would undoubtedly have entered Brown.

I was once more the youngest and the smallest boy in school. The oldest boys were some of them full-grown, wore side-whiskers and moustachios, and came from wealthy or aristocratic families. Doctor Lyon, a remarkable teacher, took a personal interest in me, and suddenly I developed a fierce and unquenchable thirst for learning. We were in school about six hours daily except Saturday and I often studied six hours a day at home. I was making fast progress in Latin, French, History, English composition, public speaking; and if I had stayed at that school two years I should either have learned more than I learned in the next six years or I should have had some kind of break-down.

Friday mornings we had 'Declamation exercises,' when every boy, except those excused for some reason, spoke a piece he had learned by heart. I had no difficulty in learning the eighty-eight stanzas of 'Horatius at the Bridge,' and I remember it took me twenty minutes to speak them. It must have bored the school almost beyond endurance. Here too I had the opportunity to speak Browning's poem 'Hervé Riel' before he published it. Browning, abandoning his usual custom, printed it in the *Cornhill Magazine* in 1871, and gave the hundred pounds he received to the suffering inhabitants of Paris. Later, in the year 1876, he published it in the volume *Pachiarotto*. Well, I was turning over the pages of Monroe's *Sixth Reader* to find a good

poem for declamation; and I found that. I had never heard
of the author but the poem pleased me; and I recited it in
1875. As in my later professional career I spent more time
teaching Browning than any other author, it interests me
to recall this early episode.

It may be that my extraordinary progress in the acquisition of knowledge came from the blessed fact that in the
University Grammar School, I was, for some unknown
reason, free of mathematics, the curse of my subsequent
life at school and at college. Apart from an hour called
'Mental Arithmetic' which seemed more like an amusing
game than anything else, I had no mathematics. All my
studies I found absorbing, exciting; they made an equally
strong appeal to my interest and to my ambition.

In this school I was also getting a much-needed social
education, though it did not last long enough to reform
my bad manners. Possibly because the other boys were
so much older or because they had all been so well brought
up, I cannot remember hearing any bad language during
the winter of my stay. They seemed to me young gentlemen
of finished elegance, and I felt uncouth; like a savage who
had wandered into a civilized home. Perhaps I was more
like a savage who had been converted by some missionary;
I was very religious, but devoid of tact or even the rudi-
ments of good social behaviour.

For my own sake, I am sorry that my earliest sermons
are lost. It would amuse me to read them. I wished to
imitate my father; I wanted to be like him in every way.
I wanted to excel at athletic games, I wanted a gun to go
shooting, I wanted a desk of my own and solitude for
writing, I wanted to be a preacher and public orator. When
I was eight years old, I began to preach sermons to the
family on Sunday afternoons and I kept this up for two or
three years. I wrote these sermons out on 'sermon paper'
and every Sunday afternoon I conducted a regular service,

the audience consisting of my father, mother, and two brothers. I remember how desperately hard it was for me to think up enough material to fill four pages of manuscript. The family assembled, with a perfectly straight face, for I was tremendously in earnest; I read the hymns before they were sung, and preached a sermon, which whatever it lacked in literary merit, was uncompromisingly orthodox. The family managed to listen seriously, until, one afternoon while reading a hymn I came to the line

Deep horror then my vitals froze

and I had the misfortune to pronounce the word as 'vittles.' The family burst into roars of uncontrollable laughter. I was hurt and I believe that ended my first efforts as a preacher. I could see nothing funny in it, and their attempts to explain the connotation of cold storage were lost on me, as I had never seen the word *victuals*.

My other early attempts at public recitals were more fortunate; I became every summer a public entertainer. In those days two classes of people went to Saratoga Springs—race-track gamblers and ministers of the Gospel. In common with other ministers, my father stayed in boarding-houses; the race-track people, whom we never met, stayed at one of the three enormous hotels that were famous all over the world, The Grand Union Hotel, The United States Hotel, and Congress Hall. It was solemnly whispered to me that at these hotels some of the millionaires paid five dollars a day!

The larger boarding-houses had some kind of entertainment every evening—music, elocution, and what not. I had learned a comic song, part sung, part recited (wasn't it by Gus Williams?) called 'Mygel Schneider's Party,' and the Manager of the boarding-house, hearing me singing it for fun one day, got me to sing it in public every night for the entertainment of the guests. I was devoid of self-consciousness, and sang this absurd piece nightly without the slightest embarrassment or fear. If I had to enter a room containing people engaged in animated conversation, I was overwhelmed with embarrassment; but I could get up before a big audience and speak or recite or sing without even a shadow of fear. I have never had stage-fright, possibly because I began to speak so early.

Henry Ward Beecher said he never walked on a platform or a pulpit without stage-fright, though it disappeared the moment he began to speak. I often say to myself just before walking on the stage in a crowded auditorium, 'Why am I not frightened?' but even that question does not disturb me. I reflect, 'You ought to be scared; you would have more respect for yourself if you were scared;' but try as hard as I may, it is all in vain. I am straining at the leash.

Beginning with 1895, I have given every year many public lectures outside of my work in the classroom; and my annual *courses of lectures* in New Haven, New York, Brooklyn, Philadelphia, and Connecticut cities I have particularly enjoyed. I think everyone who lectures frequently to large audiences enjoys it; but I think very few feel such thrilling delight as I invariably do. Whether I give it or not, I always receive inspiration. Furthermore, I love these audiences; I have for them an intimate, almost a family affection. I call them my children; in the Brooklyn Institute my Sunday children; in the Town Hall, Manhattan, my Saturday children; in New Haven, my Tuesday children; in the Forum, my Philadelphia children. Often while I am travelling in Europe or in remote parts of the United States, some person will speak to me saying, 'I am one of your Sunday children,' and it is like meeting a relation or a college classmate. There is an intimacy between my audiences and myself that adds much to the pleasure of addressing them. I am grateful to them and to all the people everywhere who have honoured me by their presence and attention. It has also been an especial pleasure to speak to academic audiences in various universities; and to conventions of school-teachers and librarians, all of us engaged in a common cause and proud of our profession.

3

BOYHOOD EXPERIENCES

At Providence, 12 November 1875, when I was ten years old, I was examined by Dr. Emory Lyon at the University Grammar School, in *Eaton's Common School Arithmetic*; and a day or two later by Harmon S. Babcock in Latin and Geography. I was examined also in French by Dr. Lyon.

I wrote the following note at Providence, 14 March 1876. 'I was examined by Deacon Hall, Mr. Benson, and Papa, to be baptized. This happened Thursday, Feb. 24, 1876. I told my experience to the church, Feb. 25, 1876. I was baptized with Miss Whaley, Mrs. Allen, Lincoln Rose, my brother Arthur, on Feb. 27, 1876, Sunday eve. Papa preached the night I was baptized on Sodom and Gomorrah. It was a very solemn sermon. The text was "And Lot pitched his tent toward Sodom." He repeated some poetry of Arthur Coxe's. I remember that the sermon was so interesting, that I utterly forgot all about the baptism.'

After the sermon when my father called for the first person to come forward to be baptized, no one moved. Finally he said 'Let the first one come!' No one moved, so I stepped forward. I should have been baptized last, because the water in the baptistery would not have been nearly so deep; the clothes and the robes of each person take up a great deal of water. I remember distinctly that when I put my foot in, I gasped aloud, and the lady playing the organ looked at me in amazement. My father led me and the water came up to my chin.

Two years later, when I was graduated from the

West Middle District School at Hartford, the Principal, Mr. D.P.Corbin, addressed the graduating class as follows:

'Don't be so *foolish* as to study Saturday, so *wicked* as to study Sunday, and so *crazy* as to study early Monday morning.'

Thursday, Friday, Saturday, 26, 27, 28 October 1876, my parents took the whole family to the Centennial in Philadelphia. I kept a diary while there. The things that I remember most distinctly are the huge Corliss engine, which Mr. Corliss would not allow to run on Sunday, and the delicious taste of butter at a French restaurant. We were wandering about the grounds and entered a French restaurant for lunch; I could not imagine why the butter tasted so much better than any I had ever known. It was the first time I had ever tasted saltless butter; but during the last sixty years I have got saltless butter whenever possible.

On top of the Ohio State Building appeared one day in the open air before an enormous crowd, Rutherford B.Hayes, candidate for President of the United States. He was introduced by General Hawley, Senator from Connecticut. Near me, on the ground, and in the midst of this throng, sat a woman suckling her child. It was the first time I had consciously seen a woman's breast; and it was a strange spectacle. The mother was as indifferent to Hayes's eloquence and to the enthusiasm of the crowd as was her child.

One of the sights of the Centennial was in Agricultural Hall, where on a perch stood a bald headed eagle called Old Abe. He had gone through the four years of the Civil War, as a pet of the Union Soldiers, and had escaped unscathed. 'Some of the rebels had shot at him,' I wrote. Again: 'Then to Machinery Hall, then to Main Building, where I saw a model of Chaos (*sic*) the greatest pyramid of Egypt.'

The glass-blowers were surrounded by throngs, and thousands of model glass slippers were sold. We brought home two. One I have now; the other, some thirty years after its purchase, I threw against the wall and smashed, in a rage at losing a game of billiards.

I did not see another World's Fair until 1893, when my wife and I went to Chicago. I do not believe there has ever been an Exposition anywhere in the world that compares with that one in beauty and dignity. No witness will forget the Court of Honour at night.

Incidentally, our first view of the new University of Chicago was from the top of the Ferris Wheel; and the one Gothic quadrangle looked academically impressive. The only person we met in front of it a half-hour later was the President, William R. Harper. He was, as usual, full of enthusiasm for the future of the university, for the future of Chicago, for the future of the human race.

The following letter is worth reading, because it reveals the character and personality of my father, and because it shows some of the difficulties that have always beset young ministers in small churches. The man to whom my father wrote this letter was so discouraged by the smallness of his salary and the conditions accompanying it, that he was considering leaving the ministry altogether and accepting an agency as a travelling salesman.

NEW HAVEN, MARCH 13, 1851

DEAR BR. GORHAM:

I have been to the Board Meeting at Norwich, & would suggest that they have unanimously appointed you as the Minister for Humphreys-ville, & very anxious for you to remain there. I also procured for you an order on the Treasurer for the amount of your salary up to the present time *Eighty-four Dollars*, & what money was on hand then, *Fifty-five dollars*, was paid for you & I have it here awaiting your order. The rest you can get any time on application to the Treasurer. Now this $84 is a snug little sum for your labors for less than two months & a half. At least it is better than nothing. And with your present salary, *due to be paid promptly*, you may not complain very much, till Providence gives you a better portion.

Your letter received Tuesday morning I liked very much, with some slight exceptions. You say you know or I know that I would not consent to do as you are doing, that is preach for the salary & the people you are preaching for. I will tell you what I did do, after I got ready for the Ministry. I was invited to settle with a little church worshiping in a poor hall, a small congregation, & on a salary of less than four hundred, & I considered it a fair chance to begin with. But for reasons, disconnected with the salary, place etc., I engaged to supply another church for nearly six months at the rate of about $300 a year, & I did so; & there preached a year for the church of which I am now Pastor at $400. And if I were not a Pastor, I would again, yes preach at Humphreysville, as you are doing, unless called else-where by Providence. I had as much debt to pay as you, & paid it faster on a small salary & few expenses, than it would be possible for me to do now.

I fully believe you will rue it, if you accept any agency, even if a larger salary is proposed. Think of increased expenses; what if you should be sick among strangers! If well, you would have no certain dwelling place. You would often get the cold shoulder, or your cause would, & if you didn't have the *blues* worse than anything you have yet experienced, then you would be more fortunate than some I know of. Suppose you should take an agency, at $600 a year. Depend upon it you would not be as well off at the end of the year as you would to remain where you are. I do not think your temperament suited to an agent. It is not absolutely necessary to stay in Humphreysville. Pas-toral relations change in the Spring often, & if duty calls elsewhere I presume some favorable opening will be presented for you. Besides, things are not to be in your village as they are now long. A good House of Worship is very soon to be built & paid for, & then there will be a good congregation, & soon a flourishing Church by God's blessing. Your present improved style of preaching, & your determination to excel, will attract no doubt a delighted audience for you, & result in the conversion of many. You know it wants a strong man, & faithful Minister just at your point in the Naugatuck Valley, where there is so much ungodliness, practical infidelity. No place in this world is a Paradise, & the most favored of God's ministers meet with things that almost crush their hearts. Suppose I should tell *all* my experience even as it is at this time. My present salary does not cover all the expenses of my family, & I am compelled to deny myself in many things that I feel as though I ought to have. But if God blesses my labors, I *hope* for improvement.

I would not put the slightest obstacle in the way of any blessing for I have the kindest & deepest interest & affection for you. But I was surprised & pained, on hearing from you, just after you had commenced a new era in the manner of preaching, etc. that you were writing to your friends in different parts, proposing to abandon the ministry for the sake of *expecting* a little more salary. I felt that you were doing what would be an injury to you & disastrous to some extent to the cause of religion. Your motives may be good; but others would not look with your eyes. May God speed you in the right course, with his richest blessing.

Yours affectionately,

S. D. PHELPS

4

INTERLUDE ON CATS

I HAVE always been an idolater of cats. Idolater is the accurate word; and perhaps only those will understand my devotion in whom, as in me, the love of cats is inborn. I once heard a famous scientist in a public lecture say that most children are afraid of anything that has fur on it; and their fear, he explained, is owing to the fact that some forty thousand years ago furred animals were dangerous to the hairless human children; and a feeling therefore rose which had become instinctive, persisting long after the original reason for it had ceased to exist. This statement, like many other remarks of scientific men, I heard with profound scepticism.

My father, my mother, and my aunt took no interest in cats, and would have been undisturbed had they known they would never see one again. Yet I cannot remember the time when any cat, no matter how humble in origin and in social station, failed to arouse in me breathless adoration. Even the dirtiest alleycat was an object of worship.

Many persons love cats; but have they had these intimations of felinity in earliest childhood? How shall I describe this cat-worship? As a baby I loved every piece of fur. My oldest brother had a fur hat; night after night I slept with it. I called it the cat-hat. My aunt Libbie had a tippet of ermine. I used to hug this article, and kiss it frantically. My aunt at first was touched when she came into the room and found me kissing her ermine, because she thought it was evidence of my love for her. She discovered it was

28

nothing of the kind; and she was even more puzzled than disappointed. I loved my aunt and she was good to me; but when she asked me if I kissed the ermine because it was hers, I shouted with the disconcerting candour character-istic of childhood, 'No! No!' and kissing the fur with re-newed vigour, I called it ' Kitty! Pussy!' Even today I long to stroke every piece of fur I see. No doubt many visitors thought I was insane. Perhaps they were right. Only if I was, I have never recovered. In addressing women I ad-mired I added the termination *cat* to their names; thus Elizabeth became Lizcat, Olivia Livcat, Madelene Mad-cat, Alice Alleycat, and Helen Hellcat.

I have always envied professionals I have seen enter the cages of lions and tigers and stroke cats eight feet long!

Of all domestic animals the cat is the most beautiful and the most graceful. His anatomy is precisely adapted to his needs; and although he takes only a hundredth as much athletic exercise as a dog, he is always in perfect condition. Whoever saw a housemaid exercising a cat? There is no other beast who from a position of absolute relaxation can spring with accuracy and with no preliminary motion. The cat does not have to wind up like a baseball pitcher, or get 'set;' he transmutes potential energy into kinetic energy with no visible effort.

When a cat aims at the top of a fence or the surface of a table, he usually succeeds at the first effort, unlike the dog, who will try and continue to try long after the impossibility of attainment has been demonstrated to a spectator. The cat's economy of effort is as remarkable as his judgement of distance; you cannot persuade him to try for any mark beyond his reach. The cat catches birds on the ground by outguessing them and by a final spring faster than flight; but if the bird has risen in the air, the cat makes no attempt at pursuit, which he knows to be futile and undignified. But the dog will run after flying birds to the limit of exhaustion.

The amazing activity of the cat is delicately balanced by his capacity for relaxation. Every household should contain a cat, not only for decorative and domestic values, but because the cat in quiescence is medicinal to irritable, tense, tortured men and women. In spite of all the physicians and hospitals and books that are endeavouring to induce men and women to 'relax'—continued energy seems to be required in order to keep quiet—few human beings understand the art of repose. They cannot let go.

Now when the cat decides to rest, he not only lies down; he pours his body out on the floor like water. It is reposeful merely to watch him. The average man looks up from the morning newspaper and roars at the folly and stupidity of our law-makers; then he happens to see the family cat, who seems to put to the householder every day the Emersonian question—'*So hot, my little Sir?*'

The beauty and grace and agility of the cat's body are equalled by his intellectual and spiritual nature. It is often said by those who have no affection for cats that cats have no affection; this is a slander. A youth tried to convince an old man that cats were without affection, saying the cat loves you only because he wishes to get something out of you. It isn't really love. 'Ah,' replied the sage, 'when you are as old as I am, you will call that love.'

The dog is a good fellow and jolly companion, but he does not compare in intellectual power with the cat. The cat has an acute mind, an inflexible will, and a patience almost divine. If the cat wishes to leave the room, he makes no fuss about it and does not annoy you with vocal importunities; he selects a position near the door. Now you may change his position but you cannot change his purpose; his purpose is to leave the room; and he knows that opportunities come to those who are ready. He pretends he has dismissed the matter from his mind; but when someone happens to open the door, the cat departs.

The patience of the cat in hunting is one reason why he seldom returns empty-clawed. A hole in the ground will arouse terrific enthusiasm in a dog; he will bark frantically and dig vigorously; but unless something happens within five minutes, his ardour cools; he goes away and forgets. If a cat decides there is game in a certain spot he does not advertise his presence; he waits for the prey to make the first move and he can outwait any other living thing.

One reason men have always liked dogs is that the dog flatters us with fawning servility; it is agreeable to be received with such demonstrations of affection. But the devotion of the dog has been overpraised. What a dog wants is entertainment. He is easily bored, cannot amuse himself, and demands excitement. His ideal is a life of active uselessness. That the dog is devoted only to his master is a myth. He is devoted to anyone in whose company he finds entertainment. I had to be disillusioned before I accepted this truth. My first dog was a noble Irish setter who apparently could not bear to have me out of his sight; he cared nothing for guests or strangers; if I left the room he instantly followed me. I felt proud of this, and often thought what a noble, faithful fellow he was. But one day I fell into a sickness and had to stay in bed two weeks. For an hour or so on the first day he remained in my room. But there were other men in the house. One of them took the dog for a walk and alienated his affections. The dog never came near me, but pretended to be pleased when I recovered.

Even the famous 'one-man' dogs are fed by the one man. Yet I feel like a traitor in calling attention to these moral defects. How can I help loving a creature so affectionate, so demonstrative, so responsive? I can't. It is only my love of truth that compels me to say that in dignity and neatness the dog does not compare with the cat. The dog is a jolly good fellow; he leaps joyously upon you, places his muddy paws on your shirt-front, and after swimming, postpones the shaking of his frame until he is within close range. Indoors he wags his tail violently, knocking down vases and ornaments and leaving a trail of wreckage. The cat, on the other hand, after delicately showing affection by rubbing gently against one's ankles, springs without apparent effort to a narrow shelf covered with fragile objects and never displaces anything. His extraordinary mental and physical poise is shown by the astounding fact that he can sleep with assurance on the top of a fence only two inches broad, or indeed far aloft on the trim branch of a tree.

The superiority of the cat is shown most convincingly in his intellectual resources. You may love a dog but the cat commands your respect. His infinite capacity to keep still makes him good company for many quiet hours. The dog, as someone has said, is always on the wrong side of the door.

The ability of the cat to entertain himself was shown in a striking essay which appeared about forty years ago in the *Yale Literary Magazine*; it was written by an undergraduate, Ray Morris, who later demonstrated his ability to write equally well on other themes. He emphasized the cat's intellectual resources.

I have observed this fact so often that it may be in my comments I shall unwittingly borrow from my memory of Mr. Morris's essay. If you leave the dog outside the front door only for a moment, while you are looking inside for something, he is in a flutter of nerves; he barks, whines, and scratches in an agony of desolation. But if you kick the cat out of the house with a kind of final gesture, he remains thoughtful a moment as if to say, 'Now I *had* planned to spend the afternoon indoors; but it is possible that it is more hygienic in the garden. I will sleep until there are further developments.'

The cat, although he has not the super smelling power of

the dog, has an astonishing faculty of finding his way to the place he has chosen to reach. A man who owned a magnificent cat was told by his neighbours that if he did not kill the animal before Saturday night, they would do it for him; for the cat had shown a fondness for their chickens. He was at a loss what to do. A friend advised him to take the cat to the most complicated corner in the city of Boston, somewhere near Scollay Square. There the streets are so crooked and twisted that no stranger has ever found his way without enquiry; he should leave the cat there, would never see him again, and would have no cause for worry, since the place abounded in grocery shops where someone would gladly take in the animal. The owner was asked a month later if he had done this and with what result. He replied, 'What a place that was! if I had not followed the cat, I should never have got home.'

To a man individual liberty is the greatest blessing; to a dog it is the last word in despair. He is happy only in slavery. Hence he sticks to a master even though he is treated badly. The more one beats him, the greater is his servility. If you wish to keep a cat you must treat him with respect. The cat is essentially free. He has never been entirely tamed. He will not stand physical ill-treatment and you must not laugh at him when he comes down from a tree, the only thing he does ungracefully. The Egyptians, with their endless patience, were the only people who succeeded in turning him into a domestic animal, and heaven only knows how many centuries they spent on the task.

Men resemble dogs; women are more like cats. A large part of men's activity is physical; they spend much time in running around, and they demand excitement. Women manage somehow to entertain themselves in a way incomprehensible to the male mind.

It is a pity that dogs take no interest in washing themselves; it would help in passing the time. It is a constant resource for a cat. If there is nothing else going on or if the cat is wakeful, he can always wash himself. To a cat self-washing is a means of cleanliness, an athletic exercise, a pastime, a fine art, a religious ritual. I have seen a cat go into a frenzy of ablution.

How strange it is that to a cat's tongue, corrugated like the blade of a golf-niblick, heat should be unendurable. The cat always waits for hot food to cool.

You can guess what a dog is thinking about and what he will do next, both of which divinations fail with the cat. The eyes of a cat do not betray his mind. He has such a patrician reserve that when he does show affection it is enormously flattering. When you want a dog to come to you instantly, you shout at him. Try that on the cat.

It is often said that the dog is more intelligent, because he learns tricks so easily. But is this good evidence? You command a dog to 'sit up' and the poor fellow thinks he has to do it. The average cat throws off, pretends unconquerable limpness of body and stupidity of mind, and an inability to understand what is wanted. Of course he understands only too well. Why sit up? There is nothing in it.

But cats, alas, are as mortal as dogs. It may be that they have nine lives, but as my friend George Stanleigh Arnold says, it is always the ninth that they lose.

No man in the world understood cats better than the famous playwright, William Gillette. After I had printed an article on cats, I received from Mr. Gillette the following letter:

Surely it must be evident to you that those who attack a person for appreciating the wonderful traits and beauties of cats are grossly and absolutely ignorant, and also pitiably prejudiced regarding them, and in addition are the resident members of a class which prefers abject unreasoning worship and cloying servility to unconquerable independence and rare judgment of character.

And surely you know what good company you are in—and I am

not referring to myself alone in reminding you of this—in the appreciation of cats. Even old Voltaire took the trouble to say 'Beware of the
woman who does not like cats'—and although I have sometimes
failed to beware of her, I nevertheless enjoy having that testimony to
Mr. V.'s attitude on the question.

What I really wanted to say was not the foregoing (which is really
foregone, as there can be no argument about it)—but the following:

There are three things which I really think you would do well to
touch upon when you next take up this subject:

1. The absolute necessity of cats for the preservation of birds. There
is unlimited testimony from scientific sources that, for the few birds
that are caught and devoured by cats, there are millions whose lives
are saved by the destruction of their enemies.

2. The unquestionable possession of some sort of extra 'sense' which
enables cats to be aware of the attitude—or even more than the attitude, of a human mind, where it concerns themselves. I have experi-
mented a great deal in this direction, and cannot avoid the conclusion
that cats are either mind readers (when they want to be) or that they
have such a wonderful appreciation of exterior symptoms that they
arrive at the mental processes via that route.

3. I have forgotten this one for the moment; but I want to tell you
this; it was very important and it would be a good thing for you to
consult me before you do anything further on this subject—and also
possibly (for all I know) on any other.

P.S. Although I have taken considerable time in trying to remember what the third point was, it has not yet occurred to me. For a substitute, however, let us say that it was the exquisite sense of comedy
possessed by the family under discussion—comedy of the very highest
known altitude. Though I have not considered the matter, it seems to
me that no other animal is possessed of such an exquisite and fastidious
sense of humour—not even man himself.

Finally, although there are many persons who are afraid
of dogs, they are not really afraid of dogs—they are afraid
of being bitten. But the uncanny and unearthly nature of
the cat is shown by the fact that many brave men and
women are in terror if there is a cat in the room. It is not
fear of what the cat might do—it is fear of the Cat.
Lord Roberts, the great soldier, had an unconquerable fear
of cats. Cosmo Hamilton wrote (*Unwritten History*),

He dined once at the country house of a mutual friend, rose in the middle of dinner, ran out into the garden, and stood trembling on the lawn because a yellow-eyed Angora kitten had poked an inquisitive head around the door. His fear was well-founded; for the next moment the kitten would have leaped on his knee. Cats have a sure instinct for those who fear or dislike them, and they will invariably leap upon them or rub against them, in the endeavour to dispel prejudice.

The late Doctor James Hosmer Penniman of Philadelphia wrote an exquisite little book on cats called *The Alley Rabbit*. He received a letter from William Gillette, written in his castle, 'Seventh Sister.'

> I have bestowed upon you the highest honor in the repertoire of the Seventh Sister Establishment. I have named a cat after you and it wasn't a gelding either but a fine sturdy Thomas cat. This superb animal has been baptized, not with the name of James alone but with your middle and last names as well. Also we call him Doc for short, and the old boy seems perfectly delighted, throwing his tail about in the air with joyful jerks—which is a darn sight more than you could do. Ever since we have been addressing this cat as Dr. James Hosmer Penniman, he has been leaving carefully selected rats on the Seventh Sister Penniman Memorial Library.

On 21 January 1928 I received the following letter from Mr. W.A.Way, from Grey Institute, Port Elizabeth, Cape Colony.

> I wonder whether you noticed in Mr. Fletcher's Memoir of A.D.Godley which appears in Godley's *Reliquiae* (Oxford University Press) the concluding words 'he shared with many wise persons a most intelligent and comprehensive affection for the whole race of cats.' Godley, who was editing the Oxford Magazine when I was up, is I suppose the happiest and cleverest and most scholarly of all writers and parodists. (He died at 70 in 1925) so that you are again in excellent company!

I received the picture of a cross-eyed cat, the pet of Mrs. Muriel Frey, of San Francisco. Had anyone knowledge of any other cat thus peculiar? My own white cat,

Miss Frosty Evans of Philadelphia, had one blue and one green eye, attracting the attention of biologists. Men and women with one blue and one brown eye are not uncommon, but the blue-and-green combination is rare.

Only a few years ago I was delighted to learn from a philosopher and scholar, author of many books, and my intimate friend, the late Dr. Henshaw Ward, that a cat had been named after me. He wrote from North Carolina in the winter of 1933:

MY DEAR BILLY:

This afternoon, when I called on Professor C.A.Lloyd of the Biltmore Junior College, I was astonished to hear Mrs. Lloyd say, 'Oh, here is William Lyon Phelps.' Then a gray cat trotted from behind me, and I was amused.

But after I had heard the story of the name I realized that it is not amusing. It is an idyll—as I will show you. When this cat was a kitten and before he was christened, the boy who owned him happened to read some passage of yours in which you express your admiration for cats. The boy exclaimed, 'Any one who can write so understandingly about cats ought to have one named after him.' The boy was entirely serious. The animal is always called 'Dr. Phelps' by the whole family.

5

RUFUS H. PHELPS

I HAVE never owned any dog except Irish setters; three of whom have been named Rufus. The one whom I describe here was the second to bear his name, and he belongs in this autobiography because he was the most literary dog in the world. Rufus was Irish, he was red-headed, he was a good fighter after he had exhausted diplomatic formalities; therefore it was natural that he should have been born during the World War, and on the anniversary of the Battle of the Boyne, still celebrated as a bellicose occasion.

He was born 12 July 1917 and died 28 June 1931, having nearly attained the venerable dog's age of fourteen.

Bernard Shaw celebrated 12 July 1928 by writing his own name for us in one of his books and under it 'Rufus's Birthday.' But the two never met.

When we had the honour of entertaining Joseph Conrad in our house in New Haven, Rufus displayed adoration. He fawned upon him, shook hands, and gazed into the face of the seaman with intense earnestness. Mr. Conrad responded with strokes and caresses. That was an unforgettable scene when the old seadog conversed so intimately with the dog of the fields.

On the first occasion when John Galsworthy entered our library, and sat at my desk, Rufus came in. He ran to Mr. Galsworthy, and although he had never seen him before, greeted him as if both were intimate friends. Mr. Galsworthy, who had an Irish setter of his own three thousand miles away, immediately knelt on the floor, clasped the dog around his neck, and kissed him fervently on the brow.

Hugh Walpole, on various visits to America, established a close friendship with Rufus, and told him many interesting facts about dogs he himself had written in England, to which Rufus listened with attention.

When Mr. and Mrs. G.K.Chesterton stayed at our house, Rufus immediately showed recognition of the genius of the famous Englishman, putting his paw up as if to say, 'We understand each other perfectly.'

Joseph Conrad was not the only amphibious writer who appreciated Rufus. When the dog was hardly more than a puppy—though he had already given unmistakable signs of coming intellectual distinction—John Masefield happened to be in my library. The two had not conversed more than a few moments when it seemed as if they had grown up together; and W.B.Yeats greeted Rufus as a fellow-countryman.

Rufus admired men of letters; and his taste was by no means narrow. It was all one to him whether his friend was a poet, a dramatist, a novelist, or essayist; all Rufus asked was that he write *something*, and that something of international fame. In this one respect, it is possible that he incurred the obloquy of being regarded as a snob. Socially speaking, all dogs are snobs; but I prefer to regard the particular homage that Rufus paid to distinguished writers, not as a mark of snobbery, but as penetrating literary criticism. He discriminated between the near-great and the great; reserving his highest favours to those who stood highest.

After his death, Rufus became a legendary figure. The story of his filling the post of librarian is well known. We have many new books lying on our library table; our neighbours and friends enter at the front door, select what books they wish to read, and depart. It was reported that those who showed literary discrimination in their selections were affectionately greeted by Rufus; those who took inferior books received snarls and snorts. This is, I regret to say, apocryphal.

6

THREE BLESSINGS

EARLY in the year 1876 my father received an invitation from Hartford, Conn., to become editor and proprietor of the *Christian Secretary*, a weekly periodical representing the Baptist denomination. Among denominational periodicals this stood high, having been founded in 1822. My father had always been a contributor, having caught at an early age (by seeing his contributions in type) what Oliver Wendell Holmes called 'lead poisoning.' His first work as an editor was in his schooldays at the Connecticut Literary Institution at Suffield, when he and another boy edited the school paper. My father loved everything that had to do with a newspaper office; he knew how to set type, and in our house in New Haven, he had a printing press and several cases of type.

He was sixty years old, and though he was in constant demand as a preacher, he knew the average congregation preferred younger pastors; there was every reason why he should go to Hartford. Accordingly, in the Spring of 1876 the family moved to the capital city of Connecticut, where he rented a house at 137 Sigourney Street.

Although the break in my formal education, in my being forced to leave the University Grammar School at Providence, set me back at least two years, in every other way the move to Hartford was for me fortunate; and in three definite ways.

My father had always had a large private library, but apart from some standard sets of classics, the library was almost entirely theological. Now, however, as he was in charge of a weekly journal with a good circulation, the publishers sent him for review new books on every subject. So our house was filled with the latest novels, essays, poems, histories, biographies, and books of travel. What this meant to me it is not necessary to emphasize. I had always read everything I could lay my hands on; and now, for the next fifteen years, from the age of eleven to the age of twenty-six, I had God's plenty. But my efforts were not confined to reading. When I was fourteen, I read among the new books, Higginson's *Young Folks' Book of American Explorers*, and my father asked me to review it for the paper! He put in a prefatory note giving the name and age of the new literary critic. This was the first book I ever reviewed in print; the first of many thousands, for I never stopped from that day to this.

When I was sixteen, seventeen, and eighteen, some books which had an influence on me were the successive volumes of the American Statesmen Series, edited by John T. Morse, Jr., who was still active at the age of ninety-six. I was led by these to read other works in American political history, and when, at the age of seventeen, I read Daniel Webster's speech of the Seventh of March 1850, I was completely converted to Webster's point of view; although I had been taught by my parents and by everyone else who mentioned the subject, to believe the opposite. It pleases me today that the best authorities on American history believe that the speech of the Seventh of March, which ruined Webster in New England, was the wisest, most far-seeing, most patriotic, most unselfish action of his career.

I shall never forget the evening in 1882 when I sat down under the gas-light to read Froude's *Life of Carlyle*. This book became a lifelong inspiration; Carlyle's writings and books about Carlyle have had a continuous influence on me. I read *Sartor Resartus* before going to college; in a later chapter I shall speak of the effect of Carlyle's *Heroes*; in 1884 when I was a sophomore appeared *Obiter Dicta*, the book that made Augustine Birrell famous; the first essay in it was on Carlyle, and I read it with excitement. About forty years later, when I was slowly recovering from a nervous breakdown I began to read David Alec Wilson's monumental *Life of Carlyle*; it had a good deal to do with my convalescence, because I became so absorbed in it I forgot my despondency; I read every word of the six volumes as they appeared in successive years. Although Mr. Wilson hated Froude I cared nothing about that controversy. I have always been grateful to Froude for arousing my interest in Carlyle when I was seventeen, and grateful to Mr. Wilson for bringing out his work just when I needed it most.

Not only do I owe my initial reading of Carlyle to Froude, but it was through this biography that I began to read a far greater writer, Goethe. Carlyle talked so much of Goethe that I read his translation of *Wilhelm Meister* before I was eighteen. It interested me enormously; the first composition I wrote for the Yale undergraduate *Literary Magazine* was on Philina. I have always been very fond of Philina, and think Wilhelm failed to appreciate her. She was not morally impeccable, but she illuminates every scene in which she appears and when she leaves the story it is like the death of Mercutio.

In my Junior year at college I went to hear the Emma Abbott Opera Company in *Mignon*. I had no idea the Mignon was the Mignon of my beloved novel; but when I saw the characters (so intimately familiar to my mind) appear on the stage, Wilhelm, Philina, Laertes, Friedrich, and the rest, I had a succession of thrills, and this opera has always had for me an especial fascination.

While I was still a schoolboy, I read Bayard Taylor's

translation of *Faust*, not only the best of the numerous translations of that work, but one of the greatest translations of any work. Of course I could not understand much of *Faust*; but it is well for boys and girls to read some authors and some books that are beyond their stage of development. I was conscious of greatness, as one obtains through shifting clouds transient views of the Matterhorn.

I *live* with Goethe as I live with Shakespeare and with Browning. Browning made the poet Cleon say that after his death his soul would be in men's hearts. Although Cleon himself got no comfort out of this, Goethe's soul has been in my heart for fifty years. I suppose I think of him every day of my life.

I have the highest intellectual respect for those three towering men of genius of the eighteenth century—Goethe, Voltaire, Benjamin Franklin, all of whom, fortunately for the world, lived to be over eighty. They were lovers of liberty and were more civilized than the majority of educated persons today.

Incidentally, in my boyhood I became fond of the offices and composing room of the *Christian Secretary*. I used to go there many times outside of school hours, set type from a 'stick,' distribute type, and fold papers every Tuesday afternoon as they came from the big press.

Like many boys of those days, I owned a small printing press, run by hand, on which I printed cards and various trivialities. My first appearance as an editor was at the age of twelve. With the assistance of another small boy, Charles A. Kellogg as 'publisher,' I edited *The Midget* and indeed wrote the entire first number, including the advertisements. I contributed an original poem, the first instalment of a novel called *Captain Chas. Plympton* (a naval officer who got into action in the first paragraph) and various items of local news. We returned the money extracted from subscribers, as the first number was also the last.

The second definite benefit that I received from our residence in Hartford was social, and of great value. The difference in the public schools in Hartford from those I had attended in New Haven and Providence was as great as if I had been in another world. I do not believe there has ever been any Grade School or any Public High School anywhere in America, equal to the West Middle District School and the High School of Hartford in the seventies and eighties.

My parents were more concerned with my spiritual and intellectual development than they were with my social behaviour; rather the opposite of most parents today, who think that if their children are healthy and have good manners, nothing more will be required. In my case what I needed was dancing-school, and my aunt in vain implored my parents to send me there, for I was the only boy among my playmates in Hartford—literally the only one—who did not know how to dance. But my parents believed that dancing, along with theatres and cards, was wicked. I could not help learning something about social behaviour from the boys in the Hartford schools; for while some of them were dissipated and smutty in conversation, nearly all of them were well-dressed and had what seems to me now (by comparison with my own) the manners of French diplomats. Perhaps I can give an idea of the social prestige of the Public High School when I affirm that there was not a single boy or girl in Hartford eligible to enter the High School who was anywhere else, except for one reason, deficiency of brains. It was emphatically *the thing* to go to the Public School.

The third definite benefit that I received from outside was the intimate friendship and influence of Frank Gay. When my father took over the *Christian Secretary*, one of the young men who worked in its office was Frank Gay, who was then about eighteen. He became a member of our family; he had a room to himself, and ate his meals with us. He was mainly self-educated; but although I spent two years at Harvard and over forty at Yale and came into intimate contact with the finest specimens of American youth, I can say honestly that I have never known a more perfect gentleman than Frank Gay. He was intelligent, was widely read, had an almost infallible taste in literature and the fine arts, was good-natured and full of fun, and yet had a quiet dignity that made him, wholly unconsciously, a model of good behaviour. Six or seven years older, his influence on me was very great. I never heard him mention religion, but he was a church-member, and he adored my mother; he could not have loved her more if he had been her own flesh and blood.

Having had to work hard for his living when many other boys of his age were in High School preparing for college, he was not an athlete; he never played any games; but I, who have always been a playboy, got plenty of that recreation at school. Frank Gay used to talk with me about books, music, the theatre, and other matters of serious import; and his example was as powerful as his precepts. He was ambitious, and after some months in our house and at the office, he secured a position in a Hartford Library, where he was rapidly promoted, soon to be the head of the Watkinson Library, and became one of the famous Librarians of America.

When I was twelve, I went to the Library one day, to take out the *Outward Bound* Series of Oliver Optic, and Frank Gay asked me why I read so much trash. I replied that I read it because I liked it. He then suggested that I read Shakespeare; I rather resented this, because I thought he was like a physician giving me a prescription. He then proposed that I should read one play by Shakespeare and that if I did not like it, he would never ask me to read another, and furthermore would keep me informed as to every new book by Oliver Optic that came to the Library. This seemed to me a fair proposal. He gave me *Julius Caesar*. I read this with such excitement that I went on to read others, and then, after reading fifteen or twenty plays, partly because I wanted to, partly out of bravado, I read the Complete Works. My taste was not very good; I enjoyed *Titus Andronicus* more than I enjoyed *Hamlet* and for obvious reasons; but the stories in Shakespeare filled me with delight; and became part of the furniture of my boyish mind.

These three influences, the new books that came for review, the social manners of my schoolmates, and the direct guidance of Frank Gay, deserve especial mention.

7

FIRST DIARY

HERE are extracts from a diary I kept in 1879, aged 14. I printed in large inky letters the following on the first page:

DIARY OF WILLIAM LYON PHELPS
CONTAINING WITHIN ITS PAGES A PERSONAL ACCOUNT OF
HIS EVENTFUL AND INTERESTING (to him) LIFE

I certainly had a happy childhood in Hartford. Over and over again I wrote, 'I had a splendid time all day.' 'Lots of fun today.' Occasionally these happy reflexions were interrupted by adverse comments on school and on my teachers, who for the most part, were kind enough. 'Miss K——, (big fool), thought I was doing something, and moved my seat. I think she is a FOOL. . . . Had a tremendous snowfight on Asylum Ave. After supper, sung some. I read *Little Lights Along Shore*. I finished the book. The next book I intend to read is the *Odyssey*.'

I attended a boys' prayer-meeting. 'I led. I read the 53d Chapter of Isaiah. We had 18 there. Sam Coit said, "How splended it would be if we could say, as Paul said, 'I have fought the good faith.'" He got matters mixed up.'
Saturday, Jan. 11, 1879. 'Played all day. Too tired to write any more.'
Sunday, Jan. 12. 'Went to church this morning, and Mr. Emerson preached, but I did not give good attention.'
Monday, Jan. 13. 'This evening, just before supper, I got caught in Berryman's sled, and accidentally, the word

48

(Damn) escaped my lips. Berryman said something about speaking in meeting. I told him I did not mean to swear, that the word was accidental, but I must see him some more about it.'

Tuesday, Jan. 14. 'Saw Berryman, and fixed it all right.'

Here are other entries for the same month.

'Studied a very little on my Algebra this evening, and could not get a single example. Yours truly.'

'This evening, a mouse ran in the buttery, and I nearly hit him with a boot. We must have a cat. When I think of the dear departed Thomas, I feel as tho' no cat could equal him in catlike beauty, skill and strength.'

I bought a book from my brother about this time, and on the flyleaf I wrote, 'Sold to him by his darling brother.'

The Principal of the Hartford High School was Joseph Hall, and he surprised me one day. 'However cross or strict Mr. Hall may be in school, he is a bully fellow out of it. At the junction, he and Joe came along in a sleigh, and Mr. Hall asked me if I did not want to hook on. He waited for me, and then we went off. I got off a little beyond the Congregational Church.' (Rev. Joseph Twichell's.)

Every day we took our sleds to school and tried to hook on sleighs. We usually succeeded and thus got hauled through the snow all the way to school and back again, both for morning and afternoon sessions; a method of locomotion not to be sneezed at.

The silver lining. 'It rained a good deal last night, spoiling the sleighing, but making it splendid for snowballing.'

And here is an entry (28 *Jan.* 1879) that, apart from the original spelling, expresses my present sentiments. 'Finished the *Odyssey* this evening. I like it very well, though it is not near as much to my liking as the ILEAD.'

Sunday, Feb. 2, 1879. 'Ed Tuller asked me to lead the young people's meeting, and after some hesitation, I accepted . . . I hope I shall lead well. My voice is changing.'

Feb. 6. 'Been sick all day, and did not go to school. I went out and snowballed a little this p.m. . . . I went to the Institute and got *Love me little, love me long,* and *Hard Cash,* both by Chas. Reade.'

Friday, Feb. 7. 'Headache still continues, and I did not go to school.'

Saturday, Feb. 8. 'Headache does not trouble me today. I went sliding on Dummy's Hill . . . At 9 o'clock p.m., I took a splendid bath, not having bathed since before Thanksgiving.'

Feb. 13. 'Drydie (my brother) brought home from the Institute *White Lies,* by Reade, and *Frank, the Young Naturalist,* by Fosdick. Mama will not let me read any more of Reade's, but I read the other nearly thro'.'

Feb. 19. 'I read the entire book of Psalms today. This morning I finished *Jean Teterol's Idea,* (by Cherbuliez), and in the afternoon and eve. read 2 books of *The Gunboat Series.* (*Frank on a Gunboat,* etc.) . . . Mama and Papa went to Governor Andrews' party, and Mama looked beautiful dressed in green silk.'

Feb. 21. 'This p.m. I finished my Bible for the 2nd time, and got $1.28 for it.'

Feb. 24. 'I don't know what *is* the matter with me. I have a headache every day from morning till night. To the horrors of headache was added the thick darkness of toothache.'

7 *March.* 'Went to prayer meeting at Tyng's house. Something was the matter with me, for I laughed all through. I felt very bad, but it could not be helped.'

2 *May.* Mr. and Mrs. John M. Ney took us with their children for a long drive to Glastonbury, where we got trailing arbutus and ate wintergreen. 'I think I shall always

remember this afternoon with pleasure, I had such a splendid, nobbie, bully, etc. time.' (And I always have remembered it.)

10 *May*. 'Yesterday Papa got me a bully spring suit, that only cost $5. I don't see how he got it so cheap. Everybody guesses about $10 as its price.'

14 *May* 1879. 'Miss Kipp, to whom we recite Grecian History, is bully. I thought she was going to be duced bad. We recite Caesar to Childs, who is quite good. Algebra to Knibloe. They have got an infernal idea in regard to Latin this year. They make us learn the Latin by heart. No use in it whatever.'

23 *May*. 'Bought and ate a pound of dried apples, which nearly made me puke and be sick.'

8 *June*. 'Ajax (our white cat) had a fight with a rat, killing him. Her eye is so swollen it is almost closed, and she is so weak and sick this morning, that she can hardly walk and won't eat. She is better this p.m., and eats. I hope she will live.'

9 *June*. 'I am about sure Ajax will live. *Beata et felix Felis!*'

10 *June*. At a church supper. 'After supper, some of the ladies played Fan Drill, charging 20 cents admission. Mama treated us to it, and I thought it was worth about 2 cts. They made over $20 on it.'

11 *June*. 'Bullard fell off a fence and hurt his arm, tomorrow or today, I forget which, as this diary was written some days after.'

9 *July*. Our literary club. 'Kellogg's composition was on Forepaugh's Difficulties in getting animals for his show. Bullard's was on The Youth of Washington. Mine was on Capt. Pedge Hash. Kellogg roared several times at his own wit. It was a pretty fair meeting.'

13 *July*. 'Finished *Little Men* this p.m. I think it spoilt both *Little Women* and *Little Men* not to have Jo marry Laurie.'

Wednesday, 16 *July* 1879. This was the day of the famous
tornado at Wallingford, Conn., the only one in our history until 1938. 'Today it was the hottest day it has
been in 25 years. It was intolerable. Bronson and I had
our lemonade stand out at 7 o'clock, to get the start of
Paton and Berryman. They were terrible mad when
they found us there. We hauled in 63 cents. Went swimming at about 10'clock, and stayed in 2 hours and a half.
The water was bully. The weather was still and hot,
when suddenly the clouds covered the sky, and there was
a tremendous wind. It was one of the most fearful winds
I ever saw. A great tree was blown down across our
swimming place and one near Cushman's factory. Anna
Bullard was reading a book on her piazza, when the
wind dashed the book out of her hand, for 5 or 4 feet.
The Bullards gave me some lemon ice and cream, which
was very good. There were several tornadoes out West,
and heavy thunder-storms.'

17 *and* 18 *Oct.* 'This morning, George Peters (afterwards
astronomer at the U.S. Naval Observatory in Washington) and I walked to Cottage Grove. We lugged a
hatchet, two infernal blankets, lunch, and my gun, with
ammunition. On the way, we killed a ground sparrow, a
warbler. When we got there, we felled trees, and built a
hut, in the thick woods. I killed a Downy Woodpecker.
We slept comfortably all night. We heard an animal and
loaded our gun in the night. The next morning shot a
ground sparrow, a warbler, and a bluebird. We got home
about one p.m. I shot an English sparrow on the way
home. Had perfectly splendid fun.'

19 *Oct.* 'Dr. Stone's father was suddenly killed, and he
has left town for the place where his father lived. So
Mr. Minor preached today. I think he looks like an
owl.'

31 *Oct.* 'Our Greek teacher, Mr. Perrin, is a bully fellow.'

17 *Nov.* 'Arthur and I have had headaches all day. Arthur got his from football. But I'll be darned if I know how I got mine.'

About this time my brother Arthur and I learned Hog Latin, where each word is spelled out and is unintelligible unless one knows the key; for example: SUSHASHYOU-TUTYOUPUP means Shut up. 'As I was standing at the foot of the staircase in Batterson's Block, a group of factory or office girls came out together, and to my surprise they were all cursing and swearing in Hog Latin. GUGOD-UDDADAMUMYOU means G—— D—— you! As they did not imagine anyone could understand what they were saying, they were very much astonished when I called out in the same language, "Shut up!"'

24 *Nov.* 'I began a small manuscript paper this morning, entitled the *Hartford Daily*. I got 4 subscribers.'

26 *Nov.* 'Edited my paper this a.m. Kicked football this p.m.'

27 *Nov.* Thanksgiving. 'Had a bully day. Skated all the morning on Sharp's. It is splendid.' One of the boys who skated with us was Charlie Dillingham, who afterwards became the famous theatre manager. Even as a boy, he had the enthusiasm so characteristic of his later years. I remember his saying that day at Sharp's, 'I'd rather skate than eat.'

3 *Dec.* 'Read *Castle Foam* all day. It is a dreadfully melancholy book. If I owned it, I'd pitch it in the fire.'

11 *Dec.* 'Read *The Woman in White* all day, pretty near.'

28 *Dec.* A rather pessimistic story of this particular Sabbath Day. 'Went to Church, Sunday School, and both meetings in the evening. As old fool —— would not be superintendent any more, old Bullet-headed —— was elected. Other officers the same. Weather warm. A tremenjous thaw. Spoilt sleighing. Spoilt coasting. Spoilt skating.'

2 *Jan*. 1880. 'My birthday today. (15.) Got splendid presents. From Mama, a checker-board and men, a great box of tools, fifty cents, two books, and a candy. Dryden, an elegant pocket-book. From Papa, 1 doz. collars. From Arthur, figuring pack, his watch and key. Papa also gave me a watch chain.'

9 *Jan*. Here came melancholia, which lasted some weeks. 'This noon and afternoon I felt dreadfully. Awful bad, somehow. I was glad when Libbie came.' (My aunt Miss Elizabeth Linsley, who came for a visit from her home in Stratford.)

10 *Jan*. 'Had the same horrible feeling this a.m. Finished Jules Verne's *Tribulations of a Chinaman*. Went hunting with Al Talcott. Shot a nuthatch and a sparrow. I hope Libbie will stay a great while.'

15 *Jan*. 'Could not eat anything, hardly. A very sick feeling. Dr. G. Pierrepont Davis gave me a prescription, and after school, I got the stuff in the shape of one enormous pill. Had to wait for it about three-quarters of an hour, and wound up by losing it. Drydie got it over again in l'evening. Took huge pill. Went down like a bullet.'

16 *Jan*. 'O how much better I feel!'

2 *Feb*. 'February has 5 Sundays this month, which has not happened for 30 years, and will not happen again for forty years.' Forty years seemed an immense distance ahead, at that time. But the year 1920, which produced its five Sundays in February according to my prophecy, now seems a good while ago.

We never paid any attention to climate or to seasons but went out shooting in ice and snow and rain and mud.

28 *Feb*. 'Frank (Hubbard), Pete (George Peters) and I had a good hunt today. I killed two warblers, one bluebird, and a nuthatch. Frank knocked over a magnificent robin. He picked him on the wing. His breast and guts were a bright red. Frank also shot a bluebird and blue jay, the

latter falling into a mudpuddle, and receiving some hurt thereby. When we got home I stuffed Frank's bluebird and my robin which Frank gave me. I could not get the wire through the knee joint, so I did not mount them.'

Much of our shooting was done in what is now a densely populated part of Hartford. Curious that we should have found robins and bluebirds, etc., in February.

8 *March.* 'This morning I cleaned out my meadow-lark, preparatory to stuffing him. This noon I fixed his eyes with shoe-buttons. Fred Keep came over this evening and put the wires up his legs. I then finished him up, and mounted him on a board. He looks splendid, and is in a natural position.'

14 *March.* 'Read *Hal, the Story of a Clodhopper,* by W.M.F.Round, all the p.m.' Round was a popular author in those days.

People who lived in Hartford many years ago will remember that when the horse cars came up the hill from the railway station to the junction of Farmington and Asylum Avenues, an extra horse was put on for that brief climb. The man in charge of him had to walk back and begin over again with the next car. This he did all day, and it was not what one would call 'a rowdy life,' which may explain his ill temper.

18 *March.* 'Clad Wiley accidentally hit (with a snowball) the old Irishman that takes up the extra horse to go up the hill with the horsecar. The old devil immediately turned around, and picking up a couple of rocks, hurled one at my head. I managed to dodge it, but he came running up, and nabbing me by the throat, he drew back his fist, and I thought I was a gone-cat. I told him over and over again that I didn't hit him, but that only made him wilder. *Denique* he went away, leaving a track of mud across my face, where he had hit me. We got it off.'

20 *March*. 'Did not go hunting today. Why not? None of your bizness. Snowballed all day. Had bully fun. Finished *In Silk Attire*, by William Black.'

Beginning with January of this year 1880, my marks at school, which had been low for three years, suddenly jumped up to nearly perfect, and I never had any trouble with school or college marks the rest of my life (except that I was not good in mathematics in college).

25 *March*. 'Rec'd my marks for this month today. 9.9 in Latin, 9.9 in Algebra, 9.8 in Latin (another course), 9 in Reading. Reading does not count. Whole average, Nine-Nine!' Perfect was 10.

Thus one continual worry and terror, which had pursued me like Black Care for three years, was permanently eliminated.

1 *April*. 'Glory of glories! Miss Snowball Jackson Diable, alias Mrs. Tiger Tomcat, hatched precisely one kitten today! It is an image of its father, Mr. Tiger Tomcat. In the Geyser Box! The kitten's name is Epaminondas Alcibiades Pentacosiomedimni. It is awful cunning.'

17 *April*. 'Fished all day in West Hartford with Rich Hubbard. We caught 15 bullheads and three eels. One or two of the bullheads were a foot long.'

Some difficulties with a prayer-meeting at the High School.

25 *May*. 'We had a boys' meeting in the little German recitation room, as of yore. Jim Reynolds led, and Lou Robinson, Hiram Loomis, Wilson, Dan Bidwell, Shipman Major, Ned Fellowes and some others were present. The meeting was ruined by Dan, who made funny speeches, called Jim " Mr. Goodell," and so forth, throughout the meeting. I spoke and prayed.'

5 *June* 1880. 'I saw the ball game between Company K and the nine made up with Sedgwick pitcher, F. Johnson catcher, W. T. Redfield 1st base, Henry Welch, 2d base,

Rob Way 3d base, Dan Glazier shortstop, Deming left
field, Arthur Shipman and later Jim Reynolds right field,
and Kong, center-field. Company K came out one run
ahead.' 'Hen' Redfield was one of the stars for Company K.

9 *June*. 'Went to Christian Home for supper tonight. Had
stacks of fun. C. Abell, Goodnow, Derrick, Josh Allen,
Frank and Charles Cooley, Hooker etc. were there.
Good supper.'

8

REFLEXIONS ON ANIMALS

PERHAPS the surest test of civilization is man's attitude toward animals. Ill treatment of animals is not necessarily the sign of deliberate cruelty in the torturer; it is more often an indication of a defective imagination, an inability to understand. Francis Parkman in *The Oregon Trail* spoke of the cruelty to birds and other animals by the Indians, especially by the Indian children, who showed no remorse or shame after those abominable practices. Many peasants with primitive minds treat animals badly; the paradox is that we call it brutality. Also, the sense of humour in some children needs cultivating; they laugh at insanity, at the sound of a foreign language, at a dog with a can tied to his tail.

Of course, it is possible for children to become over-sentimentalized. This attitude is well indicated by the familiar anecdote of the small boy looking at the picture of Christian martyrs delivered to the lions: 'Oh, look, Mama, that dear little lion in the corner isn't getting anything!' When I was a child, I woke up one night, and wept when I thought of the warm comfort of my bed and my kitten on the hard kitchen oilcloth. In the same way, those who condemn quail, partridge, and duck-shooting are, I think, over-sentimental. The only consistent attitude would be that of the vegetarian to abstain from fish, flesh, and fowl. And even then it would require only a slight stretch of the imagination to sympathize with potatoes which possibly suffer horribly when torn up by the roots.

If it is wicked to shoot quails for the table, then it is more wicked to eat chickens; for one keeps and feeds chickens only to betray them. One might easily work oneself into a frame of mind where one who eats chickens is a traitor and a murderer. After all, the child and men and women are of more importance and value than any animal; there is no sentimentality in the New Testament on this or on any other point. After reminding his audience that God never forgets a sparrow, Our Lord remarked that we are of more value than many sparrows.

When Robert Browning and others said that they would rather die than have any dog or cat suffer in order that they might be relieved from pain, these men of genius were not squarely meeting the issue. What they should have done was to balance their own children against dogs and cats.

Yet as we grow older, we are less and less willing to take the life of any animal wantonly. Why is this? Is it because we know the value of life, is it because toleration—live and let live—is the result of intellectual development, or what is the reason? Recently as we were playing golf, a large, harmless, black snake crawled across the fairway. The caddies were unanimous for death, and the four players for acquittal.

I used to wonder why it was as a small boy that I delighted in shooting and killing birds, any bird, edible or otherwise, for I was not cruel by nature, and could not bear to see any animal ill-treated or in pain. Yet, when I was too small to own a gun, I would get up at dawn, armed with David's implement, and try to kill robins and bluebirds. On the rare occasions when I succeeded, I felt thrills of joy, unshaded by regret. Later, when I owned a gun, it was much the same. It was only in riper years that I never shot except at something that I wanted to eat, or at something predatory. Apart from the pleasure of hunting, which is instinctive in every boy, I finally found the true explanation; I found it in an early novel by Zona Gale. A girl is out walking with one of 'nature's noblemen,' and when he killed a beautiful bird, she rebuked him sharply, much to his bewilderment, for he was no more conscious of guilt than was Parsifal when he killed the swan. In response to her question, he said that he wanted to see the bird *nearer*. Zona Gale's explanation is the true one. Not only did I feel a thrill when I shot a bird, but another, keener and quite different thrill when I held the dead body in my hand. The bird is an elusive creature, apparently inaccessible; one never has him near enough to examine completely and leisurely; hence the desire to hold him.

Now those were the days before the Kodak; hunting with opera-glass and camera is better for the boy and much better for the birds. Yet that same element of destructiveness characteristic of boys is also characteristic of adults who have matured only bodily. Every deserted building has its windows broken. Small boys and stupid men really do love to smash things. I was impressed when a contractor, who employed thousands of workmen, told me that when his men were engaged in construction work of any kind, work that meant creating and developing something, most of them worked mechanically, slowly and without zeal; but when the order came to demolish a tall building, they worked with enthusiasm—smashing, tearing, destroying.

9

EARLY FRIENDSHIPS, MARK TWAIN, AND BILLIARDS

WHEN my parents in the Spring of 1876 decided to move to Hartford, they unconsciously arranged my marriage, which was to take place nearly seventeen years later. I first met my wife when I was eleven years old.

At the West Middle School in Hartford there was a boy two years older than I whose name was Frank Watson Hubbard. We became friends and there has never been a cloud on our friendship during sixty years.

His father, Langdon Hubbard, was living in Huron County, Michigan, whither he had gone originally from Connecticut as a pioneer, and was engaged in an extensive lumbering business. There were no facilities out there for education; hence he had sent his three children, Frank, Richard, and Annabel to Hartford, where they lived with three maiden aunts, and had entered the West Middle School.

Frank and I became inseparable. We were both fond of outdoor games and especially of shooting. He owned a long, single-barrel, muzzle-loading shotgun, and equipped with this primitive implement, we spent entire Saturdays in the pursuit of robins, meadowlarks, yellowhammers, and other songbirds, which, I hasten to add, we always brought home, cooked, and ate with relish. I remember one winter day, when we were out in the fields and woods, we became very hungry, and made an excellent meal off English sparrows. The wild country over which we hunted extended from Woodland Street to Talcott Mountain.

The next year when I was twelve, my father allowed me to buy a double-barrelled muzzle-loading shot gun, which I bought from Charlie Shepard for six dollars. My conservative breast crossed by straps holding powderhorn and shotpouch, I thought I resembled Hawkeye.

It was owing to this gun that I became a criminal, sought by the police and by detectives, and that for the first and last time in my life, a price was set on my head. It happened in this way. I was shooting with a schoolmate, George Peters. We became separated in the woods along the banks of Hog River. Suddenly I saw, sweeping around a bend in the stream, a flock of white ducks, which I supposed to be wild. I let them have both barrels, killing two and mortally wounding three. Attracted by the report, George came up, and was overcome with horror. I fully expected him to be envious of my wonderful good luck; but instead of that, he cried, ' What have you done? Those are Mark Twain's prize ducks. If you are caught, he will put you in jail. Run for your life!'

My flush of joy turned to the icy sweat of fear. I slipped around through the woods to Frank Hubbard's house, and told him he was the only friend I had in the world. He advised me to reach home by roundabout ways, and not to come near Hog River for some time. I got home safely.

The next morning I read in the Hartford newspaper a prominently displayed notice from Mark Twain, offering a substantial financial reward for the apprehension of the 'miscreant' who had killed his white ducks. Here I was, a criminal, sought by the police, with a price set on my head. For several months I avoided Hog River and was in terror. Years later, when I became acquainted with Mark Twain, I never dared to tell him of this particular episode; for although he was the world's greatest living humorist, there were certain subjects to which his sense of humour did not extend.

Mark Twain's house stood on Farmington Avenue, near Forest Street; his neighbours were Harriet Beecher Stowe, Charles Dudley Warner, and William Gillette. His house had been built according to his own ideas, with the kitchen in front, so that the cook and housemaids would not have to run through the living-rooms and hall to see a procession go by. The billiard room was on the top floor and a tiny balcony projected from one of the windows; nearly all dwellings built in the eighteen-seventies had abscesses of that kind. I often used to see Mark Twain standing in his shirt-sleeves on that balcony, the eternal cigar in his mouth and a billard cue in his hand. While his opponent was playing, Mark would come out for air. Billiards was his only athletic exercise; he always said, 'Never stand up when you can sit down; never sit down when you can lie down.'

However, I frequently saw Mark Twain on the street; for although he was fond of driving with his wife and children in an open carriage, he must have walked down town every clear day, for I saw him often. He was so conspicuous that the jest of G. K. Chesterton applies perfectly. Some admirer said to the Englishman, 'It must be wonderful just to take a walk and have everybody know who you are.' 'Yes,' replied Chesterton, 'and if they don't know, they ask.' The Englishman had been made noticeable by nature; the American by deliberate choice. His dark brown hair was long, and fell in masses around his neck, having apparently received his personal attention. In cold weather, instead of an overcoat, he wore a jacket of sealskin, with the fur side outside; in walking, he had the rolling gait of a sailor. He was distinguishable a long way off. People stopped when he passed them, and remained as if hypnotized, staring after his diminishing figure. Those who had seen him before found him well worth seeing again; those who had never seen him asked the nearest by-stander (sometimes me) who he was, and their already awakened curiosity received a lift by the answer.

Although the name Mark Twain was familiar to all Americans, he had in those days more notoriety than fame. I do not believe there was anyone in Hartford who knew then what we know now, that he is one of the world's great literary artists. He was a funny man, and people were fond of him because he made them laugh. His most intimate friend was the Reverend Joseph H. Twichell, pastor of the Asylum Avenue Congregational Church; and Mark, though he had lost all religious belief, usually attended church. Mr. Twichell was universally beloved in Hartford for his sincerity and courage.

At church-meetings, held on some weekday night, Mark frequently entertained the audience, which crowded the room every time it was announced that he would speak. I remember on one occasion, as Mr. Twichell preceded him up the stairs leading to the platform, the audience burst into tumultuous applause. Mark, pointing to Twichell's back, called out to the audience, 'He thinks it's for *him*.'

Three of these occasions I remember very well indeed, though none of us knew that we were listening to a man of genius. First, I heard him read in 1876 from the novel just published, *Tom Sawyer*; he chose the episode of Tom's fight with the citified boy. Second, I heard him read from *Huckleberry Finn* from manuscript, some time before the year 1885, when it was published. Third, I heard him recite his own ghost-story *The Golden Arm*, and I remember the shriek of surprised horror that rose from the audience when he reached the climax.

He was the greatest master of the art of public reading then living, though we did not know it. It was an art he studied with infinite pains, and later wrote about with great detail, telling others who wished to cultivate it of the immense importance of the *pause*. The same scrupulous accuracy that made him so careful of dialect and italics in everything he prepared for publication (I have examined many of his pencilled notes on the margins of his proof-sheets) made him pay the utmost attention to the proper emphasis in reading aloud. He told us in *Tom Sawyer* and elsewhere of his disgust with pulpit-reading of the Bible and of hymns, where no attention was paid to the meaning of the passages.

In the seventies and eighties Mark's favourite poet was Browning; he used to say he could make any so-called obscure passage transparently clear merely by reading it aloud. His daughter Clara allowed me to examine his copies of Browning; they are covered with his pencil marks to indicate how they should be read. In Hartford a club was formed which met regularly to hear him read Browning's poetry. How I wish we had gramophone records!

On 23 February 1887, he wrote in pencil, ' Remark dropped after finishing "Easter Day"—& requested to "write it down."

' One's glimpses & confusions, as one reads Browning, remind me of looking through a telescope (the small sort which you must move with your hand, not clock-work): You toil across dark spaces which are (to your lens) empty; but every now & then a splendor of stars & suns bursts upon you & fills the whole field with flame.'

Here is a letter he wrote, first printed a few years ago by Benjamin De Casseres in a thin volume called *When Huck Finn Went Highbrow*—limited to 125 copies.

HARTFORD, DEC. 2/87

MY DEAR MRS. FOOTE:

Well, people & things do swap places in most unexpected ways in this world. Twenty years ago I was a platform-humorist & you a singer of plaintive Scotch ballads that were full of heart-break &

tears. And now we have changed places. You are platform-humorist (among other things), & I am reader to a Browning class! I can't imagine a completer reversal of roles than this. I hope you find your changes as pleasant as I do mine, and that you are as willing as I to let the thing remain as it is; for I wouldn't trade back for any money.

Now when you come to think of it, wasn't it a curious idea—I mean, for a dozen ladies of (apparently) high intelligence to elect me their Browning-reader? Of course you think I declined—at first; but I didn't. I'm not the declining sort. I would take charge of the constellations if I were asked to do it. All you need in this life is ignorance & confidence; then success is sure. I've been Browning-reader forty-two weeks, now, & my class has never lost a member by desertion. What do you think of that, for a man in a business he *wasn't* brought up to?

I wonder if—in one particular—your experience in your new avocation duplicates mine. For instance, I used to explain Mr. Browning—but the class won't stand that. They say that my reading imparts clear comprehension—& that is a good deal of a compliment, you know; but they say the poetry never gets obscure till I begin to explain it—which is only frank, & that is the softest you can say about it. So I've stopped being expounder, & thrown my heft on the reading. Yes, & with vast results—nearly unbelievable results. I don't wish to flatter anybody, yet I will say this much: put me in the right condition & give me room according to my strength, & I can read Browning so Browning himself can understand it. It sounds like stretching, but it's the cold truth. Moral: don't explain your author; read him right & he explains himself.

I wish you every possible success, & shall be as glad as your own heart to hear that you have won it.

Sincerely your friend

S. L. CLEMENS

It seems strange today that his literary reputation was so long delayed. He would undoubtedly have been more famous if he had not been so funny. Calvin Coolidge, who was Class Humorist on his graduation from Amherst, observed that funny men never got anywhere in politics; he made up his mind he would never be funny again.

Mark in the eighties and even in the nineties was so

generally regarded as a professionally funny man that contemporary critics and historians of American literature ranked him with Josh Billings and Artemus Ward and Petroleum V.Nasby, never where he belonged—with Emerson and Hawthorne.

Yet his humour often had an undertone of either common sense or philosophy or both. I can see him now as I saw him when I was thirteen years old, addressing the graduating class at the West Middle School, saying in his slow drawl, 'Boys and girls, the subject of my remarks today is Methuselah. Methuselah lived to be 969 years old; but what of that? There was nothing doing. He might as well have lived to be a thousand. You boys and girls will see more in the next fifty years than Methuselah saw in his whole lifetime.'

There was probably more universal interest in the personality of Mark Twain than in any other American writer, living or dead. The whole world read him and the whole world loved him. No other writer ever succeeded in making an assumed name so truly a household word. George Eliot and Anatole France had nothing like the range of his reputation nor do they seem so sure of immortality. George Eliot belongs to English literature and Anatole France belongs to French literature; Mark Twain belongs to the world.

Had he lived and died as a pilot on the Mississippi, his personality might have made him a legendary figure; had he succeeded in his mining enterprises in Nevada, he might now be remembered as one of our Western pioneers. It was only by an accident that he became a literary man; and it was only when the colossal force of his mighty genius found its full expression in *Tom Sawyer* and in *Huckleberry Finn* that he was able to produce imperishable masterpieces.

He did everything possible to escape his fate and fame. Had the Civil War not stopped passenger traffic on the river, he would have continued contentedly as a pilot, for he had reached the summit of his ambition—the pilot was the king of the Mississippi. Had he not failed of becoming a mining millionaire by a few minutes, he would have enjoyed his fortune with his friends on the frontier.

Even as a writer, Mark Twain almost always miscast himself. He thought that *Joan of Arc* was his masterpiece, for he had done his best to make it so. (Barrett Wendell said shrewdly that Shakespeare probably thought his own finest work was *Coriolanus*.) Mark Twain wanted to be a philosopher, but somehow cheerfulness kept breaking in.

The worst case of stage-fright I have ever witnessed happened at Unity Hall one night in the presence of Mark Twain. George W. Cable, from the deep South, a writer quite unlike Erskine Caldwell or William Faulkner, had acquired a national reputation through his novels, *The Grandissimes* and others. He made his first appearance as a lecturer and reader in Hartford, and was brilliantly introduced to the crowded house by Mark Twain. The applause was deafening. Mr. Cable stood up, looked at the audience, and could not even open his mouth. He was petrified by fear. He stood there motionless for what seemed an eternity, and he would have been there yet if Mark Twain had not risen, seized one of Cable's books which was fortunately on the platform, opened it, found a place, thrust it into Cable's hand and told him to read.

The only respect in which I resembled Mark Twain was in my passion for billiards. Unfortunately billiards was inseparably associated with the saloon, where I went seldom and always furtively. But when I was fourteen, Frank Hubbard discovered a man who wished to sell a small billiard table—it had rubber tubes for cushions—but the price was prohibitive, twenty dollars. Our total assets were seventy-five cents. Frank told me that his younger sister, Annabel, had received from her father, on his latest visit, a present of a twenty-dollar gold piece. He had vainly tried to induce her to part with it, for, as he said, of what possible use could it be to a girl? He made the tactical error of the brother-and-sister *motif*, and when that failed, he attempted stronger measures with even less success. Then he asked me to talk with her, saying 'You are more soft-hearted than I am.' He thought that while he had exhausted logic and threats, my powers of persuasion might be greater than his; and he thought accurately, for I subsequently persuaded her to become my wife.

I have never forgotten this diplomatic errand. It was Saturday night; pitch-dark and bitterly cold. I went to his front door, while he hid outside, and as she came to the door herself, I placed my face about two inches from hers, and began in tender whispers. I told her I knew how much she thought of that twenty dollars, and how natural it was for her to keep her money, after her brother had spent his; but that I myself felt it would be simply marvellous on her part to make this supreme sacrifice. 'Remember you are not doing it merely for him; my own happiness depends on getting this billiard table. We have no resources. I shall remember your kindness as long as I live.'

I made only one error in this entreaty. I told her we should regard it as a loan. The gentle expression on her face turned for a moment into one of incredulity; this was too much for even a girl to believe; we could no more have repaid that twenty dollars than we could have liquidated the national debt.

Instantly I saw that I was stating something which was not only incredible, but which also chilled the eternal woman's desire to sacrifice herself for a man. I went back to the wind-harp stop, and she whispered, 'Just wait a minute.' She went upstairs and returned with the twenty-dollar gold piece, actually looking almost as radiant as if she were receiving it. I gave her in return something of no value; and I also told her there was no girl like her in the whole world.

Armed with this twenty dollars, we hired an expressman to transfer the table from the place of purchase to my house, we agreeing to pay seventy-five cents. He asked for more after the somewhat difficult move was made, but we had wisely made our contract beforehand. The table was hoisted up three flights of stairs, and placed in a small room. It was nearly midnight, too late to play. The next day being Sunday, I was not allowed to touch it, and on Monday morning I had to go to school, from which I was not free till four o'clock. Then we made straight for that billiard table, and played till eleven o'clock, not stopping for the evening meal.

We played for large sums of fictitious money. Frank was taking the regular course in Hannum's Business College, preparatory to a banking career in Michigan. As he was bookkeeper, he secured funds amounting to about thirty thousand dollars, which looked like real money; we divided this into three parts, one for me, one for Frank, and one for a schoolmate, Francis R. Pratt. We used to play billiards for stakes of anywhere from one hundred to five hundred dollars; and I remember on one afternoon Frank Pratt won all my money; whereupon I suggested that we shake dice. I got all my money back and then all of his; he went home penniless and in tears, I having won something like twelve thousand dollars.

If older people had known what we were doing, they would have predicted an evil fate for us in later years. But we had enough excitement gambling with this imitation money to last us for the rest of our lives. I have never played any game for money.

I have played billiards and pocket billiards (pool) all my life and regard it as the best of indoor games. It seems strange to me that when we have taken so many sports from England we should have taken billiards from France. The English game of billiards is almost unknown in America and I have never seen an English billiard table in the United States. Even cricket is more popular with Americans than British billiards.

Not only do I enjoy playing, but also there is no indoor game that I have more pleasure and excitement in watching. When Frank Hubbard and I were small boys in Hartford we saw a great match at the Allyn House between the famous French champion Vignaux and Jake Schaefer (father of the present expert) at the beautiful game of cushion caroms. The highest run ever made was 77, by Sexton, but that night Schaefer ran 70. The masters of billiards in those days were Schaefer, Slosson, Sexton, Sutton, and a little later Napoleon Ives, who some believe was the greatest of them all. The excitement of the game, the bad air, the chalk dust were not good for him; and he died of tuberculosis. He was, I believe, the first expert to use a heavy cue. In the twentieth century I saw many great games played by Willie Hoppe, Schaefer the younger, Horemans, Hagenlacher, Walker Cochran, and others. Willie Hoppe has probably had a longer career in the first flight than any other player in history and seems today unbeatable at 18.1. When he was in Michigan in 1937, he was kind enough to come over to our house and play on the worst table he had ever seen. On the same day he enjoyed golf much more. Like many men who have reached the top in any form of sport, he is a very interesting person, modest and unassuming, full of good talk.

I wish the cushion carom game might be revived. Long runs are sometimes monotonous; long runs are impossible in cushion caroms, and every shot is interesting.

Watching pocket billiards I find equally exciting. I attend the championship matches every year when they are held in New York. Greenleaf, Caras, Ponzi, Rudolph, and others give me continuous thrills. Four hours of this spectacle seem like four minutes.

The champion billiard player, like the concert pianist (and the poet), is born and not made. Continuous practice is essential; but such co-ordination cannot possibly be acquired. I asked Willie Hoppe about this and he said all the practice in the world and from early childhood to maturity could not by itself make a champion.

The most famous men of letters whose sole recreation was billiards were Herbert Spencer and Mark Twain. I should like to have seen a match between them. Spencer I believe swore only once in his life; but the anecdote about his loss of a game to a young man is a classic. His billiard cue is preserved as a sacred relic in London. He was not devoid of humour; for when asked why he would not marry, he replied he was willing to marry any suitable woman. Accordingly they brought a woman to him saying she had a great mind; and left them together for several hours. Spencer said she wouldn't do at all. 'Instead of having a great mind, she has a small mind in constant activity.'

10

ASTRONOMY

AMONG my extra-curriculum activities in school at Hartford, was astronomy. I have forgotten how my interest in this subject began, but among the new books sent to my father for review was a copy of Simon Newcomb's *Popular Astronomy*; I read that book over and over again. Thomas Mills Day, son of the former editor of the *Hartford Courant*, was a boy at the West Middle School, and his family had come into the possession of a good telescope. I used to go to his front yard, formed by the intersection of Farmington and Asylum Avenues, and there spent many evenings gazing at the firmament.

I wanted a telescope of my own and had no funds. My schoolmate, Arthur Perkins, who had such a talent for scientific pursuits that his subsequently being forced into the practice of the law was a lifelong tragedy, offered to make me a telescope if I would provide the materials, the total cost of which was less than three dollars. He made a tube out of cardboard, painted it black, made a tripod, and with an object glass of two and one-half inches at one end, and an eye-piece at the other, I could see the moons of Jupiter, the crescent of Venus, occultations of stars, and such phenomena. I could not afford an achromatic eye-piece, so I had all the colours for nothing. For years I was passionately devoted to astronomy, and my interest in the subject lasted until I was compelled to take a course in astronomy in college, which was devoted wholly to mathematical calculations; the stars were neither seen nor mentioned. I was so disgusted that for years afterwards I did not consider the subject.

In 1881 I stayed up all night to observe a total eclipse of the moon; and I saw through my telescope two occultations of stars during the eclipse.

But the greatest day with my telescope came when I was seventeen—the sixth of December 1882, when from about nine in the morning till about four in the afternoon I observed the transit of Venus. Hartford was in the best position for this spectacle; two astronomers had been sent over from Germany, and were to cable WOE if the day were cloudy, WONDERFUL if it were wholly clear, and WONDERFUL-WANTING if they missed a contact and yet saw most of the transit.

My schoolmates, Day, Peters, and I had been talking of nothing else for weeks; I carried my telescope to Peters's yard where there would be a more unobstructed view of the sun. His interest in astronomy became professional and permanent, and in later years he was one of the astronomers at the United States Naval Observatory in Washington; Day has a very fine telescope in his home in New Jersey.

The transit of Venus is a very rare spectacle, coming one might say in pairs, with long intervals. There had been one in 1874 about which I knew nothing; there was this one in 1882. The next one will be in 2004, followed by one in 2012, when again there will be an interval of more than one hundred years.

Accordingly on the day before, 5 December, I asked my Latin teacher at the High School if he would kindly excuse me for the next day, as I wished to observe the transit of Venus. Like most persons, he had never heard of it, and viewed me with suspicion. He refused. Then I begged him to let me off, telling him I *must* see it. 'Oh, wait for the next one,' he said. Whereupon I asked him, 'Do you know

when the next one is coming? It will be in the year 2004.'
Then he got stuffy, and said, 'Well, I won't excuse you.' I
determined to be a martyr for the sake of science, and
stayed away from school all day, expecting to be severely
punished and possibly expelled; but I think my teacher
must have looked up the matter or consulted the Principal,
who knew something about astronomy, for when I returned to school no reference was made to my deliberately
defiant absence.

When the black disc of the planet approaches the outer
limb of the sun, the moment the two curves touch is called
the First Contact; when it touches the inner side at the last
moment before beginning its journey across the flaming expanse, it is the Second Contact; when, about seven hours
later, it has almost completed its transit, and touches the
inner curve on the other side of the sun, it is the Third Contact; and when it has fully completed its journey, and
touches the outer limb of the sun, not to repeat this performance for nearly 122 years, that is the Fourth Contact.
(I am glad that the horrible verb 'to contact' was then
unknown.)

The last two contacts show an apparent link or drop
uniting for a moment the small disc of Venus with the huge
disc of the sun, as if they shook hands on meeting and again
at parting. On this December day in 1882, the First Contact, at about nine in the morning, was partially cloudy;
but then the sky cleared and was cloudless all day, making
observations perfect. The 'link' or 'drop' in the afternoon
was very distinct.

All day long, the black disc of Venus, looking like a
smaller tennis ball, stood out plainly on the face of the sun;
many years later, 14 November 1907, I observed a transit
of Mercury, which looked like a golf ball. Transits of Mercury are fairly frequent, the next one occurring 11 November 1940.

That day in 1882 was one of the great days of my life; the spectacle was amazing in itself, and the thought that no one living would ever see it again lent a peculiar air of solemnity to the scene.

When I became a member of the American Philosophical Society, founded by Benjamin Franklin, I immediately associated myself with the astronomers, telling them I was the most enthusiastic non-mathematical astronomer in the world; that I loved the sea and sailing ships, but could not understand navigation; that I loved the stars, but could not comprehend even elementary mathematics. They received me with affection if not with respect; and I am pleased to be the only person not an astronomer making the annual dinner-pilgrimage at the hospitable home of Mr. and Mrs. Gustavus Wynne Cook, where there is probably the finest amateur observatory on the face of the earth.

In 1937 I made a pilgrimage with these astronomers to see the great telescope being made near Philadelphia for the California observatory; and as we were looking at this giant and meditating on the fact that in these days of mass production, here was one individual mechanism that took years to build, I told Harlow Shapley, Head of the Harvard University Observatory, that I, as an astronomer, had two advantages over him. This telescope costs about seven million dollars, whereas mine of 1882 cost less than three dollars; secondly, although his astronomical knowledge compared to mine was in about the same ratio, I had seen a transit of Venus, which he had never seen and never would see, even if he lived to be a hundred.

Logically, although not chronologically, I might mention here some other experiences with astronomers; for I have known many astronomers intimately. My lawn tennis partner in New Haven, Frederick L. Chase (we won second prize in the open doubles in the New England championship tournament), was an astronomer, and could play whist with us only on stormy evenings.

When I was lecturing at the University of California in the summer of 1908, I had the pleasure of visiting the great Lick Observatory on the top of a neighbouring mountain. The late Dr. W.W.Campbell and Robert Grant Aitken were Heads of this observatory and intimate friends of mine, whilst one of their predecessors, E.S.Holden, was one of the best friends I ever had, with whom I kept up an epistolary conversation until his death. Well, on my visit in 1908, Dr. Aitken told me that when in April 1906 San Francisco was slowly being destroyed by fire, he turned the great telescope directly on the city and felt as if he were looking down into Hell. There was no wind; immense districts of the city were steadily and inexorably being consumed by unconquerable and prodigious flames. He looked on with horror, unable to help.

The great astonomer George Ellery Hale was a very dear friend. He and Mrs. Hale were exceedingly kind to us when I was lecturing at the Los Angeles branch of the University of California in the summer of 1919. They took us to the summit of Mount Wilson (5,900 feet) where we saw and looked through the largest telescope in the world, the 100-inch reflector. That was the first time I saw the moons of Saturn; and the cluster in Hercules was a marvellous spectacle. We had a jolly supper with the staff; and as we descended the mountain late in the night, the lights of Pasadena made almost as gorgeous a display as anything we had seen aloft. Two bonds united Dr. Hale and me, apart from his knowledge and my love of astronomy. He worshipped cats, owned a magnificent feline; and he read a good many detective novels every month.

At one of the regular meetings of the American Philosophical Society, Professor Miller of Swarthmore College told me a remarkable story of Richard Croker, one of the most famous politicians of America, for many years the inscrutable Chief of Tammany Hall and absolute political boss of New York. Prof. Miller was Professor of Astronomy at the University of Indiana during the years when Croker was at the height of his fame in metropolitan politics; one night the telephone rang, and Miller was informed that Richard Croker was speaking. 'You don't mean Richard Croker of New York?' 'The same.' 'What can I do for you?' 'I am passing through Indiana and I thought you might be willing to let me look through the telescope.' He was cordially invited and the two men went into the observatory. Mr. Croker's remarks showed a fair knowledge of amateur astronomy. After the telescope had been turned on various objects, Mr. Croker wished to see the nebula in Orion, and was informed that would not be visible until about two o'clock in the morning. 'I shall be glad to wait for it,' said the Tammany Chief. Accordingly they stayed and after seeing it, and expressing his thanks, Mr. Croker remarked, 'I like the stars; they are dependable.'

To turn from the sublime to the ridiculous aspect of astronomy: the late Judge Elbert Hamlin, one of my pupils in the class of 1896, took as an undergraduate the course in astronomy offered by Professor William Beebe. On the final examination one of the questions was 'How many moons has Saturn?' Hamlin guessed, wrote down too many and was flunked. About fifteen years later, he happened to see in the morning paper that some additional satellites had been discovered, making the total number what he had placed on his exam paper. Immediately he sent a long telegram to Professor Beebe, quoting the newspaper cutting. 'Fifteen years ago you flunked me not knowing that my knowledge of Saturn exceeded yours. And your flunking me was a tragedy for Yale. There was the golden opportunity which would have given Yale University immortality in science by announcing a discovery fifteen years ahead of all other institutions of learning. I can forgive you for the personal insult, but it is difficult to forgive you when we remember what my discovery would have meant in adding prestige to Yale.'

Professor Beebe was delighted with this telegram; and I wish I could remember his reply.

MOODY AND SANKEY

WHEN I was fifteen, D.L.Moody and Ira Sankey came to Hartford and for many weeks held evangelistic services in the Rink. Although Americans, their great reputation had been made in England, and they came to the United States in the full flush of fame. Sankey had an uncultivated, almost hoarse baritone, but his singing was indescribably affecting. An audience of thousands in absolute stillness heard him sing 'The Ninety and Nine' or 'What Shall the Harvest Be' or the terrifying 'Almost Persuaded,' and no one ever forgot him. Moody was the greatest professional evangelist I ever heard. He had no mannerisms, very few gestures, and seldom raised his voice to a shout; but his deep and unaffected piety, his apposite figures of speech, his humour, his solid common sense, his thrilling earnestness, made him amazingly effective. He did great good and as he hated hysteria and sensationalism, he never did any harm. He was a man of genius. In later years I got to know him intimately, both at his school at Northfield and during his visits to Yale; it was impossible to talk with him without feeling his sincerity and his knowledge of human nature. The following incident changed the life of Sir Wilfred Grenfell, who as a young medical student had attended a big revival meeting out of curiosity. Moody asked a local clergyman to lead in prayer. The man went on praying until Grenfell started to leave. Suddenly, in the midst of this prayer, Mr. Moody spoke out in a loud voice. 'While the Rev. Dr. —— is praying, let us unite in singing

Hymn Number —.' It was sung with gusto. Then Grenfell
stayed for the sermon. When Moody was old, I asked him
one day if he would preach the following Sunday in our
church. He said, 'I will give you the answer a girl made to
a young man. He asked her, "Will you marry me?" and
she replied, "You have good judgement but bad luck."'

When I was an undergraduate, he preached one Sunday
at Yale. Attendance was compulsory and the attention to
the average sermon was not very keen; and most sermons
were no longer than twenty minutes. Mr. Moody preached
for one hour, and held the breathless attention of the students.

One of the best effects of his prolonged visit to Hartford
in 1878 was on the various pastors of the city; they were
roused to new zeal and the increase of membership was evident in every church.

The meetings conducted by Moody and Sankey were followed in Hartford by those directed by the Rev. George F.
Pentecost and the singer George C. Stebbins, who composed many tunes that became well known and in the
twentieth century are frequently sung over the radio. He is
still living and on 26 February 1938 celebrated his ninety-
second birthday.

83 HIGH STREET
CATSKILL, N.Y.

DEAR PROF. PHELPS.

Your gracious telegram of birthday greetings touches my heart
very deeply, and your recalling the meetings in Hartford conducted
by Dr. Geo. F. Pentecost, just 60 years ago at this time of year, gives
me great pleasure, and I am deeply grateful to you for it.

You do me great honor to speak of the singing in those meetings so
kindly, and also of the contribution I have made to the service of song
in the intervening years, and I thank you for it most sincerely. If you
can recall any of the songs I sang alone in those meetings, it occurs to
me it would be 'The Green Hill,' for that is the one most called for that
whole season, partly because the musical setting was new, it having

been composed for a special service in the Baptist Church of which Dr. Pentecost was then pastor in Boston in late 1877. By way of parenthesis, as you might say, I have very often seen recently that song referred to as being used in broadcasting programs of my songs by various radio stations in honor of my birthday, which has not been the case in former services on my birthday, to such an extent I had thought it had dropped out of the thought of the people.

Coming back to the meeting in Hartford, it was at that time that 'Evening Prayer'—Saviour, breathe an evening blessing—had its first introduction by its being sung by the large Male Choir that had been assisting Moody and Sankey in their great meetings there. The music of which is the first of all my compositions that came into general use. Dr. Pentecost followed Moody and Sankey there, as already intimated, and also in New Haven in the spring following. While there I had the pleasure of meeting your honored father, who gave me the opportunity of visiting with him on several occasions and who gave me copies of several hymns, which I appreciated very sincerely. I have many times recalled him and those occasions when singing his justly famous hymn 'Saviour Thy Dying Love' which, with the splendid musical setting by Dr. Lowry, I have sung uncounted number of times and always with blessing to myself, for it is one of the best hymns for the regular church service and for prayer meetings, and all deeply spiritual services to be found in any church hymnals, certainly of those I have known.

With hearty congratulations to Mrs. Phelps and yourself for having known and walked with each other since your early years, I am sincerely and gratefully yours,

GEO. C. STEBBINS

An immediate effect of these services on my schoolmates and me was that we organized and kept up for years 'The Boys' Prayer-Meetings,' which were held for an hour one evening every week at private houses. My father and mother highly approved of these, but my aunt Libbie was ironically amused, though she was astonished at their continuance for so long a period.

12

CHINESE SCHOOLMATES

THE fact that in Hartford, both in the District School and in the High School some of my most intimate friends were Chinese boys seems strange as I look back. When I entered the West Middle School, I found a considerable number of Chinese boys there; it seemed natural to have them for playmates. This may have been partly owing to the attractive qualities of these Orientals, and their genius for adaptation.

A distinguished Chinese gentleman and scholar, Yung Wing, was living in Hartford, and it was through his influence that this large group of Chinese boys came there to study and to learn American ways. Every one of them was a patrician, of good family in China, and had as a rule much more spending money than most of the Americans. They had excellent manners, were splendid sportsmen, alert in mind, good at their studies, good at athletics. I do not think I have ever known a finer group of boys and young men. After graduating from the High School at Hartford, they entered Yale, when suddenly the command came from China, and they were all forced to return home.

These boys were dressed like us, except that they wore long queues. When they played football, they tucked these queues inside their shirts and sometimes tied them around their heads; for if the queue got loose, it afforded too strong a temptation for opponents. All our games were of course new to them, but they became excellent at baseball, football, hockey on the ice, then known as 'shinny,' and in fancy skating they were supreme. When the bicycle was in-vented, the first boy at school to have one was Tsang; and I can see him now, riding this strange high machine up Asylum Avenue.

I remember them individually; King, Kong, Se Chung, Kai Kah Wong, Chuck, Cho, Tsang, and all the rest. Mun Yew Chung, a little older than the majority of them, was in the class of 1883 at Yale, where he was universally re-spected. He became coxswain on the Yale crew, and steered the boat in the races as coolly as if he were out for a prac-tice spin. It is said that he was told he must swear at the oarsmen to make them row their best; for he usually sat in his place in silence. Swearing did not come naturally to him, for he was grave and impassive; but finally, being told he must curse them, he would, at the most unexpected mo-ments, and without any emphasis mechanically utter the monosyllable 'damn!' whereat the crew became so help-less with laughter, they begged him to desist. He was cox-swain of the victorious Yale crews of 1880 and 1881; and at some Yale-Harvard meeting many years later, when a Harvard man expressed doubt as to whether Mun Yew Chung had even seen a university boat race, much less taken part in it, the Chinese suavely confessed he had never seen a Harvard crew row; and after a pause, ex-plained that they were always behind him. Mun Yew Chung became a prominent statesman in China, and occa-sionally visited the United States as a diplomatic repre-sentative of his country.

I can well remember, when we used to 'choose up sides' at football, how the first choice invariably went to Se Chung, a short-thick-set boy, built close to the ground, who ran like a hound and dodged like a cat. What Se Chung had in grace and speed, Kong had in bull strength. Built broad and strong, eternally good-natured and smil-ing, he would cross the goal line, carrying four or five

Americans on his shoulders. In baseball, Tsang was a great pitcher, impossible to hit; King was a tower of strength to any nine, and even little Chuck, much younger than the others, took to a baseball as an infant takes to the bottle. My most intimate friend at the High School was a splendid Chinese boy named Cho—dignified and serious, who even at that time was more a sophisticated man of the world than I shall ever be. To hear that young gentleman translate Caesar in the classroom was a liberal education. Every Saturday Cho and I used to go shooting in West Hartford, after meadowlarks and yellowhammers. He had a huge gun that weighed over twelve pounds, which he would carry uncomplainingly all day long; and bring down birds on the wing at a prodigious distance. When these boys, to our infinite regret, were recalled to China, Cho gave me his great gun as a pledge of eternal friendship. In China he entered the Navy, and where he is now I wish I knew. We kept up a fitful correspondence for some years.

These boys not only excelled us Americans at athletics; you should have seen them cutting the double eight and the grapevine! They cut us out in other ways that caused considerable heart-burnings. When the Chinese youth entered the social arena, none of us had any chance. Their manner to the girls had a deferential elegance far beyond our possibilities. Whether it was the exotic pleasure of dancing with Orientals, or, what is more probable, the real charm of their manners and talk, I do not know; certain it is that at dances and receptions, the fairest and most sought-out belles invariably gave the swains from the Orient the preference. I can remember the pained expressions on the faces of some of my American comrades when the girls deliberately passed them by and accepted the attentions of Chinese rivals with a more than yielding grace. Personally, I rather enjoyed this oft-recurring situation, for my father and mother would not permit me to learn to dance, and this racial struggle appealed to my dramatic instinct. And the Orientals danced beautifully.

Thus the pleasant recollections of my boyhood are full of Chinese memories: and although, by the time I entered Yale, these fine fellows had gone home, I vainly hoped they might return. There was only one Oriental in my college class, Yan Phou Lee, who had an amazing command of English, and whose articles in the '*Lit*,' and speech at the Junior Exhibition, and later on the Commencement stage, attracted attention far outside academic walls.

13

MY AUNT

I HAVE often wondered why a maiden aunt is more worldly-minded than one's mother, but it is usually the case; I was pleased to read in Alice James's *Journal* under date of 1 December 1889, 'Prof. Farlow asking at the club table one night "Why is every man's aunt so entirely different from his mother?"'

The Reverend James H. Linsley, whom I mentioned, had only two children, Elizabeth Lyon Linsley, born 1821, and my mother, born 1823. Elizabeth was never married, refusing many offers, for after her father died in 1843 and my mother was married in 1847, she stayed home and took care of her mother, who lived until 1865. We children never called her anything but Libbie; she would not have allowed us to call her Auntie. Libbie had certain peculiarities and oddities, as nearly all people have who live alone; and after 1865 she lived alone in the great house in Stratford, Conn., where she and my mother were born. She paid us frequent visits and some of the happiest days of my life were spent at her house, when my brothers and I went there for weekends.

Her influence on me (and on my brothers) was wholly beneficial, for she supplied everything I did not get at home; and if she had been permitted would have accomplished much more. Although she lived from 1821 to 1896, she belonged in her mind and tastes to the eighteenth century. At heart she was a rationalist, thoroughly disliked evangelicanism, thought revivals vulgar, and although she

invariably attended divine service and was a good judge of
sermons, never joined any church. She kept Saturday
night as faithfully as any Puritan; and gave supper parties
Sunday evening to show her colours. Pope seemed to be her
favourite poet. She never surrendered to any form of Vic-
torianism. She kept all the beautiful early eighteenth-
century furniture with which her house was filled (it is in
my house now); and although all her neighbours and
friends (including us) thought she was eccentric and per-
verse in not liking the massive ugliness of the Victorian period, nothing had any effect on her. She was right and she
knew she was right, though she fought a solitary battle.
She went to the theatre and to the opera, and tried in vain
to induce her sister to let us go; for month after month she
implored my parents to send us to dancing-school, for she
knew that although our souls were saved, our bodies were
gawky and clumsy. It is entirely owing to her that my
teeth are regular and good; for when we were small boys,
she took more interest in our teeth than in our souls, and
took us to the dentist frequently and stayed with us there
many weary hours. She was interested in every detail of
our lives, and longed to have us happy and natural, and did
her best to make us so. She studied the art of conversation
as she studied the art of singing, and she seemed to prize
good manners and good breeding and good taste above
everything. She was proud of her ancestry and of her home;
and she had a will of iron. I think she loved us three boys
more than she loved anything else on earth.

Among other things I learned from her, I learned some
consideration for others. When I was about eight years old,
spending a week-end at her house, a middle-aged man
called one evening, and after a polite skirmish with my
aunt, he devoted his attention to me. At that time I happened to be excited about boats, and the visitor discussed
the subject in a way that I found charming. After he left, I

spoke of him with enthusiasm. What a man! and how tremendously interested in boats! My aunt informed me that he was a New York lawyer; that he cared nothing whatever about boats—took not the slightest interest in the subject. 'But why then did he talk all the time about boats?' 'Because he is a gentleman. He saw you were interested in boats, and he talked about the things he knew would interest and please you. He made himself agreeable.'

Libbie was thoroughly familiar with Shakespeare. When she came to our house for a prolonged visit, I always—at her request—slept with her. She was a lonely woman, no doubt, and liked to have me in the room. I slept with her till I was fourteen or fifteen, and took it for granted, though like most elderly people, she woke up early, and woke me up too. I had recently read the complete works of William Shakespeare, and from five in the morning until six-thirty, we discussed the characters and plots with ardour. We did this on every one of her visits for several years; I learned a great deal. She used frequently to mention 'his profound knowledge of the human heart;' this remark meant nothing to me, for I knew and cared nothing about the human heart; what interested me in Shakespeare were the good stories and the dashing gentlemen. The only time I ever shocked her was once when I expressed unlimited enthusiasm for the *Taming of the Shrew*, and for the way in which Petruchio treated Katherine. This pleased my small boy nature immensely, to see this smarty girl put in her place. On this question my aunt reasoned with me in vain.

My aunt used to tell me again and again that I was a combination of a small boy and of a man of forty; and I now see that she was right.

One day I had been reading in the Bible the story of Jephthah's daughter and how she went upon the mountains to bewail her virginity. I did not fully understand this; but I was impressed by it, and still more impressed by the sensation I caused in a room full of people on that evening, when I regarded my aunt, who for some reason seemed to be depressed, and suddenly in the general silence I shot at her this question—'Are you bewailing your virginity?'

Long before the days of popular magazines which told an ignorant public what to wear, what to say, and what to think, how did she, living alone in a village, become infallible on the proper appearance of boys? When we received from somebody a few brightly-coloured silk handkerchiefs, and thought them far more 'tony' than white linen ones, she earnestly although vainly tried to persuade us they were vulgar; and where did she learn the following fact—which distinguishes as by a label the gentleman from other males? She solemnly told me, 'When the barber cuts your hair, never, never allow him to shave the back of your neck!' and I never have.

How I wish that by some miracle we might when we ourselves are old, talk with our parents and our aunts and uncles from an equality of age! There is always this gulf of generations. I suppose the attitude of a man or woman who was born when his parents were twenty-one, must be different when he is forty-five and they are sixty-six, from that of one, who, like me, cannot remember either his father or mother except when they were grey. Yet even so, does any boy ever regard his mother as a woman or remember she was a girl? Barrie brought this out in *Alice Sit by the Fire*. She isn't a woman; she is 'mother.' That is why Hamlet was so unspeakably shocked by his own mother's sensuality.

14

EXPERIENCES AT GRAMMAR SCHOOL

ALTHOUGH the transfer from Providence to Hartford was in many ways so beneficial, much loss came through the change of schools; for no matter how much parents may gain by removing from one city to another, there is almost always a loss for the children. The rapid growth in positive learning that I had made in a few months at the University Grammar School in Providence was balanced by a loss of two years in Hartford. And indeed during the next three years, with the exception of some brilliant flashes, I was, for the first and last time in my life, rated among the dull, backward, incompetent schoolboys, receiving very low marks, and finally, having to drop back a year. This was a strange and unpleasant experience; and even now, as I look back upon it, not altogether explicable.

It is possible that puberty had something to do with it. For it was during the years from twelve to fourteen that I was at my worst so far as getting good marks in studies was concerned. Or it may be that poor teaching had something to do with it, for my brother Arthur, two years older than I, who was for a time in the same classes and with the same teachers, had a somewhat similar experience; from this he as suddenly emerged, went on to graduate from High School with honours, writing an original Greek poem, and to take Phi Beta Kappa at Yale.

Mathematics always helped to keep me back; they were the curse of my life at school and college, they had more to do with my unhappiness than any other one thing, and I bitterly regret the hours, days, weeks, months, and years that I was forced to spend on this wholly unprofitable study. I shall return to this later with more venom.

In Hartford the school year began in April; we had just arrived in the Spring of 1876; and my brother Arthur and I were placed in Room Number Ten of the West Middle District School. Outside of school hours I was a great reader; and my head was stuffed full of battle-romances. I used to draw with my pencil on the inside covers of my text books two knights fighting, with one of them impaled by the spear, while the blood flowed copiously from the wound. One day, the teacher walking down the aisle, spied these pictures; and to my amazement she burst into a violent rage; in the presence of the well-filled room, she called me a dirty, vile, filthy boy, and expressed as much abhorrence for me as if I had been a criminal. I could not understand such an explosion of wrath; but she had a bad temper anyhow, and I supposed she was angry because she had caught me wasting some of my time in nonsensical drawings. It was not until years later that the real reason for her rage came to me. This teacher thought my pictures were obscene! She took the spear-head and the flow of blood for something else. She never forgave me; she hated me after that, and I found it impossible to please her, or to get anything like a good mark.

If she had asked me to stay after school, and quietly talked to me about my supposed obscenities, my frank amazement would have convinced her; but no, she had to condemn me publicly. This, and other unjust treatment that I received occasionally, convinced me that it was better in dealing with pupils, to make any mistake rather than punish the innocent.

I think during the two years that I spent at the West Middle School and the first year at the High School, my inability to get good marks puzzled my teachers more than it did me. I read aloud so easily, I wrote such good compositions, I spoke more intelligently than most of my classmates, I remembered the words and music of every song and hymn we were taught, and yet I got low marks. Some of my teachers used to talk with me outside of school hours; I can see now that they were impressed by my general intelligence and by my low standing.

A curious thing happened at the end of the first year. We had a written examination in ten or eleven subjects. We had been told that if we got a total mark above Five we should jump a room and go into the highest room, Number 12. That if we got above Four we should advance one room, and that if we fell below Four we should remain another year where we were. I announced myself as a candidate for leaping to Room Number 12. Well, the first examination was Arithmetic. I worked and wrote steadily during the allotted two hours. My mark on this examination was .04, four-tenths of one; nobody received a lower mark. I remember that the Principal, who was not an unkind man, came to me and said it was ridiculous for me to think of leaping a room; that I should probably remain where I was for the rest of my life. I made no reply, for what was there to say?

The next examination was in history, and I received the highest mark in the room. History was as real to me as my own life, and I described the death of General Wolfe on the battlefield of Quebec as if I had been an eye witness. When the Principal was shown this paper, he was flabbergasted. My total average for all the exams was 5.5, and together with my brother, I landed in the highest room, and became a Senior. During the whole of the next year, my curse was Arithmetic; I remember working four hours one evening on a question in 'Partial Payments' for the next day, and getting it wrong. I believe the standard of graduation from the West Middle School was *relatively* higher than that of any other institution I have seen. We had to take three complete exams *in all the studies*, and unless one's total was above five, one was not allowed to graduate, and one could not receive a diploma. Many failed every year. I squeezed through with an average of 5.2.

The twenty-four hours before 'graduating exercises' were among the unhappiest of my life. The reason for this may seem ridiculous, but my agony was real. All the boys and girls who were to receive diplomas were carefully drilled to march in to the auditorium two by two, first the girls, then the boys. The Principal, in addressing us, said there was an odd number of boys and an odd number of girls. Instantly I had the presentiment that he would select me to walk in with the odd girl. My worst fears were immediately confirmed. 'The girls will walk in two by two, then Willie Phelps and Alice Post will follow arm in arm, then will come the boys.' I could not have felt worse had he announced my execution.

My own sufferings in childhood and boyhood from bashfulness and self-consciousness were so acute, that I have ever since had profound sympathy for any bashful boy or girl. Older people laugh at this, which is brutal; one might as well laugh at a boy writhing in physical torment. I went to the Principal immediately after this meeting, and begged him to give the assignment to some boy who would not mind; but the Principal, probably thinking I was cowardly and needed discipline, refused to let me off. That afternoon, at the dress rehearsal, we went through with this processional. I have ever since been grateful to Alice Post (now Mrs. Haight). I supposed of course she would approach me with loathing. She came with the most gracious smile, as if she regarded walking in with me as an honour and a delight! I did not like to be rude to her, for of course there was nothing personal in my attitude. She took my arm as if I were a duke, and we went through with it. She talked with me like a woman of the world. Yet all that night I saw myself entering the auditorium, the only boy with a girl, and the entire audience grinning at me. I seriously thought of running away. But just before the exercises were to begin, I learned to my overwhelming joy and relief, that one of the girls was taken ill, hence Alice was to walk in with one of her own sex, and I marched in alone, at the head of the boys. I was thirteen years old, and the smallest boy in the class.

I did not dislike girls; they seemed to me remote and mysterious beings; in their presence I was hopelessly confused and tongue-tied. Sometimes while walking on the street, if I saw one a hundred yards away whom I knew and to whom therefore I must take off my hat, I would dive into a side street, or hide in a yard until she had safely passed. I longed to meet girls on equal terms; I longed to talk and laugh with them, and be at ease in their presence; and how I envied the boys who managed this with no embarrassment! With me it was the moth and the star.

On the stage at graduation exercises that day I suffered from another difficulty that often afflicted me, and from which I learned to understand others. I could not stop laughing. There was as much mirth in this laughter as if I had been over a slow fire; I did not want to laugh, but I could not help it. It was sheer nervousness. I understood then and I understand now why there are certain people who laugh in church, laugh at funerals, laugh during serious conversations.

It must not be thought that I was an unhappy, morose, or solitary youth. Quite the opposite. I felt absolutely at ease with other boys of my age, I played all the outdoor games with enormous gusto, I went swimming 'with the gang' every day in warm weather, I loved expeditions in the woods, camping out, and all that sort of thing. I was one hundred per cent Boy—but in the presence of girls or on solemn and formal occasions, I often did the wrong thing. I was often afraid in the church prayer-meetings that I should laugh, not because anything struck me as funny, but just because I did not want to laugh. This is a curse that particularly afflicts bashful, self-conscious, imaginative boys and girls.

So far as scholarship is concerned, my life as a schoolboy was so remarkable in its brilliance and in its stupidity (for at one time I was at the head of the class and at another at the foot) that it may be worth recording. Ten and eleven years old, at the school in Providence, I attracted amazement from both teachers and schoolmates by brilliant achievements; I seemed far ahead of my years in intellectual maturity. At the age of fourteen I was so low in standing, though working desperately hard, that I had to go back a whole year, and join the class below; a bitter humiliation. Then suddenly everything became easy again, and with the exception of mathematics, I had no more difficulties, but stood among the leaders at school and college.

The autobiography of the famous playwright and actor Sacha Guitry called *If Memory Serves* (translated by Lewis Galantière) has such interesting comment on boyhood education that it is worth consideration by parents. It seems that the boy Sacha was frequently transferred from one prep school to another; he went to *eleven*. And so, from the age of six to the age of eighteen, he was without any real education at all, and after that, made no pretence of seeking any. His peregrinations however gave him opportunities for observation of teachers, pupils, lessons, and methods; and his summary is

> The time we lose in school is lost during the most precious period of our lives. . . . I am convinced that we are extremely intelligent between the ages of eight and fourteen years, and that most of us are less so between fourteen and twenty, much less. . . . I am quite ready to agree that the professors in our institutions of higher

education are superior people, but I insist that it is at the beginning of our education that we should be confided to remarkable men. If, from our earliest years, we were given the taste for work, we should thereafter learn soon enough what our needs are; for I believe that we learn easily and usefully what we need. . . .

All the originality that we possess between the ages of eight and fourteen—our natural aptitudes, our individual gifts—are dead at the time of our eighteenth year. Of course these gifts may return later, but what time lost!

There may be another reason apart from inefficient teaching; for Goethe, in *his* autobiography says children 'generally promise more than they perform: and it seems that Nature, among the other roguish tricks that she plays us, here also especially designs to make sport of us. . . . The child, considered in and for himself, with his equals, and in relations suited to his powers, seems so intelligent and rational, and at the same time so easy, cheerful, and clever, that one can hardly wish it further cultivation. If children grew up according to early indications, we should have nothing but geniuses; but growth is not merely development; the various organic systems which constitute one man spring one from another, follow each other, change into each other, supplant each other, and even consume each other; so that after a time, scarcely a trace is to be found of many aptitudes and manifestations of ability.'

I wonder if this does not partially explain the disappointment many parents and teachers feel in so many cases of unfulfilled 'promise,' and the regret that so many old persons feel as they look back on their own life. When I was a child, I could amuse groups of other boys and even of adults by telling long stories improvised without hesitation; if early promise meant later performance, I ought to have been a novelist or dramatist. But, unlike the late A.C.Benson, I do not feel broken-hearted. Of course I envy distinguished creative writers, but why cry for the moon? I have had too good a time to cry for anything. Goethe's words of wisdom comfort me, and perhaps they may comfort others.

Yet why so many brilliant little boys and girls, and why so many dull old men and women? Who explains it more accurately, Guitry, Wordsworth, or Goethe?

Mr. Guitry also says something that applies I think not only to the education of children, but to that of college undergraduates. It seems to me ridiculous that in most colleges today lectures and recitations are regarded as a penalty for the dull and lazy; all the students are trying to get on the 'Dean's list' which means that if they are sufficiently intelligent or industrious, they will not have to attend classes regularly. The implication, of course, is that they are more brilliant than their teachers; and should not have to be forced to listen to the stupidity of specialists. I had always insisted that college classes should be so conducted that those who are dull or lazy or incompetent should be refused the privilege of attending them. They should be forced to study alone or with a private tutor until they can show sufficient ability to be readmitted. Therefore I was pleased by Sacha Guitry's statement,

> Classwork should be passionately interesting. Of course for this we should have to have passionately interested teachers, people convinced of the beauty of their mission—and not poor crocks whose chief characteristics are their mediocrity and commonplaceness.
>
> I dream of the time when a master will be able to say to a pupil, 'You behaved badly, and I shall punish you. You will not be allowed to attend class.' *Vous n'avez pas été sage, tantôt. Pour votre punition, vous n'assisterez pas à la classe.*

My standing in graduating from the West Middle District School was so low and my scholarship record during the preceding years (1876-7) had been so poor, that the Principal said I was not fitted to enter the High School and that I ought to remain at West Middle and take its Senior year over again. This was a gloomy prospect, for in spite of my miserable marks, I was ambitious. Although the Principal was a man whom we respected, in this particular matter his judgement was not so good as that of a boy only a little older than I, whose own marks were so low he had difficulty in remaining in the High School. This was Morris Penrose, and I shall always be grateful to him. He advised me to enter the High School; saying that even if I were dropped and forced to spend five instead of four years there, it would be far better for my development to spend them in the High School in a more mature environment than to repeat a year with the little boys and girls in the District School. This advice seemed to me sound and seems so still; I determined to follow it if it should be possible. But the immediate problem was, could I enter the High School?

I had supposed, unless one had the permission of the District School Superintendent to enter the High School, one was not allowed to try the entrance examinations; and he would not give permission either to my brother Arthur or to me. Thus, for two weeks after leaving the West Middle, we were despondently looking forward to re-entering the class at our old Grammar School.

I shall never forget the April morning in 1878, when a boy came running to our house in Sigourney Street, and told us that any boy or girl in Hartford was free to try the entrance exams for the Public High School; they were open to anyone, and they would begin in fifteen minutes! If he had not found us at home that morning or if he had come later, we should have lost a year. We ran down Asylum Avenue as fast as our legs would carry us, got there just in time, took the whole series of entrance exams—found them much easier than the ones we had had at the West Middle —and so both passed triumphantly into the High School.

15

THE HARTFORD PUBLIC HIGH SCHOOL

I ENTERED the Hartford Public High School in April 1878, and found it difficult to keep up with my studies. There was a printed monthly report, which gave the exact standing of every pupil in the school. This report was public, was sent to all the parents, so that the precise position in scholarship of every boy and girl in the school was known. If one's average fell below Five for three months, one was dropped into the lower classes; and if one was in the lowest class, one was dropped from the school. In the next Spring my average fell below Five. The Principal, Joseph Hall, sent for me, and told me I should have to go. I suggested we were nearly at the end of the school year, when everyone had to take the final examination; that I be allowed to try this. He immediately granted my request and to his amazement I successfully survived this ordeal and entered the next class.

But in the Autumn of the following year (1879) I fell so low in my studies that my case was hopeless. There seemed to be a cloud over my mind, so that I could not properly learn anything, though I tried hard. I became discouraged; and I had bad luck with one of my teachers who was anything but sympathetic. She thought I was a shirker and a loafer. I withdrew from the school in November, feeling my disgrace keenly. My parents must have been terribly disappointed, but they were unbelievably kind. Not a word of reproach; perhaps they saw how disconsolate I was.

In January I re-entered the High School, and in the

100

lower class. For some weeks I suffered from a depression so profound that I should have been glad to die. To see my former classmates going to their recitations, while I was doing the first year over again, seemed intolerable. But, by the mercy of God, I was assigned to a room presided over by Miss Mary Mather, a young and very attractive woman. She must have observed my sorrowful countenance, for while she never asked me what was the matter, her attitude was extremely sympathetic. She was kind; she was encouraging. Suddenly a cloud seemed to pass from my mind.

Studies that had seemed impossibly difficult became easily comprehensible; I obtained high marks with less than half the effort it had previously cost me to get low ones. I astounded my parents, teachers, and former classmates by going to the top row; my name frequently came at the head on the monthly reports, and from that time, shortly after my fifteenth birthday (1880) to the age of twenty-six, when I passed my last examination, I was always among the honour students.

Miss Mary Mather was as shy as she was kind. She suffered from acute nervousness, and it must have been torture to her often in the schoolroom. I think I was the only one of her pupils who came near understanding her. Some days she would begin to laugh, would vainly try to stop, would shake with laughter, and once or twice have to dismiss the class. The other boys were naturally amused by this; but I knew what hell she was passing through. Some years after this she was overcome by a nervous affliction, and died.

But I can say of her what the Pope said of Pompilia, that not even in Heaven could she be any more of an angel than she was on earth. It is one of the innumerable mysteries of life that a woman like Mary Mather, who was wholly kind, sympathetic, and lovely, should have had to suffer such nervous depression.

In Junior and Senior year at the High School, we had a teacher who made a profound impression. This was Winfred R. Martin, six feet four, with a large red beard. He was the exact opposite of a routine hearer of recitations; and at first we boys rebelled against his methods, because 'he asked questions that were not in the notes.' He was one of the most learned men I have ever known and he never published a line. He had an overwhelming passion for the acquisition of knowledge; and had no other ambition. To publish would have taken time which he used to learn something more. Every Saturday he took the train to New Haven, to study Sanskrit with the greatest scholar in the world, William Dwight Whitney. And after he got to the point where he could not endure High School teaching any more, he went to Tübingen and stayed there until he had won his doctor's degree. Later he became Professor of Ancient and Modern Languages at Trinity College, Hartford, where he was happy. He taught Sanskrit, Arabic, the Semitic languages, Greek, Latin, French, German, and Italian. He was never married and his highest happiness was in learning.

Occasionally I went to his rooms in Hartford and called on him, something I never did with any other teacher. I bored him horribly, but I came away from those interviews feeling inspired. I can see him in my mind's eye as plainly as I saw him in the classroom nearly sixty years ago. I remember his translation of the famous passage in Virgil's eclogues. He spoke it just once in the classroom, and it printed on my mind in imperishable type. The passage begins

Tale tuum carmen nobis, divine poeta

'O divine poet, your song is to me as deep sleep upon the grass to the weary, as in summer's heat to slake one's thirst from a springing rivulet of clear water.'

When I was an undergraduate at Yale, I became acquainted with Floyd R.Smith of the class above me, a famous half-mile runner. Fifty years later I met him in New Jersey, and discovered that before Martin came to the High School at Hartford, Smith had him as teacher of Latin and Greek in the High School at Jersey City. Replying to my request, he wrote me as follows:

I remember well the day he told us that he was going to leave, to go to the Hartford High School. So you were the looters that pilfered our treasure chest. Boy, but he was a teacher, the best of all we met on our way. He embodied for me all of the romance and service of teaching.

When, on one occasion, we were fed up on the Gallic Wars, he closed his textbook and turned to Froissart with some such comment as this: 'Froissart would have described in detail each of these patriotic murders. Caesar disposed of all of them with one ablative absolute, omnibus occisis (I believe), and devoted the rest of his column to the glorification of Julius Caesar—a great reporter, that Caesar.' He took us with Froissart on his journey through England, Scotland, Italy and finally to Aquitaine in the retinue of the Black Prince.

Our reward for enduring the monotony of Xenophon's parasangs was his personally-conducted tour to Jane Austen's pre-Victorian England. *Sense and Sensibility*, *Pride and Prejudice* for a time at least, displaced *Diamond Dick* and *Murderous Moses*.

One of the most dramatic and enduring by-products of that course in Latin and Greek was our introduction to the old Norse Vikings. Romance in golden trappings. I used to stare at him in a transport of admiration. He seemed to me to be one of them, with his six-foot stature, his commanding brow and his blond beard. We boys spoke of him as Old Man Martin, for he must have been at least thirty when we knew him—past ninety now if living. I wonder who else remembers him.

I met him in my Freshman year, on Chapel Street, and he took me to lunch. He was then taking a post-graduate course in Sanskrit, I believe. Why didn't Yale grab him?

16

WALKING, WORKING, FROGS, LOVE

SEVEN years after I was graduated from the High School I was again to meet Martin—not in New Haven but in Paris—and we had more than one meal together. Of that meeting, more anon.

When I was in the High School, George William Curtis, one of the most fastidious and exquisite gentlemen who ever appeared on a public platform, delivered an address on civil service reform in Hartford. Of this address I heard only three words but I can see him now and hear his voice as plainly as if he were in the room. He appeared on the platform in full evening dress, immaculate and graceful, with the grey side-whiskers of the period. He examined his manuscript, said 'Ladies and Gentlemen'—at that moment I fell asleep and was awakened by the applause one hour later.

It was a winter night and I had been coasting all the afternoon. There was a silver dollar in my pocket and when the big sled turned over, as it did when we were rounding a curve, that silver dollar was embedded in my hip and for a month I wore on my leg the circular impression of the U.S.A.

I did an immense amount of walking in my schooldays; several times walking the 37 miles between Hartford and New Haven in a day; the first time when I was only eleven. When I was sixteen I spent the Easter week vacation with my pal, Frank Hubbard, walking 100 miles in five days, from Hartford to Norwich to New London and Saybrook, taking the boat from Lyme to Hartford at one o'clock in the morning.

In the Easter vacation of my Sophomore year in college, my classmate John Norton Pomeroy, of San Francisco, and I walked from New Haven up along the Housatonic River into the northwest corner of the State.

And a few days after Commencement in 1887, my class-mates George Pettee, Horace Hart, Tom Penney, and I walked over 200 miles from New Haven to the White Mountains; we stopped a few days at Northfield, and heard Moody the evangelist, and were also fortunate in hearing Professor Henry Drummond deliver for the first time his address *The Greatest Thing in the World*, which Moody persuaded him to publish. It was translated into all the languages of Europe.

Only one day in my life have I performed severe manual labour from dawn till nightfall, and that was enforced. When we were living in Providence, and I was ten years old, our closest friend and playmate was a boy named Lincoln Rose, whose father was a missionary in India; Lincoln was living with a deacon in the church. This deacon was a curious mixture—as perhaps we all are—of piety, coarseness, kindness, and severity. He was orthodox of the orthodox; his speeches and prayers in public were eloquent; on his farm he was a hard driver, and yet saw that the men he employed were well fed. I remember one winter night, when we were having a 'social' at our church, with abundant food and agreeable entertainment, this deacon went out on the street, and brought in the policeman who had to be out all night, found him a place at the table, and said 'Captain, you sit here and make a good meal.' I remember plainly how that policeman gratefully ate that hot oyster broth.

Yet one day when I saw this deacon directing work on his farm, I was amazed to hear him use obscene language in shouting at a dog. It was many years before golf had caused devout people to curse fluently, and I had forgotten how such apparent inconsistencies had always been true of human nature. 'Out of the same mouth proceedeth blessing and cursing,' wrote the apostle St. James. At a football game in New Haven one day, an undergraduate left his seat and came near a friend of mine, and said 'I don't mind ordinary profanity; but that old man up there with whom I was sitting has kept up such a stream of blasphemies that I can't stand it. I don't know who he is.' On pointing him out, he was told that was the Reverend Doctor —— a sincere and devoted clergyman from another city, who exerted a particularly fine influence on boys. He was well known for his terrific excitement at all athletic games; but this undergraduate could not believe he was really a clergyman. He was, though.

Well, about that day's work. After we had moved to Hartford, Lincoln Rose wrote to my brother and me, inviting us to spend a day with him on the farm managed by the deacon, and where he worked every day for the same wages customarily paid boys. 'Sonny, how much do you get for hoeing those potatoes?' 'Don't get nothing, but get hell if I don't do it.'

We arrived in the evening, stayed the night, rose early, and we supposed that as we were visitors, the deacon would let Lincoln off for one day, and we would all three have a good time playing together. Quite otherwise. The deacon told us to come right along to the hayfield. We did not return to the house for noonday dinner; a lunch was brought to us in the fields. We pitched hay until dark and my hands were covered with blisters; as the twilight finally came on, and we took the last load to the barn, we were sent up to the upper storey of the barn to level off and smooth out the enormous heaps of hay. I can feel now the hot, close, stuffy air of that barn-room in the gathering darkness, and the stifling feeling of the hay and straw in my eyes, ears, and throat.

Of course we received no money for this work and no thanks. Either the deacon thought it was good for us to be made to work, or he thought he had a good opportunity to get two more hands for nothing. And how he did drive us all day! 'Hurry up there, I'm right on your heels!'

The next morning, as we returned to our home in Hartford, we were so stiff and sore we could hardly move; but our physical aches and pains were nothing to our bitter resentment. It seems funny enough, now, our planned holiday with Lincoln; but it was not funny then. I have never done a day's work since, so far as manual labour is concerned.

Some of the happiest hours in my boyhood in Hartford I owe to the late Pliny Jewell. His brother Marshall Jewell, several times Governor of Connecticut, was the handsomest old man I ever saw. To see him on horseback, with his ruddy complexion, snow-white hair and pointed white imperial, with his unassuming patrician elegance, looking like a Duke of the *ancien régime*, was a sight never to be forgotten. His brother Pliny, a charming, kindly old gentleman, lived in a beautiful house on Farmington Avenue, with extensive and well-kept gardens. On this estate was a pond which froze solid every winter. Mr. Jewell had printed a number of cards inscribed SKATING TICKET and he gave one to every boy in the neighbourhood he felt would not abuse the privilege. What fun we had on that pond! I remember when I was twelve years old I finished one evening *David Copperfield*. I went over to the pond in the bright moonlight. I was alone. I skated around and around repeating aloud over and over again, 'O Agnes O my soul!'

I used to go over occasionally to the pond in the summer twilight, to see Mr. Jewell with his frogs. A servant would bring out a large armchair and place it on the border of the little lake. Then the old gentleman came, took his seat deliberately, and began to ring a large dinner-bell. As the mellow tones filled the air, the frogs would emerge from the water and group themselves expectantly yet respectfully around Mr. Jewell, who fed them with bits of bread, which they received courteously. I had never discriminated among frogs; but to this gentleman every one of those frogs was an individual, and he had named them all. The largest was called Laura Matilda, and was his favourite. I have seen Laura draw near his armchair, take a bit of bread delicately from his fingers, eat it and then wipe her mouth daintily, like the Prioresse in Chaucer.

In my Senior year at the Hartford High School, I was elected Class Orator, and on Class Day I delivered my oration, 'Perils of the Republic.' I thought this was filled with original ideas; and I was chagrined when an older man asked me what subject I was going to discuss, and on hearing it, he said, 'Poor old Republic; it always catches it at Graduation Exercises!' I was then a convinced Federalist, believing in a strong centralized national government. My four perils were the Saloon, the polygamy threat in the State of Utah, a too small navy, and illiteracy among our Southern people. This speech was delivered with sincere passion in the Spring of 1883; and the first paragraph shows how much more fortunate our country was then than it is now.

> The country is now in a state of unexampled prosperity. Our revenues greatly exceed our expenses; the national debt is being rapidly decreased; the Treasury is overflowing.

And there was no income tax.

The two public days of graduation came later in the month. On the first, eight boys and girls were selected from the whole school to compete for prizes in declamation. I spoke Macaulay's 'Battle of the Lake Regillus.' For the boys, the first prize was awarded to Clarence A. Barbour, later President of Brown University, and one of the foremost platform speakers in America; the second prize, to my delight, was awarded to me, and now I am Public Orator of Yale University.

On the whole, the last three years of my life in the High School were very happy. It is true that I suffered from love-melancholy; but as Sienkiewicz said there were some physical tortures so horrible that they seemed at moments like monstrous delight, so this love-melancholy was so profound that it had a certain grave charm like the loneliness of mountain scenery at twilight.

My two love-affairs were both hopeless. I fell in love with a girl at school and remained in love with her for more than two years, without ever meeting her or speaking to her. How amazed she would have been had she known! Later in Senior year there was another, whom I knew and talked with awkwardly and tongue-tied, who seemed to me incredibly beyond my low level of existence, although she tossed me frequent notes and once when she did not know I was looking at her, I saw her kiss a sprig of pussy willow I had given her. But I was a faint-heart.

I always think of the Hartford High School with loyal affection; it was a first-rate school. And I can understand how Maurice Baring felt about Eton. As it is quite the fashion in modern novels to look back with disgust at one's days in school and to represent the atmosphere there as barbaric, cruel, and stupid, the loyal strain in Maurice Baring's temperament comes as a refreshing change:

I cannot deal with the experience of others. I can only deal with my own. I haven't the slightest pretence of impartiality, nor the slightest desire to see the question steadily, and, seeing it whole, I am a violent, an unblushing, an unrepentant partisan. About my own experiences and my own feelings with regard to Eton I have no doubt whatsoever. I enjoyed Eton wholeheartedly and unreservedly: I enjoyed it all from the first to the last moment. If I had my life to live over again, I should like all that piece back with nothing left out. . . . I do not want Harrow to win the Eton and Harrow match either this year, next year or ever. I do not believe that any other school is as good as Eton—not nearly as good. I do not believe that Eton is quite different now from what it used to be. I believe that Eton is just the same; but even if she is not, even if she has changed for the worse, I believe her to be better than any other school. (*Lost Lectures*)

His saying he did not want Eton ever to lose the cricket match will be understood by most school and college graduates. Although the great poet Alfred E. Housman failed to get his degree at Oxford and was Professor at Cambridge so many years, he always wanted Oxford to win the boat-race. In microscopic imitation of so mighty a genius, I was never more emotionally devoted to Yale than while I was teaching at Harvard and enjoying its intellectual and social atmosphere; never more wild with partisan fervour than when the Yale athletic teams came to Cambridge. Returning to the Harvard Yard from a Yale victory, one of my Harvard pupils said, 'Mr. Phelps, I never saw anyone look so happy as you do now.'

17

GOING TO THE THEATRE

My mother never allowed me to attend any theatrical performances. As I had read all of Shakespeare at the age of twelve, I was eager to see a Shakespeare play, especially as Edwin Booth was then in his prime, and appeared annually in Hartford. Ordinarily, parents would be pleased if their children wished to see a play by Shakespeare; not so with ours. Finally, when I was eighteen, Thomas W. Keene, a melodramatic actor, came to Hartford to play *Macbeth*. I had a private interview with my father, and told him how passionately I desired to see this play. Finally he gave me fifty cents and said I might go, only I must say nothing about it to mother. 'We men must stand together.' Accordingly, that night I sneaked off, and with some other boys sat in the gallery and for the first time in my life saw a play on the stage. I was thrilled. When I came home, I found my mother sitting up for me; she had discovered where I had been; her sorrow was great and sincere; she felt that I had committed some dreadful sin; I saw it was no use even to consider the matter further. It is difficult to write about this without giving a false impression of my mother. She was never grim, never harsh; she was all tenderness and also full of fun; but the theatre was wrong, and Christians did not deliberately do what they knew was wrong.

That autumn, however, I entered Yale; and as I had never promised that I would not go to the theatre, I went fairly often. I saw George C. Miln play *Hamlet*. It has often been said that no one has ever entirely failed who has played the part of Hamlet. After having seen Miln, I know this statement is not true. It was interesting to see an actor deliver Hamlet's advice to the players while breaking every rule so definitely expressed.

Of the thirty-seven plays of Shakespeare, I have seen all but five, and I hope to see them all before I die. I have not seen *The Two Gentlemen of Verona*, *Timon of Athens*, and the three parts of *King Henry VI*.

The Shakespearean performances that made the deepest impression on me: Richard Mansfield as King Richard III, Edwin Booth as Shylock, and Maurice Evans as King Richard II. Evans's unabridged *Hamlet* in 1938 I regard as the greatest production of the greatest play in the world.

With the exception of the Passion Play at Oberammergau, I have never been more thrilled than by Sarah Bernhardt in *La Tosca*; hers was the finest exposition of the art of acting I have ever seen. That was in 1892.

Among other theatrical performances I shall never forget are *Les Caprices de Marianne* at the *Comédie Française*, Maeterlinck's *Schwester Beatrix* and Gorki's *Nachtasyl* in Germany, Ernst von Possart in *Faust* and Henry Irving's production of *Faust*, Féraudy in *Les Affaires sont les Affaires*, Mrs. Pat Campbell as Magda, Hermann Bahr's *Das Konzert* (Munich), Maude Adams as Peter Pan, Nazimova as Hedda Gabler, William Gillette, Louis Calvert, and Helen Hayes in *Dear Brutus*, Katharine Cornell as Elizabeth Barrett and Saint Joan, *Die Fünf Frankfürter*, *The Old Lady Shows Her Medals*, *Mary Rose*, the New York New Theatre Company in Galsworthy's *Strife* and in Maeterlinck's *The Blue Bird*, Louis Calvert's stunning performance in Besier's *Don*, Granville-Barker's production of *The Doctor's Dilemma* and *Androcles*, Granville-Barker's play *The Madras House* at the Neighborhood Theatre in

New York, the Theatre Guild's production of St. John Ervine's *John Ferguson* and *Jane Clegg*, Mr. Hampden's
Cyrano, and I suppose I could mention forty or fifty more.

The theatre has been one of the greatest pleasures of my
life; and I have been a drama critic fifty years. When I
reached the age of twenty-one, there was no more audible
objection to my going to the theatre, and I celebrated my
freedom by publishing a long criticism of Wilson Barrett's
Hamlet in the *Yale Literary Magazine* for March 1887.

I have had the good fortune to see and hear most of the
great actors of the world. On the whole, I think the combination of play and acting that made the deepest impression was the Passion Play at Oberammergau, which I saw
for the first time in 1890. Everything combined to make
this occasion memorable. It was my first journey in Europe; I was twenty-five; there was no railroad to Oberammergau; no shriek of the locomotive stabbed the sacred silence; and the peasants had not lost their pristine simplicity.

Furthermore I sat down in front, directly before the
stage, with nothing over my head but the sky. When it
rained, as it did three or four times during the day-long
performance, we let it rain. We did not know or care
whether we were wet or not. When one sits twenty or
thirty rows back in the more expensive seats, as I did on a
subsequent occasion, one has hundreds of tourists with
their opera-glasses between one and the stage. But sitting
directly in front, I forgot it was a play. I was in Palestine.

And of all the events in the tragedy, from eight in the
morning till five in the afternoon, the supreme moment for
me was not the Crucifixion, for I had steeled myself in advance. It was a moment during the procession to the cross.
There were seven hundred actors on the stage, from the
smallest children to the oldest men and women. On not
one face did I see indifference, inattention, or any assumed

expression. They themselves were *living* the scene, which is why I was living it with them. The small boys, as they picked up stones to throw at the Son of God, screamed, 'To the cross with the Galilean!' I have beheld many mob scenes, but none like this. The turbulent, frenzied throng moved incoherently and noisily along with their victim. Directly behind him was a group of women, shaken with grief, and sobbing. Suddenly the weary and blood-stained Sufferer stopped and turned around; and at that moment the raging, excited mob became still. In this awful silence Jesus spoke to the women:

> Daughters of Jerusalem, weep not for me, but weep for yourselves, and for your children. For, behold, the days are coming in which they shall say, Blessed are the barren, and the wombs that never bare, and the paps that never gave suck. Then shall they begin to say to the mountains, Fall on us; and to the hills, Cover us.

Omitting the Passion Play, which is produced with a sincerity founded on faith, a sincerity beyond the reach of the most consummate art, I think one of the supreme moments on the professional stage was that when Edwin Booth as Shylock advanced on the helpless Antonio. This I saw in Detroit in the year 1887; and I knew then why Booth was called the greatest American actor.

It was the trial scene; the judge had apparently given the relentless Shylock full power over his victim. Shylock had been whetting the shining knife on the sole of his shoe; looking up from time to time at the face of Antonio with hellish hatred—impatient of the legal delays, and of the appeal for mercy. When the judge apparently granted the final permission, saying:

> And you must cut this flesh from off his breast;
> The law allows it, and the court awards it—

Shylock, baring his wolfish fangs in a frenzy, cried out: 'Most learned judge! a sentence!' and then, with an expression of ferocity that I can never forget, he sprang at Antonio, screaming:

'Come, *prepare*!'

So long as I live, I shall see that face and hear that word, '*prepare*!'

One of the greatest of modern actors and certainly the most intellectual, was Richard Mansfield. When he was a young man, I saw him as King Richard III. It was a stunning performance all through; but the high moment came in the dawn ushering in the last day of the usurper's life. King Richard had been tormented all night by terrible dreams, in which appeared the apparitions of the men and women he had murdered. Finally, in the doubtful twilight preceding sunrise, Catesby called him.

The king came to the front of the tent, so obsessed by the awful ghosts of his dreams that he was not sure whether this figure in shining silver armour was real or merely another horror. The king said nothing; he advanced slowly, slowly toward his retainer, and finally reached out his groping hands; the moment he touched the solid armour and knew the figure was real, he embraced him and in a voice of indescribable relief he whispered, 'Oh, *Catesby*!'

The greatest woman actor I ever saw was Sarah Bernhardt, who made a deeper impression on me than Duse. I saw the divine Sarah many times, in classic and in modern plays. She was surely at her best in melodrama; for while she had all the resources of a magnificent artist, and her voice of gold could give significance and beauty to any poetry or prose, she was primarily a tragedian of action; the more passionate the scene, the more effective she became. I shall never forget *La Tosca*. She was inspired; she seemed to rejoice in the plenitude of her powers. Even in her tenderest love scenes she purred like a tiger, and her fingers clasped and unclasped in her lover's hair with the lazy movements of a great cat.

She was at her best in the dinner scene with Scarpia. She had reluctantly promised to grant Scarpia's demands if he would write out the paper which would save her lover. As he turned his back to her while writing out the note, she looked wildly over the wreck of the dinner table. Suddenly she saw a knife. Her eyes glared. She seized the knife and in order to steady her nerves, poured herself a glass of wine, which flowed over the top of the glass and all over the tablecloth. Then with the knife behind her back, she awaited the approach of Scarpia. He came toward her, smiling in the security of triumph. As he extended the paper toward her, she sprang at him like a wildcat and drove the knife into his breast.

Henry Irving never impressed me as a Shakespearean actor; like Sarah Bernhardt, he was at his best in melodrama. Those who, like me, had the good fortune to see him in *The Bells, The Lyons Mail, Louis XI*, saw Irving at the height of his power. I think his finest scene came in *The Bells* when he sat gibbering on the floor with the accursed sleighbells ringing in his ears.

Ellen Terry during many years was the favourite actress among English-speaking people; but although I saw her many times, she never gave me a thrill. She always seemed to be her charming self. I saw her as Margaret in *Faust*, yet I cannot remember her appearance or her voice.

Magda, by the late Hermann Sudermann, is a grand opportunity for the display of acting. The title role was played by Duse, Bernhardt, Modjeska, Mrs. Pat Campbell, by all the feminine stars. A supreme moment for me occurred at the beginning of the second act, one fearfully hot summer night in the uncomfortable little Royalty Theatre in Soho. Mrs. Campbell's acting was so magnificent that we forgot the heat. She was the prima donna who had left Main Street a long time before, and fresh from her triumphs, revisits her humble home. It is a stuffy little parlour, where it is clear nothing interesting has ever happened or can happen. Magda's mousey sister, a commonplace 'home-body,' dressed in unbecoming and cheap attire, is waiting alone in this depressing environment. Suddenly the opulent, voluptuous Magda foams into the room. She stops. She looks at the dreadful changeless furniture. Then she looks at her sister. Then she kisses her. Not a word was spoken, but I found that I was crying.

Louis Calvert was an actor of genius. I saw him many times—in the New Theatre as old Anthony in Galsworthy's *Strife*, in the Theatre Guild, as the butler in Barrie's *Dear Brutus*, as Andrew Undershaft in Shaw's *Major Barbara*. Under Winthrop Ames's direction in the New Theatre, he appeared in Rudolph Besier's play, *Don.* He was describing his conversion to Christianity, although at the moment he held a pistol in his hand:

> When I found salvation after many years of sin—oh, the blessedness of it! I was walking near the Marble Arch on a winter's afternoon, and I stopped to listen to a poor man who told of the Lord's infinite goodness and mercy. And all of a sudden, like a sunrise at sea, God lit up my soul. . . .

At that moment I actually saw the sunrise on Calvert's face, and I can see it now.

The most beautiful woman I ever saw on the stage was Mary Anderson as Rosalind. By a bit of bad luck, I missed seeing Coquelin as Cyrano, although I had the pleasure of meeting Coquelin at dinner in New York at the house of Mr. George A. Glaenzer. He was most gracious. John Bigelow, over ninety, was smoking a fat cigar and chattering vivaciously with Coquelin in French at one o'clock in the morning.

One day in New York in the Autumn of 1887, I saw Irving's fine production of *Faust* in the afternoon, and Possart's production in German in the evening. The scenic effects in Irving's performance I have never seen equalled, despite the advance in mechanical devices during the last fifty years. Mr. Alexander was good as Faust, Ellen Terry unimpressive as Margaret, Irving at his best in the tragically ironical part of Mephistopheles, as he conceived it. That evening I went down in the Bowery to the old Thalia Theatre, and there saw a totally different conception of Mephisto; for Possart made his chief characteristic *Roguishness*. The audience roared with laughter and relished the interpretation. Here God was seen on the stage as plainly as in the old Mysteries or in *Green Pastures*. The curtain rose showing cloudy effects; there was God, a man with a white beard and a sonorous bass voice, with the three archangels—buxom German girls. Later, when I saw Possart in the same role in Munich, the government did not allow God to appear in person—his voice was heard. Herr Possart told me the Catholic Church would not permit it.

That night when I heard the play in New York, the German audience was in a state of continual excitement; they gave demonstrations in mirth, and in vociferous applause. The audience seemed to be religiously divided, the Catholics downstairs, the Protestants in the gallery; and once I thought there was going to be a fight. When Mephisto spoke of the Church's having a capacious stomach for the receipt of money and treasure, the people in the gallery greeted this with loud laughter and tremendous applause; the people on the floor with hissing and imprecations which were kept up for some time. The passage that aroused this rumpus was

> Die Kirche hat einen guten Magen,
> Hat ganze Länder aufgefressen,
> Und doch noch nie sich übergessen;
> Die Kirch' allein, meine liebe Frauen,
> Kann ungerechtes Gut verdauen.

Years later, in Munich, I became well acquainted with Possart, who was the Intendant of the Royal Theatres. I told him of the day in New York when I had seen Irving's Mephisto in the afternoon and his in the evening. He laughed and said that Irving, wishing to show him a courtesy, sent one of his representatives to the Thalia Theatre, had him placed in a box with a huge wreath which he was publicly to present to Possart. Now in Irving's version as in the opera, the first scene is Faust alone in his study. So when the curtain rose, and the first scene was the Prologue on the theatre and that was followed by the Prologue in Heaven, the bewildered emissary left and reported to Irving that they were not playing *Faust* that night but some other piece the name of which he did not know.

On one of Irving's appearances in New Haven, I had the pleasure of meeting Mr. Bram Stoker, then known as Irving's manager, now far better known as the author of *Dracula* (1897). Mr. Stoker was genial; he apologized for not taking me upstairs in the hotel to see Irving; the actor had left word that no one under any circumstances was to be permitted to see him. Mr. Stoker died in 1912, and twenty years later I had the pleasure of meeting Mrs. Stoker on a Hellenic pilgrimage in the Aegean Sea. She kindly invited me to come to tea when we should both be in London. I spent a delightful afternoon at her house, meeting among other interesting people, Mr. Cunninghame-Graham, for whose literary art I have absolute reverence. He was then over eighty, tall and slender, with an Elizabethan pointed beard, and looking like a great Elizabethan gentleman. It was difficult to realize, talking with this quiet, unassuming patrician, that for many years he had played so great a part in the wildest and most dangerous frontier life. I remember when the conversation turned on Bernard Shaw, his saying, 'No one can form any accurate estimate of Mr. Shaw without emphasizing first of all his most characteristic trait, his personal *kindness*.'

Here is a letter Cunninghame-Graham wrote me from Ceylon:

THE HOTEL SUISSE
KANDY, CEYLON
JAN. 30, 1934

DEAR WM. LYON PHELPS

Your too kind letter & the press cutting have just reached me. I hasten to reply & to apologize for delay. In answer to your far too flattering reference to our brief too brief meeting, I can only say, that the pleasure was mutual, & that I felt extremely honoured in making your acquaintance.

Again thanking you & hoping we may meet again

Yrs sincerely,

R. B. CUNNINGHAME-GRAHAM

P.S. A jolt on a bronco, in early years, has made my writing very bad.
R. B. C. G.

During the last seven or eight years, exclusive of opera and motion pictures, I have seen about fifty plays annually; my appetite grows by what it feeds on. Though I suppose I am the only white man who has never written a play, some of the happiest afternoons and evenings of my life have been passed in witnessing plays—pure, flawless delight that remains as a permanent addition to memory. The theatre is one of the greatest blessings of humanity, and I feel an unpayable debt of gratitude to dramatists, managers, and the innumerable actors and actresses who have given me so much pleasure. I shall never become sufficiently sophisticated to lose the keen anticipation of a night at the play. I am not ashamed to confess that I love the preliminary moments, the crowded house of men and women, who have left their troubles; the lights, the proleptic music; the sudden darkness; the ascent of the curtain;—these will thrill me so long as I am conscious.

Of all the pages of Addison, I like most the famous description of Sir Roger at the play. 'As soon as the house was full, and the candles lighted, my old friend stood up and looked about him with that pleasure which a mind seasoned with humanity naturally feels in itself at the sight of a multitude of people who seem pleased with one another, and partake of the same common entertainment.'

And perhaps no one has ever better expressed the purpose and goal of entertainment in the theatre than Doctor Johnson when he said of his friend Goldsmith's new play *She Stoops to Conquer*, 'I know of no comedy for many years that has so much exhilarated an audience, that has answered so much the great end of comedy—making an audience merry.'

18

CLYDE FITCH

ONE person who unites in my memories schooldays and
the theatre was Clyde Fitch, a classmate in the High
School, who appeared on the monthly reports as William C. Fitch. He was even at the age of fourteen a complete individualist; he was unlike any other boy I had ever
seen. He hated outdoor games and would have nothing to
do with them; instead of speaking our dialect, he spoke
English accurately and even with elegance; he was imma-
culately, even exquisitely clothed; he made no friendships
among the boys and it was evident that he regarded us as
barbarians, which we were; we showed it in many ways and
particularly in our treatment of him. He seemed to be an
impossible person. We treated him exactly as the undergraduates at Oxford ten years earlier had treated Oscar
Wilde; they threw him in the Cherwell and wrecked the
beautiful decorations of his rooms in Magdalen.

Every morning at 'long recess' we ran out into the school
yard and played football furiously for twenty minutes;
Fitch remained in the schoolroom, writing notes on per-
fumed paper and tossing them to the girls; he seemed to be
deep in correspondence during most of the school hours.
I remember sitting next to him in the class in Caesar,
and despite the ever imminent danger of being suddenly
called upon to recite—which he did easily and well—I
observed he was engaged in the rapid composition of a
letter on light blue paper; when he had finished it to his
satisfaction he tossed it with surprising accuracy to a

maiden who was waiting to receive it. He was fourteen years old.

To us he seemed quite impossible; but how offensive we must have seemed to him! When we came in from football, streaming with sweat, stewing in our own juice, and sat down beside this immaculate person, whose very hair looked clean, what inner repugnance he felt we never knew; he never betrayed his soul to boys.

Once, while I was talking with him in his house in New York, he went back of his own accord to our schooldays. 'I knew, of course, that everybody regarded me as a sissy; but I would rather be misunderstood than lose my independence. The only concession I ever made was this: on stormy days, my mother forced me to wear overshoes to school, which I hated, and I knew it would not do to appear rubbershod before the other boys. So I always hid these offensive things before reaching school, and put them on again on my way home. I hated football, baseball; was bored to death by all sports; and I did not see why I should do things I hated to do merely to conform to public opinion.'

Judged by the standards most people use in estimating success, he was right and all the rest of us were wrong; for in later years we are credibly informed that his annual income was $250,000 a year. So he finally won the respect of the Philistines. The wife of Andrea del Sarto thought her husband was an ass, because he spent his time painting pictures, instead of acting like a man; but other people, she must have reflected, were even greater asses, because they paid real money for these things.

If my memory serves me, Miss Elsie de Wolfe once expressed her amazement that Clyde Fitch should know more about women than they knew about themselves. She said that at a rehearsal her cue was to walk upon the stage in high emotion; she did so; but her inner complacency was jarred by the playwright's voice coming out of the dark auditorium: 'That isn't the way to walk in order to express your feelings in this scene; I'll show you.' He did; he walked on, and she saw immediately that he was right and she was wrong. She could not understand his insight; but I could, for I went to school with him. During the long recesses when we were playing football he was spending those minutes with the girls, for he instinctively knew that they had more to teach him than we. That is where he laid the foundation of his success as a dramatist, even as Richardson learned how to write novels by composing letters for the village maids.

After High School we did not meet again until about 1900. He had gone to New York, earned a living as a private tutor, wrote some short stories, and finally succeeded in getting one or two curtain-raisers on the stage. In 1890 he became famous with his play *Beau Brummel*, superbly acted by Richard Mansfield.

In 1900 or 1901 he invited me to his house in New York and we were intimate friends for the rest of his life. I succeeded in inducing him to lecture at Yale, and the enthusiasm of the undergraduates pleased him.

Fitch was one of the best talkers in private or in public I have ever heard. One night in New Haven, I invited a group of ten undergraduates (The Pundits) to meet him at dinner in my house. After dinner, the students sat literally at his feet in my library, while he kept up a stream of brilliant talk until one o'clock, when it was time to take his train to Boston.

He told me an interesting story of Oscar Wilde. Before the public scandal Wilde's perversion was known by many men of letters. One day when Fitch was driving in his victoria along Piccadilly, he was hailed from the pavement by Wilde; he drew up to the kerb, and Wilde entered the carriage saying, 'Why is it, Clyde, that you don't come to see me any more?' and Fitch replied, 'Oh, Oscar, you know the reason perfectly well.' They conversed for half an hour in friendly fashion, and Fitch did not see him again until after his release from prison. Then some friend told him that Wilde was living in a small cottage at Dieppe and that he would appreciate it if Fitch called on him. Accordingly Fitch crossed the channel and found Wilde all alone in a small building near the sea. In the evening Wilde said, 'I'll read you a poem I have just written.' A tremendous storm of wind and rain was raging and to the accompaniment of rain and hail beating on the windowpanes, Wilde read from manuscript the whole of *The Ballad of Reading Gaol*.

In June 1909 Fitch spoke to my Yale undergraduate class in contemporary drama. He had just completed a new play, *The City*. He described the plot and characters, saying that on his return from Europe he would begin rehearsals. On 4 September he died in France; and when *The City*, the most successful of all his successes, had its first performance in December, the following lines had for me a tragic significance unintended by the author:

Why, it was only a minute ago he was there, talking with me! It doesn't seem possible——that now——he's dead——.

19

LOOKING FORWARD TO COLLEGE

THE only subject on which my father and I ever violently disagreed was on the place where I should 'go to college.' Indeed, for a short time during my second year in High School, discouraged by mathematics, I told him I would not go to college at all; he was so horrified that I never brought up the matter again. But as to the particular college, we had a daily combat for three years before he gave in, and that for the Biblical reason—it was because of my importunity. My father was not only a graduate of Brown University, he was also a Trustee; he regarded his election as Trustee as the highest honour of his life. My oldest brother Dryden had been graduated at Brown in 1877; and in the midst of my struggle with my father, my brother Arthur was sent to Brown, only one year before I was due. But this fact, instead of putting a quietus on my hopes, stimulated me to further efforts; so that I gave my father no rest, day or night.

I wanted to go to Yale. As a little boy in New Haven I had seen the undergraduates walking the streets like gods. Any allusion to Yale in the newspapers made my heart beat faster (it does still), and I followed every athletic event from afar, once in a while going to New Haven to see a game. But there was much more in my longing than athletic sentiment. I *knew* I needed the intellectual and social stimulus of a great university. I had never been away from home; I was brought up strictly in the Baptist denomination; I was backward in everything that is included in *savoir vivre*, and my intellectual life was more intense than broad. Brown is a great university today, and even in the eighties its long and noble history—it was founded in 1764— and its Faculty gave it high standing; but as compared with Harvard or Yale, it was then parochial; and I knew Yale was a better place for me. When I began my fight to enter Yale, my father never dreamed I should be successful; he told me at the beginning to dismiss the subject from my mind. He quite reasonably said that as a Trustee of Brown, one of his duties was to persuade as many parents as possible to send their boys there; and what if his own son went to Yale? My mother thought I ought to go to Brown, because its religious influence would be better for me than the more liberal atmosphere of Yale. The only ally I had was my aunt Libbie; and she could give no practical support.

I cannot remember the exact moment when my father capitulated; but I think he weakened in July 1882, the year before I was to graduate from the High School. My brother, with some other boys, was to camp out at Lake George, where we had both been the preceding summer. I volunteered to remain in the office, give up camping and my vacation, and work on the paper with my father, if he would finally consent to let me go to Yale; the consent could not have been final, because it was not really settled till some months later. But I remember with what a sinking of the heart I saw my brother and my friends leave for the camp. Alas, for my good resolutions! after about ten days in the office, I became very ill with an attack of malaria, and as soon as I got better, the doctor ordered me off to Lake George.

The hardest of all for my father to endure was this; when in the Spring of 1883 it was finally decided that I could go to Yale, my brother Arthur, who was then finishing his Freshman year at Brown, felt he must be treated as well

as I. So my father had to explain to the authorities at
Brown that as I was going to Yale, he would have to take
Arthur out and remove him also to Yale. This really was a
terrible blow; and I must say the President at Brown
seemed fully to understand and made it easy rather than
more difficult for the transfer to be made. Arthur's standing
was so high that he entered the Sophomore year at Yale
without any difficulty, his year at Brown receiving full
credit, and he was graduated from Yale in 1886, a member
of Phi Beta Kappa.

20

THE ROBBER

FRANK HUBBARD, my playmate at the West Middle School in Hartford, had gone to Michigan, to begin his life-work with his father; he wrote, asking me to come out and spend the summer of 1883 before I was to enter Yale. I had never been west of the Adirondacks, and was glad of this opportunity. I took a train to Niagara Falls, sat up all night in the day-coach, and spent the morning at the Falls, where the greatest of all swimmers, the famous Captain Webb, had lost his life in the whirlpool a few days before; many of the residents still believed he would turn up safe and sound. At noon I took a train across Canada to Sarnia, and as that was long before the railway tunnel had been made, I reached Port Huron on the ferry, stayed at the old Huron House overnight, and at six the next morning took the steamer *Milton D. Ward* for Huron City, my destination. The boat stopped at Lexington, Port Hope, etc., and reached Huron City at six in the evening, a voyage of exactly twelve hours. There the dock was half a mile long, and after my long trip from Hartford, I was glad to see Frank at the landing place.

The most exciting thing that happened during this summer in Michigan was a 'hold-up' and robbery. There was a country store, owned by Frank's father, and managed by the bookkeeper, Austin Case. Every evening Frank and I spent in this store, talking with Mr. Case, with customers, and casual visitors. One Saturday night, between nine and ten, when every one else had left, and we three were in the back office engaged in conversation, we heard the outer door of the store open, and footsteps approaching. We thought nothing of this, for the store contained the United States Post Office, and we supposed some farmer had come for his mail. Imagine our amazement when there came into the small enclosure where we were huddled in the corner, a masked man! He was tall, and just below his eyes hung a copious black false beard, which masked his features. Pointing a revolver at us he uttered quietly three words, and I can hear them now—'*Open that safe.*' During the day fifteen hundred dollars had been deposited in the safe; he must have known this, and he must also have looked in the window, and seen that we were together in one corner, so that he could command our position as easily as if he were controlling one man. For a moment I thought some yokel was playing a practical joke, because the beard was so grotesque; but I was quickly undeceived. The robber was directly in front of me; behind me was Mr. Case, and a few feet to one side stood Frank.

Was I afraid? I was in mortal terror. The blood in my body seemed to change into ice water, and my fear was horribly accentuated by the screams of the bookkeeper, who implored the robber not to shoot. The revolver was not more than three feet from my face; looking at it, I could see the bullets in the chambers; I saw also that the hammer was raised and the man's forefinger on the trigger. I did not dare to make the slightest motion, for fear the robber might instinctively or even accidentally press the trigger, in which case I should have died at the age of eighteen. Mr. Case was ten years older, he was well-dressed and we were in old muddy clothes, having spent the day out shooting; it never occurred to the robber that anyone but Mr. Case would have the key to the safe, whereas it lay in Frank's pocket. The robber could not bear to go away without the money he had come for; and repeatedly declared he would kill the bookkeeper if the safe were not opened. But the bookkeeper, in complete hysteria, finally convinced him that he did not have the key; and Frank was so calm that fortunately the robber did not guess its location. Finally, after what seemed an eternity, the robber asked for my watch. He did not allow me to give it to him. I placed it on the counter and he shovelled it into his pocket, while keeping the muzzle of that accursed weapon on my face; he took Frank's watch, and then backed into the store, telling Mr. Case to follow him. The till was opened and he took the eighteen dollars it contained. Then he backed out of the front door, and immediately we heard the galloping hoofs of his horse. I never saw him again, though we looked far and wide in the days and nights that followed. Some months later, however, as I was sitting in my college room in New Haven, the postman brought me my watch. The robber had been caught and sentenced to prison for twenty years.

I have read many detective novels where men remain calm while facing a loaded pistol; and I had often imagined myself getting the best of a burglar, if he should ever attack me. But on this one occasion I was so afraid, that I was careful to do or say nothing that might make the situation any worse.

My first sensation after he had left us was one of rage; had it been possible to kill him, I should have shot him without any compunction. In looking back on it, however, I am not sure whether that black rage was because of our being robbed or because I was ashamed of having been so afraid. I lost my watch but I also lost my self-respect; yet I do not really see what I could have done. The wild thought passed through my mind while I was facing the pistol—'suppose I leap right upon him, the three of us will overpower him, only I shall be dead.' Today I am glad of two things; I am glad I did not spring at him, and glad also I had no opportunity to kill him.

21

COLLEGE DAYS AT YALE

Ihr bringt mit euch die Bilder froher Tage,
Und manche liebe Schatten steigen auf.

IT would be difficult to exaggerate the eagerness with which I looked forward to college. If I had been away at boarding school, the transition would not have been so violent. But I had always come home every day from attendance at public school; and it seemed to me that going away from home to college, and living there with the other undergraduates, would be paradise. I was happy at home, I loved my parents who were very kind to me, and yet I longed to get away. Boys and girls long to leave home; boys love to go away to college and girls love to have a separate apartment with the key in their sole possession.

There are two reasons, which only partially explain it. The first is that although the average child loves his parents, he does not love them half so much as they love him. This is true, as he will find out when he has children of his own. The tragedy is that the presence of children is necessary to the parents' happiness, while the son or daughter, though loving the parents, gets on very well in their absence. The greatest novel ever written on the eternal theme of the Younger Generation is Turgenev's *Fathers and Children*; and although individual parents and individual sons may be quite unlike the parents and their son Bazarov, the feeling on both sides is about the same. The love of many parents for their children is mingled with terror; terror that the youth may outgrow the parents' point of view, fear that he may be bored at home, fear that the solicitude shown to prevent this may only increase it.

The second reason is that young people hate the round of expected events, hate a routine; they love the absence of restraint; and they find this freedom more with their mates than with their family.

However this may be, no prisoner ever desired freedom more than I desired to go to college. On the few occasions when I went to New Haven at the age of fifteen or sixteen to see a football game, my excitement during the contest, great as it was, was not nearly so great as it was while I was walking down Chapel Street after the game was over. I was in this huge crowd of undergraduates; then when we reached the college buildings, I had to keep on to the railway station to take the train for Hartford, while these marvellous beings entered the college gates. If I should ever see the blessed angels entering Paradise with myself shut out, I could hardly envy them more. To think that these young men lived together in dormitories, ate their meals together, shared their studies and their sports!

And here again, at least during the first year, realization was not inferior to my hopes. Later there came something of a disillusion which Browning expressed so perfectly in his poem *Pauline*, written when he was twenty; the first part of the passage does not overstate my glow of anticipation as I gazed afar at college towers, but the second part—the disillusion—was in my case only partly true.

> As some world-wanderer sees in a far meadow
> Strange towers and high-walled gardens thick with trees,
> Where song takes shelter and delicious mirth
> From laughing fairy creatures peeping over,
> And on the morrow when he comes to lie
> For ever 'neath those garden-trees fruit-flushed
> Sung round by fairies, all his search is vain.

First went my hopes of perfecting mankind,
Next—faith in them, and then in freedom's self
And virtue's self, then my own motives, ends
And aims and loves, and human love went last.
I felt this no decay, because new powers
Rose as old feelings left—wit, mockery,
Light-heartedness; for I had oft been sad,
Mistrusting my resolves, but now I cast
Hope joyously away.

My brother Arthur and I roomed on the top floor of North Middle College, in the Old Brick Row; his company was of course congenial to me, but it was a bad arrangement for him. He should have roomed with some member of his own class; it was hard enough for him to enter at the beginning of his Sophomore year, but it made conditions much harder to be surrounded with Freshmen.

I found college life wildly exciting; and the differences between this and my previous school experiences did not lose their novelty. The four classes were forced to attend morning chapel at ten minutes past eight—a splendid thing; there we Freshmen sat in our assigned places, saw the mighty Gods of the football field come down the aisle, and realized that we too, belonged; we were a part of all this. To me it was exciting to have college classes on Saturday morning and on other afternoons at five o'clock, in rooms illuminated by gas jets. Never in my life had I attended school on Saturday; and to go to a class at five in the afternoon was almost as remarkable as if we had gone at five in the morning.

Class sentiment at Yale was then at its height; in our class rush against the Sophomores, in our crew race against the other classes, in our class baseball game against Harvard, I would at any moment gladly have died for my class flag. (This sentiment is obsolete today.) When our class crew beat the Sophomores, we carried every member of our eight up Chapel Street, and had a huge bonfire on the campus. In the Rush against the Sophomores, held on a field more than a mile from college, I had all my clothes torn off, except my shoes and socks. A Junior lent me a linen 'duster,' and clad only in that, I walked a mile through the streets to college, thrilled with pride and delight; on the campus, one of my Professors looked at me as if I had been a decayed fish. But I had fought for '87!

It was an interesting spectacle in New Haven, in the days when attendance on daily morning chapel was compulsory, to see, between five minutes and ten minutes past eight, the throngs of students sprinting toward the university house of worship. With many of them the art of dressing, eating breakfast, and running to chapel illustrated the irreducible minimum of time.

As the philosopher Thales in the seventh century before Christ said that the most difficult thing in the world was to know oneself, I think it pertinent to state that there was one undergraduate, who, although consistently unable to know his lessons, knew himself better than most philosophers. Having been informed that no further absences from chapel would be excused, he placed a placard on his bedroom door to attract the attention of the janitor. In large letters was printed the command, 'Wake me up at a quarter before eight; it is important; never mind what I say or if I make no response; be sure and wake me up at quarter before eight.' Then under this injunction, 'Try again at half-past nine.'

It was well for me that I went to Yale. I had never met anyone from our Southern States until I entered college; I had never heard the Southern accent on the lips of a white man. I remember how strange and yet how pleasant that accent sounded when spoken by my classmates from Louisiana, South Carolina, and Georgia. There were also five men in my class from San Francisco; every locality in the country was represented.

Among the most agreeable and most profitable hours in my four years were those I spent in long walks with classmates; we thought nothing of twenty miles. These long journeys on foot, with good conversations and amusing adventures, are as obsolete nowadays as Roman chariots.

Persons who live in magnificent scenery do not always appreciate it. I remember one late afternoon on our New Hampshire excursion, as we entered a vale between mountains, a young farmer asked us where we came from. I answered, 'Connecticut.' He uttered *Connecticut*! as if it were Mesopotamia! and added, 'I wish I could see Connecticut.' 'But,' said I, 'we have no mountains like these in Connecticut.' 'Oh, damn these mountains!' And it appeared that he had never been outside of that valley.

I had entered college intending eventually to become a lawyer; I read some law in leisure moments, and occasionally visited city courtrooms. I had visions of myself winning great cases in crowded courtrooms, and then entering politics, and becoming a United States Senator; for a boy of eighteen, I was deeply read in American political history. There was no moment in my college course when with a theatrical gesture I 'renounced the law,' but becoming more and more interested in literature, I was, in spite of my ambitions, slowly, at first imperceptibly, but finally, drawn entirely away from legal studies or ambitions.

Most of our classrooms were dull and the teaching purely mechanical; a curse hung over the Faculty, a blight on the art of teaching. Many professors were merely hearers of prepared recitations; they never showed any living interest, either in the studies or in the students. I remember we had Homer three hours a week during the entire year. The instructor never changed the monotonous routine, never made a remark, but simply called on individuals to recite or to scan, said 'That will do,' put down a mark; so that in the last recitation in June, after a whole college year of this intolerable classroom drudgery, I was surprised to hear him say, and again without any emphasis, 'The poems of Homer are the greatest that have ever proceeded from the the mind of man, class is dismissed,' and we went out into the sunshine. Two Freshmen instructors shone by contrast; a young teacher of Latin named Ambrose Tighe, who left Yale in a few years, and had a fine career as a lawyer and member of the legislature in Minnesota. He tried to teach us Roman history as well as Latin grammar; he talked about Horace as though Horace were a man about town, and he himself looked and acted like a man of the world. I remember his saying that he would like to teach us Lucretius, but that he did not know enough; 'for,' said he, 'in comparison with Lucretius, the entire works of Horace and Virgil sink into insignificance.' The older members of the Faculty looked upon Mr. Tighe with suspicion. He made Latin interesting; and they got rid of him.

One of our instructors in Greek, the opposite in all respects of the Greek teacher I have mentioned, was Horatio Reynolds; he had a defective leg, and was by us affectionately called 'step-and-a-half,' shortened to 'Steppy'— while later college generations always spoke of him as 'Limpy.' He was universally beloved. He told us we ought to read some Greek history outside of the classroom. Therefore for several months, I stayed up one hour later, and every night from ten to eleven, I read Grote's *History of Greece*—one of the best things I ever did.

We had only Latin, Greek, and Mathematics until the last few weeks of Freshman year; then Professor Cyrus Northrop taught us Hill's *Rhetoric*. It was Northrop's last year at Yale, as he had just been elected President of the University of Minnesota, where he made a great reputation. He was universally respected and beloved, and died at nearly ninety years of age. I called upon him in Minneapolis when he was eighty-seven; remembering the opening of Plato's *Republic*, I asked him how it felt to be so old; was he as happy as he was in youth or middle age? He said, 'I am just as happy now as I ever was, only there is such a short time left.' That night he made a speech at the Yale Alumni Dinner; it was a masterpiece—brief, witty, incisive.

Well, in the Spring of 1884, when he was teaching us Freshman Rhetoric, he announced that every one must select some essay—any essay— write a synopsis of it, and bring it to the classroom. I had never read Carlyle's *On Heroes and Hero Worship*; and I chose for my 'effort' the chapter called 'The Hero as Man of Letters.' I chose this because I thought it would be good for me. It was.

There are spiritual experiences we would not have missed for anything. They are worth more than years of routine existence. In an hour the soul rises to a higher plane, and, despite temporary lapses, one can never live again permanently on the lower level. The mind leaps to an elevation. That afternoon in my room on the top floor of old North Middle, as I absorbed 'The Hero as Man of Letters,' I was caught up into an ecstasy. There is no other word which truly describes my state of mind. The pages of the book seemed to me aflame, and the fire consumed me utterly. When I came to read my paper in the classroom, the spell was still upon me. I trembled with excitement, and could hardly read the words I had written. Professor Northrop, who had probably expected a perfunctory report, looked at me with astonishment. His talent for ironical comment had made him a terror both to slackers and to gushers; if he had chilled my holy enthusiasm with his famous icy disdain, I should never have forgiven him. But apparently he discerned that my uncontrollable enthusiasm was sincere; that I was really under the domination of the genius of Carlyle. I have not forgotten his brief but emphatic word of commendation.

At the end of my first year in college, my parents decided to move from Hartford to New Haven, so that my brother and I were to live at home while continuing our studies. This was the worst thing that ever happened to me during the four years at Yale. I heard their decision with dismay, a sinking of the heart. It was impossible to explain this feeling to them, without hurting their feelings intolerably. Yet I went as far as I dared. I begged them not to give up their pleasant social life in Hartford. Besides, my father would have to take the train every morning to Hartford and the train back in the evening, in order to continue his editorial work. But in those days every editor had a pass on the railway, so transportation cost him nothing. There were two reasons which induced them to make this change of residence. One was the expense; it was cheaper for them to have us live at home than to pay for our board; but the strongest reason was the unhappiness of our mother in our absence. She could not bear to have us away.

Those seemed good and sufficient reasons to my parents; and how could I explain that they were destroying my college life? For surely the curriculum to which I was faithful was only a part of a great experience; I wished to be independent, to live in a college dormitory, and be master of my time. Furthermore, a student in New Haven was at a serious disadvantage among his mates; the others, who came from afar, belonged to the college; he merely attended recitations and went home like a boy in High School. How I envied the students who came from San Francisco!

Nearly all undergraduates enjoy Freshman year the least and Senior year the most; with me my happiest year was the Freshman, for it was the only time when I had an actual share in the full life of the place. It was a very humble share, for I was a Freshman, and I was obscure; but after all, I belonged.

In our Freshman year two distinguished visitors from England were introduced by the President at morning chapel. One day Lord Chief Justice Coleridge spoke to us a few moments on the study of the classics; and I remember his saying that *every day since he had been graduated from Oxford*, he had read something in Greek or Latin; and he was one of the busiest men in the world. He was then sixty-three.

One morning the President introduced Matthew Arnold; all I can remember is a large man with conspicuous dark whiskers, a strong English accent (I had never previously heard any one so pronounce the word *years*) who made a complimentary remark saying that young men like us would be carrying the burden of civilization in future years.

Oscar Wilde had given a lecture in New Haven the year before I entered college; he was entertained by the daughters of Professor Whitney, who took him to a masquerade ball, where three persons came dressed as Oscar Wilde. He did not seem to mind. They asked him if he would like to dance. He replied, 'No; I used to dance; now I dine.'

In Sophomore year I had three memorable experiences, which are comparable to the excitement I had as a Freshman with Carlyle. In our Greek course we studied Sophocles's *Oedipus Rex* with Professor Frank B. Tarbell. He was then in his thirties, and the type of man more common at Oxford or Cambridge than in an American university. He was an elegant and fastidious scholar, precise and dignified in his manner and speech. He never had a frivolous moment. He was not popular with the undergraduates and for two reasons; he had only contempt for laziness and stupidity; and the depressing Faculty atmosphere of official formality, which I shall speak of later, prevented him from sharing with the students the riches of his mind. Yet he had already been discovered by some of the more ambitious undergraduates; they had sought him out, and got him to meet a few of them informally. These were in the class above ours, so that we were prohibited from attending these meetings; but rumours began to circulate about college that Professor Tarbell was a quickening intellectual force. In my Senior year he gave three courses open to only a few students; two of these, *Ancient Philosophy* and Mill's *System of Logic*, I count among the most powerful inspirations of my mental life. The third was an oddity which Tarbell gave only once, and no one has ever repeated. It was called *The Logic of Chance*. I loved the study of logic and hated the study of mathematics. Alas, I soon found this course was largely mathematics. Among the few students was Irving Fisher, today a famous mathematical economist. Even as an undergraduate he knew much more about mathematics than Mr. Tarbell, and constantly corrected the instructor in the classroom; to Tarbell's credit, so far from resenting this, he gave every sign of appreciation.

I have always regretted the lack of one course which perhaps I might have had. In our Junior year Mr. Tarbell announced a course in Greek history, open to the one hundred and fifty members of our class. As I was the only one who elected it, it was withdrawn. But if I had only gone to him, and insisted that he give it for one pupil! It would have been a tremendous experience.

He was too independent for the Faculty standards of those days; his superiors told him he was teaching the students philosophy when he should be teaching Greek grammar; and they refused to reappoint him, just at the time when he was becoming an intellectual stimulus to many. I think his departure was the most severe loss Yale sustained for many years. To him it was a tragedy. He was a lonely, awkward bachelor, diffident and shy; we were afraid he would obtain no position anywhere. And he loved Yale with all his heart.

He secured a subordinate post in the Classical Faculty at Harvard; and a few years later, when I went to Harvard as a graduate student, I renewed my acquaintance with him. He told me the number of students at Harvard electing Greek was so rapidly diminishing that he had received notice his appointment could not be renewed; he had been offered the five-year directorship of the American School at Athens, but he could not bear to leave America for so long a time.

President Harper was about to open the University of Chicago; I wrote him about Tarbell; he immediately telegraphed Tarbell, offering him a professorship. Tarbell accepted, and spent the rest of his days until the age of retirement at the University of Chicago, where he was honoured and beloved and happy. I do not think Tarbell ever knew the source of that telegram, but I look back upon it with unalloyed satisfaction.

It may be that Tarbell's unorthodox views on religion had something to do with the unwillingness of the Yale authorities to retain his services. There was an annual Day of Prayer for Colleges; many of the recitations were omitted, and a speaker from the Faculty, chosen by the students, addressed each class separately. The Freshmen had first choice, and invariably chose Professor Northrop, who was very impressive; in our Sophomore year we had Professor Frank Abbott, who later had a distinguished career at Chicago and Princeton; in Junior year we had Tarbell, and I shall never forget the sudden shock in one of the sentences of his address. After giving us valuable advice, he said, 'And then you must remember that in all dangers, depressions, and difficulties you have always one Friend; one Friend always faithful, to whom you can go with confidence at any time, in the assurance that you will find solace and inspiration; a Friend that will never desert you, a Friend always accessible; I refer of course to—*Books*.'

In the Autumn of my Sophomore year, we were studying the *Oedipus Rex*; Tarbell gave out a number of subjects for essays, which we were required to write and submit to him. He assigned to me the subject 'Does Sophocles represent Oedipus as suffering for sin?' In preparation for this, I sat down and read through at a sitting the entire play in the original; a memorable experience. Then I read many of the commentaries of various British scholars and liked none of them until I found the Irishman Mahaffy's, which seemed to my young mind full of common sense. I wrote an essay in which I maintained the negative position; there was no sin here, it was a tragedy of fate. I was requested to read it in the classroom. Professor Tarbell asked me to come to his dormitory room and talk it over, and he began by saying, 'Well, the highest compliment you can pay any essay is to say it is worth criticizing.' And he proceeded to criticize it, greatly to my edification. He hated exaggeration in any form. He hated inaccuracy. I have never known anyone else who combined to so high a degree the love of truth with the ability to speak it. Once I heard a rumour that a friend of both of us had been drinking too much; I asked Tarbell for the facts. At first he said the circumstances were so unusual that it might not be possible to contribute anything of value to the discussion. But I insisted, whereupon he replied, 'I think it must be admitted that excessive indulgence in potations has temporarily impaired his health.' The man eventually made a complete recovery.

After Tarbell died and his brother John died, his watch and his Phi Beta Kappa key came to me; they are among my most treasured possessions.

The other powerful influence in the Autumn of my Sophomore year was in English literature, and probably had much to do with my turning from law. There was no instruction in the English language and literature in the first two years at Yale, except a few months in Rhetoric with

Professor Northrop in Freshman year and three months in a manual of English literature in the winter term of Sophomore year.

But one November day in Sophomore year the entire class was rounded up in one room and addressed by Mr. McLaughlin, tutor in English. He placed on the board twelve subjects and announced that every member of the class must hand in before Christmas an original essay on one of these topics; furthermore, there would be first, second, and third groups of prizes. None of these subjects appealed to me; and as we were leaving the room, I asked my classmate John Pomeroy, which subject he had selected. He replied, 'The twelfth, of course.' Now the twelfth and last was 'Tennyson's analytical power as shown in *Maud*.' I said, 'But I have never read *Maud*.' 'Neither have I,' he replied, 'but it is the only subject worth the attention of an intelligent man.' That was the way we used to talk about the Faculty!

I decided, with some eccentricity, that before writing my essay, I would read the poem. I shall never forget the afternoon in my father's house when I read *Maud* for the first time. I entered the room one kind of man and left it another kind of man. When one passes through a profound spiritual experience, although one is apparently unaware of one's surroundings at the time, they are indelibly impressed on the memory. I thought nothing of it then, but I remember now the weather of that cold November afternoon, the location of the desk in the room and the angle at which I sat in my chair at that desk. I had always been fond of narrative verse, I had read all of Shakespeare, but I do not think I had any real appreciation or understanding of pure poetry until the day I first read *Maud*.

It did not come on the first reading. I read the poem through rapidly from beginning to end, and was not impressed. But I was ambitious; I wanted to win a prize. I knew I must feel intensely about this poem if I were to write well about it; accordingly I began to read it through the second time, and with more attention.

I cannot tell why one particular line converted me. But in the beginning of the second part, the duel scene, after the neurotic hero has shot Maud's big brother, the line

Was it he lay there with a fading eye?

suddenly transformed me from a Philistine to a lover of poetry. I saw the scene at dawn; I heard the singing birds; I breathed the odour of the woods and flowers in the garden; I saw the white figure of Maud in her party dress fleeing in horror through the shrubbery; I saw the handsome big brother dying, and the lover standing stupidly with the smoking pistol in his hand. I knew in that moment the significance of poetry; that the poet is the interpreter for us of the beauty of nature and of the passions of man. There was another garden in front of me, besides the one described in the poem. It was the garden of Poetry; the gates opened wide, I entered, and I never came out.

I shall always be grateful to this poem, for it was the means of my conversion; I escaped from the gall of bitterness and the bond of Philistine iniquity, into the kingdom of light. And after all, it is a great poem. In his novel, *The Old Man's Youth*, William De Morgan, speaking of passionate love, called *Maud* 'the poem which goes further to describe this frame of mind than anything else in English, or out of it.'

I felt an exaltation when in morning chapel President Porter read aloud the names of the four men in the Sophomore Class who had won first prizes—Kent, Lee, Phelps, Pomeroy. William Kent was the best natural writer in college; in later years he became a member of Congress and a philanthropist; Lee was a Chinese student of remarkable ability; John Pomeroy became a professor of Law.

Because I was a first prize winner, I was asked by one of the Editors of the *Yale Literary Magazine* to write an essay for that journal; there was nothing I wanted to do more than that; accordingly I wrote an essay on Philina, the coquette in Goethe's *Wilhelm Meister*. But the editors from the Senior Class rejected it, saying none of them had ever heard of the novel.

With the ten dollars prize money, I bought Mommsen's *History of Rome*. And I read it.

In the second term of our Sophomore year we took up the study of *The Clouds* by Aristophanes. On the first day we were met by our instructor, Doctor Walter Bridgman, whom we never saw after that first meeting; he took typhoid fever. A graduate student, only two years out of college, filled the vacancy and taught us for six months. His name was Joseph Lewis, a brilliant man. He had a brother among the undergraduates named Charlton M. Lewis, who later became my beloved colleague as a professor of English literature. Young Joseph Lewis was then in perfect health and Walter Bridgman had typhoid fever; but in two or three years Lewis was dead of tuberculosis and Bridgman is alive today at the age of nearly eighty.

I did not admire the way Aristophanes treated Socrates in *The Clouds*; I had read Plato's *Apology*, *Crito*, and some other works, and Socrates was my hero. I was delighted when I discovered that Aristophanes's play was voted a failure by what corresponded to the Pulitzer Prize Judges of that year, 423 B.C. Accordingly, when it was suggested by Mr. Lewis that we write essays on any subject connected with *The Clouds*, I called my essay 'The Didactic Methods of Aristophanes as Shown in *The Clouds*.' I have not often been thrilled by my own compositions, either while writing them or afterwards. But I finished my essay with this paragraph, and a thrill came over me while I was writing the last sentence. I was twenty years old.

There is therefore no reason why we should reverse the decision of the Athenian judges, who pronounced the play a failure. Its wit and even its earnestness do not save it. The man who is befouled is to us almost the incarnation of virtue. The figure of the poet, piteously begging the Athenians for the prize, contrasts harshly with the solitary grandeur of Socrates standing before his accusers, perfectly calm in the contemplation of the grave.

I left the essay at Mr. Lewis's rooms, and the next day I received an urgent invitation to visit him; he was quite overcome by that last sentence, and asked me how in the world I had ever happened to think of it. I could not tell him; while I was writing, I *saw* those two men addressing the Athenians, one pleading for a prize, the other refusing to plead for his life.

In my Sophomore year I was not very happy. These three essays were the three most important events for me. Mathematics were the curse of my existence. For six months, three hours a week, we had a course in Mechanics. Toward the close of every hour, the professor gave out a problem, and said that as soon as we had finished, we were to hand it to him, and leave the room. I tried every time, three times a week for six months; I never shirked it and never took a 'cut.' Not once in the whole six months did I obtain a correct solution.

It has always seemed strange to me that in the revolt against the required studies of Latin and Greek—a revolt that began in America in the eighties, and became successful in the early years of the twentieth century—no one ventured to attack the requirement of the study of Mathematics. It was thought Latin and Greek were useless and mathematics valuable and practical. The truth is that for every occupation except one for which higher mathematics are a prerequisite, like civil engineering, Greek and Latin are more *useful*. For the preacher, the lawyer, the physician, the journalist, and for nearly all business men, the classics are definitely more important than mathematics. Training in the ancient languages, with the accompanying culture and history, with the aid given to the mastery of expression in English—where in comparison stands the binomial theorem?

I believe in the equal dignity of all studies. But it is absurd for a university to require neither Latin nor Greek for a degree and yet insist on the higher mathematics. I have no doubt that for those who have a natural aptitude, mathematics are valuable as intellectual discipline and training, whether one will make practical use of them or not. But for those who have no gift and no inclination, mathematics are worse than useless—they are injurious. They cast a blight on my childhood, youth, and adolescence. I was as incompetent to deal with them as is a child to lift a safe. I studied mathematics, because I was forced to do so, faithfully and conscientiously from the age of three to the age of twenty-one, through my Junior year in college. After 'long division,' nearly every hour spent on this subject was worse than wasted. The time would have been more profitably spent in manual labour, in athletics, or in sleep. These studies were a brake on my intellectual advance; a continuous discouragement and obstacle; the harder I worked, the less result I obtained. I bitterly regret those hours and days and weeks and months and years which might have been profitably employed on studies that would have stimulated my mind instead of stupefying it!

I remember after a year spent on Chauvenet's *Geometry* in college, I looked up the name of the author to discover whether or not he was still living; and when I found that he was no more, I wrote on the title-page of his accursed book, 'Thank God, he's dead!'

I was always an ambitious student, and wished to excel; therefore it was necessary for me to put more time and effort on mathematics than on any other study. Even so, my grade in mathematics was never distinguished in college, and I could not possibly have been graduated with honours had I not in other studies stood very high.

But while I was unhappy, my fate was not nearly so tragic as that of hundreds of other boys. There have been hundreds who were deprived of the advantage and the privilege of a college education because of their inability to obtain a passing mark in mathematics. They were sacrificed year after year to this Moloch.

I am aware that Henry Adams lamented the fact that in his education there had not been more and higher mathematics; but surely his view of life was sufficiently pessimistic without that added bleakness.

I am glad that of all the essays and compositions I wrote during the four years in college, and I wrote a great many, I never submitted one before handing it in to any other person for correction, suggestion, or advice. No doubt my essays would have been improved had I done so; but I am glad I depended only on myself.

In the summer vacation of 1885, at the end of my Sophomore year, I went to Michigan on a visit to my friend Frank Hubbard; his sister Annabel had come there to live in the Autumn of 1884. And here I am, fifty-three years later, in the summer of 1938, writing at my desk in this same Michigan house, with my wife Annabel in the next room.

My greatest single ambition in college was to become a member of the editorial board of the *Yale Literary Magazine*. This is not only the oldest college journal; it is the oldest monthly magazine in America. It had been founded in 1836 by a group of students, chief among whom was William M. Evarts of the class of 1837; later he became one of the greatest American lawyers, and Secretary of State in the cabinet of President Hayes.

There had always been five editors, chosen from the

Junior class, who edited the *Lit.* in their Senior year. Election was by ballot, the entire Junior class assembling for the purpose; and competition was always keen. I had seen copies of the magazine before entering college, and modestly hoped that some day I might be chosen. Talking with a group of my classmates in Freshman year, I expressed my hope, but also my belief that I could never win; they were so certain of my success that I rashly promised them all a good dinner if I should be elected two years later; they remembered this promise at the proper time. Yet at the beginning of my Junior year, with the election only five months away, I had abandoned hope. I had submitted compositions in Freshman and in Sophomore year, and none had been accepted. But at the opening of the Autumn term of Junior year, one of the editors, Arthur Shipman, urged me to try. To my delight, I succeeded in getting two compositions into the October issue, and an original story into the November one; but as all three of my compositions, a story, an essay, and a poem, were rejected for the December number, my hopes sank again.

It was not considered proper for any candidate to attend the meeting of the class when the election took place; I waited in my room for news of the balloting. In an hour two or three of my friends came shouting under my window that I was elected; and although, of the five successful candidates, I received the least number of votes, I was elevated to the seventh heaven of bliss. John Norton Pomeroy and William Kent of California, Andrew F. Gates of Connecticut, and Charles H. Ludington of New York, were the other four; of the first two I have already spoken. Ludington became a high official in the Curtis Publishing Company of Philadelphia, and Gates a successful lawyer and member of the State Legislature; Gates and I are the only ones yet alive.

As a rule, editors wrote less after the election than before. It was the other way with me; and once safely on the board, I wrote continuously for a whole year, essays, stories, poems. It was good practice. In studying the play *King Henry IV*, the character of the Welsh chieftain, Owen Glendower, whom Hotspur ridiculed so cruelly, took hold of my imagination, and to one of the numbers of the *Lit.* I contributed the following Sonnet:

GLENDOWER

'I can call spirits from the vasty deep:'
The starry fires are under my control;
To me the future is an open scroll
Unfurled by angels in my golden sleep.
Kings tremble at my name; and women weep
In piteous terror as my chariots roll
To bloody battles; the funereal toll
Foretells the harvest I am come to reap.
I have a part in God's almighty power!
My voice will calm the surly ocean's swell,
And hush the boisterous winter's icy breath.
My joy is in the combat's dreadful hour:
I fear no foe in earth or heaven or hell;
And laugh in mockery at grinning death.

In the Spring of Junior year I competed with other members of the class for the Junior Exhibition prizes; eight men were chosen, who delivered their successful compositions in public, the winner to receive the Junior Exhibition (later called the Ten Eyck) prize. No subjects were announced; one could write on anything one chose. I wrote on 'Goethe as a Religious Teacher;' for although I was then forced to read Goethe in translations, I had, since I was seventeen, been reading *Wilhelm Meister*, *Faust*, the shorter poems, *Truth and Poetry*, *Iphigenia*, *Götz von Berlichingen*, *Werther*, and many other works. This competition aroused great excitement in those days, because the winner was usually elected to a Senior Secret Society. I was chosen among the eight and spoke my piece; I did not win, but the work in preparation for this essay was of great value.

I was told by some of the judges afterward that I should have won had I spoken better; and indeed, I spoke very badly, in a monotonous manner, and as if I did not believe what I was saying, though it came from my heart. I learned by my failure the importance of earnestness and emphasis in public speaking. The reason for my dullness on the platform was that a member of the Faculty (who for some cause I never discovered disliked me intensely), ridiculed me before the other men, while we were getting instructions from him about the preparation of our pieces for the great day. The unexpectedness of this attack and the virulence with which it was uttered, destroyed my confidence.

In my Sophomore year, after I had definitely given up the idea of becoming a lawyer, I wasted a good deal of time wondering what I should do; and one day I asked an older man for his advice. 'You have nearly three years before you graduate; you should not give the matter a thought; you cannot make any decision until the emergency comes; haven't you got a lesson for tomorrow? Sit down and study it.' This was the first I had heard of the advice, 'Live one day at a time.' It seemed to me sound, and I followed it.

So in the last term of my Senior year, with Commencement only a few weeks away, I could not make up my mind what profession to follow. But I had narrowed it to three things—the ministry, journalism, teaching. In those days there was no unemployment for any man of average health and intelligence, who had no bad habits; so one really could choose. I talked with the editor of a daily newspaper, who offered me a job as reporter then and there —take it or leave it—at twelve dollars a week; but as he would not wait one month for me to graduate, I left it.

As it turned out, however, my life has been spent in the practice of all three professions; and indeed at this moment, I am a teacher, a preacher, and a journalist.

22

THE YOUNGER GENERATION

I HAVE known six younger generations. I have looked forward, I have looked around, I have looked back. I may add that I have looked back only professionally, in the endeavour to understand the young men whom I teach. Personally, I have looked back very little. When I was a child, I wanted to be a man. When I was a young man, I wanted to be a mature man. And after I had descended into the vale of years, I did not, as apparently many do, look back with longing to the days of my youth. It is always the new experience I am seeking; I am wasting no time in the vain endeavour to recapture the irrecoverable past.

It does not disturb me that the body grows old. But when does one himself grow old? I think I can state accurately the exact moment when a person passes into old age. It is the moment when in solitude one's thoughts regularly turn more to the past than to the present or future. In the matchless Shakespearean phrase, the *stealing steps of age* overtake our slowing bodies; but they can never catch up with an alert mind.

When I was a little boy in the grammar school, the seniors looked to me like demi-gods; no truly great man today can seem to me quite so wonderful as those giants. They were fourteen years old. As a child, playing in the streets, I looked with envy on the college undergraduates. They were dressed in those days like a modern stage caricature of a professor. They wore frock coats, tall hats, and whiskers, yet they were in the heyday of their youth.

Good, bad, and indifferent they were. One degenerate offered me an unpardonable insult; another seemed angelic. I lost the ball I was playing with; and seeing my dismay, he bent down to me, gave me a quarter, and told me to go to the nearest store and buy a new ball. In an instant I rose from despair to rapture. I wonder if my benefactor is still alive. I wish I knew his name.

Fifty years ago I knew the younger generation by personal and intimate contact; I was among my contemporaries. Today, although I am with them every day, what do I really know about them? When someone asks me if the young men of today drink more than formerly, I am the very last man to possess the necessary knowledge. That some of them get drunk is certain; but they never came into my classroom drunk, they never called upon me while drunk.

Those who believe the present younger generation have bad habits should consider former times. In the eighteenth century, excessive drinking was the rule. Faculty and students got drunk together. Before the Civil War in America there was an immense amount of drinking. The growth of athletic games has had much to do with the improvement in personal habits. When I was an undergraduate, there was certainly a good deal of drunkenness, though not comparable to the excesses of earlier days.

The younger generation in my time had a narrow and provincial outlook. They were interested mainly in the affairs of their own little world. They were mainly Philistines: they had little respect for scholarship, were innocent of culture, knew nothing of good music or art, and cared not at all for international affairs.

A large number of modern undergraduates have travelled in Europe; they are acquainted with good literature, good music, good plays; they know not only books, but the editions of books; many of them indulge in intelligent conversation. In all these things there has been an advance.

A lady from out of town told me she came to New Haven to attend an important concert. She hurried into a restaurant to get a hasty meal. She had happened to enter one filled with students; and she supposed the conversation at the tables around her would be devoted to athletics, motion pictures, and automobiles. She was amazed to find that most of the talk was excellent, interesting conversation on interesting themes.

There is a straightforward frank honesty about young people today that commands admiration. Outwardly they are not so religious; it would be impossible to maintain prayer-meetings and religious exercises, which, even though they were slimly attended in the old days, were still a recognized part of college life. But I suppose the younger generation today *think* more about religion than they used to. They are eager to find out the truth about everything, and cannot be put off with any subterfuge. If people today are worried about the large amount of religious scepticism in college, they should remember that youth has always been more or less sceptical. It has outgrown some of the things it has been taught in childhood, and it has not yet reached a maturer view. The *Yale Literary Magazine* for the year 1879 contained an article called 'Religious Skepticism in College,' written by an undergraduate, which, if printed word for word today, would be considered up to date. There is an attitude toward religion worse than either scepticism or hostility; indifference. There is certainly today a good deal of outspoken scepticism and a certain amount of downright antagonism. But there is not so much indifference.

Dr. Cyril Norwood, Headmaster of Harrow School, in his book, *The British Tradition in Education*, mentioned five pillars as its foundation: religion, discipline, culture, athletics, public service.

Whatever we may think of the first four, there is no
doubt that the last is an essential article in the creed of
modern youth. They do not want to lead a selfish life. They
really long to be useful to their community, to their country, to the world. They may not always listen eagerly to
the gospel of orthodox religion; but to the gospel of sel-
fishness they will not listen at all. If you should tell them
merely to make the most of themselves, that the wisest life
is a life of personal aggrandizement, they would look upon
you with scorn. My hope is that life in the world will not
dull the beauty and freshness of their ideals; that they will
not become callous; that they will not compromise with
their conscience. When they have reached middle age, will
they still hold fast to these ideals? If so, the world will be
safe in their hands.

We must remember that in every age the average member of the older generation has looked with distrust on the
new. Why is this? Is it because as we grow older, we grow
out of sympathy with youth, forget our own youth, and de-
lude ourselves with the idea that boys and girls should be
as sober and self-restrained as their teachers? Remember
the splendid warning of Browning, which he put into the
mouth of the great Pope of Rome:

> Irregular noble scapegrace—son the same!
> Faulty—and peradventure ours the fault
> Who still misteach, mislead, throw hook and line,
> Thinking to land Leviathan forsooth,
> Tame the scaled neck, play with him as a bird,
> And bind him for our maidens! Better bear
> The King of Pride go wantoning awhile,
> Unplagued by cord in nose and thorn in jaw,
> Through deep to deep, followed by all that shine,
> Churning the blackness hoary.

Is it because we are jealous? We must soon leave active
participation in the great game of life, and we cannot bear

to have the game go on, played by our successors? The younger generation, said Ibsen, are knocking at the door. Shall we wait for them to break it down, or shall we admit them gladly?

I think the chief reason older people shake their heads dubiously over the younger generation is that there has been a steady increase of informality. Easy intimacy of manners seems to many serious elders akin to promiscuity in morals. 'I don't know what our girls are coming to!' If any one is depressed today over what one thinks may be a shocking loss of modesty, if any one thinks that our boys are irresponsible and our girls without reticence, let me insist that this is the way the younger generation has always seemed to venerable eyes. Now if the typical representatives of the older generation had always been right, the world would have gone to the dogs long ago; for in every period of history, prophets have announced that the world is bound dogward.

Homer remarked constantly on the degeneracy of the young men of his time, as compared with their noble and splendid ancestors. Someone dug up a rock in Egypt that had been buried about three thousand years. On it was an inscription, which a scholar interpreted. It announced that contemporary young men were effete, not at all like the hardy fellows of the good old times.

Before the Great War, I heard constantly from older men the statement that college boys were no good; that they were lazy, irresponsible, not serious, unfitted for an emergency. Then came the war, and these same boys endured hardships that no Spartan or no Roman could have sustained. Furthermore, if they were used to luxuries, think what they gave up; whereas, in the days of our ancestors, going to war was in many respects like going on a picnic. The difference between ancient wars and the Great War may be summed up in a phrase: *From campfires to poison gas.* Yet there was only one thing modern boys were afraid of; they were afraid they would not get there in time.

There is a passage in the gospel of St. Luke older people should consider. It is a prophecy of the coming young man, John the Baptist: 'And he shall go before him in the spirit and power of Elias, to turn the hearts of the fathers to the children.'

Some fathers are trying to make their sons resemble them. Is it not possible that one reason for the misunderstanding between the older and the younger generation arises from the fact that we do not turn our hearts to them?

If a son or a daughter shock the parents by announcing he has lost his religious faith, it will not do to sneer or to laugh. Profound sympathy and intellectual respect are what will help.

And there is something that will help far more. If a son says he no longer believes in the Christian religion, what is the only convincing reply? *It is, to live like a Christian.* This is more difficult than any verbal rejoinder. But the life is the only proof. From love and dependence on parents, children quickly pass to criticism. If fathers and mothers will illustrate the standards they profess, they will not have to worry.

To those numerous members of the older generation who fear that the young people are going to the devil, I recommend the following paragraph in a letter I found in the *Memoir of Lady Rose Weigall*, written 24 July 1862. The italics are hers.

> I sat at dinner by the Duke of Hamilton, who inquired much after you. He is still wonderfully handsome, and I was much struck by his *gracefulness* in dancing, which he did with several other middle-aged after dinner. It was a contrast to the *slouching walk* which the young men call dancing.

One day when I was expounding to undergraduates Tennyson's 'Locksley Hall Sixty Years After,' in which he lamented the loss of female reticence, reverence, and modesty, for the 'maiden fancies' were 'wallowing' in 'Zolaism,' I threw out the general query, 'Why is it that the older generation have always thought the younger generation were going to the devil?' and one of the students, Dana Von Schrader of St. Louis replied, 'Perhaps the younger generations would have gone to the devil, if the older generations had not always thought they were going there.'

And at about the same time, another undergraduate sought my advice alone after class. He was a good fellow, neither affected nor priggish. He spoke quite seriously. 'I am going home for the Christmas vacation, and I wish you would tell me what to do. I have no desire to drink; I simply don't like it and don't want to drink. But what shall I do? I don't want to hurt father's feelings.'

No satisfactory novel has ever been written of college life, and only one first-rate story of school life, *Tom Brown's Schooldays*, which combines local realism with the spirit of eternal boyhood.

As there is no good novel of college life, so is there only one good play, *Alt Heidelberg*. And never did a successful drama start less promisingly. When the curtain rose on the opening night, managers, actors, and author feared the worst. The playwright remarked, 'If this piece has as many performances as it has had rehearsals, I shall be content.' But to the amazement of all back of the curtain, the play scored a smashing success, and is apparently an immortal classic. It is not only frequently produced at the repertory theatres of Germany, it has also been translated into many languages. Richard Mansfield and later the New Theatre Company played it in America, and in 1924 it had a long run at the Porte-Saint-Martin in Paris. Like *Tom Brown* it has the perfect combination of realistic local conditions with the undying spirit of youth. Any man or woman who can see *Old Heidelberg* without a lump in the throat has ceased to be human.

The social life of America has changed so much since the eighties that those times seem almost as remote as the Middle Ages. And as the colleges are close to the national life, they have been borne along on the current. What were once regarded as luxuries are now considered necessities—how many who are sixty years old had the custom in the eighties of ordering in a hotel a 'room with bath'? Compare the number of city-dwellers who formerly owned a horse and carriage with those who now own an automobile.

Toward the end of the eighties, the colleges lost their monastic character, and became huge 'business propositions,' the change being noticeable in the daily activities of the College President. President Hadley's immediate predecessors at Yale were Noah Porter and Timothy Dwight. He said when he called upon President Porter, he usually found him reading Kant; when he called on President Dwight, he found him reading a balance-sheet. It is unfortunate that the modern undergraduate so seldom has an opportunity to see or speak with the President. Over a hundred years ago, Timothy Dwight the First used to meet the members of the Senior Class once a week—they asked him questions on any subject in the universe, and he answered them. Some of these were published, and it is interesting to see that they were largely the topics that are discussed today—freedom of the press, religious scepticism, war, international relations, censorship of the theatre, etc. Despite the size of modern classes, I think the College President might meet once a week all Seniors who cared to come, and conduct a question box. The President is usually a scholar and a man of the world; a weekly meeting of this kind might be of value, and ought to be a relief to the President from the importunate cares of finance.

Although the undergraduate today has a wider range of

activities than in the eighties, in one respect the earlier age was happier. College life ought to be different from the life of the world, and in those days it was. The men depended on one another for their chief happiness; they took long walks, and had interminable discussions. Football was an *athletic* event. For days before it, they discussed it, and after the game, if their college won, they celebrated together; if they lost, they analysed the tragedy. Today in practically every college in America, a football game is not primarily an athletic event, it is a social event. The game is a two-hour interval in forty-eight hours of dancing.

Changes in social life have affected the professors more than the students. Nearly all of my college teachers wore frock coats made of broadcloth, and their manner to the students was icily formal; today the professor appears in the classroom in sport clothes, talks and dines familiarly with students, plays golf and tennis with them, and comes into close and friendly relations. There was one way in which the old-time professor got into 'closer contact' with the undergraduate than now. Every member of the Faculty was then a policeman; it was his duty to stop disorder, and there was plenty of it to stop. The Reverend Ezekiel Robinson, President of Brown in the eighties, was over six feet in height, with long legs and arms; one winter night he heard a disturbance in front of his house, which stood at the top of a steep hill. He rushed out; the students scattered; he ran after one luckless individual, and just as the fugitive rounded the corner, the President caught him in the seat of the pants with a kick of such force and accuracy that the student was projected down the slope with terrific speed. In that sense the Faculty then came into close contact with the 'student body.'

23

INTERLUDE: *HIC ET UBIQUE*

When I was seven or eight years old, as I was walking up Chapel Street, New Haven, amid the crowd of shoppers, I saw an old man, with a white beard, old and ragged and looking feeble and cold and hungry, asking individuals in a piteous tone, 'Won't you give an old man a penny?' Feeling very sorry for this wretched beggar, I stood and watched him. All of a sudden he came over to me and bending down low to my little face, he whispered, 'Don't you worry about me. I'm all right and I've got plenty of money.' Then he raised the lower part of his beard, revealing the face of a healthy young man. He followed this gesture by drawing from his pocket a canvas bag containing a pint of cash, filled to the brim with silver coins. I looked at this in amazement. At that moment another passer came along; and my beggar went right up to him and said in heart-rending tones, 'Won't you give an old man a penny?'

This was my first revelation of human duplicity. I did not give him away. But why did he take this chance? Was it because he could not endure the expression on my face? Was it merely because I was a child?

Many years later, as I was standing in line to buy a ticket at a railway station, I marvelled at the sublime patience, the sweet courtesy, the undeviating politeness with which the ticket-seller answered foolish questions. Three or four women preceded me and each one of them asked this man repeatedly superfluous, almost idiotic questions. To each

one he gave a sweet smile and answered with perfect courtesy. When I finally reached him, I said, 'I can't help admiring the courtesy and patience you show in answering so
many unnecessary questions.' A transformation came over
him. He said, 'Jesus Christ! Jesus Christ! some day I'll
break their Goddamned necks!'

My remark seemed to touch a nerve in this apparently
calm man.

Why do oral corrections of our manners so enrage us?
Mr. William Walker of Albany sent me a cutting from an
English newspaper. A municipal orchestra concert was
being given at Folkestone. Mr. C.E.Mumford, an alderman, a borough magistrate, and member of the Kent
County Council, entered the room, took a seat at a table,
ordered coffee, and began to read a book. In order to get a
better light, he turned his back to the players, and was
quietly enjoying himself, reading and listening to the
music. Two men immediately approached him; one called
him a damned cad, and the other said he was insulting the
audience and the orchestra by sitting with his back to the
stage, and insisted that he be forcibly ejected. Alderman
Mumford, like many men in a similar predicament, became more and more angry the longer he reflected on this
lesson in etiquette. He said to a reporter:

> I am a peaceful old man of 71, but at the time I felt like hitting
> both men. I went into the building to enjoy the music, and to read my
> book, and I did not think that I was doing any harm by reading or
> sitting as I did. I am taking legal advice in the matter.

Self-constituted censors of other people's behaviour are
irritating. It is curious into what a frenzy of rage they can
drive their victims, and how lasting is the sense of injury. I
met a man who told me that in a New York restaurant occupied only by men he removed his coat, whereupon a

waiter told him to put it on. He swore horribly while telling this. When Sir Sidney Lee was in this country, he lit
his pipe while sitting in a man's club. He was told that
pipes were not allowed. He never recovered from the shock.
Many years ago I had finished my meal in a hotel 'coffee-
room' in Norwich, England, and while waiting for the
waiter to bring my bill, I lit a cigar. An Englishman at an
adjoining table came to me and said: 'You should remember there are ladies present.' I was too astonished to make
any reply. But as soon as I got outside, I found I was boiling with rage. Even now I cannot think of the incident with
calm. I suppose there is so much vanity in all of us we resent fiercely unsolicited lessons in etiquette.

But why should any one regard it as an insult to be mistaken for one who does honest work? Coming down to
breakfast at seven in a Philadelphia hotel, I saw a man
bending over the unlighted newspaper stand. I asked:
'Are these today's New York papers?' He turned around
resentfully and said: 'I don't know any more about it than
you do.' He thought I thought he was the paper man. The
more the idea penetrated his mind, the angrier he became,
and he added stuffily: 'How would I know any more about
it than you?' Of course he ought to have said, 'How *should*
I know?' But the time for giving him a lesson in English
grammar seemed inopportune; so I merely said: 'Sir, your
face seemed so intelligent that I thought you could answer
any question I should be able to ask.' He snorted. But why
should he be angry? Once, when I entered a theatre and
stood at the top of the aisle, a man and his girl approached;
he shoved his tickets into my hands and demanded that I
show him his seats. I answered: 'I'd do it in a minute, if I
had the least idea where they were.' Then he profusely
apologized, and his companion becomingly blushed. But
why apologize? I was not angry—why should I be? At a

social function in New Haven, a freshman handed the plate containing the remnants of his food to a New York multimillionaire, thinking him to be the butler. The great capitalist, leader of Newport society, instead of throwing the plate in the boy's face, took it without comment and carried it away.

Many 'good' Americans seem to be troubled by the vast number of English authors who come here to lecture, are eagerly and copiously entertained, return to their native land with much money, for which in some cases they have given nothing except their digestion. The thing certainly has its amusing side, especially when the 'lecturer' knows nothing of the art of public speaking, looks at the audience quizzically, begins his remarks by saying he has nothing to say and takes an hour to prove it. But why be offended? Attendance is voluntary. Some say acidly, that if we sent our authors over there, they would not receive either money or hospitality. Perhaps not; yet Mark Twain found it easy to obtain both. At this moment we have no Mark Twain; and while reading Franklin, I hit upon the possible reason why Americans entertain overseas visitors so energetically. In a note appended to his *Remarks concerning the Savages of North America*, Franklin said, 'It is remarkable that in all Ages and Countries Hospitality has been allow'd as the Virtue of those whom the civiliz'd were pleased to call Barbarians. The Greeks celebrated the Scythians for it. The Saracens possess'd it eminently, and it is to this day the reigning Virtue of the wild Arabs. St. Paul, too in the Relation of his Voyage and Shipwreck, on the island of Melita says the Barbarous People shewed us no little kindness; for they kindled a fire, and received us every one.'

Europeans generally believe that American wives are too dominant; but Doctor F.T. Wright of Arizona told me he saw the following framed motto in the window of a house in Berlin:

Ich bin der Herr im Hause und was meine Frau sagt, wird gemacht!

ARNOLD BENNETT AND THE EDUCATION OF GIRLS

My friend and former Yale pupil, Thomas E. Murray, Jr., of Brooklyn, gave me a photostat of this letter; a reply to one his brother Joe had written Mr. Bennett, describing the accomplishments of his five daughters.

75, CADOGAN SQUARE, S.W.I
21st December 1929

DEAR MR. MURRAY,

Thank you for your letter. Your story of your father is very interesting. Your story of the young ladies is more than interesting. It is, to me, distressing. Young ladies ought in my opinion to be brought up to do something more than play the piano and dance and ride and talk French. My view is that everyone, however rich, and beautiful, ought to be brought up to earn his or her own living. Also that all women who have any notion of getting married ought to learn to be professional housekeepers in every department of this vast and difficult task.

All good wishes,

Yours sincerely,

ARNOLD BENNETT

Quite often one hears the expression 'I don't know anything about music, but I like, etc.' An unexpected variation on this well-worn theme saluted my ears from a clever woman in a town in northern Connecticut. She had returned from the service at church, and remarked casually: 'I don't know anything about music, but I hate our choir.'

I do not pretend to have any ability as an architect, plumber, or carpenter. But if I were making the furniture and furnishings of a house, I should lower all the desks and elevate all the wash-basins. This applies also to the kitchen sink, where many good women have strained their backs. A great number of people get writer's cramp and neuritis by writing either in too low a chair or on too high a desk. The effort of writing is increased by every additional half-inch added to the height of the desk. That ought to be self-evident, yet every desk I see is too high.

On the other hand, one bends over double to wash one's hands; wash-basins should be elevated. Furthermore, nearly all faucets just barely project over the rim of the basin, so that it is impossible to get one's hands under them to catch the falling water. They should stick out at least three inches.

I advise those who dislike puns not to read this. Our tennis-courts in New Haven are near Bradley Street, where among many other members of the college faculty lived my friends Professor and Mrs. Frank Porter. One day, while I was playing tennis with my colleague Jack Crawford, a strong south wind brought an appetizing odour of grilling beefsteak from the direction of Bradley Street. I wondered from which house so delightful a thing came, and Jack said it must be coming from the Porter house.

The most embarrassing question I ever received in public was from the late Don Marquis, whom I greatly admired. I asked him to give a lecture at Yale on the Francis Bergen Memorial Foundation, and a huge audience appeared. After introducing him, I left the platform, and took a seat in the auditorium. In the middle of his lecture, he remarked that some writers had declared that they found first-rate composition not only delightful but easy; that all the common talk of the terrible and distasteful labour was absurd; that the satisfaction of having written well made the work pleasant. 'I do not agree with them,' said Marquis; 'to write well is extremely hard work. *Don't you find it so, Mr. Phelps?*' This is like the question in court, 'Have you stopped beating your wife?' You cannot answer either Yes or No. Nor did I.

The relativity of immorality in books is shown by the following.

While visiting at the house of a friend, I happened to open idly a volume of the *International Cyclopædia* and came upon this article on Alexandre Dumas, who gave the world the incomparable story of *The Three Musketeers*.

> Altogether it may be said that the appearance in literature of a writer like Dumas is a portentous phenomenon; and the avidity with which his immoral fictions are devoured, is the most severe condemnation of modern, and especially French, society that could well be pronounced.
> *Dumas Fils*. Who has unhappily followed in the footsteps of his father. . . . His principal work is *La Dame aux Camélias*—a novel on which is founded the notorious opera *La Traviata*. It is one of the most audaciously immoral works in existence.

This volume is dated 1892.

There is a whole philosophy of life in a missed short putt, and it makes for pessimism. One does not need to know what a putt is to understand what I mean. For what I mean is this. It is strange that men and women should be so constituted that they can do things easily when the doing of them is of no importance; whilst the moment it becomes essential the doing of them becomes a thousandfold harder. To knock a golf-ball into a hole two feet away is so easy that the ordinary man or woman, while practising alone, could probably do it two hundred times successively; but when a championship depends upon sinking a two-foot putt, there is no one who is not in danger of missing it.

There seems to be a curse on humanity, which lessens ability when it is most needed. Why should the intense desire to do a thing reduce a man's ability to do it? In a perfect world, it would be just the other way around; the more important the crisis, the greater would be the performer's skill. But among the children of men, a consuming eagerness to accomplish something—no matter what it may be—usually makes its accomplishment far more difficult. This is why ' Casey at the Bat' is at once one of the most pessimistic poems in the language and one of the truest to human nature. Why is it easy to walk on a plank at an elevation of two feet and difficult at higher elevations? Why do the most skilful surgeons turn from operating on members of their own family? Why do the greatest orators only seldom rise to an occasion? Why is it that in the complete works of Wordsworth, only a fourth part is good? Why is it that Shakespeare, who had a command of language so marvellous that he seemed to be able to find the right word without effort—why is it that only about seven of his plays are generally read and about thirty neglected? Why is it that the greatest humorists cannot be funny when they most strenuously wish to be? Why did Richter say that every great poet goes to his grave with his best poems unwritten? Why are so few happy retorts made in conversation? Why does the after-dinner speaker make his most brilliant speech on the way home?

I am entirely of the opinion expressed by Heywood Broun in his *Pieces of Hate* concerning after-dinner oratory. I regret that this institution survived the war. It will, I am afraid, survive everything except the treatment recommended by Mr. Broun. Most speakers hate it, most audiences hate it; it has no real friends, and yet it goes on its devastating course. Having to speak at a public dinner in Chicago, I found my place at that pillory of torment, the speakers' table; and there, seeing a magnificent man in evening dress, I gave him my name and grasped his hand with what cordiality I could command. He replied: 'I'm the head waiter, sir.' 'Shake hands again, old man,' I cried; 'you don't know how I envy you!'

Instead of having a long stupefying dinner, followed by long, stupefying speeches, how much better it would be, if we really wished to hear the senator, or the ambassador, or the captain of industry, if we could meet and hear him and, at the conclusion of the oratory, sit down together and enjoy a good dinner! And we should all have a subject for conversation. Furthermore, the speaker would not dare to talk indefinitely. I remember being obliged on one occasion to preside at a 'business men's banquet;' there were five speakers; the third spoke two hours and thirty minutes. I was sorry for the fourth and fifth, but still more sorry for myself, for my post of honour made escape impossible.

Sitting next to one of the other speakers at a public banquet, I observed he ate nothing, and in reply to my enquiry, he said he spoke better from abstinence. 'Ah, but what an error,' I replied; 'for then, if your speech is a failure, you have lost everything.'

At the famous dinner in honour of the seventieth birthday of Mark Twain, he stated that he bought his cigars by the barrel; that some of them had belly-bands, and some not. The little paper band around the cigar is a nuisance, and in endeavouring to pick it off with the fingernail, one frequently inflicts on the cigar a mortal wound. Years ago I made an attack in public on the cigar-band. Among the many letters I received was one from Tampa: 'This nefarious practice was begun years ago by manufacturers of the famous 5-cent variety. Gradually it was imposed on the better grades as an act of protection. Now, however, there is a tendency away from it. I live in Tampa, where we make over 1,500,000 cigars every day. You will find many styles of the better sort coming out now without bands.'

Dr. W.C.Hovey of Nokomis, Illinois, wrote that the bands came from Cuba, where Spanish ladies smoked cigars, so that 'Their pretty fingers might not be stained by coming into contact with the tobacco.'

What has become of the spelling SEGAR, so common in America fifty years ago? To my astonishment, it appeared in *Action at Aquila* (1938), by Hervey Allen.

A poignant sorrow is that I cannot blow rings. I have given the matter serious attention and prolonged practice; and by making horrible grimaces, I can once out of fifty times emit a circle. Yet some of my friends, without looking any worse than usual, can send ring after ring into the air. Professor Barrett Wendell of Harvard, after shooting a succession of rings, would, with astonishing muzzle velocity, shoot a final one through the whole row,

> As right through ring and ring runs the djereed
> And binds the loose, one bar without a break.

In my youth only Catholic and Episcopal clergy could smoke with impunity; others would lose their posts. I remember my own contrition and my respect for a Congregational clergyman, the Reverend Edward Reed of Holyoke, Mass., father of Professor Edward B.Reed of Yale, who, after dinner lit a cigar and I stupidly said, 'I suppose you find a smoke soothing after a day's hard work,' and he replied with a laugh, 'No, that has nothing to do with it; *I love the nicotine.*' This reply would have pleased Mr. Chesterton.

Why is it that a tailor is usually eager to please his men clients, whilst a dressmaker tyrannizes over her woman customers and treats them with royal disdain? A pretty question that might lead to much speculation.

One of the worst foes to human happiness is the fresh-air crank. I love fresh air as much as anybody, but I love it where it belongs—outdoors. I do not like too much of it in the house, and I particularly hate the combination of in-and-outdoor air, because the ingredients are never kindly mixed. I hate a wind blowing across a library-table, and I hate a draught down the back of my neck. One of my grievances against the fresh-air crank is that he has a positive genius for the inopportune. Just when I am absolutely comfortable in a warm interior on a winter day, and can laugh from my security at the cold, some crank is sure to say: 'Don't you think it is very close here?' He walks across the room and opens a window on the back of my neck, letting in the poisonous chill. For in a public meeting or anywhere else the fresh-air crank always opens the window on somebody else's back. He then returns to his safe chair, and says: 'That's better.' Once a friend of mine remarked on closing an open window, 'I've got only one drop of blood in my whole body, and I want that to circulate.'

A reprehensible habit is that of a host who gives a dinner-party and arranges that the guests immediately after the feast is over shall repair to a room that would answer admirably for cold storage. After eating, one is naturally cold, and should go into a warm room. This is proved by the fact that if an open fire is burning on the hearth of the room to which the dinner-guests adjourn, every one instinctively makes for that fire. Usually a large man reaches it first, stands with his back to it, and addresses the company.

Dining-rooms and their successors should never be cold. (There is only one thing worse than a cold dining-room, and that is a cold bathroom.) I felt a strong affection for a convivial and cheerful guest, who, at a dinner-party, in the midst of winter, when the host enquired, 'Shall I open

a window?' replied: 'No! Shut all the windows and open
all the bottles.'

We are told it is unhealthy to be in a warm room. But
how much better it is to be unhealthy and comfortable,
than to be healthy and miserable. My advice to the fresh-
air crank is to stay outdoors, where he belongs, for he has
never been civilized. If he must enter the house or the
hall, and must have fresh air, let him open the window on
his own back; and let us hope that he catches a terrific cold.

I have often admired the placidity and repose of the
American cow. She has a philosophical calm never attained
by man. In a forty-acre lot I saw one cow sitting in quiet
dignity, and in an unruffled manner contemplating not
only the sole item on her eternal bill-of-fare, but *all the
meals* she would eat during the next four months. Suppose
you or I between breakfast and luncheon were compelled
to gaze at the entire accumulation of food we were to eat
during the next hundred days! and not only gaze at it, but
be surrounded by it! Yet the cow did not seem to mind.
She looked off and beyond her food, apparently absorbed
in agreeable meditations. Victor Cherbuliez, in his charming novel, *L'Idée de Jean Têtérol*, said: 'All cows are alike;
there is in their eyes something fixed and eternal, a silent
dream of fresh grass.' Men and women can dream of food
only in its absence; but the fortunate cow has both her
dreams and their realization.

Yet here is a curious thing. If I had the same food for
lunch and dinner every day the monotony would become
intolerable; yet I have the same bill-of-fare for breakfast
every day and enjoy it so much that I should not like it
changed in any particular. And breakfast is my favourite
meal. I am hungrier for that than for any other repast.
I know in advance what I am going to have not only on a
particular morning but on every morning for the rest of my
life. If I knew now that I was to have the same breakfast

every morning for the next six hundred years, I should rejoice.

Browning's Pied Piper refuses to remain in the misty mid-
region of legend. Recently in Budapest a piper appeared
who, according to the press despatches, saved a section of
the city from a plague of rats by bewitching the animals
with music. Then the city authorities refused to pay the
piper. The *New York Herald Tribune* informed me that a
young veteran of the A.E.F., John Rogoff, is the Pied
Piper of the East Side. Mr. Rogoff goes into a cellar,
whistles in a peculiarly compelling fashion, and out come
the rats. They stream towards him and eat from his hands.
He gave a demonstration of his power to a sceptical observer, who, after counting seven rats in thirty seconds,
incontinently fled. He was afraid, not of the beasts, but of
the whistling. 'It had a strange influence on him. He was
afraid he'd get up and snatch a piece of bread himself.'

Why do old people eat so much? Many families have some
aged and worn-out member, who has to be supported, and
who seems to the supporters a prodigious consumer of food.
Old Isaac was swindled by that unscrupulous mother-and-
son combination, Rebekah and Jacob—swindled through
his lust for meat. The reason the aged and the idle eat so
much is that meals are the chief events in the day. To an
active man or woman good food is agreeable, but the eater
is not primarily interested in it; he has been busy up to
meal-time, and is thinking of what he has to do the moment
the repast is over. Sometimes indeed, no matter how excellent the luncheon, it is an interruption in an absorbing
occupation, which is why most Americans could not endure
afternoon tea. Do you think I would stop my work or my
golf for that? But to venerable and idle persons, who have
nothing to do except look forward to the next meal, this is

a sacred rite, not to be taken carelessly or hastily. Observe how particular everyone (except the seasick) is about food on an ocean liner, or while travelling anywhere. Some unsympathetic critics say that those who complain about their meals on shipboard probably have not very good ones at home. Of course; that is precisely why they complain when meals are all-important. It is not so surprising that tourists often remember a certain place in Europe because there they had a marvellous dinner. And there is point to what Oscar Wilde said: 'I hate people who are not serious about their meals.'

Nothing is more astonishing to people of the twentieth century than to read of the enormous meals consumed by people in the eighteenth. Those who have read *The Diary of a Country Parson* edited by John Beresford, were astounded by the huge dinners and yet they were part of the daily programme. In his case it was almost pathetic to see how as he grew old he increased his daily doses of rhubarb and began vaguely to wonder if it were not just possible that a quart of port wine might not be good for the gout.

But as late as July 1859 in the extreme heat of midsummer the following dinner card shows what a Yale class consumed at the Old Tontine Hotel in New Haven.

SOUP

Mock Turtle

FISH

Salmon, boiled; Lobster Sauce

ROASTS

Rib of Beef, Chicken, Giblet Sauce; Spring Ducks, Apple Sauce
Ham, Champagne Sauce
Broiled
Leg Mutton, Caper Sauce. Smoked Tongue. Capon, Oyster Sauce

COLD ORNAMENTAL DISHES

Boned Turkey, au Truffes, garnished with Jelly
Mayonnaise de Volaille, à la Parisienne
Langue de Boeuf, decorated
Lobsters, au Naturel
Pig's Head Cheese

CONDIMENTS

Spanish Olives, Worcestershire Sauce, Chow Chow, Brandied Cherries
Pickles   French Mustard

ENTRÉES

Côtelettes d'Agneau, grillé, au Champignons
Fillet de Boeuf, piqué, au Purée de Pomme de Terre
Spring Chicken, broiled, à la Hollandaise
Lambs' Frie, breaded, à la Printanière
Tame Pigeons, stewed in Port Wine
Vol au Vent, garnished with Oysters

VEGETABLES

Stewed Tomatoes   Green Corn   Squash   New Beets
New Potatoes   Mashed Potatoes

PASTRY AND CONFECTIONERY

Montauk Lighthouse
Champagne Jelly, Charlotte Russe, Currant Jelly Slices, Fancy Jelly
Peach Tartelettes, Cup Custards, Vanilla Candy, Swiss Meringues
Fruit Pudding, Wine Sauce; Apple Pie; Peach Pie; Blackberry Pie

DESSERT

Pyramids of Vanilla Ice Cream, Forms of Pine Apple ice
Almonds, English Walnuts, Filberts, Brazil Nuts, Figs, Prunes
Raisins, Peaches, Blackberries
Tea and Coffee

Those who believe that contempt is an indication of intellectual superiority should remember a saying by Alfred De Vigny: '*Il n'y a pas un homme qui ait le droit de mépriser les hommes.*'

It is curious how differently people regard human beings. Some, upon entering a trolley-car, hate every one else in the vehicle; some look upon the crowd at a street corner with disgust; it must be wonderful to have such a sense of superiority. It is amusing to enter a fashionable hotel, and as you advance to the office desk, followed by your travelling bags, to glance for a moment at those individuals who, having already been there some days, now gaze at you from their settled and comfortable chairs. They look at you as though you were garbage. In the same way, many people, travelling in foreign lands, hate all fellow-countrymen whom they meet. This scorn used to distress me, just as I used to be disturbed by the contempt of a waiter in a hotel or a butler in a fashionable mansion; now I am only amused.

When one thinks of the vast folly displayed in human history, it is easy to despise human nature; but when one thinks of the many individuals who, with little money, little education, little ability, nevertheless put up a brave front and meet the day's work with uncomplaining serenity, human nature seems sublime.

Still, there is an intellectual pleasure in reading a brilliant review of the human scene which Bunyan called Vanity Fair. Rose Macaulay's novel, showing that the younger generation is always just that, is well worth an attentive perusal. Satire is valuable provided we apply it first of all to ourselves; then we shall not only enjoy it, but make it profitable. I found Miss Macaulay's *Potterism* delectable; I perceived that there was not only a streak of potterism in every human being, but a large percentage of it in my own mind.

The most agreeable place to read books is on the train. One is comparatively safe from interruption, one cannot be annoyed by the telephone, one almost always has a good light both by day and by night. Two suggestions: in general in the U.S.A. sit on the right side of the train; then you will usually have no track outside your window. On the left side, freight-trains, running in the same direction, keep intervening between you and the light, and it usually seems as if every freight-train were at least four miles long. When your railway car has finally passed it, and you hear the maddened snort of the freight locomotive, maddened because you have escaped, your own train then stops at a station just long enough to permit the entire freight-train to pass, when once more you begin the tedious process of overhauling it. Therefore, sit on the right side of the train. Secondly, ride backward, if you can. It is easier on the eyes. In this attitude, the trees, poles, and landscape fade gently and gracefully away, whereas sitting forward, they rush furiously and directly into your defenceless face.

Of course, there are exceptions to this. A stranger, walking through the grounds of an American university, encountered a tall, magnificent specimen of young manhood, and enquired, ' Do you row on the University crew?' ' No,' replied the student, 'it makes me sick to ride backward.'

Apart from typographical errors, modern books contain many misspellings. The word most often misspelled by the best authors and publishers is *ecstasy*; and the *name* that suffers most often is Shakespeare's *Jaques*. There is no authority for writing *ecstacy*; and to write *Jacques* is not only to give the wrong name, but to ruin Shakespeare's rhythm. Yet in a work by that arch-corrector of other men, the late J. Churton Collins, I found *Jacques*; and in his book on *Hamlet*, published in 1922 by Professor Clutton-Brock of Oxford, I note the same ghastly blunder. There are two quite different men in *As You Like It* named *Jaques*, but there is no *Jacques*.

I am appalled by the soggy weight of nearly all books published during the last ten years. There has been a steady change for the worse. Before the war, I could tell whether a book were published in America or in England, merely by 'hefting' it; British books were light, American heavy. But then came a great improvement on the part of our American publishers; books on this side of the water were as light as those in England.

About ten years ago, both English and American books became equally detestable in their stupendous weight. To read them is not an intellectual, but a gymnastic exercise; one needs the wrists of an orang-outang to hold them. And as everyone reads in bed, there is a chance for a serious accident. Should the book fall out of one's hands while one is sleepy, it might easily kill or permanently injure the half-conscious victim.

Furthermore, such excess baggage prevents one from carrying many books when travelling, thus lessening the sales; and until recently prevented one from buying them as presents and sending them to distant friends, for the postage often cost more than the book.

Aesthetically, these heavy volumes are vulgar, and the publishers should be ashamed of them. There is a charm in a light-weight volume; it invites perusal; it seems attractive, congenial, well-bred, a valued guest in the house. But these heavy-weight elephantine tomes are as depressing as soggy porridge.

Even as we have many humorous books consisting only of the 'boners' made on exam papers, I think an anthology of typographical errors would be side-splitting. One of the most diverting was given by Charles Towne in his entertaining autobiography. Ella Wheeler Wilcox had sent to the magazine which he edited a poem in which the climax was contained in the following line:

My soul is a lighthouse keeper

but it was printed in the magazine

My soul is a light housekeeper

Mrs. Wilcox told him exactly what she thought of him and of his magazine.

Perhaps the most fascinating typographical error I ever heard of was described, curiously enough, by Herbert Spencer. A devout Christian woman wrote a book upholding self-sacrifice and toward its close came this sentence. '*Pour bien comprendre l'amour, il faut sortir de soi.*' In the irrevocable book it appeared thus: '*Pour bien comprendre l'amour, il faut sortir le soir.*'

Which reminds me of an incident that happened to the American novelist William Henry Bishop at a restaurant in Belgium. He told me that the waiter brought him a lobster so small that Bishop was disgusted. He lifted it up and said, '*C'est pour rire.*' The waiter then also lifted it up, to his amazement smelt of it and said gravely, '*Vous avez raison, Monsieur; c'est pourri.*'

An excellent typographical error (sent me by Clayton Crawford) was in Hearst's *Seattle Post-Intelligencer*: 'The Missionary Sisters of the Sacred Hearst.'

I suppose the only publications in the world containing no typographical errors are the Authorized Version of the Bible and railway time-tables.

The late Walter Raleigh, Professor of English literature at Oxford, was seventy-eight inches tall and every inch a man. He chafed terribly under academic forms and restrictions, and seemed always to wish to speak his mind. When, after his death, his letters were published, we found he hated Gladstone, Morley, God, clergymen, Thackeray, Augustine Birrell, George Borrow, Carlyle, Ibsen, Macaulay, Shaw; his black-list is a roll of honour. But he was sincere; and his judgements often shrewd. I heard him lecture in Oxford and later at Yale, and he was so conventional and mild, I was quite unprepared for the downrightness and humour of the unofficial man.

Occasionally, however, in these epistles, he wrote comments of extraordinary ineptitude. Of a book by Barrett Wendell: 'a work that might have been begotten by a German Doctoral Thesis on a Young Men's Christian Association.' In the entire universe the two things most alien to Wendell's mind and tastes, the two things he hated most, were German Doctoral Theses and the Y.M.C.A.

After Raleigh lectured at Yale he departed for Princeton, and we sent word that whoever should meet him at the train could not miss him on account of his great height. Well, there was another big fellow on that train who had an American sense of humour and ready speech. The train drew in at dusk; a huge man stepped off, and the Princeton Professor asked, 'Are you Sir Walter Raleigh?' Instantly the man replied, 'No, I am Christopher Columbus.'

A distinguished physician who has spent his entire life in the South and has always had negro servants devoted to him, told me that all the white man knows of the negroes is what the negroes are willing to impart. He said that negroes, when among themselves, talk in a manner entirely different from the way in which they speak to white men.

Shortly after this conversation, I read in one of Somerset Maugham's books that white men really know nothing about the thoughts of Orientals, and in response to a question of mine as to whether the dark-skinned men know us any better than we know them, I received the following interesting letter.

MAY 21 (1936)

Victoria Palace Hotel
Paris

DEAR PROFESSOR PHELPS

Thank you for sending me your brief article. The answer to your final question—do the dark-skinned men see right through us?—is no. I am convinced of that. Do you think I, who was born in France and have lived here for years, know a Frenchman as a Frenchman knows him? Not for a minute.

Yours sincerely,

W. S. MAUGHAM

Perhaps the best retort I have ever heard of occurred when Thackeray was a candidate for Parliament, and was opposed by Edward Cardwell. The two competitors happened to meet in the course of the campaign, and after a friendly discussion, Thackeray said it would be a good fight, 'and may the best man win.' 'Oh, I hope not!' said his rival.

As a rule Barnum knew the American public loved to be gulled. It was a shame *not* to take the money. His genius consisted in knowing exactly how to swindle them. He swindled them in a way that called forth their admiration, affection, and delight. When I was a small boy in New Haven, one of the sideshows in his circus advertised 'a cherry-coloured cat,' which you had to pay extra to see. No one had ever heard of such a phenomenon, and accordingly crowds streamed into the tent. What they saw was an ordinary black cat, a common enough sight on any street. 'What does this mean?' they enquired of the attendant; receiving the dry answer, 'Some cherries are black.' Now Barnum had accurately known in advance exactly what would happen. Instead of becoming enraged and demanding their money back, they all grinned foolishly, ejaculated

the then equivalent of 'Stung again!' immediately went
out and implored every one they met on no account to miss
seeing the cherry-coloured cat. The result was an enormous
intake. In this case I happened to know the cat. It lived in
a house at the corner of York and Chapel Streets, belonging
to Mrs. Sanford. The day before the circus reached town,
the cat disappeared. The day after, the cat was returned to
the house, with a ribbon around its neck, bearing a card,
'With Mr. Barnum's compliments.' So that his 'overhead'
was nil. Every cent he took in was as 'velvet' as the cat's
fur.

On another occasion he put up inside a part of the tent a
large sign TO THE EGRESS which pointed to an alley in canvas. Crowds streamed there expecting to see some wild
woman; they reached the outer air and found they had to
pay their entrance fee over again. The result was as the
great man had foreseen. 'Isn't that just like him?'

If, on leaving a shop in Paris, you say 'Bon Jour,' the person addressed says 'Au Revoir' and if you say 'Au Revoir'
the rejoinder is 'Bon Jour.' Parisians dislike parrot talk.

This reminds me of the laconic inscription on a tomb in
Vevey, Switzerland:

LOUIS BONJOUR

1841–1896

AU REVOIR

I heard of an American who had a fanatical hatred of
superfluities of speech and who requested the shortest possible inscription (in verse) on his tomb. It is a pity he
could not have lived long enough to see it.

THORPE'S

CORPSE

The Gentleman ought not to become obsolete. John Galsworthy, in his fine drama *The Skin Game*, emphasized the real danger of fighting. The danger is that in a skin-for-skin contest, gentility will prove to be worth nothing; for it will be sacrificed in the desire for victory. Or, in other words, if the enemy cheats, we must cheat too. During the World War the worst possible argument for reprisals always seemed to me to be one constantly urged; namely, that we must treat the enemy as he treats us. In other words, we must allow our foes to determine our own moral standards, and imitate them in the very things that gave us the reason for fighting them. There is where we can take a lesson in manners from Julius Caesar. In that interesting little volume *The Marginal Notes of Lord Macaulay*, containing extracts from the comments Macaulay jotted down on the margins of the books he read, Sir George Otto Trevelyan quoted the following: Cicero had written Caesar a letter expressing his grateful appreciation for the clemency shown by the latter to his captured foes, and Caesar replied to this epistle in words which contained, so Macaulay used to say, the finest sentence ever written: 'I triumph and rejoice that my action should have obtained your approval. Nor am I disturbed when I hear it said that those whom I have sent off alive and free will again bear arms against me; for there is nothing which I so much covet as that I should be like myself and they like themselves.' And on the margin of the book by that sentence, Macaulay wrote: 'Noble fellow!'

Yet for over fifty years it has been the fashion to sneer at Macaulay. When I was a Freshman at Yale in 1884, I remember that Professor Cyrus Northrop, who was the embodiment of dignity, yet who was always called affectionately by the students 'Guts' or 'Gutsy,' saying impressively in the classroom, 'Gentlemen, I am somewhat behind the age in my admiration for Macaulay.' I quoted this remark in print a dozen years ago, and Dr. Lawrence Abbott, Editor of the *Outlook*, wrote me that he was ignoble enough to find great pleasure and satisfaction in his writings. He had recently read all through again Macaulay's *History of England*. At that moment I received a letter from the fastidious scholar T.S. Perry of Boston, who mentioned his suddenly renewed enthusiasm for Macaulay. He added that he had just called on a friend, who said, although the matter had not been brought up in the conversation, 'I have had a sudden reversion to the worship of Macaulay!' Mr. Perry added

> It is certainly a curious bundle of coincidences. Now does T.B.M. perhaps just released from Purgatory, try to boom his reputation in this world, working in some mysterious way through our exceptionally open minds? Or do our thoughts just flow into our minds (and out again) from some great sea of thought, entirely without our control? I have often wondered whence come the thoughts that flow into my mind entirely without my doing anything about it. They flow in like a tide. Just now a certain T.B.M. matter seems straying in the universe and gets into our thoughts.

I am grateful to Macaulay for many things; and I admire him for saying that he would rather have written two lines in Goethe's great lyric than anything else in the history of literature.

> Und Marmorbilder stehen und sehen mich an:
> Was hat man dir, du armes Kind, getan?

Most professional pessimists are happy men (except Swift); most professional humorists are not. Josh Billings usually cried copiously while composing, God knows why. A man who called on him in a newspaper office while he was hurriedly writing manuscript for the importunate printer, was told he must wait; Billings was writing and crying. His friend was sympathetic and wished to know the cause of his grief. 'Oh, nothing; he always cries while writing.' At that moment the boy came out of the room with the fresh copy; the manuscript was doubly wet with ink and tears; his friend glanced at it and read, 'Nothing can cure a man of laziness; but a second wife will sometimes help.'

I am sorry for those whose work has in it nothing of the spirit of adventure; but I remonstrate with those who, although their work is individual and creative, still regard it as drudgery. I was talking ten years ago with one of the leading singers of the Metropolitan Opera House. She said: ' The public have a completely mistaken idea of the life of a prima donna; they think it must be wonderfully happy, filled with pleasure, meeting the gayest people, having constant excitement, being taken out to dinner every night. As a matter of fact, it is a life of the hardest and most unremitting toil, scarcely any fun at all.' Did she not make the cardinal error of forgetting that the chief fun of her life lay in the work itself? It ought to be a delight to interpret before enthusiastic audiences masterpieces of music.

Most persons are afraid to confess either that they are happy or that they enjoy their work. Some are superstitious, and fear that if they say they are happy, some jealous and mysterious force will take their happiness away; others are so afflicted by the insidious disease of self-pity that they have acquired the habit of regarding themselves as protagonists in tragedy. Two weeks of influenza would make their ordinary daily activities seem more alluring.

Like millions of others, I have often wondered what was the expression on Pilate's face and the tone of his voice as he uttered the famous question *What is truth?* Bacon wrote 'What is truth? said jesting Pilate.' Surely he was not jesting. He may have been indifferent or impatient, but not jocose. I feel certain that Bacon had in mind there the

Pilate of the Mystery Plays, which he, like Shakespeare, had seen in his youth, for in them Pilate was sometimes represented as a jester. Even as Shakespeare took his Herod from the Mysteries, Bacon probably took his Pilate. Pilate was a Roman, a practical politician, and was confused and dismayed that in this terrible emergency, instead of thinking of some way to save himself from a horrible death, the prisoner began to talk about truth. 'What's truth at a time like this? Don't you see you are in terrible danger? You don't want truth. You want a practical scheme to get you out of this fix.'

In August 1924 my elder colleague, Professor Henry A. Beers, wrote me the following letter about this:

It happened that I was occupying the same cottage at Chatham that I had occupied in 1917. The lady who owns the shebang has a library consisting of four volumes; two copies of the Bible, a book about Cape Cod, and the biography of a whilom missionary and sea captain. In 1917 I read the book of Job. This summer I was reading Isaiah when your commentary arrived. I have been intrigued like you, about those words of Pilate, 'What is truth?' I do not believe, in spite of Bacon, that they were spoken in jest. It may be that the translation ought to run 'What is the truth?' i.e., 'What is the truth in this particular case? the truth which you say you have come into the world to teach?' But if the translation, as we have it, is idiomatically correct, may not Pilate have meant something like this: 'You say you have come to preach the truth, but what *is* truth? Truth, my young friend, is a hard thing to discover. Here are the Jews who believe in Jehovah, and who want me to crucify you: and there are my countrymen who believe in Jove; and the philosophers and poets of Greece and their Roman followers who don't believe any popular mythology or theology. There is Plato e.g. and there is Lucretius who thinks the universe a concourse of fortuitous atoms, etc. I tell you, my young friend, truth is hard to come at.'

When Madame Nazimova first came to this country in the Russian company headed by Orlenev, and played Ibsen in Russian, the company were in financial straits. Not one of them could speak a word of English; but their performance of *The Master Builder* was so impressive that the opaque language was really no obstacle. Nathan Haskell Dole, of Boston, who translated the works of Tolstoy, gave an afternoon reception for the company in Boston; and with the hope that they might be patronized by society and thus receive some financial support, he invited to meet them the Cabots and the Lowells and the rest of the fashionable Back Bay. This meeting began under difficulties; none of the Americans could speak Russian and no member of the company could speak English, but after some smiling and amicable gestures, a fashionably dressed lady appeared who spoke fluently both Russian and English. She was called Mrs. Brown, or something like that, and saved the situation by her charm and grace of manner and by her continual flow of good talk. Finally she departed with the Russian company and, after she had gone one of the Cabots or Lowells asked, 'Who was that charming woman who spoke so beautifully and showed such ease of manner?' and Mr. Dole replied, 'Why, don't you know who that was? That was Emma Goldman.'

If there is at times a certain condescension in foreigners, the Europeans are even more fanatical worshippers of American movie stars than we. In 1924 little Jackie Coogan arrived in London and went to the Savoy Hotel. I took a short walk in the Strand, and on my return I thought the hotel was on fire. There was an enormous crowd in front of it, which blocked the pavements. Later in the day he was taken to the place where occurs daily the picturesque changing of the guard. His motor-car was rushed by women; they climbed onto the running-boards, and insisted on grabbing his small frame. Four policemen finally succeeded in pushing them off; and it was necessary to take the actor into the building, whence he escaped by a secret passage. Such is the appeal of Soloism; such is the power of advertising.

When years ago Charlie Chaplin arrived at Southampton, women broke the windows of his taxi so that they might take hold of him.

My beloved senior colleague at Yale, Professor Henry A. Beers, could have been one of the best short story writers in America if he had had any ambition. He published one volume of short stories called *A Suburban Pastoral*. The title to the book was the title of the initial story. This story, when I first read it, made an indelible impression because it was so true to life and so contrary to the typical magazine story. He described how a young man took his girl in New Haven for a walk out on the salt marshes near the city. The hero was not an athlete; he was unfortunately obliged to wear spectacles. He had not yet asked the girl to marry him but it was evident they were in love with each other and sooner or later a formal engagement seemed certain.

They were botanizing on the meadows and stayed out a little too long so that as they walked into the city dusk was already falling. They had to pass through the slums before getting into the civilized part of Chapel Street. In front of a saloon stood a group of toughs and as the man and girl approached, an ominous, premonitory silence fell, the calm before the storm. The man felt this danger keenly and attempted to hurry their footsteps but the girl, apparently unaware of any tension, seemed positively to saunter. Just as they got opposite the group the crowd of toughs began to hurl insults. The man made no reply but finally one of the men took a quid of tobacco out of his mouth and threw it. It caught the girl on the cheek. She wiped it off with loathing. Her escort turned around and faced the crowd in impotent rage. The crowd dared him to come on, calling him 'four-eyes' and 'sissy' and then the girl made the one unforgivable remark which closed their romance for ever. She said, 'Oh, how I wish a man were here!'

The difficulty was that her escort had imagination. He knew he was no match for that crowd. Through his mind passed the impulse to attack them, in which case he knew that he would be knocked down and trampled on and the girl would be at their mercy. He saw so plainly the results of action that there was no action. Nothing further happened. They walked home together without the exchange of a word.

Now there is the essence of tragedy; pure realism. In the magazine story her escort would have been a magnificent athlete. He would have acted instantly; he would have knocked down two or three of the toughs and escorted the lady home in triumph. But this happens as a rule only in magazine stories. In real life the toughs will not play up to the hero and allow him to have his will. What does a woman expect of a man at such a time?

Of course there are certain persons without physical fear who would have commanded the situation. Had the girl been accompanied by a genius like Lord Clive, he would have emerged from this ordeal in triumph, but her escort was just an ordinary gentleman who thought more of the girl's ultimate welfare than of his own reputation. Hence he lost her for ever.

I thought of this situation one Sunday evening when I was an undergraduate taking a walk about dusk outside of New Haven with a classmate of mine, Ernest Caldwell, who I think was entirely without physical fear, but lacked imagination. Furthermore he was strong. We happened to walk by a group of tough boys who were younger than we, but there were a good many of them. One of them hurled an insult. I thought it best to take no notice of this but Caldwell turned instantly, walked into the middle of the group and hit the biggest boy a blow on the face. For one moment I had the horrible impulse to run, to which fortunately I did not yield. The curious thing is that not a single word was spoken. Caldwell said nothing, he simply struck, rejoined me, and we walked on together. I expected every moment a stone in the back but nothing happened. The crowd was so overawed that they not only did nothing, they said nothing. Now if Caldwell had hesitated even half a second, we should have been torn to pieces but it was his instant resolution that gave him command of the situation.

When I was ten years old, at Sunday School in Providence, there was indelibly impressed upon my mind the folly and futility of *farewells*; and since that day I have never indulged in the luxury of emotional language as an accompaniment to a supposedly final separation. Sunday Schools opened and closed with 'General Exercises;' and on one Sunday, after the lessons were over, the Superintendent (Mr. Horton) rang the bell and called the whole assembly to attention. A young man who had for some years taught a class was about to leave us and he wished to say a few words of farewell. He had secured a position in New York and this would be his last day with the School and with his class. He was sincerely affected; although we should never meet again in this world, he hoped we should all see one another in Heaven. I did not feel the bourne from which no traveller returns was adequately represented by New York; it did not seem to me beyond the range of possibility that somebody in this large Sunday School might at some time once more see Mr. Blank. He, however, thought otherwise, and took an affecting farewell, as he looked into our faces for the last time. Well, during the week he lost this job in New York and the very next Sunday was back in his accustomed place teaching his class; I myself felt like a fool to see him there, and could only dimly imagine how *he* must feel.

Saying Goodbye is one of the fine arts; Maupassant has demonstrated what might happen to one who after a prolonged farewell, returns for his forgotten umbrella; but even where the hosts are really sorry to have the guest depart, it is best not to stretch the scene. How often one says goodbye with thanks, and then the hosts say, 'But we are coming to the station with you!' 'Now don't do that,' I beg; 'I shall find the train all right.' But with a mistaken sense of hospitality, they insist, and accompany me to the railway station; the train is an hour late; it is one of the longest hours in life, mine and theirs; one finally descends to idiotic remarks, 'See the steam coming out of that engine!' and when one's train 'at long last' arrives, the relief is equally welcome on both sides.

'Ten Men Love What I Hate'

I am amused when I see myself described as one who likes everything. Here is a partial list of things I hate: Musical comedies, over-long novels in the shape of trilogies, free verse when it is not poetry, all forms of simplified spelling, especially *thru*, female legs in the daily news, personal items from Hollywood, hypocritical enthusiasm from radio announcers, books written by 'tough guys,' biographies where the author feels more important than his subject, night clubs, postum, buttermilk, cauliflower, parsnips, vegetable marrow, panatella cigars, good meat plastered with thick gravy, paint on young faces, pageants, the pronunciation of JOAN with two syllables, the spelling *Vergil*, the substitution of hand-me-down words for thinking, such as *complexes*, *mother-fixation*, *defence-mechanism*, *escapist*, *wish-belief*, accenting of *positively* and *evidently* on the third syllable, and the following words: *Angle* (used inaccurately), *message*, *gubernatorial*, *pools* for *eyes*, *wailed* for *replied*, *contact* as a verb, *wistful* (for Charlie Chaplin). I particularly hate the word *gotten*. I was pleased when a man telegraphed his wife 'Have gotten tickets for the theatre' and the telegram was received 'Have got ten tickets for the theatre' and she showed up in the lobby with eight eager friends.

And I hate the whole group of novelists whom I call the Medlar Novelists—the medlar is a fruit that becomes rotten before it is ripe.

24

WILLIAM GRAHAM SUMNER

THE two most brilliant teachers on the Yale Faculty were both in the department of Political Economy, William Graham Sumner and Arthur Twining Hadley, later President of the University. Sumner was then in his prime, in the middle forties; he was a tremendous personality. His classroom was a battlefield; he encouraged intellectual resistance from the students, and loved to fight out every disputed point. As his greatest pupil and literary executor, Professor A. G. Keller, used to say, 'It was an eager and nipping air that blew on those heights. If you brought any bit of research to Sumner, he would ask three questions: Is it true? How do you know it? What of it?'

Sumner frequently gave us statements from the newspapers and printed books, asking us to point out their fallacies. He hated sentimentality, vague idealism, and would tolerate no loose or untidy thinking. If the main purpose of the teacher is not to impart instruction, but to arouse and increase the power of thinking—and I believe it is—he was the best teacher we had. I elected every course he offered in my Senior year and in the two graduate years that followed. Later, when I became a member of the Faculty, I got to know him very well. We went together one night to see the Russian actress Madame Nazimova, in Ibsen's *Master Builder*, which some humorist has called 'the piece that passeth understanding.' As we came out, he said, 'All I can make out of this play is, that a young woman induced a man to climb a tower; he was fool enough to do it, and broke his neck.'

Because he was an absolute free-trader, and taught free trade and constantly ridiculed the doctrine of protection, many of the older alumni feared he would corrupt our minds, and letters came frequently to the authorities, urging that he be expelled from the University.

Sumner was as severe with himself as he was with others. He told me that when he was in his thirties he used to smoke ten cigars a day; on a certain occasion, he was looking over the household bills for expenses, and found that for the preceding three months his own bill for cigars was exactly equal to the amount he had spent on groceries for the family; 'and I was a professor of political economy. I paid that bill and never smoked again.'

His course on the Political and Financial History of the United States I took for two years as a graduate student; the political part interested me greatly; the financial part was beyond my comprehension. I have never been able to understand any treasurer's report. The two columns always come out exactly even at the bottom. One day he put on the board a bank statement; suddenly he singled me out and said, 'What do you think of that, Phelps?' I ventured the remark, 'Professor, the bank seems to me in an excellent condition.' Professor Sumner replied, 'We are all grateful for your valuable opinion; that bank closed its doors that afternoon.' In financial matters I seem to be exactly the opposite of Daniel Webster. He was the greatest authority on public finance but was unable to pay his bills. I cannot understand public finance but have never been in debt.

Sumner had the same attitude toward the study of philosophy and metaphysics as that previously held by Benjamin Franklin, who said, 'I quitted that study for others more satisfactory.' Only, while Franklin parted from it genially, on good terms, Sumner never forgave himself for the years he spent on it in his youth nor could he ever forgive professional philosophers. He was always ridiculing them.

Years later, when I was a member of the Faculty, I was sitting directly behind Sumner, when the calling of a new professor of philosophy was the subject under discussion. In his customary downright manner, Sumner addressed the meeting. 'Philosophy is in every way as bad as astrology. It is a complete fake. Yale has a great opportunity now to announce that she will take the lead and banish the study of philosophy from the curriculum on the ground that it is unworthy of serious consideration. It is an anachronism. We might just as well have professors of alchemy or fortune-telling or palmistry.'

The Faculty would not agree to this, so the discussion was resumed. The professor who was making the report on the candidate said he was not sure of the new man's position on Pragmatism. While he was talking, I observed that the back of Sumner's neck was becoming a fiery red, sure indication of a coming explosion. He turned around, looked at the speaker and barked 'What's that you say?' 'Pragmatism,' was the reply. Sumner gave a derisive snort—'Pragmatism!' Then a professor of Greek thought it time for a rebuke, and said reproachfully, 'I think it very unworthy for any of us to ridicule the terminology employed in any other study. All our specialities have their terminology, and I must say—' Sumner grunted, 'Huh, I feel as if I were in Sunday School.'

One day I was at a railway restaurant and took a seat directly behind Professor Sumner. He was quite unaware of my presence. He was eating a large wedge of mince pie, growling over it like a fierce dog. Suddenly he stopped eating, and soliloquized aloud, 'The less I eat of that pie the better I shall feel!' I laughed; he whirled around and

said, 'What, you there?' To change the subject, I remarked that I had seen in the papers his name mentioned
as a candidate for the Presidency of Yale. 'Nothing in it;
nothing at all.' 'Aren't you in the hands of your friends?'
'I should say not! Nothing on earth would induce me to
give up the freedom of a professorship for such a job as
college president.'

On the very first day we met him in an undergraduate
class, he alluded to Henry George's *Progress and Poverty*
and stated that a certain paragraph in it contained a fallacy. Toward the close of the hour, he said that we must
bring in the next time a written comment on his lecture. I
looked up the passage in Henry George, thought (at that
time) that Henry George was right and Sumner wrong,
and said so on my paper. He read my contribution aloud
(without embarrassing me by saying who wrote it) and
remarked, 'Although this man is mistaken, I am giving
him the highest mark in the room; because he looked up
the reference in order to verify it.'

On other occasions, however, he treated me with devastating irony, which I deserved.

25

HENRY DRUMMOND AND SCHOPENHAUER

In the Baptist denomination one could receive a preaching licence from one's church; so a few months after graduation, I went to Hartford, preached a trial sermon in the Asylum Avenue Baptist Church, and was given a licence to preach.

About this time, a woman asked me how I should like to spend my life if I could fashion it according to my desire. I replied that I should like to work hard at some form of intellectual activity from breakfast until luncheon; to spend the afternoon in violent athletic exercise, playing some game; and in the evening to enjoy myself socially, going out to dinner, attending the theatre, conversing, or quietly reading; and that is in general the way I have spent my whole life.

Not knowing exactly what line to take after graduation, and suddenly being offered the position of Secretary of the Yale University Young Men's Christian Association, with an attractive room—which later George Santayana said was the best room he had seen on his visit to Yale—the opportunity to spend half my time as a graduate student, and a salary of seven hundred and fifty dollars, I accepted this, and have never regretted it.

In a few weeks after the opening of the Autumn term, I became intimately acquainted with Professor Henry Drummond of Scotland, the most effective university speaker on religion I have ever heard. His book *Natural Law in the Spiritual World* (1883) had made a sensation;

so in 1887, when he came to America on a speaking tour among the colleges, there was widespread curiosity to hear him. He happened to be at Hartford; I went by train there, had an interview, and he agreed to come to Yale and give a series of addresses. He particularly wanted to speak at Sunday morning chapel, where all the students were required to attend. But the President of the University would not allow him to conduct this service, because he was not an ordained clergyman. He was so disappointed at this refusal, that he came near staying away altogether; but I persuaded him to come, and there was a tremendous crowd at the Sunday afternoon voluntary service. He spoke again that evening, and every night the next two weeks.

I have never seen so deep an impression made on students by any speaker on any subject as that made by Henry Drummond at Yale in the Autumn of 1887. He was a gentleman and a scholar; his method was new, fresh, original. He spoke in quiet, conversational tones, never raised his voice, made no gestures, but was intensely in earnest. He changed the emphasis from death to life. 'We come not to save your souls, but to save your lives. We want you to be Christians, not because you might die tonight, but because you are going to live tomorrow.'

After fifty years, I can still see his face and hear his voice. Mommsen said the eloquence of Cicero was the eloquence of rounded periods, whereas the eloquence of Caesar was that of deeply felt thought. Could any comparison more fitly describe the difference between conventional pulpit oratory and that of Henry Drummond? Every word he spoke was born of years of thought and study and knowledge and meditation. We hung on his words as though they were the Bread of Life.

He told us too much introspection was bad; to keep our eyes not on ourselves, but on the Master. By contemplation of Him, we might gradually be transformed into His likeness. He told us of a little group of young missionaries who went into a far country and never mentioned religion either in speeches or in conversation. They engaged in business and tried to live like the Master. After a year of this, the natives kept coming to their house to find out the guiding principle of their lives, what they believed that made their daily conduct different from others and kept them so cheerful.

Drummond said the reason a consistent Christian seems eccentric to the man in the street is because he *is* eccentric; his life revolves around a different centre from the common centre of self-interest. *Take my yoke upon you.* The yoke is not a badge of servitude, but a convenience, a method of carrying the burden in an easier manner, so that the burden seems light. Jesus had been a carpenter. He made yokes. He knew what He was talking about. He did not mean we should take an additional burden but that we should adopt His method of carrying the burden. The yoke is not an infliction on the ox; it helps the ox to draw the burden without being galled and with less effort. And what is our burden? Some calamity or sorrow? No; the burden is the burden of everyday life, with its cares, perplexities, problems, and worries. If we take the easy yoke and adopt Christ's way of life, the burden will be lighter.

For Drummond's whole emphasis was on Christianity as a way of life. At Northfield in the summer of 1888, Mr. Moody invited him to take a daily, active part in the meetings. Nothing could have better illustrated 'church unity' than that partnership; nothing could have been better evidence of the common sense and spirituality of both men. Moody was an uneducated Fundamentalist who believed every word of the Bible was true; Drummond was a professor of geology, who had been educated in the universities of Scotland and Germany. No two men could have been wider apart in their attitude toward theology. But both were sincere and devout followers of the same Master; and each had deep respect and affection for the other.

The influence of Drummond's visits to Yale—for he came several times in the next few years—lasted from 1887 to the World War. Those successive generations of students had usually as their undergraduate leaders men who took a prominent part in the religious life of the University. I have never seen anything like it; a foreign student told me it would have been inconceivable if he had not witnessed it.

Drummond sought out the leaders of undergraduate life, the principal athletes, the most popular men socially; many of them became earnest, devoted Christians; I can see now a big fellow, member of the University crew, standing up, giving his testimony, with the tears running down his face. Drummond was persuasive; he said we do not need advocates for the Christian religion, but *witnesses*. He kept conference-hours every day, and individual students talked with him. There was no hysteria, no undue excitement, but hundreds of men were really converted, and a good many members of the Faculty.

Drummond persuaded the students to organize little groups of what he called deputations; these went out to other colleges and preparatory schools and talked; the work spread all through the Universities of the East. In the Spring of 1888 three undergraduates came from Princeton to address the students at Yale. They had been carefully chosen by Drummond. One was Winthrop M. Daniels, the valedictorian of his class and now Professor at Yale; one was Robert M. Speer, member of the football team, who was to have a splendid career in the ministry; the third was the most famous football player in the country, Hector Cowan, who could not make a speech, but who was a national hero in athletics. These three men were true to form. Daniels made a brilliant intellectual speech, full of closely reasoned thought; Speer made a charming, persuasive talk, with the very grace of oratory; Cowan, an enormous fellow, stood up, with the sweat running down his face. There was much curiosity to hear what he would say. He stood looking at us a long while, overcome with stage-fright. Then he said, 'I feel more at home on the football field than making a speech; and I guess that'll be about all,' and sat down. But the sacrifice he had made in coming, and his evident sincerity, made a deep impression.

The greatest spiritual influence in my life during my first year as a graduate student was the contact with Henry Drummond; the greatest intellectual stimulus the philosophy of Schopenhauer.

Professor George T.Ladd gave a course on Schopenhauer's work *The World as Will and Idea*. There were about twenty-five students and nearly all of us became college professors. I had always been fond of reading philosophy; and at this time I thought seriously of devoting my life to it. What stopped me eventually was my lack of knowledge of the scientific side in physiological psychology. My interest in philosophy was and is largely literary. I would rather read the writings of Santayana than those of Wundt.

With the single exception of Plato, Schopenhauer is the most interesting writer on philosophy I have ever read. *The World as Will and Idea* is a masterpiece of thought, beauty, wit, humour, and literary style. It is a treatise on human nature and the fine arts; it opened my eyes, and the world has never seemed the same since. While studying that work I could almost feel myself passing from boyhood to manhood. I grew up. I have always been grateful to Lord Haldane and to his collaborator Mr. Kemp for translating Schopenhauer; we should not have studied the original. I hate to think what my life would have been without Schopenhauer; this great pessimist added so much to my happiness. He illuminated every subject he touched and he touched them all. The sincere pessimists—Swift, Schopenhauer, Hardy, Housman—give me extraordinary pleasure. Mentally, I have lived with Schopenhauer fifty years, and find him a charming companion, brilliant and stimulating.

In my serious philosophical studies, I loved Schopenhauer, I had deep respect for Kant, I thought Eduard von Hartmann crude, and Fichte incomprehensible.

In that short-lived London weekly periodical of the nineteenth century, *Literature*, I read a diverting dialogue in the Elysian Fields between Edward King and Arthur Henry Hallam. One of them said to the other (I haven't seen the article for forty years) something like this. 'What lucky fellows we are! we died too soon to accomplish anything, and we should have been forgotten, if we had not had the good fortune each of us to be the friend of an immortal poet; thus we are both immortal figures on earth; and incidentally, I like my mausoleum much better than yours.' 'I can't possibly agree with you on that,' replied the other with some heat; and a long controversy followed which took the form of a comparison of the literary merits of *In Memoriam* and *Lycidas*.

I myself would suggest that *In Memoriam* is a horizontal poem and *Lycidas* a vertical; the former covers far more ranges of human nature and there is in it something that appeals to everyone. *Lycidas* is an austere solitary peak, reaching a height not only quite beyond Tennyson, but beyond any other English poet except Shakespeare. As a rule, I love the poetry of human nature much more than poetry rising into sublimity from meditative rapture or through an ethereal imagination. Thus, of the four greatest poets of all time, I read Homer and Shakespeare and Goethe far more than I read Dante. Yet to *Lycidas* I make an unconditional surrender; in the presence of its perfection other great poems seem for the moment second-rate.

Yet for eternity I do not think I should choose for a travelling companion either Tennyson or Milton. Tennyson was a great poet, but I do not think he had an interesting mind; and as for Milton, well, I would rather talk with Benjamin Franklin than with George Washington.

If it is possible to do so in the next world I should like to give a succession of small dinner parties where Browning and Schopenhauer could discuss the philosophy of music, for they held and advanced the same views on this subject; the question of optimism and pessimism would in the new environment have a humour all its own; where Barrie and Strindberg, both masters of the theatre, could discuss the eternal feminine in the new light thrown upon that interesting subject; where Hardy and Chesterton could discuss literature and G. K. C. could say, 'I told you so;' where Goethe and Dr. Johnson, who respectively hated and loved controversy, could discuss the respective merits of Eckermann and Boswell—what did Johnson really think of Boswell?—and agree on one theme anyhow, that conversation and not oratory is a true revelation of intelligence; where Rostand could tell Ibsen that he was the only great dramatist in a half-century on earth who owed him nothing; where Dickens could tell Emily Brontë that if he had lived long enough to finish *Edwin Drood* and she had lived long enough to read it, she would have liked it; where Housman and Francis Thompson would at first look at each other and say nothing; but after awhile they would begin to discuss the name and nature of poetry; where Henry James would analyse the motives of angels and Dumas exaggerate their resulting actions; where Stevenson would tell Moore a romantic tale and Moore forget (until too late) where he was; where Mill would wonder how the other half lived and Carlyle would say it served them right; where Swift, looking back on earth, would say that they were a pernicious race of little odious vermin, and Emerson would smile serenely and say, 'But you see everything worked out perfectly according to the divine plan.'

26

BROWNING

INASMUCH as I have read books since I was four years old, it is natural enough that various authors have profoundly affected my mind and character. I have already expressed something of the debt I owe to Shakespeare, to John Stuart Mill, to Carlyle, to Tennyson's *Maud*, to Goethe, to Schopenhauer; to the Authorized Version of the Bible it is impossible to express similar indebtedness. The individual authors just mentioned came at a time in my boyhood and adolescence when they supplied what was needed; but the Bible was from the start an integral part of myself; and it would be as absurd to attempt an estimate of what I owe to it as it would be to appraise what I owe to my lungs or to my heart.

I shall always be grateful to Mill and Carlyle and Schopenhauer, although I was never the disciple of any one of them. It was the influence of Browning's poetry that became paramount. His view of life irresistibly appealed to me. So far as a humble individual can share the philosophy of a mighty genius, Browning's philosophy is my own; his ways are my ways and his thoughts are my thoughts. He was and is for me what Bentham was for Mill. I am a Browningite.

I have mentioned that when I was ten years old I declaimed at school his poem 'Hervé Riel'; but the author's name meant nothing to me then or for the next ten years. In my Senior year at college, in a general course in English literature, we had three or four lessons in Browning, which aroused in me definite aversion. This aversion was increased by the widespread adoration of the poet, by the notoriety of the Browning societies in London and in Boston, and by other eccentric propaganda. The disciples of Browning whom I met were acutely uninteresting.

I was still sufficiently a Philistine to believe not only that Browning was far from being a great poet; I thought also that his influence on the art of poetry was evil. Yes, I was like thousands of my elders who should have known better; the same critics who maintained that whatever Browning was he was certainly not a poet were those who insisted that Wagner could not write music and that Ibsen could not write plays. This attitude toward these three men of original genius seems idiotic today, but in the eighties (among English-speaking people), it was not uncommon. Professor F.J.Child of Harvard, then the foremost English scholar in America, told me seriously in 1890 that Wagner was a charlatan who would soon be forgotten and that those who admired him were full of ridiculous affectations.

In 1886 the famous American tragedian, Lawrence Barrett, was announced to appear in New Haven in *Julius Caesar* (his most successful Shakespearean role was Cassius). I bought a ticket, and was looking forward to the performance, when members of the Yale Faculty and some other citizens got up a petition and asked Mr. Barrett to substitute Browning's *A Blot in the 'Scutcheon*. I was furious at seeing the work of this impostor preferred to a Shakespearean masterpiece. I went to the box-office, got my money back and boycotted the show. I regretted that piece of folly for fifty years.

My father, as Editor of the *Christian Secretary*, received for review the new Riverside six-volume edition of Browning's works; and I decided to read them. They, and they alone, were the means of my conversion. The way to appreciate beauty is to keep looking at it, to appreciate music is to keep listening to it, to appreciate poetry is to keep reading it. I read and read, and gradually changed from aversion to an admiration not much this side of idolatry.

For a few weeks in 1890 I acted as private tutor of the two sons of the railway king, George M. Pullman. They were about ten years old; and I lived with them in a house on the seacoast of New Jersey. After they went to bed, I read every night in *The Ring and the Book*. The *Athenæum* was right when it saluted the poem on its first appearance (1869) with these words: 'It is the most precious and profound spiritual treasure that England has received since the death of Shakespeare.'

We have the greatest affection for those authors who have contributed most to our spiritual development; who have added to our faith, courage, and happiness. A great deal of my *happiness* I owe to Browning.

It was natural, therefore, as soon as I became free to teach at Yale what I wanted to teach, that I should have devoted more time to the teaching of Browning than to any other author. I began in the session of 1897–8 with a course in Chaucer and Browning, remembering what Landor had said to his young contemporary:

> Since Chaucer was alive and hale
> No man hath walked along our roads with step
> So active, so inquiring eye or speech
> So varied in discourse.

Landor had made the exception of Shakespeare, who belonged not to England, but to the world.

Thirty-four students elected this course. The next year I changed it to *Tennyson and Browning*, known to successive generations of Yale undergraduates as 'T and B.' In the last year I gave it, 1932–3, it was elected by 550.

From 1898 to 1933, I had the pleasure of introducing the poetry of Browning into the lives of hundreds of young men; and while naturally not all of them shared my enthusiasm, a large number of them kept up their reading of Browning in after years. It has been good for them, as it was for me.

27

BEGINNING TEACHING

ONE day in the Spring of 1888 Doctor John Meigs, Head Master of the great Hill School at Pottstown, Pa., entered my room and offered me a position as teacher. I told him I had no experience. 'You will get it with us.' At that time the Hill School had no superior in America and I was flattered by the offer, especially as a good salary came with it. We talked it over, and I was about to accept, when I thought I had better ask what subject he expected me to teach. 'Mathematics.' Then I knew the Hill School was not for me. I told him I was incapable. 'But these are elementary mathematics.' I said there were no elementary mathematics; I had had a wide experience, and had never seen any. 'Can't you teach arithmetic?' 'No, Sir; it would be taking money on false pretences.' He laboured with me for a long while, and finally went away sorrowful. I was not very happy myself; but in two or three weeks Mr. William Lee Cushing entered the same room, and said he was about to found a new school for boys at Dobbs Ferry, N.Y., to be called Westminster School, and wanted me to teach there. 'What subject?' 'Anything you like.' I liked all the history and all the English, and we came to an agreement in a few minutes.

The salary was even better than that from the other school. As there were practically no expenses, I saved enough to help me through another year of graduate study, to give me three months bicycling in Europe, and to leave five hundred dollars for my wedding journey.

I now had the opportunity to try teaching as a career; to find out whether or not I could do it, and whether I should enjoy it.

One afternoon in September 1888, I stepped off the train at Dobbs Ferry on the Hudson River and entered Westminster School. This was the first time I had ever been inside a boarding school, and now I came as a teacher. The next day the boys began to arrive, and although with only one exception they were under seventeen, they were for the most part more sophisticated than I. They were certainly more at home away from home; for I had never been away from home except during my Freshman year in college.

The Headmaster was a big, powerful athletic man in the late thirties. I have never known a more honest, upright, sincere, straight-forward individual; all the boys respected him, and I cannot conceive of a more satisfactory Head. There was at the beginning only one other teacher besides me; this was Edward Farrington, who had just been graduated from Yale. After Christmas, another teacher joined the staff—Mr. Buffum of the Amherst class of 1884, a great baseball player. The first night at school Mr. Cushing called Farrington and me into his study, and divided the entire work into three equal parts; thus taking, in addition to all the executive work and cares and responsibilities, exactly as much teaching, discipline and supervision as was assigned to Farrington and to me.

My first night at Westminster School I lay broad awake until it was time to get up in the morning; it seemed to me there were trains every few minutes and the freight-siding near the school gave me the opportunity to hear each freight car start separately after the pull of the engine. But these continuous noises never bothered me again.

During the school year I was busy nearly every waking moment. The only time I had free was Tuesday and Sunday afternoons. We rose at seven, and at every meal I presided over a table of boys. Teaching was from eight till one; in the afternoon, games and athletic exercises. In the evenings, presiding over study hour, where absolute quiet had to be maintained; then the supervision of the small boys with their nightly baths. Thus from seven in the morning until ten at night I had not a free moment, except on Tuesdays and Sundays. Sometimes I became weary of the companionship of so many little boys, though I was fond of them; and merely to relieve my mind, I would take a train on Tuesday afternoon to New York, walk the streets and mingle with crowds of men and women.

Sunday mornings I took a group of boys to the Episcopal Church, where I was supposed to maintain order. They never gave me any trouble; and I enjoyed the Episcopal service, which never previously had I heard on two consecutive Sundays. Immediately after church, I taught a class of girls about fifteen or sixteen years old, in the Presbyterian Sunday School; they were quick-witted and clever and I enjoyed it. The cleverest of them, Isabel Niven, subsequently became the mother of Thornton Wilder, the novelist and dramatist, and is now a fellow-citizen of mine in New Haven.

In going to Westminster School as a teacher, I had two main objects—to earn some money and to find out whether or not I could teach. I did not expect to enjoy the year. I thought it would be drudgery and that I might be a failure. But I enjoyed the year enormously. I had not the slightest trouble maintaining discipline, I had a warm affection for the boys, I kept in magnificent condition through constant physical exercise, and I had the subsequent life-long friendship of Mr. and Mrs. Cushing and their children, one of whom today is Tom Cushing, the playwright. He was a little boy during my year at the school; and he used to beg me to read aloud the blood-curdling stories of Edgar Allan Poe, to which he listened with delight.

It was fortunate that I was even more fond of outdoor games than the boys themselves, for half the day was spent playing. I was never quite good enough to become a member of the Varsity during my undergraduate days, but I had tried for various teams; and I could play baseball, football, lawn tennis, and hockey better than any boy in the school. In those days teachers were allowed to play on prep school teams; thus I was not only the coach of all the athletic organizations in Westminster School, I was also pitcher on the nine, half-back on the football team, etc. We practised every afternoon and no boy enjoyed it more than I. We won all our football games with other schools and lost only one baseball game.

Mrs. Cushing was exceedingly kind to me, and I owe much of my musical education to her. She played Beethoven for me on the piano, and occasionally took me to a concert in New York. There for the first time I heard the Ninth Symphony, conducted by Walter Damrosch. On another occasion, she took me to hear the great Hans von Bülow, who played Chopin's nocturne in G Major. Altogether, this was a rich year in my life; although I was so busy I did not read three books through.

She also did a good deal for my social education, for I was still crude, very crude indeed. She begged me to stand up straight, and added, 'But I know you won't; only idiots stand straight.'

The year was also memorable for me, because I had one accident and one narrow escape from instant death. In the early Spring, workmen were cutting down trees to clear the ground for an addition to the school buildings. I begged them to let me cut down one tree; I succeeded in doing this, and when the tree was felled, thought I was through. But one of the workmen told me I must trim all the branches.

My heart was beating at a great rate, and I was covered with sweat. My axe went through one of the twigs, through the lacing of my shoe, and down deep into my foot. The blood gushed out in floods. I got to the piazza, and for the first time in my life, fainted clean away. I went through the experience of dying; it was interesting. Mr. Cushing and Mr. Farrington were bending over me, binding up the wound. Suddenly the distant trees and the landscape began to fade; and the curious thing is, that although for some time I could hear every word spoken by those near me, I could see absolutely nothing. Then I said to myself, 'I am dying,' and passed away completely. I have since learned that it is a common experience for very sick persons not to be able to see anything, but to have their hearing if anything sharper than normal. A man will lie on the bed apparently totally unconscious, and yet hear every word spoken by anyone in the room. Wills have sometimes been altered as a result of this.

Browning, who noticed everything, has two parenthetical stanzas in 'Childe Roland to the Dark Tower Came' which ironically illustrate this interesting fact.

> As when a sick man very near to death
>   Seems dead indeed, and feels begin and end
>   The tears and takes the farewell of each friend,
> And hears one bid the other go, draw breath
> Freelier outside, ('Since all is o'er,' he saith,
>   'And the blow fallen no grieving can amend;')
>
> While some discuss if near the other graves
>   Be room enough for this, and when a day
>   Suits best for carrying the corpse away,
> With care about the banners, scarves and staves:
> And still the man hears all, and only craves
>   He may not shame such tender love and stay.

My other experience at Westminster School, the escape from instant death, though it left me uninjured, was terrible. One morning after Mrs. Cushing had gone to the station to take the train to New York, Mr. Cushing gave me a note for her, suggesting that if I ran straight down the bank to the tracks and along to the station, I could reach her before the train started. This short cut we had occasionally taken.

It was a crisp, cold, windy morning. I ran at full speed down the steep hill to the tracks. On the opposite track an express train was coming along very fast, making a tremendous clatter; I had my foot out to spring on the empty track between me and this train, when a drop of water came into my eye. I made an impatient ejaculation and waited a tenth of a second, to wipe my eye before running ahead; and in that speck of time, another express train, running at full speed in the opposite direction, and which I had not heard on account of the racket made by the train on the other track, came within two inches of my body. I was blown over backwards by the wind of its advance. Had it not been for that drop of water in my eye, I should have stepped directly in front of the locomotive. Even as it was, my foot was within a few inches of the track. That was fifty years ago. I should have missed a great deal.

28

GRADUATE STUDIES AND SPORT

IT is commonly said that during the first few years after birth we learn more than in any later period of equal duration; but it seems to me that during the ten years from 1883 to 1893 I made more mental progress than in any other decade of my life.

I passed from boyhood to manhood. I entered the University in 1883, was graduated in 1887 with special honours in English and in Philosophy and with Phi Beta Kappa; then followed a year's graduate study with the tremendous experience of Schopenhauer; and during that year my religious faith was permanently directed and inspired by Henry Drummond. The next year I taught in a boys' school, a valuable experience which also determined my life work; another year of graduate study with a summer in Europe, and on a bicycle; then came residence at Harvard, the first year as a graduate student. I took the degrees of M.A. at Harvard and Ph.D. at Yale; in my second year at Harvard began my professional work as a college teacher. In 1892 I began teaching at Yale; in 1893 published my first book, *The Beginnings of the English Romantic Movement*; and in the Christmas vacation of 1892-3 I was married.

As I look back on those ten years, a great deal seems to have happened. I began them as a boy, uncertain of the future; I ended them as a married man, living in my house, a member of the Yale Faculty, and the author of a book.

I enjoyed my year of teaching so much at the Westminster School that it settled for me the question of my
life-work. I had no further doubts; only I felt sure I should
be more happy and more successful teaching in a university than in a secondary school. Accordingly, I declined
the urgent invitation to remain at Dobbs Ferry, and having obtained a scholarship in the Graduate School at Yale,
I went there for the academic year of 1889–90.

On the whole, this was the unhappiest year of my life;
and mainly because of one misfortune. My living with
those little boys had made me hungry for learning. I was
in splendid physical condition. I was twenty-four years old,
and I was free to devote myself exclusively to my studies,
looking forward to them with unspeakable eagerness. On
the very first night of the term, and without any preliminary warning, my eyes suddenly gave out. I had never
worn glasses in my life, and had hardly ever been conscious that I had eyes. I had never taken the slightest care
of them, studying all through college under a flaring jet of
gas. Now I suddenly found that after reading three or four
minutes, my eyes felt as if they were full of needles; and
even when I was not reading they were abnormally sensitive to light, so that I could not face any artificial light or
even a window. I had no idea what was the matter; but of
course it was a case of acute conjunctivitis; and if the
treatment for that had been understood at the time, I
think I could have found complete relief. I went to the
leading oculist in New Haven, who said I had astigmatism,
put bella donna in my eyes which kept them out of action
for two weeks, and prescribed glasses, saying that when the
accommodation of the eyes became normal and I used the
glasses, I should be all right. He did nothing to relieve the
inflammation. Well, I found at the end of those two weeks
that my eyes were just as bad with the glasses as they had
been without them.

For five or six months I was miserable. In perfect health otherwise, I could read only ten minutes at a time. I could not go to the theatre, to evening entertainments, to anything; lights tormented my eyes. Thus, after four o'clock in the afternoon, I simply sat in a chair in the darkest corner of the room, waiting for bedtime.

After nearly six months of this, I went to the greatest oculist in America, Doctor Knapp in New York. After an hour's minute examination, he said 'Throw away your glasses; there is nothing whatever the matter with your eyes.' When I told him that the New Haven physician said I had astigmatism, he replied 'That's nothing; everybody has astigmatism.'

I went back to New Haven without the glasses and that night at a dinner-party, for the first time in many months, the lights did not hurt my eyes. I hoped they were cured; but after a few weeks, the trouble returned; and I went back to the glasses, after trying others that were even worse. The following summer I spent in Europe, and when I went to Harvard in the Autumn, I paid a visit to the famous oculist in Boston, Doctor Myles Standish. I told him that my whole career and lifelong happiness depended on my getting relief; and indeed I had thought that I should probably have to give up my plans for the life of the mind, and get a job as lumberjack or something like that in the Far West. Doctor Standish said the astigmatism was so slight that many persons with much more of it never wore glasses; but inasmuch as I suffered so intensely, he would have frankly to guess at prescribing glasses which might or might not be of assistance. I left his office with a heavy heart; but as a matter of fact, his glasses helped me more than anything else I had tried, and I found I could do a reasonable amount of work. The magnifying power of these glasses was so slight that I was constantly forgetting them as I saw exactly as well without them; but if I left them off for reading, the eyestrain began again. I have never understood why my eyes should have been so intolerably weak that year, or why I could not get relief. But I would rather go through life without legs than with such eyes.

And here is a strange thing, which may help to explain some of the almost miraculous effects wrought by Christian Science, by the teachings of the late M.Coué, by hypnotic suggestion, and by other forms of mental influence.

One evening in that unhappy winter, when my eyes were at their worst, I was invited to address two or three hundred undergraduates. At the appointed hour I took my seat on the platform. The hall was illuminated by a huge ring of gas-jets suspended from the ceiling. The lights hurt my eyes so that while sitting on the platform I was compelled to look at the floor. Yet during my speech, which lasted from thirty to forty minutes, my eyes felt absolutely strong and without a semblance of pain, and I could look directly at these lights without any blinking whatever. Then when the assembly was over, my eyes were again weak.

I thought then, that if some way could be found by which my mind could be kept strongly concentrated on something, not for forty minutes but for a week, I might be cured. For clearly it was a case of the mind triumphing over a bodily illness.

For I have had similar experiences. Crossing the ocean in June 1935, I had an attack of lumbago so severe that I could walk only with great difficulty and could not stand up straight. I was asked to give a lecture on shipboard. I spoke for one hour. As soon as I began to speak, every trace of pain and stiffness left my body; I stood up straight, moved about with perfect flexibility while talking, and when the lecture was over, walked away to my stateroom with ease. For a moment I thought I was cured. But the trouble then resumed its sway.

In one respect the misfortune with my eyes may have been a good thing for me; on that account, my work as a graduate student the second year at Yale was not brilliant, and the College Faculty, who had the power of appointment, did not reappoint me to a scholarship. I needed one more year of graduate work to get my degree of Doctor of Philosophy, and told the Faculty that if I did not get a scholarship at Yale, I should go to Harvard. I think they believed I was bluffing; for my father and mother lived in New Haven, I could stay with them, and I had no friends at Harvard. I shall not forget the night toward the end of June and the close of the academic year, when I called on President Dwight—to discover the results of the Faculty meeting on scholarships. He was very kind and considerate, but said there were only a few scholarships and they must be distributed around. I told him I should write to Harvard that night. 'Oh, I wouldn't do that,' he said; 'you can get along here and you have only one more year.' I wrote to Harvard at once and got Professor Henry A. Beers to write a letter of recommendation. By return of post, I received a letter from the Harvard authorities, saying that I should be given a Shattuck scholarship, which would pay my tuition, and that if I had only applied earlier, I should have received something better. This was the first of many favours received from Harvard; and with these favours there was always a hearty encouragement.

Thus, it is possible that if the miserable condition of my eyes had not prevented me from doing first-rate work, I should have received another scholarship at Yale; and thus never would have studied at Harvard. While I am certain that my going to Yale as an undergraduate was the best thing I could possibly have done, I am equally certain that after six years of Yale, my going to Harvard was for me

the best thing imaginable. Out of my disappointment
came a tremendous benefit; for my life at Harvard was
greatly advantageous. I cannot find words to express
what this change in academic residence meant in my development.

In the summers of 1888 and 1889 I went to Chautauqua
at the invitation of George E.Vincent, then the executive
manager, who later has had such a distinguished educational and professional career. Professor (afterwards President) W.R.Harper, who was giving regular courses of instruction at Chautauqua, also urged me very strongly to
go. But although I took courses there in French and German, and listened to lectures and concerts, my real reason
for going was the splendid opportunity the place offered
to play baseball. The most famous college athlete in America was my intimate friend and Yale undergraduate associate, Amos Alonzo Stagg, the greatest baseball pitcher in
Yale's history and an All-American end in football. He was
the Captain and Coach of the Chautauqua nine, and in
1888 offered two prizes, one in fielding and one in batting
for the whole season. Herbert Moore won the fielding
prize and I won in batting. My prize was a copy of the
Complete Poems of Byron and I still look with pride on
the inscription on the flyleaf.

> W.L.Phelps
> From his Friend
> A.A.Stagg
> Chautauqua 1888. Batting average, 389.

In the summers of 1937 and 1938 I visited Chautauqua
for the first time in nearly fifty years and met Bert Moore,
who won the fielding prize on that nine in 1888; and
Emmet Flanders, the catcher. He showed courage and skill
in catching Stagg's pitching.

Among speakers who visited Chautauqua in those two

summers, were Professor H.H.Boyesen of Columbia and
Professor J.P.Mahaffy of Trinity College, Dublin. The
former gave a lecture on George Eliot, in which he said
that he once had a conversation with the Russian Turgenev and George Eliot's husband, George Henry Lewes.
The discussion turned on the novels. Boyesen thought
Middlemarch was the best, Turgenev said *The Mill on the
Floss*, and Mr. Lewes, like a loyal husband, said *Daniel
Deronda*. Boyesen said that George Eliot was totally without physical charm. 'She had a face like a horse, and if you
will imagine a very sad horse, you will get her expression
correctly.'

The Irishman Mahaffy, then about fifty years old, gave
a course of lectures in Chautauqua, and I had many good
talks with him. We attended a public banquet together
and he scandalized the crowd by calling for wine, and saying in a loud voice that it was ridiculous to have a dinner
without wine. At that time nearly everybody at Chautauqua was 'temperance' and not a drop of liquor was ever sold
on the premises or permitted. I walked back from the dinner with Mahaffy in the moonlight, at two o'clock in the
morning. I told him that in my Sophomore year at Yale I
wrote an essay on Sophocles, and that I had read many
criticisms written by professors at Oxford and Cambridge,
and found them all more learned than sensible; at the last
I had got hold of his essay which seemed to me full of wisdom. 'What is the matter with those scholars?' I asked.
'Why,' said Mahaffy, 'they live secluded lives; they are
pedants; they know Greek perfectly, but they don't know
anything whatever about human nature.'

I then told him how much I had enjoyed reading Schliemann's *Troja* and how greatly I admired A.H.Sayce's Introduction. 'Yes, Sayce is a fine scholar and a good man;
but the poor fellow is dying of consumption. He will hardly
live out the present year (1889).' Sayce lived till 1933,

dying at the age of 88! He survived Mahaffy fourteen years, Mahaffy dying in 1919 at the age of eighty.

Sayce's *Reminiscences* (1923) is an interesting autobiography. In the first sentence he says he was born coughing and had coughed ever since. Probably the constant exposure in the open air in his archaeological expeditions kept him alive. After he retired from his professorship at Oxford, he spent the last years in the impossible climate of Scotland. *Venienti occurrite morbo!* Sayce's *Reminiscences* is full of good stories. Herbert Spencer, as everyone knows, told the whole world about his ill health, and particularly about his insomnia, which he dwelt on frequently and with unction, representing himself as a martyr. Sayce says that one night he and Spencer had to share the same room in an inn, and that the moment Spencer got into bed he must instantly have fallen asleep, for he began to snore and kept it up with such volume all night, that Sayce could not sleep a wink. In the morning, Spencer got out of bed wearily, and said he hadn't been able to sleep at all; he had lain awake the entire night.

I wrote to Sayce expressing my admiration for his autobiography.

> 8 CHALMERS CRESCENT,
> EDINBURGH
> June 9 '26

DEAR SIR,

Somewhat belatedly let me thank you much for your kind & encouraging letter of April 2. I am but just returned to my Scotch residence from the East & your letter has now been put into my hands. It makes me feel that my work has not been altogether in vain.

Yours sincerely

A. H. SAYCE

29

BICYCLING IN EUROPE

Travelling was cheaper then than now; and the dollar of course bought more. I set apart five hundred dollars for my first trip to Europe. First class fare round trip, $105; purchase of a bicycle in Brussels, $80; clothes bought in London $50; all travelling expenses in Europe, $250; and I had fifteen dollars in my pocket when I arrived in New York.

We sailed on an old, small, and cheap steamer of the Red Star Line, the *Waesland*, Captain Grant. We left New York harbour Wednesday, 25 June 1890, at eleven in the morning.

There were five in our party; my Yale classmates, George D. Pettee and Horace Hart, and two graduate students at Yale, John Strong and H. Austin Aikins. All are now living except Hart.

Pettee became Head Master of the University School in Cleveland, Aikins professor of philosophy at Western Reserve University, and Strong a clergyman. I shall always be glad that my first voyage to Europe was on a very small steamer with only one deck and that we sailed directly from New York to Antwerp *without any stops*.

On the modern luxury liners, it is quite possible to spend every day on one of the decks and never see the ocean. But with our small ship lying low in the water we lived very close to the sea, and the deck was frequently awash. On the fourth day out we had the biggest storm I have ever seen; one day four or five of us on deck were hit by a terrific wave, knocked down, and all went sprawling and submerged, coming to a sudden stop somewhere in the scuppers. In the midst of this storm a little boy died, and was buried at sea; only a very few of us could attend the funeral on account of the violent motion of the ship. I stood by the Captain while he read the funeral service; and I could hear only an occasional word through the screaming wind and the roaring waves.

It was a voyage of eleven days; I shall never forget the landing at Antwerp. On Sunday afternoon, we sailed up the Scheldt with the beautiful green grass on both sides and the picturesque windmills turning. We docked at Antwerp at five o'clock; landed (it seemed) almost in front of the cathedral.

In addition to the pleasure of having on board five Harvard students, equalling in number our five Yale men, with whom we played exciting matches of shuffleboard and sang songs, there were several members of college faculties whose conversation I listened to with keen enjoyment.

One of these was an extraordinarily shy but exceedingly learned research scholar in linguistics, Philippe Marcou of Harvard, to whom I became attached, and whom I saw frequently during the following year at Cambridge, Mass. One day the conversation turned on favourite passages in poetry and music, and I remarked that I could not explain my preference, but that there was one passage in the Ninth Symphony coming immediately after the divine *Adagio Molto e Cantabile* which Beethoven gave to the second violins, that affected me more deeply than any other phrase in music. Doctor Marcou said, 'That has always been my favourite.' Nothing perhaps unites people more than such preferences; and from that moment I loved the man. There were two professional musicians on board, Professor Amsberg and Professor Himmelsbach of

Philadelphia. One day there was a grand debate between them on an ideal subject for discussion, because the propositions cannot be proved. Herr Amsberg said Mozart was as great a composer as Beethoven; that *Don Giovanni* was the greatest opera ever written; and that anyhow vocal music was greater than instrumental. All three of these propositions were vigorously denied by Professor Himmelsbach, who insisted that everything in human nature could be found in the first eight symphonies of Beethoven, and that instrumental music could express emotions far beyond the range of the voice. They argued with abundant illustrations for two hours, at the end of which each had convinced himself; an interesting discussion, coming from professionals.

For the first time in my life I met men who spoke various languages fluently; and how I envied them! Marcou spoke English, French, German, and Spanish with ease. A Belgian merchant who seemed to have travelled everywhere spoke six languages fluently and went from one to another without apparent difficulty. It was interesting to me to meet these cosmopolitans, because most Americans, when they do speak a foreign language, speak it as if it *hurt*, as the average tenor sings.

Although I have always been sensitive to new impressions and increasingly so with advancing years, I must confess I have never been able to recapture the rapture of that first voyage to Europe. To me the arrival in the Old World was such a succession of thrills that I cannot find words to express my emotions; the landing, the walking about Antwerp that first Sunday night, the journey to Brussels and Cologne, the beginning of the bicycle excursion,—I was in a continuous excitement. The first night of our bicycle excursion we spent at Bonn; and I remember looking out of my hotel window before going to bed, and wondering if it were not all a dream from which I should awaken. 'Is it possible that I am really here in a German city?'

In Brussels for the first and last time in the whole three months we engaged a guide to show us the town. This man took us immediately to the house of ill fame. It was apparently in a respectable part of the city, certainly not in the slums; there was nothing to distinguish this house from any other; it was simply one in a rather long block of good-looking residences. A well-dressed woman came to the door and we were shown into an empty room where there was a piano. In a few moments seven girls appeared, one of whom was a negro; they were suggestively dressed, but to me and I believe to my companions they were not in the least tempting though they tried to be. Whenever I read of the beauty and grace and charm of harlots—for I suppose there is no class of women described more sentimentally—I think of these Brussels prostitutes. They were dull and stupid; they had no conversational gifts; they were devoid of charm; a man would have to be quite drunk to desire them; and we were very glad indeed, after paying a few francs for a bottle of wine, which seemed to be expected as tribute, to leave the girls and the room and house and breathe the open air again. Our guide was sadly disappointed by our virtue; I suppose he had a commission from the house.

In Brussels we bought our bicycles, and took the train for Cologne. Here we entered the cathedral about eight in the morning and did not emerge for five hours. We listened to a religious service which lasted about an hour; then we explored every nook and cranny of the vast structure and climbed to the top of one of the towers, over five hundred feet.

It is not matter for astonishment that the modern drama had its origin in the Catholic Church of the Middle Ages; the difference between worship and drama is a difference

mainly of *intention*. I had an opportunity that morning at
Mass to witness the distinction. It so happened that I
sat between a devout German Catholic and some foreign
tourist. The German worshipped reverently; the tourist
had a pair of binoculars which he turned curiously on the
priests and the choir from beginning to end.

From Cologne we bicycled along the bank of the Rhine
and near Bingen *an early dream came true*. When we were
Sophomores in college, Pettee and I had attended an
illustrated lecture by John L.Stoddard, probably the most
successful lecturer who ever lived. When it was announced
in any American city that his course of six illustrated
lectures would be given, the line used to form in front
of the auditorium forty-eight hours before the box-office
was opened.

Pettee and I were in the top gallery and the lowness of
our purse may be known by the altitude of the seats. When
the stereopticon picture showed the river Rhine, I turned to
Pettee in the gallery and whispered, 'I'll shake hands with
you to stand on that very spot within seven years.' We shook
hands solemnly. Neither of us had any money; my father
was a Baptist minister and his father kept a general store
in a New England village. But that night we knew that if
we were both alive, we should see the Rhine. Five years
later we leaned our bicycles up against the roadside,
looked out on the river, and the dream came true. 'Remember that night in the dark theatre? Well, here we are!'

At the University of Heidelberg we heard a lecture by
the famous Kuno Fischer. It was a hot summer day and
there seemed to be no air at all in the lecture room, very
much as Browning described the German university in
'Christmas Eve.' All the windows shut tight; I think they
had not been opened for thirty years. I had supposed that
German professors lectured to their students in a dry, im-
personal manner. I was in for a surprise. At precisely

quarter past four Fischer walked briskly into the room to
the accompaniment of foot-applause from the students;
he hung his hat on a peg, began speaking almost before he
reached his place behind the desk, and without a scrap of
notes, poured out a lava-like flow of burning eloquence,
gesticulating violently, reaching tremendous heights of
oratory, descending to the most bitter ironical denuncia-
tions; and occasionally being overcome by sentiment, his
voice would break and his eyes fill with tears. The subject
was Leibniz, and I have never seen anyone before or since
get into such a storm of passion over Leibniz.

Kuno Fischer was an old man then, short, fat, with
scanty white hairs on the two sides of his bald head. His
face was clean shaven, his mouth very wide, his nose
hardly bigger than a button. But his bearing had such
dignity and sincerity and his broad forehead gave such intellectual power to his expression that his nose was unable
to spoil his face.

Toward the close of his lecture he reached a climax of
eloquence; his eyes blazed; his voice thundered. Suddenly
as the clock in the hall struck five, he stopped almost in
the middle of a sentence, and walked swiftly out of the
room while the students stamped. In delivering his lecture he spoke with such torrential speed that I understood
hardly anything; and yet, after the space of more than
forty-five years, that lecture remains vividly in my mind.
I can see and hear him as distinctly as if I were now in the
room.

We wheeled along through the Rhineland to Strassburg,
and from there through the Black Forest; in the little
village of Offenburg I was impressed by a huge statue to
Sir Francis Drake, erected in honour of his having introduced potatoes into Europe.

One day, the weather being very bad, we took a train
for some thirty miles, and there being no one else in the

compartment, we all began to sing; the guard came along, and said that if we sang, we must pay fifty pfennigs extra.

On Saturday afternoon, 26 July, we went to Oberammergau; in those days the train went only part way, and we climbed the mountain in a springless wagon, receiving a series of terrific jolts. The next day Sunday dawned clear and bright. We rose at five, and after coffee and rolls in the kitchen of the cottage where we stayed, we went to Mass, and at half-past seven entered the theatre. Our seats were in the second row, directly in front of the stage, with nothing over us but the sky. The play began at eight, with a recess from 11.30 to 1.30, and closed at 5.15. Then we walked and ran all the way down the mountain and caught a train for Munich.

During the last fifty years I have seen the most famous actors in the world, from Salvini to those now living; but I have never seen any play or any acting that affected me so uncontrollably as the Passion Play at Oberammergau. I shall always be glad that our seats were close to the stage, in spite of the fact that during the showers that fell at intervals, we were drenched. During the entire day in 1890, I felt not as if I were seeing a play, but as if I were taking part in the most tremendous series of events in human history.

The Crucifixion was not the most effective part of the play; it was marred by the too realistic breaking of the legs of the thieves, which was grotesque. But the scene in the morning when Jesus bade farewell to his mother, and she asked, 'When shall I see you again, my son?' and we knew it would be on the cross—the spectators close to me were sobbing aloud and the tears rolled down my face.

There was also one moment in the performance not rehearsed. Heavy clouds came up during the conversation between Jesus and Herod; and when Herod with a sarcastic smile asked Jesus a question, the Saviour looked silently at the sky and there was a tremendous crash of thunder. An answer from heaven.

In this year of 1890 there was a tragedy within the tragedy. Every young man in Oberammergau hopes some day to be chosen for the part of Christus; and every young girl hopes to be chosen for the Blessed Virgin. This year the girl selected for the role was engaged to be married; her lover insisted that the marriage take place that Spring, in which case she could not appear in the play. She begged him to wait until the Autumn, explaining that to appear as Mary the Mother would glorify her whole life. The young peasant became very angry at this and told her she must choose between the play and him; she chose the play. His pride was greater than his love; he forsook her and made a hasty marriage. All summer long she played the part of Mary with her own heart pierced with sorrow, and in the Autumn she took the veil.

From Munich we went to Switzerland and in dare-devil mood we pushed our bicycles up to the top of the Furka Pass. At the beginning of the climb the temperature was about ninety; at the top, where we stayed over night, it was midwinter, snow all around and the road frozen solid. It was the first day of August. The next morning we started bicycling down the mountain, making the spiral curves with the greatest difficulty. Some native bicyclists hitched a small fallen tree to the rear mudguard, dragging that after them as a break. We strapped the brakes down; the whole thing was a foolhardy proceeding and I know I had two or three very narrow escapes from going over the precipice. Once I fell on the very edge and looked straight down some two thousand feet.

When we first started in Germany, I noticed that the German wheelmen all carried a whip in a socket attached to the handlebar; and I was informed it was for defence against dogs. We soon found out that some form of preparedness was necessary. I do not know why the dogs hated cyclists with such fury. Everywhere we met men with carts drawn by huge and savage dogs; these dogs would frequently break away from their masters and come tearing after us, hauling their carts after them. And free dogs seemed equally hostile. I tried the whip, I tried carrying a pocket-full of stones, but the best expedient I finally discovered to be the simplest. When the wild dog got very close and tried to bite my leg, I leaned over and spit in his eye. With some practice I became accurate. It never failed. Dogs that paid no attention to whips or stones stopped instantly when they got this dose.

During that whole summer I never got over my amazement at the excellence of the roads. Except in cities and in private estates, there was not a single good road in America in 1890. Ruts and dust and mud but never anywhere a hard smooth surface. When I was told that in Europe the roads were good everywhere and that for hundreds of miles the macadam was perfect, I did not believe it, and every day it was a fresh surprise. I had taken so many long tramps in America and had never seen or expected to see a good road that these magnificent highways astounded me. They were much better then than they are now, for the automobile had not been invented and there were no trucks or lorries to spoil the surface. The best of all the roads were the great *Routes Nationales* in France, made by Julius Caesar and improved by Napoleon. We travelled many miles through the deserted French countryside without seeing a house or a man; yet five of us could ride abreast on a road as smooth as a billiard table.

The only dangerous wheeling we had was in Switzerland, and as I look back on that I wonder I escaped with my life; but coming over the Jura mountains from Geneva into France we had some tedious climbs and some thrilling coasts—running down for miles. Auxonne is a town I never heard mentioned, but I shall never forget our entrance into that tiny mediaeval city; it was heavily fortified; we pushed our wheels between two immensely thick walls and over several moats to effect an entrance. Americans on the roads in 1890 were an object of intense interest; all the school-children everywhere stopped to ask us questions, and near Auxonne a poor old woman who had been gathering herbs was so fascinated by our having come from far away America that she talked with us for a long time. She asked if I would accept a glass of wine, whereupon she fetched a bottle from some corner of her clothing. I drank and she refused to take any compensation. The kindhearted old girl said she had a son in the wine business.

When we entered Dijon, we went to the Hotel de la Cloche, and found that Phillips Brooks had just registered. I asked the clerk if it were really the great preacher and he said volubly, 'Yes, Dr. Brooks has just arrived with his two daughters!' What a public scandal if it had been true! And what ammunition it would have furnished to his antagonists the next year when they endeavoured to prevent his election as Bishop.

At Montbard, the birthplace of the famous eighteenth-century scientist Buffon, we stopped for the night. After dinner, I wandered out alone in the twilight, and came to the castle. The great gates to the estate being open, I entered and found a land of enchantment. Never have I seen any allusion to the Castle at Montbard so that its beauty came upon me as a stunning surprise. I thought the place more beautiful than Heidelberg; and the extensive park and gardens were in perfect order. No one was visible. I had the beauty of the place to myself; and

in the deepening dusk the gardens about the ancient grey
walls seemed to be filled with friendly ghosts.

> A moment after, and hands unseen
> Were hanging the night around me fast.

I expected to see these *revenants* but I saw neither the quick
nor the dead. Surely the *Genius Loci* must be there, but
he gave no visible or audible sign.

Near the Castle Tower in the dusk, I had a beautiful
prospect of the town, with the lights beginning to appear
in the houses. I longed to stay in the Enchanted Ground
another hour, but fearing that some retainer might close
the gates, I returned reluctantly to the inn. But 'I had
caught for a moment the powers at play.' It is indeed
impossible for me adequately to describe the emotion I
felt in that crepuscular solitude.

In Paris a few days later we went to the opera to hear
Faust. Before the curtain rose a gentleman with a big
beard whose seat was directly in front of us, turned around
and said he had recognized my voice. It was Doctor
Winfred R. Martin, my inspiring teacher of Virgil in the
Hartford High School nearly ten years before. He told us
we were in luck that night, because a beautiful American
girl from Maine named Emma Eames, who had just made
her début and was the sensation of Paris, was to sing
Marguerite. She was indeed passing fair to see and her
glorious voice haunts me still. She had not then sung in
America but in the years to come I was to hear her over
and over again; and in later years was to have (as I have
now) the privilege of her intimate friendship. She has always been my favourite prima donna, even though her
contemporaries were the most extraordinary group of
sopranos the world has ever known. I shall always remember that night in Paris, when I first saw her in the
radiance of her youth and beauty (she was twenty-five)

and heard that voice of gold. By great good fortune, the Mephistopheles was young Pol Plançon, one of the greatest bassos of all time, whom also I was to hear so many nights in America. They sang in that sensational trio in the last act with such wealth of tone that the audience insisted on an encore; I was shocked by their acquiescence.

In Rouen, a city I was to visit often in the future, I found that I did not agree with those who had told me the church of Saint Ouen was more beautiful than the Cathedral—beautiful they both are, but I found the Cathedral, outside and in, overwhelming. We crossed the Channel from Dieppe so that we might first enter England in Newhaven, for both my companion and I, Horace Hart, were natives of New Haven in America. In London at Westminster Abbey the grave of Browning was covered with fresh flowers. He had been there only about six months.

In London I had my first subway journey in the world, in the London 'Underground' as it was called. The smoke and smell and din were terrific, but it was exciting. At a Promenade Concert in Covent Garden a woman, fat, fair, and more than forty, appeared on the stage, and I wondered why that ancient ruin was permitted to exist. But when she opened her mouth, a flood of gorgeous tones filled the room. It was magnificent singing; and finally, in response to repeated encores, she sang 'Home, Sweet Home.' It was Belle Cole, of whom I had never heard, and whom I have never forgotten. Sims Reeves, the great tenor, very old, sang in a way that charmed the vast audience, who idolized him.

I rode my bicycle the whole length of Piccadilly without a dismount, a feat I should not attempt in these latter days. But I loved those wood pavements of London. In our boarding house at Portman Place, an English physician sat next me at dinner, and said 'You an American? Why, you don't talk through your nose.'

On a Sunday, I went across the river to Newington Butts, to hear the Rev. Charles Spurgeon, most famous Baptist preacher in the world. His Tabernacle, built to accommodate his audiences, held an audience that morning of about six thousand. There was no organ and no instrument; the congregation sang with gusto. His text was, 'Lord, I am unworthy that thou shouldest come under my roof.' The language of the sermon was simple and sincere; his manner intensely earnest; his voice could be distinctly heard. I remember his saying something like this: 'Did I earnestly follow God many years ago? I don't care tuppence whether I did or not. I am following Him *now*.'

I came across the river on top of a bus over Westminster Bridge, thinking of Wordsworth's Sonnet which he composed 3 September 1802 on the roof of a coach on that same bridge. But the 'mighty heart' of London was never lying still in my time.

On 3 September 1890, however, I found myself as solitary as Wordsworth. Since 25 June, when we set sail from New York, I had had jolly companionship. But here, Horace Hart only being left of the original five, and he wishing to go to Edinburgh and caring nothing about Stratford-on-Avon, we separated, and words cannot describe my melancholy loneliness, from which, however, I completely recovered in two days. I would no more have visited England without seeing Stratford than I would have read Shakespeare and skipped *Hamlet*. That night I went again to Covent Garden and a young girl, Miss Grimson (where is she now?) was the piano soloist in Mendelssohn's Concerto in G Minor, which, curiously enough, I have never heard since. It was her first appearance; she was horribly nervous, and toward the end, she forgot. The orchestra stopped, and her music was handed to her. A few hissed, but this hissing was drowned in tremendous applause; and at the close, she was recalled three times. The audience did their best to cheer her, but how she must have suffered! Years later, while sitting with my friend, the late W.J.Henderson, music critic of the *New York Sun*, the great Madame Samaroff, who was giving the cycle of Beethoven Sonatas, forgot the music in the middle of the Hammerklavier Sonata. She laughed aloud, asked the audience to excuse her, went back stage and returned in excellent humour with her music, and finished the piece triumphantly. Bill Henderson told me he had more than once seen a famous pianist forget; but that they had always tried to fasten the blame on the piano or on somebody else; this was the first time when the artist frankly confessed to a lapse in memory. She was so great she could afford to do it; anyhow, she did, and won the devotion of the audience.

Cardinal Newman had died on 11 August, nearly ninety years old, and the shop windows were full of his portraits, and the hymn 'Lead, Kindly Light' was being sung and quoted every day. It is interesting to remember that Charles Kingsley and John Henry Newman, whose public debate attracted so much attention, and who wrote so many volumes in prose, will both be longest remembered for one lyrical poem by Newman, and three by Kingsley. The greatest hymn in our language is *Lux Benigna*, and 'The Three Fishers,' 'The Sands o' Dee,' and 'O that We Two Were Maying' will live forever. Newman's hymn, like the Lord's Prayer, can be sincerely uttered by anyone who feels religious aspiration, no matter what his theological position may be.

I had just bought a copy of a new edition of Rossetti's *Poems* and his lyrical translation of songs in Victor Hugo's *Burgraves*, one of the finest translations ever made by one great poet from another, haunted me so that I kept shouting it aloud when alone.

I

Through the long winter the rough wind tears;
  With their white garment the hills look wan.
      Love on: who cares?
      Who cares? Love on.
My mother is dead; God's patience wears;
  It seems my chaplain will not have done.
      Love on: who cares?
      Who cares? Love on.
The Devil, hobbling up the stairs,
  Comes for me with his ugly throng.
      Love on: who cares?
      Who cares? Love on.

II

In the time of the civil broils
  Our swords are stubborn things.
A fig for all the cities!
  A fig for all the kings!

The Burgrave prospereth:
  Men fear him more and more.
Barons, a fig for his Holiness!
  A fig for the Emperor!

Right well we hold our own
  With the brand and the iron rod,
A fig for Satan, Burgraves!
  Burgraves, a fig for God!

I spent several evenings in Hyde Park and found the
speeches tremendously interesting. It was a strict case of
the survival of the fittest. Every orator had a group around
him, but if he for a moment lost his inspiration, a rival
speaker only a few yards away, would capture half his
audience. One speaker asserted loudly that he did not believe in royalty—'Of course I have nothing personally
against the Queen; she does her best, according to her
lights,' to which the crowd listened with indifference. Not
far away a debate was in progress between a venerable

white-bearded atheist and an evangelical Oxford undergraduate. Here was Radical Old Age against Youthful Conservatism. Each man was accompanied by seconds, who
held books for his principal, while a third man held a lamp,
so that each of the antagonists could refer to and read from
his particular authority. The crowd took a deep interest in
this; but it was a sporting interest, exactly like that in any
athletic struggle. The skill of the contestants was more interesting than the question at issue; controversies are usually uninstructive.

Saturday 6 September was a red-letter day. I started out
alone on my bicycle at ten o'clock, wheeled through Hammersmith, Hounslow, and Colnbrook to Windsor, crossing
the Thames at a lovely place where there was a fine view of
the castle; and I soon saw the landscape from the top of the
Round Tower. After walking about Eton, I bicycled to
Stoke Poges, where I saw the churchyard of Gray's
'Elegy' as one sees visions in a dream—for my spirit
seemed to leave my body, and I was elevated into ecstasy.
The time and the place. The lovely September afternoon
was drawing to a close; there was not a breath of wind and
in this twilight calm I saw the churchyard, the yew tree,
the rugged elms, the graves, and the whole quiet scene not
changed since Gray described it. I fell on my knees, carried
away by my emotions.

On that same afternoon I did homage at the grave of
William Penn. He is buried in the small enclosure of a quiet
country house and lies with his family, a small headstone
containing only the words

WILLIAM PENN: 1718.

Nearby I entered the cottage at Chalfont St. Giles, where
Milton wrote part of *Paradise Lost*, and where the furniture
remains as he left it. I also made a pilgrimage from the tiny
cottage of the uncompromising Milton to the spacious man-

sion of the compromising Waller, and read the inscription; thirty-eight years later I read it again in company with G. K. Chesterton, whose house was only a few feet away.

That evening in the Red Lion at High Wycombe I met an English gentleman who was also an enthusiast on English poetry, and we talked till a late hour. Next morning (Sunday) I bicycled to Oxford, entering the town as the bells were knolling men to church. I took a seat in All Saints, and heard the Public Orator preach a dry sermon. It was the Rev. Dr. W. W. Merry, whose name at any rate was quite familiar to me, as he was the editor of the text-book of Homer that I had studied in my Freshman year at Yale. I remember perfectly after all these years the expression on his face in the pulpit. He looked very unhappy. The subject of the sermon was *Gratitude*!

Oxford was even more beautiful than I had anticipated. At the hotel I met Billy Brown, who was graduated from Yale the year before me (now the Rev. Professor Dr. William Adams Brown, of Union Theological Seminary, author of many admirable books). Billy and I went out for an evening walk at Oxford and found ourselves in the midst of St. Giles's Fair. Two or three damsels pushed feather dusters in our faces, so we bought similar weapons and enjoyed the occasion. Universal licence prevailed in the thick crowds, but with the utmost good nature everywhere. This was my first experience of an English Fair, and it reminded me every moment of Ben Jonson's *Bartholomew Fair*, which I had studied at Yale.

Wheeling on to Stratford, I stopped to read on a big monument the following inscription:

6 MILES

To Shakespere's town whose name
Is known thro' all the earth
To Shipston 4, whose lesser name
Boasts no such poet's birth.

I saw all the sights at Stratford and fell in love with the town. In the twilight I hired a rowboat and rowed for an hour on the Avon.

Next day I walked to Shottery and talked with an old lady in the famous cottage; she was Mrs. Baker and claimed to be a descendant of the Hathaways. On my way I passed many children going to school, with shining morning faces. In my inn at Stratford I had in my bedroom gaslight, the first time I had had anything except kerosene or candles in a bedroom since leaving New York in June.

I wheeled on to Coventry, seeing Warwick Castle and Kenilworth on the way and at dusk came in sight of the 'three tall spires.' Next day I visited the George Eliot country, seeing the little farmhouse where she was born, the church at Astley, which I suppose is the one in *Scenes from Clerical Life*, and entered the spacious grounds at Griff, where she lived for twenty years; her brother was living there then. The old gardener, who remembered her perfectly, was well supplied with anecdotes, and I found his conversation interesting.

On the way to Birmingham I had an alliterative lunch by the road, consisting of Crackers, Cheese, Cakes, Chocolate, and Cider. At the Theatre Royal I heard Wilson Barrett in *Hamlet*, whom I had heard in New Haven three years before. The house was jammed and when he appeared the cheering was tremendous. I sat in the top gallery among crowds of men, many of whom had never read the play and were ignorant of its plot. How I envied them! they were spellbound. When Hamlet drew his sword on the King at prayer, a man next me whispered, 'Now he's going to kill him!' and his disappointment was acute; and Hamlet's reasons seemed to him flimsy.

In Shrewsbury I had cakes and ale with a young Welshman, who was so hospitable that he invited me to come to his house near Snowdon and stay there till I sailed for

America; and I should have been glad to accept, if only I had had the time. I visited the scene of the Battle of Shrewsbury (1403) and thought of Falstaff and Hotspur.

I heard an organ recital in Chester Cathedral that impressed me more than any similar performance in my life. Curiously enough, there are in the cathedral two battle-flags brought from Bunker Hill!

On Sunday morning, 14 September, in company with three young Englishmen, we wheeled to Hawarden to see Gladstone in church. Mr. Gladstone entered at a side door and sat in the chancel. If only he had read the lessons, and I could have heard that marvellous voice! Just before the sermon he took a seat in the front pew in order to hear better. The preacher was pompous, well nourished, red-faced, and said nothing worth remembering; yet I remember his saying that if people gather together and put up a meeting-house, that cannot possibly be called a Church; the only true Church is the Church of England. After service I hurried around in front. Mr. Gladstone soon appeared. As he came out he recognized some acquaintance with a smile on his old face, that reminded me of sunlight on a cliff. As he came close to me, I took off my cap, and he acknowledged the salute. He was then nearly eighty-one and walked with the ease and grace of youth. As I was looking at his receding figure, an Englishman whispered in my ear, ' You are looking at the greatest man England has ever produced.' I knew better than that; but I thought then and I think now that I was looking at the greatest living statesman in the world.

In the afternoon I wheeled away into Wales, passing into a wild and desolate country, with grand mountain views in the distance. Passing through St. Asaph, where Mrs. Hemans is buried, I coasted along down to the seashore, with splendid mountain views on the left and the wide sea on the right. Wheeling through a rocky defile past a castle,

I caught up with a young Englishman and we travelled along side by side, and that night we shared the same room in the Stanley Hotel at Llandudno. Walking out together, we saw sitting at an open window, Carmen Sylva, the famous poet-queen of Rumania. Ellis and I spent the next day climbing around Llandudno in magnificent weather, enjoying the holiday crowds and the stunning views of mountains and sea. I bade farewell to him in the late afternoon and took the boat for Liverpool and the bicycle trip was over.

My journey alone through England was in some respects the most interesting of the summer. I was really almost never alone, for I was constantly running across Englishmen who in five minutes seemed like old friends. English people in their own country are perhaps more friendly than anywhere else. It would be impossible anywhere to find any persons more so; it was my daily experience.

Aikins and Hart, who had started with me in June, appeared, and we all three embarked on the small *City of Chester* on 17 September, and in nine days we reached New York.

30

LIFE AT HARVARD

L'amitié jette des racines bien profondes dans les cœurs honnêtes.
—Vingt Ans Après.

On the first day of October 1890 I arrived in Cambridge and went to my rooms at 22 Winthrop Street. My roommate was Arthur Gordon (now the Reverend Doctor) who was a son of the Reverend Doctor A.J.Gordon of Boston, one of the greatest pulpit orators in America, and an intimate friend of my father. Arthur was six or seven years younger than I, and was in the Junior Class at Harvard College; thus he used the rooms only during the day, returning to Boston every evening. He was the best of company, always cheerful; and I wished very much he could have lived in the rooms as I did, for I missed him in the evenings, and was lonely. Fortunately he had two lovely and charming sisters, Elsie and Helen.

In going to Harvard I made up my mind that I would learn all I could, not only from my studies and teachers, but also from my new associations. There were many Yale men studying in the Harvard Law School; it was a strong temptation to see them, but I resolutely avoided them and all former friends and everything that in any way reminded me of past years. This life at Harvard was a new experience, and I determined to get the most out of it. Thus I ate at a table in Memorial Hall, roomed with a Harvard undergraduate, cultivated Harvard acquaintances, and altogether behaved as if I had never heard of Yale.

245

The one exception to all this was a fortunate one; my own beloved Yale classmate, William A.Setchell, later for many years Head of the Department of Botany at the University of California, was then beginning his famous career as a teacher of botany at Harvard. He was at my table in Memorial Hall, and his assistance and advice during those first few months was of the greatest value to me. He and I had been devoted friends at Yale, and had taken midnight walks together; it was delightful to find this one old friend in new surroundings.

On my second day at Harvard I called on the professors under whom I was to study; and first of all on Professor Francis J.Child, known to the students as 'Stubby' Child. He hated to be interrupted in his home in Kirkland Street, but he was kind and considerate. At that time it was considered both by the Faculty and students in the Harvard Graduate School, that everyone who took advanced studies in English must spend nearly all his time on philology. Thus I found the students were all studying Anglo-Saxon, the history of the English language, Historical English Grammar, Old Norse, Gothic, and what not; furthermore, the Doctor's theses were on linguistic subjects. I asked some of these men if they really preferred to write on such themes. 'No, of course not; but you can't write a doctor's thesis in literature.' I replied that my thesis would have nothing whatever to do with philology. They regarded me with a mixture of incredulity, wonder, and envy.

Now when I called on Professor Child, he began to make out a programme for me consisting of the unpalatable subjects mentioned above. I told him I had had one year of Anglo-Saxon at Yale, and that would have to last me all my life. But he said I must have these other linguistic studies. I told him I had the highest respect for those studies and for the professors who taught them; but that they did not interest me. I wished to confine myself to English literature. He was so astounded at this and perhaps thought I was not taking graduate work seriously or was lazy or dilettantish or something, that he became rather severe; and my career at Harvard very, very nearly came to an end on the second day. I finally said, 'Professor Child, I have come to Harvard to study literature under you and your colleagues; if you refuse to allow me to take the studies I came here for, I shall take the first train back to New Haven.' Suddenly his whole manner changed. 'You go ahead and take anything you like. It is refreshing to find a graduate student who knows what he wants.'

Accordingly the first year I took Shakespeare with Professor Child; the History and Principles of English Versification, with Dean L.B.R.Briggs (God bless his heart!); Elizabethan Drama, with Mr. George Pierce Baker, who nearly forty years later was to be my colleague at Yale and Head of the Department of Drama; and a course in research in eighteenth century literature, where I reported my results every week or so to Professor Barrett Wendell. In the following year I took Chaucer under Professor Kittredge; Elizabethan literature (outside drama) under Professor Wendell; and English literature of the seventeenth century, under Dean Briggs.

This was the last year of my life that I was exclusively a student; I remember what a strange sensation it was in June 1891, when, on taking my examinations on the year's work at Harvard, I reflected that I had been going to school and taking examinations from the age of three to the age of twenty-six, and now I should never have to take an exam again! One chapter in my life had closed. Preparation was over. The professional work of my life would begin in the Autumn.

Although this was my last year as a registered student, it was the only year when I had been able to concentrate on my favourite studies; thus, until my breakdown in health, it was the happiest year of my life since my Freshman year at Yale. As an undergraduate at Yale, there were hardly any courses in English literature; and even in the Yale Graduate School, there were not sufficient courses in English, so that I took philosophy, history, and economics as well. But now, at Harvard, I had only the studies I wanted. My eyes grew better all the time, and although I lived like a hermit, had hardly any exercise and no recreation, I was happy.

Once more, as has so often happened in my life, realization was better than anticipation. I went to Harvard as an experiment, thinking it would be good for me, but not expecting to enjoy it. It was like a new lease of life. I felt like Andrea del Sarto at the court of François Premier. There was a keen intellectual atmosphere created not only by the members of the English Department, but by a Department of Philosophy which I suppose was the most brilliant that has ever existed—William James, Josiah Royce, George Santayana, George Herbert Palmer, Hugo Münsterberg; I knew these men and heard them give public lectures. On Sunday afternoons I went occasionally to the house of Professor Nathaniel Shaler, who was a brilliant talker on anything and everything; Charles Eliot Norton was in his prime, and his *obiter dicta* in his famous course in Fine Arts were reported all around the place. There was a vitality indescribable. Bliss was it in that dawn to be alive.

At our eating table in Memorial Hall, we had good conversation. My seatmate was John Matthews Manly of South Carolina, now one of the foremost English scholars in the world. Other men were Charles Davenport, now the famous biologist, and Charles M. Bakewell, subsequently my colleague at Yale and a member of Congress. Nearly all the men were from the South, and they were so good to this particular Yankee that they elected me an honorary member of the Southern Club and on the occasion when they gave a public dinner to Thomas Nelson Page and Hopkinson Smith, I was the only Northern man present. I remember how queer old Professor Toy looked with his enormous white beard; because while he might have been the model for a portrait of Hosea, his cigarette in that beard seemed incongruous. The Southern students at my Harvard table were Logan H. Roots, now Bishop in China; Andrew Patterson, later Dean at the University of North Carolina; David Houston, later University President and member of President Wilson's cabinet; Francis Caffey, now United States District Judge for Southern New York; William J. Battle, later Dean at the University of Texas; Augustus Long, later of the English Department at Princeton; and Collier Cobb, later Professor of Geology at the University of North Carolina. These Southern young gentlemen became my most intimate friends, and perhaps being such an unmitigated 'damyankee' I may have been in a way as good for them as they certainly were for me. One day, with that brilliant young Southerner, whose early death was such a loss to his country, William G. Brown, we all walked together from Cambridge to Salem, and visited the historical places.

Other men at the table and good friends of mine were Brace Chittenden, later a professor of Mathematics, and his brother Percy, one of the very few who did not enter academic life; Dickinson Sargent Miller, later Professor of Philosophy; his eccentric friend Hodder, afterwards professor at Bryn Mawr; and William E. Ritter, later Professor of Zoology at the University of California.

The Harvard professor with whom I came most closely in contact was Barrett Wendell; we became intimate friends; he was very kind to me, and I shall always think of him with grateful affection. In many ways he was the most peculiar man on the Harvard Faculty and President

Eliot waited a good many years before promoting him to a full professorship. It speaks well for Harvard—it is indeed meant by me to be the highest possible compliment to Harvard, both to the authorities and to the undergraduates—that in the nineties Harvard was the only university in America that could or would have kept Wendell. There have been some universities (not Yale and not Harvard) where the oddities, indiscretions, and other characteristics of professors as revealed in the classroom have been a source of revenue to students whose love of money has been more acute than their sense of honour. These students, ignoring the fact that things said in the classroom are not for publication, have furnished to the papers sensational statements made or supposed to be made by their teachers; and as college professors are generally 'news,' these indiscretions form what the newspapers call a 'story.' To the everlasting credit of Harvard undergraduates, I never knew of a single one of Wendell's remarks or acts being supplied by them for public consumption. They had much good-natured fun with him in the articles and in the pictures of the *Harvard Lampoon*, but that was all in the family; and if there had been any talk of letting Wendell go, these students would have been the first to rise in his defence.

A stranger meeting Barrett Wendell for the first time would have thought he was impossible. He had the most exaggerated 'English accent' I have ever heard either from an Englishman or any one else. He spoke like the stage caricature of an Englishman. Where he originally acquired this accent I do not know; but it had become a part of himself. I never caught him off his guard; nor did I ever hear him speak in any other fashion in the classroom, on the public platform, in general conversation, or in the bosom of his family. On the street people stopped and stared at him, arrested by these strange sounds.

Apparently he never was aware of the attention he commanded.

In describing the exaggerated 'English accent' of some Englishmen, H.G.Wells called it the 'whinnying voice.' I have sometimes wondered if the great Jonathan Swift had not chosen his Houyhnhnms after first hearing the conversation of cultivated Englishmen. Now Wendell had that whinnying voice; beginning very high with a slight stammer, and then descending in a rapid cascade of sound.

Wendell was like the English too, in his love of a cold room. His famous 'office' in Grays 18, in the Harvard Yard, never had steamheat, only an open fire, and even in winter the windows were open; so that later, when we had meetings of the English Faculty there, the aged Professor A.S.Hill, famous as the author of Hill's *Rhetoric*, always wore his fur overcoat.

Wendell's peculiarities seemed at first like affectations; yet I have never known any teacher of English composition who showed more common sense. For many years he carried the all but intolerable burden of reading and correcting themes, day after day. His room was filled with these compositions; they were all over the table and on the chairs, and when he lay down on the sofa, to get a little rest, he used a bunch of themes for a pillow. However picturesque and bizarre his own manner and way of expression, he never tolerated affectation in the compositions of his students. Ruthlessly he combed out of them every bit of 'fine writing,' every trace of insincerity, and taught them how to express themselves clearly and with economy of words. His book *English Composition* is the best treatise on the art of writing I have ever seen, and certainly the only one I read through from first page to last with undiminished interest.

Furthermore, Wendell, although very sensitive, was extraordinarily modest; so modest that it was almost painful;

one hardly knew what to say. At my first interview with him, when I came as a graduate student, he said 'I don't know anything,' and a few days later he said, 'You have probably already taken my measure.' It took me some time to find out what he meant. He meant he felt out of place in a modern German-trained American college Faculty, surrounded as he was by research scholars and philologists. He had never studied Anglo-Saxon, he knew no German, he had never studied for the degree of Doctor of Philosophy, which had in general become the sole gateway to college teaching. But he knew English literature thoroughly, was an admirable critic, and was thoroughly at home in the Latin, French, and Italian languages.

On that Harvard English Faculty, one could hardly imagine five men more unlike than Professor Francis Child, A.S.Hill, L.B.R.Briggs, George Lyman Kittredge, and Barrett Wendell. But they got along together beautifully, with mutual respect, admiration, and affection.

During my first year at Harvard I saw Wendell frequently; during the second year I saw him every day. Except at meals, or in the lecture-room, I never saw him when he was not smoking or preparing to smoke; at a time when in many colleges it would have been fatal for a member of the Faculty to take a drink, Wendell insisted on having alcohol—as he called it—with his meals; and how he shocked Professor Coy of Andover, at a school dinner there, by taking a bottle from his pocket! Wendell hated hypocrisy; and he said no one should refrain under any circumstances from drinking at a public dinner, if it was his custom to drink at all.

Probably no man ever loved his children more than he; but he loved also not to show this emotion. I came into his room one day and the following dialogue took place.

P. 'How are your children, Mr. Wendell?'
W. 'Oh, just at this moment I believe they have scarlet fever.'

P. 'Why, that's terrible!'

W. 'Yes, and you know scarlet fever is often followed by Bright's disease, idiocy, and such things.'

P. 'How fearful!'

W. 'Well, that's the sort of thing that lends interest to the game, you know.'

They all got well.

At another time he was explaining to me that he very seldom saw his children, as he left the house so early and came home just at dinner-time, when they had had their supper and had gone to bed.

P. 'Do you really love your children, Mr. Wendell?'

W. (After a long period of consideration) 'Ye-es, but not when the first one came. It was so exceedingly rudimentary.'

Once, when I was in his room, Dean Briggs came in.

B. 'How are you getting on with your book, Wendell?'

W. 'I shall finish it next Sunday.'

B. 'Why, do you work on Sunday?'

W. 'Of course; it's the best day to work; the only day free of interruption.'

B. 'Well, merely putting it on the lowest possible ground, Wendell, the lowest possible ground, that of health, I should think you would find it well to have one day of rest.'

W. 'My dear fellow, that's the highest possible ground.'

He came at my invitation to Yale to speak at the banquet celebrating the sixtieth anniversary of the founding of the *Yale Literary Magazine*. Unfortunately there was one Yale student present who was quite drunk. I introduced Wendell saying that he had consented to come to the enemy's country. Wendell rose and whinnied, 'The enemy's country! My God, what is that?' and immediately the drunken man, catching the pitch with precision, gave loudly a perfect imitation. I suffered agony; Wendell paid no attention to the interruption and went on with an admirable speech.

At the celebration in 1901 of the two hundredth anniversary of the founding of Yale, for which elaborate preparations had been made, we had invited as guests at our house William Dean Howells, Thomas Bailey Aldrich, Dean Briggs, and Professor Wendell. Wendell's *A Literary History of America* had recently appeared and only a short time before the celebration, the *North American Review* contained an article by Howells attacking this book with such severity that it would be impossible for the two men to meet. Howells thought the book was the work of a snob, and being very democratic himself, he said what he thought about it and its author. Fortunately neither Howells nor Wendell knew that the other had been invited; so the University authorities arranged for Howells to go elsewhere, and Mr. and Mrs. Wendell came to us.

Wendell loved life intensely; he loved his family, his home in Boston, his colleagues and students, and his friends in the Tavern Club and elsewhere; and I remember his saying to me on the occasion of this 1901 visit, 'Do you realize we've got only about fifteen more years of all this?'

The well-deserved honours that came in later years were most gratifying to him. The famous Clark lectureship at Cambridge University, his residence for a year in France as Exchange Professor, his election to the American Academy of Arts and Letters. He died in 1921.

It seems trivial enough now, but in the year 1896 Harvard and Yale had some dispute over athletics, so that for a brief interval there was a suspension of contests; in that same year Wendell and I collaborated on an edition of the play *As You Like It* to be used in schools; he wrote the introductory matter and I supplied the notes. At his suggestion, we both signed this dedicatory sentence, written by him.

At a time when such differences as declare themselves between the two oldest colleges of New England are unduly emphasized, it is a

singular pleasure to bear part in any work which shall help to show
how truly Harvard and Yale are at one.

B. W.
W.L.P.

February, 1896.

Professor L.B.R.Briggs was then about thirty-five and
had recently been made Dean of Harvard College. At a
little distance he looked like an undergraduate, and to the
very end of his long life he had a certain boyish charm. It
has been my good fortune to know many men of upright
and unselfish and indeed of noble character; I never knew
a better man that Dean Briggs. He was a Saint; and his
saintliness was equalled by his modesty and his common
sense and his effervescent humour. His sympathy for the
weaknesses of humanity was matched by his sensitive
conscience. Hence he was an ideal Dean. He loved the
undergraduates and he believed in discipline. He was universally respected by his colleagues and by all classes of
students; and some of those whom he expelled from Harvard remained his friends for life. The influence of this
man on innumerable individuals cannot be exaggerated.

He was never robust and he had a chronic trouble with
his throat. It seems to me he had a sore throat for fifty
years. But he allowed nothing to interfere with his duties;
and we met him outdoors in the worst of sleety weather,
clad in his long overcoat with the flying cape, bent on some
errand of duty or unselfishness.

One of the best things in my life was my intimate friendship with Briggs. Just as I always felt ignorant when talking with Professor Kittredge, so I always felt morally unworthy while talking with Dean Briggs; yet both men
somehow or other made it easy for me.

After I had been at Harvard as a graduate student two
months, I was awarded a Morgan Fellowship, a great

honour in itself, and yielding an income of five hundred dollars a year. I did not find out until much later, that Dean Briggs, hearing there was to be a vacancy, had spent an entire afternoon in snow and sleet, walking about Cambridge, calling on various members of the Committee, and obtaining their support for this Fellowship.

Usually, when men are driven by an inflexible sense of duty, they are somewhat grim. The extraordinary thing about Briggs was that although no Puritan was ever more uncompromising, no sinner ever had more personal charm. What Mr. Morse said of John Quincy Adams would apply to Briggs—'the temptation to perform his duty was always strong; and if the duty were a particularly disagreeable one, the temptation became ungovernable.'

When Rollo Brown's *Life of Briggs* was published, I wrote to Briggs about it; and received the reply, 'I told him to wait until after my death and then not to do it.'

When Briggs reached the age limit of retirement and became Professor Emeritus, he carried out a plan that I recommend to all lonesome or unoccupied Emeriti. I would do it myself if I were not so busy. He elected two courses in the classics at Harvard exactly as if he were an undergraduate, attended every class exercise, and faithfully prepared every lesson.

As I was a graduate of Yale and had had comparatively little training in English studies, and at Harvard was competing with graduate students who had had four years of English, I expected to be outstripped by some of my competitors. Imagine my satisfaction, then, at the end of the year in June, when the marks of all the students were printed for distribution, to discover that not only did I have an 'A' in all four of my graduate courses, but that in three of them, I was the only person with this distinction. One of my fellow-students, now a professor of English, said to me, 'Damn you! it's owing entirely to you that I got a B instead of an A. I was told that in any ordinary year my work was good enough to have won an A; but that yours was so much better he had to put you in a class by yourself.'

In the Shakespeare course Professor Child addressed the class just before returning the bluebooks containing our exam papers, which he had himself corrected, annotated, and marked. He said, 'Many of you no doubt think you are going to get a good mark; but in this exam absolute accuracy is essential; I cannot give a high mark except to those papers that show a thorough and precise knowledge.' I thought to myself, 'This means that probably the best I can expect is a C plus.' My book was handed back to me. It was marked A, and under this letter Professor Child had written

Excellent book!

And it was legible, so there could be no mistake. His handwriting was so bad that once a student, on receiving a composition back from him, said, 'Professor Child, I did not think my composition was anything remarkable, but was it so horrible as all this?' 'What do you mean?' asked the professor. 'Why, Sir, look; at the end of my composition you have written *My God*!' Child looked at it and said, 'That isn't *My God*; that's *Very Good*.'

During my first year at Harvard I lived more like a recluse than ever before or since. I worked three hours a day on my doctor's thesis; then I had in addition the regular courses of study to carry through. As soon as I had finished a meal in Memorial Hall, I returned directly to my room or went into the College Library. Feeling that such a life was too selfish, I used to go on Sunday mornings with Logan Roots and Francis Caffey and a few others to the Boston docks where we visited the ships, and attempted some evangelistic and other helpful work with the sailors. Usually we were received kindly by these men, though with some bewilderment mixed with commiseration; and once we were emphatically told by a sea-captain to get out and stay out. Although this was rather humiliating, I secretly sympathized with him. He had not asked us to call.

The other philanthropic work I did was in connexion with the Boston Associated Charities. I was assigned to take charge of a destitute family, to visit them regularly, and find out their needs and how much assistance was necessary. I kept this up for two years and how I did hate it! But the people in charge of the organization were invariably kind to me, and when I told them that I could not see that I was accomplishing anything, they assured me that I was. The poor family at any rate were always affectionate, and the Irish widowed mother paid me a charming compliment, saying, 'I hope you'll live till I'm tired of yer!'

My room at 22 Winthrop Street faced the North; no ray of sunlight ever entered it. It was imperfectly heated by a defective furnace in winter, as the poor woman who kept the house could not afford sufficient fuel. Studying hour after hour in this gloomy room I acquired malaria, which I had not had for five or six years. Every day I suffered from what Burton is always talking about in *The Anatomy of Melancholy*—flushing and chills. I had what the country people used to call 'dumb ager.' I felt my face and head getting hot and chills creeping up my spine. I was taking no exercise and had no recreation. I was absorbed only in study, determined to finish my thesis by the first of May.

A woman on the other side of the double house, whose room was next to mine, was learning both to sing and to play the piano. When her voice became exhausted she rested it by her piano exercises until it was sufficiently refreshed to begin singing again.

In addition to these difficulties, the husband of the woman who was my landlady was dying of tuberculosis. This was in the year 1891, and none of us knew—certainly not his physician—what to do. What they actually did was to keep the windows of his room where he sat all day hermetically sealed so that no draught could injure him. Being entirely ignorant of the danger of infection,I used to go into this close and stuffy room, and sit by this man's side and have long talks with him. I must have inhaled ten thousand germs but nothing happened to me; he was evidently dying, and did die while I was staying in the house.

In the early Spring, obsessed by the work I was doing on my Doctor's thesis and by the fear that I should not finish it in time, I became afflicted with insomnia. This became so severe and so long-continued that finally I went back to my parents' house in New Haven to rest. But what people need who suffer from sleeplessness is not rest but diversion; and there was no diversion. I suffered so much that I really do not care to write about it. But it was a remark made by Professor Beers of Yale that did me more good than any physician or any medicine. I went to him and said that I had hoped to have my thesis completed by the first of May, which was the time for submitting it, but that I feared I should have to give up my degree that year, as I was in such poor health. He merely remarked, 'You have already done enough work on your thesis to deserve your degree, and you will get it anyway. Hand in your incomplete work at the proper time, and you will receive your degree at Commencement. You can polish it and if necessary add to it next year.' I do not think that he ever knew what he did for me; for I might have had a complete and prolonged breakdown.

But his statement took a tremendous load off my mind. I returned to Harvard immediately, and although I felt that I wrote that thesis not in ink but in blood, I finished it some time before the date, and did not have to ask any favours.

During those weeks of depression, before temporarily

giving up and going to New Haven for rest, and while at New Haven, although in no danger of suicide, I constantly longed to die. If any robber then had pointed a pistol at me in the night, I should have regarded him as my best friend. I am always sympathetic with sufferers from 'nerves' or from melancholia or depression, for I know the particular part of hell they are in. And I feel when any young person commits suicide that if someone could only have been with him or if he could only have got through that month of misery, he might have had before him forty or fifty years of happiness.

DR. EDWARD CONSTANT SEGUIN (1843–98)

One day in the early summer of 1891, while I was slowly recovering, I wrote to Dr. Seguin in New York, asking for an appointment. He telegraphed that he was sailing for Europe on the next day; he could see me if I called early in the morning. I got to his house before his office was opened, and was the first in what soon became a long line of patients. I was tremendously impressed in the hour's conversation with him. He apparently took a great interest in my case, and asked if I had, when in good health, been a sound sleeper. I told him that never since childhood had I slept both long and well and that only once in my life had I slept until nine o'clock in the morning. 'You are a man who requires comparatively little sleep; it is an error for you to go to bed early. Do not go to bed before midnight; but get up early.'

As I was going to Harvard that autumn to begin my work as a teacher and would have a college room, he told me to be sure and have a roommate so that I would never be alone at night. He urged me also to have a lighted candle always by the bedside (electric lights were very rare then) because one usually has to get up to extinguish a gas light and that brings one too fully awake. 'Read until you are sleepy, the moment you feel sleepiness blow out the candle, and if you wake in the night, read some more.' Then he gave me a prescription of sulphonal, telling me not to use it except for severe and prolonged insomnia. Merely talking with Dr. Seguin did me so much good that I took no drug for several weeks and then used his prescription only once. There was something about him that seemed to give me new courage and strength.

I did not know then of the terrific tragedy he had suffered about nine years before, when his wife killed herself and her three small children, but that tragedy lent additional force to his remarks when I later reflected on them. He said with quiet emphasis, 'I am a great believer in the power of the human will. The will can be cultivated and strengthened so that one can actually control not only one's conduct but one's thoughts. For example, I can decide when I go to bed the exact hour when it is necessary for me to wake and I wake exactly at that hour; whether it is four or five or seven or eight. I never have to be called no matter how necessary or important it may be for me to get up at a certain hour, and I have never used an alarm clock.'

I tried this myself but the difficulty was that if it were necessary for me to rise at five or six to catch a train or for any other reason, and I depended on my will, I always woke up two or three hours too soon.

Dr. Seguin made as great an impression on me as did any specialist I have ever consulted. He was born in Paris, the son of a distinguished psychiatrist. His father brought him to the United States when he was seven. He was a graduate of the College of Physicians and Surgeons in New York and he became profoundly interested in the study of nervous diseases. He went to Paris in 1869 and studied under the greatest specialists in the world, Charcot and others. In 1894, three years after I had consulted him, he had the first symptoms of an illness of the brain. He knew it was fatal although he lived four years. He made a special study of his own disease for the benefit of others.

A curious, disagreeable, and for many years inexplicable effect of taking sulphonal or any of its kindred soporifics I will mention, because although I feel sure it is unusual, there may be others who are similarly affected and do not know the cause.

I took one dose of the sulphonal in a glass of hot milk at four in the afternoon. I noticed absolutely no effect. I went out and about as usual, took a walk with a friend that evening, and went to bed without feeling sleepy at ten. But the next moment (as it seemed) it was seven in the morning; it was the best night's sleep I had had in years, and I experienced no unpleasant effects.

Nearly ten years later when I was in London, I had a prolonged case of sleeplessness, and took sulphonal from a new prescription. In a few days I began to itch terribly; far worse it was than mosquito or flea bites. Then big discoloured blotches broke out on my ankles and wrists. I consulted a London physician, a good general practitioner. He did not use the word but it was clear he thought I had syphilis. He told me my condition was serious; he thought I was going to be an invalid. I was certain it was not syphilis, because never in my life have I run any chance of taking it; I told the physician that in two weeks I was planning a bicycle trip, and he said that would be entirely out of the question. Well, I knew he was mistaken. In a few days the trouble entirely disappeared and I was perfectly well. Three years later I took some sulphonal with exactly the same result; but I did not connect the itching and blotches with the sleep-mixture. It never occurred to me. Some years after that, the same thing happened again; and being at that time in the company of one of the most distinguished physicians in the world, Dr. William Welch of Johns Hopkins, I showed him the blotches on my wrist, and asked him if he knew of any cause for such things. He was entirely at a loss to account for them; I doubt if even in his long practice, he had ever seen anything just like them. It is possible, of course, that *he* thought I had syphilis. He had no solution to offer and no remedy.

But a few years after that, the same result following the same medicine, I discovered the cause for myself. I suddenly remembered that whenever in previous years I had taken sulphonal or trional or anything like that, it was followed by this horrible itching and hideous blotches. I knew then that I must never take these things, for the results of the remedy, although temporary, were worse than the malady.

Yet in conversation since then with many excellent physicians, it is clear to me that they are for the most part unacquainted with the cause of these symptoms, so that I think such results are rare. But if some other persons have had them, heaven only knows what remedies the doctors have prescribed! The medicines—both external and internal—prescribed for me by that London physician did no good at all.

The Yale and Harvard Commencements in the year 1891 came on the same day; and on that day I received the degree of Master of Arts from Harvard and Doctor of Philosophy from Yale. Although I had looked forward to the doctorate for years I decided to take my degree in person at Harvard; for I had already had one degree at Yale and had never seen a Harvard Commencement. So on that June day, in Sanders Theatre at Cambridge I received my diploma from President Eliot and became an alumnus of Harvard as well as of Yale.

I had determined to stay at Harvard another year; and in the Spring of 1891 I had been reappointed to the Morgan Fellowship. But only a few days after receiving this honour, Professor Wendell asked me if I would be his Assistant during the coming year and read all the daily themes in his course which was known as English twelve, at a salary of six hundred dollars. There were two reasons—apart from the pleasure of the work and Wendell's company—which induced me to accept. It was a six hundred dollars clear because tuition was free to teachers; this would turn out therefore to be two hundred and fifty more dollars than I should have from the Fellowship. But the chief reason was that it made me a member of the Harvard English Department, on the teaching staff. I had no position elsewhere, thought it probable that I should get a job in some Western university, and I could get a better position if I went from the Harvard Faculty rather than as a student without experience.

All appointments at Harvard—great and small—were made by President Eliot; and I had an interesting interview with him. Although a good many Yale graduates went to the Harvard Law and Medical Schools, very few went there for anything else; he was interested in the reasons that brought me to the Harvard Graduate School and in my impressions of the life there. He asked me many questions, and told me I was appointed. I asked him 'Is my title to be Assistant or Instructor?' 'It will be Assistant.' 'But, Sir, it will be a great deal better for me if I can have the name *Instructor*; for I suppose this will be my only year at Harvard. I must be on the lookout for a full-time teaching position somewhere, and if I can call myself an Instructor at Harvard, it will be of great value.' He smiled and said 'Your title will be Assistant.' 'But, Sir, the man who has just had this very same job is called on the Catalogue Instructor.' 'No he isn't, he is Assistant.' 'If you will look him up, Sir, you will see that he is Instructor.' He rang and ordered a copy of the Catalogue brought to him. 'To my very great surprise, Mr. Phelps, I find you are right; he is called Instructor. It must have been an error, and I will see that it never happens again.' Then we both laughed.

Thus I began my work in the Autumn at Harvard as Assistant in English; but after about three weeks, I received a letter from Yale, informing me that I had been appointed Instructor in English at Yale, and suggesting that I begin my work immediately. During the two years preceding, I had hoped for this appointment more than for anything else. Now I felt it had come too late. I was settled in my room at Harvard, 54 Thayer Hall in the College Yard, I had begun my work as a member of the Harvard teaching force, and although I felt that if I refused this Yale offer it would kill my chances of ever going there, it seemed to me right to refuse.

I called on President Eliot. He was rather astonished at my receiving such an offer in the midst of term, and this is what he said: 'You are entirely free to go if you wish; whenever Harvard appoints a man for a certain term, the University is bound, but the man is not. The University must keep you and pay you till the expiration of your term, but every man who teaches at Harvard is free to go anywhere else, at any moment, and without notice. I will therefore not urge you to stay; but if you do decide to stay at Harvard, we shall raise your salary to the amount equal to that of the Yale offer, for which of course you will do some more work.'

'*And my title will be Instructor?*'

He laughed and said 'Your title will be Instructor.' I replied, 'I am grateful for your kindness and I shall stay this year at Harvard.' So before the first of November my salary was raised to one thousand dollars (my college room was free) and my title was Instructor in English.

I wrote the Yale authorities, thanking them for the offer, saying I should have accepted had it been offered before the opening of the term, explaining that I felt I should now remain for the present year where I was. And when I had posted that letter, I felt that I should never have the chance to teach at Yale.

Getting my roommate that second year at Harvard was rather interesting. Several men I had met at Harvard asked if I would room with them, but for various reasons I declined. Then a man from Bucknell University said a friend of his was coming to Harvard from that college to spend his Senior year, and take the Bachelor's degree the following June. He spoke in the highest terms of the great ability of this young man, added that owing to his aggressive personality he might be difficult to get along with, but if I waived that, I should find him interesting. I have never seen anyone I could not get along with, so I wrote a letter to him, remembering that Schopenhauer had said that a man's character is more clearly revealed by a letter than by an interview. His name was Ralph Charles Henry Catterall.

The letter I received pleased me; and we immediately agreed to become roommates at Harvard. I never saw him until we were in the room together. The following September (1891) he reached Cambridge a few hours before me, and when I entered the room, there he was; we introduced ourselves, and from that moment until he died in my house in Michigan in 1914 there was no cloud on our friendship. We were absolutely congenial. He was specializing in history, saying he loved literature too much to make the study of it professional. He had an astonishingly good memory. If I quoted any passage from English poetry, he immediately gave chapter and verse. He had an exceedingly interesting mind; I was always happy and contented in his company, and it pleases me to remember that his becoming my roommate changed the course of his life. I introduced him in Boston to the girl who became his wife. At the end of the college year, I wrote to President Harper of Chicago, urging him to grant Catterall a fellowship in the Graduate School. This was given; Catterall went there, took his doctor's degree, became Instructor and Assistant Professor of History at the University of Chicago, and some years later was called to a full professorship at Cornell, where he had enormous success as a teacher and as a member of the community. He made a tremendous impression on the students. His wife was Helen Honor Tunnicliff of Macomb, Illinois; she had studied law at the University, had taken her degree, and was an accomplished musician. I had met her while she was studying music in Boston. They were married in 1896 and often visited us in our country home in Michigan. We spent part of our Sabbatical year with them in Paris in 1903. In 1912, while travelling in Europe, he had a stroke; from this he seemed to have recovered, and with his son, Ralph T. Catterall, now a lawyer in Richmond, Virginia, he came to our house in Michigan in July 1914. On that first evening he seemed to be in excellent health, but during the night a second stroke came and in two days he was dead.

He was one of the most interesting men I have ever known; and one of the most brilliant.

One day, near the close of my first year at Harvard, Charles Davenport, now the famous biologist, asked me if I would accept the Presidency of the Harvard Graduate Club. This was a club of graduate students, who had regular meetings for social and intellectual purposes, and invited members of the Faculty to address them. I felt flattered and accepted with alacrity. I enjoyed my administration; it brought me into close contact with students in a variety of departments and also with some distinguished men who spoke to us. During the year, I secured as speakers President Eliot, Charles Eliot Norton, Thomas Sergeant Perry of Boston, Frank Tarbell, and others. President

Eliot seemed surprised that the Presidency, instead of being given to one of the two hundred Harvard graduates, was given to the only Yale man in the Harvard Graduate School; and this led to frequent and rather intimate conversations with him.

One of the most interesting young men on the Harvard Faculty was Lewis Gates, Instructor in English. He was a recluse; he lived in his room on the Yard, never took any exercise, never went into society, and stayed up nearly all night with his books. His only release from his studies was music; he played the piano well, and had a good knowledge of instrumentation. He was one of the best classroom lecturers at Harvard; and I think would have become one of the distinguished literary scholars of America, if it had not been for the tragic mental disease that eclipsed his splendid intelligence. I told Wendell how much I admired Gates, and asked some questions about him. Wendell replied that while everyone admired Gates, no one knew him; that it was impossible to know him; that he resisted every attempt at acquaintance. It seemed to me that while Gates doubtless valued his independence, his seclusion was the result of shyness. I therefore called upon him, and discovering his love of music, proposed that we go to the opera together. We became intimate friends; several times we went to Grand Opera in Boston and walked back to Cambridge at one o'clock in the morning, a good time for intimate talk. I shall never forget those conversations. I became immensely fond of him, and I really think I brought a little happiness into his solitary existence. I have found very often that men who are said to be averse to society or sour-minded, are really only shy; I have never known one who did not gratefully and affectionately respond to friendly advances.

One night at the close of *Lohengrin*, as Jean de Reszké departed for the magic land whence he had come, Gates whispered to me, 'There goes the Ideal! it can never stay!'

A few years later, being in Cambridge for the day, I called on Gates, and to my amazement found him with a tennis racket in his hand; 'Why, I thought you hated all games.' 'I cannot begin to tell you how I hate them; I loathe tennis; but the doctor tells me I must let up on work, and have some exercise every day.' He looked very despondent; it was the beginning of his decline.

I made the most of the propinquity of Boston. Although my financial resources were slender, I never missed a good opportunity at the theatre, at concerts, and at the opera. During the season of 1890–91, Booth and Barrett made a prolonged stay, and I heard them in *Julius Caesar*, *Othello*, and other plays. With about forty other Harvard students, I acted as supe, being a Roman senator, one of the 'skin' guards, a gentleman-in-waiting on Desdemona, etc. Lawrence Barrett was exceedingly kind to us. While waiting to go on, he talked to us in the wings about Harvard, about our plans for the future, and was most gracious. The regular Boston stage hand who had us in charge was an abominable and foul-mouthed ruffian. We hardly knew what to do with him; but once, just as Mr. Barrett was going on as Cassius, and this brute shoved three or four of us out of his way, he immediately took the man by the shoulder and said, 'It is fortunate that you are dealing with young gentlemen; if they were as brutal and bestial as you are, they might seriously injure you; the only thing that saves you is their good breeding. I advise you not to put it to any further strain.' The bully was cowed and slunk off. It was as dramatic as anything on the stage. We were all in the wings, the play was going on; there was Mr. Barrett in full Roman armour, speaking in an impressive whisper to this tough, while we, clad as ancient Romans, looked on in amazement.

Lawrence Barrett's greatest part was Cassius; he completely dominated the stage in the famous tent scene. As Othello he was also very fine. But as Iago—for one night Booth and Barrett exchanged roles—he was curiously miscast. He almost never took that part; the great combination was Barrett's Othello and Booth's Iago. However, he noticed everything; one of us, as a Roman senator, kept his eyeglasses on, and Mr. Barrett whispered in the midst of the scene while we were all on the stage, 'Take off those eyeglasses!'

A popular slogan at Harvard in those days was 'To Hell with Yale!' Some Harvard Freshmen had it printed on their stationery. One evening, when I went in with about forty Harvard students to supe in *Julius Caesar*, one of the actors, who knew more about acting than about undergraduates, coached us in the wings. 'Remember you are the Roman mob; be rough, unruly, turbulent, jostle each other!' Imagine saying that to a group of students. No sooner had we got on the stage than our 'mob' in the Forum degenerated into a free fight; we slugged and shoved each other unmercifully. The actor who had coached us looked from the wings aghast at his too faithful pupils; he kept shaking his fist at us and stage-whispering 'You damn fools! you damn fools! behave yourselves! what the hell do you think you are?' This roused us to fresh efforts; and the audience at all events showed no lack of appreciation. I thought we were going to steal the show.

This same actor had told us that when Mark Antony mentioned the will of Caesar, we were to shout hoarsely in unison,

We'll hear the will! we'll hear the will!

I cannot say whether these Harvard students had deliberately prepared the following effect, or whether one happened to say it and the others joined in; but whether

planned or impromptu, no sooner had Antony mentioned
the will, than these rascally academic supes all shouted

To Hell with Yale! to Hell with Yale!

If the essence of humour be incongruity, I do not know of
any more incongruous spectacle than this mob, clad in
Roman togas, shouting that famous slogan. The audience
in the first seven or eight rows, hearing it distinctly, went
into convulsions.

I was selected among the supes as one of six, called the
'skin guards,' as we were dressed only in rough, furry, and
horribly filthy skins, to carry the dead body of Brutus from
the stage. We had of course the utmost reverence for the
great Edwin Booth; and I am glad to remember that in
this rather difficult undertaking we made no mistake. In
full view of the audience we picked him up, and carried
him tenderly back into the wings, and deposited him in a
large armchair. He put his hand affectionately on my
shoulder and said, 'Well done, boys!' which made us very
proud. Thus I have not only appeared on the professional
stage with Edwin Booth but have literally supported
him.

I attended two meetings of the Harvard Religious Union,
a group of undergraduate and graduate students who met
to discuss matters concerning religion. At the first meeting,
Professor Toy, the famous scholar in the Semitic languages, who I believe taught in the Harvard Divinity
School as well as in the Graduate School, was the speaker
of the evening. He threw overboard everything usually
associated with Christian theology. In answering questions
from the audience, one student asked 'Do you believe in
prayer?' to which, after some consideration, Professor Toy
replied 'No; prayer is unscientific; at any rate, if any words
are used. Perhaps the nearest approach to a true prayer
would be a sigh.'

Yet at another meeting, Professor George Herbert Palmer was the speaker. He defended belief in the miracles recorded in the New Testament, saying he thought there was a real difference between those in the Gospels and those in the books of the Old Testament. A man might rationally reject the latter, and yet believe in the stories of the Gospels.

With reference to Professor Toy's remarks on prayer, there was a story current at Harvard in my time, which may be apocryphal, and yet is pertinent and amusing. The number of students in the Divinity School was so small that about half the rooms in the dormitory were occupied by Sophomores in the College. The Divinity students were often shocked by the alcoholic enthusiasm of Sophomores, returning from Boston late at night; but the shock was nothing to that received by the Sophomores, when they asked the candidates for the Christian ministry about their religious beliefs. At the end of the year, the Sophomores, on being asked if they wanted to continue occupying rooms in the same building with the Divinity men, answered, 'No! we don't want to room with those damned atheists!'

The professors in the Philosophical Department were so distinguished that there was general and frequent discussion of philosophical questions by undergraduates and indeed by all members of the academic community. It was announced that Professor Royce would give a series of lectures on metaphysics; on the opening night the spacious hall was so crowded that many were standing and many could not get in at all; the second lecture was given in a much larger room with the same result; all the subsequent lectures in the series were given in Sanders Theatre.

Although I shall always be grateful to Harvard for giving me an appointment as Instructor, and although my year of teaching was advantageous to me in every way, nothing would have induced me to consider a reappointment. I did not believe in the Harvard system of compulsory English compositions or in the enormous labour required of the instructors. The only subject required of Harvard undergraduates was the writing of compositions; this was required of every Freshman, every Sophomore, and at least for part of the year, of every Junior. The result was that a large number of men on the Faculty spent nearly all their time and energy in reading and correcting these themes; it seemed to me that this work was not University work at all, and that any primary schoolma'am would probably have been more efficient in the correcting job. That a man should graduate from Harvard with honours, spend two years in advanced study in the Graduate School, then a year of research in Europe—only to correct spelling, grammar, paragraphing, etc., seemed to me a hideous waste of time and energy. Furthermore, although many of these Freshmen and Sophomores wrote abominably when forced to sit in a room and compose a theme on an assigned subject, whenever they wrote a letter asking excuse on account of sickness, their style was correct and respectable. I knew of no work anywhere that so well illustrated the law of diminishing returns as this forced English composition.

I believed then and I believe now, that *elective courses* in advanced composition for men who wished to cultivate the art of writing and loved it, were exceedingly valuable; there were such courses at Harvard offered to picked men by Professor Briggs and Professor Wendell which were most profitable. After I had taught at Yale a few years, I sent up to Professor Wendell a collection of themes written by my Yale Sophomores, in connexion with their studies in English literature; these men had never received any college training in English composition; but I felt sure that technically their themes would be as good as those written by Harvard Sophomores, though the latter were thoroughly trained in technical composition. Mr. Wendell read them and wrote me that they were in every way equal to the work of Harvard Sophomores.

The only men on the Harvard English Faculty who were excused from reading themes were Professor Child and Professor Kittredge; and these men, with Wendell, did not believe in the required system. The most bitter expressions came from the venerable Professor Child, usually regarded as the foremost English scholar in America. For many years he had been forced to read hundreds and hundreds of undergraduate compulsory compositions; he said the system was bad for both students and teachers. He regretted the enormous amount of time and energy he had thus wasted. One day I met him in the Yard, and he asked me what I was doing; I replied, 'Reading themes.' He looked at me affectionately and said, 'Don't spoil your youth.'

During the entire academic year at Harvard, I read more than eight hundred themes every week; I read all day and a good part of the night. Once I was sick for two days, and a substitute read for me, because even one day's lapse made it impossible to keep up.

Now I do not regret this one year; far from it. I had the most pleasant associations with my colleagues on the Harvard Faculty, and my principal work brought me into close contact with one hundred and thirty representative Harvard Juniors and Seniors. Professor Wendell gave a course, where the men wrote long themes for him every two weeks and a one-page theme every day. My job was to read the dailies; and as these students wrote a diary I became intimately acquainted with them; furthermore, many came to see me for individual conferences. A splendid group of young men—frank, honest, humorous, they wrote of their daily doings and of their thoughts on all subjects. It was a great experience for me—I became devotedly attached to these Harvard undergraduates.

Professor Briggs said I was the only man in the world intimately acquainted with both Harvard and Yale undergraduates. Some of these men became lifelong friends. Frederick Winsor, Head of the Middlesex School at Concord; Osward Garrison Villard, editor of the New York *Nation*; David D.Wells, a young novelist who died at the dawn of his fame; H.G.Pearson, Professor at the Massachusetts Institute of Technology; De Lancey Howe, author of *The Star of Umbria* and other books.

Among my Sophomore theme-writers, I gave out at the end of the year only two ' A's;' one of these to Lindsay Todd Damon, now Professor of English at Brown University; the other to Edwin F.Edgett, later the accomplished literary editor of the *Boston Transcript*.

Another great delight of that year of teaching was the weekly meeting of the English instructors in Wendell's room at Grays 18—A.S.Hill, Briggs, Gates, Lathrop, Hurlbut, Arthur Carey. We had good times discussing the work.

PRESIDENT HARPER

During that year of 1891-2, Doctor W.R.Harper was travelling about the country, visiting all the Universities, selecting men for his Faculty for the new University of Chicago, which was to open in the Autumn of 1892. There was a fluttering in academic roosts, whenever it was rumoured he was coming; for he offered to Heads of Departments the then extraordinary salary of seven thousand dollars; and there were many stories of fabulous things that were going to happen. I spent a whole day with him at Harvard and accompanied him on his successful expedition to Newton, where he captured Professor Burton, a Biblical scholar. President Harper offered me an instructorship at fifteen hundred dollars, which I accepted. Two months later I received an offer from Denison University at Granville, Ohio, at eighteen hundred, with living expenses fifty per cent lower. I wrote to President Harper about this, and I gathered from his reply that I was entirely free to accept that offer if I wished. I declined it. In the Spring I was asked by President Dwight of Yale to come to New Haven for a conference. He immediately offered me fifteen hundred dollars, with the stipulation that I should not be required to do any teaching of English composition, but only of literature. He said however, 'You must decide now, on the spot, whether you will or will not take this position; I do not want you to go to President Harper, and then come back here, with a larger offer from him.' I replied, 'I will take the position.' I began work that year, September 1892, and remained at Yale forty-one years, automatically becoming Emeritus in June 1933.

When I wrote to Doctor Harper, I got a telegram telling me not to accept the Yale offer until I had talked with him; but I explained it was settled. He did not like this, but I wrote him that I had fully understood from our correspondence on the Denison matter, that I was free to accept any offer. Thus the offer from Denison University, in all probability, changed the course of my life. If I had not had Dr. Harper's letter as a precedent, I should of course have felt bound not to accept the offer from Yale until I had communicated with him; he might have told me that I was not free to go; thus I should have begun teaching at the University of Chicago, and might never have received another offer from Yale. Or if I had, the financial inducements at Chicago would perhaps have been so great that I should have felt compelled to remain there.

William Rainey Harper, the organizer and first President of the University of Chicago, was in educational affairs a man of genius. Although he died in his fiftieth year, he had lived longer than most men. He took his B.A. degree at the age of fourteen, his degree of Doctor of Philosophy at the age of nineteen, and was married in the same year. He was the hardest worker I have ever known, and I have known many. He went to bed at one, and rose at six. He never took a vacation; he played no games, had no hobbies or avocations, and no recreations of any kind. He was always apparently in high spirits, enjoyed himself enormously, and was boiling over with enthusiasm. I suppose there never was a greater teacher. For some years he was on the Yale Faculty, teaching Hebrew to the Divinity students and the English Bible to the undergraduates. He revolutionized the study of the Bible in America; and gave courses of public lectures on the subject at various universities and large cities. His students were aflame with enthusiasm. He started more young men studying the Hebrew language than any ten teachers have ever done before or since. He made them think the Hebrew language was more important than any other subject, ancient or modern. I asked him once how many times he had taught the first verse of the Hebrew Bible; and I forget how many thousand times he mentioned. I asked, 'Are you always full of enthusiasm for it?' 'Not always; but when I am not enthusiastic, I create the enthusiasm.'

He was tremendously happy in his home life. He told me that he was married at the age of nineteen, with no resources. 'During the first few years of our married life, there were a number of times when neither my wife nor I was able to write a letter, because we could not buy a postage stamp. But we never regretted the marriage.'

To enter any of the classes he taught at the Divinity School was a memorable experience. The students crowded into the room as eagerly as men go to a great athletic contest or to hear a great opera singer.

No other man could have accomplished what he brought

to pass at the University of Chicago. Starting with no buildings, no library, no Faculty, no students, in a very few years the University of Chicago became one of the leading universities of the world.

President Harper died of cancer; when the case was hopeless, he exhibited magnificent courage; but his son told me, 'I have never known any man who wanted to live so much as my father.' For several months he lingered, giving everyone an example of faith and uncomplaining cheerfulness.

I saw him often during his years of administration; he was always the same—full of gusto. Before any plans were known, and while he was engaged in active teaching at Yale and I was a student there, he had astonished me one day, when I was alone with him, by telling me that Mr. Rockefeller had provided funds for the founding of a great American university; then he asked, as if my opinion were important (it was a way he had with everyone) 'Where should this University be founded?' I replied without any hesitation, 'Chicago.' 'Oh, no,' he said, 'by no means; that's not the place at all. Try again.' 'Well, then,' I said, 'if Chicago is impossible, some place in the Mississippi valley.' 'Why, you're still further off. Can't you do better than that?' 'No, I give it up.' Then Doctor Harper said, 'There is only one place in America for this new University, if it is to be the institution I have in mind; it must be in New York City.' I was amazed. 'New York? Why, there are three great universities there now.' 'All the better,' said he, 'all the better.' What caused the change in plans I never knew; but once Chicago was selected, 'there is no place in the world like Chicago!'

In some way, President Harper combined immense courage and unlimited energy with extraordinary modesty. It was a rare combination of assurance of success without even the faintest trace of conceit. He always had what the poet Vaughan called high humility. A very beautiful character.

31

TEACHING AT YALE

I BEGAN regular work as a full-time Instructor in English
at Yale in the Autumn of 1892. The College was nearly
two hundred years old, but this was the first time that
English literature had ever been taught to Freshmen. I
was given one-third of the class from September to Christmas, another third from Christmas to Easter, and the last
section from Easter to June; so that I was to meet intimately in small divisions, three hours a week, all the members of the incoming class of 1896. I was twenty-seven
years old and looked eighteen. When I came to the door of
the lecture-room and found it locked, one or two Freshmen
waiting there, naturally taking me for a classmate, said
'Oh, the Prof hasn't got here yet.' When I took a key from
my pocket and unlocked the door, they looked at me in
amazement.

I taught the Freshmen *As You Like It*, *Macbeth*, and
King Henry IV, *Part I*. I enjoyed the work unspeakably;
and at the end of the Autumn term, when the first alpha-
betical third of the class found that they were to have no
more English until Sophomore year, they sent to me a dele-
gation headed by John Berdan (now Professor of English at
Yale) asking me if I would continue to teach a volunteer
class in the evening. I agreed to this—though it was an unprecedented thing at Yale. Accordingly for the next three
months, I met a large group of Freshmen one evening a
week and taught them English poetry of the nineteenth
century.

279

At the end of Freshman year, I was directed to continue the teaching of English to this same class of 1896 in their Sophomore year. It was for Sophomores an elective study, but all except three men took it. I had one-half of the class until February and the second half for the rest of the year. Our friendly and intimate relations were still further strengthened. Then, when they became Juniors, I began to offer elective courses in addition to my work with the lower classes; many took these courses, so that I really taught them for four years. When they graduated in June 1896, they presented me with a large silver cup.

I suppose there has never been a member of the Yale Faculty who knew intimately every member of a large class as I knew these men; and although they are now over sixty, my friendship with them has only been strengthened by time. As it happened, this class, the first I taught at Yale in regular daily work, contributed more men to the Yale Faculty than any other class in Yale's history; so that a considerable number of my first pupils became my colleagues.

The intense affection between these undergraduates and their young teacher was refreshingly exceptional because of the traditional teaching at Yale. To me my methods seemed simply natural and unaffected; to some of my older colleagues on the Faculty they seemed revolutionary, deliberately sensational.

About a year before I began my work at Yale, an older member of the alumni asked me what profession I had chosen, and I said, 'Teaching.' To which he replied, 'Oh, that's too bad. The novelty of the thing will appeal to you during the first year, and you will think it is fine; then you will fall into a rut, teach in a routine fashion like all the rest, and become merely mechanical. Furthermore, you will be cut off from active life among men and women, and will never know anything about the world.'

I have always been glad that I received that challenge before I began work; for I made up my mind then and there that I would never allow myself to become a routine teacher, that I would try to make every recitation an event in the lives of the students, and anyhow, an event in my own life. Despite innumerable errors and shortcomings, I can honestly say that although I have often taught and lectured badly, I have never done it mechanically; and in my last year of teaching, at the age of sixty-eight, I found it as thrilling and delightful as during the earliest days.

During those early days, the students were eighteen and I was twenty-seven; during the last year, the students were twenty and twenty-two and I was sixty-eight. Between us there was that immense gulf of years; in addition to which, the after-war morality and new points of view would seem to make it impossible for the students and me to stand on common ground. Thus, during those last few years, if the undergraduates had regarded me as an amiable anachronism, I should not have liked it, but I should not have resented it. But, as my own enthusiasm for teaching was if anything stronger in old age than in youth, I found—really to my amazement—that my intimate relations with the members of the classes of 1933 and 1934 and 1935 were about what they had been with those of 1896. Perhaps nothing pleased me more than an editorial in the *Yale Daily News* during the Spring of 1933, which said that the students then in college were probably closer to Professor Phelps than had been the men of the early nineties. Whether this were true or not, I loved to hear it!

The reason my teaching in 1892 seemed to my older colleagues revolutionary was that Yale was a place where traditions counted enormously. In the traditional teaching at Yale, formality was the rule. Nearly all the members of the Faculty wore dark clothes, frock coats, high collars; in the classroom their manners had an icy formality;

humour was usually absent, except occasional irony at the expense of a dull student. It was quite possible to attend a class three hours a week for a year, and not have even the remotest conception of the personality of the man behind the desk. The teachers seemed to believe this was the only method by which discipline could be enforced and maintained.

There was a blight, a curse on the teaching, unfortunate both for teachers and pupils. Instructors who were thirty years old had the classroom manner of old men; I remember how astounded I was at discovering that one whom we all believed to be venerable was thirty-eight. These men certainly gave no indication of enjoying teaching; and of course the students found no joy in learning.

I will give two illustrations. There was one of our professors who was like the rest in merely hearing recitations and marking them; he never made comments and never betrayed emotion. One day I happened to meet a lady who was his contemporary, who had known him well when he was an undergraduate. She told me that he was the life of every party, outdoors or in; that whenever there was a picnic or an excursion anywhere, if they could get him, success was assured; that he was the finest and wittiest and most delightful conversationalist she had ever known. I told her she must be thinking of someone else; but no, this was the man. It was incredible. Officially he was one person and on other occasions he was another.

The most extraordinary case however, and yet different from the majority only in degree, was that of a professor whom it was my misfortune to have in Freshman, Sophomore, and Junior year. He never gave the slightest indication of having any human emotion, like sympathy, humour, consideration. He was a remorseless machine in the classroom, holding us down by iron discipline; it was impossible for me or any other student to penetrate the barrier between this man and the class he taught; and there was a steadily disagreeable attitude on his part that made us hate him. If he had died during my undergraduate years, I should have rejoiced greatly. Not only was this man icily contemptuous in the classroom, he made himself obnoxious to the students by interfering with many of their extra-curricular activities; so that for at least thirty years successive generations of undergraduates regarded him with hatred.

It was not until some years after my graduation, and after I had become a member of the Faculty, that I discovered he was generous, kind, considerate. He was also full of fun, delighting in jokes and ridiculous puns. The special papers that he used to write for a club were full of original wit.

Now this man was Jekyll and Hyde. Unofficially he was absolutely lovable; officially he was detestable.

He was a martyr to his theory of discipline. He ought to have been admired and loved by all those generations of youth; and how they would have loved him if he had given them a chance, and how he would have appreciated their affection and their esteem! Instead of that, this tender-hearted man had the tragedy of knowing that year after year he was hated and despised.

I mention these things because they help to explain why my teaching seemed revolutionary and sensational; I simply made up my mind that I should be exactly the same man in the classroom as out of it; there would be no detectable difference. I would assume that the undergraduates and I were equally interested in the subject, and that we were studying it together. Thus I was not sensational; I was natural.

But as in the old days of rhetorical oratory, when any exceptional individual spoke from the platform in a natural, easy, conversational manner, it seemed astounding; when an actor on the stage, dispensing with conventional mannerisms, spoke and acted with unaffected naturalness, the result was amazing; so my natural manner in the classroom produced an effect that must be called startling. The response from the students indicated it.

Informality in college teaching is common enough now; but in the nineties at Yale, it was almost unheard of.

Informality does not necessarily mean any loss of dignity; it may mean simply that one throws away all pretence. I began to teach with absolute naturalness; later in my public addresses, in my sermons in church, in my dinner speeches, in my orations at funerals, I have never changed. Whether I am talking to two persons or to two thousand, my manner is exactly the same. As a great deal is said about the technique of public speaking, I will say that this is all the technique I know. But whenever I address a strange audience, there is always that same opening shock. I can feel it; it is not unpleasant. I never begin with conventional platitudes and generalities; no matter how large the audience may be, I always feel as if I were talking to each one separately. 'This only is the witchcraft I have used.'

The year 1892 was memorable personally. I finished my year of instruction at Harvard in June. I began my career as a teacher at Yale in September and remained in active service until retired by age in 1933. After finishing reading my first exam papers as a teacher in December, I took the train to Michigan. On Wednesday, 21 December 1892 at high noon, I was married to Miss Annabel Hubbard in the house at Huron City where I am now writing (1938), and we have lived happily ever after. The Rev. Jacob Horton of Port Huron, assisted by my brother, the Rev. Dryden W. Phelps, performed the ceremony.

Neither my wife nor I had ever been South, so we decided to take our wedding journey in what was described as the

Sunny South. We went to Asheville, North Carolina; and the day after we arrived, the thermometer fell to zero and stayed there for a week. We therefore went to Boston, where we were comfortable, stopping at Washington on the way.

On our return to New Haven, early in January, I was pleased to find that the Freshmen whom I had taught from September to the Christmas vacation had made us a beautiful wedding present, the *Complete Works* of James Russell Lowell.

After I had been teaching a few weeks, there was a meeting of the Freshman Faculty, most of whom were much older than I. I was informed that my marks were too high. To which I replied that the Faculty were at liberty to make a horizontal reduction if they wished, but that this Freshman class was very remarkable and I believed they had earned those grades. The older men naturally were amused and wished to know how I could pronounce the class to be remarkable, when it was the first class I had taught. I told them I was sure of the fact. They decided to let my grades remain. Two years later this very class entered more members of Phi Beta Kappa than had ever been known at Yale, and in the years following, as I have said, this same class contributed more members to the Yale Faculty than any other class in Yale's history before or since.

I have always been grateful that my first experience in Yale teaching should have been with this really amazing class of 1896; and in later years I had as my colleagues in the English Department Professors John Chester Adams, John Milton Berdan, George Henry Nettleton; in other departments Herbert E. Hawkes in Mathematics, now and for many years past the famous Dean of Columbia University, known and admired by all men; Albert G. Keller, Professor of the Science of Society, the distinguished

successor of W.G.Sumner; Hollon A.Farr, Professor of
German, and for many years a high official in the Dean's
office; Rudolph Schevill, who taught romance languages,
and for many years has been Professor at the University
of California; Professor Christopher Coleman, Professor of
History in Butler College, Indianapolis; Rowland Cox,
Instructor in Surgery, Columbia University; Sherwood O.
Dickerman, Professor of Greek at Williams College;
Edward L.Durfee, who became Instructor in History at
Yale; Jay G.Eldridge, who for many years has been Pro-
fessor of German and Dean of the University of Idaho;
Clarence V.Fowler, Instructor at the U.S.Naval Academy;
Herbert E.Gregory, Professor of Geology at Yale; William
M.Hess, for some years Recorder at Yale; Frederic B.
Johnson, Bursar of Yale; Robert S.McClenahan, President
Assiut College, in Egypt; William C.Morgan, Professor of
Chemistry, Reed College, Oregon; Henry A.Perkins, Pro-
fessor of Physics, Trinity College, Hartford; Fred O.
Robbins, for some years Instructor in French at Yale;
L.R.Scarborough, President of Southwestern Baptist The-
ological Seminary, in Texas; Charles P.Sherman, for many
years Assistant Professor of Roman Law at Yale Law
School; M.J.Spinello, for some years Instructor in Romance Languages, University of California; Douglas Stewart, Director of the Carnegie Museum, Pittsburgh; Canon
Anson Phelps Stokes, for many years the famous Secretary
of Yale University; Chauncey W.Wells, Professor of English at the University of California.

Haec sunt mea ornamenta! and I have mentioned only
those who became members of College Faculties. Many
others became teachers in Secondary Schools. I believe
such a scholastic record for a college class after graduation
is extraordinary. It was a good class for me to meet in my
first essay at teaching at Yale.

During the whole four years my relations with this class

remained intimate. Outside of the classroom I played tennis and hockey and whist with them. The famous 'Bridgeport Tennis Tournament' will be remembered by every man who took part.

When they came to graduate, Elbert Hamlin headed a committee who called at my house and said the Class wished to present me with a Cup. I told them I was deeply gratified, but that there must be no public presentation and no announcements in the papers. I did not tell them, but the reason was that my popularity with this class had aroused jealousy and hatred from some older members of the Faculty, and that a public ceremony of presentation might cost me my position. Hence the magnificent cup was left at my house by a small group one afternoon when I was away.

There is no doubt that in those days (1880–1900) popularity with the students was a serious handicap; if promotion to professorships had been in the power of the President and Corporation, as it was in most other American universities, it would have been otherwise; but the Permanent Professors on the Faculty had the power of election; thus it was in some ways like being admitted to a very select club. It was easier to be elected if one were an 'available' candidate; that is, if one had not attracted undue attention; but extreme popularity made the ruling powers feel that the candidate must have stooped to conquer. Professor Sumner used to say it was often easier for a man from another college to receive an appointment than for a man on the ground; 'the latter's faults we know, and all we know of the distant man is that he has faults, but as we do not know what they are, we forget their certain existence.'

I had already as an undergraduate witnessed what I have always regarded as disasters for Yale. Mr. Ambrose Tighe, who taught us Latin in our Freshman and Sophomore years made his classroom so interesting that he incurred the displeasure of the higher powers, and was released. Frank Tarbell, our Instructor in Greek and Logic, was released just when his influence was becoming really profound. Tarbell later was very happy at Chicago, with his colleagues in the classics and in archaeology, and with his intimate friends Robert Herrick, William Vaughn Moody, Robert Lovett, and John Manly, of the English Department.

Now, after I had taught at Yale for seven or eight months, I was warned by several professors that my stay would be short; some were friendly, and merely told me to look out; others were quite the reverse, and gave me distinctly to understand that I could never look for promotion. Every time I received an offer elsewhere, I was earnestly advised to take it. I do not believe any member of the Faculty ever received so many invitations to leave Yale that came *from the inside*. One of my superiors told me that if I went on, I should be like Ambrose Tighe (my hero) whom he mentioned with contempt, and would share his fate.

After four years as Instructor, however, I was promoted to an Assistant Professorship, but only after a fierce battle in the Faculty, which was not settled until Commencement Day! Three years later an endowment for a Professorship in English Literature was given to Yale, and it had to be filled; a younger colleague of mine, and one who had had much shorter service was appointed. (I am glad that my friendship with him was never injured by this; we were dear and intimate friends till his untimely death.) But when this appointment came up to the President and Corporation, they, feeling it to be unfair to me, ratified it and at the same time unanimously elected me as well, and sent the two names back to the Faculty. The Faculty rejected me, and the letter I got from President Dwight that evening was one of the severest disappointments of my life. He said that his own disappointment was very great; and I knew that he had pleaded with the Faculty during a long session urging that I be appointed along with my colleague. And he added in his letter to me that what distressed him most was that he believed that now I could never become a Professor at Yale. This letter I received at night and my suffering was so intense from the shock of it that I was actually in physical agony. Nor did I get a good night's sleep for many weeks.

There were, however, two Professors, Frank K. Sanders and E. H. Sneath, who wrote me personal letters, telling me they were sure I should eventually win promotion. And two years later (1901) the election took place.

Apart from the jealousies, heart-burnings, and whisperings, which are characteristic of every University community as they are of every military post, I think that the older professors in those days honestly felt that what every young instructor needed was repression, 'taking down,' that encouragement and praise would be bad for him. Certain it is that for years the affection and enthusiasm I received from my students was balanced by the hostility that came from those who had my Yale future in their power. Words of encouragement were few and far apart.

Fortunately for me, the Senior Professor of English Literature at Yale College when I began to teach was Henry A. Beers. He was nearly twenty years older than I, had entered the law after he had been graduated from Yale, and after a brief and uncongenial experience in New York, had been called back to the University. Although he had spent a year of study at Heidelberg, he was totally unlike the conventional German-trained English scholar typical everywhere in America during the twenty years preceding the World War. At Heidelberg he had studied both Goethe's *Faust* and metaphysics with the eloquent Kuno Fischer;

and he had thoroughly enjoyed himself with the students. Professor Beers was a man entirely without ambition, without the slightest itch for publicity, without any talent for self-advertising. He never professed to be a research scholar in the approved Germanic style; but in reality he was one of the most profound and accurate scholars on the Faculty. He was thoroughly at home in Greek, Latin, Italian, French, German, Anglo-Saxon. In addition to courses covering all the range of English literature from Chaucer to contemporaries, he gave courses in Italian on the *Purgatorio*, and in Anglo-Saxon. And for an entire year I attended with immense profit a voluntary course that he gave in *Faust*, where he read the entire poem aloud in German, translated it, and commented.

He was entirely free from the meaner vices, so commonly found among actors, singers, military officers, and college professors. *He had absolutely no jealousy*. It made not the slightest difference to him what anybody thought about anybody else. Although he never made a religious profession of any kind, he loved only the best in men and in art. He was quietly pessimistic about life, never asking or expecting much, and viewing the world with an unobtrusive and infallible sense of humour. I have never seen him emotionally excited about anything; I never heard him raise his voice; I never heard him roar with laughter. His profound knowledge of literature and his fine taste were a good corrective for me when I was a graduate student. I was too easily excited and given to exaggeration of loves and hates.

I have never known a more agreeable companion. He was perfect; only one had to draw him out. He never cared for games of any kind; he loved to be at home with his wife and numerous children; and like some other men who were near-sighted, he was an excellent amateur botanist. He loved dogs and cats and was kind-hearted. It is really impossible to describe him; I have never known any one like him.

But it was a good thing for me that this quiet-tempered, reticent man, so innately noble, should have been my Senior officer.

Had he had any ambition, he would have been one of the best known of contemporary creative writers. His volume of short stories called *A Suburban Pastoral* is written with delicate art; his volumes of original poems are full of beauty and quiet music; his humorous publications, *The Ways of Yale* and others were a delight to the vast number of Yale graduates. His most important work on scholarship, *History of Romanticism*, was a contribution to the subject.

After I had taught Freshmen and Sophomores for two years, 1892–4, Professor Beers gave me permission to offer an elective open to Seniors and Juniors, members of the class of 1895 and 1896. Accordingly I offered a course in Elizabethan Drama, which was taken by one hundred and thirty men. Thus I had the pleasure of becoming acquainted with the Seniors and also of carrying on my work with the class of 1896 in their Junior year.

One day after I had finished a lecture on Marlowe's *Doctor Faustus*, and had spoken incidentally with enthusiasm of the playing of Mephistopheles in Gounod's *Faust* by Edouard de Reszké, who was on that very day appearing in New York, an undergraduate told me of his own rapturous admiration for that great artist, and asked my advice. He said that he was to take his degree in June, and that the one ambition of his life was to be an opera singer. His parents, however, were bitterly opposed to this, thinking it was not a career for a young American. 'What do they want you to do?' 'They want me to be a business man.' 'Very good; as soon as you graduate, go to New York, get a job in some business; then hire a first-rate teacher, and take singing-lessons at night. In a few months he will tell you whether you have only a parlour voice or whether you really can aspire to the operatic stage. If the former be true, you will be glad to remain in business; if the latter, your parents will certainly consent to your professional career, and if they don't, what of it?'

He followed my advice; and before six months he was well started as a singer, in a few years he was invited to become a member of the Metropolitan Opera House company, and after the final departure of Edouard de Reszké, he not only took his role as the King in *Lohengrin*, but also showed me with pride his royal robe—under the collar was written the name Edouard de Reszké. The mantle of the great Polish basso had thus literally descended on Herbert Witherspoon.

Herbert had a brilliant career on the stage, later became the Head of a school of music, and in 1935 was chosen Manager of the Metropolitan Opera; but before he could begin his work, suddenly died.

There was another undergraduate in this first course I gave in Elizabethan Drama, a Junior named Alexander Smith Cochran. He was shy and reticent; and I had no means of knowing whether or not the course had made any impression upon him. Nor did I know anything about him personally; or that he was a millionaire in his own right.

Some ten years after his graduation he wrote me from England, saying that the course in Elizabethan Drama had awakened in him an acute interest in the literature of the period; that he had amused himself with collecting some rare books; and that in a few days he would send me his manuscript catalogue. I really was quite unprepared for what followed; for every month I receive letters from persons who think they own books of great value, which are worth perhaps five dollars.

When I got Cochran's catalogue, I was astounded. He

had books that were worth several hundred thousand dollars, Shakespearean quartos, a copy of the first edition of the *Sonnets*, of Bacon's *Essays*, and so on. The next year he wrote me again, saying he was coming to America, that he had in mind an original plan, and would wait until we could discuss it together. His plan was a good one. He wished to found at Yale an Elizabethan Club, because the one thing he had most missed at Yale was good conversation; that if there were an undergraduate club, with a remarkable library as a nucleus, he thought students who loved literature and the arts would be glad to meet there, and talk informally and naturally about literature, both with their contemporaries and with congenial members of the Faculty. He would donate the club building, the library, and an endowment.

He asked me to find a suitable building. I found one and told him the owner wanted seventy-five thousand dollars. 'I'll buy it,' said Cochran, and he did. A vault was built for the books, one hundred thousand dollars was given for endowment and the Club opened its doors in the Autumn of 1911. It is one of the most successful organizations connected with the University. Later Cochran went over to England on a special journey, and in advance of the auction, bought all four folios of Shakespeare from the Huth Library.

The club has been addressed by many distinguished men of letters from Europe and America. No one who was present will ever forget the address by Sir William Osler on Burton's *Anatomy of Melancholy*.

From the start, the club has been fortunate in having the services and counsel of Andrew Keogh, the distinguished librarian (now Emeritus) of Yale University.

I regard the late Alexander Smith Cochran as one of Yale's greatest benefactors.

Commemorating the one hundredth anniversary of the

death of Keats, the club invited Miss Amy Lowell to address the members. The undergraduates were interested in
what she would say and also hoped that she would run
true to form and smoke a cigar; for most of them had never
seen a woman with a cigar in her mouth. Miss Lowell made
an admirable and scholarly address and described her
Keats original manuscripts and early editions, after which
the meeting became informal. It is difficult to describe
what followed without giving an impression of vulgarity;
and Miss Lowell was downright but never vulgar. She lit
and kept in her mouth during conversation a huge black
cigar, which fascinated the group of students who surrounded her. One asked her, 'Miss Lowell, what do you
think of Rabindranath Tagore?' Without removing the
cigar from her mouth, Miss Lowell said 'He's a charlatan.'

The reading of exam papers was the only part of my
academic work that I disliked; it was drudgery. Until I
was sixty, however, I read every paper myself, over five
hundred twice a year. Once in a while a gleam of humour
brightened the task. In discussing the Mediaeval Mystery
Plays, I had described the costumes of the players, God,
the Devil, Pilate, and so on, and the realistic jaws of
Hellmouth, in front of which were the damned souls, persons dressed in black tights with yellow stripes. Several
months later, in setting the exam, I put down as one of
the questions, 'Describe the costumes worn by the players
in the Mysteries,' and one man wrote 'The Damned Souls
wore Princeton colours.'

On another occasion, in the course in Tennyson, I in-
nocently set the question, 'What ultimately became of
Dora?' and a student wrote 'She died.'

For only one year the Freshmen were required to listen
to a series of lectures on Oriental history; they did not
suppose there would be any final examination. But being
told about two weeks from the end of the course that they

Our House in New Haven

Westminster School Baseball Nine, Dobbs Ferry, N.Y. 1889
Mr. Phelps in centre

Attending Yale-Harvard ball game, Alumni Day, 1933

Huron City, Michigan

William Lyon Phelps and Thornton Wilder
110 *Whitney Avenue, New Haven, 5 March* 1929

Professor Henry A. Beers, '69, and
Professor William Lyon Phelps, '87 (1915)

Reading. Seven Gables, 1938

Rufus and I, 1938

must all be ready for a written test, most of them decided
to substitute imagination for memory. I wish I had a complete collection of the written answers. They ran somewhat
like this:

Q. Enumerate the four members of a certain dynasty.
A. I will enumerate them: Number One, Number Two, Number
  Three, Number Four.
Q. Can you give the ancestors of Cleopatra?
A. I can.

The senior class statistics, where every member of the
graduating class had to write a series of answers to a questionnaire, used to be a general release of humour. To the
question, How far back can you trace your ancestry?
Jimmy Jenkins replied, I can trace my ancestry about a
mile, after a light fall of snow.

To the question, 'How many athletic prizes have you
taken?' Stevenson ('Nutty Steve') replied, 'I took three
of my roommates' cups, but I returned them.'

There were these replies to the question 'What is your
favourite character in fiction?' 'Saul of Tarsus.' 'Yale
Democracy.' 'Napoleon, as conceived by Professor——.'
One of the humorists wrote, 'It is ridiculous to say there
is no democracy at Yale. Why, even the most aristocratic
Yale student will speak to a poor working girl, right on the
street.'

After I had been teaching at Yale for about a year, I received a letter from the President of Bryn Mawr College in
Pennsylvania saying that I was being considered as a possible member of the English Department at that institution, with the request that I would meet the President at a
certain day and hour in a hotel in New Haven. The letter
was typewritten and signed in a bold hand, 'M. Carey
Thomas.' I supposed the President was a man, and I replied, beginning my letter 'Dear Sir,' that I should be very

glad to be at the appointed place at the appointed time. I got there first and when the lady walked in, I saw that I had made a blunder, and remarked that after such an unpardonable mistake I supposed there would be no use in negotiations. Miss Thomas brushed this aside, saying that it was a mistake that happened so often in her correspondence that she had ceased to pay any attention to it.

She was a business-like woman and told me exactly what she expected of me in case I was invited to Bryn Mawr and accepted. She had read my book *The Beginnings of the English Romantic Movement* and liked it; from what she had heard of my teaching at Yale she was favourably impressed. She then asked me many questions about my ideas of scholarship and of teaching English literature. We talked for over an hour and got along very well. Then as she rose to end the interview, she said, 'Well, I like your ideas very much, and there is only one more question. What are your views on religion?' I smiled and replied, 'I don't think there will be any difficulty on that point. I should not have been regarded as orthodox by the old-fashioned Calvinists of fifty years ago, but I am a Christian and a member of an evangelical church.' To my amazement, a look of intense disappointment, almost of horror, came over her face. 'I am deeply distressed to hear this. I am most anxious that our girls be left with entirely free and open minds. I do not want them unduly influenced by religious doctrines or biased by any theological or superstitious views. This is a serious drawback, Mr. Phelps. Do you think, if you should be called to our Faculty, that you could keep your religious prejudices out of the classroom?' I replied that I understood that I was to be hired as a teacher of English, and not as an evangelist.

We parted amicably, although the interview had begun inauspiciously with my blunder and ended with her disappointment. However, in a few days I received a very kind letter from President Thomas, offering me a good position. I considered it carefully and declined, mainly because I preferred to teach young men rather than young women.

A short time after this, I told President Dwight of Yale confidentially of this interview. He was very much astonished and laughed heartily as he replied, 'It has always been my experience that those teachers who are religious never mention it in the classroom, whereas those who are antagonistic to religion are always talking about it to the students.'

President Thomas was at that time beginning her career as Executive even as I was beginning as a teacher. She became one of the most distinguished of American college presidents and her intellectual ability combined with her capacity for leadership gave her a permanent place in the history of American education. Apparently, however, she never got over her dislike of religious enthusiasm; for a friend of mine, sitting at the same table with her many years later, in the dining-room of an ocean steamer, observed that while she was enjoying her meal, she had propped up in front of her a novel by A.S.M.Hutchinson, which she was reading apparently with increasing disapproval. All of a sudden Miss Thomas spoke in a determined voice: 'Steward, take this book and throw it out of the window!'

One day in the Spring of 1895 I called on Professor Beers and told him that I should like to give a course on Modern Novels, confining the subject-matter entirely to contemporary works. Rather to my surprise and greatly to my pleasure, he gave his immediate assent to this, saying there was no reason why the literature of 1895 could not be made as suitable a subject for college study as the literature of 1295.

Thus was inaugurated what I believe was the first course in any university in the world confined wholly to contemporary fiction. I called the course *Modern Novels*. It was open to Seniors and Juniors, and was elected by two hundred and fifty men.

It was a good time to begin the serious academic study of contemporary prose fiction, for the preceding year 1894 was remarkable for the appearance of new novels many of which belong to literature: *Trilby*, *Lord Ormont and His Aminta*, *Esther Waters*, *The Ebb Tide*, *The Jungle Book*, *Life's Little Ironies*, *Jude the Obscure* (serially), *Pudd'nhead Wilson*, *Pembroke*, *The Prisoner of Zenda*, *The Dolly Dialogues*, *Under the Red Robe;* and Conrad's first novel *Almayer's Folly* was in press. Hall Caine's *The Manxman* and Mrs. Humphry Ward's *Marcella* also appeared in this same year. Although they both attracted immense attention from the public and intellectual respect from the critics, both novelists were unimportant and ephemeral, and for exactly opposite reasons.

When I gave the first lecture in the Autumn, I hoped the course would attract no attention outside of academic halls; for in those days, newspaper notoriety was often fatal to a university career. It is hard to say just how this publicity began, for I gave out no interviews, nor did I mention the subject anywhere; but a notice in the New Haven newspapers was quickly followed by a whole column in the *New York Times*, and it seemed as if every newspaper in the country followed suit. The usual headline was

THEY STUDY NOVELS

and a page was devoted to the revolutionary theme. Editorials usually appeared in the same issue. The vast majority of newspaper comment was favourable; but there were some editorial writers who looked with disapproval on the course, the separate novels studied, and the young instructor. The news of this amazing addition to the curriculum travelled across the ocean; the course was gravely condemned in a full column editorial in the London *Daily*

Telegraph, and the following delightful parody appeared in *Punch* (Autumn 1895), called

A NOVEL EDUCATION

The tutor of St. Mary's, Cambridge, was sitting in his rooms after Hall interviewing a succession of undergraduates.

'Sit down, please, Mr. Jones,' he said to the last comer; 'I wish to speak to you very seriously on the subject of your work. The College is not at all satisfied with your progress this term. For instance, Professor Kailyard tells me that your attendance at his lectures has been most irregular.'

'Well, Sir,' said Jones, fumbling with the tassel of his cap, 'I didn't think they were important—'

'Not important? How do you expect to be able to get up difficult authors like Crockett and Maclaren unless you've attended a course of lectures on Scotch dialect? Do you know the meaning of "havers," "gabby," or "yammering"? I thought not. Then your last paper on "Elementary Besantics" was very weak. Have you really been giving your energies to your work, or have you been frittering away your time over other books?'

Jones looked guilty, but said nothing.

'Ah,' resumed the Don, 'I see how it is. You've been wasting your time over light literature—Homer and Virgil, and trash of that sort. But you really must resist temptations of that kind if you wish to do creditably in the Tripos. Good evening.'

Jones departed, to be succeeded by another undergraduate.

'I sent for you, Mr. Smith,' said the Tutor, 'because—though your work on the older writers is pretty good—your acquaintance with modern realism is quite insufficient. You will attend the course of anatomy lectures at the hospital, please. You can't study your "keynotes" intelligently without them.'

A third student made his appearance in the doorway.

'Mr. Robinson, I'm sorry to say that your work is unsatisfactory. On looking at your Mudie list, I find that you've only taken out ten novels in the last month. In order to see whether you can be permitted to take the Tripos this year, I'm going to give you a few questions, the answers to which must be brought me before Saturday. You will find pen and ink on that table. Kindly take down the following questions, as I dictate them.'

The tutor cleared his throat, and began:

'Question one. Explain "P.W.D. accounts," "a G.T.," "G.B.T.

shin-bones." Trace the bearing of the history of Mowgli on the Darwinian theory.

'Question two. "The truth shall make us free." Give context, and comment on this statement. Conjugate, in accordance with the library catalogue, *The Woman who—*, noting which of the tenses are irregular.

'Question three. "There were two Trilbys" (Trilby, Part VIII). Explain this statement. What had Mr. Whistler to do with it?

'Question four. Give the formulae for the employment of (a) the Mad Bull; (b) the Runaway Horse; (c) the Secret Marriage. What would you suggest as the modern equivalents of these?

'Question five. Rewrite the story of *Jack and Jill*,—(a) in Wessex dialect; (b) as a "Keynote"; (c) as a "Dolly Dialogue."

'That will do for the present,' concluded the tutor. And, as his pupil left the room, he seated himself at the writing-table and began Chapter XXIX of his 'Prolegomena to *Three Men in a Boat*.'

Then letters began to come in from everywhere; I could not afford a Secretary and I had no time to answer them. So I had printed an answer, which I had to send out at least three times every day for a year.

When I gave the semi-annual examination at Christmas on the material covered during the first term, the best paper I received was from a member of the Senior Class, Clarence Day, who forty years later was to become universally known as the author of *Life with Father*. Clarence was regarded with affection by his classmates but the chief impression he made on them was as an eccentric; he was voted on graduation the most eccentric member of the class. He had an extraordinary collection of pipes. I felt quite sure of his success in literature and told him so. Not long after graduation, however, he became afflicted with a lifelong disease, arthritis, which had the double effect of completely crippling him and at the same time being exquisitely painful. For over thirty years he showed daily heroism in not allowing this tragedy to conquer his spirit or destroy his creative energy. Yet during the few years that elapsed between graduation and the arthritis it is somewhat surprising that he was not murdered. He journeyed into the States beyond the Mississippi, carrying several hundred cards that he had had beautifully printed. When accosted by strangers in the train, he would after a little conversation silently present one of these cards; they bore inscriptions like this—'I will not take up any more of your valuable time. That remark of yours about the weather is very original,' etc.

Although the undergraduates apparently enjoyed both the course and the writing of a weekly critical theme, which I made obligatory, and although the newspaper comment was on the whole highly favourable, the majority of the older professors gave me distinctly to understand that unless I dropped the course at the end of its first year, I should myself be dropped from the Faculty. President Timothy Dwight, always the best friend I had among my superiors, sent for me, and advised me not to continue the course another year. I told him that I fully believed in the value of the course, but that I had no illusions as to my place in the university. 'You are the President—you are my chief and it is only a pleasure to obey you.' I knew that he had only my welfare in mind. Then the Dean of the college, Henry P. Wright, sent for me and made the following remark: 'If your course had been a failure there would have been no objection to its continuance.'

I had no desire to pose as a martyr and I hoped that the silent omission of the course for the following year would not be observed; but unfortunately it was. Learning that emissaries from the New York papers were on their way to New Haven to interview me, I left town and for a week only my wife knew where I was. On my return, the teapot-tempest had somewhat subsided, and to all the newspaper men I stated that I had voluntarily given up the course for one year. This was at least technically true; for the President had told me that I had a perfect right to continue it if I wished, only he advised me as a friend to conform to the judgement of my superiors.

Two years later I gave a course in American literature, in which I included all the American novels I had discussed in the previous course; and five years later I gave a course, the first of its kind, I believe, in any university, which was confined to contemporary dramatists.

My term as Instructor expired with the Novel course; and the Professors, perhaps relenting, perhaps pleased with my determination to avoid publicity connected with the withdrawal of that course, promoted me to an Assistant Professorship for five years. I learned this fact on Commencement Day. So that I began my work as Instructor at Yale with the Freshmen of the Class of 1896, and on the day this class was graduated, I ceased to be an 'Instructor' and became an Assistant Professor. At the expiration of my term in 1901, I was promoted to a full professorship, and a few months later, was made Lampson Professor of English literature, which position I held until my retirement, when I became Professor Emeritus.

William Lampson was a Yale graduate of the class of 1860, who lived at Leroy, N.Y. He left in his will money for three professorships, one in Greek, one in Latin, one in English, the balance of his estate to pay for the erection of a Yale building for lectures and recitations. This was an admirable bequest, as it provided for the foundation of three professorships and released money for current expenses. Thus for thirty-five years my salary came from the estate of a man whom I had never seen. I did what I could to make his name known, and kept a large portrait of him in my college office. I have always felt grateful to him and wished that I could have known him personally. His estate provided for an annual salary for every one of the three professorships of four thousand dollars a year. This was in 1901 the maximum salary for a full professor at Yale.

I was told on a cold morning of February that the professors were to meet that afternoon and recommend me for a professorship. I had to lecture at Madison, New Jersey, that evening. I came back over the ferry at New York near midnight; the river was filled with huge blocks of ice. I reached New Haven at half-past two in the morning. My wife greeted me with the glorious news of my promotion and had a supper ready of oysters and champagne. I wrote in my diary, 'I am very happy. My future is settled.' A number of professors called on me the next day, and said that whatever opposition there had been to me in the past was entirely dead, and that the Faculty were wholly appreciative. This gave me unspeakable delight.

Although their discussions were secret, several of them told me of one amusing incident that was too good to keep. A dignified and elderly Professor of Latin said in the meeting, 'Well, I am going to vote for Mr. Phelps, but there is just one thing about him I don't like. I wish he had a little more dignity. Everyone calls him Billy.' There was a moment's pause which was suddenly broken by the decisive and harsh voice of Professor William Graham Sumner, 'They call me Billy, too!' Everyone roared with laughter, and that remark made my calling and election sure. Professor Sumner was regarded as the most distinguished man on the Faculty; the students and his colleagues were somewhat in awe of him; yet by the undergraduates and alumni he was always spoken of as 'Billy' Sumner.

President Eliot of Harvard used to say that as he grew older he became in the eyes of the undergraduates steadily younger. When at the age of thirty-five he was elected President of Harvard, he said everyone called him 'Old Eliot'; but when he was eighty years old, walking across the Harvard Yard one night, two undergraduates passed, and he heard one of them say, 'I wonder what Charlie is doing out so late?'

A typographical error gave me an unexpected honour. A Boston newspaper alluded to me as *Lampoon* Professor at Yale. The Harvard *Lampoon* quoted this item, and said, 'With pardonable pride Lampy points out that his favourite son has been doing rather well, even at Yale.' Well, I am proud to represent a Harvard institution *in partibus infidelium.*

On Saturday 2 November 1895 I gave a lecture on ' The Modern Novel' before the Saturday Morning Club of New Haven, which was the beginning of my work as a public lecturer. On the same day I received twelve guineas from London for my editorial work on the plays of Chapman (Mermaid Series).

Early in my career, I was introduced to a large audience by a chairman who said, 'Several times we have secured distinguished men and their lectures have been a total failure; tonight we decided to get a man who is not distinguished but who we know can speak well;' and while the first half of the last clause was certainly true, it aroused general merriment. I certainly enjoyed it.

Introductions are an art. 'We had hoped to have Mr. Phelps here last year, but fortunately he could not come.' 'He is a speaker of word-wild fame.' One rather pompous chairman asked me what he should say. 'Please don't make a speech; just say that the speaker of the evening is Mr. Phelps of Yale.' But unfortunately he had prepared a series of superlatives, at the close of which he said, 'I now have the honour of presenting to you Mr. Yelps of Fale.'

Many poets confine their public appearances to reading from their works, often very badly; the best public reader of his own poems I have ever heard is Alfred Noyes. Yet once in a while, when I have persuaded an author to give a lecture, he has enjoyed the occasion enormously; he had not known what a thrilling experience it can be.

I am inclined to think that while writing helps lecturing,

lecturing is bad for writing. The same applies to teaching. A man's teaching is improved if he writes books, but his style in writing is apt to suffer by teaching often or before large classes. Of the mighty army of school and college teachers, how few are successful novelists, poets, or playwrights! The art of teaching and the art of writing are alike only in that they use the same alphabet. There the resemblance stops. One profound difference is that in composition a man is solitary, he is alone in the room; whereas in teaching and lecturing the more crowded the room, the greater the stimulus.

Many writers, whose compositions are boldly aggressive, are very shy, reticent, bashful, almost timid in conversation; which is natural enough, though at a first meeting one cannot repress a feeling of surprise.

I remember, after reading many things by Rebecca West, I had the pleasure of meeting her, and it seemed incredible that this shy, timid, tiny creature with the whispering voice, could be the author of such defiances. By the way, Mr. Van Druten's play made from her story *The Return of the Soldier*, which I saw in London, affected me more uncontrollably than almost anything else I ever saw on the stage. I not only wept copiously during the scenes, I sobbed aloud between the acts!

Although the art of writing is probably deservedly regarded as superior to the art of public speaking (and the writer may be remembered by the preservation of his words in print, whereas the lecturer, like the actor, will be forgotten) it is certain that a really good lecturer is rarer than a really good writer. There are ten expert writers to one expert public speaker. First-rate public speaking is uncommon.

In my work as a college teacher, apart from my continuous interest in the subjects I have taught, ranging from Chaucer to contemporary writers, perhaps the most gratifying thing is the number of intimate friendships with those who have been my undergraduate pupils. I taught at Yale forty-one years, averaging four hundred students a year. If we multiply four hundred by forty-one, we shall come near the number of personal friends that I have possessed. Some deductions from this large number must of course be made. There are some students on whom I have made no impression; either because they did not care for the subjects I taught, or because they did not care for the way in which I taught them. There have been some—not many, I think—who have hated me. As I look back over these years, I see clearly why I must unavoidably have produced on some students an unfavourable impression. My ebullient enthusiasm, however sincere and unaffected, rasps the nerves of temperaments wholly unlike mine. If a man be cold, sceptical, or cynical, anyone with high-hearted emotional fervour cannot help arousing irritation. Some of these adverse critics have had good minds and some have had dull and sluggish minds; but I know that I have succeeded in arousing from them only hostility. I cannot take credit for this, as a teacher might if he were hated for his austerity. I am sorry for it, yet I could not, in order to please a few, change either my nature or the methods of teaching that seemed to me both natural and in general, effective. If I had pleased only the loafers and did not have the intellectual respect of many good students, then I should know that I was unworthy, not fit to hold a professorship in a great university.

But it is certain that the vast majority of the men that have been in my classroom (including the able students) have enjoyed being there, and have had for the rest of their lives a strong affection for me. I am just as certain of this as I am of the dislike of the (comparatively) very few.

This means that in every town of any size (and in many tiny villages) in the United States I have at least one intimate friend. This is surely an immense reward for the years of teaching.

A temperament like mine, that is easily excited, accompanied by an equally easy loquacity, has the defects of its qualities. But, however much or little I may have contributed to the happiness of others, my almost infinite capacity for appreciation has enormously contributed to my own happiness.

I do not know that I could make entirely clear to an outsider the pleasure I have in teaching. I had rather earn my living by teaching than in any other way. In my mind, teaching is not merely a life-work, a profession, an occupation, a struggle: it is a passion. I love to teach. I love to teach as a painter loves to paint, as a musician loves to play, as a singer loves to sing, as a strong man rejoices to run a race. Teaching is an art—an art so great and so difficult to master that a man or a woman can spend a long life at it, without realizing much more than his limitations and mistakes, and his distance from the ideal.

In a novel published in 1930, *Green Isle*, by Alice Duer Miller, I found the story and the characters interesting, but the following paragraph more interesting than either:

> Strangely enough there is nowhere the average person can go to learn how to live his daily life. Children are taught Latin and astronomy, but no school or college tells them how to clear their mind for a decision, how to tell certain psychological, or even psychopathic types, and how to deal with them; how, for any individual, to draw the line between idleness and serenity, between overwork and fullness of life, between sweet charity and being every man's dupe. Everybody needs such instruction, something halfway between religious precepts and practical talks to salesmen. Women need it particularly, for they do not get, as early as men do, the experience of the business world.

It is quite true, that even among the prodigious number of things professionally taught in some universities today, like cream-separating, nursing, scene-painting, advertising, fertilizing, short-story writing, and among the increasing number of 'business colleges,' 'schools of journalism,' 'schools of the drama,' there are no graduate schools devoted to the art of living, and no professional teachers employed to specialize in Life.

Yet the paradox is that the less practical, the less 'efficient' the particular subject and the particular method of teaching may be, the more the average person will learn how to live his daily life. In a course on electrical engineering, taught by a first-class teacher to a picked class of superior pupils, there will probably be little knowledge gleaned on how to prepare one's mind for a decision, and how to distinguish between sweet charity and being every man's dupe. But in a course in Greek literature, the students may learn little if their proficiency is determined by the ease with which they can read Greek at sight; but they cannot help learning something—and some of them will learn much—about the art of living.

It is curious that many people believe in the importance of what they call vocational and practical courses, and regard the study of great literature as merely ornamental, a pretty accomplishment in seminaries for young ladies. As a matter of fact, nothing is more essential in the proper furnishing of a man's mind than a knowledge of the world's best literature. Literature is the immortal part of history. Literature is the interpretation of human life.

It is unfortunate that the majority of pupils in high schools and colleges do not study literature with the concentrated attention they give later to vocational and professional studies. They do not see the connexion between 'liberal' studies and success in life, but they ought to.

I asked a successful engineer in Boston, a man who is at the head of enterprises with scores of young engineers working under him, this question: 'What studies in college would you advise for one who intends to become a civil engineer?' He replied without any hesitation, 'Anything so long as it has no connexion with engineering.' He told me that those who came to him from technical schools with no liberal education began at first to surpass those who had studied literature and other general subjects. But in a few years the truly 'educated' young men went ahead, because they had imagination, interesting minds, and a knowledge of human nature.

I should not urge boys and girls to read good books because it will make them successful lawyers, physicians, engineers, business men; it is better to be a good father, a good husband, a good son, a good brother, a good friend, than to achieve material success; it is better to be an interesting personality than to be an efficient machine. But just as a physician who has an admirable 'bedside manner' is more successful than one who carries an atmosphere of chill, so it is certain that a knowledge of human nature, with the sympathy, tolerance, and understanding that should accompany such knowledge, is an asset for success in any calling where one comes into contact with people.

I had a conversation some twenty years ago with a cultivated Englishman, Mr. E. Nelson Fell. He attended one of the most famous schools in the world, Eton, which prepares one for the university. But Mr. Fell did not proceed to the university. He found that Eton prepared him for life. He became a business man, and was sent into a remote part of Russia, where as Superintendent of a vast enterprise, he had under his direction several hundred Russian peasants, *muzhiks*. His educational preparation for this undertaking consisted of the Greek, Latin, Mathematics he had at school.

He not only was obliged to have a thorough knowledge of the immense construction work on which he was engaged; but also he had to manage these peasants, who had adult bodies and infantile minds. Every day he had to make sudden and important decisions; every day he had to draw the line between charity and imposition; every day he had to diagnose correctly psychological and even psychopathic types. His efforts were crowned with success; the enterprise was profitable from the financial point of view, and the peasants, despite occasional outbreaks, were devoted to him heart and soul. He told me that he regarded his years at Eton as the most valuable training he could possibly have had for this particular task. He thought it more valuable than any special training in business management, the psychology of labour, or 'personality.' Apparently he learned at Eton something that was not part of the curriculum—he learned the very things that Mrs. Miller says no school or college imparts.

No matter how many false prophets have gone out into the world, no matter if some of them are in University faculties, no matter if every fundamental principle not only in religion, but in morals and, what seems to some more important, in economics, is publicly challenged, there is no doubt in my mind that schools and colleges are now, even more than ever, the homes of idealism. And this idealism shows itself particularly where there is freedom of thought and liberty of expression. The ideal of service does not mean an enforced and standardized patriotism. I believe the best patriots are those who have the courage and the brains to think for themselves and to declare their opinions, even though those opinions may run counter to received community sentiment. No university is worthy of the name, that does not, with all its discipline and culture, encourage its students to think for themselves. Let them in later years sacrifice their money for the public good; but they should not sacrifice their convictions for anything.

This matter was expressed with his customary felicity by Sir James Barrie, in his address called *The Entrancing Life*, delivered on his installation as Chancellor of Edinburgh University in 1930, and now available in print. He discussed the aim of Scottish universities: the 'needs of the genius of the Scottish people.'

> Those needs are that every child born into this country shall as far as possible have an equal chance. The words 'as far as possible' tarnish the splendid hope, and they were not in the original dream. Some day we may be able to cast them out. It is by Education, though not merely in the smaller commoner meaning of the word, that the chance is to be got. Since the war various nations have wakened to its being the one way out; they know its value so well that perhaps the only safe boast left to us is that we knew it first. They seem, however, to be setting about the work with ultimate objects that are not ours. Their student from his earliest age is being brought up to absorb the ideas of his political rulers. That is the all of his education, not merely in his academic studies but in all his social life, all his mind, all his relaxations; they are in control from his birth, and he is to emerge into citizenship with rigid convictions which it is trusted will last his lifetime. The systems vary in different lands, but that seems to be their trend, and I tell you they are being carried out with thoroughness. Nothing can depart more from the Scottish idea, which I take to be to educate our men and women primarily not for their country's good but for their own, not so much to teach them what to think as how to think, not preparing them to give as little trouble as possible in the future but sending them into it in the hope that they will give trouble.

So far from being a dull routine, teaching is to me the most adventurous, the most exciting, the most thrilling of professions. It has its perils, its discouragements, its successes, its delights. Browning says, 'It's an awkward thing to play with souls;' and whenever I enter a classroom filled with young men, I think of them not as a class or as a group, but as a collection of individual personalities more complex, more delicate, more intricate than any machinery. Not only is every student an organism more sensitive than any mechanical product; every student is infinitely precious to some parent or to some relative who may be three thousand miles away. That is why the teacher should never use irony or sarcasm or the language that humiliates; that is why he should never take the attitude of suspicion or depreciation. The officials at the United States Mint, the Head of a diamond mine, the President of a metropolitan bank are not dealing with material so valuable as that in the hands of the teacher. Their mistakes are not so disastrous as his; their success is not so important. The excitement of teaching comes from the fact that one is teaching a subject one loves to individuals who are worth more than all the money in the world.

In the year 1896 the daily round of lectures and recitations was enlivened by a manuscript poem received from one of the foremost living poets. Two undergraduate literary clubs had been formed and were holding regular meetings—the Stevenson Club and the Kipling Club. The members were confined to Sophomores of the Class of 1898. I was asked to be a member of the Stevenson Club and I accordingly met regularly with them. We contributed together fifty pounds toward the Stevenson memorial in Edinburgh. The Kipling Club did much better. Its President was Gouverneur Morris, now and for many years a popular American novelist. This Sophomore wrote to Mr. Kipling in Vermont, inviting him to attend the 'annual' banquet of the Kipling Club. One day young Morris came racing up to me on the Yale campus waving a manuscript. Perhaps no man of genius ever made a more gracious and generous response to an invitation from a college undergraduate than Rudyard Kipling had made with this poem.

Morris had the poem printed in the issue of the *Yale Literary Magazine* for May 1896; and that issue immediately became enormously valuable as a genuine first edition of Kipling. This whole matter has been admirably

discussed in a pamphlet written by the distinguished journalist, Julian S.Mason, of the Class of 1898 and a member
of that Kipling Club. This pamphlet was printed in 1937
by the Yale Library Associates of the Yale University
Press, together with a photostat copy of Kipling's handwriting, for the entire poem was written in pen and ink and
signed by the author. Here is the poem.

> Attind ye lasses av Swate Parnasses
>   An' wipe my burnin' tears away
> For I'm declinin' a chanst av dinin'
>   Wid the bhoys at Yale on the foorteenth May.
>
> The leadin' fayture will be liter-ature,
>   (Av a moral nature as is just an' right)
> For their light an' leadin' are engaged in readin'
>   Me immortial Worruks from dawn till night.
>
> They've made a club there an' staked out grub there
>   Wid plates an' napkins in a joyous row,
> An' they'd think ut splindid if I attinded
>   An' so would I—but I cannot go.
>
> The honust fact is that daily practise
>   Av rowlin' inkpots, the same as me
> Conshumes me hours in the Muses' bowers
>   An' laves me divil a day to spree.
>
> Whin you grow oulder an' skin your shoulder
>   At the World's great wheel in your chosen line,
> Ye'll find your chances, as Time advances,
>   For takin' a lark are as slim as mine.
>
> But I'm digressin'. Accept my blessin',
>   An' remember what ould King Solomon said,
> That youth is ructious an' whiskey's fluxious,
>   An' there's nothin' certain but the mornin' 'head.'

On 25 March 1898 I accompanied the Yale undergraduate expeditionary force of debaters in an invasion of

Princeton. Yale won the debate; but the 'most notable feature' as the newspapers correctly stated, was the banquet that followed; at the head table sat two Presidents of the United States, though we thought there was only one. President Patton of Princeton presided; at his right sat Grover Cleveland, at his left James H. Eckels of Chicago, who had been Controller of the Currency; the Honourable William L. Wilson, who was in Cleveland's cabinet, and at this time President of Washington and Lee University; Woodrow Wilson, professor at Princeton; the great historical scholar, J.F. Jameson, then of Brown; the Hon. Everett Wheeler of New York; and the Hon. James Alexander, President of the Equitable Assurance Society of New York; last and least, myself. All made speeches, and when I was called on, it was three o'clock in the morning. I was brief.

I obtained the signatures of the distinguished speakers on my dinner-card. The only writing implement I had was a tiny gold pencil, no bigger than a match. I shall never forget Cleveland's quizzical look as he took that tiny pencil in his enormous hand; he looked at the pencil and then at me, before he looked at the space where he was to write.

MR. CLEVELAND'S SPEECH (*NEW YORK MAIL AND EXPRESS*, 26 MARCH 1898)

My association with Princeton is so new that, with that devotion which generally characterizes a new investiture, I am much cast down. I supposed when I was honored by Princeton in their request to come to the debate tonight that it merely foretold pleasant things. I did not suppose I would be called upon to mourn for a Princeton defeat. But I am in that position. In law when we are defeated there are two courses open. We may either appeal or go to the hotel and swear at the Court. We cannot appeal in this case, however, and as for swearing at the Court, the proprieties of the occasion demand that it should be done in such a private way as to make it hardly worth while to undertake it at all. I take considerable comfort out of the debate tonight—that is, I take all the comfort I can. I am, however, just like the old woman who, at her husband's funeral, said that inwardly she was as mad as anybody.

I was glad they did not introduce us to the grill room of this inn to-night instead of the dining room. Indeed, there remains a bare chance that I may save a little of moral character and a slight vestige of good Presbyterianism. Yale had to work for all she got tonight. But we take joy in the fact that there are other days, and we can feel like the old confederate going home, who said his people had killed as many of the enemy as they had of them.

I am proud of our boys. I am very proud of them; and we shall not forget them. I am proud of the character of this contest, which was a contest of wit and brains and practice and mental work. We can say to our friends of Yale that they cannot carry home an exclusive pride in their men. We feel a pride in them, too. They belong to the brother-hood of collegians, and they have demonstrated, along with our boys, that they are not behind-hand in developing talent that is sure to tell in the future for the good of our fellow beings and the welfare of man-kind. I know the character of collegians too well not to know that after an occasion of this kind there is no sharpness in defeat nor any undue glorification in victory. Such contests as tonight fit men for good citizenship, and I hope hereafter that this sort of contest will have its proper number of innings, as it certainly should have, and we promise our friends of Yale that we will give them additional in-nings, and under new circumstances in the future.

32

MY FIRST BOOK

THE title of my Doctor's thesis and of my first book was *The Beginnings of the English Romantic Movement. A Study in Eighteenth Century Literature*. It was really the fulfilment of a boyish dream; for the first literary problem to arouse my interest made appeal in my schooldays at Hartford. I was reading a good deal of literature of the Age of Anne, comparing it in my mind with the romances of Walter Scott. What caused that extraordinary change in the tone and fashion of poetry and prose? As a boy, I made up my mind that some day I would find out.

In the Spring of 1890 Professor Beers at Yale suggested that I take for the subject of my thesis the history of English Romanticism. No subject could possibly have interested me more. That summer I was enjoying my first visit in England; and I went to the British Museum to read for a few days. Although I was twenty-five years old, I looked like a boy, and was dressed in bicycle clothes. The man in the Librarian's office at first refused to give me a ticket, telling me that English schoolboys were not allowed in the Reading Room, and that I must not come there to read for my exams. I told him I was an American and a college graduate and was twenty-five years old. He did not believe this; and finally asked, 'Will you swear that you are over twenty-one?' Accordingly I swore, and signed on some dotted line, and was very reluctantly given access to the Reading Room for two days.

At the time I was amused but amused very much more

MY FIRST BOOK 317

three years later; for in 1893 appeared the book for which
I had begun reading on that September day in London,
and to my delight, Doctor Richard Garnett wrote me a
long personal letter of congratulation, saying he had read
the new book, had ordered a copy for the British Museum,
and wished to congratulate the author.

I did all the research work on this book in the Harvard
College Library, but Professor Beers was kind enough to
send me the manuscript of his lectures on English Romanticism, which were of especial help to me in order and
method. When my thesis was finished and before it was
taken to Yale, Professor Barrett Wendell read it, and insisted that I must publish it as a book. I had had no intention of publishing it, being content to have finished it; for
as another graduate student remarked, 'I have finished my
thesis; and if God will forgive me, I will never write another.'

The next year I asked Professor Beers if he had any objection to my publishing it, for although my thesis confined itself to beginnings and closed with the year 1765,
and his lectures extended all through the nineteenth century, I felt I might be stealing some of his thunder. He
immediately urged me to print, saying he might never
publish and that if he did, it would be some years hence.

Professor Wendell gave me a letter to Scribner's, and the
manuscript was given to the famous critic, W. C. Brownell,
to read. I had a pleasant talk with him and with Mr. Charles
Scribner, not knowing how closely intimate would be my
friendship with both men in later years. Mr. Brownell declined the book as he thought it a work of special research
and not suited to the general reader. It is the only book of
mine ever declined by a publisher. His judgement seemed
good and yet the future proved him mistaken, as the book
after forty years continues to sell some copies annually. It
had to be reprinted many times.

When Professor Kittredge heard it had been rejected, he wished to read it, and he urged Ginn and Company of Boston to publish it, which they did in the autumn of 1893. I well remember my excitement when the first proofs arrived. Kittredge's kindness did not stop there; for he reviewed the book in *The Nation*.

It received a very good press in the United States, Great Britain, France, and Germany. The only qualifying clause in the chorus of praise was that the book was too mechanical. Professor Edward Everett Hale in his review said that no scholar henceforth could get along without it, but that Doctor Phelps treated books as if he were cataloguing shells. And a very favourable French review (by Joseph Texte) said the style of the book was *un peu sec*, something no-one has ever said since of anything I published.

I conclusively proved in this book that the English Romantic movement began, not in the last quarter of the eighteenth century, but before 1750; that its beginnings were unconscious and instinctive, in contrast to the French romantic movement in the nineteenth century. For the French movement was a fight, led by some men of genius, against the national literary instinct, whereas the English movement was the assertion of the national romantic temperament in literature, held in bondage for a short time by men of genius in the Age of Anne. Even at the zenith of their glory, the signs of revolt were plainly visible.

I shall never know whether, after this gratifying initial success, I ought to have continued in research work in literary history or not. I had the satisfaction of having made an addition to orderly knowledge, which even the most fanatical believer in 'special research' was compelled to treat with respect.

As I look back, the thing that I most regret was the amount of time during the best years of early middle age that I gave to the *editing* of authors; this was sound scholarly work, but it took an immense amount of time, and it would have been better if I had devoted those years to writing original works.

But I was asked to edit the Selections from the Works of Thomas Gray, and although I succeeded in making my text closer to the originals than any edition that had appeared since Gray's death, and although the value of my book was greatly increased by a fine chapter contributed by Professor Kittredge on 'Gray's Knowledge of Norse,' in which he pointed out some appalling errors by Gosse, I doubt if the whole year I spent on this book was worth while. One of the best things about it was that it brought me a close epistolary friendship with the late Reverend D.C.Tovey of Worplesden Rectory, Guildford, England. In his edition of Gray's poems, he expressed his gratitude to the edition by Professors Phelps and Kittredge of Yale College (*sic*), and in his later edition of Gray's *Letters* he began his preface as follows:

> If I had their permission, I should like to dedicate this volume to four kindly correspondents whom it has never been my privilege to meet, but to whose encouragement in this, or comments on my previous work on Gray, I am much indebted. These are Professors Hales and Dowden on this side of the Atlantic, and Professors Phelps and Kittredge on the other. I am able to face once more some adverse and captious criticism, in the belief that my labours on Gray seem to them neither superfluous, nor, in spite of errors and oversights which, of all students of the poet they are best able to detect, unscholarly.

This led to a correspondence that lasted until his death. The most interesting statement in the following letter is the allusion to his son Donald, who more than justified his father's faith in him. He is now Sir Donald Francis Tovey, Reid Professor of Music in the University of Edinburgh, music editor for the *Encyclopedia Britannica*, composer of many pieces of music and author of important books.

WORPLESDEN RECTORY
GUILDFORD
May 4, 1901

MY DEAR SIR,

Ever since the receipt of your kind letter I have been alternately reproaching myself for not acknowledging it (or *did* I acknowledge it after all) and invoking a murrain on the yokels who misinformed you about Worplesden. I am on the way from Guildford to London. You must have passed my station in going up to town. It would have been a real delight to me to welcome you and Mrs. Phelps to my parson's fare, if you would have stayed to accept it.

I am sending you a few *errata*. I have sent the like to Professor Kittredge. Are you coming here again?

Yours ever

D. C. TOVEY

Are you a musician? My son Donald is making a name for himself both in England and Germany, as a pianist and composer. I daresay you will see him in America in a year or so.

The allusion in this letter to the misdirection was owing to the fact that my wife and I, bicycling from Devonshire to London in 1900, in passing through Guildford had in vain tried to find Worplesden Rectory and were sadly misdirected.

The Reverend Mr. Tovey, Professor Kittredge and I were in complete agreement about the standing of Sir Edmund Gosse as a scholar. As a literary critic, Gosse had a deservedly high reputation, but his immense British reputation as a scholar seems mysterious and inexplicable. Mr. Tovey, himself a scrupulous scholar, was never given to over-statement. In one of his letters he wrote me: 'I have gleaned more misinformation from the works of Edmund Gosse than from any other writer, ancient or modern.'

My edition of Gray led me into a series of editorial tasks which used up a vast amount of time and energy. Thackeray's *English Humourists of the Eighteenth Century* of which the British Museum did not contain a first edition, the Complete Novels of Samuel Richardson, the Works of Jane Austen, Stevenson's Essays, the Best Plays of Chapman for the Mermaid Series (I was pleased to be in that company) were some of the tasks that occupied my spare time in term and in vacation for fifteen precious years between 1894 and 1909!

My revolutionary course in Modern Novels at Yale had a permanent effect on my life and career; and it is impossible for me to say whether I chose rightly or wrongly. What I am certain about, however, is that the way I chose contributed to my happiness and to a less extent, naturally, to that of others.

In 1907, Mr. George P. Brett, head of the great publishing firm of the Macmillan Company in New York, asked me to call. He suggested that I write a book on Modern Novelists, for which he would give me a favourable contract on the spot, without waiting to see a page of manuscript. This subject appealed to me, for while it could scarcely be called research, it was more interesting to me than reading the works of authors who were not worth reading at all, whose sole value lay in their possible indication of literary movements. For in the summer of 1900, I had done an immense amount of work in the British Museum and in the Bodleian at Oxford, on the history of the English Drama in the eighteenth century. I do not regret this, because the conditions of work were delightful, and the field, from the point of view of research, was sufficiently rich. But from every other point of view, the material was dust and ashes.

So, two years later, after due reflexion, I accepted Mr. Brett's generous offer—I shall always be grateful to him—and wrote a book called *Essays on Modern Novelists*. There were separate essays, most of which I first printed in the *North American Review*, the *Forum*, the *Independent*, and other periodicals, on Thomas Hardy, William De Morgan, Mark Twain, Kipling, Alfred Ollivant, Howells, Stevenson, Björnson, Sienkiewicz, Sudermann, and Mrs. Humphry Ward. All of these authors were living, except Stevenson.

I admired these novelists, except Mrs. Ward. My essay on her novels was the ungracious attempt to destroy her reputation as a great novelist. It seems strange enough today that she ever was so regarded; but when I wrote my essay, she was almost universally considered, both in England and in America, as a writer of genius, and as one of the permanent figures in the history of the English novel. I had the highest respect for her mental ability, for her literary conscience, for the nobility of her character; but I thought her novels showed more industry than inspiration, and were without a spark of genius.

I have always enjoyed appreciative rather than destructive criticism; Goethe said the prime qualification of a critic was enthusiasm. But the contemporary appraisals of the novels of Mrs. Ward seemed to me ludicrously wrong. I will quote here the first and the last paragraphs of my essay.

It is high time that somebody spoke out his mind about Mrs. Humphry Ward. Her prodigious vogue is one of the most extraordinary literary phenomena of our day. A roar of approval greets the publication of every new novel from her active pen, and it is almost pathetic to contemplate the reverent awe of her army of worshippers, when they behold the solemn announcement that she is 'collecting materials' for another masterpiece. Even professional reviewers lose all sense of proportion when they discuss her books, and their so-called criticisms sound like publishers' advertisements. Sceptics are warned to remain silent, lest they become unpleasantly conspicuous. When *Lady Rose's Daughter* appeared, the critic of a great metropolitan daily remarked that whoever did not immediately recognize the work as a masterpiece thereby proclaimed himself as a person incapable of judgement, taste, and appreciation. . . .

Mrs. Ward is an exceedingly talented, scholarly, and thoughtful woman, of lofty aims and actuated by noble motives; she is hungry for intellectual food, reading both old texts and the daily papers with avidity. She has a highly trained, sensitive, critical mind,—but she is destitute of the divine spark of genius. Her books are the books of today, not of tomorrow; for while the political and religious questions of today are of temporary interest, the themes of the world's great novels are what Richardson called 'love and nonsense, men and women'—and these are eternal.

My book appeared in January 1910. It went through a number of editions, had a large sale for some years, and has not yet joined the overwhelming majority of the extinct. After twenty-eight years, the publisher's statement shows that during the last year many copies were sold!

Among the reviews that greeted its first appearance, I liked best the one written by Francis Hackett in Chicago—even if he did say that I occasionally hit the walls of my own mind.

Most of the reviewers were amazed that a book of essays on contemporary writers should come from a university professor; and indeed there were still many, probably the majority, of the academic men who did not know and did not care anything about living writers.

Of the senior professors of English literature at Yale, Professor Beers and Professor Thomas R.Lounsbury held exactly opposite views concerning the work I was doing. Mr. Beers gave me encouragement, and Mr. Lounsbury thought I was wasting my time on trivial matters. He wanted me to edit the complete works of Ben Jonson, or write a biography of old Ben, or if I must be modern, to write a biography of Browning.

Mr. Lounsbury enjoyed a great reputation as a scholar. He was an ornament to Yale, and we were proud of him. Furthermore, he was full of humour and common sense, a delightful companion, and favourite among the New York literati; but he cared nothing for European contemporaries. I do not believe he ever read a line of Ibsen, or of Tolstoy. His anthology of American poetry (1912) called the *Yale Book of American Verse*, will still delight the judicious reader by the wit and irony of its preface; he ridiculed Longfellow's 'Psalm of Life,' saying, 'The last place a rational man would choose for leaving a permanent footprint would be on the sandy beach bordering an ocean. . . . this particular young man seems to have been very young. He is advised by his heart to be a hero not only in the battle but in the bivouac. If the psalmist had thought it worth while to reply, he would doubtless have informed the young man that the bivouac, in the modern sense of the word, affords little opportunity for one to show himself a hero, and that the best thing he could do would be to act like one of the dumb driven cattle which his heart warns him not to imitate, and lie down and go peacefully to sleep. Yet with these views about the poem itself, I insert it in this collection in deference to a sentiment in which I do not share.'

For the same reason he included Bryant's 'Waterfowl' which he rightly regarded as second-rate.

The 'bivouac' particularly got on Mr. Lounsbury's nerves, for he fought as a private soldier at the battle of Gettysburg. He told me that in the roar of the battle, when his brigade were told to lie down for a few minutes, nearly every man fell asleep!

Yet, despite the wit and humour and common sense of this preface, the fact remains that the anthology included seven poems of Aldrich, seven of Gilder, seventeen of Holmes, nine of Stedman, and one of Whitman, and that one 'O Captain!' When someone praised that poem to Old Walt, he exclaimed, 'O *damn* My Captain!'

I mention all this because Mr. Lounsbury was the furthest possible from the dry-as-dust pedant, which makes his attitude toward contemporary writers and contemporary criticism all the more evidential of the then academic mind.

I well remember also his saying to me over and over again, and always with emphasis, that it was ridiculous to judge of the value of a college professor by what his students thought of him. They were not qualified to judge. It was only what other professors thought of him that should count; for they were his peers. Certainly, from the point of view of research, that is true. But, alas, their opinions were often affected by vanity and by jealousy.

It seemed to me that there were a sufficient number of professors dealing with the remote past, and doing 'original research.' While it would be a calamity for any university if all the professors of English literature were like me, I felt there was room in this vast body of scholars for one man who should devote at least part of his time to contemporary literature; even as the professors in every branch of *science* knew the latest discoveries. I therefore decided to go ahead.

In 1911 I published *Essays on Russian Novelists*, the first American critical work dealing with this subject. Not knowing Russian, I had to read many of these novels in French and German. Constance Garnett's incomparable translations of Dostoevski and Tolstoy and Chekhov had not appeared; Artsybashev's sensational *Sanin* I read in German. However, I knew that all the books I dealt with would soon appear in English; and my aim was to induce American and British readers to become familiar with some of the greatest works in the history of prose fiction.

The volume included separate essays on Gogol, Turgenev, Tolstoy, Dostoevski, Gorki, Chekhov, Andreev, Artsybashev, Kuprin, with some remarks on Garshin.

The value of these two books was increased by the

bibliography supplied for each by my friend, Mr. Andrew Keogh, Librarian of Yale University.

In 1915 I produced a critical work on Browning, and in 1932 I republished it with enough additional matter almost to double its size. It is meant to be both a commentary on many of the short poems and an introduction to the study of the poet; intended for the general reader. A review that gave me particular pleasure was by the Irishman Robert Lynd, who said, 'This book will introduce readers to a new world of excitement,' for that is exactly what I hoped to accomplish.

Other books I have published are *The Advance of the English Novel*, *The Advance of English Poetry in the Twentieth Century*, *Human Nature in the Bible*, and *Essays on Books*. The last-named appeared in 1914, just after war broke out in Europe. It drew a favourable review in *The Nation*, written I suspect by Paul Elmer More. He headed his review with the caption

REST AMONG THE PEDANTS

and went on to say that during the shambles in Europe pedants showed us how and where to take refuge. To be called a pedant in that particular journal gave me keen pleasure.

In addition to more than twenty-five original books, only one of which was intentionally humorous, I have written articles in a great variety of periodicals.

Most of my writing has been done in the Long Vacation in my summer home in Michigan, where we enjoy isolation and the absence of a telephone. We rise at six every morning, which gives me five good hours at my desk before lunch. If there were only no letters to write! The absence of letter-writing, said Mark Twain, was one of the things he was most eagerly looking forward to in hell.

Inasmuch as I have owed so much in my development

to the series of volumes called *American Statesmen* which I read when I was seventeen, edited by John T. Morse, Jr., I had an intense desire to meet this famous biographer.

16 FAIRFIELD STREET
BOSTON
April 3 1929

MY DEAR PROFESSOR PHELPS:

I have often wished that I might have the pleasure of meeting a gentleman of whom I have heard so much, and so pleasantly, as I have of you. Your scheme for giving me that opportunity is most welcome, and I shall await you next Saturday forenoon.

Very sincerely yours

JOHN T. MORSE, JR.

This letter was written in longhand, legible as large type. Mr. Morse was then 89. When I knocked, he was playing the typewriter vigorously; he seemed to spring across the room. I had an hour's good talk. His sight and hearing were perfect, his movements around the room were as active as if he had been thirty, and his mind equally alert.

33

PROFESSORS

IT is rather exciting to live in a small town like New Haven or Cambridge and to be aware of the fact that there is no field of human knowledge, no frontier of speculative thought, no department of the fine arts, where some member of the university faculty is not an authority. If you stand at one street-corner long enough, you will meet a fellow-citizen who can converse intelligently with Einstein, another who knows the latest discoveries in astronomy, another who can tell you about the electron, another familiar with the so-called prehistoric animals, another who can give an intelligent opinion on ancient or modern literature, another who can conduct a symphony orchestra without the score, etc., etc. The 550 members of the Yale faculty, for example, include experts on every department of knowledge. Any time I want to know anything about anything, I use the telephone, and I do not have to tackle the toll line. The amount of actual knowledge possessed by a group of men living in New Haven is almost as vast as the universe itself.

Sometimes, while my students in English literature were entering the classroom, I could not help thinking what an immense variety of instruction was to be imparted in various rooms during the next hour—in physics, chemistry, anthropology, economics, painting, architecture, law, musical composition, biology, zoology, botany, theology, metaphysics, ancient and modern languages, physiology, anatomy, calculus, drama, theatre, government, international

328

politics, constitutional and financial history, and so on.
And the life-philosophies of the professors are almost as
different as their fields of instruction. One is a strong
nationalist, and believes in big armies and navies; one is an
ardent pacifist; one is a free-trader, one is a protectionist;
one believes in the capitalistic form of government, one is a
communist; one is an orthodox Christian, one is antagonistic to all forms of religious belief; there are also Roman
Catholics, every shade of Protestant, and Jews. The university world is a microcosm of the world of thought.

And in practical affairs there is almost as much diversity. There are professors who can sail a ship across the
ocean, there are those who can drive the Twentieth Century locomotive from New York to Chicago, there are
those who can run a bank, stock-exchange, or machine
shop, build a suspension bridge, preside over a court of law,
paint a portrait, construct a cathedral, compose a sonata.
It is exciting to live in such a group.

Today the pews and the pulpit, the students and the
teachers, the voter and the office-holder, are nearer together.

The curious thing is, that in those olden times, when the
members of the faculty displayed a front of dignified authority, there were frequent outbreaks of disorder, in the
classroom and out of it. Teachers were often chosen for
their ability as policemen. Now the question of order and
good behaviour is never even considered, because there is
no occasion for it. Students are as well-behaved in the
classroom as in church. In those days, it was so customary
to throw coal through a tutor's windows, that he used to
say, 'My salary is a thousand dollars, and coal thrown
in!'

When I was an undergraduate, it was part of every instructor's duty, if he had a room on the campus, to maintain order. It was not an uncommon sight, in the midst of

an uproar at night, to 'spot' a professor in his nightgown, hiding behind a tree, and taking down names of those unfortunate students whose faces were revealed by the bonfire. Then someone yelled, 'Faculty!' and there was a scattering.

Imagine President Seymour or President Conant making such a connexion!

The old-fashioned 'stage' professor has gone forever. The familiar caricature expressed what was the common conception among the populace; a professor was a learned fool. He was a dungeon of remote and unimportant knowledge, without common sense, at home only in the classroom or in his researches. He might be treated with outward respect by the unregenerate, but with a secret contempt—at best, tolerance.

Now that the professor is a man of the world, conforming in appearance and manners to the conventions of society, there is perhaps some danger that he will go too far toward the other extreme. Religion and morality used to be generally associated with teaching. Many modern teachers are so eager to avoid the odour either of learning or of earnestness, that they sometimes adopt an air of flippant sophisticated ironical scepticism. Whatever place irony may have in certain forms of literary composition, it should never characterize the teacher. Teaching should be productive; irony is sterile. A teacher should believe in the subject and in the object; he should believe that his subject is all important, and that the pupil is worthy of his best efforts.

J. M. Barrie told me that he thought jealousy, rather than the love of money, was the root of all evil; he had seen so much misery caused by it. And I suppose jealousy is the love of oneself. High-minded scholars ought to be above such weaknesses; but there are many teachers who cannot endure to hear a colleague praised. Often, when some member writes a fine book or attains success in the classroom, he receives praise from every one except from his fellow-teachers.

In Germany I once saw an amusing play, *Privatdozent*, where, to the infinite entertainment of the audience, college faculty meetings were a part of the show, and what was still more amusing, meetings of professors' wives who took a hand in college politics. Here the really estimable and successful teacher was turned down, and an unworthy man promoted.

But of course there are weaknesses, sin, and vices, wherever there are men and women. And for my part, I rejoice that my life has been spent in an academic circle. We often hear of college friendships, the word being invariably applied to relations between undergraduates. But there are friendships equally strong among members of the faculty, and more enduring as well, for they live together longer. Living with college teachers is to live with men who are intelligent, cultivated, sympathetic, attractive, and on the whole, better and happier than the general run of men in other occupations. Especially *happier*. I brought a New York business man to take lunch in the Graduates Club in New Haven, and he said, 'How happy everybody seems in this place!'

President Hutchins of the University of Chicago recently made an address, which deservedly received wide comment, in which he praised the wisdom and foresight of college professors. They are indeed a fine body of men, because they are searching for the truth and eager to impart it. I am happy and proud to be in their company.

34

GEORGE SANTAYANA

In the Department of Philosophy at Harvard in 1891 were William James, Josiah Royce, George Herbert Palmer, George Santayana, and Hugo Münsterberg, a quintet of striking personalities, each differing from the other four in many convictions and opinions, while dwelling together in fraternal harmony. Apart from their distinction as scholars, every one was a literary artist. They all knew how to write, not merely with force and with what clearness is possible on such themes, but with that beauty of expression that belongs only to consummate mastery of style. And the best *writer* among them, although he was overshadowed by the reputation of his older colleagues, was George Santayana.

I was invited one evening to attend the regular 'experience meeting' held periodically in the nineties by the Department of Philosophy. At these small assemblies—which were analogous to confessional prayer-meetings—various teachers and students in philosophy gave in the frankest manner a history of their bringing up, and a statement of their present attitude toward life, thought, and religion. The evening it was my good fortune to be present was a red-letter occasion, for the three speakers were young Santayana, still in his twenties, a fiery evangelical preacher, and a Japanese Buddhist. It was like a world's congress of religions on a small scale. Mr. Santayana, who seemed to me the last word in culture, refinement, and suavity, gave in quiet tones, half-smiling all the while, a beautifully expressed statement of a philosophical attitude which would have cost him his job at any other American college. 'If I had to define my position, I should call myself an atheist and a pessimist.' During this flow of exquisite language, it was clear to me that a storm was brewing in the evangelical mind, whose owner, by the way, was a German. As soon as the testimony was completed, this preacher was asked for his 'experience,' and he exploded. 'Before beginning my remarks, I wish to say emphatically that I regard Mr. Santayana's attitude with thorough contempt.' This made a small sensation; but the face of the gentleman attacked betrayed nothing except polite interest. The speaker was passionately sincere, but as Dryden wrote of Jeremy Collier, 'I will not say "The zeal of God's house has eaten him up"; but I am sure it has devoured some part of his good manners and civility.' He was, however, permitted to proceed without protest. 'I have been *converted*'—he glared around the room—'oh, I know how ridiculous that word sounds at Harvard, but'—at this point Professor Royce interrupted, and asked, 'Won't you tell us exactly your experience of Christian conversion, so that we can understand it psychologically?' which, indeed, he did. When he had concluded, the Buddhist, whose Oriental face had, to an Occidental observer, remained inscrutably impassive during the entire evening, gave a statement of his religious philosophy. In one evening, then, I heard a Spaniard, a German, and a Japanese express with commendable frankness points of view as far apart as the cluster of Hercules from the Charles River. Such was the quickening and exciting intellectual atmosphere in the Harvard Philosophical Department, in which Mr. Santayana was developed and to which he contributed. He remained an instructor nine years, an assistant professor another nine years and then, shortly after he had been promoted to a professorship, voluntarily withdrew, and went to live in Europe, where I had much good talk with him. He left Harvard to the sharp regret both of the students and of his colleagues.

Perhaps Mr. Santayana's breadth of view and intellectual charity are shown most of all in the fact that he has always honoured me with his friendship, which, as it has survived so many things, I hope will survive this book. I really believe in the Incarnation—that the Son of God is not only the Saviour of the world, but that He will eventually save it—and I can conceive of no mental or religious outlook that could be to my friend more crude or naïve. Possibly he enjoys points of view so different from his own, being quietly conscious of rational superiority. I remember his visit to me after I returned to Yale. He had never 'stopped off' at New Haven, and perhaps he had much the same idea of Yale as was not uncommon at Harvard. Berlin looked down on Oxford, Oxford looked down on Harvard, Harvard looked down on Yale, Yale looked down on— anyhow he came. We had splendid Autumn weather, the regular thing at New Haven (*advt.*), and I took him through the buildings, to college chapel, to a football game. I took him to the top of East Rock and showed him all the kingdom of Yale, and the glory of it. When he returned to Cambridge he published a charming article in the *Harvard Literary Monthly*, which called forth an immediate protest from the *Harvard Crimson*. 'Why, if a stranger should read Mr. Santayana's essay he might think Yale was superior to Harvard, which of course it isn't.'

Mr. Santayana was born in Madrid and brought up as a Roman Catholic. His parents were Spanish; he came to America when he was nine years old and was graduated from Harvard in 1886. While his father was living, he used to spend every summer in Spain, and he is as bilingual as it is possible for anyone to be. He began a translation of *Don Quixote*, which I am glad he abandoned; it would have been beautifully done, but what is the use of translating books when you can write masterpieces?

Logan Pearsall Smith, one of the best of anthologists, made judicious extracts from the writings of Santayana. He found in Mr. Santayana's books

> much writing like that of the older essayists on large human subjects, which seemed to me more interesting and in many ways more important than anything I found in the works of other contemporary writers. I soon fell into the way of copying out the passages that I liked, and thus I gradually formed a collection of little essays on subjects of general interest—art and literature and religion.

My only regret is that Mr. Smith did not include some of the author's poems. Not only is Mr. Santayana, even in his prose and in his philosophy, essentially a poet, but he has written and published many of the finest sonnets to be found in contemporary literature.

All honestly written philosophy is difficult reading for the average mind; it therefore gains by being presented in short pieces, the intervals allowing the reader to rise to the surface to breathe.

There is, indeed, a certain resemblance between Schopenhauer and Santayana; both have a passion for the life of reason, for art, literature, and music, and both have such a control of literary style that they make expression of thought a thing of beauty. Both belong more to literature than to philosophy; there is no doubt that the prodigious influence of Schopenhauer is owing more to the charm of his writing than to its truth. His style—admirably rendered into English by Lord Haldane—is a pliant slave to the author's will, now sparkling with wit and humour, now imperiously impressive with solemn earnestness.

Mr. Santayana's Essays are the fruit of long contemplation and of original thinking. They could not have been written by a pure Anglo-Saxon; they come from a mind essentially Latin in race, Catholic in training, and saturated with mediaeval scholastic philosophy.

He loves serenity and dignity of mind; it is not surprising, therefore, to find him unsympathetic to the turbulent and passionate Browning. But why should the hostility to Browning's philosophy make him incapable of appreciating Browning's poetry? I do not care much for Mr. Santayana's philosophy, but that does not prevent me from enjoying and admiring the literary art with which it is dressed. It is a corpse arrayed in shining garments. The faint suggestion of intellectual snobbism is seen in the following remark on the works of the great British poet. 'They not only portray passion, which is interesting, but they betray it, which is odious.' How plainly I can hear him say that! No man can understand everything, and I fear that Mr. Santayana does not understand Browning, though he thinks him particularly easy to understand. Browning had a gust for life, enormous vitality—qualities that in all civilized society have irritated the patrician; and Mr. Santayana cannot endure Browning's love of life; Browning must seem like a vulgarly cheerful fellow who slaps you on the back. To our philosopher a wise man will never covet immortality in the Christian sense; he might not accept the offer of any life anywhere. This is true pessimism; with all the author's delight in reason—an amazing gift to man—it is quite possible that he would prefer non-existence:

> Nothing can be meaner than the anxiety to live on, to live on anyhow and in any shape; a spirit with any honour is not willing to live except in its own way, and a spirit with any wisdom is not overeager to live at all.

If Mr. Santayana really understood the art of Browning, he could not have said 'the love he describes has no wings.'

> O Lyric Love, half angel and half bird,
> And all a wonder and a wild desire—

It would seem to me that if love is half angel and half bird it can hardly be said to lack wings.

Of religion he always speaks tolerantly, believing that the religious instinct represents man's ideal; there should never be such a thing as religious controversy, any more than we should argue with a lover about his taste. Hence Mr. Santayana has little sympathy with the 'liberal' element either in the Catholic or Protestant Church. The liberals are talking as though there were some basis of truth in religious belief, whereas, of course, it is a matter of poetry and emotion, like love of country. Why bring Raphael up to date? He himself loves the Catholic Church and its beautiful ritual, and in his own interpretation believes that every man should be religious, but not for a moment will he admit that the Catholic Church or any other has a fact foundation. As it is impossible to represent fairly the position of a philosopher on any subject, I had better quote,

> It could never have been a duty to adopt a religion not one's own—any more than a language, a coinage, or a costume not current in one's own country. The idea that religion contains a literal, not a symbolic, representation of truth and life is simply an impossible idea. Whoever entertains it has not come within the region of profitable philosophising on that subject.

It is much the same with his view of immortality. He is an unbeliever in any life beyond the grave, or in the continuance of personality; but he believes that the best part of us is immortal—that is, our influences and our share in the scheme of the universe; and he seems to take comfort in this thought. But, according to this system, the worst part of us must be equally immortal with the better; in order to believe that such immortality was agreeable, one would have to believe that the majority of human actions and thought make for goodness, which I am quite sure he does not believe at all. This is sentimentalism; if the better part survives in our friends, family, or influence—it is really they that survive, and they only for a short time. We do not survive. To Shakespeare himself, in this philosophy, it can make no possible difference five seconds after his death whether he wrote *Hamlet* or whether he spent his days as a drunken sot. Mr. Santayana says that we all ought to be willing to die for our children, or for art, or for our country; but Renan said, 'I am quite willing to die; only I should like to know whether death will be of any use to me.' And surely he was an honourable man.

I am not sure whether Mr. Santayana now calls himself atheist or not; but his philosophy is anti-Christian. To him man is a very small part of the universe, and it seems to him vulgar and conceited to think otherwise; but the whole stress of Christianity is on the importance (to God) of every individual man, woman, or child. In practice, Mr. Santayana believes that everyone should cultivate his mind to the utmost, in order to reach a position of philosophical quietude whence he can survey (like God) all human history and the vain passions and delusions of men, himself serenely (and consciously) superior to the common herd; but Christianity teaches that all men are brothers, and that the highest happiness consists in helping others rather than ourselves. He is better than his creed, as I am worse than mine.

But just as he finds religion beautiful, so do I find his books beautiful like lovely architecture, painting, or music. And it is the honest and noble effort of a man who is determined to make the best of the worst; who wishes to live the life of pure reason, but who is at heart a poet, loving everything beautiful and radiant.

His position in our day seems to me not unlike that of the poet Cleon created by that 'barbarian,' Robert Browning. Cleon summed up in his own person and achievements Greek life and thought; the intellect and art and beauty of the ancient world. He despised St. Paul, as Mr. Santayana despises evangelists. Only, so far from finding his philosophy a means for removing the sting from death, he said (quite correctly) that death was much more terrible to the cultivated philosopher than to the savage.

> Say rather that my fate is deadlier still,
> In this, that every day my sense of joy
> Grows more acute, my soul (intensified
> By power and insight) more enlarged, more keen;
> While every day my hairs fall more and more,
> My hand shakes, and the heavy years increase—
> The horror quickening still from year to year,
> The consummation coming past escape
> When I shall know most, and yet least enjoy—
> When all my works wherein I prove my worth,
> Being present still to mock me in men's mouths,
> Alive still, in the praise of such as thou,
> I, I the feeling, thinking, acting man,
> The man who loved his life so overmuch,
> Sleep in my urn.

So, if I were to look over the world today to find one man who summed up in his mind the best of human culture, both ancient and modern, who knew how to express his ideas in language that gives delight to the eye and to the ear, who represents the highest point attainable by study, thought, and contemplation—I should take the author of those books, which represent so much that is dignified and splendid, the last word of modern civilization, powerless to save the world. For, in the power of changing human lives, this beautiful book is like the Northern Lights, making darkness visible; whereas the simple words of the Gospel are like the genial sun at noonday, giving illumination and warmth to the meanest creatures on the globe.

Doctor William Fogg Osgood, for many years Professor of Mathematics at Harvard, now Emeritus, remembers Santayana very well as a boy, for they were in the same class at the Boston Latin School for four years. As seems natural enough, Santayana cared nothing for athletic games, and showed little ambition at that time to excel in scholarship. He was of course interested in the English language and in the history of Rome. 'Latin came easily to him, and French was like a dialect of Spanish.' I can understand that he cared nothing for mathematics or physics and did only enough to pass; but I am rather astonished that in those boyhood days he showed neither brilliance nor ambition in Greek, especially as 'we had the world's best teacher, Arthur Irving Fiske, Harvard '69.'

In Paris I had good walks and talks with Santayana. He is a philosopher, and lives what I suppose is the true life of a philosopher, though I should find it intolerably lonely. Still, he has what very few people have today, leisure for meditation. All his books are born of long hours of solitary, uninterrupted thought. Though I think he enjoys his own society better than that of other people, he is an admirable conversationalist and a perfect table companion. In a rather dingy restaurant on the Boulevard S. Michel we talked of literature, morals, and religion.

The English are the leanest race in the world; one seldom sees a fat Englishman, yet many of them eat four square meals every day. And when you do see a fat Englishman you will find that he carries his weight remarkably well. Mr. Santayana told me a new story of the famous Oscar Browning, of King's College, Cambridge. He ate seven meals a day. There are people who wake up in the middle of the night and cannot fall asleep again until they have eaten something. But O.B. set his alarm clock at three in the morning in order that he might wake and eat a herring! Then at seven o'clock tea and various eatables were brought to his bedside. At eleven he had a snack two hours before lunch. At four-thirty, high tea with plenty of food. He then ate nothing till dinner, an elaborate affair in many courses, and with a variety of wines. His seventh and last meal was a hearty supper, which he took just before going to bed. He lived to be eighty-three.

In August 1920, the *New York Times Book Review* published a long article by me on Mr. Santayana's *Little Essays*. In this I said his position among English and American philosophers was somewhat similar to that of Schopenhauer in German philosophy, since both of them owed their great reputation largely to the beauty and charm of their literary style, Schopenhauer being one of the few really great masters of German prose and Santayana having no living superior in his mastery of English style.

I then, perhaps mistakenly, compared Mr. Santayana's statements about immortality and religion with those of Lord Morley, as it seemed to me that Morley was absolutely frank in his complete disbelief of any future life, while Mr. Santayana's phrases about it seemed to me not absolutely frank. I also thought it strange that, when he had such a love for Dickens, he should have such a strong dislike for Browning. In all these matters he very courteously and very clearly shows that I somewhat misrepresented his position.

PARIS, SEPT. 8, 1920

DEAR PHELPS

I am much pleased to have your letter and your review of the *Little Essays*. All the first part of it makes me feel as if I were reading an obituary notice by anticipation, and I can almost imagine some Phi Beta Kappa orator, in the not very distant future, spreading this sort of roseate sunset glow over my uneventful history and limping personality. I don't object to the headlines; Harvard in the 1890's being me, and America Today being you: and I think the view of the Yard has much the same quality of cautious idealization. Yours is not a cubist portrait of your humble servant, nor yet a Dutch inventory of his features and circumstances. I think it is very good and fair, if one allows for the friendly partiality you do not disguise, and also for a certain glamour or pathos of distance that already bathed our memories of youth. The only fact that is wrong is your saying that my mother was an American: she was Spanish—we never spoke English together—but had been first married (in Manila) to one of the Boston Sturgis's, so that my half-sisters and half-brother belonged to that once prosperous and always agreeable tribe: and it was in consequence of this connection, and money matters concerned in it, that we went to live in America. A point of interpretation where I feel you are also somewhat misled, or at least reticent, is in regard to my reasons for leaving Harvard. Weariness had something to do with it, but weariness with lectures and with the "problems" of technical philosophy rather than with college committees, on which I seldom appeared. They knew I was no good at business! But my chief motive was a lifelong desire to live in Europe and—which is only possible here—to be left alone. In respect to higher things, most of what you say pleases and satisfies me greatly, especially your mention of Schopenhauer: that is to hit the nail on the head. There are only two points in which perhaps you don't understand me: it seems to me unfair to suggest that, unlike the wizzened Morley, I am not frank about immortality; a scholar like you ought to know that the platonizing or Spinozistic things I say about it, taken in an ideal sense, are the *original motif* of this doctrine in the European tradition: the notion of ghosts or of resurrection has been merely confused with it, and it is no compromise or hedging on my part to separate the two views once more. The other point is about liking life, and the poets who relish it. My disgust at Browning is not because he loves life or has it abundantly, but because he doesn't love it (as Dickens does, for instance) for what is *good* in it, but for what is bad, tawdry, and pretentious. I protest against being called a snob; what I love is what is simple, humble, easy, what ought to be common, and it is only the bombast of false ambitions and false superiority, that I abhor.

Before the war I was on the point of going to give some lectures at the University of Wisconsin and at Columbia, but I doubt now whether I shall ever cross the Atlantic again. I have my head-quarters here, and go away at intervals. Last winter I was in Italy, now I go to Spain, and I was in England throughout the war. All places, where there is an arm-chair within and something human to see without, are much the same, and I lead the same life everywhere. You will find me somewhere on the beaten track whenever you next come to these parts.

Yours sincerely

G. SANTAYANA

In 1928 Mr. Santayana told me he had begun writing a novel but that it would not be published until after his death. At Harvard in the old days he had been conspicuous in social life in Boston, and much sought after; but in Europe he was leading the life of a true philosopher, very simply and never going out in the evening. He was however most genial and affectionate. On 17 August we lunched in a restaurant and talked about ethics, Goethe, Schiller, and Emerson. He said that an ethical life could be lived much better without religion than with it.

In the autumn I preached a sermon at Yale, in which I quoted his Sonnet beginning

> O world, thou choosest not the better part!
> It is not wisdom to be only wise,
> And on the inward vision close the eyes,
> But it is wisdom to believe the heart.
> Columbus found a world and had no chart,
> Save one that faith deciphered in the skies:
> To trust the soul's invincible surmise
> Was all his science and his only art.

I wrote him that I had quoted this poem in the pulpit and he replied

ROME, NOV. 2, 1928

DEAR BILLY—

You always bring with you, even if you come only by the post, a sort of Gulf Stream of warmth and kindness. I have said that old Sonnet (written in 1884) over to myself—I find that I still remember it—and although the words are too much spaced, thinly scattered over an empty waste, like the scrub oaks over a ploughed field, which in Spain are called a wood, yet the whole is perfectly limpid, and I can imagine that emitted in a rotund voice in a hushed religious atmosphere (do people still cough in the Yale Chapel?) it might have a good effect. In any case, I appreciate your appreciation, and I hope our combined exhortation will encourage your young people to have Faith—in themselves!

I have been in Spain—no harm resulting—and afterwards at

Strong's in Fiesole: now I am trying to bend all my remaining energies to finishing vol. II of Realms of Being.—Affectionate greetings
to you both from your old friend

G.S.

In February 1932 my wife and I sailed to Greece, but
before starting I wrote, hoping to meet him in Rome. We
met there in April and he invited us for lunch at a restaurant, the windows of which commanded a magnificent
view. Every afternoon I took long walks with him and his
conversation was, if possible, more stimulating than ever.
As a rule he was visible only between four and six; he wrote
steadily in his room from early in the morning until four,
and after six he retired. But he was kind enough to break
his rule for that one luncheon, and he seemed to enjoy
being with us. Tea and long walks in the afternoon he particularly enjoyed, for I am sure he knew that he had done
a good day's work. I asked him again about the novel; he
was proceeding rapidly with it, but he still felt sure it would
not be published until after his death.

HOTEL BRISTOL, ROME,
Jan. 4, 1932

DEAR BILLY—

Much better than a hurried cruise in a moving, rolling, smoking
and crowded boat would be a quiet luncheon on one of the Eternal
Hills (we may forget that the Vincinal has been removed) of Rome,
namely, the Aventine, to which I invite you both in advance, without
prejudice to other meetings. All that is necessary is that you should
come here on your way to Naples, as I presume you would in any
case.

Your journeys are so many and so energetic that you must often
have been in Rome before; but you will find the old sights probably
mellowed in an eye that has kept watch over New Haven, Conn.
(you see I can quote poetry too, and better than Browning's) and
also many new improvements. I confess I envy you going to Athens
and the Greek islands; but not in the *Queen Mary*. If I were younger

I should go, alone and solitary for several months; but as it is, I try to make up in memory and fancy what is wanting in leg-power.

I will not give you any news of myself, or ask for any of you, in the hope of soon seeing you.

Yours sincerely

G.SANTAYANA

I knew that he had delivered a lecture at the invitation of some learned academy at The Hague, but I thought it was about Erasmus. I am glad I made the error, for it drew from him the following letter.

HOTEL MIRAMONTI,
CORTINA D'AMPERESSO
July 10, 1933

DEAR BILLY—

Not Erasmus, Spinoza! But even that is not accurate. I went last September to the Hague, where they had a meeting in honour of the tercentenary of Spinoza's birth, and I read a paper which is only attached to Spinoza by way of the zenith: for, mind you, though physically every zenith is at a hopelessly different point from every other, spiritually the nearer anyone gets to his own zenith, the nearer he is to everybody else's. This paper is to appear in a polyglot volume entitled *Septimana Spinozana* which was to have been issued last November, but is still delayed. Perhaps it will appear by November next.

As I approach 70 (December next the venerable number will be complete) I feel that I may abandon the future more and more to Providence. I go on working, but without being at all confident that it will be possible, or would be best, for me to accomplish anything special. At present, I am crawlingly proceeding with my 'novel': this is something nobody else could do, since it gives the *emotions* of my experiences, and not my thoughts or experiences themselves: whereas *The Realm of Truth* or *The Realm of Spirit* might perfectly well be described by some future writer better than I should do it. However, I am very well, and not worried by the crisis or the collapse of the dollar: it makes me much poorer on paper, but I had a broad margin to my budget and as yet have no need of changing my way of living; and it is not impossible, if I should live ten years more, that I might finish my whole programme.

This place—where I have spent three previous summers—is really delightful: warm enough in the sun to make the system exude its waste substances, and cool enough at night to kill all mosquitoes and even flies. Besides the Dolomites are highly picturesque, the peasants also, and the people at this hotel very tolerable—since I don't have to speak to them. The trouble is that on September 1st winter sets in, and I shall have to move to Venice or elsewhere until it is time to return to my Roman diggings.

Well: You at Great Yale are probably being carried sky-high on the crest of twenty enthusiasms at least. Don't break your neck, and God bless you!

Kindest regards.—Come again to Rome: it is improving yearly more than if it were in America. You will be astonished.

Yours ever

G.S.

He changed his mind about publishing the novel, for-tunately for the public; and in the winter of 1935–6 it ap-peared first in England and then in America. Curiously enough, although he has a very high reputation in England, the novel did not make a sensation there; but in America it had an enormous sale, and received favourable reviews from the leading critics. I was enchanted with the literary style and with innumerable observations, because they re-vealed the great artist and the great mind; but I thought his characters lacked vitality. I wrote a long review for *Scribners* and the following correspondence took place.

HOTEL BRISTOL, ROME
Feb. 16, 1936

DEAR BILLY—

Your letter about *The Last Puritan* was one of the first that reached me, but I have put off thanking you for it until others began to come, so that I could have a certain background on which to place your judgement, other than my own necessarily internal or *a priori* view; because the hardest thing for an author, especially when he has lived as long as I have with his characters—45 years—is to conceive how they will seem to other people, when conveyed to them only by *words*. I have pictures, quite as distinct as memories; and my characters *speak to me*, I don't have to prompt them. This doesn't contradict the fact which you mention, and I point to in the *Epilogue*, that these characters speak my language, and are in some sense masks for my own spirit. On the contrary, that makes, or ought to make, them more living, since they are fetched from an actual actor on the stage, for their social parts. And I think you are partly wrong, like so many other critics, when you suggest that my characters are ghostly and not 'living.' Even the admitted literary character of their talk is not incompatible in the drama, with individuality in tone and temper. Of course, I don't always succeed; yet I think, if you drop all preconceptions or clichés, you will find that there is a good deal of individuality in the way my characters talk, within the frame of what you might call my *metre*. It is my writing, but it is their sentiment. Only the book is very long, it can't leave distinct images if not allowed to settle. The great point is, as with poetry, to get the mind docile and free for suggestion, and then the dramatic spell will work. At least, that is what I can't help feeling, and what is confirmed by various witnesses. One notices Mrs. Darnley's special speech; another tells me he can *hear* Rose talk; . . . surely Irma and Mrs. Alden are not echoes of myself.

However, that isn't the point that matters most in the book or in your letter. You say I don't love life, and that faith is necessary. Very true: I don't love life unconditionally; but I enjoy the 'mere living,' (as Browning has it) when I am in good health, which is most of the time: and I enjoy the episodes, unless I am rudely prevented from doing so. If you have my *Dialogues in Limbo*, and will look at pp.156–161, you will find Socrates and me defining the matter exactly. It was Oliver, not I, who didn't love life, because he hadn't the animal epicurean faculty of enjoying it in its arbitrariness and transiency. He was a Spiritual man, incapacitated to be anything else, like Christ, who wouldn't be a soldier or athlete or lover of women or father of a family (or, even, though I don't say so in the book, a good believing Christian). Now that is a magic vocation, like the vocation of the poet: it demands sacrifice and devotion to a divine allegiance: but poor Oliver, ready for every sacrifice, had nothing to pin his allegiance to. He was what the rich young man in the Gospel would have been if he had been ready to sell his goods and give to the poor, but then had found no cross to take up and no Jesus to follow. Faith, as you say, is needed; but faith is an assurance inwardly prompted, springing from the irrepressible impulse to do, to fight, to triumph. Here is where the third sloppy wash in the family tea-pot is insufficient. And without robustness an imposed intellectual faith wouldn't do: it would only make a conventional person. You say you can't understand how I seem to hold my own in the world without faith, and almost without the world. It is quite simple. I have the Epicurean contentment, which was not far removed from asceticism; and besides I have a spiritual allegiance of my own that hardly requires faith, that is, only a humorous animal faith in nature and history, and no religious faith: and this common sense world suffices for *intellectual satisfaction*, partly in observing and understanding it, partly in dismissing it as, from the point of view of spirit, a transitory and local accident. Oliver hadn't this intellectual satisfaction, and he hadn't that Epicurean contentment. Hence the vacancy he faced when he had 'overcome the world.' *Basta*. Thank you a thousand times for your friendship.

G. SANTAYANA

On receiving this admirable letter, I asked his permission to print it in *Scribners*, as it made the best commentary on the book that I had seen.

By his lack of 'faith' I meant not only faith in God, but faith in life, such as, for example Sacha Guitry has, who dedicated his autobiography to *La Vie*. I also said that not one of the characters in his novel was what I should call 'good.'

HOTEL BRISTOL, ROME
March 16, 1936

DEAR BILLY—

Yes, of course you may print my letter; not that I remember what I wrote, because my memory disdains to record recent events, but I can trust you to leave out any indiscreet passages. . . .

There is something which I probably didn't say in my letter that I wish you would discuss some day in your 'As I Like It' articles. An important element in the *tragedy* of Oliver (not in his personality, for he was no poet) is drawn from the fate of a whole string of Harvard poets in the 1880's and 1890's—Sanborn, Philip Savage, Hugh McCulloch, Trumbull Stickney, and Cabot Lodge: also Moody, although he lived a little longer and made some impression, I believe, as a playwright. Now, all those friends of mine, Stickney especially, of whom I was very fond, were visibly killed by the lack of air to breathe. People individually were kind and appreciative to them, as they were to me, but the system was deadly, and they hadn't any alternative tradition (as I had) to fall back upon; and of course, as I believe I said of Oliver in my letter, they hadn't the strength of a great intellectual hero who can stand alone.

I have been trying to think whether I have ever known any 'good' people such as are not to be found in my novel. You will say 'There's me and Annabel: why didn't you put *us* into your book to brighten it up a little?' Ah, you are not novelesque enough: and I can't remember anybody so terribly good in Dickens except the Cheeryble Brothers, and really, if I had put anyone like that in they would have said I was 'vicious,' as they say I am in depicting Mrs. Alden. But Irma was what I think good: she wasn't sillier than we all are, except that we keep our silliness quiet. And Oliver was very good: I don't think you like *good* people really, only *sweet* people—like Annabel and you!

G.S.

My acquaintance and subsequent friendship with Mr. Santayana I count among my blessings. Despite our divergence in *Weltanschauung*, I honour him and I love him. His essay on Dickens (in *Soliloquies in England*) is the finest interpretation I have ever read; I have never recovered from my astonishment at his admiration for that particular author. It was natural that Chesterton should love Dickens; but Santayana? I thought Santayana would be repelled by what he would consider Dickens's vulgarity. But no critic has ever written of Dickens with more sympathy and enthusiasm. I asked him how these things might be; and he told me that during the war he was in England. In spare moments he tried to do some reading and soon found that Dickens was the only writer he could read. His essay tells us why.

35

THOMAS SERGEANT PERRY

WHILE I was a boy in high school, I read Mr. Perry's admirable book *English Literature in the Eighteenth Century*. His treatment of the subject produced a permanent impression, and about eight years later when I was a graduate student at Harvard, he was kind enough to invite me to lunch at his house in Boston. Mr. Perry was a great linguist and after he was seventy years old learned Russian and finally read it with ease. He said he thought he had accomplished more than Cato, who learned Greek at eighty. Mr. and Mrs. Perry brought up their children to speak European languages; I remember my amazement at this lunch at their house when the baby girl had a tantrum and was removed from the room, crying and protesting *in French*. I had not supposed any American children took French so seriously or so naturally. That baby is now the wife of Mr. Joseph C. Grew, the accomplished American ambassador to Japan; formerly ambassador to Turkey and to France.

Mr. Perry was a scholar who loved learning for its own sake; he had little ambition and disliked publicity. His intellectual curiosity was insatiable and his letters to me were always interesting. In the seventies he had known Turgenev well in Paris and at that time he produced an English translation (from the French version) of one of his novels. He had an unqualified admiration for the writings and for the personality of Chekhov; and as he grew older he felt that America was intellectually immature and steadily growing more vulgar.

Mrs. Perry, a niece of James Russell Lowell, was a painter, whose professional career extended over many years. In the early days Howells was an intimate friend and in the twentieth century Edwin Arlington Robinson. She painted their portraits.

The Perrys lived abroad for years, and in 1906 we spent a day with them at Giverny. We had tennis doubles and Perry, who was sixty-eight years old, said he preferred singles. I asked if he were not afraid such a contest might kill him. 'But what a glorious death to die!' He (like me) read with avidity all the accounts of the great tennis matches. He read every word in *American Lawn Tennis*, which he called the best magazine in America.

When letter-writing had become almost a lost art, Mr. Perry was a master; his letters, of which I received at least one every week for fifteen years (how I miss them!) were full of charm. One day he had been reading Chekhov's letters to his wife (the famous actress Madame Knipper), and while Mr. Perry felt that they were too intimate to print, he could not help enjoying them.

> Since the letters are printed I most gladly read them. I find them touchingly delightful. You know my sworn devotion to Chekhov, and now it is renewed. They sent me the book from the Public Library, and along with it one that treats of certain states of mind among our fellow-citizens. Its title is 'The Raven on the Skyscraper,' by Veronica and Paul King. . . . It is a ghastly record of our sins, and a confirmed optimist like you will feel its injustice, but a professional pessimist like me will revel in it. Of course it is one-sided, but even then there is a lot of one-sided vulgarity and indecency and brag in this half-ripe, half-rotten country and we are all miserable sinners. Look however at the Chekhov book. It is delightful.

In response to my request, he wrote to me about Emerson: 'I wonder if any one knew him well, as men commonly know one another. I certainly did not, though I saw him several times, first as a boy of 10 when I saw him lecture and he looked like his early portrait, long, lean, lank but with the face of a communicative angel; then in 1862, a Freshman taken to the shrine by his son, a classmate. When I was a tutor, he came to my room on some vaguely understood overseer business. A friend of mine, a senior, was in my room who, I told him, fell on his belly with awe and wriggled from the room like a serpent, for there was, with all his simplicity, his habit of rocking, of eating pie, of coddling each elbow with the other hand, an aura of greatness that was most imposing. Every one felt it. He and Monet—very unlike—gave me the impression of greatness—it's a splendid feeling. Then soon after our marriage L. and I paid a visit to R.W.E. and I could give you details of his talk (about Swinburne e.g.) if writing were easier. Then I heard his lectures (though earlier) at Harvard College.'

Mr. Perry told me of one conversation with Emerson that made a tremendous impression. Emerson came into the room where he was, and began speaking with animation of a friend who had suddenly fainted away. His eyes glowing with excitement, Emerson said 'He fell in a swound,' pronouncing the word to rhyme with *ground*. Swound is a word one *sees* often, but for the first and last time in his life, Perry heard it spoken. The greatness of the speaker, his 'sad sincerity,' his utter unconsciousness of using an unusual expression, combined to make the remark unforgettably striking.

HANCOCK
NEW HAMPSHIRE
June 25, 1927

DEAR P,

If you want to read a real book (as you have probably done already) take *Trader Horn* (Simon & Schuster); it will delight you. It is full of the real stuff & makes almost all other bks. seem like theatre programmes. I am tired or I wd. go on for half an hour.

I reproached Robinson for giving you & not me the *Torrent*, the rare first egg he laid. I bo't the other bk. Dec. 12, '97, I believe,

having taken it up in the bk. shop & found it worthy. I can't remember what exact lines fascinated me, for soon after I was off to
Japan.

T.S.P.

I had written him that I possessed autographed copies of
the first two books by Edwin Arlington Robinson.

36

PLAYING GAMES

I HAVE always been a playboy and have wasted (if you like) a large proportion of my life playing games, but I have had such an enormous amount of fun in competitive sport that I find it difficult to regret the time I have given to it. I began playing baseball when I was five and kept at it until I was forty-five; then, although broken tendons in the leg quickly healed, I decided to quit. I have never played any game, outdoors or in, for money; for my excitement in games, my joy in winning, my sorrow in defeat, have always been so intense that no additional stimulus has been necessary.

I do not really regret the lost time. I regret in learning games that I did not take them more seriously. If I were to live my life over again, I should get early enough good instruction in golf and lawn tennis, especially in the latter. I have never risen above mediocrity in any sport except long distance running, though I have won a fair share of prizes. In 1887, when I was twenty-two, I won the cross-country championship of Yale, running nine miles in fifty-four minutes. There were twenty-three starters. I ran in fourth or fifth place for half an hour, then I increased the pace, and passed every man but one, who was so far ahead of me I could not see him. And indeed, if he had not been an inexperienced Freshman, four years younger than I, he would have won. I did not get a sight of him until about three-quarters of a mile from the finish, when I not only saw him but also saw he was running well. I knew then the only way I could beat him would be to pass him just once, a hundred yards or so from the finish, and to pass him with a burst of speed so that he would think I had much in reserve. With great difficulty I gained on him; then as I got nearer to him, although I was completely exhausted, I summoned my will power, and on sheer nerve, I dashed past him. He gave a grunt and acquiesced, evidently thinking I had saved everything for the home stretch. In reality, although 'all in,' I went 'all out,' and fell across the finish line, not unconscious, but unable to move. In a few moments he came in relatively fresh.

I did no training for this race; I was always in good condition and in those days never smoked or drank. An hour before the race, I ate a hearty meal, finishing with a large wedge of apple pie.

In college I was not good enough to win a place on the University nine, but I made the 'second' nine, called the Yale Consolidated.

The summers in Huron County, Michigan, where I am now writing these words, were largely spent in playing ball until I was over forty; and our nine, the Huron City nine, made up chiefly of members of the U.S. Coast Guard, won the championship of the County in 1897.

The most exciting moment in all the years I played baseball, happened one summer day in 1893 at Harbor Beach (then called Sand Beach) when I played third base for Bad Axe against the Sand Beach nine. Many times have I struck out with men on bases; and here was the stage set for great drama, which happens so often in story-books and so seldom in life. It was the last half of the ninth inning. Our opponents were exactly three runs ahead. We had three men on bases, but two were out when I went to bat. I got two strikes. Apparently no chance of our winning! I can hear the voice of the enemy catcher now (Al Knapp remembers it as well as I do; he was the catcher and I see him every summer). 'Put one right over; the big stiff can't hit it!' I saw the pitcher wind up and the ball approaching. I had no confidence left; I fully expected to strike out. But with the strength of despair, I swung my bat with all my might. To my amazement I saw the ball going on a line over the centre fielder's head. It brought in four runs and won the game, and as I crossed the plate, I had the greatest single thrill of my life. This famous hit made history; it is still talked of and written about in that part of the world.

The love of most men for sport and their absorbing interest in it cannot perhaps be defended rationally; it is an instinct going deeper than reason. Men like W.H.Hudson, Bernard Shaw, and others to whom sport was abhorrent, were without 'sporting blood.' Yet the fact that the majority of men turn first of all to the sporting page in the newspaper can be accounted for on the ground that the first page is usually a record of failures—failures in business, failures in the art of living together, failures in citizenship, in character, and many other things; whereas the sporting page is a record of victories. It contains some good news, a commodity so rarely found on the first page. During the World War, I was travelling somewhere on the train and in the early morning the Chicago newspapers were brought to us; we all grasped them eagerly. Sitting next to me was an Episcopal clergyman in clerical dress. He paid no attention whatever to the war news, but turned feverishly to the sports pages.

In 1892 I was reading aloud the news to my father. My father was an orthodox Baptist minister; he was a good man and is now with God. I had never heard him mention a prize fight and did not suppose he knew anything on that subject, or cared anything about it. So when I came to the headline CORBETT DEFEATS SULLIVAN I read that aloud and turned over the page. My father leaned forward and said earnestly 'Read it by rounds!'

I began to play lawn tennis in 1882, played a good deal, but not regularly, in college, and after I became a member of the Yale Faculty and joined the New Haven Lawn Club in 1892, I played daily. On 30 May 1896 Dr. Fred Chase (the astronomer) and I reached the finals in the New England Tennis Championship, and won second prizes; we were beaten by Malcolm Chace and Arthur Foote, both of them famous players. In 1904 I entered the Bavarian tournament at Munich, and with my partner Bernhard Fünfstück won first prize in men's doubles (*Herren Doppelspiel mit Vorgabe*). We received handsome silver cups. In this same tournament I won first prize in Veteran singles, open only to those who were more than thirty years old! I was thirty-nine. In the finals I played against an Austrian Count, who had me five–love in the first set. He never won another game, however, as I defeated him 7–5, 6–0. I got another silver cup, first prize singles, *Veteranenspiel*.

In 1912 at Mentone, in Southern France, with my French partner M. Arnal, I won first prize in the men's handicap doubles. Although I was forty-seven years old, this was the best playing in doubles I had ever performed; we had a long, hard road to the finals, every match being close.

The New Haven Lawn Club was the only club in America, so far as I know, where tennis was played in the open air with deep snow on the ground, and a temperature at zero or below. We had a court made of wooden planks, laid down every Autumn at the end of the season. The snow was shovelled off, and I have never enjoyed tennis more than in the crisp winter air. I do not know why other clubs did not follow our example. Later, we built two concrete courts, and continued to play tennis all through the winter.

Although in all games I have always played to win, have been elevated by victory and depressed by defeat, the playing has always been mingled with abundant hilarity. My delight in games has made it impossible for me to keep my mouth shut. I am afraid that persons playing tennis on adjoining courts have often been annoyed by the stream of talk and nonsense. My innumerable tennis partners and opponents will remember (not unkindly, I think) the laughter and talk and bad puns that have accompanied our games of tennis and golf. The almost oppressive silence in which most persons play games is foreign to my nature. This silence is characteristic not only of great experts, but of ordinary players and duffers.

I have had the pleasure of seeing many of the greatest players of the world, not only in tournaments but in practice; the only ones who talk and laugh a good deal are Tilden and Perry and Borotra. I remember watching Crawford and Quist playing practice sets with others for several hours. Crawford never smiled and when he spoke, at rare intervals, it was almost a whisper. Quist had the expression of a chief mourner at a funeral. No doubt they enjoy playing and prefer silence; but with me, physical exercise in outdoor games has always stimulated an irrepressible effervescence.

Many of the happiest afternoons of my life were spent playing tennis with my colleagues on the Yale faculty and other friends at the New Haven Lawn Club. For thirty years I gave a series of twenty Tuesday afternoon public lectures in New Haven which began at quarter past four; so every Tuesday afternoon I used to play tennis beginning at two and watch the clock carefully to see just how much time would be left to bathe and change and reach the lecture hall. During the month of September, while we were living in Michigan, I looked forward to these tennis matches with such eagerness that I used to write to Professor Jack Crawford, my regular partner, to Mr. Stanley Williams, to Mr. Lewis Bronson and others, so that on the first Tuesday of the term three men would be sure to be there at the Lawn Club at two o'clock for our first game.

We had a special terminology for various strokes. Because a famous Yale football player, Otis Guernsey, had won a game with Princeton in the last moment by a long kick that trembled on the cross-bar and finally fell on the other side, every net-cord shot was called a 'Guernsey,' and was greeted by shouting that word—unintelligible to spectators. Innumerable other expressions known only to the initiated were employed to punctuate exciting moments in our games, so that these doubles, in which I took part until I was seventy, mingled violent physical exercise with a continuous torrent of vocal hilarity. Even now when I look at that clock on the Lawn Club grounds which I used to watch with such intensity, I feel a pang that I shall never again take part in these exciting and joyful contests. Of all the things I regret most at being forced to abandon because of old age, lawn tennis would come first and I shall always be grateful to the following men, colleagues of mine on the Yale faculty, whose companionship in this magnificent sport gave me such intense pleasure for more than twenty years: Jack Crawford, A. K. Merritt, George Nettleton, A. G. Keller, Fred Luquiens, Stanley Williams, Arthur Corbin, Stewart Mims, Charles Warren, Jack Adams, Karl Young, W. C. Abbott, Howard Church, and others.

On 1 Sept. 1905 my brother-in-law, Frank W. Hubbard, and I went to Brainerd, Minnesota, to visit Alfred K. Merritt, the Yale Registrar, and there for three days we had the finest prairie-chicken shooting I have ever enjoyed. Although these birds are as big as hens and rise from short stubble, it is impossible to see them until they do rise. Of course no sportsman would ever shoot them except on the wing; but why are they never seen ten yards away in stubble two inches high?

I have never been a bridge player because learning the modern game takes more time than I am able to give, but I am devoted to the old-fashioned game of duplicate whist, which almost no one plays today. For thirty years three of my colleagues on the Yale faculty, A.K.Merritt, the Registrar, A.G.Keller, Professor of the Science of Society, and John M.Berdan, Professor of English, have played duplicate whist, Merritt and I playing against Keller and Berdan. We have never played for any stake because we are so eager to win and so anxious not to lose that the excitement needs no further stimulation. Furthermore we never play in the evening because if I should play this game in the evening, I should not sleep all night. None of us can afford to waste a morning at it, and if the weather is good we should rather be outdoors than playing any game inside. But when the weather is bad and we all four have an afternoon free we play; to play the twenty-four boards back and forth takes about three hours. We have had an enormous amount of delight out of these stormy afternoons and candour forces me to admit that Keller and Berdan have, during a period of thirty years, won more games than Merritt and I, though not enough to prevent a continuous white-hot excitement every time we begin.

We have a formula for telephonic invitations to these whist battles. When the weather is horrible, I call up these three colleagues, announcing *This is the day the Lord hath made!* which is immediately understood as an invitation. Professor Keller cut that text in Hebrew out of some Semitic journal, whereupon my friend and colleague, Professor Charles C.Torrey, was kind enough to letter it out for me in the original Hebrew, on a long card, and this placard stands over us as we play.

In later years we added to this Faculty Whist Club Mr. Edwin Oviatt, Professor J.C.Adams, Professor F.B. Luquiens, Professor C.B.Tinker; it is an interesting fact

that a majority are members of the class of 1896, whom
I first met in 1892 and with whom I kept up intimacy all
my life.

Speaking of cards, the former pastor of our church in
New Haven one morning when I was present unconsciously
demonstrated his own innocence and the guilt of the congregation. In the middle of his sermon, he remarked,
'Members of this church should never play bridge for
money. It is not the amount that matters, it is the principle of the thing. It is wrong. Even if you play for a very
small stake, it is still wrong. Even if you play for a trivial
stake, for a merely nominal stake, even if you play for *only
five cents a point*, it is still wrong.' The gasp of horror that
went over the audience gave them away. I have often wondered what would have happened to this excellent man if
he had ever followed the example of Dean Inge. The Dean
said he did not believe in playing cards for money, but
that just a few times, to help out a party, he had played
for very small stakes. I am sure the Dean knew exactly
what he was doing, but the American. . . .

All men can be divided into two classes; those who are
excited over playing games and those who are not. It is,
of course, from the rational point of view absurd to feel
bad because one is beaten; and absurd to rejoice over a
victory. No one knows better than I that what one should
chiefly enjoy is the pleasant exercise, the good companionship; and after the match is over one should not then care
either for victory or defeat. But how impossible such a
philosophical attitude!

One illustration will suffice for all. When I was an undergraduate perhaps the greatest scholar on the Yale faculty
was William Dwight Whitney, who was regarded both in
Europe and America as the leading authority on Sanscrit.
His home was constantly visited by students because of its
hospitable, social, and stimulating atmosphere; no better

conversation could be had anywhere in New Haven. I remember when a Freshman I first entered their sitting room and found not only the three charming young girls, his daughters, and their sweet-tempered and affectionate mother, but the great scholar himself. He looked the part, with snow-white hair and beard and unaffected dignity. He rose from his chair and greeted me, a humble Freshman, as if I were somebody.

Now this gentleman was, as I remarked, one of the most famous scholars in the world and his speciality was in the remote field of Oriental languages. In manner he was calm, self-collected and courteous. But I discovered that his physician had forbidden him to play any game whatever—croquet, halma, checkers, or cards—because he was so excited and so depressed by defeat that it was bad for his health.

I don't know how others would feel on receiving such information; but my respect and affection for the man, when I heard this, were increased an hundred fold.

I know how to enjoy demonstratively and how to enjoy in silence. In playing games I am noisy, except when another is addressing or hitting a golf ball; but my intense, ecstatic enjoyment of symphony orchestras and the operas of Wagner finds me immobile and silent. Never have I committed the mortal sin of nudging my neighbour at music; for there is only one sin worse than that, which is humming a melody when it is sung or played on the stage. Apparently there have always been persons who either consciously (to show off) or unconsciously, commit this unpardonable sin. Chard Smith, in his entertaining and valuable work, *Annals of the Poets* (1935) reminds us of what Dr. Johnson said of the poet Matthew Prior: 'One day he sat at the Paris opera by a man who was so transported that he accompanied the principal performer with his own voice. Prior began to vituperate the actor so loudly and eloquently that his French neighbour, ceasing from his own song, began to protest, saying that the performer was among the greatest singers of the age. "I know all that," replied Prior, *"mais il chante si haut, que je ne sçaurois vous entendre."*'

The first game of golf I ever played was at Providence, my companions being Professors John M. Manly and Edmund Delabarre, of Brown University, on 17 May 1896. Our scores for the nine holes were Delabarre, 68, Manly, 95, and mine 87. I did not play again until the summer of 1897, on a course of four or five holes at Port Austin, Michigan. In the Spring of the next year, 1898, I joined the Golf Club in New Haven and on 21 October 1899 I won the championship of the New Haven Country Club, defeating T. S. Woolsey, Jr., in the final round of 36 holes.

I became a fanatical golf player and forsook lawn tennis altogether. For those first years of the century, 1900–03, we paid no attention to the season or to the weather. We played golf in rain, hail, snow, sleet and in every week of the year. If the snow was very deep, we wore hip rubber boots and used a red ball. We were insane and had a good time.

In 1903 my wife and I went to Europe for a year. There was no golf either in France or Germany, so I took up tennis again, and grew to enjoy it so much that when we returned to Yale in the Autumn of 1904 I played only tennis for some years. Then I took up golf again, and gave about an equal amount of time to both games until I was seventy years old. I should have played either one of these games better had I given up the other; but I should not have had so good a time.

A few years ago I wrote an article on golf, which some day I hope to expand into a small book, with the title *Thirty Years of Looking Up.* One of my former students,

Leonard Kennedy of the class of 1909, gave me the perfect quotation from Browning's *Childe Roland*.

> For, looking up, aware I somehow grew
> 'Spite of the dusk, the plain had given place
> All round to mountains—with such name to grace
> Mere ugly heights and heaps now stolen in view.
> How thus they had surprised me,—solve it, you!
> How to get from them was no clearer case.

In the year 1925 we spent nearly four months at Augusta, Georgia, while I was convalescing from a breakdown. I played golf in foursomes about three times a week with the great Walter J. Travis. He was the first American-trained golfer ever to win the amateur championship of Great Britain; that was in 1904, and it was many years before an American succeeded again. The English, in those days, were not accustomed to see invaders win championships, and his victory was regarded as a national disaster. After his death, the following fine tribute appeared in the London *Times*.

> He never came back again, and among the thousands who watch golf today there are few who saw him play; but that ominous, almost sinister little figure with the black cigar and the Schenectady putter is still familiar to the imagination of all British golfers.
>
> Mr. Travis had a formidable rather than an engaging personality. He kept himself to himself; he played silently and dourly: . . . we were inclined to say that he ought to have been beaten. Yet one solid, uncompromising fact sticks in my head—namely that when Mr. Travis had reached the final, we were afraid, mortally afraid, that Mr. Travis was going to win. . . .
>
> It is his putting that has become legendary, and it was wonderful. . . . I never have seen, however, such utter consternation as was produced by Mr. Travis's putting in that final at Sandwich, nor any putting that had about it such a suggestion of black magic. This was enhanced, no doubt, by the man himself. As he stood there after the stroke, still as a statue, watching the ball with those in-

scrutable eyes of his pursuing its inexorable course, he seemed a wizard to be burned at the stake. . . . As a game-player he had essential greatness.

As he stood there after the stroke—many players walk right after their putt up to the hole; Mr. Travis knew better than that. Indeed, most golfers would have profited by playing with Mr. Travis, for he believed in adhering rigidly to the rules of the game, not conceding putts, and not allowing other players and caddies to stroll ahead of the man who was to make the next shot.

But, after all, the best thing about Mr. Travis was not his golfing—the best thing was himself, his mind, his character. He had an interesting mind, a great range of information on many subjects, and was one of the best conversationalists I ever knew. I loved the man, and do honour his memory.

It is possible that playboys like myself are intellectually inferior to those whose main delight is a solitary walk; botanical strollers at all events are self-reliant; they have resources of their own. They need no companions and no apparatus; they commune with nature, and instead of trying to escape from themselves, they do just the opposite; they loaf and invite themselves; and yet—heaven forgive me!—I glory in my shame. For while the pleasure of sport consists largely in human companionship, still I love the sport for its own sake. I have reached an age where in playing golf I put the weather first, the company second, and the game third. I had rather play a rotten game in good weather than a good game in rotten weather. Yet even so I had rather play golf alone than take a walk alone.

I respect all men who love to potter around in a garden, but for me such diversion would be a bore. When I talk with a respectable citizen and ask him the familiar question what he does for exercise or recreation, and he says he spends an hour in the garden before breakfast and another hour when he returns home from the day's work, I look upon him humbly as a superior intelligence, but I would not imitate him. If I were obliged to mess around in a garden, even though I were so successful as to behold the desired fruit of my labours, I should feel unutterably depressed.

Alex Herd, perhaps better known as Sandy Herd, the famous professional and golf teacher, author of that admirable book, *My Golfing Life*, wrote me a letter so full of enthusiasm for the game that it must be quoted:

> I can assure you when I was a boy at school in my dear old home in St. Andrews, I used to follow all the old champions around the links, watching every shot they played, and admired their skill, and also as men I admired them. It used to give me pleasure once when I was old enough to carry their clubs; what an honour I thought it was! Then they used to gather outside old Tom Morris's shop at night and talk of the great matches that they had played and how they had lost and won championships. I used to stand with my ears and mouth wide open, drinking every word in.
>
> I used to dream of golf. I would get up at four o'clock every morning and play a round of golf before work, and after my hard day's work was over, I would play another round at night. And every putt I played, I would say to myself, 'Got this to win the championship,' little thinking that one day I would achieve that honour.
>
> Golf is a game one must have at heart. One must love it and think it all out as to how to become a champion. One must practise for everlasting, and we can never quite master its wonderful illusive ways.
>
> I love America. I like the kind way I was received. I was treated with kindness itself and given all hospitality beyond my dreams.

I love fresh woods and pastures new, but I love them more with a golf club in my hand. If, instead of going out with three good fellows to play golf, I went out alone to find the trailing arbutus or something like that, I should not be happy.

And there is another thing about solitary walking in which I am sure my experience is not unique. I can play eighteen holes of golf, which means three hours of walking, I can play three sets of tennis doubles, which means an hour and a half of violent exercise, without fatigue; over and over again I have felt less tired at the end than when I began. But if I go for a slow saunter with or without companionship, I become exhausted. My back aches horribly, and my legs feel as if they were going to sever their connexion with my frame. And when at last I do sit down, instead of a pleasant fatigue, I feel as if I should never smile again. There is only one fatigue worse than that; it is where some obliging person shows you the 'sights' of a town, or the interior of a museum.

The majority of creative writers are not playboys; they care nothing for outdoor or indoor games. So far as I can find out, Browning never took part in any athletic contest; his chief physical exercise was playing the piano, horseback riding, walking (he never took a cab if he could help it), and, up to the time of his marriage, dancing. Elizabeth expressed her surprise that the author of *Paracelsus* should dance the polka all night. Tennyson played no games; his chief exercise consisted in booming out his own poems in his sea-captain's voice, or taking the dogs for a walk on the edge of the cliffs. In answering the stock question, ' What is your chief recreation?' Bernard Shaw wrote, ' Anything except sport,' and George Moore wrote, ' Religion.'

My oldest brother, Dryden William, eleven years older than I, was entirely different from my brother Arthur and me, for he hated all games, never learned how to swim or even to whistle, never fired a gun or a pistol; but had an accomplishment in which he excelled anyone I have ever seen or heard of. He could definitely remember something that had happened *every day of his life* after the age of five. For example: in the year let us say 1890, if you asked him 'What did you do February 17, 1868?' he could tell you within three minutes.

Once in a dime museum I saw a man, regarded as a freak, who received a good salary for his ability in calculation. If you told him the day of the month and the year when you were born, he would in a few minutes give you the day of the week. By this accomplishment alone, he earned his living. I told him I was born on the second of January 1865. He turned to a big blackboard, made calculations with a piece of chalk, and said 'You were born on Monday,' which was correct.

I mention this because what he succeeded in doing with the help of a blackboard, my brother Dryden did much faster in his head. 'What did you do on February 17, 1868?' By some mysterious process inexplicable to me, but which lasted only about twenty seconds, he would say 'That was a Wednesday' (if it was) and he would then describe the weather and something he had done. I never knew him to fail. Nor was he ever mistaken. One of his favourite tricks was to visit the New Haven cemeteries and correct by his memory dates that were cut on the tombstones. He was invariably right.

Dryden was a tremendous walker; and occasionally my brother Arthur and I went out with him. When I was a small boy, we walked from New Haven to Hartford in one day, nearly forty miles by road. I did that repeatedly before and during college. One day in Freshman year, my classmate, George D. Pettee, and I rose at three in the morning to see how far we could walk in one day. If it had not been for unfavourable weather conditions, we should have done seventy-five miles. As it happened, fifty was the best we could manage. It turned out to be the hottest day in the year; and along about three in the afternoon, we were caught in the severest thunder-storm I ever saw. Before we could reach any shelter, we were drenched. The lightning seemed to play all about us, and a ball of fire struck the ground not fifty yards away. We crawled into a shed, and when the storm ceased, we felt like Rip Van Winkle waking from his twenty years of slumber; we were so wet, so soggy, so cramped, and so stiff, we could hardly move.

When I was sixteen, in company with one of my Chinese schoolmates, I used to run two or three miles every evening. I had read with interest Blaikie's then famous book, *How to Get Strong and How to Stay So*, and one of his recommendations was to run three miles daily. Accordingly, this Chinese boy and I would meet after dark and run out to West Hartford and back. I am glad I did this; it has had a beneficial effect all my life.

In 1882 I saw my first University football game, Yale against Columbia. Yale won easily, but the feature of the game was the number of drop-kick goals made by E.L.Richards, Jr., of Yale. His father was Professor of Mathematics at Yale, and Chairman of all athletic committees. In fact, he was far more interested in athletics than in mathematics. He maintained that activity in athletics could always be accompanied by success in scholarship if the students would plan their time properly. He was proud when his son, Eugene, of the class of 1885, gave such a magnificent illustration of his father's precepts! For Eugene was Chairman of the *Yale Literary Magazine*, Captain of the University football team, and Phi Beta Kappa with philosophical oration (highest honour group).

He and his mate at half-back, Wyllys Terry, were sadly missed after they were graduated in 1885; and that autumn, Frank Peters of the class of 1886 had to develop a green team. Henry Ward Beecher, grandson of the famous divine, was quarter-back; freshmen like Woodruff, 'Pa' Corbin, Charley Gill, Billy Bull, before they were graduated became among the most famous athletes in America;

but it was a green team, and when Princeton came to play the final game with Yale in November, very few believed Yale had any chance at all. Yet Yale should have won. The green team outplayed the Princeton veterans. Watkinson dropped a goal from the field, which then counted five points, and the score remained Yale 5, Princeton 0, until a few minutes before the end. Yale had possession of the ball and was gaining slowly but just enough to keep it, that is, just enough to be assured of victory, when deep in Princeton territory, Yale punted, no one knows why.

The ball bounded wide to one side, and Lamar, the Princeton half-back, caught it on the run, sprinted past the entire Yale team, ran nearly the length of the field without a single Yale player near him, and made a touchdown. No spectator will ever forget 'Lamar's run.' The Princeton crowd rushed deliriously on the field; one man kissed Lamar on both cheeks, and there was pandemonium. Peters threw himself on the ground and tore his hair. I have often read in books of people in grief tearing their hair, but this is the only time I ever saw it.

The score was then Yale 5, Princeton 4, but we felt sure that the Princeton quarter-back would make his place-kick successfully. He did; Dick Hodge stepped up to the ball with as much confidence as if nothing depended on it, and kicked the ball straight between the posts; Yale 5, Princeton 6, the final score. Dick played quarter-back, his brother Hugh end. Both boys had been members of my class at the Hartford High School; their older brother Aspinwall, and their younger brother Sam, also were members of the Princeton University football teams.

At that time we of Yale were heartbroken. But in subsequent years I have always been glad Lamar made that victorious run and won undying fame. For a few years after graduation, he heroically and unselfishly lost his life in the endeavour to save someone from drowning.

Lamar of Georgia—one of the immortals in football.

Although Harvard is perhaps Yale's greatest athletic rival, no game with Harvard has been so thrilling as two twentieth century games with Princeton. I shall remember these as long as I live, and they are as bright in my memory as if they had happened yesterday.

The first of these two games that I have in mind was played 16 November 1907. Ted Coy was then full-back for Yale, Tad Jones was half-back, Howard Jones end, Ray Biglow tackle and captain. Before the game the Princeton team was thought to be superior, and during the entire first half Princeton outplayed Yale with such ridiculous ease that if they had tried a little harder they might have scored another touchdown. They went through the Yale line as easily as if they had been playing against small boys and made a touchdown and goal, counting seven points, and then, when they got near the Yale goal a second time and might easily have made another touchdown, Harlan drop-kicked a goal from the field in an almost contemptuous fashion, not even looking to see whether the ball had gone over the bar or not. This gave a score of Princeton 10, Yale 0, and it seemed as if they would defeat Yale by about 40 points.

When the teams came out for the second half, I said to my neighbour, 'Well, we hardly got hold of the ball in the first half, but, although we are going to be beaten, we shall have the ball for a few moments because Princeton has the kick-off.' But to my amazement and disgust Princeton recovered the kick-off so that Yale didn't even have that small solace.

From that moment the game was all Yale! It seemed as if the teams had changed uniforms. I have never seen such a revolution between the two halves of a football game. This was the golden day in the spectacular career of Ted Coy, one of the greatest football players of all time. He stood far back of the line, receiving a long pass from centre and then started around the end, apparently without interference. Every Princeton man who got in his way was knocked down, not by the interference but by Coy himself. He was inspired; he was a demon; he was a Juggernaut. It was not long before Yale was down in Princeton territory. Then Tad Jones held the ball close to the ground, apparently for Coy to kick, but Coy picked it up and ran over the line for a touchdown. The score was then 10–6. After kicking, Coy started again on his rampant run, and this time the entire Yale team went over the goal line, overwhelming Princeton like an avalanche. Cheers turned to groans, however, when it was learned that the touchdown was not allowed. But in a few moments Yale had the ball again and carried it over for another touchdown, making the score Princeton 10, Yale 12. Even now, looking back after all these years, it seems unbelievable and indeed it was almost miraculous. There is no explanation for it, for although Ted Coy played splendidly during the next two years of his college course, he never reached the heights of the second half of the Princeton game of 1907. Thirty years later Biglow told me that it was sheer inspiration felt by all the team as they came out for the second half.

In an address I made to the students between this game and the game with Harvard on the following Saturday, which Yale won 12–0 but which had not a single spectacular feature, I told them (all witnesses of that Princeton game) that for the rest of their lives, any time that they were despondent or discouraged, they would feel a tide of joy arising in their hearts when they thought of that score 12–10.

The other Princeton game was played at Princeton 14 November 1936. Two years previously Yale had beaten a Princeton team, which was at least twice as good as Yale, by a score of 7–0. In 1935 Princeton had beaten Yale with ridiculous ease at New Haven by the largest score ever made by Princeton against Yale. And when the teams lined up in 1936, the betting was in favour of Princeton.

I had a ticket for this game but was uncertain whether to attend or not. I lectured at Town Hall in New York at 11 o'clock that morning; the weather was perfect, and as soon as I finished the lecture I caught a train for Princeton after the excursion trains had gone, and by running from the train got a taxicab and reached the stadium two minutes after the game had begun. Here until nearly the end of the first half it was all Princeton. The score was Princeton 16, Yale 0. Then Charlie Ewart, one of the smallest men on either side, caught a punt and ran 30 yards through the Princeton team. This run had a stimulating effect. A few minutes later Clint Frank threw a pass of about 55 yards that was caught by Kelley as he was running full speed down the centre of the field. Kelley had hands that were like gigantic claws; he pulled that ball down out of the air and over his shoulder, for he was running, of course, in the same direction as the flying ball. He got rid of two Princeton opponents and went unmolested over the line. All through the second half Yale continued scoring. Yale was ahead of Princeton until early in the third quarter when Princeton got another goal. A few minutes before the end of the game Yale made a final touchdown, making the score Yale 26, Princeton 23. Then Jack White of Princeton got the ball, went through the entire Yale eleven, bound for a certain touchdown, when Al Wilson, Yale half-back, came from the extreme left side of the field, coming apparently out of nowhere, running with terrific speed, and pushed Jack White out of bounds not very far from the goal. This saved the game for Yale because there was not time to make another score for Princeton.

On the whole, it was the most spectacular game I have

ever seen, because I was certain that if the game had lasted ten minutes longer, more scoring would have been done.

All of Yale's athletic relations with Princeton, despite the intense rivalry, have been marked by unclouded friendship.

I have seen but one six-day bicycle race and then only for half an hour, which was quite enough for me, though not for twenty thousand others. It was one o'clock in the morning but I was the only man in the throng who seemed to be aware of it.

I wish that the six-day go-as-you-please on foot could be revived, as in these days of physical development and scientific training it would be interesting to see what the human body could endure. In the eighties, although there was no radio to attract the attention of millions, these six-day races in New York were first page news every day in every newspaper in America.

I remember when the English champion Charles Rowell came over announcing he would endeavour to run 600 miles in six days, something that had never been done. He trained by running forty miles daily, just a warming up. In March 1881 he started with the other competitors in Madison Square Garden at midnight Sunday night and on the first day he ran 150 miles. I have often wished that he had later tried for a twenty-four hour record, for although he meant this to be only the first of six days, no other man has ever run so far in one day. His leading competitor I believe covered 130. In the first three days, that is by Wednesday midnight, he had covered more than 350 miles and the bookmakers refused to take any more bets on him, as he seemed to have the race won. But on the very next day (Thursday) he withdrew. He was unable to continue and said it was owing to his having done too much the first day. An Englishman named Hazael won and covered 600 miles by ten o'clock Saturday night. He was an international hero. Two years later Rowell again competed in New York and this time did not go nearly so far in the first day. He completed 602 miles in the six days but alas, an Irishman named Fitzgerald did 610. Among the great six-day runners of those days were also Cameron, who called himself Noremac, Hughes and a negro named Hart. The trick of course was to find the minimum of sleep during the week. Too little was fatal; too much meant defeat.

When the Olympic Games were revived in 1896, they were appropriately held at Athens and I have always been glad that the Marathon (26 miles 385 yards) was won by a Greek and was actually run from Marathon to Athens, over the course presumably taken by Pheidippides in 490 B.C. This race immediately became popular, particularly in America, where it is run in various localities every year. A Boston shoe-maker for some years gave with every pair of running shoes a printed copy of Browning's poem *Pheidippides*. One of the most famous Marathon runners in America is Clarence De Mar, who has won the Marathon repeatedly with long intervals between victories. In 1928, knowing he was a Sunday School teacher, I invited him to come to New Haven and address a meeting of Yale undergraduates on a Sunday evening. He made an admirable speech.

On the preceding day, although I believe he was forty years old, he had once more won the Marathon race. He showed no stiffness, lameness, or exhaustion when he arrived in New Haven. He made a fine address, and when I took him to the station where he was to take the four-hour train journey to Boston, arriving late at night, he refused to allow me to buy a Pullman seat, saying he preferred the day coach!

37

JOURNEY TO EUROPE

THE last year of the nineteenth century began in Connecticut with a tremendous snowstorm in a temperature of 15 degrees. The next day I celebrated my thirty-fifth birthday by playing billiards in the morning and hockey on the ice in the afternoon and duplicate whist in the evening.

The next night I took the steamer *Richard Peck* for Providence and from there the morning train to Boston. The South Station at Boston on Summer Street, near where Emerson was born in 1803, had recently been completed and was called the 'largest in the world.' I went out to Cambridge and saw my old friends and former colleagues on the Harvard Faculty, lunching with Kittredge, dining with Briggs, talking with Santayana and Robinson and Gates and Barrett Wendell. I had a long talk with President Eliot about conditions at Yale and at Harvard; I explained the method of election at Yale, how I had been elected Professor by the Corporation but the Faculty had refused to agree, so the election was void. He wished to know what objection the Faculty had. 'Well, I had often made imprudent remarks,' to which he said, 'Prudence is not a desirable quality in a college professor.' He seemed astounded that at Yale the Faculty had more power than the Corporation, and gave me definitely to understand that at Harvard one man made all the appointments. I was never more impressed by his energy and determination and air of authority, though I had also never seen him in a more gracious and kindly and cheerful mood; so that I was astonished when, on my saying as I rose to go, 'I hope, President Eliot, I may always come and talk with you when I am in Cambridge,' to hear him reply, 'The next time you come I may not be here.' 'Why, are you going to resign?' 'Resign? Resign? Certainly *not*. But, Mr. Phelps, I am sixty-six years old.' To see him there, the embodiment of health and vigour, and yet feeling death near, made me laugh aloud. He lived twenty-six years after that, sound in body and mind, and died at the age of ninety-two.

A few weeks after I saw him, I received a letter from him, saying it was probable that I should be invited to become a member of the Harvard Faculty. He knew I preferred to remain at Yale if I were allowed to, but this letter gave me immense encouragement, for it removed worry about the future.

On the eleventh of January I heard Paderewski, then in the plenitude of his powers, play the *Sonata Appassionata* as I had never heard it before; at the conclusion of the programme, as an encore, he played Liszt's Rhapsody No. 2, my favourite. Many regard this as 'hackneyed,' but I am so constituted that works of genius never grow stale. I had heard Paderewski in Boston on his first visit to America and I heard him many times after 1900. But for some reason, I was more thrilled by this particular performance than by any other. The very next time I heard him play the Second Rhapsody was 38 years later in his famous motion picture.

On the fifth of April I was one of the Judges for the Ten Eyck Prize Speaking by men of the Junior Class. On the first ballot I voted for Arthur Gleason, and after a hot session lasting over an hour, he received the prize. After his graduation in 1901, he became a distinguished journalist, and his early death was a severe loss.

On the sixth and seventh of April Harry Vardon, being on his first visit to America, played exhibition matches at the Yale Golf Course. This was the first time Americans had had an opportunity to see high-grade golf; it was a revelation and seemed miraculous. On the second day, playing the best ball of two undergraduates, he made a 71, which no one before or since ever equalled on that course. One of his student opponents was Eb Byers of Pittsburgh, who afterwards became National Amateur Champion of America. Vardon was silent even for a golf-player; but when Tim Cheney, who played against him on the first day, put on gloves, Vardon enquired, 'What's the matter? Are the lad's hands cold?' Vardon, a big fellow, used clubs that were light and even dainty in appearance. Many bought them after his visit, but were unable to use them effectively. He had little amenity. On a certain course in Connecticut, as he and his local opponents were leaving the home green and had reached the piazza of the club-house crowded with spectators, one of the 'home players' asked him 'And what do you think of our course, Mr. Vardon?' His answer was awaited in an intense silence. After mature deliberation came the reply, 'With one exception, it is the worst in the world.'

After my bicycle trip through Europe in the summer of 1890, I did not cross the ocean again until 1900, when my wife and I spent three months in England with two weeks on the Continent. Crossing over on the slow and steady cattle-ship *Menominee*, we had some interesting fellow-passengers, Professor Jeremiah Jenks and family and Santayana.

On 11 July of that summer we saw Queen Victoria, as she drove along Constitution Hill. The Queen had come to London that morning from Windsor. In the afternoon we went to The Green Park, and stood at the kerb. A few mounted men in uniform preceded her, and then came the Queen in a little, low, open pony phaeton, coming so close to where I stood that I could have touched her as she passed. She was eighty-one years old, with snow-white hair, and wore large dark spectacles. She was herself not impressive to look at, being short, dumpy, and fat. But to me she was tremendously impressive as Queen and Empress of India, and because of her long reign—the longest of any monarch in English history, and one of the longest in ancient or modern times. As I stood uncovered, I felt both reverence and wonder; she had known all the intellectual giants of the Victorian age, in politics, in literature, in science.

That same morning we had attended a wedding in St. Martin's-in-the-Fields. The American Ambassador, Joseph H. Choate, was there, and took a seat directly in front of us. He turned around and whispered to me, 'Is the bride pretty?' 'Not very' I said. My old college roommate at Harvard, Professor Ralph Catterall, was best man. Immediately after the entrance of the bride, we all sat down, and the Ambassador fell into a deep sleep and did not awaken until the loud music of Mendelssohn at the close.

The most impressive performance at the London theatres we saw that summer was that of Mrs. Patrick Campbell as Magda. She was magnificent, and I shall remember her appearance and her voice as long as I live. Thirty-two years later I persuaded her to give a lecture at Yale; she still had her glorious voice, and she imitated various types of women merely by the quality of tone. She recited Browning's short poem *Wanting—is what?* in a manner that was better than a hundred annotations. She stayed at our house, accompanied by her dog, smoked big cigars, and said she wished to hear me give a literary lecture.

At its close she said, 'Why, you *love* people. It is unmistakable, in the way you look at the audience, in the way you talk.' When I said Goodbye to her the next day, she said 'You are going to kiss me, aren't you?'

THE BARCLAY

Dec. 10/32　　　　　　　　　　　III EAST 48TH STREET

MY DEAR DR. PHELPS,

This word is to send you and your wife my love, and beg you not to forget me.

You don't know how happy and proud I was that I pleased you. And I never told you how much I enjoyed your lecture and marvelled at your most blessed, kindly and intelligent way of meeting your fellow creatures.

I wish I had that gift. I feel always a stranger—talking to strangers —when I get on to the platform. Horrid for me isn't it?

Thank your dear wife and you for your friendliness. What a wonderful people you are for putting people at their ease, making them feel comfortable.

Yours affectionately,

(If I may)　　　　　　　　　　　BEATRICE STELLA CAMPBELL

Cyril Maude, who also in later years became a good friend and was in our house in New Haven, we saw that summer in *The School for Scandal.* A very fine performance it was, with Winifred Emery.

I worked every day in the British Museum, and among the famous scholars was the great historian Gardiner. He was very kind to Catterall, lending him his notes. One Sunday in Marylebone Church we heard the Rev. H.R.Haweis, whose books on music I had read in my boyhood. He was a curious figure of a man, apparently not more than five feet high, and very untidy. The poor fellow was also lame. But he preached with tremendous vigour on China, expressing the fervent wish that Great Britain would take a 'strong line,' etc.

On 25 July, a terrifically hot day, 96 degrees, we went to the House of Commons, where the Hon. James Bryce was kind enough to give us tickets to the gallery. He said it would be a dull day, and we looked for merely routine business. But, the Boer War was in progress, and anything might happen. In the midst of a dull afternoon, and a sparsely inhabited House, somebody got up and moved that the Secretary of State for Foreign Affairs, Joseph Chamberlain, have his salary reduced. A thrill of excitement went through the assembly; men came crowding in from the lobby, and in a few moments the House was packed. The men on the Irish benches were unruly, filled with ungodly mirth, giving every Conservative speaker except the leaders ironical applause; they were enjoying themselves tremendously.

A youngish man, in the late thirties, rose and was listened to by all with respect. He spoke with intense earnestness. The Englishman next to me in the gallery whispered 'There is the coming man, he will be famous some day. His name is Lloyd George.' Courtney rose and spoke against the war. He was interrupted by someone who called him unpatriotic. Courtney enquired 'And what is your definition of patriotism?' The answer was given and Courtney remarked 'I think patriotism will survive the gentleman's definition of it.'

Joseph Chamberlain spoke with fervour and force for an hour, defending himself, his party, and the country. He was of course listened to with attention, though with manifest disapproval from the opposition and Irish benches. Sir Henry Campbell-Bannerman from the front opposition bench, made a short speech, in which he said that on this particular question he would not vote at all, but expressed his abhorrence of the war. Labouchère, Sir Edward Grey, and Sir Robert Reid spoke. John Morley sat on the front bench of the opposition (the corner seat) and how eagerly I longed to hear him speak! He said not a word, however, but listened to the defenders of the war with an ironical smile. James Bryce spoke for the opposition, and finally Mr. Balfour rose, and in his suave, easy, cultivated, smiling fashion, ridiculed Sir Henry Campbell-Bannerman.

Who would have believed then that in a few years C.B.
would be Prime Minister?

Thirty-eight years after that field day in the House of
Commons, I was engaged in general conversation with my
friend, Charles MacInnes, K.C., of Toronto. I do not know
why I mentioned hearing that debate in 1900, but I had no
sooner mentioned it, than MacInnes exclaimed 'Why I was
there on that day myself!' We compared notes and found
that we had both been equally impressed and had remembered accurately everything.

When C.B. was Prime Minister, some important person
wrote him a letter about a political crisis. C.B. replied that
at the moment his wife was very ill, and that her health
meant more to him than the whole British empire.

My wife and I spent a month working in the Bodleian.
Mr. Fortescue, the Keeper of the Printed Books in the
British Museum, had said 'I will give you a letter to the
Librarian of the Bodleian at Oxford; he is an ass, but you
must not mind that.' He was certainly eccentric, and
looked at me as if I were a decayed fish, but I had no trouble
with him. At Oxford I had a delightful afternoon with
Morfill, the professor of Russian. His literary enthusiasms
pleased me, especially because we agreed. Turgenev was
his favourite novelist and Donne almost his favourite
English poet. He read aloud to us many of his translations
from the Russian, and also an original poem he had written
to his cat.

At Cambridge we had 'lodgings' for the first and last
time in my life; it was a new experience to have meals
brought in and served in our sitting-room. I wished to
visit the Pepys library at Magdalene, and had sent a letter
to Professor Alfred Newton, the zoologist. When I called
upon him, each was surprised by the other's appearance.
All he knew of me was that I was a university professor.
As I was thirty-five years old and looked like an under-

graduate, he could hardly believe I was the man he was awaiting. He himself looked antediluvian, and could walk only with the aid of two canes. After he had recovered from the shock of my youthful appearance, he was kind and considerate, and it was thrilling to examine the volumes in cipher in Pepys's handwriting. I was permitted to examine other books in that library; one of them had on the flyleaf the autograph of Francis Drake!

One afternoon I called on the famous scholar W.W.Skeat, and had good talk with him about Chaucer and other matters. I asked him why he, a Cambridge professor, had his Chaucer printed at the Oxford Press, calling it the Oxford Chaucer. He laughed heartily and said it was because he got more money out of it.

We went over to the Continent that summer and on 19 August saw the Passion Play. I called on and talked with many of the players I had seen ten years before, Mayer who had been Christus three times and was now Choregus, Zwink who was Judas again, though he had told me in 1890 he would not live another ten years, and the St. John who was 28 years old, taking the part for the second and last time. I was not so deeply impressed by the 1900 performance as I had been in 1890—perhaps because it was the second time.

Coming back through Germany, we were admitted to the cathedral at Speyer when they were opening the graves of the Emperors—an extraordinary spectacle. We saw the great sapphire ring of Henry IV.

On 30 August we had a perfect day on the Rhine, taking the steamer from Mainz to Cologne. As we passed Bonn, I noticed a large building on the shore, with the sign *Frauen-Klinik*. A German and his wife with whom I had been engaged in conversation, gazed on this edifice with especial attention. Then the German said to me, ' My first wife died in that building.' It was rather difficult to know how to reply to that statement. I could not say 'How sad!' for his second wife was with him. And the remark did not call for hilarity or congratulations. Suddenly I thought of one of the most useful words in the German language. I said '*So?*'

When we had entered the train at Nuremberg for Munich on our way to the Passion Play, we found in the compartment a fine looking American father and son, the boy about eighteen. The sign on the railway carriage said *Nach München*. As we were waiting for the train to start, the boy asked his father, 'Does *nach* mean *not*?' 'Yes.' 'Well, then, we must get off,' and they began to haul down their baggage. I asked them where they wished to go, and they said Munich. 'Stay where you are, then!' 'But this train says it is not going to Munich.' I explained the meaning of the word *nach*, and then, wishing to make it easier for them, I said to the boy, 'I suppose you have not studied any German.' 'Oh, yes,' said he, 'I have just passed my entrance exam in German for the Sheffield Scientific School at Yale.'

We started our bicycle trip through southern England on Sunday 2 September, wheeling down Holborn through Cheapside and crossing London Bridge without once having to dismount. The Bow Bells were striking noon. That night we stopped at Rochester, heard Dean Hole preach in the cathedral, and the next morning we called on him. While we were waiting in a room filled with books, I glanced over the shelves, expecting to see works on theology, philosophy, and literature; of the hundreds of books in that room every one was apparently on some form of athletic sport. The Dean entered, a magnificent figure. Over eighty years of age and over six feet in height, with a great mane of snow-white hair, he was gracious and hospitable. He invited us to lunch, but we could not stay. He seemed pleased to know that I came from Yale; said he had immensely enjoyed a visit to Yale, and that he thought Yale was closer to Englishmen than any other American university.

Two weeks later on our bicycle trip, we went to Moor Park in Surrey to see the place where Swift and Stella lived at Sir William Temple's. A wealthy American gentleman from Connecticut had leased the place and was living there. He was most cordial, but wondered why we were particularly interested. When I told him it was on account of Swift and Stella, he laughed and said that although he had been living there a year, he had never heard of either of them. 'I like this place because there is good shooting. I can knock down half a dozen rabbits every morning before breakfast.' He invited us to stay and take tea on the terrace and we had a most agreeable time.

Jane Austen died at Winchester, 18 July 1817. She is buried in Winchester Cathedral and the house where she died is very near the vast church.

We had a curious experience in front of this house. It was a cloudless morning. I asked my wife to take a picture of the front of the house; accordingly the camera was pointed at the front door. This door was closed and there was no one in front of it or near it. The camera clicked.

But when the picture was developed there was a woman dressed in black standing close to the door. We have no explanation whatever for this, so we have decided to call the unknown the ghost of Jane Austen. It was such a clear day that every corner of the porch and of the front door appeared in sharp relief; we could almost have seen a fly. There was absolutely nothing; but there stands the woman in the picture.

On 7 September we bicycled across the Isle of Wight; coming to Tennyson's home at Farringford in the late afternoon, we found the place closed and a care-taker said it would be open to visitors only on the regular day. He was deaf to entreaties and other more practical methods of persuasion. But while he was uttering prohibitions, I saw two ladies enter the gate; and I asked them if we might also enter in, explaining that I had the honour of teaching the poet's works to American undergraduates. They were both relations of the poet, and very kindly took us about the spacious grounds, showing us Tennyson's favourite haunts, his cliff walk, and the place where he wrote *Maud*.

Not long after that, I was talking with two nuns about Tennyson, and they told me that one day in the eighties they were looking at Farringford and that a big man with a beard and smoking a pipe, spoke to them, and asked them if they would like to enter. It was the poet. He took them over the grounds, invited them to his study, and then asked, 'Which of my poems shall I read to you?' They were too overcome to choose; so he read aloud the whole of the *Morte d'Arthur*. They never forgot that tremendous experience; but they also told me that while he was conversing with them immediately after the reading, he stood so close to them that he blew copious clouds of tobacco smoke from his pipe directly into their faces, utterly unaware of the effect; and that one of the sisters as a result was violently sick for two hours after the interview.

On Sunday 29 July I called on the famous Boswell scholar, G. Birkbeck Hill (1835–1903), whose edition of the *Life* far surpassed in value all those that had preceded it. He was 65 years old, and looked feeble; but he was working hard every day and night, and like so many other Englishmen, in the evenings did his minute textual work by the light of candles.

He insisted on my staying to supper. He said the regret of his life was that he had begun scholarly work so late and now 'there was not much time left.' He envied all young scholars. I told him of my admiration for the work of his son-in-law (Mr. Crump) for his admirable editorial work on Landor; Mr. Hill spoke of him with admiration and affection.

I shall never forget Mr. Hill's expressions of tragic grief over the Boer War; he was, like so many other first-rate men of that time, wholly opposed to it. He could not speak of it without crying. The tears ran down his face as he exclaimed 'This wicked, cruel war!'

It was of course a pleasure for me to give him the references he asked for in the following letter.

> I, THE WILDERNESS,
> HOLLY HILL,
> HAMPSTEAD, N.W.
> Nov. 18, 1902

My Dear Professor Phelps,

I should have thanked you earlier for the trouble you have taken about the quotation had I not been in the greatest affliction when I received your letter. My dearest wife died on October 30, after a long illness. We had prayed for her release, so much had she suffered, but when the blow fell it was very grievous. We were but a boy and a girl when we were engaged—forty-eight years ago.

I am supported by the love of my children—never had a man better. In my grandchildren I find also great comfort, so that I do not feel desolate. I am taking up the broken threads of my work as well as I can. During many weeks I could do nothing; but in occupation I shall find great relief. I must try to get my edition of the Lives finished, though it seems to have lost most of its interest.

May I trouble you with another question. Emerson, in Letters and Social Aims 1885, p. 55, says that Ben Jonson said that "Donne for not keeping accent deserved hanging." Can you give me the reference? My edition of Jonson is of 1756. I easily found in it your reference.

You may be interested in the following quotation from Henry Crabb Robinson's Diary, i.340 (Aug. 3, 1811): "I made use of the expression poor Coleridge. 'He is,' said Lamb, 'a fine fellow, in spite of all his faults and weaknesses. Call him Coleridge; I hate *poor*, as applied to such a man. I can't bear to hear such a man pitied.' He then quoted an expression to the same effect by (I think) Ben Jonson or Bacon."

Will you give my kindest remembrances to Professor and Mrs. Lounsbury and their son. I know I shall have their sympathy. It is a pleasure to know that you and Mrs. Phelps are to visit England next year.

Yours very sincerely,

G. BIRKBECK HILL

We returned to America in time for the opening of the Autumn term. On 20 October I went to New York to see a special matinée of Browning's *In a Balcony*. Mrs. LeMoyne was the Queen, Otis Skinner played Norbert, and Constance was played by the beautiful young Eleanor Robson (now Mrs. August Belmont). I had expected to see in Browning's one-act poem only a literary curiosity, but to my surprise the play was thrilling. After the curtain the three players were recalled ten times, and then Mrs. LeMoyne, who was too hoarse to speak, whispered something to Otis Skinner, who came to the footlights and said 'Mrs. LeMoyne wishes to tell the audience never to make fun of Browning again.' Although it was intended to give only this one performance, the success was so overwhelming that the three actors went on tour, playing nightly until the end of June, when one of the final performances was given in New Haven, and I had the pleasure of hearing the play again. In May 1912, on the occasion of the celebration of the centenary of Browning's birth in London, I heard an English company give the same play, and since then I have heard it in New York and elsewhere five or six times; and always it has made a profound impression on the audience.

On the last night of the nineteenth century, 31 December 1900, my wife and I went to Trinity Church on the Green in New Haven, and at midnight while the audience were on their knees, the chimes played *Lead Kindly Light* and so began a new century.

38

THOMAS HARDY

NEARLY fifty years ago I read my first novel by Thomas Hardy. This experience I have often tried in vain to forget. When I was feeling ill, I opened a novel with the agreeable title *A Pair of Blue Eyes*. After I had read about two hundred pages, it appeared that the heroine and the two heroes were in a most unpleasant predicament; I myself saw no way out; but I had read so many novels where unpromising situations were neatly changed that I read on in a fool's paradise, thinking the author would exert his magic in the right way. I have since often advised those who read this novel to stop when they are about two-thirds of the way through, and then ask themselves this question—What is the worst possible way in which this story can reach a conclusion? No reader can imagine an ending more shatteringly tragic than the one provided. When I came to that last page, I threw the volume across the room; I vowed I would never read another novel by Thomas Hardy; I went to bed and stayed there one week. Such was the effect produced on me by a pair of blue eyes. Within a year I had read every one of his books.

He seemed to me the foremost living English novelist and to belong to the great tradition. Hence I was eager to meet him.

As it turned out, I forced myself upon his leisure in a way that I suppose is unpardonable; and yet, although I repent some of my sins, I have never felt any regret for this.

On our bicycle tour in 1900, which had begun in London, we reached Dorchester in the moonlight Saturday evening, 8 September, and put up at the King's Arms. Sunday morning I walked to Hardy's house, Max Gate, and found a large sign on the front door, 'Not at home.' Accordingly, I knocked, and when I asked the maid if Mr. Hardy were at home, she replied with another question. She pointed to the sign and asked if I could read. I asked in turn if she could, and if so, what were her favourite books? She was taken aback and perhaps thought I was insane. I explained that I knew I had no business to be there, but that I was an American who adored her master; and if she would explain to him that I was not a newspaper reporter, that I wished to see him only for a few moments, I should never forget her kindness. I never have. She went to the door of a room that I was to enter myself twenty-eight years later and knocked. Soon she returned and said Mr. Hardy would see me at three o'clock.

At three I was at the front door again and just in front of it was Thomas Hardy. He was sixty years old. Like me, he was clad in knickerbockers, with an aged jacket and a straw hat, the only Englishman I ever saw with that head-gear. He was small and slight in stature and figure, looking rather frail and depressed, with grey face and grey moustache. We sat down on a bench in the open air. Although at this first interview he neither laughed nor smiled, he was, after the first moments, exceedingly gracious, kindly, and sympathetic. He was grave rather than sad. He spoke of the wickedness of shooting game birds, of killing any animals; 'wickedness' was the word he used. I reminded him of Emerson's poem beginning 'Hast thou named all the birds without a gun?' but somewhat injured the effectiveness of the quotation and my own reputation by confessing that I often went shooting in America.

Discussing literature, I told him that I should have

known by the structure of his novels that he had been a practising architect; even if he had not used architects as leading characters in *A Laodicean* and *A Pair of Blue Eyes*; that the structure of his novels was evidence enough, and that the manner in which buildings were described, as in *Two on a Tower*, revealed the architect. He said *A Laodicean* contained more of the facts of his own life than anything else he had ever written. That was published in 1881; during its composition he was dangerously ill, and did not believe he could recover. He thought it was his last illness, and perhaps that was why he put in so much of himself. (It would have interested him during those painful weeks of illness if he had known that he was to live on forty-seven years.)

He said he thought the novelist ought always to *tell a story*; that a novel should be constructed with a definite plot.

He then asked me what I thought of his poetry; he had published his first volume of verse, *Wessex Poems*, only two years past, in 1898, with illustrations made from his own drawings. I wish I had then liked the poems as I do now; I could not believe they stood so much higher than the novels in his own estimation, that they were so close to his heart. He was evidently pained when I told him that of course I found them interesting reading, but that I felt they were not so great as his works in prose. He spoke quite strongly about this. He thought they were far superior to any of his novels and that many of his more discerning friends had told him so. I did not know then what I knew in later years, that he had ceased to care about his novels; he did not wish to discuss them. He wished to be considered and remembered only as a poet. Instead of a great novelist writing verse as an avocation, he wished to be regarded as an English poet, who had written some stories in prose. It may be that posterity will so remember him. He had at all events the dearest wish of his life granted. His career as a novelist lasted twenty-five years; his career as a poet, beginning when he was fifty-eight, lasted thirty years. And although he did not publish poetry until late in life, he had been writing verse since boyhood.

I have always regretted that none of his subsequent volumes of poems was, like the first one, adorned with pictures by his own hand. I admire the illustrations he provided for *Wessex Poems*.

We talked for three-quarters of an hour. I had stood up to go after a few minutes, but he had urged me to stay. Finally, when I was taking leave, he asked, 'Is your wife with you?' and when I told him, he asked 'Why didn't she come?' I replied that she did not have the nerve. He cordially invited us both to tea with Mrs. Hardy and himself the following afternoon at five o'clock.

I told him I would rather do that than anything else on earth, but that we were both on a schedule, that in a few days we had to sail for America, and that we had reserved the following day for bicycling all over the country described in his novels, and I did not see how we could do that and still come to tea. He said, 'Leave it this way; Mrs. Hardy and I will be in the garden anyhow at five o'clock tomorrow. If you and Mrs. Phelps can come, we shall be glad to see you; and if you don't appear, we shall quite understand.'

Walking back to the King's Arms, I had an inspiration. The sky was clear and I remembered the harvest moon was due. I suggested to my wife that we bicycle all night through the Hardy country, reach Salisbury, and take the train back to Dorchester, thus accomplishing both objects—seeing the literary landscape and having tea with the Hardys. All we should lose would be a night's sleep. Without a moment's hesitation she agreed, and about five o'clock we mounted our bicycles and wheeled to Puddle-town (the Weatherbury of *Far From the Madding Crowd*). We entered the old church and studied the inscriptions on the graves in the churchyard. Then we went on to Egdon Heath. We reached the vast and sinister Heath just as day was giving way to darkness and saw it exactly as it is described in the early pages of *The Return of the Native*.

> In fact, precisely at this transitional point of its nightly roll into darkness the great and particular glory of the Egdon waste began, and nobody could be said to understand the heath who had not been there at such a time. . . . The sombre stretch of rounds and hollows seemed to rise and meet the evening gloom in pure sympathy, the heath exhaling darkness as rapidly as the heavens precipitated it. And so the obscurity in the air and the obscurity in the land closed together in a black fraternization towards which each advanced half-way.
>
> The place became full of a watchful intentness now; for when other things sank brooding to sleep the heath appeared slowly to awake and listen. Every night its Titanic form seemed to await something; but it had waited thus, unmoved, during so many centuries, through the crises of so many things, that it could only be imagined to await one last crisis—the final overthrow.

And while we were looking at this tremendous scene and thinking of the words describing it, suddenly the full moon rose and flooded the dark waste with silver light. That was one of the unforgettable moments of our lives.

We wheeled on through the silent night. There were no clouds, there was no wind and we never met a human being. It was as if we were alone in a dead world illumined by the moon. The outlines of churches stood out in the strong light as clear as noonday. We caught a little sleep toward dawn at a wayside inn. Then we pushed on to Salisbury, and reached the railway station only a few minutes before the train left. I gave our wheels to a man in uniform, asking him to keep them for us till the next day; and we entered the train for Dorchester.

At five o'clock we walked into the gardens at Max Gate. Mr. and Mrs. Hardy were there. Mr. Hardy said, 'Oh, then, you didn't take your bicycle trip!' 'But we did!' and when we explained, he held up both hands in amazement, and exclaimed 'These Americans!'

Mr. Hardy was almost covered with cats. Three or four cats were on various parts of his person, other cats were near at hand, and I noticed saucers of milk placed at strategic points in the shrubbery. 'Are all these your own cats?' 'Oh, dear, no, some of them are, and some are cats who come regularly to have tea, and some are still other cats, not invited by us, but who seem to find out about this time of day that tea will be going.' I said I was a fanatical cattist and was enchanted to have their company.

Mr. Hardy told me that at any time he could dig almost anywhere in his garden and find Roman remains, that once he had found the skeleton of a Roman soldier with his armour and other implements. I reflected that whenever he sat at his desk to write, he was competing not only with his contemporaries, but with twenty centuries. I think these centuries of human habitation gave to his writing a grave sincerity that perhaps it could not have had in a newly-settled land.

Mrs. Hardy was an artist, and in the house she was kind enough to show us many of her pictures. I told her I thought her husband was the greatest of living English writers. She said she liked his earlier novels better, and did not care much for the latest ones. I suppose she had in mind *Jude the Obscure*. She was a devout, orthodox Christian, and in those days some of his later work rather shocked her, I think. I then told her what he himself had said on the previous day about *A Laodicean*. 'Yes, when he wrote that he thought he was on his deathbed. He was suffering terribly, and dictated the whole novel to me, being too ill to hold a pen.'

Mr. Hardy was even more genial on this afternoon than during our conversation of Sunday. He was kindness itself, and seemed to be in almost radiant humour. We stayed two hours, and we shall never forget such kindness and hospitality.

That evening at the King's Arms we sat at dinner with a young lady who was the daughter of the famous publisher Kegan Paul. She said she would have given anything to have that interview with the Hardys, but she added 'I should never have had the brass to go there.' There was also at table a young Englishman, Mr. Eaton, of Cambridge, who walked with us to the train the next morning, and was exceedingly amiable.

Mrs. Hardy died in 1912; in 1914 he was married again. The second Mrs. Hardy not only made the last fourteen years of his life happy, but her inspiration was so strong that he continued to write and publish original poems up to the very end. He was extremely fortunate in both marriages, and in a short poem he paid a beautiful tribute.

> But soon or later, when you hear
> That he has doffed this wrinkled gear,
> Some evening, at the first star-ray,
> Come to his graveside, pause and say:
>
> ' Whatever his message—glad or grim—
> Two bright-souled women clave to him';
> Stand and say that while day decays;
> It will be word enough of praise.

Well, late one afternoon I stood by his grave at Dorchester in company with Mrs. Florence Hardy; and she told me that on the same day that his ashes were placed in Westminster Abbey, his heart was placed in this grave with his first wife.

After these two September days in 1900 I did not see Dorchester again until September 1928; then I spent a day there with Mrs. Hardy and stroked the beautiful cat that had been given to him toward the end of his life. She said that up to his last very brief illness, Mr. Hardy showed no sign of physical or mental decline. He took long walks, his hearing was perfect, he could read all he wanted to, and he composed poetry almost up to the last day. He died in his eighty-eighth year.

In May 1932 we were there again and stayed overnight at Max Gate. We had the pleasure of calling on Mr. Hardy's sister Katherine, a charming woman. Mrs. Hardy showed us the graves in the garden at Max Gate of their favourite dogs and cats. The tombstones were designed by him and the inscriptions prepared.

She told us of his last illness, and of how he asked her to read to him *Rabbi Ben Ezra*; she paused in the middle of the poem, but he signalled to her to read it to the end. He died on the evening of 11 January 1928, and she said that *an hour after his death* she came again to his bedside, and saw on his face such an expression as she had never seen on any human countenance. 'It was a look of radiant triumph such as imagination could never have conceived.'

Mrs. Hardy told us that although her husband was wholly English and wrote almost exclusively on English themes and of English people, he had the deepest conviction of the brotherhood of mankind, and lived consistently in harmony with this creed. During the war there was a large German prison-camp near Dorchester; the prisoners were assigned to various tasks in the neighbourhood. Mr. Hardy took a personal interest in every German prisoner who worked on his place. He gave food and medicines, treating them not only with solicitude for their welfare, but with respect for them as individuals. Now no one was more eager than Mr. Hardy for England's triumph in the war. But his clear intelligence was never clouded by prejudice, and his heart was too big and tender not to be touched by human suffering. It is pleasant to know that these Germans were grateful, that they wrote to their families in Germany about him, and that a letter came back saying that as a result of his consideration, the English prisoners in that part of Germany were receiving better treatment.

Mrs. Hardy told me that 'T.E.Lawrence' was one of their dearest and most intimate friends; that whenever he was in England he always came to their house and stayed with them; and she said with great earnestness, 'In his personal character and habits of life and speech and thought he is more like Jesus Christ than any person I have ever known.'

Mrs. Hardy's biography of her husband, in two volumes, is an admirable work; it tells readers all that readers have a right to know. It has dignity without dulness.

She was kind enough to take us in her motor to have lunch with Mr. and Mrs. St. John Ervine at their home in Seaton, in Devonshire. On the way we stopped at Lyme Regis, and I made the jump in memory of the famous scene in Jane Austen's *Persuasion*.

Mrs. Hardy disliked anything that savoured of chauvinism; she felt that the Religion of Nationalism was evil. At the dinner given by Sir James Barrie in 1928, I sat between Mrs. Bernard Shaw and Mrs. Hardy. I asked Mrs. Shaw in what part of England she was born; and she replied with considerable emphasis, 'Why, I was not born anywhere in England. I am an Irishwoman!'

Mrs. Hardy whispered to me, 'I don't like to hear her say that; I don't see why anyone should be so proud or so glad of their nationality. I am an Englishwoman and love England; but I have sometimes felt that I should have been glad to be of another country.' And I asked, 'Have you felt that way about any particular country?' 'Yes, I have sometimes wished I were French, and at other times I have wished I were an American.'

I think she was really glad to be an Englishwoman, but she felt that nationalism was a danger and that it led to misunderstandings and to war. She was pro-human and had boundless sympathy for humanity.

At the funeral of Hardy in Westminster Abbey in 1928 the choice of pallbearers emphasized the poet and dramatist, rather than the novelist—Sir James Barrie, Bernard Shaw, Rudyard Kipling, Alfred E. Housman, John Galsworthy, Sir Edmund Gosse. Every one of these men, except Mr. Housman, published novels; but Barrie and Shaw were known almost exclusively as dramatists, Galsworthy was as well known as a playwright as a novelist, Kipling was more distinguished for his poetry than his prose, Gosse was a poet and critic, and Housman a lyrical poet.

From the king to the humblest peasant, there was sincere mourning for the death of Hardy; his eminence in four fields of art—architecture, prose-fiction, drama, and lyrical poetry—would have made him a world figure; but the beauty of his character, his sympathy, kindliness, modesty, gentleness, made an equally deep impression.

In the *New York Herald Tribune* for 22 January there was an article by Ford Madox Ford on Thomas Hardy which contained the astounding statement that Ford heard Hardy say he was a practising member of the Anglican Church. To be sure, Samuel Butler said that his own views were the same as those held by the advanced wing of the Broad Church; but the diabolical Butler was a master of irony, and that remark was a two-edged sword. Hardy had less of hypocrisy than of anything else. If he was reported as saying that he loved the church ritual and often attended the services, well and good; he was brought up in the Church, was an ecclesiastical architect, and must have loved the old traditions. Probably no man ever had less respect for God and more respect for His house. But a practising member? Then John Morley was a Fundamentalist and Leslie Stephen an Evangelical Methodist.

I asked Mrs. Hardy about this, and she replied that he never was a practising or believing member of any church; Mr. Ford might have heard Hardy say something sympathetic or appreciative about the church service.

I have always regarded *The Return of the Native* as his masterpiece; it is a desolating tragedy as it stands, but he seems at one time in its composition to have wished to make it even more so. I received the following letter from the American publishers, Harper and Brothers.

MAY 9, 1928

Mr. William Lyon Phelps
Yale University
New Haven, Conn.

DEAR MR. PHELPS:

Mr. Thomas Wells, the editor of our Magazine, has suggested that I write to you as one who knows more about the various editions of Hardy's *The Return of the Native* than anyone else in the country. One of our authors has asked us if we know anything of a note written by Hardy to the effect that Book VI of *The Return of the Native* was added to please the public. Our author says that such a note exists, but no edition can be found which contains it.

I am wondering if you can give us any light on this inquiry.

Sincerely yours,

FRANK S. MacGEEGER

In this letter my knowledge was like Mark Twain's death. But in my copy of Professor Samuel Chew's book *Thomas Hardy as Poet and Novelist*, which had just been published that year (1928) I read the following paragraph (p.40).

One may well question the grim note which Hardy, in the definitive edition of the book (*The Return of the Native*), appended to it, to the effect that only the exigencies of periodical publication caused him to arrange an ending with the marriage of the two children of the heath and requesting readers of 'an austere artistic code' to imagine that Thomasin remained a widow and that Venn disappeared from the country-side.

My younger colleague at Yale, Prof. Richard Purdy, who *is* an authority on Hardy, was kind enough to give me the following information.

By 'definitive edition' Professor Chew must refer to the costly limited and signed Mellstock Edition. The note has not been retained in either the American Harpers or the English Macmillan standard editions—at least the current issues of those editions.

8, ADELPHI TERRACE,
STRAND, W.C.2.
26th March 1929

DEAR PROFESSOR LYON-PHELPS:

I hope that you and Mrs. Lyon-Phelps are both well. I often think of our pleasant meetings. Sir James Barrie was not well at Christmas —a sharp attack of bronchitis—but he is well now—indeed I lunched with him today. He has been the kindest friend possible during the sad days. . . .

I am so glad that you like *Winter Words*. Some of the poems I think are poignant beyond anything else that I have ever read, notably 'He resolves to say no more.' They tear my heart, because I think that if he could have recovered from that illness he could have written more. I miss him more than ever; the thought of returning to Max Gate to live alone there is almost more than I can bear.

With every good wish and my affection to Mrs. Lyon-Phelps and yourself, and my most grateful thanks,

Ever yours sincerely,

FLORENCE HARDY

MAX GATE,
DORCHESTER, DORSET
8th August 1929

DEAR WILLIAM LYON PHELPS:

So many thanks for your letter. It was like a kindly hand stretched across the ocean giving me help and encouragement.

J.M.Barrie is not looking very well, I think, but the hot weather in London has tried him very much, and also the journey to Edin-burgh and back the week before last, when he received the freedom of the city, and also he has been looking after someone in a nursing-home who had a bad motor accident. There is no one I know who exerts himself more for any friend who may be ill or in trouble than J.M.B. . . .

My love to you both,

FLORENCE HARDY

MAX GATE,
DORCHESTER, DORSET
4th January 1932.

DEAR PROFESSOR LYON PHELPS,

Your letter was the first I opened on New Year's day. It was so kind of you to write. I do send you and Mrs. Lyon Phelps my very best wishes. I hope I shall see you when you are in England. . . .

I have not seen the Bernard Shaws since that book was published, but Colonel T.E.Lawrence, who saw them off when they left England a fortnight ago says they did not mind the book (I expect that Mrs. G.B.S. disliked it) and that G.B.S. allowed it to be published for the sake of Harris's widow.

I hope you were pleased with Sir James Barrie's little story in the Times. The post that brought me your letter brought also one from his only surviving sister Margaret, and she was very excited about it. The last paragraph I thought very fine. He spent Christmas in Dorset, not here, but at Mells, the home of Lavy Horner, and he is now, I think, at Stanway. He has not been well this autumn but is better now I think—and hope. . . .

I long to go to America, but the force that seems to hold me at Max Gate may perhaps prevent me ever leaving England.

I am grateful—eternally grateful for what you say and write about T.H. I wish I could hear you lecture.

With my love and devotion to you both,

Affectionately,

FLORENCE HARDY

MAX GATE,
DORCHESTER, DORSET
TELEPHONE, DORCHESTER 43
6th November '32

DEAR BILLY—

It was kind of you to write and I loved having news of you both. I hope you are both well. I shall look forward immensely to having your new book on Browning. This is my only address at present. I may go to London later for a few weeks, but that is uncertain. Anything will find me here, and I should be backwards and forwards in any case.

I gave your kind message to my sister-in-law—Katherine Hardy—and she was delighted to know that you remembered her.

I have not seen J.M.B. for a little time, but I had a letter from him a few days ago, asking for news of me as I had not written to him or been to see him for some time. I have been too busy to go to London. But Aircraftman Shaw (Colonel T.E.Lawrence) told me last week that Peter Davies (J.M.B.'s adopted son) had told him that ' Barrie was growing old.' Almost impossible to believe. J.M.B. told me that his visit to Scotland did him a lot of good as the air there suits him so well. I *must* go to see him soon, even if I make a special journey to London for that purpose.

With every good wish and my love to you both,

Affectionately,

FLORENCE HARDY

5, ADELPHI TERRACE,
STRAND, W.C.2.
Sunday, April 29th, '34

MY DEAR BILLY:

Yes, indeed I am in the Adelphi—sitting writing at this moment by a window from which if I raise my eyes I see Cleopatra's needle just in front—& beyond a wonderful view of the Thames, with barges sliding by—& just beneath this room is the beautifully decorated room where Mrs. Garrick gave that famous party to Dr. Johnson, Boswell and others two years after Garrick's death. . . .

Enough of my flat. Thank you so much for sending that cutting, & for the kind words. I did not select the poems. T.H. did. He certainly asked my advice but I think he always held by his own judgment. E. Gosse always thought that *I* selected the poems—but he was wrong.

I am sorry you & Annabel are not to be in Europe this summer as I should have loved to see you both. However, I shall hope to see you in 1935—all being well. Barrie has been keeping pretty well this spring—much better than he was last year. . . .

On Wednesday I go back to Max Gate for a few days but I shall be back here before you receive this I hope—& Max Gate is always a safe address—at least for this year. I do not know about next.

I often think of your jump from the Cobb at Lyme Regis.

All good wishes & love to you both.

Ever sincerely,

FLORENCE HARDY

On 15 May 1937 Mrs. Hardy wrote me she was going into a nursing home 'for a little while.' I thought she had no suspicion of the serious nature of her illness; but my colleague, Richard Purdy, believes she was quite aware of it. It was like her not to complain. Professor Purdy, an admirable research scholar, frequently visited Dorchester in preparation for his studies in Hardy's works; and Mrs. Hardy gave him every assistance possible. He saw her during her last illness. She died of cancer in the Autumn.

Apart from her position as the wife of Thomas Hardy, she was extremely interesting because of herself; she was one of the finest women I have known.

MAX GATE
DORCHESTER, DORSET
16th August 1936

DEAR BILLY:

Your letter, with its generous and characteristic writing was a joy to receive. I hope you are well, and your Annabel. It was so sad that I missed you when you were in London last year. I do not know how that happened. I wish you were coming this summer.

Richard Purdy is on his way to England—indeed I think the boat arrives tonight—for he is due to be in London tomorrow, and I believe he is coming to see me on Tuesday or Wednesday.

I had a visit from Sir James Barrie three weeks ago, and he seemed very well indeed. He did not say much about his play, except that it is to be produced in London in October.

Margaret Kennedy (Mrs. David Davis) asked me some while ago to go with her to the first performance in Edinburgh that month, but I think I will wait until it comes to London. I sincerely hope that Elizabeth Bergner's health will not fail her again.

My husband's sister Katherine Hardy is quite well I rejoice to say, though she has had some slight illnesses early in the year. I see her very often. I told her you had asked after her in your letter, and she was very pleased that you had remembered her, and she said 'I was thinking of him only the other day.' I, too, think of you often, and always when I hear or speak of the Cobb at Lyme Regis, where you walked, and from which you jumped. I hope you will walk there again.

With greetings to you both,

Yours ever,

FLORENCE HARDY

39

ROOSEVELT AND RILEY

AT the Bicentennial celebration of Yale University (founded in 1701) in October, Theodore Roosevelt, who had within a few weeks become President of the United States (McKinley died 14 September) received an honorary degree and made a characteristic speech. In the afternoon he was like a caricature of himself; and yet evidently sincere. I was Head Usher and presented individually to him an interminable line of men. He was not allowed to shake hands with anyone, because McKinley had been shot while doing so; he held his hat in both hands and it was evident that he chafed under the enforced restraint. Whenever a famous athlete appeared in the line and I mentioned his name, the President would release one hand and grasp him around the neck and say 'It's a darned shame I can't shake hands with you, old man!'

Among the men of letters who received honorary degrees, Howells, Aldrich, etc., Mark Twain received the loudest and most prolonged applause.

One of the most picturesque figures was Archbishop Ireland; in his ecclesiastical robes, he attracted much attention.

While I was standing near President Hadley at the evening reception, a delegate from Sweden, covered with medals, was presented. He addressed Hadley *in Latin*, making a fairly long speech. The moment he finished, Hadley replied in equally fluent Latin.

I first met Riley at Indianapolis in the late nineties; some ladies took us to lunch at the Country Club, and before we started, they said the shortest and pleasantest way to drive was through the cemetery, asking us if we had any objection. 'I should like it very much,' said Riley; 'because some day I shall drive there and won't have to come back.' Not long after that, I persuaded Riley to give a reading from his poems at New Haven. I went to his room at the hotel about five o'clock, and found him in a state of absolute hysteria. He was walking up and down in his room like a caged wild beast, shouting out his woes, 'Oh, my God, why did I agree to do this, why, oh, why?' I said, 'After you have had a good dinner, you'll feel better.' 'Dinner? Hear him talk! dinner! I haven't eaten a mouthful all day. I could not possibly eat.'

I thought I had better go, and he screamed 'Don't leave me! stay with me! What will happen to me if you go?' It is impossible to exaggerate his agony of mind; and I wondered why he ever consented to appear in public when it produced such suffering. I tried to tell him that he wasn't going to lecture, did not have to think of anything to say; all he had to do was to recite his poems. It was no use. He remained in this excruciating torture until it was time to go to the lecture, and he was exactly in that same frame of mind behind the curtain, so I feared he would break down. But the instant he appeared before the immense audience, he was wholly at ease, gave a marvellous recital of his poems, and seemed to enjoy doing it; and certainly enjoyed the tumultuous applause. After the lecture, I took him to the Graduates' Club, where, not having eaten anything all day, he ate a huge dinner and was in the highest spirits. I could not help asking him if he always suffered agony during the hours preceding his appearance in public. 'Always.' 'But I should think you would remember that you had done it before and always enjoyed it.' 'No, that doesn't do any good at all.'

Riley was the man of his works. He was kindly, lovable, full of fun, generous, a loyal and devoted friend. He was one of the best men I have ever known, and although he kept up a stream of profanity in conversation, his profanity never seemed vulgar; it was lyrical; and spoken in that soft, gentle voice, seemed a natural manner of emphasis. He never could see anything in the poetry of Walt Whitman. Without raising his voice, he would purl along, 'Old Walt found the —— —— stuff he wrote wasn't worth a —— ——; so he mixed up a lot of —— —— nonsense, and fooled the whole —— —— world.' He was laughing all the time he said this.

The National Institute of Arts and Letters gave Riley the Gold Medal for his poetry. At that time he was very ill, and the medal was sent to him with an appropriate message. I was present at the Institute meeting when the matter was being discussed. It was suggested that at the end of the telegram, three words be added—'God bless you.' Some members objected to this, thinking it was not dignified; but finally the blessing was added to the telegram. Riley unexpectedly recovered from this illness; and when I was talking with him one day about the vote on the medal, I remarked that some men thought the message 'God bless you!' was lacking in dignity. 'Then,' said Riley, laughing, 'why didn't they simply send the message "You have been awarded the gold medal for original poetry. God damn you!"'

Riley thought both pessimism and the philosophy of defiance were either affectations or mere arrogance. After he was crippled, someone read aloud to him Henley's familiar lines and when he had finished the last words,

> I am the Master of my fate,
> I am the Captain of my soul,

'The *hell* you are,' said Riley with a laugh.

After Riley had had a stroke, he spent a good deal of time in his automobile being slowly driven around town in Indianapolis. On one of these days, I was with him, when a car passed us containing four or five ladies, everyone wearing the broad hats of the period tied down with veils. Riley looked at them wonderingly and then murmured 'Why do they wear those —— —— hats?'

I asked him if he believed in immortality. He looked at me in amazement. 'Why, of course, we aren't going to die. I shall live right on after my body is buried. There isn't any doubt about it.' And there wasn't in his mind. He had never been interested in spiritualism or in 'messages;' he simply had absolute faith in personal survival.

In response to a request from him, I sent him two essays I had printed on Jane Austen and on Stevenson, and received the following letter:

INDIANAPOLIS, NOV. 28, 1906

DEAR FRIEND: . . . thanks for your just and fine Austen tribute— though her genius is subtly ingenuous as that of Irving in his real characters on the stage—(as hers are on the page). The Stevenson book is just here—so I've barely struck hands with it yet and clapped it on the shoulder. What a man of kidney was R.L.S. No intellectual Bright's disease about that lovely cuss! Lor' don't you love him! Sir Walter, even—for all the start he's got—won't outlast him! And now the pawkie twa o' them are aye toegither! Oh, it's hame!— hame!—hame!—It's there I'm goin' to be, Wi' Weelum Lyon Phelps himsel to gang along wi' me!

All best hails to you and your household, and to your friends that are mine down around 'The Academic Works.' As always your fraternalest,

JAMESY

John Sargent's portrait of Riley in the gallery at Indianapolis is a work of genius. It has that *diablerie* characteristic of his expression when swearing volubly; for I never heard him swear when he was not also laughing. 'When you say that, *smile*.' He looks in the portrait exactly as he must have looked when he described his vain attempt to meet me at the railway station in Indianapolis. He was as helpless as a baby in everything to do with trains or topography. He wrote me that he had gone to the station one hour ahead of time in order to be sure of seeing me, and after all, he failed. He added, 'I could have wept, had not the Almighty given me the blessed gift of cussin'.'

The prophet without honour in his own country was never true of Riley. He was more beloved and honoured in his own town than anywhere else, even though he received a tremendous reception in England. The better he was known personally, the more he was admired. The State of Indiana keeps his birthday as a legal holiday.

In 1902 Yale gave Riley the honorary degree of Master of Arts, the first academic recognition from a great university. I had arranged to entertain him at my house in New Haven, when I had a sudden recurrence of the malady that had laid me low the preceding winter. The physician told me to leave immediately for our summer home in Michigan. My mother and my brother Dryden entertained him, and the Dean of the College, Henry P. Wright, told me that Riley received more applause at Commencement than all the rest of the 'honorary degree' men put together.

NEW HAVEN,
June 26, 1902

Dr. William Lyon Phelps

My Dear Friend:
   This is all pure magic—Dr. Riley here in your own library writing to you whose presence is so longed for! But Heaven bless you for so promptly going in your health's behalf—besides here in your lovely home I have found your gentle welcoming mother and brother, who gave your home over to me, though I offered them fairest opportunity

to leave me quartered at the hotel—for we arrived late at night and there lodged—going to find your people and explain at 10 next morning.

Well—I just *cannot* realize all that has followed. It is *exchantment*, simply! Professor Beers has been a very brother through it all—and your brother likewise. Dr. Hadley was an inspired man throughout all the ceremonies of yesterday—yea, and last night at reception at Art Building, where your brother took me, 'and the world went well with me then, then, oh then!' But you'll hear of the success of everything through the press and your friends—never a hitch in any particular that I'm aware of. Even read a poem (bran' span fresh and new) though in no wise pertinent to the occasion—which I priorly explained to committee, and they said *Give it*—and I done give it and it seemed to 'go' in really very great shape! We may be going on to New York today, where (utter confidence) I've a new book in press. . . .

All your home-folks send love to you and Mrs. Phelps with this most grateful greeting of your affectionate old friend,

JAMES WHITCOMB RILEY

In 1888 I had seen Riley in the distance at Chautauqua, and this interview with him (author unknown) contains material not easily available elsewhere. It is taken from the 'Walks and Talks' column in Chautauqua Assembly *Daily Herald* of August 1888.

James Whitcomb Riley is a new name on the Chautauqua program, but a name firmly entrenched in public favor by two entertainments which must be counted among the hits of the season. He proved himself such a genius in the field of dialect poetry that he might safely be called the Robert Burns of America. One thing is certain—he is sure of a hearty welcome should he ever visit Chautauqua again. I had a chat with him in his room at the hotel after his last entertainment. I asked him, "How did you happen to choose such a peculiar field." He replied to my question, "I wanted to be an actor, from the time I began to take part in school entertainments in my little native town. When I was a child my father, who was a lawyer and an eccentric man, used to dress me up in quaint clothes and take me to the Courtroom. Left to myself I studied the faces of country lawyers and witnesses from the farms, and unconsciously acquired their peculiar dialect. Afterwards I joined a strolling company of actors, but my sense of the histrionic exactness prevented me from reciting what another man had written. I began to create my own characters, language and all, and now and then would acknowledge the authorship. Sometimes I would publish a dialect poem, but no one would give me anything for it until I received a letter from the poet Longfellow concerning one of my poems, in which he said: 'I believe it shows true poetic faculty and insight.' After that it was easy enough—I had at last gained recognition." This interview closed with the remark, "I cannot travel with a trunk. I am continually haunted by the fear that it will be lost; and so I go about the country with a grip. I keep a tenacious hold upon it all day long, and never feel quite safe about it at night. In case there is ever a fearful railway accident, and among the debris is discovered a valise with an arm attached to it firmly, they may bury it without further identification as the fragments of the Hoosier Poet."

40

EVENTS IN 1902

SICKNESS, MAETERLINCK, WISTER, WHITTIER

ON 3 January 1902, looking out of the windows of the railway berth as we crossed to St. Louis, I saw the Mississippi River for the first time. The broad stream was filled with huge masses of ice.

When I was returning East, W.J.Bryan occupied the seat in front of mine, and wrote incessantly—probably an editorial for *The Commoner*. As I left the train I wished him a happy New Year, and he shook hands cordially.

On Saturday 8 February I played hockey on the ice at Lake Whitney all the afternoon. I was never to play that game again. The next morning I was unpleasantly surprised by a sudden appearance of acute kidney disease. I went to my family physician, Dr. J.P.C.Foster, in whom I had well-placed confidence. He told me, after a laboratory analysis the next day, to take no exercise in the way of games or violent exertion, to give up all outside work except teaching in college, and not to worry. He said he could take me to a New York specialist, but it would not be necessary. Although I did not expect to recover, I went ahead with my regular work in the university, giving up outside engagements; and with occasional setbacks, I became entirely well. But I did not play golf until April and no tennis until the next year and never hockey.

One reason I trusted Dr. Foster, a G.P., was because I knew of the experience of an undergraduate friend of mine a few years previously. He told me he had some trouble and wished to know of a good physician. I sent him to Dr. Foster and said, 'Do exactly what he tells you.' The Doctor found he had acute Bright's Disease, but insisted he could cure him. The boy felt he was not progressing rapidly enough, and wished to see a specialist. Dr. Foster took him to the most famous man in New York, who after examination, asked him if he wanted to know the truth. The boy did; and the specialist told him he could not live six months. Two years later, he won the mile run in the university track meet; and is alive and well today.

A grimly amusing thing happened while I was being examined that first evening in Doctor Foster's office. I was pretty sure that my trouble meant death; I thought I was doomed. While he was examining me, his daughter in the next room began to play Chopin's Funeral March. I burst out laughing and said, 'Doctor, I admire your daughter's skill on the piano; but do you think she selects the most appropriate pieces for your office hours?'

On 3 April we had an interesting and beautiful river journey. We took the steamer *Pocahontas* leaving Norfolk, Virginia, at seven in the morning, and travelled the whole day on the river James, reaching Richmond in the evening. We passed the old tower at Jamestown, thinking of Captain Smith, saw charming old colonial residences like Westover, and enjoyed the cloudless sunshine.

On 19 April I was a Yale delegate to the inauguration of President Nicholas Murray Butler of Columbia; the President of the United States, President Eliot of Harvard, and Harper of Chicago, made addresses.

On 20 December I went to Denver for the first time, to address the Yale Alumni dinner, presided over by Ex-senator Wolcott, who was full of good stories. The weather at Colorado Springs on Christmas Day was unbelievable. In the same latitude in Kansas (neighbouring state) it was two below zero; here it was 80 in the shade, people sitting on the grass, as in summer.

Going out on the old Union Pacific, which I took for sentimental reasons, I was impressed by the immense prairies of western Nebraska, as majestic as the illimitable sea. Returning from Denver, I took the Burlington; the train left at sunset, and as I looked back on Denver, the whole western sky was aflame—El Dorado. There were four or five poor fellows in my car who were sufferers from tuberculosis; I remember particularly one agreeable young man with the too red complexion, who said cheerfully, 'They think I'm very ill; there is really nothing the matter, only a little stomach trouble.' That night he died in his berth.

The hospitality of the Yale men and others in Colorado was warm and generous; and I found it the same when I next visited Denver, 34 years later, in 1936. Only this time what an advance in railway speed! In 1902 my train left Chicago at 5.30 p.m., and arrived in Denver the next evening at midnight. In 1936 I left Chicago at the same hour and arrived in Denver at about eight the next morning. This new stream-lined train often went 115 miles an hour.

In this year 1902 Owen Wister's novel *The Virginian* was published and immediately became a best-seller. Unlike most best-sellers, it has had a steady sale ever since, being today one of the best-known and most widely read American novels of the twentieth century. I called his attention to a tiny slip and to one or two other little specks. The following letter came, and it led to an intimate friendship, broken only by his death 21 July 1938.

SAUNDERSTOWN, R.I. OCT. 8, 1902

MY DEAR SIR:

Thank you most heartily. Shorty could *not* read, and the newspaper either was for Trompas's perusal, or for kindling their fires. The next impression shall benefit by your friendliness. I wish this were the only what you call 'speck'; I find the surface full of them—and of various sorts!

Yours faithfully,

OWEN WISTER

In 1902 Maurice Maeterlinck produced his play *Monna Vanna* which had immediate and widespread success. It was translated into many European languages and was a favourite with playgoers in Continental capitals. It was forbidden in England because the theme turned on the moral problem of whether a wife were justified in giving herself for a night to the commander of an army attacking her country, if by so doing she could save her country from invasion, conquest, and destruction. For the hostile commander promised that if she would come to his tent he would withdraw his army altogether. She agreed to this; feeling that if men were praised for giving their lives for their country, she would deserve even higher praise for sacrificing her honour. This decision, however, did not appeal to her husband who regarded her as a degenerate even for considering such an abominable proposal.

I read *Monna Vanna* early in 1903, and was astonished to see that one of the scenes was so similar psychologically to a scene in Browning's almost forgotten play *Luria* (1846), that I felt it could not be a coincidence. It is only an incidental scene and is not concerned with the main plot; but surely only Browning would ever have conceived it. The fact that both plays deal with the war between Florence and Pisa in the 15th century, that the commander of the Florentine forces is an alien (Moor) was not what impressed me; it was the peculiar psychological twist given to an interview between the Florentine diplomat and Prinzivalle, the Moorish general.

I published an article in the New York *Independent*,

not accusing Maeterlinck of plagiarism, but merely calling attention to the amazing similarity of the two
scenes.

James Huneker, at that time drama critic of the *New
York Sun*, wrote an article dismissing my absurd discovery
as typically professorial pedantic stuff and nonsense. The
London *Academy* took the same view. I therefore sent my
article to M. Maeterlinck and received the following letter
by return of post.

67 RUE RAYNOUARD
PARIS
22 Mars 1903

CHER MONSIEUR

Je viens de lire avec intérêt, ds. *The Independent*, la note que vous
avez bien voulu consacrer à *Monna Vanna*. Vous avez parfaitement
raison: il y a entre une scène épisodique de mon 2 acte (celle ou Prinzivalle démasque Trivulzio) et l'une des grandes scènes de *Luria* une
Similitude que je m'étonne de n'avoir pas vu signaler plus tôt. Je
m'en étonne d'autant plus que, loin de cacher cette similitude, j'avais
tenu à l'affirmer moi-même en prenant exactement les mêmes villes
ennemies, la même époque et presque les mêmes personnages; alors
qu'il eut été bien facile de transposer le tous et de rendre l'emprunt
méconnaissable, si j'avais eu l'intention de le dissimuler.

Je suis un lecteur assidu et un ardent admirateur de Browning qui
est selon moi l'un des plus grands poètes que l'Angleterre ait eus.
C'est pourquoi je le considère comme appartenant à la littérature
classique et universelle que tout le monde est censé connaître. Il est
donc licite et naturel de lui emprunter une situation ou plutôt un
fragment de situation, comme on en emprunte journellement à
Eschyle, à Sophocle, à Shakespeare; les emprunts, quand il s'agit de
poète de cet ordre se font, pour ainsi dire, *coram populo*, et constituent
une sorte d'hommage public.

Pour le reste, en mettant à part cet épisode, qui occupe une place si
accidentelle et si accessoire qu'on pourrait le supprimer sans que mon
drame en fut ébranlé, toute ma pièce s'écarte complètement de la
tragédie de Browning et n'a plus rien de commun avec elle. Cette
scène s'élève donc dans mon oeuvre comme une sorte de stèle isolée
que ma mémoire pieuse y a dédiée au souvenir du poète qui avait

créé en mon imagination l'atmosphère où se meut *Monna Vanna*, un souvenir d'un maître entre tous admiré.

Je vous remercie donc bien cordialement de votre amicale communication qui m'a permis d'affirmer ceci, et je vous prie de me croire votre très dévoué

M. MAETERLINCK

I asked his permission to publish his letter and received the following reply:

12 MAI 1903

CHER MONSIEUR:

Votre lettre datée de 26 avril, n'est, je ne sais par quelle erreur de la poste, arrivée qu'hier soir.

Je vous suis très reconnaissant de votre attitude cordiale et très correcte dans cette petite controverse littéraire et je vous en remercie infiniment.

Je ne me souviens plus exactement des termes de ma première lettre—mais comme j'y dis simplement une vérité que je tenais à dire, je ne vois nul inconvenient à ce qu'elle soit publiée telle quelle. Je crois seulement me rappeler que j'y disais que la scène entre Prinzivalle et Trivulzio avait été *empruntée* à Browning. Il serait plus exact de dire qu'elle m'a été *inspirée* par la lecture de *Luria*. C'est d'ailleurs ainsi que ma nouvelle pièce *Joyzelle*, m'a été inspirée par La Tempête de Shakespeare.

S'il semble naturel de chercher un point de départ et un motif d'inspiration dans Shakespeare, pourquoi s'étonnerait-on qu'on le cherche dans Browning?

Merci encore, et croyez-moi, cher monsieur, votre très dévoué

M. MAETERLINCK

The following December (1903) I was in Paris and wrote M. Maeterlinck requesting an interview. He gave me an appointment for six o'clock in the evening. He was living at 67 rue Raynouard. A maid showed me through many long dark corridors and passages, which reminded me of the early plays of the author; finally she knocked at a door, a hearty voice cried '*Entrez!*' and there in a brightly-lighted room, with a pleasant open fire sat the famous Belgian at his desk, writing. In view of the mystical dramas by Maeterlinck, I had expected to see a dreamy bard. But Maeterlinck was just the opposite. He looked like a man fond of beefsteak and ale; he was robust and hearty and genial; perhaps the best word to describe him would be the word *jovial*. He was most cordial. He offered me a cigarette, which I lighted and in my embarrassment I stuck the lighted end in my mouth. Maeterlinck roared with laughter at my discomfiture, which was the best possible thing he could have done, for I immediately felt on intimate terms with him, and we had free and intimate conversation for over an hour. Directly behind him so that he could reach the books without leaving his chair were the Elizabethan Dramatists in the then famous Mermaid Series. The only one missing was the Chapman, which I had edited myself; and I completed his set the next day, for which he was grateful. The bookcase seemed to be full of English and American books; I knew that he had written an introduction to a French translation of Emerson.

I amused him very much by telling him of the account of his French translation of the Elizabethan play by Ford (*'Tis Pity She's a Whore*) which he had translated under the title *Annabella*, and how the news of the Parisian performance had been given in the *New York World*.

THE CARROLLTON
981 MADISON AVE.
Oct. 5th 1903

MY DEAR PROFESSOR PHELPS

Pardon my seeming rudeness—I only read your kind letter yesterday on my return from a six months trip in Europe. I saw Mr. Maeterlinck in Paris and he quite agreed with you; what more can a friendly critic say on the subject!

In action 'Monna Vanna' is much less suggestive of 'Luria' than in the book. The beautiful—and for me the instructive—part of the affair is Maeterlinck's modesty. I'm glad, however, you made us all acknowledge you are in the right, especially as you are!

Sincerely

W.L.Phelps Esq.　　　　　　　　　　　　　　JAMES HUNEKER

This certainly is a handsome letter and it gratified me; I was a little surprised two years later, to read in Mr. Huneker's book *Iconoclasts* (published 1905) on page 428 the following:

> Then I brought up Browning's Luria and the opinion of Professor Phelps of Yale that Maeterlinck had profited by reading the English poet when he composed Monna Vanna. M.Maeterlinck smiled.
> 'Naturally I read Browning; who does not?' he said, with the naive intonation that becomes him so well. '*Luria* I have known for a long time, but *Luria* is not a stage play'; which, coming from the author of *Les Aveugles*, I considered sublime. He is quite right—*Monna Vanna* and *Luria* have little in common except that the scenes of both are laid at Pisa, and that both Luria and Prinzivalle were treated badly by an ungrateful country. But then, so was Coriolanus and a host of other historical patriots.

During the term of 1901–2, I was lecturing to my class in American literature, and the subject for the day being Whittier, I remarked that the Quaker poet had never been married and so far as I knew, had never wished to be. One of the undergraduates, Charles C.Russ of Hartford, came to the desk at the close of the lecture and said, 'I dislike to contradict you, but Whittier proposed to my great-aunt.' I asked him for proof, and he said the family had the letter. In response to my request, young Mr. Russ brought me the letter of Whittier's in which he certainly did propose marriage to Miss Russ. The family kindly gave me permission to print it, and it appeared in *The Century Magazine.*

Mr. Samuel T.Pickard, the leading authority on Whittier, stated in the newspapers that he thought the letter was a forgery. I took the train to Boston, showed him the epistle, and he immediately declared it genuine.

On 12 November John Drinkwater, whose play *Abraham Lincoln* was then attracting universal attention, gave a lecture at Yale. Professor Tarbell told me he had never seen a man whose face exhibited more integrity, more nobility. He made a fine address on the encouragement of good feeling between Great Britain and the United States, and that evening told us about his terrific struggles with the Birmingham Repertory Theatre. At long last success had been attained; had he known what difficulties he was to encounter, he would not have undertaken the thing at all. I thought Drinkwater was not a natural dramatist, and that the play on Lincoln was a fluke; yet his light but charming comedy, *Bird in Hand*, ran for two years in London and in New York.

41

1903

On 9 January in New York I heard for the first time Eleanora Duse, in D'Annunzio's *Francesca*. In order to make money, the play was given in the Metropolitan Opera House, unsuitable for spoken drama. I was bored. And indeed I was never fortunate in hearing the great Duse. During her last journey in America, I heard her in Ibsen's *Ghosts*, and she must have been ill, for she was uninspired.

On 16 January I heard Edward H. Sothern give a commendable performance of *Hamlet* and after the play, John Corbin and I had a pleasant supper with him at the rooms of Miss Purdy. We talked till four o'clock, and Mr. Sothern was very agreeable. Next day we lunched with him at his New York house; he showed us a MS. play by Percy Mackaye, of which he spoke with enthusiasm. I have never met a famous actor more modest and more unaffected than Mr. Sothern. He seemed, however, to be impressed by a book called *It was Marlowe*, which tried to prove that Marlowe wrote Shakespeare's plays. He begged me to read it, so I took it and read it and found it worthless.

On 5 February about ten members of the Yale Faculty went to Bridgeport as guests of Professor Sam Sanford— an elaborate dinner. When the champagne came on in swaddling clothes and before it had been served, Professor Sanford, addressing President Arthur Hadley, said 'I'll bet you can't tell what brand of champagne this is.' To which the university President replied, 'I will tell you not only the brand but the year.' When the wine reached him, he took one sip and immediately gave correctly both brand and year. This seemed to me miraculous, and on the way home I asked the President if he had bluffed. 'Oh, no, I had no difficulty whatever in telling the brand; and I knew that Professor Sanford, being a rich man, would have the best year obtainable. The difficulty was that for this particular brand there were two best years. I admit that I did guess between the two and got it right.' This feat, which still seems to me amazing, was only one more instance of scores illustrating Dr. Hadley's astounding memory. He never forgot anything he had ever seen, heard, tasted, or read. He was the only man on the University Faculty who could have passed the entrance examinations to Yale.

Before the war, he was Roosevelt Exchange Professor at the University of Berlin; he spoke German fluently, having taught it at Yale in his younger days. One night at a state dinner given by the Kaiser, a high official asked Hadley if he could tell the brand of wine that was being served. 'No,' said Hadley, 'because I have never tasted it before.' 'How do you know that?' 'If I had ever tasted it, I should remember it. But although I have never tasted it, it seems to me as if it must have come from an area'—and then he gave a small area near the junction of the Rhine and the Moselle. The official was astounded. 'But that is exactly where it comes from, and the reason you have never tasted it before is because all the wine from that region is reserved for the Kaiser. It is never sold.'

The only allusion I have ever seen referring to any one's ability to discern by tasting it the locality whence came any particular wine is in Goethe's *Wilhelm Meister* (Chapter VIII of the *Travels*). In a letter from Lenardo to his aunt, 'By the wares I sent, you would see how and where I was. By the wines, I doubt not my uncle has tasted out my several places of abode.' (Book I, Chapter VI in German original.)

President Hadley's knowledge was as varied and voluminous as it was exact. He could have filled a professorship
in half a dozen departments, though his speciality was
Economics. He could pour out a stream of information on
widely different subjects. Once, on a ship coming back
from Europe, a lady was so fascinated by listening to his
conversation with his friends, that she finally interrupted
and said 'Sir, I have been listening to your instructive remarks for several days; and I should like to ask you one
question. Of all the things you have studied and upon
which you have reflected, what is the one thing in the
world you think you know best?' Hadley considered this,
and replied, 'I think I know best how to discard at piquet.'

President Hadley was justly proud of his skill at games.
He was admirable at chess and at difficult card games like
skat; he was an excellent lawn tennis player, and fair at
billiards.

In the Spring of this year Sidney Lee gave several lectures at Yale and I had long walks and talks with him. He
was pleased that I had bought both the *Dictionary of
National Biography* and the Oxford Facsimile copy of the
First Folio of Shakespeare, which he had edited the previous year. He had in 1891 succeeded Leslie Stephen as the
Editor of the D.N.B. He told me interesting anecdotes of
Carlyle, Browning, Jowett, and others. He was sometimes
shocked by my American accent. As we were walking, he
asked for the name of a certain building, and I said it was
a physics laboratory. 'Why do you say labora*tory*?' 'Well,'
I replied, 'I don't think I do; but we always accent two
syllables of that word; what do you call it?' He said
'La*bora*try.'

I gave a dinner in his honour, attended by President Hadley, Professor Lounsbury, and others. And on
this visit a friendship began which lasted until his death.

In 1906 I sent him a copy of an article I had written in

the *Yale Courant* containing photographs of various pages of the MS. of Browning's *Dramatis Personae,* then the property of Dr. and Mrs. John Meigs, of the Hill School, in Pottstown, Pennsylvania. This complete manuscript, which Browning had sent to the publishers, and which bears the finger-marks of the type-setters (1864) is now in the Morgan Library in New York. It is interesting in many ways; *Rabbi Ben Ezra* has hardly any corrections; evidently a fair copy. The long poem *Mr. Sludge, the Medium* which infuriated poor Mr. Home so fiercely, is covered with corrections. It must be the only draft in existence; Browning never took the trouble to copy it.

LONDON, 26 DEC. 1906

DEAR PHELPS,

All good wishes for the New Year. I am very much obliged to you for your kindness in sending me the Yale Courant, with your most interesting and valuable article on 'Browning's Dramatis Personae.' It is of great service to know where the MS. is, and I congratulate the Head Master of the Hill School on his good fortune in acquiring it.

I am going through a troubled time. The illness and death of one of my most intimate friends W. J. Craig proved coincident with the falling-ill of my sister who is still in a serious condition. I am at work on some articles for Scribner's Magazine. With very kind regards and pleasant memories of Yale, I am Yours very sincerely,

SIDNEY LEE

In 1913 he was appointed Professor of English Literature in the East London College, and held that post until 1924. He had been knighted in 1911, and died 3 March 1926, at the age of sixty-six.

In the Spring of 1903 there were exciting meetings of the Yale College Faculty, when after long discussions, it was finally voted to give eight elective courses in Freshman Year from which could be chosen five. The bone of contention was whether or not Greek, Latin, and Mathematics should continue to be required studies. On 7 March we

came to a vote, and I give it here because some of the men
who took part were so well known. Affirmative: Dean
Wright, W.G.Sumner, A.Wright, Charlton Lewis, Phelps,
G.M.Duncan, Charles C.Torrey, Hanns Oertel, Gustav
Gruener, James Pierpont, E.H.Sneath, Henry Lang,
H.S.Williams, John C.Schwab, Charles F.Kent, C.H.Smith,
George B.Adams, E.G.Bourne, F.A.Gooch, Henry A.
Beers, Henry C.Emery, Irving Fisher—22. Negative:
Willard Gibbs, Tracy Peck, Thomas D.Seymour, E.P.Mor-
ris, B.Perrin, Horatio Reynolds, Thomas D.Goodell,
A.W.Phillips—8. All but Gibbs and Phillips were profes-
sors of Latin or Greek. This was one of the last appear-
ances of the mathematical genius, Josiah Willard Gibbs,
whom Einstein has called the greatest mind in American
history. He died during the next month, on 28 April.

President Hadley used to say that Gibbs's knowledge of
mathematics began where that of other specialists left off.
I know nothing of what he knew, but I knew him; he was
a quiet, modest sweet-tempered man, with a beautiful
head and face. There is no other adjective to express it. He
was never married, and lived alone with his brother-in-
law, the Yale Librarian, Addison Van Name. He was born
in New Haven, was a Yale graduate, and after some years
of study in France and Germany, was made Professor of
Mathematical Physics at Yale in 1871, and held that position till his death in 1903. He lived only a few doors from
my house in New Haven, and I used to see him taking his
solitary walks; and I thought what an exciting life he
really must be leading, away out on the remote frontiers
of speculative thought. For, as Henry James said, ' There
are no adventures like intellectual ones.'

On Monday 13 April 1903, at nine o'clock in the evening, my mother died. Had she lived until November, she
would have been eighty. Her death was the severest loss
and most bitter grief I have ever felt. She had had a cold,

but colds were common in the last years of her life and there seemed no occasion for alarm. My oldest brother Dryden was living in the house with us, and we also had her cousin Nellie Hubbard, to take care of her. So there seemed to be no reason why my wife and I should not go to Virginia for a few days when the college Easter vacation began on Wednesday 8 April. On Sunday we received a telegram that my mother had pneumonia. We took the night train and were in New Haven about ten the next morning, to receive the greatest shock of my life. My mother was dying; three physicians and two nurses were there, but I shall never know whether or not she recognized me, as she could not speak, even with the aid of the oxygen. I had never believed it possible that my mother, whom I had talked with in the most natural fashion on Wednesday, should in four days be so tragically changed. She died that same evening, and Doctor Walter Judson, whom she had known since he was a boy, said 'There dies the best friend I have ever had.' I could not forgive myself for being absent those last days; I could not forgive myself for a thousand other small things where I could have shown her more tenderness or more consideration. I was overwhelmed. Among the letters we received, the one I liked best was from a Yale undergraduate, Paul Ney. He wrote. 'Ten years ago my mother died; it is just as hard for me to bear now as it was then; and I am glad it is.'

On 8 May I lectured on 'The Novels of Thomas Hardy' at Williams College. Among the undergraduate listeners was Stuart P.Sherman, though I did not know it. In later years he was Professor of English at the University of Illinois and still later, the Editor of the weekly *Books* of the *New York Tribune*. He was the author of many books of literary criticism, and he told Dr. Henry S.Canby that he was first inspired to a literary career by that lecture of mine at Williams.

42

FIRST SABBATICAL YEAR

(1903–1904)

GIVING college professors a free year at half-salary is good for all concerned. As a friend of mine expresses it, 'You can go abroad and acquire a few ideas, and with half of your salary the college can hire a better man to take your place.' In my own instance the college hired nobody to take my place and saved the money for some possibly more useful purpose. Upon reflexion, I found this wholesome. Had the garbage-collector taken even a month off, someone would immediately have been appointed to take his place; but when I went away for a year, it seemed that the college proceeded well enough without me. Thus the garbage-collector was more essential to the community than I.

On 20 June, having left our Irish setter Rufus with Fred Lockwood, our brother-in-law in Norwalk, and our grey cat Tiger Tuesday with our neighbours, Mr. and Mrs. Sloan, we sailed from New York on S.S. *Pretoria*, on our first Sabbatical, to be gone fifteen months. It was a slow, heavily-laden ship, twelve days to Cherbourg. We went directly to a pension at 117, rue Notre Dame des Champs, where we found our old friends, Professor and Mrs. Ralph Catterall of Chicago. At this same pension were also Professor and Mrs. McGiffert, and Dr. Philip Churchman, a Princeton graduate, now Professor of French at Clark University.

I used to wonder how it was possible for Americans to

live for months abroad and learn nothing of any European language. But on this Sabbatical year we discovered that it was not enough to live in France and to be with French people; a will of iron was necessary, if one wished to acquire the art of speaking French, for nearly all the foreigners one meets wish to learn English. We accordingly made a vow and kept it; we might not learn French and German, but we determined *not* to teach English. This involved eternal vigilance and frequent rudeness; but we explained to those foreigners who wished to talk English with us, that if they would travel to America, we should be glad to oblige them. Thus we never conversed in English with Frenchmen or Germans except on the rare occasions when they spoke our language with absolute ease. Professor Beljame, head of the English Department of the Sorbonne, was very kind to us, and spoke English like a native; when we took dinner in his Paris apartment and in his country house, it would have been ridiculous to converse in French. I asked him one day how it happened that he, a Frenchman, spoke English without an accent; the only foreigner I had ever heard with that accomplishment. He replied, 'It is because I have spoken English every day for forty years. It takes that long to master the pronunciation.' He forgot to add that his mother was an Englishwoman.

Some of the best friends we made at this pension were also eager to learn French; Mr. Hans Escher and his sister, German-Swiss from Zürich, and two German lieutenants, Schiemann (son of the Berlin professor) and Remmets. I suppose both these men were killed in the war. But when in 1914 I read that every German military officer was a degenerate brute, I could think only of these two young gentlemen, so kind, so considerate, so generous and affectionate.

With Remmets we made excursions to Fontainebleau

and elsewhere, and also to the theatres; and our efforts at conversation on trains and tramcars fascinated the passengers. Whenever we began to converse, they would go into convulsions of uncontrollable laughter; we did not mind; how indeed could they help it? Their facial expression seemed to say, 'Why on earth don't those people converse in their own language, instead of butchering ours?' But we couldn't. Remmets could not speak English, and we could not speak German; thus we afforded innocent delight to fifty million Frenchmen.

I remember our horrible disappointment when, along with the good Remmets, we first went to a matinée at the Théâtre Antoine, to see how much we could understand. We understood nothing; and I can still see the expression of despair on the face of Remmets, as he whispered to me, '*Je suis désolé.*' So were we.

I remember how amused a French lady sitting in front of us at the theatre one day was, when, after a long speech in some classical drama, I whispered, 'Je n'ai pas compris un mot; mais c'est superbe, *c'est épatant*!'

When I hear people say, as I have so often, that they cannot speak French but can understand it, I think they are lying. For the average person, it is more difficult to understand a foreign language than to speak it. The exceptions to this are of two varieties; those who have learned French thoroughly in their childhood, and have not spoken it for years—and those few individuals, usually women, who are content in any company to remain silent, but have cultivated the art of listening. I was glad to see in a book by Somerset Maugham the statement that his servant could not understand English though he spoke it easily.

Long after I could speak French and German fluently, I had difficulty in understanding it, except in a conversation where someone was speaking directly to me, or in a lecture, or on the stage where I had previously read the play. For, when I spoke, I knew what I said, and could rapidly make up correct sentences; but what was the other fellow saying? I have invariably found this to be true with foreign professors and lecturers in America; they speak English easily (except for pronunciation) but it is clear they have not the remotest idea what we are saying, if we speak as we should to another American.

Indeed, I am certain that Joseph Conrad, who wrote English as well as any contemporary English man of letters, did not easily understand English conversation. I have seen him at dinner, and in social groups, and it was quite clear he did not know what was being said. Of course he understood if you spoke to him directly and with clear enunciation.

One of the best gifts parents can give their children is to have them taught by governesses French and German in their childhood; then they learn these languages naturally and without drudgery; and if care is taken so that they do not cease to use them as they grow, the accomplishment will add enormously to their happiness.

Mademoiselle Desfaveries, who taught us French, told me there was a distinguished American professor who had employed her to teach him, and he was so humiliated by not being able to understand, that he would often pretend he did, by nods and becks and wreathed smiles and various grimaces. So she cured him of this hypocrisy one day by telling him an agonizing story of a little child run over in the street by an automobile; while she told it, she kept laughing, and he joined heartily in this laughter, as if he were enjoying a very funny story. When he found the laugh was on him, he was disconcerted.

An amusing pun was made by an American woman whose wit triumphed over her sufferings. A Parisian dentist was trying to extract one of her teeth, and broke it. He exclaimed, '*Quelle tragédie!*' To which she calmly replied, '*Une tragédie de Racine, n'est-ce pas?*'

Among the lost opportunities of my life which trouble me like Rossetti's spilt water in hell, is the failure to see Coquelin in *Cyrano de Bergerac*. During that month of July 1903, he was playing it every night; but we decided to postpone going until our ears were more attuned to spoken French. At the end of the month he departed, was away from Paris all the rest of the year, and died in 1909. I had heard him in New York in *Thermidor* and I often heard his brother, Coquelin Cadet, who died ten days after Constant, at the Comédie Française.

I heard Richard Mansfield play Howard Thayer Kingsbury's translation of *Cyrano* and Walter Hampden play Brian Hooker's translation; I heard it in Italian at Rome, and I heard Le Bargy play it in the original at the original theatre in Paris. I suppose the finest translation of it is in German and by Ludwig Fulda. It was Ludwig Fulda who told me that a schoolgirl wrote on her exam paper that Goethe, after winning Frederike's affections, suddenly left her 'and was never heard of again.'

In 1913, being in Biarritz, I wished very much to call and see M. Rostand at his home in Campo; accordingly, I wrote, asking for an interview, and his secretary called me up on the telephone, saying the dramatist had just returned from Paris, was weary from his work there and from travel, but that I could see him in a few days. A cordial letter came a few days later inviting me to call, but I had given it up, and was at the Puy de Dome. I had supposed I should have another opportunity but he died in 1918.

On the day the great Pope Leo XIII died, 20 July 1903, we were in the cathedral at Chartres. As we entered it, I heard a French tourist whisper *C'est écrasant!* The interior of Chartres is the most impressive of any church I

have ever seen, but the plain tower, over which the architects and critics become ecstatic, seems to me no better
and no worse than the average steeple on any Methodist
church. I know well that such a remark means damnation;
but I have looked at that tower in different seasons and
under varied skies, and the wonder and beauty others feel
are hidden from me.

At the end of July we went to the village of Carolles
near Mont St. Michel, to 'escape the heat of Paris,' and
we nearly froze; there was day after day of bitter wind,
driving horizontal rain. However, we made pleasant French
acquaintances, as we were the only foreigners in the little
town. All the Frenchmen in those days, young and old,
wore beards; and in church on the day of the Assumption,
15 August, a Frenchman behind us whispered 'That man
is either an actor or an American—he has no beard.' It
was the growth of lawn tennis and other outdoor sports,
then almost unknown in France, that eliminated the silky
French beards. To play tennis with a full beard is grotesque,
and a serious handicap on a windy day.

To see Carolles a little way off with the ancient church
surrounded by the cluster of houses, reminded me of
Guy de Maupassant's remark that the church in every
French village looks like a hen surrounded by her
chickens.

Carolles and that whole Norman coast in the neighbourhood has an atrocious summer climate; no wonder
the Normans are a dour, hard-bitten race. We made various excursions, to Coutances, to Avranches, and saw the
place where the English King, Henry II, did penance in
1172 for the death of Thomas à Becket in 1170. We stayed
over night at Madame Poulard's at Mont Saint Michel,
and took the two-hour steamer journey on the charming
river Rance from Dinan to Dinard; and at St. Malo across
the mouth of the river, saw the scene immortalized by

Browning in *Hervé Riel*. Although the rain fell in torrents all day, there was a steady stream of pilgrims to the tomb of Chateaubriand; I was told this happened every day in the year.

We made a number of delightful acquaintances with French people. M. Boulay, a haberdasher from Paris, who had been a French soldier in Madagascar, was most agreeable. He and his wife hired a little donkey named Rigolette for the season, and took us on many an afternoon drive to abbeys and old churches. I amazed and delighted him by curing him instantly of a case of hiccoughs that had lasted two hours and had given him great alarm. We were far out in the country and I told him I should cure him as soon as we could secure a glass of water. He would not believe he was to be instantly cured. I told him to place his two thumbs tightly in his ears, closing the ears hermetically; and with the forefinger of each hand to close both nostrils; whereupon I held the glass of water to his lips, and told him to swallow once. He did so and the hiccoughs ceased immediately. I have never known this simple method to fail.

When the weather permitted, we walked on the shore of the sea; and I remember one September afternoon we watched the sun hanging low over the horizon and then saw it sink into the ocean; exactly as Browning describes it in *Saul*.

> Than by slow pallid sunsets in autumn, ye watch from the shore
> At their sad level gaze o'er the ocean—a sun's slow decline.

In the midst of September we decided to escape from this accursed climate; we had paid in advance for our rooms till the first of October, and we knew that if we told our teacher we were going, it would involve us in a long explanation, as the French people do not believe in wasting money. So we eloped. We disappeared early one

morning and spent three heavenly days on the Island of
Jersey; the weather was fair, the climate was mild, and
the place more English than England. It seemed incredible
that a few miles could make so complete a change. From
there we went to the Loire and once more were favoured
during the last ten days of that September by mellow,
lovely weather.

We followed the Loire to its mouth on a Browning pilgrimage, spending two days at Pornic, the scene of *Gold
Hair*, and visiting Le Croisic, the home of Hervé Riel.
His statue was erected nine years later, in 1912 on the
occasion of the hundredth anniversary of Browning's birth.

Then we spent three months in Paris, from the first of
October to the last day of the year. Here we revelled in
the theatres, going four or five times a week. The Ministry
of Public Instruction gave me free admittance to the
Comédie Française, the Odéon, the Opéra, and the Opéra
Comique; and I received the same privilege at the Théâtre
Antoine. On 14 October the King of Italy (then young)
drove on the Champs Elysées with the Queen and with
President Loubet whose black simplicity of dress con-
trasted dramatically with the gorgeous raiment of royalty,
and as the equipage passed I shouted ' *Vive le roi!* ' A
Frenchman asked me why I did that, since I was an
American. 'That is just the reason; I have never had a
chance before,' and I let out another whoop.

My friend Lewis Einstein was Secretary at the American
Embassy and in October he took me on a three days'
automobile journey to Meaux, Château-Thierry (to see
where La Fontaine was born), to Reims, to Laon, the
enormous military tower at Coucy (destroyed in the World
War), and to Soissons. Near Soissons we saw that astounding façade of the great Abbey. The façade with its two
towers stood up like a stage set; the walls of the nave
had disappeared long ago. In the World War, the tip of

one of these towers was knocked off by a shell. When we got to Reims, it was dark; the cathedral was closed; but the sacristan, after a little financial persuasion, unlocked one of the doors, gave us a single candle, and departed. We spent an hour in that vast interior, illumined only by the light of our little candle, amid grotesque and gigantic shadows.

Einstein had a fine automobile and an excellent French chauffeur; near Laon he 'let her out' and the car reached the dizzy speed of thirty-six miles per hour, which at that time seemed miraculous.

In the Paris theatres, we frequently heard the classic plays and the actors Mounet-Sully, Sarah Bernhardt, and Lucien Guitry at the dawn of his fame. However great was the excitement when *Hernani* was first produced, modern audiences were impressively unimpressed. During the long harangues of Mounet-Sully, there was a steady accompaniment of coughing accompanied by unrestrained guffaws.

On a November evening I spoke at the annual dinner of the Yale Alumni in Paris; the famous Yale rowing coach, Bob Cook, was present. He told me that when he was in college he asked Professor Packard what his mark in Greek was. The Professor replied 'I don't know.' 'You don't know, Professor? Why not?' 'Because I haven't got a microscope. Your standing is so low I can't see it with the naked eye.'

One day at the Sorbonne, I had an interesting conversation with Emile Faguet, one of the most prolific authors of modern times; he was very agreeable. I asked him about the vogue of English poets in France; he thought Browning was little read. Faguet gave regular lectures at the Sorbonne, was the drama critic for the daily *Journal des Débats* and produced several books every year.

An amusing incident that led to a long friendship began with a letter of enquiry in the Paris edition of the *New York*

Herald. 'Where is Professor Wm. Lyon Phelps?' The signer said he was a Princeton man, had heard that I was somewhere in Paris, and that it was most important for him to meet me. The address he gave was two houses from ours! I went to see him. He was a wealthy young American gentleman, recently graduated from Princeton; he said he had told his friends he was going abroad *to study*, which seemed to amuse them (indeed they went into peals of laughter) for he had not distinguished himself by enthusiasm for work. 'Well,' I said, 'and why do you wish to see me?' 'Because you can tell me how to get a doctor's degree in literature from the Sorbonne. Mind you, I don't care a damn about scholarship. The only reason I want a degree is to fool my friends. I will work day and night, I will do anything, but I am going to get that degree, and you can show me how.' Never had I seen an advanced degree pursued with that motive; but he had three things in his favour; he had time, money, and determination. I told him I was not able to give any supervision; but the thing for him to do was to take an Elizabethan play, make a correct and variorum text, write a sufficient amount of annotation, take a few courses in the Department of English at the Sorbonne, and he might come through. The next day he departed for London, bought up all the expensive early editions he could find, critical works on the author, old and recent, and returned to Paris with his spoils. I introduced him to Professor Beljame, and then I stepped down and out. In two years this indefatigable young man of fashion got his *Docteur ès Lettres* at the Sorbonne, and published his edition of the play. Professor Beljame said the candidate had a tough time at the oral exam, but they finally decided to let him through, as he had done a prodigious amount of work, and had established a text.

On 20 December with our friend Philip Churchman, we

set out on a few days' journey by train, arriving at Rouen
that evening. The next day in a fog we took the train for
Le Petit Couronne, and visited the house where Corneille
and his brother lived many years. It is kept as a museum.
Then after visiting Flaubert's grave in the cemetery, we
took a tiny steamer for Croisset, to see the cottage where
Flaubert wrote *Madame Bovary* and where Turgenev used
to stay with him. The little inn adjoining was kept by
M. et Mme Colange, formerly members of Flaubert's household; they told many anecdotes, and proudly exhibited the
signed photograph he had given them. It was also appropriate, considering my own name, to see in Rouen the
mediaeval gate *William Lyon*. That evening we took the
train for Amiens, and the next day we called on Jules
Verne. The maid said we should probably find him walking
near the cathedral. And there he was, a kindly old gentleman with a white beard. We stopped him and paid our
compliments; he was gracious; and showed to us individually that warmth of affection which he displayed so frequently to Americans in his romances. The next time we
came to Amiens (1913) we found his statue.

At Beauvais we were filled with amazement at the colossal proportions of the choir, the only part ever completed.
That architect had set out to build a cathedral that should
dwarf every other one in the world. They never got farther
than the choir, but he erected a tower 500 feet high, which
stood at the junction of choir and future nave; it fell down.

During our stay at 110 rue Notre Dame des Champs,
the news came of the death of Whistler on 11 July. The
next week in the *Revue Bleue*, a French critic stated that
Whistler was the greatest painter of the nineteenth century. On 28 December George Gissing died at St. Jean de
Luz, and the French journals gave him more recognition
than he received elsewhere.

Looking back over those months in the theatres at Paris,

nothing impressed us so much as the new play *Les Affaires sont les Affaires* by Octave Mirbeau, played at the Comédie Française by the incomparable Féraudy. We saw it three times and with increasing enthusiasm. It was the success of the year and the theatre had to repeat it often; it was translated into all the languages of Europe; we saw it in German at Munich. It was Mirbeau's only striking success. There are interesting anecdotes about the hard-bitten Mirbeau in Sacha Guitry's memoirs. He remarked that many men of letters met Mirbeau and said they did not like him; but the truth was the other way around; he did not like *them*. It was Mirbeau, so difficult to please, who first saluted Maeterlinck and made him famous in Paris. He called him 'the Belgian Shakespeare.'

While *Les Affaires* was the most dramatic of the new plays, the most beautiful performance we saw (also at the Comédie) was Alfred de Musset's *Les Caprices de Marianne*, with Madame Sorel. This was a flawless production; it was like lovely music; it was like a tranquil sunset, serene and unforgettable beauty.

On the last day of the old year, we said goodbye to our hosts at the pension, Pastor Fuster, his wife and daughter; it was sad to leave them. Down at the train to see us off were Martin Telleen, a former student at Yale, Philip Churchman, our Rumanian friend Orescu, who embraced me fervently, and the Scot Miss MacInnes, a fine French scholar. We took the noon train for Munich, 31 December 1903.

43

THE CITY OF MUNICH

1904

NEVER shall I forget our invasion of Munich on the first day of January 1904. We had spent three months in Paris, and most of the time in drizzling weather. When we stepped out of our train at Munich in the morning, the sky was cloudless, the air was sharp, with some snow on the ground. It was a holiday; military bands were playing, the people looked radiantly happy, and the keynote of the place seemed to be cheerful animation. We drove up the broad Ludwigstrasse, turned to the left near the University at Schellingstrasse, and at No. 3, found the Pension Nordland, where we were to remain for months. It was kept by two charming German ladies, Fräulein Lammers and Fräulein Junkers, who were never separated until the former's death in 1937. They showed us to our rooms, which faced the South, and which were flooded with sunshine; in the corner of each stood a stove taller than Grandfather's Clock.

We had not been there five minutes before we felt at home, and Munich has seemed to me ever since *eine deutsche Heimat*.

Many novelists have written out plans and specifications for a Utopia, the city of their dreams. But while the Munich before the war had its imperfections like everything else on earth, it seemed to me then and seems to me in retrospect to be nearer the ideal city than any other.

439

Munich is nearly as large as Boston and yet as quiet as a country village. Where the people are I don't know, but those who are familiar with Boylston and Tremont Streets in Boston will see nothing like that in Munich. The streets are calm, the sidewalks uncrowded, the highway uncongested by traffic; there is no Great White Way; there are no flaring lights; there is no hurly-burly. You can hear your own footsteps. My colleague, Professor Emery, arrived at Munich at nine o'clock in the evening, and observing the silence of the streets, asked his taxi driver to take him somewhere. The driver said, 'Isn't that rather indefinite?' 'You know what I mean—take me where there is a lot of noise and a lot of people.' The driver answered, 'What you want is the railway station.' And indeed that is the only place in Munich that fulfils those requirements.

There was everything in Munich to make a cultivated foreigner happy, cheerful, and content. I have never seen any town that has so much to give to the visitor. In the first place, everything one wants to see is within easy walking distance. If one rooms in a boarding-house on a side street off the Ludwigstrasse, one can walk in a few moments to the university, to the public library, to the concert halls, to the State Opera House, to the State Theatre, to the Play House, to the art galleries; and the English Garden, an enormous tract of land, is in the centre of the town and close to all of these other delectable places. In the English Garden in summer one may take long walks or one may sit down and hear music as one sips coffee or beer. In the winter one may skate on the frozen lake. Those who are fond of winter sports have the mountains close at hand. It is estimated that on Sunday mornings in winter 100,000 people take early trains to the mountains for skiing and other amusements. In the summer the environs of Munich are beautiful. There are lakes where one may take excursions in a little steamer or in a rowboat;

where one may visit famous old castles and see their treasures.

If one is fond of tennis, there are three or four tennis clubs in the heart of the city where one may become a visiting member at a nominal fee and find plenty of agreeable companions. The golf links are ten minutes by trolley, and there again the entrance fee is nominal. The only objection that I have to the golf links is that the magnificent mountains are so near that one is constantly tempted to lift up one's eyes to the hills, and however valuable it may be for one's spiritual development, it is fatal to one's efficiency.

Every night in Munich there is something interesting to hear at the opera, at the theatre, or at the concert hall. Every morning there was published a little paper devoted exclusively to theatrical and musical affairs. This paper gave every event that would take place in the city in the afternoon and evening, with the exact time of beginning, the exact time of closing, and a list of the actors, singers, and performers.

One of the chief attractions of the theatre and the operas in Munich is the fact that they began early. The opera began at six o'clock and was always over before ten, except in the case of a very long one. The plays began at seven-thirty and in nearly every instance were over at nine-thirty. In other words, the opera and theatres were not run for the benefit of members of a leisure class who do not have to get up the next morning, but for the ordinary citizen and his family who are obliged to rise early and go to work. In New York, in Paris, and in London theatre-going and opera-going are in the nature of a dissipation. The theatres in Paris do not close until midnight, and in New York and London one does not usually get to one's domicile before that. The result is that one is exhausted, and, 'There is nothing certain but the morning head.' To go to the theatre or opera four nights in succession in London, Paris, or New York—unless one is able to rise very late the next day—is an exhausting ordeal, but in Munich, during a period of seven months, we averaged five nights a week at the opera and theatre and never felt fatigue.

There is another advantage about beginning early. Instead of going to the opera or theatre stuffed with a soggy dinner and made somnolent by food, one takes tea before going and when the entertainment is over one goes into a cheerful café, has a hot supper in delightful company, and is in bed before eleven.

What does going to the theatre mean in New York, London, and Paris? It too often means something like this. One attends a dinner party where half the guests arrive late; one then has a long course dinner, hurried toward the end; the company is hustled into automobiles and arrives at the theatre or opera a half-hour after the performance has begun and in a condition that precludes mental concentration.

After we had spent two or three months in Munich, we fell in love with the place, with the temper of the town, and with the people. After we had spent four months there, we went in April to Italy. There we lived in sunshine and enjoyed the glory and beauty. But after a while we became homesick for Munich, and, although on the morning of our return it was raining and the weather in general was doing its worst, our hearts were singing, for we were home again.

New Year's Day in 1904 was Friday; on Sunday evening, with my former pupil Alfred Ernest Richards, who took his doctorate at the University of Munich and is now Professor of English at the University of New Hampshire, we heard at the *Hoftheater* a splendid performance of *Die Meistersinger*, which began at six and closed at eleven. My

friend at Paris, the German Lieutenant Remmets, told us
that if we wished to know the inner spirit of the German
people, the true heart of Germany, we must hear two
operas—*Die Meistersinger* and *Der Freischütz*. We were
fortunate in being in Munich in 1904, for the opera
was like New York's in the nineties, distinguished by a
constellation of stars. Fräulein Morena, Herr Knote,
Herr Feinhals, Herr Bender (all of whom sang later at
the Metropolitan in New York), were in their prime; and
the Wagner performances were magnificent.

Among Americans living in Munich in 1904 were Gertrude Atherton, Poultney Bigelow, Doctor Coit (formerly
of St. Paul's School), Professor and Mrs. Homer Eaton
Keyes of Dartmouth, and others; and although we avoided
English-speaking people as a rule, we had good times with
these congenial friends.

Among those studying at the pension were several young
Polish gentlemen, students at the University—Count
Zoltowski, Count Stadinicki, and Pan Glabisz; we became
intimate friends, and although they spoke French and English fluently, they were kind enough to speak only German
with us; this was a sacrifice we appreciated, for like all Poles
in those days, they hated Germany, Austria, and Russia.
They were the best of company, at the theatre, on country
excursions, and later in lawn tennis.

Among Shakespeare's plays I had never heard before in
any language, I heard at the Royal Theatres *King Lear*,
Measure for Measure, and *Pericles*. The Intendant of the
Royal Theatres was the famous Ernst von Possart, the
idol of Germany, almost a legendary figure. He gave me
the entrée to the three theatres of the kingdom. Exactly
forty years before, he had made his début at Munich in
Schiller's *Die Räuber*; accordingly on the night of the anniversary, he played it again; and after the performance
University students took the horses from his carriage, and

drew him in triumph to his house on the other side of the Isar, a mile away.

I took regular courses at the University, and became intimately acquainted with Schick, the professor of English, Muncker, the professor of German, who smiled when I showed him a volume of the magnificent complete edition of Lessing, which he had edited. He said that although he had edited it, he had never been rich enough to buy it. The *privatdozent* in English, later professor, Ernst Sieper, was a good friend. He was to be as truly one of the war casualties as if he had fallen in battle; for he had devoted his whole career to increasing the good feeling and understanding between Great Britain and Germany, and when the war came, it broke his heart, and he died.

I saw the great Professor Röntgen, who had discovered the X-rays, frequently at the University, but I never had an opportunity to meet him.

One of the most intimate friends of my life was and is Doctor Jules Simon, a Belgian, lecturer in French at the University. Wishing to keep up our practice in hearing and speaking French, we attended his lectures; and a friendship began which will last until death do us part. A few years later he was married to a young lady of Munich; and now Barbara and Jules are grand-parents. Our friendship is kept alive by continuous correspondence. It was at a dinner-party at their house that I made a terrific German pun. Someone was saying that an acquaintance had got a divorce; he begged his wife to let him go. He was a dentist; whereupon I said that if he was a dentist, he could with double emphasis in making such a request of his wife use the language of Tannhäuser to Venus:

O Königin! Göttin! lass mich *ziehen*!

We went frequently to the Münchener Schauspielhaus; at the house of the Director, Herr Stollberg, we met the actors and actresses of the company. This little theatre is attractive and comfortable; it was interesting to be there on first nights, because the German audiences were so sincere that no matter how popular the actors and actresses were, if the play did not please, the final curtain was greeted with such hissing and such a tumult of disapproval that the piece could not be repeated. I remember one night at the first performance of *Hans Sollenstössers Himmelfahrt*, there was both cheering and hissing; finally the cheering was drowned in loud, derisive laughter; whereupon a stately German gentleman rose in the middle of the audience and shouted 'Es ist eine Roheit zu lachen!'

This is the piece that had in other cities of Germany only a moderate success and much opposition; but when Mr. George Kaufman and his collaborator remade it for the American stage, calling it *Beggar on Horseback*, it had an enormous success. I saw both the original and the American version; and I hope the German author got something from the immense receipts in America, for the idea and the plot were certainly his own.

44

LITERARY PILGRIMAGE IN ITALY

ON 21 March 1904 we left Munich for Italy by way of the
St. Gothard Tunnel—deep snow giving way to sunshine;
after visiting the Lakes, and staying three days at Genoa
with our friends the American consul William Henry
Bishop and his wife, we visited Rome, Arezzo, Florence,
Milan, Asolo, and Venice. I have never understood what
Bishop Burnet meant by his comment on Milan cathedral
—'The cathedral hath nothing to recommend it in the way
of architecture.' We were in St. Peter's on Maundy Thursday, Good Friday, and Easter; and I can still feel the
warmth of the body of the stranger tourist jammed tightly
against me for hours as we stood up during the long service
on Easter Day. On Thursday the famous Cardinal Ram-
polla was under the baldachin; it is that baldachin that
gave me the feeling of immense space in the church. It is
90 feet high and yet seems no more out of place than a
writing-desk in a private library.

We were on a Browning pilgrimage, verifying the places
the poet so definitely describes; 'those lancet-windows'
jewelled miracle' in the cathedral at Arezzo, and Caponsacchi's church Santa Maria della Pieve; the house where
Petrarch was born 20 July 1304 we had all to ourselves.
But I wished I might have been there three months later,
when delegates came from all over the world to celebrate
the six-hundredth anniversary of his birth. My Yale colleague Professor Kenneth McKenzie was delivering his
address in fluent Tuscan, when the official souvenir post

card photograph was taken; a great day for Arezzo, Petrarch, Yale, and McKenzie!

In Florence I wished to repeat as definitely as possible Browning's experience when he found the *Old Yellow Book*, which was to produce such a tremendous impact on his mind and to give the world the incomparable *Ring and the Book*.

> I found this book,
> Gave a *lira* for it, eightpence English just,
> Across a Square in Florence, crammed with booths,
> Buzzing and blaze, noontide and market-time,
> Toward Baccio's marble,—ay, the basement-ledge
> O' the pedestal where sits and menaces
> John of the Black Bands with the upright spear,
> 'Twixt palace and church,—Riccardi where they lived,
> His race,—and San Lorenzo where they lie. . . .
> (June was the month, Lorenzo named the Square)
> I leaned a little and overlooked my prize
> By the low railing round the fountain-source
> Close to the statue, where a step descends:
> While clinked the cans of copper, as stooped and rose
> Thick-ankled girls who brimmed them, and made place
> For marketmen glad to pitch basket down,
> Dip a broad melon-leaf that holds the wet,
> And whisk their faded fresh.

Well, if one goes there on market-day—for on every other day of the week the Square is empty—one will find an exact reproduction of this scene. As the bells of Florence were striking noon on Thursday 7 April 1904, I entered the Square; I stood at the foot of the statue by the little fountain; and as I stood there, a marketman came up with a basket of vegetables, dipped a broad melon-leaf into the water, whisked his faded wares fresh, and went on his way; as if he had been rehearsed for a Browning pageant.

The only child of Robert and Elizabeth Barrett Browning, Robert Wiedemann Barrett Browning, was born at Florence, 9 March 1849, and died at Asolo, 8 July 1912.

When Nathaniel Hawthorne visited the Brownings at Casa Guidi, he said that Browning had an elfin wife and an elf child. 'I wonder whether he will ever grow up, whether it is desirable that he should.' On this occasion the little elf flitted about the room, merrily handing strawberries to his father and mother, Nathaniel Hawthorne, and William Cullen Bryant. He grew up, entered Balliol College, Oxford, but left without taking a degree, his chief interest being in art. In 1887 he was married to Fannie Coddington of New York, and for the rest of his life lived mainly in Italy. His paintings and sculptures were sometimes exhibited in London and on the Continent, and he might have reached a high reputation if he had not carried the burden of his parents' fame. When I visited the Palazzo Rezzonico in Venice, the house where his father died, the rooms on the top floor were filled with large paintings by the son, some of them beautiful and interesting, but without any striking originality. I saw there, too, the original pen-and-ink sketch of Tennyson reading *Maud*, made by Dante Rossetti on that memorable evening at London, in 1855, when the Tennysons, the Brownings, Dante and William Rossetti were gathered together in an upper room. Tennyson, with one leg curled under him on the sofa, chanted *Maud*, the tears running down his cheeks; and Browning read *Fra Lippo Lippi*, both poems published that year.

After Browning's death in 1889, his sister Sarianna went to live with her nephew. She died 22 April 1903, in her ninetieth year. Barrett Browning took devoted care of her, and seriously injured his health, and particularly his eyes, in doing so. Up to the last few months of her life, she had that extraordinary vitality and vivacity characteristic of her famous brother. Her nephew, with considerable pride and evident affection, showed me a photograph that he took of her. I saw an old face full of strength and intelligence.

It was on a beautiful day, the twelfth of April 1904, that I saw and talked with Barrett Browning. He had sent me a cordial invitation to visit him, and I took the tramway at Giotto's Campanile in Florence. After several miles of steep ascent, I reached the terminus, and entered the carriage that Mr. Browning had sent for me. A few more miles of stiff grade, and I came to La Torre all' Antella, his lovely and romantically situated home. Mr. Browning greeted me with unaffected and charming friendliness. He was a short man, like his father, rotund and red-faced, and the red veins traced patterns on his cheeks and brow. He spoke with what we Americans call the English accent, and when I said that he must feel like a native Italian, he quickly and vigorously replied, 'Oh, dear, no; I'm an Englishman.'

The expense of this home, and that of buying the place in Asolo, where, in accordance with his father's wishes, he had built 'Pippa's Tower,' supply reasons enough, I think, why he was later forced to sell the Palazzo Rezzonico in Venice. He had a strange collection of exotic birds, some of which he would hold in his hands, while they screamed with ear-splitting screeches, and kept their formidable beaks in what seemed dangerous proximity to his eyes. Over the tea-cups we talked of his father and mother, for I had frankly stated the object of my visit.

I lamented the fact that there was no adequate biography of Robert Browning; this was before Griffin and Minchin's scrupulous work had appeared. When I particularly condemned the *Life and Letters* by Mrs. Orr, he cried out, 'Oh, that is a very bad book!' 'None of the family liked it,' said he. After Browning's death, the question of an authorized biography was discussed by his sister and his son. Mr. Browning declined to write it, and as Mrs. Orr had known Browning intimately, and as her *Handbook* to his works was excellent—he glanced at me here, and I nodded emphatic approval—she was selected to perform the task.

She was supplied with all available material. She never showed her manuscript either to Mr. Browning or to his aunt Sarianna, but at last sent the proof. They were both bitterly disappointed and corrected the worst and most glaring mistakes, and made many suggestions. Mrs. Orr brusquely replied, 'I cannot change the proofs.'

Mr. Chesterton's book had recently appeared, and it was anything but pleasing to Mr. Browning. He said the work was filled with errors; the mistake that apparently perturbed him the most was the statement that Browning was in weak health and 'declining' in the last years. On the contrary, he insisted that Browning was tremendously vigorous up to the last; that no change had taken place in his appearance, manner, or habits. He had caught a bad cold walking on the Lido, but refused to take proper care of himself. Instead of staying in, he set out for long tramps with friends, constantly talking in the raw autumn air. While suffering with this heavy cold, he ran rapidly up flights of stairs, the son vainly trying to restrain him. The result was bronchitis with heart trouble, and he died at ten in the night of 12 December 1889. That very afternoon he had risen from bed and walked about the room. During the last few days he told many good stories and talked with the utmost vivacity. There was never any 'decline,' and the son seemed almost fiercely to resent Mr. Chesterton's statement.

Robert Browning inherited excellent health from his father, who died at the age of eighty-four, without ever having known a day's illness. Mr. Barrett Browning told me that until the last sickness he had never seen the poet in bed during the daytime. He had a truly wonderful digestion; it was his firm belief that one should eat only what one really enjoyed, desire being the infallible sign that the food was healthful. 'My father was a man of *bonne four-chette*; he was not very fond of meat, but liked all kinds of Italian dishes, especially with rich sauces. He always ate freely of rich and delicate things. He could make a whole meal off mayonnaise.' I reminded him that Emerson used to eat pie for breakfast. Both men were optimists.

Late in life he was very fond of swimming, though he did not learn early. The son taught him how to swim at Pornic, in Brittany, and he was venturesome for a man well on in years. He learned with great eagerness, and swam far out with boyish delight. The poet alludes to this in the prologue to *Fifine at the Fair*.

Browning's eyes were peculiar, one having a long focus, the other very short. He had the unusual accomplishment (try it and prove) of closing either eye without 'squinching,' and without any apparent effort, though sometimes in strong sunlight on the street his face would be a bit distorted. He did all his reading and writing with one eye, closing the long one as he sat down to his desk. He never wore glasses, and was proud of his 'microscopic' eye. He often wrote minutely, to show off his powers. When he left the house to go for a walk, he shut the short eye and opened the long one, with which he could see an immense distance. He never suffered with any pain in his eyes except once, as a young man, when, in imitation of Shelley, he was trying to be a vegetarian.

He was amazingly vivacious and impulsive, with a great flow of talk. He constantly acted on impulse, and was boyish and enthusiastic even in old age. If he liked anything, he spoke of it in the heartiest manner. He was very generous in his appreciation and praise of other men's work. He always tried to see what was good. Occasionally he was enraged at reading a particularly hostile criticism of himself, but generally stood abuse very well. He had not been soured by the long years of neglect and ridicule. A great admirer of Tennyson's poetry and of Tennyson's character—they were dear and intimate friends—he never liked the stock comparison. He had no jealousy, but he said,

'Tennyson and I are totally unlike.' The son admitted that perhaps the desire to be original and different from other writers sometimes led him into excesses and eccentricities in his poems.

What was said of Browning's impulsiveness is borne out by the general testimony of his friends, and particularly by a letter from Mrs. Browning to Mrs. Jameson. The manuscript of this letter was bought by an American in London and went down with the *Titanic*. An extract from it appeared in the bookseller's catalogue: 'You must learn Robert—he is made of moods—chequered like a chessboard; and the colour goes for too much—till you learn to treat it as a game. He was very tired that evening.'

In conversation he was perfectly normal. He loved to talk, but no one would ever have guessed that he was a poet. He was interested in multitudinous things, and never spoke of his poetry if he could avoid doing so.

In later years Browning hated to write! His work became so distasteful to him that he would rather do almost anything else. He rose early, before his son; they had coffee together; then the father was never visible till lunch. He did all his composition and letter-writing in the morning. After lunch, he would not touch a pen if he could help it, and seemed relieved to have the morning's work over. He gave the impression of liking many things in life much better than poetry or literature. 'Yes,' repeated Mr. Browning, after a moment's hesitation, 'he really hated to write.'

Contrary to the oft-repeated statement, Browning was not a really fine pianist. As a very young man, he used to play several instruments, and perhaps then he played the piano well. In Casa Guidi he taught his little son piano-playing. 'Much to my regret,' said Mr. Browning. 'It took up a lot of time and did no good.' In later life Browning became ambitious to improve his own skill on this instrument, but it was of no use, for his fingers were clumsy and stiff. Still, when old, he rose at six, and practised finger-exercises for an hour!

He loved first-class music ardently, had a profound knowledge of it, and was a good judge. If the performance was fine, he was delighted, and would express his praise with the utmost enthusiasm; but bad work gave him intense pain. Sometimes at a concert he would put his fingers in his ears, his suffering apparently being uncontrollable.

Robert Browning often talked of *his* father, a wonderful man, with an extraordinary range of knowledge and culture, but without one particle of literary ambition. He wrote reams of poetry, which he destroyed. Browning said his father had amazing facility in verse composition—that he could compose much faster than he himself. Robert Browning's education was the elective system pushed to the extreme limit. His education depended absolutely and exclusively on his inclinations; he was allowed to study anything he wished. His father gave him perfect liberty, never sent him anywhere, and allowed him to do exactly as he chose. He provided competent instruction in whatever line the youth expressed any interest.

Mr. Barrett Browning told me that he remembered his mother, Elizabeth Barrett Browning, as clearly as though he had seen her yesterday. When she died in 1861, he was eleven years old. Her ill health, both before and after her marriage, had been greatly exaggerated. She *was* an invalid, but did not give the impression of being one. She was able to do many things, and had considerable endurance. One day in Florence she walked from her home out through the Porta Romana, clear up on the heights, and back to Casa Guidi. 'That was pretty good, wasn't it?' She was of course the idol of her household, everything revolving about her. She was intensely loved by all her friends. Her father was a 'very peculiar man,' who grew more stubborn with advancing years.

The origin of his own nickname, 'Pen,' had almost always been stated inaccurately. It came about in this way. When he was a child, he stuttered (he stuttered, indeed, in telling me about it), and in trying to pronounce 'Nini'—the name Italians give their children—he said, 'P-n-n-n-nini.' English visitors called it 'Pen-nini,' and this led to 'Pen.'

In later years, at London, he often saw Carlyle with his father. 'Carlyle was always exceedingly kind and thoughtful and sweet.' He took tactful interest in the pictures painted by the young man, and made a point of speaking often about them. The traditional surly side to Carlyle never appeared. Mrs. Carlyle was the 'terror' of that household. One day Robert Browning, while calling on the Carlyles, took up the tea-kettle while talking animatedly. Mrs. Carlyle cried shrilly, 'Put that down!' The poet obeyed, but unfortunately placed it on the carpet. After that she hated him.

With reference to his own publication of the love-letters that passed between Robert Browning and Elizabeth Barrett in 1845–6, Mr. Browning told me that he was in a difficult position, but had to make a decision, and did not dare postpone it. In 1887, when Browning moved from one house to another in London, he destroyed an enormous mass of correspondence. It is probable that the uproar occasioned by Froude's printing of the Carlyle letters was one reason why Browning was determined to leave as little material behind him as possible; but if he had not moved his household effects, it is certain that thousands of letters would have been preserved. Still, Browning did not like to have his personal letters read. He told his son to be sure to destroy every letter that he received from his father, and the son had faithfully done this. Now, the love-letters were the sole exception. He not only had not destroyed them, but had taken special pains to preserve them, had numbered every one in its chronological order, and had placed them in a receptacle specially prepared for the purpose. The son had to do one of two things; he must either destroy them, which seemed really impossible to do, since his father had preserved them with such loving care, or he must print them himself. To make no decision, simply to leave them alone, would be to run the risk of having someone in the future print them inaccurately, 'edit' them, or omit certain portions. Mr. Browning therefore took the responsibility. He would never have printed them had he not been able to print every word exactly as it was written. There was no alteration from the manuscript, not a word omitted. He had been loudly abused for having given them to the world, and he felt this hostile criticism keenly, but he believed the verdict would ultimately be in his favour. Perhaps it was already.

Mr. Browning told me that horses were his passion, and invited me to go with him to the races at Siena. How I wish I had been able to accept this kind invitation! I know nothing whatever about horses, but I should have been glad of the opportunity for further intimate talk. The time had come to say good-bye and Mr. Browning himself drove me three or four miles toward Florence. A smart pair of horses, hitched tandem, carried us along at high speed; they were spirited and skittish, but were beautifully handled by my host. I shall remember Mr. Browning not only because he was his father's son, but because he was an exceedingly kindly, courteous, hospitable Englishman. As Dr. Kenyon said, 'It is not only as the breaking of a link with the two great poets that his death will be regretted both in England and in Italy.'

Mr. Browning's charitable work for Asolo, a pious tribute to his father, should not be forgotten. When Browning visited Asolo for the last time, in the summer of 1889, the silk-mill where Pippa worked was still standing, containing the obsolete wooden machinery. Mr. Barrett Browning bought the building and tried to re-establish the silk industry. This proved to be impossible; he therefore changed the institution into a lace school, thus providing remunerative occupation for thirty Asolo girls of about Pippa's age. When I visited Asolo, the school was flourishing, and I obtained a specimen of the work. Mr. Browning also brought to life an old industry of the little town, the 'hand-loom weaving of linen.' He built 'Pippa's Tower,' and lived to see in Asolo the celebration of his father's centenary, when a new street was formally named for the poet, and all the inhabitants came out to honour the memory of Robert Browning and show their hearty affection for his kindly and generous son.

Friday night 8 April we were present at the début of Clara Clemens as a concert singer; she sang from *Semiramide* with glorious tones. In the audience was her father Mark Twain. I spoke to him and he said in mock solemnity, 'Yes, I am passing off the stage, and now my daughter is the famous member of the family.' I asked permission to call at his villa and he told me to come early on the following Thursday 14 April; so that we could talk together before his weekly reception of visitors, which began at four o'clock. His daughter Jean was with him. He was 68 years old, but looked older; his wife was desperately ill and indeed died in this villa Sunday 5 June. During this hour's interview, Mark smoked three cigars; there was a constant twitching in his right cheek and his right eye seemed inflamed. He was excited about the Russo-Japanese War, and was an intense partisan of the Japanese. I told him that Edith M. Thomas had published a poem calling on Americans to support the Russians because they were Christians and the Japanese heathens; and he replied, 'Edith doesn't know what she's talking about.' He pretended to believe the Russians had made a fatal error and shown lack of judgement in not sending a sufficient number of ikons with their soldiers. 'Why,' speaking with great emphasis, 'I read that they have sent out only eighty holy images with their troops! General Kuropatkin ought to have carried at least 800!'

The conversation changed to literature. I asked him which he thought the best of all his books. He said, 'What do *you* think?' and I replied '*Huckleberry Finn*.' He thought a moment, and then said, rather unwillingly, I thought, 'That is my best.' I felt as if he had yielded to popular opinion, and in his own mind he did not agree with it. Probably he thought *Joan of Arc* his masterpiece. Knowing how profound and complete was his pessimism, I ventured to say, 'Mr. Clemens, when you look back on your life and realize what you have made of yourself without any assistance and without any lucky accident, that entirely by your own genius you have risen from obscurity to a position where you are a desired and welcome guest in any royal court in the world and in any intellectual society, I should think you would feel some pleasure in it.' In his inimitable drawl, he replied very slowly, 'Well, I do look back upon my career with considerable satisfaction.'

In Munich on 27 July with about thirty Americans, we took the train to Wolfratshausen, and there we embarked on an enormous raft of logs, and came down to Munich on the Isar rolling rapidly, driven only by the current. No oars, no engine, no sails; one steersman. It was the very poetry of motion. We glided past lovely meadows, through villages, through deep woods; and sliding down the occasional waterfalls lent additional excitement.

About a month later at Bayreuth between the acts of *Tannhäuser* we saw Frau Cosima Wagner walking about and I had some interesting conversation with her son Siegfried Wagner, the conductor of the orchestra. He was most agreeable. The Wolfram was the American Whitehill.

Next day (*Parsifal*) we happened to sit at the restaurant next to Madame Nordica, who had come to see the interpretation of Kundry, as she was studying it. She did not want anyone to know she was there, but of course we recognized her and she was in high spirits. She was just 'one of the crowd' after the performance and would not allow me to get her a cab; I could not help thinking how different was her exit from this theatre, jostled by the throng, from what she was accustomed to. But she liked it! She said the man who sang Parsifal had dirty fingernails, which seemed to her unnecessary. At luncheon I asked her if she thought George Moore's novel *Evelyn Innes* contained valuable criticisms of Wagner and of music, to which she replied it was worthless—exactly the opposite of the opinion given me by Professor Horatio Parker.

Our stay at Weimar was interesting, as I have been a fanatical admirer of Goethe since I was eighteen. The Römisches Haus seemed full of memories and on the wall hung the Calendar for the year 1828! It was the last year of the life of Duke Karl August. In the garden at Jena I was deeply moved seeing the table where Goethe and Schiller talked, which bears the inscription, taken from the words spoken here by Goethe to Eckermann on 8 October 1827: 'Sie wissen wohl kaum, an welcher merkwürdigen Stelle wir uns eigentlich befinden. Hier hat Schiller gewohnt. In dieser Laube, auf diesen jetzt fast zusammengebrochenen Bänken haben wir oft an diesen alten Steintisch gesessen und manches gute und grosse Wort miteinander gewechselt. . . . Das geht alles hin und vorüber: ich bin auch nicht mehr der ich gewesen.'

At Berlin we saw the opening play of the season at the Deutsches Theater; it was Shakespeare's *Troilus and Cressida*, which I had never had an opportunity to see in English; it was extremely well done; the next evening we saw Ibsen's *Lady from the Sea* and on the next Oscar

Wilde's *Lady Windermere's Fan*. The Berlin audiences at all three of these plays seemed cold, after the enthusiasm of Munich.

On 17 September we sailed from Hamburg on the same steamer we had taken from New York about fifteen months before, the slow *Pretoria*. We stopped several hours at Boulogne, because one Frenchman had taken the boat to England thinking it was the ship's tender, and we had to wait until he returned. The most famous authority on whist in the world, Mr. Foster, was on board, and it was amusing to play with him, for he knew what cards I held better than I did myself. There was one diverting episode; I had been asked to make up a party of four but told them they had better get someone else, as I never played for money. At the moment they could not find a fourth man, so they agreed to play 'for fun,' although 'it would not be exciting.' On the first hand my partner (not Foster) accused one of his opponents (not Foster) of reneging. This enraged the other, and he said he would bet five hundred dollars he had not. The other man got out his pocket-book and they both began to count from huge rolls of bills. Foster finally succeeded in pacifying them; they put up their pocket-books, but my partner said 'You *did* renege.' The other shouted 'You are a —— —— liar!' and they began to fight; we had considerable difficulty in separating them; and we did not play any more. And this was a game 'for fun' that was not to be exciting. It nearly ended in bloodshed.

45

EVENTS IN THE THEATRE

On 2 January 1905 I wrote in my journal, 'I am 40 years old today. Hard to realize it—that I shall never see the thirties again. I have no regrets, however, am wholly content with life, and don't mind being 40.' Being content with life is quite different from being self-satisfied. It is perhaps more common for persons to be dissatisfied with everything except themselves, than it is for them to be content with life.

On 2 May of that year Richard Mansfield produced *The Merchant of Venice* in New Haven. The house was sold out and we waited expectantly for some twenty minutes, wondering why the curtain did not rise. Finally the local manager appeared and read a statement dictated by Mr. Mansfield that ran something like this: 'Owing to my incredible and unpardonable stupidity and negligence, the lights have not been properly arranged for the performance. Mr. Mansfield has finally consented to play, under protest, but he wishes the audience to understand that the bad lighting is my fault and not his.' The audience would have noticed nothing amiss if this statement had not been read. Between the acts I found out that Mr. Mansfield had insisted that no performance be given and that the money be refunded to the spectators. His own acting was of course very fine; I think his death some years later the greatest loss the American stage ever suffered. After the performance that evening, a few of us met him at dinner at the Graduates' Club and talked until three in the morning. I asked him if it were true that he had refused to play. 'Of course it is true, and I ought not to have played.' 'But, Mr. Mansfield, people had come from all over the state to see you; they would have been bitterly disappointed if there had been no performance.' 'I can't help that,' he said, 'no true artist should appear unless the conditions are right.' He spoke bitterly about Joseph Jefferson, saying Jefferson had refused to help him at a critical moment in his career. Mansfield was difficult to get along with, but he was a great actor. When he played Shaw for the first time in America, the Irishman wrote him how a certain passage should be spoken to bring out the love interest, and Mansfield cabled him, 'Love interest be damned.' And Shaw cabled, 'The same to you.' Mr. Shaw told me in 1935, that when Mansfield was playing *The Devil's Disciple* in New York, a lady said to the playwright in London, 'Mansfield ought to get down on his knees and thank God for such a play,' to which Mr. Shaw replied, 'Yes, but he wishes to God someone else had written it.'

I saw Mansfield in many plays; his *Richard III* was magnificent. On this evening in New Haven, although he was amiable and charming, he expressed peculiar views. I had always wondered why he did not play Hamlet; he said Hamlet was an ass, and that morally Shylock was the best character in *The Merchant of Venice*.

The centenary of Schiller's death was celebrated at Yale on 9 May. The German department asked me to make the address, for which I made careful preparation.

At a dinner at Professor Sanford's 19 June we had the pleasure of meeting Sir Edward Elgar and his lady. He had been overcome by the heat (American weather) but was gracious and affable.

On 27 October in New Haven came the first public performance in the world of Shaw's *Mrs. Warren's Profession*, with Arnold Daly, who made a speech. I wrote a favour-

able review for the local newspaper. But the next day, by
order of the Mayor, the afternoon and evening performances were prohibited. This made a sensation, because the
first presentation of the play in New York was to occur only
two days later. After one night in the metropolis it was
suppressed although some of us protested in print. It was
soon produced in Russia and the audiences called it conventional and old-fashioned and Philistine!

On 15 March 1905 Herr Conried brought from the Irving
Place Theatre in New York, his German company to Yale
in *Kabale und Liebe*. At the banquet following, I read the
following original poem. A few days later I received a poem
from my colleague Professor Albert S.Cook, one from
Professor Hanns Oertel, then Professor at Yale, now Professor Emeritus of Sanscrit at the University of Munich,
and one from my colleague, Professor Henry W.Farnam.

KABALE UND LIEBE

New Haven, d.15. März 1905

I

Wir grüssen Sie, vortreffliche Schauspieler!
Sir waren heute Abend kolossal!
Den Geist des grossen Dichters, Friedrich Schiller
Sie haben mitgebracht in diesen Saal!

II

Die besten Künstler schmückten unsere Bühne,
Der Präsident, sein Ferdinand, der Wurm:
Und Lady Milford, mit der edlen Miene,
War wie ein Stern in einem wilden Sturm.

III

Wir sahen auch den rohen Geiger Miller
Mit seiner geizigen und dummen Frau:
Und alle beide sahen aus wie Schiller
Hat sie zuerst geschöpft, und ganz genau!

IV

Der Hofmarschall, mit seiner fremden Sprache
Hat uns gefallen, und wir lachten viel:
Obgleich wir weinen über Walters Rache,
Ein bischen Lachen hilft dem Trauerspiel.

V

Wir müssen auch die Sophie nicht vergessen,
Als Kammerjungfer war sie riesig gut:
Und auch, in diesem knappen Abendessen,
Ich möchte denken an Luises Mut.

VI

Zum ersten Male tritt sie auf die Bühne!
Ohne Verlegenheit die Rolle spielt:
Sie spielte nicht wie eine stumm' Maschine,
Sondern wie Menschenskind, das Liebe fühlt.

VII

Von ganzem Herzen danken wir Herrn Conried,
Dem guten Freund und auch dem grossen Mann:
Wie Wagner sonst, in seinem Hause Wahnfried,
Fangen wir hier die Lebensfreude an.

VIII

Wir müssen plaudern, lachen, singen, trinken,
Allezusammen sind wir fröhlich hier:
Und wie die Steine in dem Meere sinken,
So sinkt Frau Sorge in dem dunklen Bier.

KABALISTISCHE LIEBE

Wie wird man nach und nach zu einem Dichter?
Durch deutsche Biederkeit und deutsches Bier;
Aus ihnen sprudeln Geniefunken-Lichter!
Glaubt man es nicht, er 'mal, wie Phelps, probier'!

A.S.C.

New Haven, d.20. März. 1905.

Hurrah! Der Phelps besteigt das Ross
Dressed up wie ein ' Kuhjunge,'
Er schwingt sich auf den Pegasos
Schont weder Haut noch Lunge.

Es bocket das alte Musenpferd
Es kickt und schlägt gar munter;
Dochendlich wird es ja belehrt:
''s kriegt Wilhelm doch nicht "runter."'

Erstaunet stehn der Goethe da,
Der Lessing, Schiller, Heine:
' Nee, so wat war ja noch nich da!'
' Die Kraft in die zwee Beine!'

Der Dichter-Schar (glaub mir, o Freund,)
Von Neid erfüllt ist gelb se,
Der Phelps sitzt oben auf dem Pferd,
Das Pferd'st nicht auf dem Phelpse.

H.O·

Wilhelm dem Löwen, dem tüchtigen Dichter, ihm danken wir schön,
Schmeichelnde Reime, geschickt und gesellig, geschunden zu haben.
Kälber und Würmererringen das Lob des Königs der Tiere;
König der Dichter! Was du uns gebrüllet, Dir flüstern wir's nach.

Dem hoch geehrten Verskünstler

Wilhelm von Löwen-Fels, resp. Löwen Pelz (nicht zu verwechseln mit
dem Schafe mitten im Süden. im Löwenpelz).

H. W. F.

On 2 February 1906 Sarah Bernhardt came to New
Haven. The undergraduate President of the Yale Dramatic
Association was Chauncey McCormick of Chicago, now
the famous art critic, largely responsible for the magnificent art exhibition at the Century of Progress Exhibition
in Chicago in 1934. A group of students went with me to her
private car at the railway station, to pay our compliments

and invite her to take tea that afternoon at the University. McCormick entered and she said 'Your mother brought you up very well, you speak French so beautifully.' She was in ebullient spirits but the day was so bitterly cold, 12 above zero, with an icy wind, that she gave him a little manuscript note on her writing-paper with the engraved legend *Quand Même*, saying she could not go out. As it had been stated in the college paper that she would appear on the campus, one of the undergraduates dressed in woman's clothes, with an enormous hat and veil, and was driven about the college grounds, throngs of students reverently standing uncovered and cheering with tremendous enthusiasm. That night she appeared in *La Dame aux Camélias*. After the play, we went back stage and I introduced a score of students and professors to her, calling her 'la plus grande actrice de deux siècles,' which seemed to please her. When I presented to her Professor McKenzie (now at Princeton) she held his hand and said 'McKenzie! comme le nom est drôle!' I asked her if she would like to hear the college football 'yell.' She stood and beat time while we gave the 'long cheer.' The marvellous woman left on the train at three o'clock in the morning for Providence.

On 22 June 1906 we sailed for Europe, spending the summer in France, Germany, Switzerland, and England. At Lincoln cathedral we saw in the close Watts's colossal statue of Tennyson, only recently placed there. It represents him looking at the Flower he had just taken from the crannied wall, 'root and all.' A party of young American girls came up and asked me who it was. 'Tennyson.' 'Why is he here?' 'Because he was born in Lincolnshire.' 'Why is he looking at his watch?'

Of all the English cathedrals, Lincoln is my favourite; yet I shall not forget rowing in a little boat on the Wear, and looking up at the majestic fortress-cathedral of Durham. On 12 September we had a beautiful journey on the

river Wye; an Englishman having told me it was the loveliest scenery in England. At Ross we entered a rowboat, and
two sturdy English oarsmen, who had fought in the Boer
War, and who said the war was a mistake, rowed us down
the river all day. We passed Goodrich Castle, where
Wordsworth saw the little child that inspired 'We Are
Seven,' the royal Forest of Dean (*Geraint and Enid*), the
Seven Sisters, Monmouth (*King Henry V*), and stayed
overnight at Tintern, visiting the Abbey, after looking at
it in the light of early dawn from the windows of our room.
We sailed from Plymouth 17 September on the *Pennsylvania*, the same day, the same ship, the same port, of precisely six years before. And in the dining-room we found
we had been assigned seats next to Professor Jacobi and
family, another exact repetition!

In New Haven on 5 November arrived the English
dramatist Henry Arthur Jones, who gave a lecture at Yale
on the drama. Our friendship began then and remained
unbroken and unclouded till his death.

This autumn Mrs. LeMoyne produced on the New York
stage *Pippa Passes*, omitting only the scene between Luigi
and his mother. Contrary to my expectation the Ottima-
Sebald scene fell flat and the last scene with the corrupt
ecclesiastic was overwhelmingly impressive. Miss Tallia-
ferro made a charming Pippa.

I never saw Edward Dowden but we had an epistolary
friendship and I felt as if I had seen him because Mahaffy,
Æ., and others gave me many anecdotes of him.

HIGHFIELD HOUSE
HIGHFIELD ROAD, RATHGAR,
DUBLIN
July 9, 1906

MY DEAR SIR:
I am very grateful to you for giving me one of the 50 copies of your
Introduction to Jane Austen's novels. It comes to a true lover and

constant reader of the novels. And I find it agrees so closely with my own judgment that I cannot but think it as just as it is certainly interesting. Perhaps however as I read three or four of the novels, I think each, while reading it, the best.

Our late Provost of Trinity College, Dublin (eminent as a Mathematician and as a Biblical critic) was a devoted Austenite, and I think somewhere in Temple Bar lurks an article on some points in the Novels by him (George Salmon).

My own introduction to her was delightful. When we were very young and very ignorant my brother (now Bishop of Edinburgh) and I were walking in Co. Wicklow and by stress of weather were compelled to spend one long wet day in a little wayside Inn. But it was the shortest of days—for a copy, wanting the title and opening leaves, of Mansfield Park made the hours speed by. We had never heard of Mansfield Park in those old antediluvian days, and when we returned to Dublin we were eager to discover who this wonderful magician was. It was not long before we knew our Jane Austen better than most readers of nearly half a century ago. And how a torn copy of Mansfield Park ever came to a little Wicklow country Inn, I cannot imagine, unless some kind Angel, humourously dropped it in his flight, for our delectation. How much you must have enjoyed your pleasant task! I am glad you pull up the Dict. Nat. Biog. for its errors. It is, I fear, swarming with errors still unnoted.

With cordial thanks, I am

Sincerely yours

EDWARD DOWDEN

Every year—when I lecture my class—I am your debtor, and confess the fact.

One of the happiest occasions of this 1906 summer in Europe was our accidental meeting with our intimate friends Mr. and Mrs. George Nettleton of Yale. We went to St. Moritz and Ragaz together and played in the tennis tournaments. George won the open singles championship of the Engadine.

46

WILLIAM DE MORGAN

My wife and I had the pleasure of meeting Mr. and Mrs. William De Morgan a number of times in their home in Chelsea, London, and in their apartments in Florence, whither they went for many years in the winter. Mr. De Morgan had been a potter until he began to write novels at the age of sixty-five; his wife was a distinguished painter. He was tall, very thin, with a thin voice and a thin beard. It was a delight to talk with him as he was always in high good humour and had had interesting experiences. He began to write by accident when he was recovering from an attack of the flu; and I believe it was his wife who persuaded him to continue and finish the manuscript of *Joseph Vance*. He gave an impression of benevolence and kindness. He was deeply religious in his own way. He told me the only parts of the Apostles' Creed that he thoroughly believed were the first seven words and the last four words, but there was no man in the world, I think, who believed them with more sincerity or with more confidence. He not only believed in personal immortality or 'immortalism' as he called it, but also in a way that was partly quizzical, partly humorous, but yet somehow wholly sincere, he believed in ghosts. That is, he believed that spirits of the departed occasionally revisited the glimpses of the moon. His long story, one of the last he wrote, *When Ghost Meets Ghost*, represented an inner conviction.

Joseph Vance was published in 1906; the author was a man of sixty-five, with no popular reputation. His novel contained two hundred and eighty thousand words. He wrote it in longhand, and the MS. looked like a bale of cotton. It was of course refused by publishers. Then Mr. Lawrence, who said it was too long, but that he wished it were longer, took it to William Heinemann, and said: 'You have got to read it.' Mr. Heinemann replied: 'I'll be damned if I do!' But he did and published it, and it had an enormous sale. In spite of the fact that it is not now being read by many, I believe it will never die.

I announced as subject for the John Hubbard Curtis prize, open to Yale undergraduates, *The Novels of De Morgan*. The prize was won by H.D.Hammond of Tennessee. The successful essay was published in the *Yale Courant*, and a copy sent to the novelist.

Mr. De Morgan wrote to the young critic, 13 August 1909,

> I have scarcely an exception to take—What I have is to be found among some jotted comments on the margins of the Courant that I return to you—I daresay you will see that your irreverence (shall I call it?) for Dickens has occasioned some implication of cavil from me—But all you young men are tarred with the same feather nowadays—
>
> Your remark about the red cap in David Copperfield made me reread the chapter. I am obliged to confess that the red cap is absurd—a mere stage expedient! He would have seen the hair, like enough. But oh dear!—What a puny scribbler that rereading made me feel!

CHELSEA
September 5, 1909

DEAR PROF. PHELPS,

How I agree with you about this spelling craze! How could I else, holding as I do that to ask the way to Charing Cross is to make an *en*quiry, but that one makes an *in*quiry into the Nature of Things? My broad impression is that *en*quiries get answers, and *in*quiries don't. Please put this down to flu, if you see no meaning in it.

But surely the Marshalsea in Dorrit is fine?—Oh yes—and the death of Merdle?

I shall expect your essay with true interest—egotistic of course, but that cannot be helped.

Always yours truly,

WM. DE MORGAN

JULY 15 1912
127, CHURCH STREET,
CHELSEA, S.W.

DEAR PROF. PHELPS

It was a pleasure to get your Italian article in the "Alumni"—What a capital idea the Browning pilgrimage was!

It makes me wish I had read "The Ring and the Book." A shocking thing for a writer to say! But its all past praying for now, for me. I refer to the study of the literae humaniores. I scarcely looked in a book, unless it was about pots or mechanisms, for forty long years. There's a confession!—a little exaggerated in form from chagrin at the truth of its spirit, but substantially true for all that.

So I am really a stranger to my Browning, not having read what so many think his greatest achievement. (That's so, isn't it?) My ignorance of this poem must be forgotten, please, in consideration of my admiration of his shorter poems, within my grasp, and especially of the fact that my enjoyment of "John Jones" has rather than otherwise enhanced that admiration. Even so a friend once told me he had never really enjoyed the "Appassionata" sonata until a man wrote, and played, a caricature of it. But how that caricaturist must have known his Beethoven! What a knowledge of Browning must Swinburne's have been!

The twenty-six letters of the alphabet are very powerful. If it were not for them the chief recollection of Britannia by the States would be the discomfiture of the former's butler by Uncle Sam a century and more ago. But the mere re-arrangement of those 26 makes Browning and Shakespeare possible—even if the latter was really somebody else.

Will the rearrangements to come last forever? They will last *us* out, anyhow—and even if only

I∞∞∞∞∞∞∞∞∞∞∞∞∞∞∞∞∞∞∞∞∞∞ ∞∞∞∞∞∞∞∞∞∞∞∞∞∞∞∞∞∞∞∞
(10)

books are possible, with original matter in them, we may expect Literature to last your undergraduates out, even at the present rate of publication. Of course the number of books is large—and there may be a sort of shoddy infinity about it if we call two books different because a word is spelled differently. But an infinity got at this way won't wash.

We called on your friend Ellsworth and he was having a music party—so we did not attempt to get in—have not experienced any result.

I'm afraid you are even warmer than we are. What with the heat, and what with Lloyd George, living is uphill work in these parts.

Our kindest regards to yourself and Mrs. Phelps.

Yours always truly,

WM. DE MORGAN

OCT. 26 1914
127, CHURCH STREET,
CHELSEA, S.W.

MY DEAR PROF. PHELPS

I am sorry to say that I am barbarous by nature and catch myself gloating over slaughter—slaughter of Germans of course!—half of them men I should have liked—a tenth of them men I should have loved. It is sickening—but . . .

A friend has just left me who maintains that the Germans never do anything that is not in strict accordance with International Law. Then a devil may break loose, and yet comply with international law!

Good forecasts—good for us—are in the air tonight! I hope—but I have done some hoping to no purpose latterly. However the last rumour I heard professed to come direct from Sir John French.

We have left Florence altogether, so you will find our nest tenanted by other birds if you go there. I feel as if the World were ending up, to the sound of melinite! And yet, as Browning wrote "God never says one word."

Our very best regards to yourselves.

Yours ever

WM. DE MORGAN

DEC. 20 1915
127, CHURCH STREET,
CHELSEA, S.W.

DEAR PROF. PHELPS:

I put aside my long novel, because, with Kultur in full swing, I felt I should spoil it. I took up an old beginning—sketched in immediately after Joe Vance—and have got about halfway through, with great difficulty. The train of the poison gas is over us all here, and I can only get poor comfort from thinking what a many submarines we have made permanently so. All the same, one of my favourite employments is thinking how to add to their number—a grisly committee—coffins full of men very like our own. For all seamen are noble, because they live face to face with Death.

Always yours

WM. DE MORGAN

He died 15 January 1917.

47

QUEER SOUNDS AND SIGHTS

On the night of 25 February 1906, with the exception of
the maids on the top floor, I was alone in the house. I
had not been well for many days, and felt particularly
miserable when I went to bed. I had lain uneasily for some
hours, and had finally lapsed into semi-consciousness. At
half-past two I was startled by the loud ringing of the
front doorbell. Accoutred as I was, I descended, and opened
the door. There was no-one. For a few moments, like the
man in Poe's poem, I stood, deep into the darkness peering.
But the darkness gave no token, and wonderingly I shut
the door. I had not got half-way up the stairs, when once
again the doorbell rang with violence. It is easy enough to
tell this lightly now, but then, alone in the house, and ill,
it was worse than mysterious. I ran to the door, and flung
it wide open. Not a soul in sight, the street silent and deserted. Then I thought it might after all not have been
the doorbell, but the telephone. Accordingly I rang up
Central, only to be informed that no-one had called my
number. While I was considering this, the doorbell once
more reverberated through the empty house. Again I
opened the door. No-one.

I decided that someone with a deficient or perverted
sense of humour was making me a victim. Accordingly I
shut the front door, and crouched directly behind it, with
the intention of leaping out and seizing the humorist as
soon as he rang again. In a few moments the bell rang
loudly; I jerked back the door and sprang outside. But

there was no-one, and no sound of retreating steps.

I stood outside the door, lost in amazement and fear, for I was terrified. I gazed wonderingly at the button, half-expecting to see some spirit-finger push it; when, to my utter dismay, the bell rang shriller and louder than ever.

If I had really believed in ghosts, that would have been sufficient evidence. As it is, I shall never forget my distress while the bell continued ringing and I was looking directly at the only means of making it ring. I closed the door, and had a bad night.

In the morning I consulted a specialist, not on nerves, but on doorbells. The explanation was simple. A mouse was enjoying the flavour of the paraffin in which the wires in the cellar were wrapped, and every time he gave a particularly fervent bite, the bell rang. I hope it scared him as much as it did me, but if so, his hunger triumphed over his fear, for he kept returning to the feast.

On another occasion I was out shooting in a desolate place in Michigan accompanied by my friend, A. K. Merritt, who will vouch for the truth of the story. Dusk was falling; there was no wind. We had wandered into a scene of stagnant desolation. Dead trees had fallen in rotten ruin across the trail, and the swampy pools were covered with a green mantle of decay. Merritt was walking in front and I close behind him. The gloom and depression of the scene in the deepening dusk had affected our spirits, so that we had not spoken for some time. Suddenly I thought of the scenery of Browning's poem, 'Childe Roland.' The lines of that masterpiece of horror would well describe this place, I thought; and I began to repeat them in my mind without saying a word aloud. Methought only one thing was needed to make the picture complete. That was the horrible horse, which in the poem stood alone and sinister in the gathering night. If that horse were here, I said to myself, this would indeed be the veritable country of Childe Roland. Something impelled me to look behind, and to my ineffable surprise and horror, I was looking directly into the tragic eyes of a forlorn old horse, at a distance of six inches. I let out a yell of uncontrollable terror.

Merritt was as startled by the yell as I had been by its cause. I asked him if the horse was really there. It was bad to have him there, but worse if he were not. Merritt reassured me on that point.

I suppose the poor old horse had been pensioned off by some farmer, and had silently followed us on the spongy ground, either because he was lonesome or because he wanted salt. But he gave me the shock of my life.

I have thought much about it since, and I am unable to determine whether the appearance of the horse at the precise moment when I was thinking of him was the coincidence—or was I all the time *subconsciously aware of his presence?* That is to say, did the nearness of the horse, even though I had no conscious knowledge of it, suggest to my subconscious mind the lines from the poem? I wish I knew.

> As for the grass, it grew as scant as hair
>   In leprosy: thin dry blades pricked the mud
>   Which underneath looked kneaded up with blood.
> One stiff blind horse, his every bone a-stare,
> Stood stupefied, however he came there:
>   Thrust out past service from the devil's stud!
>
> Alive? he might be dead for aught I know,
>   With that red gaunt and colloped neck a-strain,
>   And shut eyes underneath the rusty mane;
> Seldom went such grotesqueness with such woe;
> I never saw a brute I hated so;
>   He must be wicked to deserve such pain.

On 6 March 1906 I gave an address at the University in commemoration of the one hundredth anniversary of the birth of Mrs. Browning: the newspaper report said Browning had to live in Italy on 'account of his wife's frailty.' One reason for the erroneous dates of her birth so frequently printed was that Browning himself would not tell. One day a man met him and had the impertinence to enquire 'How old is your wife?' and Browning replied, 'I don't know, Sir; I never asked.'

While we were playing golf at Farmington 18 April, a man came running to us on the links, saying San Francisco was being destroyed by an earthquake and fire, the worst disaster that had ever happened to an American city. And unlike most sensational news, the reports the next few days showed that the situation was becoming worse and worse.

On 6 June we celebrated at the University the 300th anniversary of the birth of Corneille. The French Ambassador, J.J.Jusserand attended, and made an address, after which our students acted *Le Cid* in French. The leading actor, Francis Markoe, was an accomplished French scholar, but something went wrong with his costume. M. Jusserand did his best to control himself, but finally went into convulsions of mirth, in which the audience cordially joined. I do not believe Jusserand ever laughed more uproariously in his life.

48

VARIOUS NOTES

IN January 1907 I wrote an article for the *North American Review* on Mark Twain, in which I called him the greatest living American writer, which at that time seemed to many mere hyperbole.

On 12 February the Russian actress Alla Nazimova, who had just begun to act in English ('I have burnt my battles behind me') lunched at my house and gave an address to my students in Contemporary Drama. She said she enjoyed playing Ibsen more than Shakespeare because Shakespeare was statuesque (here she drew a statue in the air) and Ibsen was complex (she rolled her arms up dramatically). She declared that Norah would never return to her husband and as for her children, Norah would think more of her own life than of them. She was in the highest spirits and charmed the undergraduates. Shortly after this, she appeared in the theatre and after the play I took some of the students and one Princeton undergraduate to her dressing-room; and after the interview, the Princeton boy (bless his heart!) asked me, 'Is she married?' and when I told him I did not know, he said, 'Oh, Mr. Phelps, I do hope she isn't married.'

On 23 February I lectured at Hartford on Keats, and discovered after the lecture that a grand-daughter of George Keats was in the audience, accompanied by her two daughters. They were not enthusiastic over my emphasis on Keats's humble origin, which I had spoken of merely to accentuate the mystery of genius.

On 18 March I was Toastmaster at the Yale Phi Beta Kappa dinner; I lectured in Stamford that afternoon and my train returning was very late. Professor Barrett Wendell was to speak at the dinner and was staying at our house. After he dressed and came downstairs he found smoke and many firemen in the library. He called to my wife, 'I think the house is on fire, but I must go to the dinner.' Then my wife came down, and seeing the firemen she told them she was already late to a dinner and went out the front door. After that, I came tearing into the house and was surprised to find it full of firemen. 'Well, put it out as soon as you can, please; I can't wait a minute,' and I departed. They extinguished the flames, but they must have been amused at the casual manner in which all three of us took it. The chief guest at this dinner was William Howard Taft. I nominated him for President of the United States and then Professor Tracy Peck nominated him for the same office in Latin! This latter speech attracted much attention in the newspapers. The next year our guest of honour was Woodrow Wilson, the President of Princeton; who followed Taft as President of the U.S.A. After that, I gave up the Warwickian job of making Presidents by inviting them to the Phi Beta Kappa dinners, for fear I might eventually make a blunder.

At the Taft dinner Wendell whispered to me to notice how healthy the President of Yale looked and all the executive officers; whereas the Professors looked unhealthy and overworked. 'This is invariably true,' he said.

At the dinner where Wilson was present I told him a story of how two men were walking to Bridgeport and after they had gone ten miles they asked a stranger how far it was to Bridgeport and he said, 'Eight miles.' After another hour's walking they asked another, and he said, 'Eight miles.' They got the same response an hour later and then one of them said to the other, 'Well, cheer up!

It's not getting away from us; we're holding our own!' I had forgotten this, but in 1912, when the Democratic convention at Baltimore was balloting and a reporter asked Wilson what he thought his chances were, he replied, 'Well, two men were once walking to Bridgeport,' etc., and added, 'I'm holding my own.'

This Spring the undergraduates at Yale gave for the first time in the world in English, Ibsen's *Pretenders*; and William Archer the translator for the first time heard his own words spoken on the stage. And this was the beginning of my friendship with him, which gave me unalloyed pleasure for so many years. We had intimate conversations in America and in London; and once, staying at my house with his son who afterwards became a barrister in London, we took long walks. Alas, when Archer and I went together to see that disastrous first night of *Macbeth* (Lionel Barrymore) in New York, I asked 'How is your son getting along?' not knowing he had been killed in the war. 'I lost my boy.'

William Archer, professional drama critic for many years who always insisted he could not write a play, *dreamed* the plot of *The Green Goddess*. He invited Shaw to collaborate, and Shaw replied, 'When I want to write for the movies, I'll let you know.' This refusal was fortunate for Archer; he wrote the play; it made more money than he had earned during his life as critic. I went with him to its first night in New York and he was delighted with George Arliss and the enthusiasm of the audience.

In 1907, on a summer afternoon in Michigan, Emily Whitney, my wife, and I composed this vegetarian sonnet-parody; my friend Professor Irving Fisher had been writing articles about diet.

> The Meat is too much with us; late and soon,
> Guzzling and bolting, we lay waste our powers:
> Little we have in nature that is ours:

We have given our taste away, a sordid boon!
The wheat that bares her bosom to the moon:
The meals that should be eaten at fixed hours
Composed of varied vegetables and flours,
For these our stomachs now are out of tune,
They move us not. Fletcher! I'd rather be
A Pagan, suckled in some creed outworn:
So might I, standing on Lake Huron's lea,
Have a digestion somewhat less forlorn:
Have sight of PROTEID rising from the sea,
Or hear old Fisher blow his dinner horn.

At that time Mr. Fletcher had caused a sensation by recommending very sparse diet, with an enormous amount of mastication; this was Horace Fletcher (1849–1919), from whom came the words fletcherism, fletcherite, fletcherizing (now in American dictionaries).

I sent this sonnet also to my friend and former Yale pupil, Clarence Day. At that very moment he happened to be dieting himself in the sanatorium at Battle Creek, and sent me his original drawing. (See p.481.)

On 30 September with Baker of Harvard we dined in New York with Henry Arthur Jones and went with him to the opening night of his new play *The Evangelist*. This was a painful experience. Mr. Jones kept his eyes on the audience and never once looked at the stage. He reminded me of a man on trial for his life, gazing steadfastly at the jury for signs of mercy. I liked the play but it was clear that it was not a success. Walter Prichard Eaton, now a professor at Yale, was then drama critic on the *Sun*; he wrote a very fine review.

On a Whittier pilgrimage in November I met at the house of her parents, Mr. and Mrs. Charles Ingham, their little daughter Katharine, seven years old; one of the most bewitching children I ever saw. She is a well-known American novelist today—Katharine Brush.

At Whittier's house in Amesbury I saw many curiosities;

ARENCE S. DAY, JR. SECRETARY
RE OF 45 WALL STREET, N. Y.

Battle Creek
XI.   9.   1907

Sonnet

You irreverent brute !

the old bachelor poet evidently had had trouble keeping buttons on his shirt; therefore he had them all made without buttons; and every morning he pinned stiffly starched collars to the neckband; how he did this without blasphemy can be explained only by invincible piety. He never liked to see a high forehead on a woman; hence whenever the admiring ladies called on him, as they did nearly every day, he pulled their hair down nearly to their eyes. In his photograph album, containing scores of pictures given him by these fair admirers, whenever a high forehead was exposed, he had taken his pen and inked the hair down.

Henry Arthur Jones (1851–1929) celebrated a long run of *The Hypocrites* (1906–7) by giving a magnificent dinner on the evening of 28 June 1907 at the Claremont Restaurant in New York. The guests around the circular table were John Philip Sousa, Daniel Frohman, A.L.Erlanger, Samuel Harris, Henry Harris, Paul Armstrong, Charles Klein, Frederic Thompson, John Mead Howells, John Corbin, and a few others. Everyone was compelled to make at least one speech, and along toward dawn many were making speeches in unison. Paul Armstrong excitedly condemned the whole company for not praising the 'Master playwright of us all, William Gillette.' Mr. Howells made a beautiful, modest, and graceful tribute to his father, the novelist. This, and Dan Frohman's reminiscences were the only dignified speeches heard that night. Abraham Erlanger amazed us very late in the night by giving an accurate summary of every speech that had been made early in the evening by every individual present, accompanying this astounding feat of memory with an estimate of the personality and character of all speakers (only half of whom he had ever seen before) that would have been the envy of a professional psychoanalyst. Just as dawn was breaking John Philip Sousa conducted an oratorio—words and music extempore—in which we all took part. It was the only time I ever sang under his direction.

On New Year's Day 1908 we had a memorable experience in Detroit. Mr. Charles Lang Freer, the famous collector of Whistler's paintings and etchings, was kind enough to show us over his house, which had been built as a box for its treasures. There we saw the Peacock Room and many other works of art, an astonishing collection of Japanese screens, and his latest acquisition, the recently-discovered manuscript of the Gospels—which he valued for its uniqueness, but which gave him a text for one of his frequent onslaughts on religion. This was the only matter, however, which seemed to arouse his antagonism; he was most gracious, though it must have been a bore to him to exhibit his works of art over and over again to strangers. Mr. Freer had been an industrial and railway capitalist, who retired in 1900 in order to devote the rest of his life to collecting works of ancient and modern art, which on his death in 1919 he left to the Smithsonian Institution in Washington.

The story is told that when Mark Twain was introduced to Whistler, Mark went up to a painting not yet dry, and pretended to put his gloved finger on some object in the picture. Whistler cried out in horror; and Mark said, 'Don't worry; these gloves are old.'

On the evening of 3 January, at a dinner of the Society of Colonial Wars, in St. Paul, Minn., I gave a lecture on 'Jonathan Edwards and Benjamin Franklin,' and while I was reading Edwards's famous description of hell, the coloured waiters were in a state of absolute terror.

In the early evening of 17 January Professor Sanderson telephoned that he had found our Irish setter 'Lad,' lying unconscious on the pavement, evidently hit by an automobile. But when we arrived at the place, Sanderson was in bewilderment—the dog had disappeared while he was telephoning. In a state of semi-consciousness, Lad had

walked a mile to a friend's house where my wife was having
dinner. We got him home and expected he would die that
night. The whole top of his head was so crushed that it
felt like a bag of peanuts; there was a hole in the forehead
bigger than a silver dollar; one eye was completely closed;
and he lay in a state of coma. We did not expect to find
him alive in the morning; but he was still breathing,
though unconscious. We sent for the veterinary, who said
a big operation was necessary; and while we were considering this, one of the greatest surgeons in Connecticut,
Dr. Francis Bacon, who had retired from practice, and
refused even the most importunate demands, came into the
house. He had heard our dog had been injured and wished to
see him. With his fingers he pulled three or four splinters
of bone out of the hole in the head, and then said, 'Do
absolutely nothing; don't touch the dog; leave him alone.
Dogs sometimes get well of serious accidents if they are
left alone.' The 'vet' remonstrated; said an operation was
necessary or the dog would die. 'He may die anyway,'
said Dr. Bacon; 'but his only chance is to be let alone.'
Then Dr. Foster, our family physician, came in, and then
Dr. Ring, the oculist, both of whom had heard of the
accident. These regular physicians held a consultation (I
had not sent for any of them) and agreed that the dog had
a chance and that he might possibly recover the sight of
the left eye; the right one was good. The next day, while
we were at lunch, the dog came down stairs, although
seemingly unconscious; and in a few weeks, he entirely
recovered. The case attracted wide attention; the New
York papers and the Paris *New York Herald* had long
articles about it; and the oculist finally pronounced the
left eye completely normal again, saying the recovery appeared miraculous. The big hole in the dog's head turfed
over in a month or so, but until it did, he flatted his barks.
He lived nine years after that and there was no mark

or scar or unevenness of contour. It was an amazing demonstration of the recuperative forces of nature. A Japanese
student at Yale, Mr. Okamoto, sent me a picture he had
drawn of the dog in bed, with his head bandaged, dreaming of a man clad in a fur overcoat driving an automobile
(just over him in the picture) and under it the Japanese
artist had written, '*He calls me beast,*' *says Lad.*

On 27 March Madame Komisarzhevsky, a great Russian
actress, took tea in one of the undergraduate rooms and in
the evening gave the best interpretation of Norah in
A Doll's House that I ever heard. Not long after this, having
agreed to appear in some town in Russia, she insisted on
keeping her engagement, although warned that smallpox
was rampant; she played as advertised, caught the disease
and died. She was not only a great actress; she gave the
impression of being a Great Lady, a born aristocrat.

This year I gave a series of lectures on literature at the
United States Military Academy at West Point. These
expeditions are among the most pleasant memories of my
life. I enjoyed the cadet audiences; and at the officers'
mess and in other meetings, I shall always remember the
remarkable conversations with Colonel and Mrs. Hugh
Scott, the Astronomer-librarian E.S.Holden, Colonel and
Mrs. C.W.Larned, Colonel and Mrs. Howze, and others.
I have never found a more interesting group of people.
At the conclusion of the course, I was offered the permanent position of Professor at the Academy, with the ultimate rank and pay of Colonel in the Army, with its per-
quisites. My devotion to Yale was all that kept me from
accepting.

One very amusing incident took place at my last lecture
in May. It was a warm and beautiful day and when the
cadets had marched in with precision, the big doors at the
end of the auditorium were left wide open. Being the only
man in the room facing them, in the middle of the lecture

I observed two large setter dogs enter; and as I was the only face they could see and the only voice audible, I felt sure they would come to the platform, which of course was what happened. These big friendly setters came down the aisle, mounted the platform and placed their paws on my shoulders. The cadets wanted to laugh, but they were in the presence of their officers and the situation was strained. I petted the dogs and suddenly thought of the right thing to say then and there, instead of on the way home. I exclaimed 'Why, these are *setters*, and I had expected to see only West Pointers!' Then the whole audience roared with laughter and the situation was saved.

In 1908 Mrs. Humphry Ward lectured in America, but I could not possibly have accepted the invitation in the following letter. I wrote it would be impossible for me to praise her and what deplorable taste I should exhibit if I came and said what I thought. Gummere told me that Mrs. Ward's novels were filled with clever and brilliant people who never said anything clever or brilliant. Here is the letter:

HAVERFORD, 31 MARCH, 1908

MY DEAR PHELPS:

We are very anxious to have you come on Monday night next, 6th April, and just talk for ten minutes as an American makeweight to Mrs. Humphry Ward, who addresses the Contemporary Club on the Peasant (it looked like peanut as I wrote it) in Literature and Fiction. It will be a turnout of all Philadelphia intellect, and we have had to take the largest room at the Bellevue-Stratford, the regular place for hoe-downs of the first magnitude. Now of course the club will pay all your expenses and that sort of thing; but my concern is of another sort. I want somebody on our side of the water to speak who really knows the subject. It is pride, Sir, pride. Mrs. H.W. has an exaggerated reputation, to my mind, but they are all capping and cringing as if 'Old Leviticus himself' were back again. Can't you just throw your cap over the mill, cut Yale, and come? Weston, the Secretary, will write you about particulars; but I wish you would wire him, at his expense, what your decision may be, without waiting to hear from him:—S.Burns Weston, 1415 Locust St., Phila.—And make it 'Yes.' It will be a good occasion for you and Yale will not regret letting you go. Weir Mitchell will be on deck, and many another; but we want *you*.

Yours faithfully,

F. B. GUMMERE

When my book appeared, in which I attacked the novels of Mrs. Ward and praised those of William De Morgan, Gummere wrote me at some length. I still hold to my high regard for De Morgan's novels; but I wonder if the present neglect of them by the public is evidence that Gummere was right? I never believed De Morgan to be the equal of Dickens, only that he was more like him than any other writer of the twentieth century.

I wholly agree with Gummere about Norris, the neglect of whose novels is unfortunate. They are indeed 'never dull.' But despite the efforts of his fellow novelists to induce the public to read him, for the best craftsmen of his time saluted him as a peer, he is still largely unread. I met Norris in Paris and found him just as attractive as his books.

I agree with Gummere too in the implication in the sentence about Hancock, although Allen is not altogether forgotten. Professor Hancock I knew well and his early death was a severe loss to academic scholarship, however much he exaggerated the merits of *The Choir Invisible*.

20 JANUARY, 1910

DEAR PHELPS:
    Your book reached me yesterday morning, and I read it last night,—all of it.
    One can't dust a woman's jacket, as Macaulay put it about his fun with Croker; but whatever the feminine equivalent may be, you have achieved it with Mrs. Ward. I subscribe to every syllable. One crowlet I should pick with you is de Morgan. *Joseph Vance* through the

initial stages,—and *praeterea nihil*, is my firm word. How can you range the man with Dickens? *Vance* was read aloud to me when my eyes were tied up; I took it steadily and all of it; and my roar of delight at the beginning changes to cries of pain for the rest.

To see what was wrong in *me*, I have just read *Somehow Good* once more; and with all the humbleness of my spirit,—for you don't talk in vain,—I could find nothing that makes for greatness in the whole extent. Get down your *Under the Greenwood Tree* and read how William Dewy and Reuben and the rest, with Leaf, visit Parson Maybold, in his study. Like the parson's own skin, that scene 'bursts out a'bleedin' afresh every time I think of it. Now go back to de Morgan,—can you draw such blood, any blood, from him? My good colleague Hancock once wrote for the *Outlook* an article 'On the Art of James Lane Allen.' And you, too, are a generous man.

Do you know that the best second-rate novelist in England is W.E.Norris? Do you like *Matrimony*? My dear old F.J.Child 'put me on' Norris, and I've read him all. Prolific, easy, mildly satiric, unexciting, but never dull. . . .

Cuss me for all this. The rest is admirable. The Hardy chapter I will swear to *jurare in verba magistri* with absolute emphasis on the magistracy.

Yours enviously,

F.B. GUMMERE

Francis B.Gummere was one of the most distinguished Professors of English Literature in America, both as scholar and teacher, and loved Haverford College so loyally that nothing would induce him to go elsewhere, though he had been offered a professorship at Harvard. His conversation was full of wit and sense; it was always a pleasure to be with him.

49

FIRST JOURNEY TO CALIFORNIA

Thirteen Thousand Miles in the West

In the year 1908 I was invited to lecture at the University
of California in Berkeley, during the summer session. Accordingly we left New Haven on 9 June, and took the
Santa Fé railway from Chicago. Near Kansas City we
found enormous floods everywhere. For many miles the
wheels were under water. It was a curious experience, to
stand on the rear platform of the train, and to see the
'wake' made by our passage; no land visible for miles.
On 14 June we saw for the first time the Grand Canyon
of the Colorado. We stayed at a hotel there three days and
saw the Canyon by sunlight, twilight, dawn, and moonlight; and took drives of many miles. The Canyon is the
most sublime spectacle I have ever seen, and the only one
of which a picture gives not even a faint representation
or conception. It seems all the more astounding because
the approach to it is so commonplace and tame. We
walked through rough grass and scrubby, dwarfed trees,
and then suddenly—But it is vain to attempt a description,
either of the vast abyss or of one's impressions.

When we left the Canyon, taking the small junction-
train to Williams, the fireman of the locomotive had a
day off, and sat down in the train beside me. I said, 'The
Canyon is the most sublime spectacle I have ever seen.
You have to make three or four trips back and forth every
day. Does it still seem to you wonderful? or is it just the

end of the run?' He replied, 'You want to know how the canyon affects me? I can tell you best by quoting poetry.' Then he recited from memory the whole of Bryant's *Thanatopsis*. 'That's the way I feel about the Canyon and about scenes of natural beauty.'

That evening as we stopped out in the desert in the moonlight, the brakeman got off the rear platform and picked a bouquet of wild flowers. He said, 'I love flowers.' I do not know whether all the train-hands on the Santa Fé love natural scenery and flowers; these are the only two with whom I talked.

Among the travellers on this train was a German military officer, Major Steinbach. He had a German Baedeker of the United States, and was assiduously verifying everything he saw. In a conversation with him, I asked him about the German army and military life, and had the temerity to ask if he thought two famous recent plays which I had seen in Germany, *Rosenmontag* and *Zapfenstreich*, where the cruelty and hierarchy of the military officers were bitterly attacked, and the fact that both plays were popular and received with shouts of approval, had any significance. Did these plays represent anything evil or that needed correction or modification in German social life? In the emphatic manner characteristic of Germans in authority, he said 'There is nothing whatever in these attacks on German army life. The plays you mention were written by Jews. No Jew is allowed to be an officer, so they attack the army. That's all there is to it. And furthermore, something will have to be done about the Jews. They are cleverer and more unscrupulous in business affairs and in civic life than Christians. It is a great question what to do with them.' This was in 1908.

We reached Los Angeles on the morning of 17 June. My brother Arthur, who lived there, and my oldest brother Dryden, who was visiting him, welcomed us at the station.

We drove out through Pasadena, played golf, and that evening I spoke at a dinner of the Yale Alumni Association. The next afternoon I spoke to 1,700 pupils at the High School.

In San Francisco there were many evidences of the earthquake, or 'fire' as it was called there, but the city was making marvellous convalescent strides. Californian hospitality was all it was said to be. After our first evening, we were invited to dinner somewhere *every night for six weeks*. My first lecture was at eight in the morning, the second at ten daily. I gave a course on American literature at eight and on Tennyson and Browning at ten. The earnestness and enthusiasm of those students—many of whom were school-teachers from California, Oregon, and Nevada—was tremendous. It was a delight to speak to such eager and responsive students.

In the American literature class, I shall always remember two incidents. One day, quite unconscious of the sacrilege, I said, 'When I get back to America. . . .' A roar of laughter went up from the audience; that sentence was never finished.

The other incident was even more embarrassing at the time, though it resulted in a friendship. I was lecturing on Bret Harte, partly biographical, partly critical. In the latter part I spoke of the genius displayed in his early tales. In the early part, I made some derogatory remarks about his character. At the close of the lecture, a member of the California faculty whispered to me, 'Bret Harte's sister is in the audience, would you like to speak to her?' 'No, I should not like to, but I will.' A sweet-faced white-haired old lady was led up to the desk. She said, without waiting for any introductory formalities, 'Young man, every word you spoke of my brother's character is a lie!'

I replied that I earnestly hoped she was right, that I hated to believe what I had said, but supposed I had it on unimpeachable authority; that if she would give me the facts, I would not only correct what I had said, but would make a humble apology. We then found a place where we could talk together in seclusion, and the result was a warm friendship that lasted until her death. She told me that Frank, as she called him, was always kind to her and to his family, that he was noble and good in every way, and that the things said about his domestic and financial habits were slanders. The next day I began my lecture by saying that although I had been informed my statements were false, I was glad I had said them, because otherwise I might not have had the pleasure of meeting his sister, Mrs. Wyman, who had given me the facts.

Several times after that, I had conversation with her. 'I know how you adore the genius of Mark Twain. I want to give you this letter.'

It was a letter of inestimable value, yellow with age, that Mark had written to Harte on the day of the publication of *The Celebrated Jumping Frog*, 1 May 1867, a few days before his lecture in Cooper Union, and shortly before the voyage to the Holy Land that was to give him immortal fame. I included it in my *Essays on Books* (Macmillan 1914), now out of print.

WESTMINSTER HOTEL, MAY 1, 1867

DEAR BRET—

I take my pen in hand to inform you that I am well and hope these few line [*sic*] will find you enjoying the same God's blessing.

The book is out, and is handsome. It is full of damnable errors of grammar and deadly inconsistencies of spelling in the Frog sketch because I was away and did not read the proofs—but be a friend and say nothing about these things. When my hurry is over I will send you an autograph copy to pisen the children with.

I am to lecture in Cooper Union next Monday night. Pray for me.

We sail for the Holy Land June 8. Try and write me (at this hotel), and it will be forwarded to Paris, where we remain 10 to 15 days.

Regards and best wishes to Mrs Bret and the family.

Truly Yr Friend

MARK

The University of California deserves credit for what seems to have been forgotten. After Bret Harte had published *The Luck of Roaring Camp* in the *Overland Monthly* (1869) the University, then only a few years old, offered to make Harte *Professor of Recent Literature*, at a fine salary. Harte declined; but if he had accepted, California would have had the honour (if you like) of giving the first university course in the world on contemporary novels; that dubious honour was reserved for me in 1895 at Yale. But so far as I know, not any university has ever had a Professorship of Recent Literature. The formal vote of the trustees appointing Harte with that title is in the records.

The climate of Berkeley in the summer suited me perfectly. I was told that I would get sick of sunshine and long for clouds and rain; I never did. It was a blessing to know in advance that one could make any outdoor arrangements with confidence. Every morning we got up early; it was like a mild winter day; a fog covered the sky; if we had not known it couldn't rain, we should have thought it was going to rain in five minutes. We turned on the steam heat, and had breakfast in a well-heated dining room. Then I went to my first lecture at eight o'clock at the University, wearing an overcoat; when I came out of the lecture, the sun was shining bright, the temperature was eighty; another gorgeous summer day. After lunch we went out to play tennis or golf, carrying an overcoat although the temperature was about eighty-five. Along about four in the afternoon the sky became overcast, the fog rolled in at the Golden Gate, and during the rest of the day the temperature was about fifty. So we had four seasons of the year every day, with the one exception that it never rained or snowed.

Although it is next door, San Francisco is colder than Berkeley; the temperature during summer ranges usually from 52 to 60, and about four-thirty in the afternoon a cold fog rolls in with an icy wind from the ocean.

I had read Stevenson's descriptions of the beauty of the fog but did not realize what he meant until we ascended Mount Tamalpais. On 18 July Professor and Mrs. Osterhout took us on an early morning ferry to San Francisco, and on another ferry to Mill Valley. Then we took the train up the mountain. It was intensely hot up there until the middle of the afternoon, when we saw the fog rolling in at the Golden Gate; apparently a solid grey mass. It covered the cities of San Francisco, Berkeley and Oakland. Overhead was the blue sky and the brilliant sun; underneath was this infinite fog, glistering, dazzling white, rising and falling at various levels like a sea of silver, one of the most beautiful sights I have ever beheld. We came down the mountain on a 'gravity' car, that is a car equipped only with brakes. It was exciting. With this vehicle we reached Redwood Canyon; and saw the superb redwood trees, given to the United States by my Yale classmate William Kent. Among these trees we met the dramatist Percy Mackaye and his sister.

A few days later, at the Bohemian Club I met Kent and Gifford Pinchot, Yale 1889, afterwards Governor of Pennsylvania. On the same day at a meeting of the San Francisco Browning Society, I met Agnes Tobin, intimate friend of Joseph Conrad, William De Morgan, and many other contemporary British novelists. She gave me an amusing photograph of 'The Worship of William Heinemann.' In the picture, the publisher Heinemann is standing in mock solemn grandeur, and on their knees, imploring and worshipping him, are William De Morgan, Edmund Gosse, Agnes Tobin and another acolyte.

We spent a delightful week-end at the magnificent country home of Mrs. Phoebe Hearst, mother of William R. Hearst, whose two little children were there. Professor

Robert Herrick, the novelist, and his son Philip, were with us. Mrs. Hearst was then sixty-five; a rather small, slight figure, very clear-cut features, keenly intelligent face. She was kindness itself, showing us the treasures of the vast dwelling. A pure white building, standing entirely alone among rolling hills with mountains in the distance, no town or village in the neighbourhood, it seemed like a feudal castle, with its army of retainers. So it was; only far more comfortable.

Professor Thomas R. Bacon of the University of California, one of the most interesting men I ever knew, discussed past members of the Faculty. Every college president is called a liar by somebody. When I asked Bacon what he thought of the astronomer E.S. Holden, who at one time was President of the University of California, Bacon replied, 'He is a very able man; but the truth is not in him.' Later I met Holden at West Point, and asked him what he thought of Professor Bacon. 'Ah, don't you think he looks exactly like a hired assassin? Wouldn't you hate to meet him on a dark night?'

The familiar story illustrating the reputation for veracity attained by college presidents is generally told at the inauguration of every new one. When Dr. Canfield was inaugurated at Ohio State University, President Eliot of Harvard said to him, 'Well, Canfield, now you are President, and everybody will call you a liar.' 'Why, Dr. Eliot, did any one ever call *you* a liar?' 'Worse than that,' said Eliot, 'they proved it.'

The difficulty any President has in being regarded as truthful comes partly from his conversations with assistant professors who seek promotions or increases of salary. It is almost impossible for him to say anything without being misunderstood. The best story on this I ever read was by Robert Herrick, my colleague in California; but when I told him so, he said he had no recollection of ever having written or published such a tale. It appeared in the *Atlantic Monthly*.

Many English visitors to California, wishing to speak the vernacular, and please their hosts, call San Francisco 'Frisco.' As this is regarded everywhere among cultivated California people as the last word in disgusting vulgarity, it is better to speak of the city with its real name, giving the full value to every syllable.

It was in San Francisco that Stevenson had his first cocktail, sometimes regarded as America's most important contribution to civilization. Stevenson said, 'I took one sip and a streak of fire shot down my right leg. Thereafter I had the sensation as of a burning coal in the pit of the stomach, not altogether unpleasant.'

On the way West, I was sitting in the smoking car one evening and a man sitting opposite kept looking at me. Finally he came over, took the seat next to mine and said, 'You *are* Lloyd Osbourne, aren't you?' I replied, 'You mean Stevenson's stepson?' He affirmed it. I told him I felt flattered but that I was not Mr. Osbourne and had never seen him. 'This won't do; you are Mr. Osbourne, and for some reason you are travelling *incog*.' Nothing that I could say convinced this gentleman. 'I don't see why you won't admit it, Mr. Osbourne; surely you must remember that night in Samoa when you and I sat out and talked together for hours.' Finally he went away sorrowful.

Some years later I met Isobel Strong, Osbourne's sister. I asked her if I looked like her brother. She scrutinized me closely and exclaimed, 'Why, yes, you do very much resemble Lloyd.' Not long after that I met Lloyd Osbourne at the Coffee House in New York and told him of the incident on the train.

I have sometimes played poker for fun, just to see which member of the party would first lose all his chips. I am the worst poker player in the world, having the opposite of a poker face. Everyone knows whether I have a big hand or whether I am bluffing.

I also have the misfortune to look guilty when I am innocent. Years ago when the Pullman fare from New Haven to New York was fifty cents, I caught the train just too late to buy a ticket. The Pullman conductor came through, and as he approached me, I remembered my total possessions were a ten dollar bill and a fifty cent piece. And I reflected that I needed to have that ten changed; but 'if I give it to him won't he ask me for something smaller and if I then produce the coin, won't he believe that the coin is bad and that he got it because he was asking for it?' All these reflexions passed through my mind as he drew near and all happened as rehearsed in my thought. I offered the ten. He asked if I had anything smaller. Looking like a crook, I produced the coin. He took it reluctantly and suspiciously, glaring at me. He tried to scratch it with his finger-nails. By now I had the appearance of a criminal. He looked at me sternly a long time. Then he went out on the vestibule of the train and I heard him bouncing the coin against metal. Every time he passed through the car he looked at me.

My last lectures in the Summer School at Berkeley were given on 31 July; it was painful to say farewell to such devoted students.

That night we took the train at Oakland for Portland. Many times I have taken a sleeper on warm evenings and felt cold in the hours before dawn. This experience was the opposite. The evening air at Oakland when we took the train was very cold; but as we went toward Sacramento in the night the temperature rose, and it was one of the hottest nights I have ever spent on a train. The next day was the hottest day, certainly. The temperature was 108 in the shade at every station and in the dining-

car, with all the fans going, it was 98. Mount Shasta was
a refreshing sight, an isolated peak, 14,000 feet, covered
with snow. Arriving at Portland, Oregon, the second morning, there was a great change; it was refreshingly cool.

Wherever we went we met former Yale students and
friends, who did everything possible to make our visits
enjoyable.

We took the train up the Columbia River to the Dalles
and returned to Portland by river steamer; I saw more
splendid scenery that afternoon than on any other river in
the world. Over and over again, looking at the innumerable
lofty mountain cascades, I thought of Tennyson's lines in
The Lotos Eaters.

> And like a downward smoke, the slender stream
> Along the cliff to fall and pause and fall did seem.
>
> A land of streams! some, like a downward smoke,
> Slow-dropping veils of thinnest lawn, did go;
> And some thro' wavering lights and shadows broke,
> Rolling a slumbrous sheet of foam below.
> They saw the gleaming river seaward flow
> From the inner land: far off, three mountain tops,
> Three silent pinnacles of aged snow,
> Stood sunset-flush'd: and, dew'd with showery drops,
> Up-clomb the shadowy pine above the woven copse.

After a visit to Seattle, we decided to make the round
trip by railway from Vancouver to Banff and back to see
the mountain scenery and Lake Louise. The scenery from
the railway was superb; enormous canyons, rushing rivers,
and mighty mountains. One westerner, being asked by a
Boston lady if the scenery along the Canadian Pacific
was good, replied 'Good? Good? Lady, on one side you
can look up ten thousand feet; on the other side, you can
spit twelve thousand.'

Yet this magnificent scenery was marred for me by a
misfortune. During the day of 10 August I suffered more

acute physical pain than in any other day of my life. It was an ulcerated tooth that finally gave me a temperature of 102; getting off the train at Banff, I found there was no dentist in the town. I telephoned to Calgary and made it clear to the dentist that he must on no account miss the train. I was sick in bed, in agony, quite unable to travel. At eight o'clock in the evening, after waiting for hours, word came from Calgary that the dentist had missed the train. We found a doctor in Banff who said he had occasionally pulled teeth for lumber-jacks. After a fearful struggle, he finally succeeded in getting mine out, unfortunately breaking the sound tooth next to it, for which I have found it difficult to forgive him. As he went out in the hall, I heard him say to a friend, 'It's a wonder I didn't break his damned jaw.'

At the dining-table in Vancouver, I met an Englishman, and I said 'You may be behind the times here in Vancouver, but why do you advertise the fact?' 'What on earth do you mean?' 'Well, look at the dinner-card. It says, *Vancouver, B.C.*' 'But it doesn't mean *that*, you know!'

We spent a day or so in Victoria, a garden-spot indeed, and more English than England. I wish we might have stayed there a long time.

On Tuesday 11 August it rained, the first rain we had seen since 14 June. To me it was not welcome.

From Seattle we took the excursion steamer *Spokane* to see the sights in Alaska, a fifteen-day trip, with marvellous scenery; the sea filled with bright blue icebergs, and tall mountains completely covered with snow rising from the sea. The boat takes the so-called inside route; one is in the open sea only four hours, in Queen Charlotte Sound, but during those four hours I saw more acute cases of sea-sickness than on any other voyage. There was an Australian gentleman who stood by the rail with a faraway look in his eyes, who erupted with such regularity that I called him *Old Faithful*. It was a fascinating spectacle, for it was possible to predict the exact moment of his next explosion. This was on a Monday afternoon and watching him, we counted back to the previous Thursday's luncheon, taking three meals for each day.

Besides this regularity, the like of which I have never seen, this Australian was a most interesting person. I told him all I knew about Australia was what I had read when a small boy in Charles Reade's novel, *It Is Never Too Late to Mend*. I asked him if he had ever read that book. He said the book had changed his life. 'I was born in Birmingham, England, and when I was nine years old I read that story. It took such a mighty hold on my imagination that I determined to see Australia. I ran away from home, grew up in Australia, was successful in business there, happily married, have two sons, and am now at the age of 45, for the first time returning to England to see my native city.'

At Skagway, our farthest north, nearly 60 degrees, I had the pleasure of meeting Mrs. Pullen, who lived there. A few months previously I had seen and talked with her son, an undergraduate at West Point. I told her she should be very proud of him. He was the fourth in his class in scholarship, Captain of the football team, respected and beloved by students and Faculty. She was quite overcome by emotion and thanked me with tears in her eyes. When we got back to the steamer, we found our stateroom filled with magnificent flowers, sent there by Mrs. Pullen.

On the way back east, we spent a week in Yellowstone Park, the most fantastic place in America; absolutely grotesque scenery. It seemed more like a comic opera than anything else, combining so much beauty, horror, and mirthful distortion. Everything is abnormal; one sees Paradise, one sees Hell, but nothing natural or human.

> Now blotches rankling, coloured gay and grim,
>   Now patches where some leanness of the soil's
>   Broke into moss or substances like boils;
> Then came some palsied oak, a cleft in him
> Like a distorted mouth that splits its rim
>   Gaping at death, and dies while it recoils.

And now that I am quoting from Browning's 'Childe Roland,' readers will remember the stanza describing the unexpected river.

> A sudden little river crossed my path
>   As unexpected as a serpent comes.
>   No sluggish tide congenial to the glooms;
> This, as it frothed by, might have been a bath
> For the fiend's glowing hoof—to see the wrath
>   Of its black eddy bespate with flakes and spumes.

Stephen Philbin, who had been an undergraduate student of mine (1910), told me that he was a guest at a luncheon given by Ex-President Theodore Roosevelt, recently returned from his hunting expedition to Africa with his son Kermit. 'At twilight one evening, we were in a jungle where no white man had ever been before; when suddenly at our feet rushed a narrow stream, going at such speed that it startled us, for we had almost stepped into it. We paused and in the silence Kermit began to recite aloud the stanza from "Childe Roland." "Why, Kermit, I did not know that you knew that poem!" Then we repeated aloud together the three stanzas about the river.'

Browning wrote that poem in one day, 3 January 1852, in his apartment in Paris, to the accompaniment of vehicles on the Champs Elysées. In the next century two Americans recited parts of it aloud in a silent twilight in a remote desolation in Africa.

50

W.D.HOWELLS

ONE day in the late nineties I had the pleasure of a long conversation with Mr. Howells at his home in New York. He was extremely kind and made an indelible impression of sincerity and nobility. He expressed his dislike of romanticism in the strongest terms; his creed was realism. I never saw him or any one else laugh more unrestrainedly than he did while discussing romantic fiction; 'he drew himself up to his full height,' etc. He laughed till the tears ran down his face.

He gave a lecture in New Haven on 19 February 1900 and the next day he came to lunch at our house. Other guests were Professors T.R.Lounsbury, Henry A.Beers, Theodore S.Woolsey, Charlton M.Lewis. Mr. Howells was particularly agreeable, courteous, and kind to my mother. After luncheon, in my library, when he saw the Nathan Haskell Dole edition of Tolstoy in many volumes, he was enormously interested, as he had not known of its existence.

40 WEST 59TH STREET
March 25, 1900

MY DEAR MR. PHELPS:

Thank you for the book which you have sent me, and I will read it as soon as I get time, and write you again about it.

I have not been very well and I have been very busy; otherwise I should have acknowledged before this the great pleasure I enjoyed at your house, in meeting your family and friends. The cordial interest with which your Mother met me was especially gratifying and hereafter I shall write nothing without hoping that she will like it. I deeply felt the kindness of your whole household, and of all New Haven.

Yours sincerely,

W. D. HOWELLS

48 WEST 59TH STREET
May 24, 1902

MY DEAR MRS. PHELPS:

The books came yesterday, and I am very glad of them, and of the privilege of keeping them a little while. I hope to return them very early next month, after I have written my paper. They are just what I wanted.

We are greatly interested in this household by Mr. Phelps's Richardson enterprise; but I have not yet had time to read Mrs. Howells the *Clarissa* introduction. Do give him my best regards and wishes for his prompt and full recovery. I feel, rather selfishly, that he cannot be spared from the kind of work he is doing to be sick long. (Thank you for not saying he was 'ill.') I have not forgotten my delightful lunch with you. Will you kindly remember me to all under your roof, especially to Mrs. Phelps, sr.?

Yours sincerely,

W. D. HOWELLS

W.D.HOWELLS
KITTERY POINT, MAINE
July 28, 1907

MY DEAR MR. PHELPS:

Nothing ever gives me so much pleasure as praise of my son, and if the praise is from you! I am afraid, however, that since you speak of him as a young man, he may have acquired merit with you by his youthful appearance. He will be 39 in a fortnight, and he has had time to go through Harvard, get to be Diplomé of the French government at the Beaux Arts, and practice his profession twelve years in New York. I tell you all this that you may discount your favor as much as you think just. But he was as much pleased by your letter as if he deserved it every word.

I am slowly 'getting round' to your beautiful edition of the divine

Jane (I read your essay with great satisfaction) and hope to do a North Am. Rev. paper about it before the summer is over.

With regards to Mrs. Phelps and yourself,

Yours sincerely,

W.D.HOWELLS

W.D.HOWELLS, 130 WEST 57TH STREET
March 4, 1910

DEAR MR. PHELPS:

I ought to have written you before; now my wife is so very sick, I can hardly think what to say. But I felt the very great kindness and fairness of what you wrote about me; you have always been kind, and more than fair. I don't think Tolstoy has affected me aesthetically; my pace was set long before his giant strides overtook me; but his moral influence was like a 'religious experience' and I hope it will never end with me.

I liked your criticisms of other people as well as of myself; though I should have put Hardy above all the other living English. Stevenson is food for babes—boy babes—in his fiction, though he is a true, rare poet.

Yours sincerely,

W.D.HOWELLS

The doctor has just reported my wife a little better, and I am sorry I don't, won't, or can't praise R.L.S.

51

MAHAFFY AND JAPAN

On 7 January 1909 Professor J.P.Mahaffy of Trinity College, Dublin, whom I had not seen since we had had many talks together at Chautauqua in 1889, stayed a few days at our house and gave a lecture at Yale; I gave a formal dinner for him, inviting only the Professors of Latin and Greek, including Ex-President Dwight. I was shocked to see how old Mahaffy looked (he was only seventy), but he was as much of a Tory as ever. In 1889 he told me that he and Gladstone used to be intimate friends; they made many excursions together; 'but now,' said he, 'if I should meet him, I should refuse to recognize him; I would have nothing to do with him.' And in view of the disclosures about Mrs. O'Shea which startled the public and set back the cause of Home Rule in the very next year, 1890, it is interesting to recall what Mahaffy said to me in 1889. 'Parnell is one of the worst libertines in England; has many affairs.' I have no idea whether there is any truth in this or not; but nobody hated Gladstone and Parnell and Home Rule more than those in authority at Trinity College, Dublin.

This time, twenty years later, I went to the railway station in New Haven to meet him; he carried a huge rug, and seemed surprised I was able to recognize him! After dinner, the Japanese servant entered and placed some wood on the fire and then withdrew. 'I don't like that,' said Mahaffy, 'these Japanese are really spies; they are studying our resources.'

In the Irish rebellion of Easter 1916, Mahaffy directed the defence of the College. He was 77 years old.

In the collection of old portraits at Yale, Mahaffy was particularly interested in the contemporary painting of Bishop Berkeley and his family. He talked a good deal about him. His conversation was always interesting. He said when Oscar Wilde was an undergraduate and he had taken him with him on a journey to Italy, the young man's wit was as brilliant and as spontaneous as in later years. A wonderful travelling companion.

On 26 January we dined at the house of Professor and Mrs. John Berdan; as I bent to stroke their large cat, the animal bit me and drew blood. Our hosts were alarmed, but I said laughingly there was nothing to worry about so far as I was concerned; but that I feared for the cat, as I was sure I was full of poison. For several days thereafter, Berdan would open the door of my college room and ask 'How are you *now*?' I told him he was disappointed not to find me in convulsions, and again I said 'Do take care of your cat: give him an antidote.' Three days later he entered my room in a state of excitement. 'The cat died this morning!' I pretended not to be astonished.

On 11 February we heard Mischa Elman, 'a young Russian violinist,' give a recital in the theatre; he was unknown and only a few persons were present. But he was soon to be the reigning sensation in America and in Europe, until Jascha Heifetz appeared.

On 30 June at Yale Commencement, I officiated for the first time as Public Orator, in the temporary absence of Professor Perrin. On the platform, as one of the regular members of the Corporation, was the President of the United States, William Howard Taft; he told me that once he was introduced by a voluble chairman who said, 'The name of this man is known in every part of the world—Willian *Henry* Taft.'

The last person I presented for the degree was William Graham Sumner. The audience rose and he received such a tribute that the tears ran down his face. He had less than a year to live.

On 6 November the New Theatre opened in New York with a dress rehearsal of *Antony and Cleopatra*, with Edward Sothern and Julia Marlowe. It lasted till one a.m. I sat next to Thomas Edison, who could not hear a word, but who remained cheerfully till the end. In the afternoon we attended the public exercises held on the stage. J.Pierpont Morgan presided; addresses were made by Governor Charles Evans Hughes and Elihu Root. Forbes-Robertson gave Hamlet's address to the players. This theatre proved a financial failure, but it had a greater effect on the art of producing plays in America than anything else. Under the direction of Winthrop Ames, plays were produced with wonderful company-acting and with appropriate scenery. It was a turning-point in the history of the American stage. Some of their greatest successes were Galsworthy's *Strife*, Maeterlinck's *Blue Bird*, Besier's *Don*, and various plays of Shakespeare, notably *A Winter's Tale*.

52

JOURNEY TO THE SOUTH

On 5 January 1910 we moved from our old house at 44 High Street, which my father had built in 1868, to our new house at 110 Whitney Avenue, ground for which had been broken in November 1908. It is on the exact plot of ground where we first lived after our marriage in December 1892; just before breaking ground for the new house, we sold the old wooden one on the premises for fifty dollars! Our new house of Colonial style was very comfortable and for the first time in our lives we had electric light. Someone told me that as this was the first house we had built, we should only learn from it how to build another; that after we moved in, we should find many disappointments. The humble truth is that we were satisfied indoors and out on the first day we moved thither, and after nearly thirty years in it, we like it better than ever. On the day we moved the thermometer fell to zero; no mud or dust entered the house and the workmen had to move with speed.

Shortly after we were settled we were visited one evening by thirty of our neighbours who gave us a surprise party as a welcome. This was one of the happiest evenings of our lives.

On 18 June in the open air on the Yale campus the students gave a fine performance of *The Taming of the Shrew*—the feature being the admirable acting of Katherine by William C. Bullitt, Yale sophomore, who during the war was assistant in the Department of State and was sent abroad on various missions, and who was years later to become famous as American Ambassador to Russia and to France.

At Commencement John Burroughs received an honorary degree and stayed at our house; he said he had never owned a gown, so he did me the honour of wearing mine.

In December we saw Florida for the first time. We reached Jacksonville some four hours late, and transferred to the St. Augustine train. It had been raining heavily in the old Spanish town, and as we drove from the tracks to the hotel, the soft, balmy air was heavy with the scent of flowers. The two following days were superb; a real whiff from the tropics. We visited the old fort, the wonderful ocean beach, the slimy collection of crocodiles, and picked splendid oranges off the trees in a spacious grove.

At St. Augustine we saw two distinguished persons, and met one of them. We saw the great railway magnate Flagler, and had the pleasure of meeting Mr. Chatfield-Taylor of Chicago. He was writing a Life of Goldoni, and was interested to hear of the Yale performance of *The Fan*.

Wednesday, 21 December, is a day I have not yet forgotten, though I have made every effort to do so. We left Jacksonville early in the morning on a train that loafed across the longest width of Florida, with the palpably hypocritical pretence of ultimately reaching New Orleans. This train moved like a snail suffering from hookworm. The locomotive made a house to house canvass. However, we had a fine opportunity to become intimately acquainted with the hamlets strung along the line, as twenty minutes were assigned to each. At Tallahassee a large covey of girls flew aboard, and although it was pleasant to see how radiantly happy they were at the closing of school for the holidays, and although youth is always glorious, still, a pack of hyenas would have made less noise.

We entered New Orleans about eleven in the forenoon of
22 December, four hours late, and were gladdened by the
sight of Stanhope Bayne-Jones, now Dean of the Yale
School of Medicine. He was our guide and philosopher during the day, exhibiting the quaint French landmarks of the
city, giving us a marvellous Gallic luncheon at Antoine's,
taking us out to the wonderful parks, the great shell road,
Tulane University, and the impressive dwellings of the
dead, all buried above ground, in aristocratic miniature
mansions of stone. That evening occurred the Yale Alumni
dinner, arranged by LaCour, '04, and gracefully presided
over by Stewart.

An additional pleasure in visiting New Orleans was that
it was the birthplace and home of Lewis C.Everard of the
Class of 1908. He had gone all the way from New Orleans
to New Haven without any friends or influence or money,
supported himself all through the four years, sent money
home to help his parents, was elected to Phi Beta Kappa
and became Champion Intercollegiate Gymnast. After
graduation he became my Secretary, later a member of the
Yale Faculty and afterwards entered the Government
Service. In New Orleans I had the pleasure of meeting his
proud parents. In the nineteen-thirties he had three sons at
Yale.

We were taken to the French opera, one of the most interesting experiences of the whole expedition, and we saw
Christmas arrive at midnight in the crowded cave of the
Hotel Grunewald. Judge Godchaux,'96, and Leon Godchaux,'09, gave us a brilliant French luncheon, and the
latter took us out Sunday afternoon to the great aviation
meet, where I saw airplanes for the first time in my life. We
witnessed several daring flights by Moisant, who was killed
a few days later. On that evening, the last in New Orleans,
I had the honour of being presented to Mr. James J.
Corbett. He entered the dining room, and I remarked

sotto voce 'That's Jim Corbett!' The waiter, misunderstanding my half-unconscious tribute to greatness, immediately brought him to my neighbourhood, and I apologetically explained the origin of the mistake. We shook hands, and then, instead of squaring off, parted in the most amicable fashion.

Sunday night we left New Orleans on a fine train over the Southern Pacific, which reached Houston (pronounced Hewston), Texas, exactly on time the next morning. We were greeted at the station by the Cleveland brothers, '94, and by Dillingham, '89, Sheff.

We spent an afternoon at Galveston, seeing the great sea wall and other wonders, and Tuesday 27 December was a red-letter day. The alumni at Houston met in the morning. We had luncheon together at the Club. In the afternoon a reception was given by the men and women of the city interested in university matters, and we had the opportunity of meeting the wives, mothers, sisters, and daughters of Yale. That evening came the Yale Alumni dinner, and I do not think I have ever heard more interesting speeches than those delivered on that occasion by the men of Texas representing Yale and other institutions. The speeches took the form of an animated discussion on such topics as whether a large university was better than a small college, whether a Southerner should go to his state institution or to Yale, and what education really means.

Wednesday, 28 December, we took the train for Abilene. The State Teachers Convention, which I had come to Abilene to address, was in full swing; there were nearly two thousand in attendance.

The next morning I took part in a heated discussion in the English group, where I found that they were just as 'hot and bothered' in Texas over the amount of time that should be given to English composition as we in the North.

There were evidences enough of a strong reaction against the terrible burden of theme-reading.

A paper was read by Mr. Wasson, of the *Dallas News*, a thoughtful and suggestive essay. The *Dallas News*, which Belo, '96, was directing at the time of his death, is one of the best newspapers in America. It is free from sensationalism, its editorials are admirable in matter and expression, and its reports accurate.

In the evening, 30 December, I made the closing address before the convention, speaking for an hour on the pleasures derived from education, taking as my text President Dwight's definition of happiness, that he gave to our Class in Senior year—'The happiest person is the person who thinks the most interesting thoughts.'

After leaving Abilene, we retraced our course in Texas travelling east and south to Austin, the State capital and seat of the University. I had good talk with Sidney Mezes the President and with William J. Battle, the Dean; both were intimate friends as we had been closely associated in the Harvard Graduate School twenty years before. John A. Lomax, the famous collector and interpreter of cowboy ballads, introduced me to many of the Faculty; one of the most interesting men was Professor Benedict, afterwards President of the University. His speciality, Mathematics, had sharpened his natural wits.

We visited Baylor University in Waco, where is now— under the care of Professor A.J. Armstrong—one of the finest collections of Browning memorabilia and manuscripts in the world.

I had heard wild stories of sudden changes in the weather in Texas; and after one experience, I did not feel they were greatly exaggerated. We spent New Year's Day, 1911, in Dallas; perfect summer it would have been in New York; seventy degrees all day long. That night we took the train *south* to San Antonio; before dawn the wind changed and blew a 'norther;' when we alighted at San Antonio, the temperature was exactly twelve degrees, a drop of 58 degrees in a few hours. I had been told of the man in Texas driving two oxen; one of them died of the heat; he went to the farm to get another; and when he returned, the survivor of the heat wave had frozen to death. I am now prepared to believe that.

53

SECOND SABBATICAL

On 16 February 1911 I persuaded Horace Howard **Furness** (1833–1912) the Shakespearean scholar and editor of the *Variorum*, to give a reading to the Yale undergraduates. This splendid old man, nearly eighty, was as deaf as Beethoven, and could not hear the applause of the students, which almost shook the building. As was his custom, he read from his own copy of the First Folio (1623). Every place in the hall including the aisles was filled with undergraduates, and how they did cheer! After he had read for nearly an hour, he announced a recess of ten minutes and withdrew to the room reserved for speakers. He told me there that he expected to see less than half of the original audience when he returned. Not a single man had left the room when he reappeared on the platform, and the enthusiasm was overwhelming. He read the famous passage in *King Henry V*, beginning

Once more unto the breach, dear friends!

Then he paused, and asked two questions. 'Just what did Shakespeare mean by that passage? But how can my puny mind comprehend the mind of William Shakespeare?'

There was proportionally not so much cheering on 19 November 1912, when I took Henry Arthur Jones, the English dramatist, to the annual football game between Yale and Harvard, the first and last he ever saw. He was disappointed when the result was a tie, neither side having scored. His emotions as a man of the theatre had been aroused by the hope of enjoying the enthusiasm caused by a touchdown and the cheering parade that follows a victory.

On 1 July 1911, we sailed for England on our Second Sabbatical. Our neighbours, Professor and Mrs. Russell Chittenden, were on the same steamer and we had a happy month together in western England. It was one of the exceptionally dry summers: we saw not a blade of green grass until we reached the Lake counties. One day on the top of a coach an English gentleman enquired of our friend, 'Are you any relation of the great Chittenden, the famous physiological chemist?' It was pleasant to see the stranger's enthusiasm when Chittenden modestly confessed.

I do not know whether the tiny corner of the planet where we live in New Haven has any special healthful atmosphere; but it is interesting that the two neighbours, whose gardens are next to ours, Judge John K.Beach and Dr. Chittenden, were both active after eighty. I played golf with Judge Beach when he was 82 and at this moment Chittenden, 82, is fishing in Maine. At the corner lived Professor Edward S.Dana who died in 1935 in his 86th year, while fifty yards from his house are living two brothers, Henry and Lewis English, both active and over eighty. In 1938 I attended a party given Henry on his birthday; he is 87. And at the next corner lived the late Henry L.Hotchkiss, also full of physical and mental activity well beyond eighty.

We said goodbye to the Chittendens in August and we proceeded to Copenhagen by way of Hamburg. The American Minister to Denmark was a distinguished man of letters, Maurice Francis Egan; he made our stay in the beautiful capital most agreeable, and in a few days we were at the same hotel with him in Christiania.

Although the University of Upsala in Sweden was founded in 1477, and the University of Copenhagen in 1479, the University of Christiania was not born till 1811. The hundredth birthday of this infant was celebrated with academic pomp and splendour during the week beginning 3 September, delegates from older institutions like Yale, Harvard, and Pennsylvania coming to pay homage. The weather, during every day of the *fest*, was like New Haven autumn weather, clear, bright, cool, tonic, reminding me keenly of the glorious sunshine of our Bicentennial.

We left Copenhagen at nine in the evening of Saturday, 2 September, passing through Elsinore two hours before the ghost of Hamlet's father was due on the platform. The next morning the train rolled along leisurely through Sweden and Norway among pine forests, slanting farms, lakes, and fjords. At one village we saw a little country church on the hillside, with a group of worshippers gossiping about the portal in the strong sunlight, exactly as Björnson pictures the scene in *Synnöve Solbakken*. We reached Christiania as the bells were knolling noon, and drove up the principal street of the city to the Grand Hotel, in the big café of which Ibsen spent so many hours of his later years.

It was Sunday in Christiania, not in London. The streets were crowded with people, spending the day in active uselessness, walking briskly, laughing and talking. Animation and gaiety were in the air and overhead was the Christiania sky, not drawn close like a tent-roof as it is in Paris, Berlin, and London, but unspeakably far aloft, with its radiant blue streaked here and there by long, thin clouds dazzling white, like snow-drifts. The sky in Christiania, at all hours of the day and night, is impressive.

The street, for a hundred yards in front of the University, was arched with bright flags and bunting. The handsome academic buildings stand a little back from the broad highway, with the big and dignified National Theatre directly opposite, and the palace of the King at the top of the hill.

During the afternoon, delegates from all parts of the earth began to arrive, and within twenty-four hours we had met many old, and made many new friends. Georgetown University had the honour of being represented by His Excellency the American Minister to Denmark. The University of Pennsylvania was there in the person of its distinguished head—Provost Smith. I had never seen him before, but it was worth a trip to Norway to know him, a specialist in chemistry, and an able executive, with the unshakable conviction that a college education which does not emphasize character and discipline is a poor thing. Harvard was represented by the American consul at Christiania, Mr. Gade, whom I was glad to see again, for he had been one of my pupils at Harvard. I wish I could believe I had helped to make him as I found him in 1911. Columbia's delegate was no less a person than its Dean, Professor Carpenter, experienced man of the world, as befits the Dean of an urban institution. These men were excellent company. My one regret was that Yale's delegate, Professor Charles Andrews (who lived across the street when we were boys in Hartford), and who would have represented Yale with such distinction, was prevented at the last moment from coming, by illness in the family. I was the regular delegate, not from Yale, but from the Connecticut Academy of Arts and Sciences, holding my commission from Governor Simeon Baldwin, the President, and George Eaton, the Secretary: on my arrival, I found a letter from Andrews, with his formal credentials, and a request that I should represent Yale in his place. I therefore stood for two groups, was obliged to mount the stage twice, and present two parchments.

At five in the afternoon of Monday, 4 September, the delegates met, and after an address from the Rector, each group held a separate conclave to elect its spokesman for the following day. This is a high honour, and when the

American University Group assembled, it appeared that
two strong candidates were in the field. After a little skirmish, we elected Minister Egan. In the other group to which
I belonged, Academies and Learned Societies, we elected
Professor W.P.Ker, of England, a notable scholar in English Literature. That night an elaborate dinner was given
to all the delegates at the Grand Hotel. We sat with a Norwegian Professor of Medicine, who spoke Norwegian fluently, but not French, German, or English. The conversation took the form of violent physical exercise, and at the
end, while we were polite and even affectionate, we were
exhausted.

The next morning, Tuesday, the first great public exercises took place in the National Theatre. The ceremony
began at eleven o'clock, with the singing, by a large choir,
of Björnson's ode, *Lyset* (light). This music was about five
times too long—in fact, it was a colossal bore. Then the
Rector made his formal address, setting forth the desir-
ability and necessity of a World-university. He spoke in
German. After this address, the various groups, eight in
all, marched successively upon the stage, while the pre-
viously-elected spokesman presented the compliments of
himself and colleagues to the Rector. Then each visitor's
name and university or society were called out, each delegate shook hands with the Rector, presented his formal
parchment, and went back to the auditorium. The spokes-
men for the delegates usually made their brief address in
the language of the country they represented. The Heidelberg professor spoke German, the Paris professor French,
and Dr. Egan English. Mr. Ker, who represented the
learned societies from various countries, quite properly
spoke in Latin. A Czech professor from Prague delighted
the audience by speaking Norwegian.

In the evening, the King and Queen entertained the
delegates at dinner in the Royal Palace. This was the first

time I had ever met a king, and I felt (like Franklin) the truth of the Scripture saying—'Seest thou a man diligent in his business? He shall stand before Kings.' This royal pair were democratic. They shook hands with each one of us (we were about six hundred, and Oh, the wild charge we made!) and actually talked with each delegate. The King asked me about the study of Scandinavian languages at Yale, and I was glad to be able to tell him of Professor Palmer's courses. As a compliment to the Americans, we were received first. Then we stood at the end of the hall and watched the others. Finally we all went in to dinner, and the King standing on the floor among the guests, cheek by jowl with the crowd, drank our health, to which we responded with a cheer. The delegates felt deeply grateful to the King and Queen for this royal invitation, and for the exceedingly friendly unceremonious manner of their Majesties.

The next morning we went to the University Aula, where the honorary degrees were to be distributed. After a brief spell of music, a general historical address was delivered in Norwegian by Professor Spang; but a French 'crib' had previously been handed to each delegate. Then the various Deans announced the list of honorary degrees. The names were read rapidly, and the recipients did not appear, as with us. The Dean of Theology came first, and delivered his remarks in German; then the Dean of Law, in English; then the Dean of Medicine, in English; then the Dean of Literature, in French; lastly the Dean of Science, in German. The last name on each list appeared to be the place of honour. Finally, to my great joy, the last name on the last list was Dr. Elkin! Then the delegate from Yale congratulated the delegate from the Connecticut Academy, and the delegate from the Academy congratulated the delegate from Yale.

That evening the Mayor and Commune of Christiania

gave a formal dinner in the Town Hall, where appropriate speeches were made between the courses. I found
my entire Norwegian vocabulary, 'Skoal!' more than
adequate.

The next day I went out to the beautiful cemetery to do
homage at the graves of Ibsen and Björnson, who lie near
together. Ibsen's monument is marked by a large hammer; Björnson had as yet no monument, no tomb, no
stone; simply a mound of grass, grown over by wild
flowers. A large fresh wreath lay upon it. . . . Before the
theatre stand two colossal statues of Ibsen and Björnson,
erected during the lifetime of these modern Norse gods.
Ibsen's coat is buttoned tightly, and he is looking downward; Björnson's coat is flung wide open and his face looks
defiantly up and out toward the world—for the personality
of one was secretive, and the other just the contrary. The
son of Ibsen married the daughter of Björnson, and their
little boy often stood before the huge statues, and said
proudly, 'These are my grandfathers!'

I heard an authentic anecdote in Christiania which I
think had not been printed. When the statesmen of
Norway were trying to arrange the separation from Sweden, Björnson, with his usual hot-headed and warm-
hearted impetuosity, wrote a letter to the leading diplomat,
volunteering his public services, and asking how he could
most efficiently assist the cause. He received a telegram,
'Hold your tongue!'

Thursday evening the formal exercises were concluded
by a gala performance in the National Theatre of Björnson's fine historical drama, *Maria Stuart*. This was particularly interesting to us, for only three weeks before we
had stood in Holyrood Castle, Edinburgh. The acting and
scenic effects were excellent, and the signal for beginning
the play was the appearance of the King and Queen in the
Royal Box, whereat the entire audience rose silently, and

were rewarded by a gracious bow and smile from their Majesties.

The whole centenary was splendidly managed by patient, courteous, and efficient reception committees, every care was taken to see that each delegate enjoyed the occasion, and I am sure all the visitors were grateful to their kindly hosts.

54

JOURNEY TO RUSSIA

1911

IT is rather surprising that the short sea voyage from Stockholm to St. Petersburg is not better known in the western world. It is enchanting. We left Stockholm at six o'clock in the evening of a fine September day, and as we drew away, the sunset light over the fair city hung a new picture on the walls of my mind. It takes some five hours to reach the Baltic, five hours of constantly changing scenery, one view melting into another like a succession of dissolving panoramas. Hundreds of tiny wooded islands, dotted with châteaux and country houses; winking lighthouse towers: the grey sea and the long black land. Yes, and to my amazement and dismay, the yellow half-moon large and low! Every year I had told my Browning classes that the common interpretation of the famous poem, which places the visit at dusk, is incorrect; or else Browning's astronomy failed him. The half-moon is never low in the early evening in English or American latitudes. But here near the sixtieth parallel in September the half-moon leered at me just over the rim of a rocky hill. To be sure, it was not a precise half, something over, in fact, but close enough to be disquieting. Although it had no business to be there, it supplied the last touch of glory to the scene. We stood on the top deck, and beheld the spacious firmament on high, thick inlaid with patines of bright gold; while the long level light of the impossible moon fell across the darkening water and the myriad islands.

Some time in the night we crossed the Baltic, and early in the morning we entered the Gulf of Finland. The air was nipping and eager, but the sun shone from a cloudless sky. All day the steamerkin nosed her way through the blue sea, twisting and turning among the countless points of the earth's surface that were just able to keep their heads above water. A few of these were covered with green grass, and supported white farm buildings where laughing children ran out to see our transit, accompanied by dignified and serious dogs; but for the most part these elevations were bald rock, with a tall lighthouse as sole ornament. At five in the afternoon we reached Helsingfors, my farthest north, and stepped ashore to see the town, the boat not proceeding to St. Petersburg until late in the night. Here I obtained a clear notion of Finland's sentiment toward Russia. Prime Minister Stolypin had been shot the day before, and the evening paper reported him much better, on the road to recovery. A Finnish gentleman, highly educated, refined, tender-hearted, said to me with a smile, 'Yes, they say Stolypin is better: but we have our hopes.'

The passage across the gulf to Petersburg was rough, the clouded sky was low and harsh the next morning, and the sea was surly. Toward noon it cleared, and before two o'clock we saw the gilded domes and spires of Holy Russia. The approach to the great capital is immensely interesting, the boat moving through a long canal, passing interminable shipping. Finally, we docked, and after some delay with the passports—it was impossible to enter, leave, or visit any town in the empire without one—we drove across one of the bridges over the Neva to our hotel on a corner of the Nevski Prospect. Although it was September, the temperature was under fifty, and seemed colder. I had a severe cold, which had its origin in a bad chill which I had caught in rashly touching a piece of toast that a waiter brought me in a London hotel.

But I was right in style. Everybody in Petersburg had a cold. The coughing, sneezing, nose-blowing, and hawking reminded me grimly of Battell Chapel, where coughing drowned the parson's saw. Many of the people had their ears and mouths bandaged, while their feet were encased in huge boots—all seemed to be suffering from the foot and mouth disease. Never shall I forget the boots and overcoats on the Nevski Prospect. This question of leg-clothes would have interested the author of *Sartor Resartus*. In Edinburgh all the men and some of the suffragettes wore knickerbockers, with stockings that seemed an inch thick, made of material feathered like the legs of a setter. Scots of all ages and degrees donned the knickers. Tottering octogenarians, with wrinkled faces lost in a wealth of white whiskers, stumbled along Princes Street in motley knickerbockers, a world too wide for their shrunk shanks. In order to avoid the glare of publicity, I bought in Edinburgh a pair of these homespun garments myself, and tramped the city in them, much to the amusement of my comrade Professor Chittenden.

I tried them just once on the Nevski Prospect. Once was quite enough. Everyone stopped to stare. Had I worn a flowing scarlet robe, I should not have been so conspicuous. I was a mark for the populace. Officers gazed at me in cold amazement, as though I had the leprosy; while the more naïve inhabitants made audible comment, which was fortunately lost upon the victim. Then I tried the experiment of conventional clothing, but wore low shoes. Everyone gazed at my feet, some in wonder, some in admiration, some in apparent terror. I felt like a bold, bad man, but declined to fetter my legs in the enormous black knee-boots, which would have been as conspicuous elsewhere as the knickers were in Russia. Some twenty years ago, I

walked the streets of Brussels with a curiously striped cap
on my head. A gentleman looked at me earnestly, and then
said in an almost reverent tone, and he said it three times,
'*Nom de Dieu!*'

Americans at home show the same interest in strange
clothing. Professor E.B.Wilson, then of the Yale Faculty,
purchased a suit in Paris, which was 'just the thing' on
the Avenue de l'Opéra. He wore it in America only once,
and when I asked him why only once, he said that he
tried it on Chapel Street. He got as far as Trinity Church,
when a citizen of New Haven gazed at him steadfastly, and
exclaimed, 'J——!'

Nearly every man on the Nevski seemed to be an officer
or an official. There were an incredible number of uniforms, and as the overcoats, boots, and swords passed each
other, the hand at the side rose to the cheek in a stiff
salute, a salute that the projection of a half-inch would
transform into the universal gesture of contempt, known
and understood in all lands. One never forgets the Nevski.
I see it as plainly in my mind's eye at this moment as I
saw it in the grey Russian autumn. The broad avenue,
crowded with the little Russian carriages, rolling with a
dull sound over the wooden pavement, a pavement springy,
as though the marsh lay just below; the almost total absence of automobiles, the roads outside the city being so
bad that this vehicle was not useful; cathedrals, churches,
and public buildings lining the sides of the street, with
the needle gold spire of the Admiralty at the end; overhead the low, sombre sky, which often descended in a thick
mist; the sidewalks always crowded with a moving mass
of humanity, the conspicuous feature being the eternal
overcoats and long boots.

The faces of the common people were sad to behold,
both on the Nevski and in the churches alongside. Not
only was there no hilarity, such as one sees in most cities;

the faces indicated an absence of illuminating ideas. They were blank, dull, apathetic, hopeless. Their religion seemed to be one of fear. I stood on the front platform of an electric tram-car, and every time we passed a church—which means every few moments—the motorman took off his cap three times. But his expression, while intensely serious, seemed to indicate that he did this to ward off bad luck, rather than from a principle of glad and active worship. Inside the churches, at any hour of the day, I saw wretched men on their knees. They would press their foreheads to the stone floor, then cross themselves, then down with the forehead again. In a corner by the altar stood a priest, holding a dirty cross: a constant procession of diseased and filthy folk trooped up, and kissed the cross. I accompanied my friend Gaylord '76, to the Russian Y.M.C.A., where a mass was held for the soul of Stolypin. Two priests chanted and swung incense, and we all got down on our knees and held lighted candles. Mr. and Mrs. Gaylord did a great work in St. Petersburg for young men, being careful to keep absolutely aloof from politics. Years ago, amid the greatest difficulties, they founded a Y.M.C.A., where religious exercises were held, lessons in modern languages and practical business and scientific work given, the building including an excellent gymnasium and reading room. Then the Gaylords went to Moscow to found a similar organization there. Today Franklin Gaylord at the age of 82 is full of vigour.

Armed with a French Baedeker (there was none in English) we saw the chief sights of the Russian capital. In the temporary absence of the Tsar, we visited the Winter Palace, the most interesting room being the study of Alexander II, with all his favourite things just as he left them before the assassination. We spent hours in the Hermitage, one of the finest art galleries in Europe—what stunning Murillos!

One afternoon I walked the entire length of the Nevski Prospect, no mean achievement in a heavy overcoat. I began at the banks of the restless, blustering Neva, to get a good running start: passed the extraordinary statue of Peter the Great, came through the garden by the statue of Gogol, and with the Admiralty at my back entered the long avenue. I followed the immense extension of the Nevski, clear to the cemetery, and stood reverently in front of the statue of Dostoevski. Here, in January 1881, the body of the great novelist was laid in the grave, forty thousand persons present as mourners. Then, in a corner of the enclosure, I found the tomb of the composer Tchaikovsky, whose harmonies will delight the world forever. I gazed on the grave of Glinka, father of modern Russian music, but I searched in vain for the earthly resting-place of Rubinstein, also buried here. On account of the marshy soil, the graves are above instead of below the ground, exactly as at New Orleans: it is really a city of the dead. I passed out of the cemetery, walked through the grounds of the convent, and came clear outside the city, on the edge of a blank gloomy wide plain.

In Moscow we stayed at a vast caravanserai, cold as Siberia. Everyone who still believes in war ought to spend an hour in the Tretiakov gallery, and see the pictures by Vereschagin. They are too horrible to describe, but not so horrible as war. I walked up the hill and took off my hat in front of the statue of Pushkin, remembering that when this statue was uncovered in 1880, Turgenev and Dostoevski made speeches to the innumerable throng, the address of Dostoevski, with its text of universal brotherhood, being as great a masterpiece as any of his books.

Twenty-four hours on the train between Moscow and Warsaw gave us only a faint notion of the Russian country. Immense forests of white birch trees, their slender silver boles contrasting exquisitely with the red and gold

flames of the leaves, the autumn sunlight glorifying them
all. Well are these feminine trees called the queens of the
forest. Sometimes, on emerging from the woods, the train
came out on a prodigious steppe, where nothing broke the
view to the far horizon. Many villages were simply a few
huts around a big church. Women were working in the
fields, bent over double to the ground, as though looking
into their graves.

In Warsaw, the Roman Catholic churches were as noticeable as the Greek. We walked through the lovely
Saxon gardens, in the shade of mighty old trees. The
statue of Copernicus stands not far away, and I thought
as I looked at it, how much greater a miracle he had
wrought than Joshua. Joshua commanded the sun to stand
still, but only for a short time: Copernicus put it in its
proper place, and it has not dared to move around the
earth once since he finished with it. Strolling toward the
hotel I almost ran into a squad of soldiers, that came
briskly around the corner: at the same moment, a very
stiff officer advanced; the men saluted, not with the legs,
as in Germany, but with a loud unanimous shout. Something struck me as irresistibly ludicrous in all this, and I
unintentionally caught the officer's eye, not six feet away.
I burst into a quite irrepressible roar of laughter, even
though I feared he would smite me with his sword for *lèse
majesté*. But my guffaw hit him on the funny-bone. He
roared too, and then all the soldiers joined in one spontaneous burst of mirth. Without speaking a word to each
other, we all seemed to agree subconsciously that this
military business was silly and out-of-date, but that one
must still go through the forms. These men had only three
or four years to live (1911–15).

55

GERHART HAUPTMANN

On Friday, 29 September 1911, we were in the Hotel
Adlon in Berlin. I took the elevator and at the third floor
I stepped directly into the arms of a man hurrying to
enter it. As soon as I released myself from the clinch, I
asked 'Aren't you Gerhart Hauptmann?' He replied with
a smile, '*Das ist mein Name.*' Then I told him I had the
honour of teaching his plays to undergraduates at Yale
University, and I should like very much to have ten minutes of conversation at his convenience. He said his wife
was in the hospital and he was on his way thither. Naturally I apologized for keeping him even for a moment. He
said if I would be in the office of the hotel the next morning at ten o'clock, he would be very glad to talk with me.
I was there of course, and he was accompanied by his son,
a pretty boy about ten years old, and dressed like Little
Lord Fauntleroy.

Herr Hauptmann was kind, considerate, charming. He
impressed me as an absolutely sincere man, modest, quiet,
with strong convictions—later, when I got to know John
Galsworthy, the two men seemed to me in their ideas and
in their manner very much alike. I asked Mr. Hauptmann,
'Which of your plays do you think is the best?' Without
any hesitation he said, '*Und Pippa Tanzt.*' This surprised
me. He added that he had never enjoyed writing a play
so much as he did *Fuhrmann Henschel.* He said the dramatist must never think of the box-office or of the possible
financial success of his work; he must write plays, as he

must write everything else, only to express himself. I believe he meant this; it was not a pose; certainly not an excuse; it was sincere. I asked him if the box-office failure of many of his plays disturbed him at all. 'Not in the least,' he affirmed emphatically, 'I write only to please myself. If the people like it, well and good; if they don't, I can't help it.' I asked, 'Do you express your own opinions in your plays? Does the character Loth in *Vor Sonnenaufgang*, for example, represent your opinions?' 'No, I do not express my opinions in my plays; but after reading five or six of my plays, anyone ought to know well enough what kind of a fellow I am.' He added that while no character, not even Loth, should express the playwright's opinions, the whole play should always express the author's personality. 'The play *Pippa* is very subjective; it came right out of my brain.'

He liked Berlin better than Munich. A better place for him to live in and work.

He said he was writing a novel, some of the scenes of which would be laid in America, indeed in Connecticut. I told him I had heard he had a brother living in Stamford, Connecticut. 'No, that is not true.' 'But you, Herr Hauptmann, you have been in Meriden?' 'That is true.' When this novel *Atlantis* appeared the next year (1912) I naturally read it with great interest. Many people thought the shipwreck in it was the *Titanic* which had gone down in April of that year; but it was the *Elbe*, which sank in the North Sea some years earlier. In *Atlantis* he also describes a journey on the railway from New York to Meriden, and he mentions the interesting old negro who for many years came on board at New Haven selling sandwiches.

He told me he intended to write both novels and dramas and in the many years since this interview, he has carried out that intention. Although his first play *Vor Sonnenaufgang* (1889) is starkly naturalistic, Hauptmann is at heart a thorough romantic and idealist, as is shown in most of his writing, and as was abundantly clear to me in this conversation.

I asked him to sign his name in my copy of his novel, *Der Narr in Christo*, which he did, and wrote under his name, '*Kunst ist Religion*' ('Art is Religion'), which interested me. Perhaps it would have been nearer to the exact truth if he had written *Kunst ist meine Religion*. Art and religion seem to me quite different.

As I was about to take my leave, he said, 'I want you to talk with my little boy over yonder; please don't say a single word in German to him; I have had him taught English, and I want you to see if he speaks it well.' Mr. Hauptmann and I had not uttered a word of English. The boy came up to me with charming grace. I spoke to him in English, and he answered in fluent and perfect English, without a trace of accent. The father listened to our conversation with an approving smile. He was evidently proud.

After that conversation, I did not wonder at the almost idolatrous admiration for Hauptmann everywhere evident in Germany. Although only a minority of his plays have been successful on the stage, there is a streak of genius in nearly all of them. And he himself is a sincere idealist—a poet at heart. In the early years of this century, some newspaper in Berlin sent out a questionnaire to many thousands of readers—'who are the ten Germans now living who are most important for Germany?' The first name was of course the German Emperor, but that was a complimentary vote. The second was Gerhart Hauptmann. Further down on the list were Koch and Roentgen, Koch who by his discoveries had saved the lives of millions, and Roentgen, who had made possible the use of the X-ray; yet Hauptmann, who had never done anything useful or a day's work, in the ordinary sense of that word, was regarded as more important than great physicians or men of science. For, while men cannot live without bread, they cannot live on bread alone.

In 1932, when Hauptmann was seventy years old, I saw in Munich the first performance of his new play, *Vor Sonnenuntergang*; it was not successful, yet it had, like all his work, that indefinable sense of latent power. The Director of the theatre told me he had to leave out an enormous part of it for the stage production; even after this amputation it was too long.

During the summer of 1911, we never heard any Englishman say a word about Germany or about the possibility of an approaching war; but when, late in August, we arrived in Hamburg, the German bellboy who showed us to our room asked if we were British or American. On hearing our answer, he said, 'Well, I want you to know that Germany can beat England in the war, and we're going to do it.' During that autumn in Germany, I heard similar talk from many Germans of varying degrees of education and social position. They all seemed to be eagerly looking forward to the war, and the hatred of England was intense and universal. When I ventured to suggest to a highly educated German that such a war would be the most disastrous calamity imaginable, he said, 'It is bound to come, and the sooner the better.' There seemed to be organized hostility to England felt by all classes of Germans. And when the war did come three years later, I do not believe any country has ever entered into a war with such united and such holy enthusiasm. It was like a release of long pent-up emotion. It is difficult to realize this now, because after the war Germany felt almost an affection for England, while her hatred was transferred to France; but there is no doubt that for the five or six years preceding the war, German public opinion was so inflamed with anti-British feeling, that one does not have to search far for the *immediate cause of the war*, whatever the remoter antecedents may have been. This hatred was like a swelling river that finally overflowed. I do not know whether anything could have been done to prevent it.

A strange thing happened that first night we spent in Germany in 1911. If we had been fanatical or suspicious, we should have believed that we had been deliberately poisoned, the Hamburg hotel waiters or cooks thinking we were British. I did not then and do not now believe it; but I know we came very near to death. We sat down to dinner and began with soup. I took one spoonful, and whispered to my wife, 'Don't touch another drop of this soup.' We had had only one table-spoonful apiece. To me there was a horrible taste in it. I called the waiter, and explained to him that there was something fatally wrong with the soup. He expressed surprise and scepticism, but I have always been glad I did not believe him. That night we were both taken ill, with every symptom of poisoning, and had to remain in bed, both with a temperature, and violent stomach disorder, for twenty-four hours. Indeed we should have stayed in bed three or four days, but we were anxious to leave that hotel. We went to Copenhagen, and got medical treatment. Although I believe it was an accident, I also believe that if we had taken half a dozen spoonfuls of that soup, we should both have died.

56

THE RIVIERA

1912

'ROUGH winds do shake the darling buds of May,' said the Englishman Shakespeare: I wonder what he would have said could he have seen the Riviera roses bending their pretty heads to the soft breath of February.

We left Munich early in the morning of the second day of February, in a blinding blizzard. All day long the snow fell, drawing an impenetrable curtain between us and the mountains as the train climbed and descended the Brenner pass. Verona was dressed in white, and the two gentlemen did not appear; when we reached Milan late in the evening, the city was buried in snow. Oh what a difference in the morning! At San Remo, the sky was a brilliant, cloudless blue, the dark-blue sea was trimmed with ermine: green grass, palms, orange and lemon trees everywhere, so that the whole place seemed to be full of gorgeous blue and green and gold. In spite of the high wind that sent tremendous waves crashing on the rocks, the air was gentle and pleasant: there were no teeth in the breeze.

We left the *train de luxe*, which like many luxurious people was six hours late, at Nice: and put up at a hotel which we could not put up with long. The food was excellent, and our rooms—it sounds impressive to use the plural—faced the splendid sea. But the table-manners of the 'guests' of that inn baffle description. I am no glass of fashion and mould of form, and do not pretend to be an authority on etiquette. Yet, democratic as I am, I was driven from that hotel at the point of the toothpick. Never have I seen such a collection of sword-swallowers. There was a dear old woman, who sat at a table close to ours: she had a face that brought to mind the portraits of our New England ancestors of the seventeenth century; her expression in repose was prim, austere, and yet not unkind. But when she gathered, with infinite pains and astonishing skill, a conglomerate mass of meat, gravy, and vegetables on the long blade of her knife, and played the game right up to the handle, I was fascinated: looking the other way, with the hope of finding someone less expert, I saw worse things. . . . A thesis should be written on 'The Decay of the Toothpick.' In the days of Queen Elizabeth, it was the height of fashion to parade the central aisle of St. Paul's, bearing a toothpick in the mouth, and twisting it without hands, as a politician worries his cigar: even a hundred years ago, the toothpick was in great vogue, for in one of Jane Austen's novels, I think it is *Sense and Sensibility*, the young exquisite enters the expensive shop to buy a new toothpick case. But things have changed. . . . The air in this dining room was so full of toothpicks that it looked as though Birnam wood had come to Dunsinane. Some kept them in the mouth while eating and drinking: but the majority, after searching each remote orifice with scrupulous care, and examining with loving interest the trophies of the chase, used the weapon for purposes of emphasis and gesticulation.

No American accustomed to a comfortable house should patronize a hotel on the Riviera where the furnace is not taken seriously. How miserable it is to be colder indoors than outside! I received an epistolary masterpiece from my colleague Clarke, who was shivering in a hotel at Cannes. 'They have central heating here,' he wrote, 'but it is much more central than heating.' From the point of view of physical comfort, I suppose one should visit Russia in the winter, and Italy in the summer. A friend of mine, who had spent the winter in Stockholm, went to Italy in the spring, and was colder there in a week than he had been in three months in the frozen north. George Ade tried Venice in January; but declared that he would spend the next winter in Duluth, where he could keep warm.

Many French folk cannot bear to give out money for fuel. They think it a wicked waste. I remember with what horror our landlady in Paris watched me jovially heaving on to the fire the neat little lozenges of coal; she saw the francs going right up the chimney. One mouse-poor student in Paris told me that he kept warm during the entire winter with one billet of wood. It seems he lived on the sixth floor. He hurled the stick out of the window, ran down six flights, retrieved it, and ran up again; this kept him warm fifteen minutes, when once more he threw the thing out of the window; by repeating this process every quarter of an hour, he got along famously.

I shall not soon forget the morning of Washington's Birthday. Our hotel at Mentone crowns a high hill, and we lived at the top of the house with a balcony commanding a marvellous view of mountains, terraces, orange-groves, gardens, town, and sea. I was awakened by the morning-star glaring directly into my left eye. The star stuck out of the sky so far I thought it was going to fall, and went out on the balcony to see it drop. There I beheld the great drama of the dawn, with the protagonist still invisible, but evidently waiting for his cue. He got it, and made a magnificent entrance. Straight out of the waves he rose in majesty, and came walking on the water, flooding the sea and the mountains with golden light.

> Full many a glorious morning have I seen
> Flatter the mountain tops with sovereign eye,
> Kissing with golden face the meadows green,
> Gilding pale streams with heavenly alchemy.

In 1911 Nice was a city with about the same population as New Haven, whereas Cannes and Mentone were like villages. We were in Nice during the heart of the Carnival, which I found not particularly interesting. It is too completely syndicated for the benefit of visitors. There was too much organized cheering and little spontaneous mirth. Even the far-heralded battle of flowers aroused no enthusiasm, because there was no gusto in it. A long and minute list of things that one must and that one must not do was carefully printed in the papers, and the zest went out of the parade. Many once quaint and beautiful customs and many charming places are now spoiled by being systematically financed and managed, before they meet the eye of the tourist. I remember even in that wonderful sea-village of Clovelly in England, much of the striking effect was lessened for me by seeing the old salts, clad in neat blue jerseys, standing about in attitudes that savoured of long and careful rehearsal. Instead of looking like those who go down to the sea in ships, they looked like a chorus in a musical comedy.

Mentone is more attractive than Nice, being situated on a little strip of land just between the ragged mountains and the blue sea. The twenty-mile drive over the hills from Nice is picturesque. And the view from the sea-front of Mentone of the long, winding, precipitous Italian coast is beautiful, and seems to change in colour every hour. One meets few Americans in this town; they are nearly all English. And although the English at this hotel are for the most part delightful companions, I overheard a conversation in the village between two sons of Albion that seemed insular. One was complaining to the other of the mistakes made by the Mentone compositors in a small bit of English printing he had ordered. 'You see they are all foreigners,' he remarked angrily. To speak of Frenchmen in a French town as foreigners, appeared to me to lack breadth of view.

The large number of English gentlemen who, from the American point of view, do nothing, is a never-ending source of wonder. In Ireland I met an English baronet at dinner. He said to me, 'I suppose you have always worked for a living, always had a regular occupation?' 'Certainly,' said I: 'I have supported myself since the summer I was graduated from college.' 'Ah,' said he, 'you are much happier than I. I have never done anything; my father, grandfather, and all my ancestors never did anything.' When I narrated this incident to an English lady at Mentone, she said, 'But most of the English gentlemen I know are very busy—busy all the time. They hunt, shoot, fish, play golf, polo, and tennis. They are not idle.' She enquired, 'You haven't any regular class of gentlemen in America, have you?' I replied, 'No, not in the sense in which you use the term.' 'But it seems strange that you have no recognized superior class. Doesn't the man who mows your lawn take off his hat to you?' 'No, he does not; and if he did, I should then take off mine.' 'How extraordinary!' said she.

The Secretary of Yale University, Anson Phelps Stokes, was staying at Cannes, and on Lincoln's Birthday took us for a superb motor excursion over the mountains. The road at first was so close to the sea that we were nearly splashed by the breakers; then we climbed the heights and far away saw the little town of Grasse, 'sown in a wrinkle of the monstrous hill, sparkling in the sunshine like a grain of salt,' as Tennyson says. Overhead the deep blue sky; below us the deep blue sea; and in the distance, tier on tier of snow-capped mountains. One afternoon Stokes and I went over to Monte Carlo, where every prospect pleases, and only man is vile. In the midst of that international crowd, an extraordinary collection of human curiosities, we appeared like Christian and Faithful at Vanity Fair. When I attempted to enter the famous gambling-rooms, I was

kindly but firmly shoved back; the guardian pointed eloquently to my *knee-breeches*, saying that no one was allowed near the tables unless properly clad. So I stood at
the portal and watched the aristocratic sansculottes pass
majestically by. My rejection seemed to amuse Stokes
prodigiously.

We had three Springs in 1912 instead of one: and it
would be difficult to say which was the most beautiful.
The roses on the Riviera in February, the bright fruit-
blossoms in Italy in April, and the magnificent horse-
chestnut trees on the Champs-Élysées in May, gave us four
months of the very pick of the season. We reached Florence
on 26 March, a day of cloudless, windless sunshine. There
we ran across one of the Honolulu Judds—may their tribe
increase—and proceeded to visit every spot in the city
associated with the Brownings. We gazed on the panorama
of the town from the height of San Miniato, and recited
the first two stanzas of 'Old Pictures in Florence.' We went
to the Square of San Lorenzo, where on a hot June noon,
Browning found the old yellow book, and we followed his
footsteps by the Strozzi, by the Pillar, by the Bridge, till
we reached his home in Casa Guidi. We grasped the iron
rings on the palace that casts the shadow, and in imagination saw Fra Lippo Lippi descending hand under hand,
and running after the girls. We regarded in another square
the bronze Duke—symbol of perpetual lack of motion—
gazing forever at the farthest window facing the east. Then
we went out to the lovely cemetery, and stood by the
graves of Elizabeth Barrett Browning, Landor, Clough,
Theodore Parker of Boston, and the American historian,
Richard Hildreth. When I was an undergraduate, I asked
Professor Sumner, 'What is the best history of America?'
Gruffly he grunted, 'Hildreth's!' So I read every word of
the six volumes, and have ever since had an enormous respect for this historian, whose sole object in writing was

to tell the truth. Twenty years after graduation, I told
Mr. Sumner that I had done homage at the grave in
Florence, and he was alertly interested. He was unaware
of the location of Hildreth's dust, and I had the satisfaction, which came to very few, of telling Mr. Sumner something he had not already known. The tombstone is like the
man it covers—simple and upright—marked only with the
name and the date of his death.

We attracted some attention on these Florentine excursions, for besides Baedekers, we carried an even better
guide, the Works of Browning. A pleasant result of this
was that we made many converts; the booksellers straight-
way sold out all their Brownings, and wondering what on
earth had happened, began to write to London for fresh
supplies. We gathered accretions as we swept along. I remember the surprise and delight of an English lady, who
annexed herself to us in front of Casa Guidi, when I
pointed out to her the little terrace where Browning paced
up and down in the night, thinking of Pompilia—and I
read aloud the wonderful lines in which the poet describes
this memorable experience. I think she had never heard
them before, but she got out her notebook, and then made
hot-foot for the nearest bookshop.

After ten golden days in Florence—I admire Rome for
what it has been, I love Florence for what it is—we set out
on the trail of Caponsacchi and Pompilia, as they fled
through the gate of San Clemente in Arezzo in the solid
black before the April dawn. Perugia is high up on the
hill, with its twisted, narrow, sinuous streets wriggling over
each other like a mess of worms—but in the midst of mediaeval memories we received a shock, for a huge placard
near the Cathedral announced a great football match,
'Perugia vs. Ancona.' Here we left the railway, and drove
southward in an open carriage on the same highway, where
on another April morning, two hundred and fifteen years

before, the young priest and the young wife rolled in mad haste toward Rome. The scenery has not changed; we saw the same miracle of the awakening year; fruit trees in blossom, green pastures, rich upturned earth with the peasants driving the white oxen; on our left, the bold mountains, carrying on their tops the last fragments of the defeated forces of winter.

We stopped some hours on the holy ground of Assisi, and visited the wonderful churches within the walls. Driving on again toward Foligno, we entered the great edifice that holds the first oratory of St. Francis, and pondered on the enormous changes in the world's history made by one lonely man. It was dark when Caponsacchi and Pompilia reached Foligno, but we passed through the gates an hour before sunset. Here we had a curious repetition of their experience on the way. The lady asked her friend

> How do you call that tree with the thick top
> That holds in all its leafy green and gold
> The sun now like an immense egg of fire?

(It was a million-leaved mimosa.)

Well, outside the walls we stood in front of an immense mimosa, and the bright sun just over the western horizon, shining directly through the thick mass of tiny leaves, seemed to be doing its very best to reproduce the picture that arrested the attention of Pompilia.

57

THE FANO CLUB

THE next day was Easter, glorious and cloudless, as Easter should be. We left for a time the Road to Rome, and carried out a project that had been in my mind for eight years. I had never met anyone of any nationality who had ever seen the little town of Fano, on the Adriatic, made immortal by Browning's splendid poem, 'The Guardian Angel.' We took the train to the beautiful city of Ancona, and then a branch road took us on the very edge of the blue sea to Fano. On the way we crossed the Metaurus, on whose banks was fought the battle that changed civilization, and in the course of an hour we came to the small city and realized our dreams.

In the Summer of 1848 Mr. and Mrs. Robert Browning left their house in Florence and travelled all night in the diligence over the Apennines to the east coast, their intention being to escape from the intolerable July heat of Florence and find solace in the cool sea air of Fano.

Fano is an old Roman town, with a Roman wall still in a fair state of preservation; by looking at the map of Italy you will see it is about thirty miles north of Ancona. It has a magnificent bathing beach, where people have enjoyed swimming for more than 2,000 years.

The Brownings found Fano even hotter than Florence; and, looking about the city for some shade, they happened by chance to enter the Church of San Agostino. There, in the chapel of the edifice, they were thrilled to discover a large painting, *The Guardian Angel* (*L'Angelo Custode*), by a third-rate painter of the seventeenth century named Guercino. For once in his life Guercino had achieved a masterpiece; but it was unknown to the world. They were so excited by the splendour and beauty of this painting that they went to see it three times.

Then at Ancona, resting in the hotel, Browning wrote one of the greatest of his poems, under the inspiration of the picture. So far as I know, he had no copy of it with him, but remembered the details.

The poem—'The Guardian Angel, A Picture at Fano'— was first published in 1855 in the collection in two volumes of *Men and Women*.

The picture represents death, birth, earth, and heaven. On a large tomb stands a little child; the angel is teaching the child to pray, holding its little hands pressed together; the angel is looking out over the earth, perhaps for more persons who need his protection; the child is looking up past the angel's face into heaven.

In the poem Browning expresses the wish that he might take the place of the child and receive the tender care of the angel; and if this were granted, he would not look into heaven, he would look into the angel's face. The last three stanzas of the poem are a postscript; he sent it to his friend Alfred Domett, then living in New Zealand.

This poem became so famous that it called the picture out of the obscurity where it had reposed for so many years and gave it a new lease of life. In many picture shops in various parts of Italy I saw photographs of it, and in some editions of Browning the picture was engraved.

But I wondered why no-one ever went to Fano to see the original. The town is easy enough to visit. Every train from Venice to Brindisi, running along the east coast of Italy, stops at Fano. Ancona is an important seaport, and there is a daily express train from Ancona to Rome. I suppose the reason why no Americans ever went to Fano was that it is off the beaten track. Americans, of course, see Florence and Venice and Rome. Many of them go to Milan and the Italian lakes; but Fano, never.

This ancient city was visited by Montaigne in his famous journey to Italy, 1580–1581, and I find in his diary the following entry (tr. E. J. Trechmann).

> I forgot to say that at Ancona, in the church of San Ciriaco, there is a low tombstone of one *Antonia Rocamoro patre, matre Valetta, Galla, Aquitana, Paciotto, Urbanati, Lusitano nupta*, who has been buried ten or twelve years. We left there early in the morning, and followed the seacost by a very agreeable road. Near our dinner-time we crossed the river Metro, *Metaurus*, by a large wooden bridge, and dined at
>
> FANO, fifteen miles, a little town in a pretty and very fertile plain adjoining the sea, rather badly built, very closed in. We were very well treated there as regards bread, wine and fish; the accommodation is not up to much. Fano has this advantage over the other towns on this coast, as Sinigaglia, Pesaro and others, that it has plenty of fresh water, many public fountains and private wells, whereas the others have to go as far as the mountains to fetch their water. We saw here a large ancient arch, on which there is an inscription under the name of Augustus, *qui muros dederat*. The town was formerly called Fanum, and was *Fanum Fortunae* (The Temple of Fortune).
>
> Almost throughout Italy they boult their flour with wheels, by means of which the baker does more work in an hour than we in four.
>
> In nearly all the hostelries you find rhymesters, who make rhymes on the spot, applicable to the people present. There is an instrument in every shop, even in those of the butchers at the street corners.
>
> This town is renowned above all those in Italy for its handsome women: we saw none, but some very ugly ones; and when I questioned an honest man of the town, he told me that the age of them was past.
>
> You pay on this route about 10 sous for the table, 20 sous a day per man; the horse, for hire and expenses, about 30 sous: which makes 50 sous.
>
> This town belongs to the Church.

In 1900 I began to ask persons who had lived twenty years in Italy if they had ever seen Fano; no one had.

Sir Rennell Rodd, British Ambassador to Italy (1908–19), wrote a little poem about Fano, but that was the only reference I could discover from any contemporary.

Accordingly, on Easter Day 1912 we stood before the painting in the little church at Fano. There was a priest who had never seen an American; we were as fantastic figures to him as if we had been Eskimos or Kanakas. He walked around us, to get a front and rear view. Then he wished to show us the church; but I told him I was not interested in the ornate church, but only in the altarpiece in the chapel. He said no one had ever come there to see that. He, of course, had never heard of the existence of Browning. But when I told him of the great English poet, who had made this picture famous in all parts of the world, and that this year was the centenary of his birth, he became excited; I wrote in execrable Italian a one-page theme on Browning.

We scoured the city for picture postcards; we finally got about seventy-five, and sent them to various friends in America. These postcards never reached their destination. They are at the bottom of the Atlantic Ocean: all went down on the *Titanic*.

There in Fano on Easter Day we founded the Fano Club. Anyone could become a life member by doing three things. One must visit Fano. One must see the picture. One must send me a picture postcard postmarked Fano. When we returned home and were talking about this club, my colleague, Professor Alexander Evans, said this was the most exclusive club in the whole world; it had only two members. He immediately left for Italy and became the third member. Since that time the membership has steadily increased. Almost every month I receive a postcard from someone travelling in Italy who has just seen the picture. There are now over five hundred members. Many of these were brought in by my friend, Professor A. J. Armstrong of

Baylor University, Waco, Texas. He has taken parties of pilgrims there, and now on the wall of the church next to the picture is a tablet placed there by the Texas pilgrims.

In 1932—exactly twenty years after our first visit—we stood once more in Fano. But this time the picture was not in the church, though it is there now. Fano had been roused from its sleep of centuries by an earthquake, which had specialized on the church of San Agostino. The picture was shaken up; the wall on which it leaned was broken.

It took many months to make the necessary repairs; and in April 1932, we saw the picture, outside of its frame, leaning against the wall in a room in the city museum. Although it looks better in its natural setting as an altar-piece, still, there was one advantage in seeing it in the museum. The light was stronger. We sent an Italian painter from Florence, who made a life-size copy of the original, and now we have in New Haven what is probably the only copy of this picture that has ever been painted.

On this last visit I went to the largest postcard shop in Fano, and found hundreds of cards on sale. The proprietor asked me why it was that so many Americans had come to his shop in the last few years, asking for postcards of *The Guardian Angel*. And there was one thing that puzzled him still more. Many of these pilgrims talked about a *Fano Club*. Could I give him any information about that? 'Sir,' said I, 'I am its founder and president.' He did obeisance; he will never forget the day when the president of this famous organization entered his shop and deigned to talk with him.

One diverting by-product gave me much amusement. So much had been said about the Fano Club that notices of it appeared in Italian newspapers. I received a questionnaire. What is the Fano Club? For what purpose was it founded? What is discussed at its meetings? Who is the president?

I forget what I replied, but I suppose I gave assurance
that the club had no political significance.

A number of my colleagues at Yale have followed the example set originally by Professor Evans. Professor Chauncey Brewster Tinker and his friend, the Rev. Dr. William
Pitt McCune of New York, both of them former pupils of
mine, arrived in Fano on a Sunday and could find only one
picture postcard on sale, which was of a ramshackle bathing
pavilion on the beach. Accordingly, they sent me this poem:

> To be in Italy and not see Fano?
> McCune and Tinker both cried, ' Ah, no!'
> For not to go, and here's the rub,
> Means missing Phelps's Fano Club.
> On Sunday at Fano shops close, all and each
> Save this poor place on the bathing beach.
> But even this we think, by Jiminy,
> Is better than a card from Rimini.

Many Yale students who had taken my course in Browning have visited Fano. At the annual dinners of the Fano
Club on 7 May, Browning's birthday, we have received
cables from high officials in the city of Fano, many tele-
grams, and delightful letters in Italian from Dean Wig-
more of Northwestern University and many others. Sending Americans to Fano has been, I think, one of the major
achievements of my life.

The Fano Club was also enriched by Henry T. Rowell, a
Punditical member of the Senior class at Yale (now on the
Faculty) and by two of Father McCune's New York pa-
rishioners, Constance A. Jones and Helena Paul Jones, who
commemorated the fact that they followed their rector and
Professor Tinker thither, in these stirring lines:

> To be in Italy and not see Fano?
> McCune and Tinker once cried, ' Ah, no!'
> So what could good Ignatians do
> But follow in their footsteps too?

And following, as you will see,
Our minds are filled with poesy.
And if the merest mortal dare
Her own poor efforts to compare,
We think we sing a better tune
Than either Tinker or McCune!

Some days after our Fano pilgrimage, we resumed our
Ring and the Book journey; we visited the dreary little
village near Rome, where the infuriated Guido came face
to face with the runaways, Castelnuovo. We saw

The old tower, and the little white-walled clump
Of buildings and the cypress-tree or two,

and as we gazed on the windows of the wretched inn, the
tragedy took on the air of reality.

Our hotel in Rome was close to the Piazza del Popolo,
where Guido and his four accomplices were executed on the
22 February 1698. We followed the track of the condemned
men as they were led from the prison cell by Castle Angelo,
across the Tiber, through the Via Panico, Via Governo
Vecchio, Via Pasquin, Piazza Navona, by the Pantheon,
through the Piazza di Colonna, and down the full length
of the Corso to the place of death. As Guido entered the
Corso on his cart, he saw plainly in the distance the obelisk
of the Square. What must have been his feelings during
the last ten minutes of that journey, as he drew nearer
and nearer to this ancient column?

We walked on other days through the Via Vittoria, the
'aspettable street' where Pompilia lived: entered the
church of San Lorenzo in Lucina, looking on the lions at
the door, that terrified her in childhood. This was the
church where she was married, and where the bodies of her
parents were exposed in front of Guido Reni's *Crucifixion*.
Every detail of the church is still exactly as Browning
describes it. And in the church of the Gesu, we saw the

huge lump of lapis lazuli, mentioned by the dying delirious
Bishop of St. Praxed's, as he gave instructions for his tomb.

On our way north again, we stopped at Chiusi, through
which Guido rushed on his chase after the young pair. He
took the shorter route to Rome and I have never understood why the fugitives took the longer one. But we remembered also that Chiusi used to be called Clusium, and
in the railway station we shouted in chorus

> Lars Porsena of Clusium
> By the nine gods he swore

our enthusiasm arousing the officials on the platform.

At Siena, remembering that one of Browning's worst
poems was written about old Pacchiarotto, we studied his
curious work with some attention. Siena is probably the
greatest cat town in the world. I counted nine cats in about
nine paces. I stopped to caress each one. It is well to do
this, for their owners immediately take a pleased interest
in their furry possessions, and are sure to treat them with
increased respect. I asked many Italians, 'How old is your
cat?' and I never failed to receive immediately the precise
number of years, showing that the animal is appreciated.

We reached London on the eve of Browning's one
hundredth birthday, and the next morning—the seventh of
May—I traversed the Southampton Street, across the
river in Camberwell, where he was born on 7 May 1812.
In the afternoon I attended the exercises in Westminster
Abbey, which were devoted to his memory. Only a few
feet from his grave, the choir sang a portion of his poem
Saul, and some stanzas from Mrs. Browning's *He giveth
his beloved sleep*. Then we went into the little College Hall,
where interesting addresses were given by those who had
known Browning personally. The son of Lord Houghton
presided; a letter was read from Browning's son in Italy; the
son of Tennyson was present, and the grandson of Coleridge.

58

HENRY JAMES

I FIRST saw Henry James in 1911 in New Haven. He had been staying with some friends in Farmington, Conn., and he seemed to enjoy motor trips more than anything else. Miss Pope, who brought him from Farmington in her motor car, said that if she asked him if he would like to meet some people at a luncheon, he would say No; but if she suggested a journey in an automobile, he gladly agreed to that, and never asked whither they were going. Accordingly on this day, 23 May 1911, she brought him from Farmington to New Haven, where he was the guest of honour at a luncheon given by Mr. and Mrs. Harry Day. Mrs. W.E.Hocking, Mrs. Kingsley Blake, and Mr. George Seymour were present.

I had supposed that Mr. James would be reserved and remote, difficult to talk with; on the contrary, he was absolutely charming. He made me feel immediately at ease, and as if we had been intimate friends. 'Come and sit here with me on the sofa,' he said, and put his arm affectionately around my shoulder. I had with me a copy of his book *The Turn of the Screw* and I told him that although his literary style had often been called obscure, there was something else in his work that was even more difficult to read. 'And what is that?' 'That is your handwriting.' He smiled and took pains to write his name very slowly and distinctly in my copy of his book. I told him I thought *The Turn of the Screw* was the most terrifying ghost story I had ever read; that I read it when it first appeared, late at night, and when I had finished it, I did not dare go down stairs and put out the hall light. However, as I did not wish to leave the gas burning all night, there was a struggle between my Yankee parsimony and my fear of the dark. Finally I got my wife to stand at the head of the staircase. 'Don't you go away for a moment! don't you take your eyes off me; for if you do, I'll never get this light out!' I extinguished it and raced upstairs as if the devil and all his angels were after me.

Mr. James expressed delight. 'Do you know, I wrote that story with the intention of terrifying every reader, and in the course of its composition, I thought it would be a total failure. I dictated every word of it to a Scot, who never from first to last betrayed the slightest emotion, nor did he ever make any comment. I might have been dictating statistics. I would dictate some phrase that I thought was blood-curdling; he would quietly take this down, look up at me and in a dry voice, say "What next?"'

It has been wittily said that Henry James conversed as if he were reading proof. This is really true. In desultory conversation on that day and on another occasion in England, he would stop in the middle of a sentence, feeling around in his mind for the right word; if he could not find it, he would abruptly change the subject, rather than use what he regarded as not quite the accurate or suitable word.

The next time I saw Henry James was on Saturday afternoon, 1 June 1912 in London, at a tea given by the English novelist, Mrs. W. K. Clifford; only Henry James and May Sinclair were present. The conversation turned on the novels of Thomas Hardy; and I expressed my feelings of many years before, when I read *Tess* for the first time. The events and persons in that story seemed so real to me, and the catastrophe so overwhelming, that for days after I had finished it, I could not shake off my depression. Miss Sinclair said that the same sense of reality impressed her in reading the novels of Mrs. Humphry Ward. This appalled Henry James, who said, '*May Sinclair, May Sinclair*, such a remark may do credit to your heart, but where does it leave your head?'

Drawn off into a corner of the room by Henry James, I spoke of testing a written style by reading it aloud; that I had found many passages in Browning which seemed obscure to the eye were transparently clear when I read them aloud. To my surprise, he became excited. With intense earnestness he whispered in my ear, 'I have never in my life written a sentence that I did not mean to be read aloud, that I did not specifically intend to meet that test; you try it and see. Only don't you tell.'

There are writers who have an immense public and no fame; and there are a few who have never had many readers yet are truly famous. It is interesting to see what has happened to many authors in the twenty years since Henry James's death. His fame is higher and greater now than it ever was; yet the number of his readers is still comparatively small. He himself would have been glad of a large constituency; it pained him that his books had so small sales; he suffered; but he would not change his method, or write in any manner except to satisfy himself.

He was appreciative of praise from individuals. I regard Henry James as perhaps the greatest literary critic America has ever produced. When his book *Notes on Novelists* appeared, I could not help writing and telling him of my enthusiasm; but I begged him not to acknowledge the letter; I told him I had the audacity to deliver a public lecture on his novels and I should advise my audience to read this latest critical work. He wrote me the following letter: and I have always been glad I had written him, because in the midst of his agony over the war—no unbereaved person suffered more—it evidently gave him a moment's gratification.

DECEMBER 15TH, 1914
21, CARLYLE MANSIONS,
CHEYNE WALK, S.W.

DEAR W.L.PHELPS:

But I *must* thank you for the pleasure given me by your generous lines about my "Notes"—letting you measure what that is by the fact that under this huge nightmare, the unprecedented oppression or obsession of our public consciousness here, pleasure (save of the grim sort that premonitions of Victory, terrifically paid for, bring) is very hard to take and very questionable even to desire. However, I rejoice without scruple in what you tell me of your so liberal appreciation of my book—and if I could only have been present in time—and in spirit—at your expounding lecture (it would have helped things even for your author), this would have represented, oh, such a blest break in the constant comprehensive ache of yours all faithfully,

HENRY JAMES

Lady Ritchie (Thackeray's daughter) told me a good story about Henry James. One day as she was entering Paddington Station and was carrying under her arm a copy of a novel by him, she had the good fortune to meet him. 'Look, Henry James, here I am carrying one of your works to read on the train, and I meet the author himself!' He simulated dismay. 'My dear Lady Ritchie, what bad luck for you! Don't you know that you have there a copy of the most expensive edition of that work, and a new edition has just been issued for six shillings?' 'Don't you worry about that, Henry James. I just bought this at a second-hand bookstall for *one* shilling.'

I coined a phrase to describe Henry James's style both in writing and in conversation—*verbose reticence*. He wrapped his meaning in layers of words, but he did not tell you much, and you had to dig it out for yourself. An incident told me by Sir James Barrie illustrates what I mean. Barrie said that one cold, dark autumn afternoon he and James went to a matinée to see a play. After the play was over, they stood on the pavement discussing it. James was describing how the play impressed him. Gradually it grew very dark; after an hour or so, it began to rain; Barrie finally suggested they enter a taxicab; the two men drove around for an hour or so, while James continued his criticism of the play; and finally, Barrie said he must leave him, as he had to dress for dinner. 'As I left him,' said Sir James, 'I gathered that he thought the play would do no harm.'

Mr. Robinson Smith tells me the following story. Henry James was saying that a bevy of young ladies had invited themselves to tea. 'Were they pretty?' asked Mr. Gosse. 'Pretty! Good Heavens! yet one of the wantons had something of a cadaverous grace!'

Mrs. Edith Wharton told me that once at a dinner-party where Henry James was among the guests, a message came from a newspaper asking her if she would verify a rumour. She read the message aloud to the assembled party—'are you and Henry James engaged to be married?' The silence was broken by Henry James, exclaiming 'And yet they say truth is stranger than fiction!'

Barrie told me that if he were in trouble, the first two men he would go to for assistance would be Bernard Shaw and Henry James. Everyone who knew Mr. James intimately had experience of his extraordinary kindness and marvellous tact. Miss Clare Benedict, in her books about Constance Fenimore Woolson and *The Benedicts Abroad*, describes the wonderful kindness of Henry James after the death of Constance. He gave up everything for six weeks, devoting himself to the bereaved family, taking on his own shoulders innumerable burdens of practical detail.

It would be difficult to imagine a more beautiful letter than the following which Mr. James wrote to Mrs. and

Miss Benedict, just before they took ship for Europe—beautiful in its sympathy and in its practical, definite assistance. He fulfilled the Scriptural admonition by really bearing their burden.

Almost by this you will have heard from me that I will meet you at Genoa—be there when you arrive. I am sure Rome will be a very soothing, softening impression to you—that after a little . . . the horror of the weeks you have been living through will be lost in the simple assenting, participating tenderness with which (in regard to her memory and deep exemption now from everything that's hard in life) you will find yourselves thinking of her—till at last you will feel almost at peace in your acceptance. Meanwhile, only I live and think of living, from hour to hour, and day to day; it is perfect wisdom and it takes us through troubles that no other way can take us through . . . Have no plan whatever, in advance, about Venice . . . there is no need for any. The whole question will simplify itself, settle itself, facilitate itself, after you get to Italy . . . May you float down fast into kindly southern waters and meet the consoling, alleviating spring!

On 12 and 13 December 1915 Mrs. W. K. Clifford wrote me from London:

I am so glad you remember that afternoon, dear Mr. Phelps, with beloved Henry James & one or two people here. This letter is so badly written I feel almost incoherent for I write it waiting for a telephone message from his illegible secretary (it is 10.30 on Sunday night) with the Dr.'s last report of him. He is very ill as the American papers I know have told you. We kept it out of the papers here till we heard it was in *The New York Times*. He had a slight stroke last Thursday week—a second one the next day, now an attack of pneumonia has developed and we fear the worst. Mrs. William James arrives at 3 p.m. tomorrow—we hope she may be in time. He is *very* dear to us. He has been so splendid too, ever since the war broke out, taking his part, & giving his share, & feeling it all intensely. He spent hours every week comforting the soldiers in Hospital—especially the French ones who were lonely in strange surroundings & found English difficult. It was in token of his love for the country he had lived in so long, & his sympathy with the allies—that he 'turned English' last summer. Not that he did not love his *own* country tho' after the

President's *first* note, which he thought fine and dignified, he has been disappointed in the attitude at Washington.

Monday 13th. I had to stop. He is better this morning but talking wildly. If he recovers we fear one side will be paralysed. Mrs. William James is expected anytime now. Her boat has been delayed by storms. All greetings to you both, . . .

Henry James died in his flat in Chelsea, 28 February 1916.

On 16 March 1916 Mrs. Clifford wrote me, and at the top of her letter she had written her name in full, with this note, 'I put my formal name thus for the benefit of the Censor. *Are* our letters to *you* opened? It is too funny or wd be if it were not sad.'

And at the end of the letter she wrote 'P.S. It is so strange. All our letters from America are opened by the Censor. Even those with the imprint of well-known names —I had one from the Century Co. & one from Harper's— both opened. Rather absurd?'

And here is the part of the letter concerning Henry James.

I do so want you to know that though it was too late to give the message in your letter to dear Henry James, I gave it to Mrs William James who was over here; and she seemed pleased and touched by it. Henry, as I think I told you, had two strokes before Christmas, and complications followed, and his head was never clear afterwards, or rather not clear for the present time; concerning things that had happened five-and-twenty years ago he was fairly lucid, but later things were all confused with him. It is a great loss. He was a great personality in London and everybody who knew him seemed to have felt his personal note, and of course in England we were so immensely touched at his becoming one of us in the darkest time our country has known for centuries. It was the most supreme proof he could give us of his sympathy and affection. But his *own* country must not for a moment think that he forgot it, for he didn't; and he left directions that his ashes, after cremation, were to be taken back to it. There was much talk of a service in Westminster Abbey; the Prime Minister approved of it and the Dean was quite willing there should be one, providing the Chapter consented (which was a matter of course). But Mrs. William James, very wisely I think, refused all idea of it. The simpler service in the little church not a stone's throw from his flat, was more in accord with his life, she said—better befitted the New Englander. So thus it was; and a most beautiful and dignified farewell took place in the little church that is now centuries old and will now forever be identified with him. I daresay you saw a letter about it from Edmund Gosse in The Times. The notices in the English and French papers have been wonderful and show how much he was thought of in Europe.

My acquaintance with Mrs. W. K. Clifford, which ripened into an intimate friendship, began in 1919. When I was an undergraduate editor of the *Yale Literary Magazine* in 1887, I reviewed Professor Clifford's book *Lectures and Essays*, which had been published after his death. Clifford was a brilliant mathematician and philosopher, who died in 1879, at the early age of thirty-four.

In 1891 I read a novel called *Love-Letters of a Worldly Woman*, by Mrs. W. K. Clifford. I enjoyed this story immensely: it made a permanent impression. I thought it would be interesting to know the author of such a book, though I never expected to meet her. In 1910 I published a book called *Essays on Modern Novelists*. To my surprise, I received a letter from her, in which she said that she supposed I had never heard of her or of her work, but that if only some critic would write about her as I had written of the novelists discussed in my book, how happy it would make her! I immediately wrote her expressing my delight in her novel read twenty years before, and also of the fact that I had reviewed her husband's book, so that she could not possibly appear to me as a stranger.

Two years later I saw her for the first time in her home near Paddington Station. A brave, gallant high-spirited woman, and almost any afternoon at her tea-parties one met some of the most interesting people in London. Sir Frederick Pollock, Dean Inge, Shaw, May Sinclair, and many others.

We enjoyed an amusing incident one night at the theatre. Mrs. Clifford had just written a vigorous letter to the *Times* asking if something could not be done to prevent people from coming late to the theatres; they climbed over people's ankles, interrupted the play, and were an unpardonable interruption. The night after this appeared, we were enjoying the first performance of a charming comedy called *Many Waters*, when, some twenty minutes after the play had begun, in came Mrs. Clifford and a friend, and climbed over a number of spectators to reach their seats, in the middle of the row, directly in front of us. She was recognized by many in the audience and there was general merriment. Between the acts she explained to us that she had quite forgotten the admirable London custom of beginning plays on first nights one half hour earlier, so that the critics would have a little more time to write their reviews.

At one of her afternoon teas I had an interesting conversation with Dean Inge, whom I found anything but 'gloomy.' He spoke with high admiration of the Quakers. When I asked him if he thought he really would enjoy their religious services as much as those of the Church of England—'wouldn't you miss the beautiful ritual?' 'No,' said he, 'for the Quakers have that in their faces.'

One afternoon in 1912 we went to the Coronet Theatre at Queen's Gate, where Miss Horniman's splendid company from Manchester were in repertory, to see Arnold Bennett's play *What the Public Wants*. In the course of the first act, Mr. Bennett accompanied by May Sinclair entered a box. In the intermission, he came down in the auditorium and took an empty seat next to mine. Interesting it was to be present at a play with its famous author beside me. I told him how much I enjoyed the comedy. He said he wished the public agreed with me, but it was not at all a box-office success. 'Do the people think it is too highbrow?' 'That is exactly what they think, and they will have nothing to do with it.' He looked seraphically happy, however, for at another theatre, his play *Milestones* was packing the house. I asked him if he had a good time at Yale during his recent visit to America. 'I had a terrible time there! I had just been at Harvard and had lost my digestion when I left for Yale. Those Harvard people gave me too much to eat. President Hadley gave me a luncheon, and oh, I was so sick, I couldn't play up to him at all, oh, not at all.' But he said he was certainly coming back to the States, as he wished to see many places and things he had missed. He never was able to carry out this plan.

Later they told me in New Haven that he was so ill at President Hadley's luncheon he could eat nothing, and asked for a cup of tea. Tea was brought to him, he took one sip, and exclaimed 'It isn't brewed!' The British can never understand why an American, handing them a cup of tea, will say, 'Will you have some tea? It's very weak.' Which in their thought is equivalent to saying, 'It's very bad.' The English novelist Miss E.M.Delafield (Mrs. Dash-wood) wisely refused tea everywhere in America, although it was constantly offered her. She always took coffee. She knew that the Americans had the best coffee in the world and the English the worst, and that she could have plenty of tea at home. Arnold Bennett talked in conversation with me exactly as the author of his books ought to talk. He was simple, natural, unaffected, humorous, friendly, with the agreeable assurance that comes from success.

One of the most charming women we met in London in 1912 was Lady Ritchie. She pointed out various interesting things in the room. 'At that table Turgenev sat one day, waiting for me to come. Finally he gave it up, and wrote me a charming note, which I found when I came in.' As we walked around her room, looking at various wonders, she took a book off the shelf, and a little note, written in thick black ink, fell to the floor. I picked it up and she said, 'Read it aloud.' It ran like this: 'Dear Annie: be sure and be home tomorrow afternoon for I am coming around to walk with you. Alfred Tennyson.'

She showed me many of her father's novels, which were covered with pictures along the margins, which Thackeray had drawn to amuse his children. She was kind and gracious and looked exactly like the drawing of her by John Sargent.

She told me many things about Browning, whom she knew intimately. One evening at a large dinner-party, when the ladies had withdrawn, she mentioned a bit of gossip that she had heard, that Browning was to be married again. It seems that a day or two later, he heard this, and enquired who had said it and was told that it was said by Annie Thackeray. She did not know that it had reached his ears.

The next evening he was assigned to take her in to dinner. She came up to him with the usual intimate greeting, and to her amazement he would not look at her. She took his arm, and as they walked from where they were toward the dining-room, she attempted to speak to him, whereupon he spiked her with his elbow. They reached the table and during the entire meal he talked only with the lady on his left, not only saying nothing to Miss Thackeray, but not even replying to her questions. As soon as the ladies withdrew, she exclaimed 'Is Robert Browning crazy?' and described his behaviour. The others told her it was doubtless because he had heard that the rumour of a second marriage had come from her, and added cheerfully, 'He'll never forgive you.' During the rest of the season, although they met frequently at dinner-parties, he never spoke to her. But that summer, when he was spending a few weeks at a favourite resort in Normandy together with his friend the Frenchman Milsand, it so happened that

Anne Thackeray was at the other end of the village. One day Milsand said to Browning: 'You are behaving abominably. Miss Thackeray is heart-broken. She never intended to hurt your feelings and she is suffering tortures.' Browning, always impulsive, said, 'Why, is that so?' and he started on the run for her lodgings. She told me she was sitting lonely at a window in the second storey, when she saw Browning running toward her panting and puffing, but making good time. 'I ran down stairs, opened the front door, leaped into his arms, and had a wonderfully good time sobbing and weeping.' They were the best of friends again, and Browning dedicated his next long poem to her.

In 1889 when Browning, impulsively again, sent that terrible 'spitting' poem to the *Athenæum* on Edward Fitzgerald, he wrote a very long letter to Annie Thackeray explaining how he came to write such a poem and why he did it. She allowed me to read this letter through; it showed that Browning was suffering tortures, but he felt he was justified.

He had opened carelessly the newly published *Letters of Edward Fitzgerald* and had the bad luck to see the sentence 'Mrs. Browning is dead; thank God! we shall have no more Aurora Leighs.' Wild with rage, he sent in hot haste a poem to the *Athenæum* in which he said it would be difficult to think of an appropriate punishment for Old Fitz: kicking is the common lot of curs, and the only reason he could not spit on him was because he could not spit through lips that had been sanctified by hers.

It is unfortunate that this poem ever appeared in print. We know now that he tried in vain to recall it before it went into type. On page 378 of the *Letters of Robert Browning Collected by Thomas J. Wise*, we read:

> Browning experienced a revulsion of feeling against the publication of these stanzas, and sent a telegram to Mr. MacColl, asking him to

withhold the lines from publication. But, though there really was still time to excise them from the copy for the printer, Mr. MacColl so managed by talking to a friend before opening the telegram as to be able to inform Browning that it was too late to keep the stanzas from appearing.

In 1911 Thackeray's centenary had been celebrated at Yale; knowing of his daughter Lady Ritchie's intimate friendship with Turgenev, I sent her a copy of my *Essays on Russian Novelists*. This was before I had the pleasure of meeting her. Her admirable book *Blackstick Papers* had anecdotes of Turgenev. Having failed to keep an appointment, he came to her next day and held up his hands. 'Look at my thumbs! See how small they are! Such small thumbs mean that their owner is always being prevented from doing what he wants to do!' He laughed gaily and his manner was so charming she would have forgiven him anything. Furthermore, his resemblance to her father was uncanny.

The great Turgenev, in some respects my favourite novelist, was, I think, a pessimist from early youth; and his pessimism deepened as he descended into the vale of years. He said that he would give all his genius and all his fame if there were only one woman who cared whether or not he came home late to dinner. Although a giant in stature and very fond of outdoor sports, especially of shooting, he had attacks of the blackest melancholia. When these came upon him, he would remain motionless for two or three days neither eating nor sleeping. Although he was wholly without prejudices in contemplating the world of men and women, he had an active and extraordinarily sensitive conscience, both moral and artistic. This conscience forced him into various activities that he hated and fortunately for the world compelled him to write books. Once when asked his ideal of happiness, he replied 'Remorseless laziness.'

Some years ago there appeared in *Red Panorama*, a weekly Russian magazine published in Leningrad, a list of his replies to the same questionnaire, first in 1869 and the second in 1880. He died in 1883. The humour of the second list does not disguise its despair.

My friend Professor Petroff translated them for me.

Question	Answer in 1869	Answer in 1880
Your favourite virtue?	Sincerity.	Youth.
Your favourite quality in man?	Kindness.	Age of 25.
Your favourite quality in woman?	Kindness.	Age of 18.
Your favourite recreation?	Hunting.	To sniff tobacco.
Characteristic feature of your personality?	Laziness.	Laziness.
Your idea of happiness?	Excellent health.	To have nothing to do.
Your idea of unhappiness?	To be blind.	To work.
Your favourite colour?	Indigo.	Grey.
Your favourite flower?	Narcissus.	Cauliflower.
Your favourite writer?	Cervantes.	I do not read any more.
Your favourite poets?	Homer, Shakespeare, Goethe, Pushkin.	I do not read any more.
Your favourite artists and composers?	Rembrandt, Mozart, Schubert.	I do not go to concerts or exhibitions.
Your favourite heroes in history?	Washington, Pericles.	The man who discovered oysters.
Your favourite heroines?	Madame Roland.	Any dark complexioned maidens.
Your favourite heroes of romance?	King Lear, Prometheus.	Falstaff, Gargantua.
Your favourite dishes and drinks?	Meat, champagne.	What my stomach can digest.
Upon what vice do you look most leniently?	Drunkenness.	All.

Question	Answer in 1869	Answer in 1880
Your favourite motto?	None.	Good night.
If you were not what you are, what would you like to be?	My dog, Pegasus.	Nothing.

59

J.M.BARRIE

EVEN as there are elective affinities between men and women, and great friendships between men (I imagine that monks in mediaeval monasteries had friendships compared to which our best college friendships are thin and pale) so there are authors who especially appeal to certain individuals. It requires no effort and no peculiarity of taste to enjoy Shakespeare; it requires oddity not to admire him, which dislike was one of the many eccentricities of Tolstoy. But there are certain authors who affect us so profoundly that we suffer physical pain when we hear them disparaged or ridiculed.

Before Elizabeth Barrett had even the remotest idea of ever meeting Robert Browning, she said that attacks on his poetry affected her like the lashing of a whip on her skin.

Of all modern British authors, I am the most deeply affected by J.M.Barrie. My own attitude toward his writings has always been quite different from my admiration for some of his contemporaries; I admire their works; but for the creations of Barrie I feel something deeper than admiration. He touches something in me that instantly responds.

> Mon cœur est un luth suspendu:
> Sitôt qu'on le touche, il résonne.

I do not like to see the works of any authors misunderstood, misrepresented, undervalued; but when this hap-

pens with Barrie, I feel something more personal than dis-
agreement. I have always felt this way, since I began to
read Barrie and since I first saw his plays on the stage.

In 1902 I began giving annually an elective course at
Yale confined to contemporary dramatists in Europe and
America. I think it was the first university course anywhere dealing *exclusively* with this theme; though there
were many courses in the history of the drama where some
modern playwrights were included. Among the foremost
living writers of plays in English, Barrie was the only one
who had published nothing. Accordingly in 1909 I sent
him the programme of my course, and begged him to make
his plays available for students and readers. I received the
following letter:

> LEINSTER CORNER,
> LANCASTER GATE, W.
> 15 May 1909

> DEAR SIR,
> I have been on the continent and hence delay in receiving and an-
> swering your very pleasant letter. I thank you for it heartily. Some
> day I shall print 'What Every Woman Knows' and some others of
> my plays, and it is an uncommon pleasure to me to think that at
> Yale you may do them the honour you speak of.
> Believe me

> Yours sincerely,

> J. M. BARRIE

As it turned out, the first play he consented to publish was
not *What Every Woman Knows*.

I felt more eager to see him than to see any other man of
genius. Being in London in May 1912, I wrote and asked
him for a brief interview. He immediately replied, asking
me to lunch; but I had promised to lunch that day with
some persons no more distinguished than myself; and I so
informed him. Then he asked me to come in the morning.

Accordingly, on the morning of 23 May 1912 I entered the lift in the building in Adelphi Terrace that took me up to his rooms. I was shown in by a servant who looked like the Admirable Crichton. A moment later, Barrie entered and greeted me cordially. A little man, very dark hair, tiny dark moustache, little hands, little feet, and with an expression on his face of profound sadness. I asked him if he were still smoking the Craven Mixture; no, he had given that up. 'But that was the Arcadia mixture that you made famous in *My Lady Nicotine*?' It was, and the book had made a fortune for the manufacturer. It appeared that he was now smoking John Cotton Number One. . . . 'Be sure and get Number One' (it was the mildest form of this tobacco). The next day I went to a tobacconist's on the Strand, and I could not remember the name of the mixture I was looking for. 'Have you the Ben Jonson smoking tobacco?' He immediately brought the desired John Cotton.

Barrie told me his work was entirely outside himself. No one could draw inferences from it about his own thoughts or opinions. Plays were harder to write than novels. At that time he had not published a single one of his plays. I besought him to print them, telling him he was the only important dramatist whose plays were not 'works.' He said that after he had written a play, and got it through the days and nights of rehearsals, and then through the final horror of the first night, he never wished to see it again, or even hear it mentioned. But I suggested that all he had to do was to give the manuscript to the publisher. 'Oh, no, there's an immense amount of work to be done. Think of the stage-directions!' I did not know what he meant by that remark, nor did I find out till his first plays were published, when it appeared that these stage-directions were in some ways the most original and striking passages (for the reader). If the reader have enough imagination to give him television, these stage directions will enable him to be present in the theatre, even while alone under the lamplight.

I kept on imploring him to print, no matter what the additional labour might be; and before I left the room he actually promised to do so. Of course it is improbable that my importunity could have changed his mind. But it is barely possible that I hastened the consummation.

For, shortly after (1914), two of his plays appeared in illustrated editions—*Quality Street* and *The Admirable Crichton*, illustrated by Hugh Thomson. Copies are now much sought after by collectors; at the time of their publication, Sinclair Lewis was working in a publisher's house in New York. He presented me with my copy of *Crichton*. Barrie then went on to publish all his other plays in small single volumes, although *Peter Pan* came much later. And finally he was induced to publish his collected plays in one tall tome.

In this same first interview, I asked him which of his plays he thought the best; without any hesitation, he answered *The Admirable Crichton*. Twenty years later I asked him the same question, and he said, 'Well, now I rather prefer *Dear Brutus*.'

He thought William Archer had done more for the elevation of the contemporary English stage than any other man.

At that time, Mr. and Mrs. Bernard Shaw lived next door in Adelphi Terrace, one storey lower. Barrie said that when he wished to talk with Shaw, he merely raised his window and called out. Sometimes, if Shaw's windows were lighted at two o'clock in the morning, both men leaned out of their windows and had long talks. If only one knew the time of these aerial conversations! they would have been well worth awaiting all night in the street below.

Once, he said, he could not attract Shaw's attention by calling; so he threw pieces of bread at Shaw's windows. It appeared that Mr. and Mrs. Shaw were giving a dinner-party. Mr. Shaw looked up at Barrie and wanted to know if he were contributing manna to the feast.

I told Barrie he ought to be the happiest man in the world; this remark caused astonishment. 'Why should I be happy?' 'Oh, I don't mean that you should be happy because you have given so much happiness to the hundreds of thousands who have seen your plays and read your novels, though that must be a source of considerable satisfaction. What I refer to is the fact that you, perhaps more than any other living writer, are able to embody your thoughts in words. Now the difficulty, even with the ablest creative writers, is to transfer the pictures in their imagination and the thoughts in their minds to the written page, without loss; even with most successful writers, there is a sad difference between conception and execution. But you sit at this desk and fantastic images and ideas come into your mind, so strange they must often surprise you and make you laugh aloud in solitude. Yet you have the divine gift of transferring them to paper so that we see them very much as they first appeared to you.'

He listened to this with polite attention, and made no comment.

Shortly after, I withdrew, feeling that he was all and more than I had hoped to find. He was the Man of his Works, and my admiration for them became almost idolatry toward him.

I had not been in my hotel more than fifteen minutes, when a messenger arrived, bringing Barrie's little book on George Meredith. On the flyleaf was written, 'W.L.Phelps, from his friend, J.M.Barrie.'

The next time I saw Barrie was in his London flat on 19 September 1924, when I had tea with him. His hair was just as black as in 1912, but he had grown stouter. He said that his short play which had aroused so much discussion, *Shall We Join the Ladies?* he originally had intended to write in four acts, as a full-length play, but now he would never finish it. He did not volunteer any information as to who was the murderer, although John Galsworthy told me it was the butler. I tried to draw him out a little about the significance of his play *Mary Rose*, but it seemed he did not wish to discuss this.

He told me that in this very flat on one evening during the war, there were gathered together sitting on the floor around one lighted candle, for on account of Zeppelin raids they were not allowed to show much light, Thomas Hardy, Bernard Shaw, Joseph Conrad, John Galsworthy, Arnold Bennett, and himself; when suddenly a tremendous bomb fell from the sky and exploded on the pavement very close to their apartment. Anyone may now verify this for himself. The bomb fell at the foot of the obelisk on the embankment, and while the pavement has since been repaired, the holes made in the base of the obelisk are as they were. It would have been a sad and sensational loss to English literature if the bomb had struck a few yards north.

We talked about Shaw's latest play, *Saint Joan*, which I had just seen. Barrie expressed the highest admiration for it, but when I told him I wished the epilogue had been omitted, he agreed with me. So did Mr. Galsworthy.

In 1928 we came over again.

ADELPHI TERRACE HOUSE,
STRAND, W.C.2
30 May 1928

DEAR MR. PHELPS,

Delighted to hear you are coming in July. This is 'As I like it,' and a warm welcome awaits you.

Yours sincerely

J.M.BARRIE

We reached London on 27 July and a telephone message greeted us at the hotel, asking my wife and me to come to dinner at his flat the following evening; that the only other guests would be Mr. and Mrs. Bernard Shaw and Mrs. Thomas Hardy.

If I had to describe the temperament of this famous Irishman in one word, I should use the word *happy*. He seemed the happiest man I had met, and I have met many cheerful individuals. He was seventy-two years old, but had the springy alertness of youth not only in his mind, which might be expected, but in his body. As Mr. Service expresses it, he had the mind of a savant in the body of a savage. He is over six feet, spare, active, and agile, so that his voluminous snowy beard seems incongruous, as though it were some histrionic mask. As a rule, beards, unless closely trimmed, look untidy; they are often discoloured in various sections, so that the general effect is unattractive. Mr. Shaw's beard, like his hair, is evenly white—it is the cleanest beard I ever saw. The whole effect of his clothes, beard, and general appearance is so clean as to look antiseptic, his only resemblance to the members of a profession he so often attacks. I observed that he ate no meat, drank no alcohol, and declined to smoke. Whatever may be true of others, he needs no wine to stimulate his dinner conversation or to elevate his spirit. He is the only person who has ever come anywhere near to converting me to vegetarianism. He is a magnificent advertisement of his dietary doctrines. If abstinence from meat, wine, and tobacco can make a man in the seventies so radiantly healthy, buoyant, and resilient, the experiment might be worth trying.

His keen blue eyes sparkled as he told one good story after another. He gave many good-humoured and diverting reminiscences of the actor Henry Irving. Irving's voice and articulation were not good; when he spoke slowly, he was clear enough, but when he increased in speed, his words turned into a series of grunts. Mr. Shaw gave a remarkable imitation. At this point the conversation turned on distinct enunciation and the correct pronunciation of English. Mr. Shaw is a member of a committee which determines the pronunciation of English for the professional broadcasters; for it is hoped that broadcasting may be used to standardize and improve the general pronunciation. He said that one difficulty arises from the fact that no two cultivated persons pronounce words exactly alike. For example, he was certain that no two persons, no matter how fastidious in their speech, would pronounce the word *Cross* in the same way. (Of course one of the most noticeable differences between American and British pronunciation is observable in the letter *o*. The average American pronounces 'motor' quite differently from the average Englishman.) The committee, which was very small, had, as I remember, one Irishman, one Scot, one Welshman, and only one Englishman.

Mr. Shaw was interested in the movietone, and spoke of it with animation and emphasis. When he was asked to appear in the movietone he took charge of the whole affair himself, directed it, managed it, used his voice according to his own judgement, and the result was a complete success. He described his method with abundant illustrations. 'I come forward through the shrubbery, blow my nose—' Mrs. Shaw enquired: 'And why, Bernard, did you blow your nose?' 'Because I wanted to give the effect of naturalness, informality.' Later we went to a London movietone, and it was immensely interesting to see him appear on the screen so soon after talking with him. He came forward in a golf suit, consulted his watch, blew his nose, and gave an entertaining monologue.

Mrs. Shaw is a charming Irishwoman, and she may accurately be described in the language Ibsen used when replying to an impertinent question concerning his wife. Ibsen said: 'She suits me exactly.'

We stepped outside on the balcony surrounding Barrie's flat, which looks out over the Embankment all along the river. This is holy ground to the lover of literature. In an adjoining street Rousseau came and lodged with David Hume. Just below us was the inn where the Pickwick Club started on their famous journey. Doctor Johnson and Boswell had many conversations in the house next door. Thomas Hardy worked in the same block for several years as an architect. A house in the next street, plainly visible, was the place where 'Milady' stayed on her famous visit to London in *The Three Musketeers*. On my expressing my unlimited enthusiasm for that series of tales, Sir James said: 'It is undoubtedly the best story ever written.'

He showed me some books owned by Thomas Hardy when Hardy was a small boy. One was a compendium of athletic games, a kind of sportsman's manual, containing also directions for fishing, the care of dogs, birds, etc. A short time ago someone gave Barrie a canary. He knew nothing about taking care of canaries, but he remembered Hardy's boy's book. Consulting it, he found complete directions for the diet and regimen of canaries. He had been following these directions, and the bird prospered. Another book, owned by Hardy when he was twenty-five, was a copy of the poems of Shelley. Hardy had marked page after page, underlining words that especially appealed to him.

I spoke of the unhappiness suffered by many writers when they see their vogue declining, and younger men taking their places, as Ibsen expressed it in *The Master Builder*, with the younger generation 'knocking at the door.' Barrie said he often felt that the love of money was not the root of all evil, but rather jealousy. That is, the jealousy felt by one artist toward another. He had seen the evil effects of it in many instances, where men, brooding over their fancied wrongs, had turned sour, and had therefore lost happiness and peace of mind. It is a vice that naturally accompanies ambition, distinction, and love of fame. He added that he had never known a man more completely free of anything like jealousy than Bernard Shaw. Even in the long years when Shaw, although writing steadily, was receiving no recognition, he was quite free from envy and jealousy. 'Shaw has a healthy mind.'

I reminded Barrie of a passage in one of the novels by Archibald Marshall, where it is said that possibly the happiest persons are those who live in the country on an income just sufficient for their needs and *who are without ambition*. 'Yes,' said Sir James, 'that may be true. But perhaps even in those instances their minds are filled with little jealousies, little grievances arising from local affairs.'

I asked Mr. Marshall himself if he would be willing to give up ambition, literary fame, and the arduous labor of writing in exchange for a mind free from all these things but filled with placid contentment. 'Not for all the world,' was his emphatic reply. He was living in London and steadily engaged in writing *Simple Stories*, a series of tales about children that had great success in England. Mr. Marshall knew his London very well indeed and we had some interesting pilgrimages together, visiting the old city churches.

On 26 July 1928 I had a long talk over the teacups with Barrie. He was gratified by the success of Helen Hayes in her revival of his play *What Every Woman Knows*. I told him of the excitement at the first night of *Dear Brutus* in New York when Helen Hayes and William Gillette appeared in the play. She was sixteen, and in that one night went from obscurity to a fame that has never diminished. Barrie spoke highly of the work that Eva Le Gallienne was doing in New York with the Civic Repertory Theatre, and I was pleased to see that it was probable he would give her permission to play *Peter Pan*. Her success in this play the following Christmas season was immense.

He talked about Henry Irving, saying there was something compelling about Irving's personality, so that when he was acting, it made no difference how many people there were on the stage, you saw only Irving.

The conversation turned on Daisy Ashford and the publication of the story written when she was a child, called *The Young Visiters*, for which he had written a preface. Many believed he had written the book himself; he said there was not the slightest foundation in fact for such a statement. He had never seen Daisy Ashford until after he had written the preface; though he had met and talked with her after the appearance of the book. My wife suggested that no adult could possibly have written the story, because it contains the expression, 'Mr. Salteena got down from his chair.' That is what a child has to do, whereas a man or woman gets up. 'No,' said Barrie, smiling, 'I could have thought of that expression, only I didn't.'

Barrie was deeply impressed with the new novel by Thornton Wilder, *The Bridge of San Luis Rey*. He said Americans should be proud of two things; first, that the author was an American, second, that over 200,000 copies of the book had been sold in the United States. 'He is a true literary artist. I am a writer, and I know what good writing is. That passage toward the end of the story "he leant against the flame,"—is abundant evidence of Mr. Wilder's great ability as a writer.' I told him Wilder was a school-teacher and that on long, lonely walks he could not only think of ideas and material for plots, but could actually compose pages of dialogue. 'I can understand that, and I think it is fortunate that Mr. Wilder is a professional teacher. It is better for a writer to have some

regular occupation besides writing. I have often wished I
had myself. But I am only a writer.'

ADELPHI TERRACE HOUSE,
STRAND, W.C.2.
26 May 1932

DEAR LYON PHELPS

Welcome to these shores. You probably just missed our summer
week, but no matter. What matters is when you are coming in to
see me. Can you come in to luncheon Wed—or Thursday next week?
Both of you, at 1.30. Just alone. Will fix something else if you are engaged.

Always Yours

J. M. BARRIE

Barrie was a true Scot and had the reserve and reticence
characteristic of his nationality; but one could not help
feeling that his sincerity was as marked in his personal
friendships as in his art; and that his sympathy was as
deep as it was unaffected. He had a positive genius for
friendship; he was one of the closest friends of George
Meredith, and during the last twenty years of his life he
was more intimate with Hardy than any other man of
letters; he enjoyed the devoted affection of Henry James,
and was a lifelong friend of Bernard Shaw.

Since I began reading the works of Barrie in 1891, I
have never wavered in my faith in his genius; but I will
add that every time I met him and talked with him, I felt
that he himself was greater than everything he has written.
And I believe there are no greater English dramas of the
twentieth century than *Peter Pan*, *The Admirable Crichton*, and *Dear Brutus.*

We talked of Arnold Bennett's new play *The Return
Journey*, which he had not yet seen. I said the first act was
excellent; then the play declined and the last act was positively bad. I asked if it were not true that the greatest

difficulty in play-writing was to make a good last act. 'There is no doubt of it; and in order to make sure of having a good last act, when I wrote *The Admirable Crichton*, I wrote the last act first.' 'Did you ever do that again?' 'No.'

On 6 June 1932, we lunched with Barrie in his flat. During the conversation, I mentioned his fine University Commencement addresses, *Courage* and —— neither of us could recall the exact title of the other. I knew the word was not *enchanting*, but like it. He thought for a few moments and said, 'Well, I can't remember it, either; but I know *enchanting* is not it.' Then the conversation turned on other themes, when all of a sudden Barrie exclaimed 'I've got it! The word is *entrancing*! *The Entrancing Life*.'

On 5 June 1935 I had tea with Barrie and we talked for more than two hours. He was in good health and exceedingly animated, laughing aloud several times—rather unusual for him. We talked about books we had read and enjoyed twenty years ago, and wondered if on reading them again we should feel equally enthusiastic. 'Usually not,' he said; 'but I have just read through Bennett's *The Old Wives Tale*. It is a very great novel. It seems to me greater than when I first read it.' Then we spoke of the tremendous rise in fame in the twentieth century of the novels of Dickens. 'He is next to Shakespeare.' Barrie had been reading Thornton Wilder's new novel. 'Perhaps it is not so good as *The Bridge*, but I enjoyed it very much indeed. It is full of humour. And remember this, even if he had never written *The Bridge*, even if *Heaven's My Destination* were his first novel, we should see right off that he was a remarkable writer. No one but a literary artist could have written it.'

I asked him about the new play he had made for the actress Elisabeth Bergner. I told him that a few months before, after her matinée performance in New York of the play *Escape me never*, I had talked with her in her dressing room. She said 'Barrie is the greatest living dramatist and his new play that he has written for me is a tremendous masterpiece.' I told her I agreed with her in the general statement and felt equally sure she was right in the particular one. 'Well,' said Barrie, 'I had not written a play for fifteen years, when I decided to write one for Miss Bergner. I had forgotten how to write plays, and wondered how I used to do it. Did I think of incidents and a plot first, or did I think of the characters? I had no idea. But the moment I sat down at my desk and took my pen, everything seemed natural and easy. It all came back.'

The death of Barrie on 19 June 1937 was felt as a personal loss by individuals in every part of the English-speaking world.

Barrie could never dictate, not even letters; and as he had never learned to use a typewriter, everything he wrote was in longhand. The result was that after many years he was afflicted with writer's cramp; he then learned gradually to write with his left hand, and perhaps the enforced slowness explains the increased legibility. For the letters he wrote me with his left hand are easier to read than the preceding ones.

Yale University several times offered Barrie an honorary degree and I naturally wrote him personal letters; in 1914 he replied

ADELPHI TERRACE HOUSE,
STRAND, W.C.

DEAR PROF LYON PHELPS,

I wish I could have arranged it immensely but I had to write to the Secretary that circumstances made it impossible for me to get away. We shd have had a good time. It was very pleasing to me to be asked at any rate. Glad you liked 'Leonora,' and hoping to see you again on that side or this,

Yours very sincerely,

J.M.BARRIE

In 1918 I published a little book called *The Twentieth Century Theatre*.

2, ROBERT STREET,
ADELPHI, W.C.2.
20 Jan 1919

DEAR PROF. PHELPS,

My hearty thanks for the 'twentieth century theatre' which I have enjoyed much. Alas, for the nice things you say of my own efforts! But in my heart I am glad that you are so kind to them, I can do the headshaking myself. I dont know whether you have had such an out-pouring of war-plays as has deluged us. A V.C. to every leading actor, and I think that if the plays were to remain the record of the war future generations would decide that we had had no casualties. How many! And indeed we sometimes feel that all the best are gone. One seems to miss them more when the war is over, as if they should come back now.

I was nearly starting for America just now, had a pleasant invitation but could not get away. All hail and much happiness to you in 1919.

Yours Sincerely

J.M.BARRIE

In Barrie's own plays included in the volume *Echoes of the War* there were certainly casualties.

In 1927 appeared the following paragraph in *The New York Times*.

A UNIQUE HONOR FOR BARRIE

For the first time in the history of the Théâtre Français a play by a living British dramatist has been selected for performance on that classic stage. Sir JAMES MATTHEW BARRIE's " The Old Lady Shows Her Medals," as adapted by the French playwright NOZIERE, is to be produced in the coming season. If it is surprising for the Comédie Française to break through its traditions in the case of a contemporary foreigner, the work selected is equally puzzling, for it is in no sense Gallic in form or treatment, and does not even show its author in his real whimsical form. Perhaps the title adopted for the French version, "La Vielle Maman," should give a clew. The war is too recent and too serious for anything connected with it, however remotely, not to be taken seriously in the home of French comedy.

In 1928 I saw this at the *Comédie* and at its close the audience rose and cheered vociferously while the tears ran down their faces. As played in America by Beryl Mercer, the effect was overwhelming. In the last scene, as the Old Lady moved in absolute silence about the stage, uncontrollable sobs were heard all over the auditorium.

In 1921 Yale made one more effort to induce Barrie to come over and receive a degree.

> ADELPHI TERRACE HOUSE,
> STRAND, W.C.2.
> 2 April, 1921

DEAR MR LYON PHELPS,

I am much honoured by the action of the Yale University Corporation and am replying formally to the Secretary from whom I have heard also. Alas, there is I think no possibility of my being able to visit America at that time, but the pleasure you all give me is as great almost as if I could be among you. I look forward to the new book and hope to enjoy it as much as the last which I liked immensely. You will gradually get me to believe some at least of the nice things you say about me. I think you may have seen in papers that I meditated going to America to produce a Peter Pan film, but the only truth is that I said No to it. Yet it might have been worth while. It is the only thing of mine that I can see being dealt with satisfactorily in that bewildering medium.

My kindest regards to you, and I wish you would revisit these shores.

> Yours Sincerely
>
> J. M. BARRIE

The book he alludes to was one called *Essays on Modern Dramatists* published that same year.

I was in London in September 1924, and I hardly expected to have the good fortune to meet him there in that month. However, I sent him a line from my hotel.

ADELPHI TERRACE HOUSE,
STRAND, W.C.2.
17 Sep

DEAR MR PHELPS,

I have just arrived in London, obviously with the express purpose of seeing you again. Anyhow it is a sufficient reason. The prospect delights me, and I hope you can come in at tea time tomorrow (Thursday) about 5 o'clock. If there is anything not suiting you in this time, almost any other day would be right for me. My telephone (not in book) is Gerrard, 9764.

Yours

J.M.BARRIE

I had a good talk with him, and when the conversation fell on authors whose books were very popular and undistinguished, he said that in every best-seller there was always something good; the things that were good, not the things that were bad, caused the popularity. Later I had an interesting conversation on this same theme with Bernard Shaw, who said that best-sellers were never written down to the public, but in order to reach a huge sale, their authors must be sincere, no matter what the critics thought of their work.

In 1925 the American publishers, Charles Scribner's Sons, wished to issue a volume of selected plays by Barrie and when they wrote asking him whom he would choose to write the Introduction, he gave them my name. The book appeared in 1926.

ADELPHI TERRACE HOUSE,
STRAND, W.C.2.
27 Sep. 1925

DEAR LYON PHELPS,

I am very pleased that you are to write that introduction. I naturally thought of you at once when Scribners put me to the question, and your letter is delightful. I take off my hat to your course of lectures and wish we had something more like it here. I am however furious with you for saying you wish 'Leonora' was available, because I thought it was. Enquiry shows it isn't, and it must now be shrinking from observation in a bursting and loathsome cupboard. Or it has gone over-board in the night with some companions too. I am reminded of a stranger whom I sat beside in a railway carriage. We stopped at a small station where an elderly woman was sitting, and after gazing at her he said "I once asked that woman to marry me, and now I cant remember her name." My pretty dears, I cant remember all their names.

All kind regards

Yours

J.M.BARRIE

Whenever I wrote him, unless a reply was necessary, I begged him not to acknowledge the letter, as I knew how completely his time was taken. But against my urgence he wrote this note in response to a little paragraph I had printed about him.

ADELPHI TERRACE HOUSE,
STRAND, W.C.2.
15 Aug 1934

DEAR LYON PHELPS,
I enjoyed the fairy poem much and the kind thought that made you send the cutting also. You dont speak of being [sic] coming over this year but if such is in your head please see that you turn in at my door. Yours sincerely

J.M.BARRIE

On 23 June 1926 Barrie received an honorary degree from Oxford, the Public Orator, A.B.Poynton, whose citations delighted University audiences many years, presenting him. I had an interesting talk with Mr. Poynton at a luncheon given at University College, Oxford, by my friend and former pupil, Arthur Goodhart. Both Goodhart

G. K. Chesterton, William Lyon Phelps, and Æ. in my house in New Haven, 1931

The American Academy
William Lyon Phelps, Dr. Wilbur Cross, Robert Underwood
Johnson, Henry Van Dyke, Dr. Nicholas Murray Butler

Seven Gables, Huron City, Michigan
August 1938

Seven Gables, 1938

Saluting the Owl at Seven Gables, 1938
Shot by Mr. Phelps, 1933

W.L.P., Thornton Wilder, and the late Ellery Walter,
author of the book Around the World on One Leg, *New Haven*

Rowing on the Cam at Cambridge
England, 1900, *aged* 35

Telling a funny story. Rotary dinner, Philadelphia. On the left William K.Huff, director of the Forum, and on the right C.Arthur White, president of the Rotary Club.

and Poynton are Fellows of that college. Mr. Poynton amazed me by saying that my citations as Public Orator at Yale were more difficult to write than his; to which I naturally replied that mine were in English whereas he had to write in Latin. 'Exactly,' said he; 'you have got to be witty, because all understand every word you say; whereas, mine being in Latin, the audience have no idea whether mine are any good or not.' However, he would certainly perform my task better than I should his. Here is what he said in presenting Barrie: (from the London *Times*, 24 June 1926).

SIR JAMES BARRIE

After allusions to *Quality Street*, *A Window in Thrums*, and other literary masterpieces of Sir James Barrie, Mr. Poynton continued: *ad insulam illam solitariam avolemus, ubi promus ille κρείττων αὐτοῦ naturae obsequens cuivis Stoico par regnat.* This inventor of *dulcissimae inanitatis* had a sure place in our hearts, *cum eorum memoria, quos infantes ita amavimus ut tamen "adultos esse" gaudeamus.*

Sir James, who received an ovation from the House, was welcomed by the Chancellor as *Vir dilectissime, qui personas tuo ingenio fictas ita ad vivum describis ut apud nos vivere videantur.*

The biographical part of my introduction I put into the first paragraph, as follows:

James Matthew Barrie was born on an island situated seven leagues west of the most western of the Islands of the Hebrides. It can be reached only by the right pair of boots. In ancestry he comes straight down in the authentic line of apostolic succession, there being two of the disciples in his name; a happy combination of works and faith. Although a mortal man, he is the father of immortal children, among whom may be mentioned Tommy, born in 1896; Crichton, born in 1902; Peter Pan, born in 1917; Mary Rose, born in 1920. So much for biography.

60

SINGING BIRDS

I SHALL have more to say of travelling in England, but I will content myself now by relating my long and finally triumphant pursuit of the nightingale. Many may think it is ridiculous to go abroad merely to hear a nightingale; but this is the most famous of song-birds; and when I remember how I had unsuccessfully chased the vocal fowl through many countries and for many years, the result is worth recording. All the great British poets for five centuries paid poetic homage to the famous bird, and it became essential to my happiness that I should hear him. Wherever I went, I found he had just left. For example, whenever I was in Florence, and went out to the Cascine or along the Arno, and listened to nothing, I was always informed that last week scores of them were in activity. Speaking of the moon in Florence, Browning said:

> Full she flared it, lamping Samminiato,
> Rounder twixt the cypresses and rounder,
> Perfect, till the nightingales applauded.

Well, many a night I walked along the Arno, and saw the moonlight on the façade of San Miniato, but heard no nightingale. It was the same way in Germany; Bremen is famous for its nightingales, but there were none for me. I asked my English golf-partner if he had ever heard a nightingale, and he replied, 'I wish I had a shilling for every bootjack I have thrown at them.' I never saw a bootjack, but it appears to be an implement used by Englishmen to throw at nocturnal soloists. I suppose every well-regulated British household has a collection of boot-jacks, which are hurled at the voices of the night, are collected again during the day, and conveniently arranged for the midnight barrage.

In an interesting conversation with the English novelist, Alfred Ollivant, I mentioned my bad luck, and he declared that if I would come down to his house in Sussex on the following Saturday, he would produce a nightingale. Accordingly at the appointed time we took the train, and I was agreeably shocked to observe that the station where we got off was Horsham, the town where Shelley was born; of course there should be singing-birds. We drove in the twilight nine or ten miles; and after we had proceeded some distance, Mr. Ollivant remarked, 'Now, this is funny.' 'No,' said I, 'this is not funny at all; this is the same bad luck I have had for years.' 'Why, last Saturday night there were scores of them all along the road.' This time there were none. After dinner we sat in the garden till midnight; nothing. I gave it up, and went to my room; but just as I was getting into bed, there was an excited knock on the door and a hurry call. At the word, accoutred as I was, I sprang to the window. It was a very dark night, no moon, no stars; I made out three big blurs rising from the lawn—three tall trees. In each of the trees there was a nightingale, and the three birds were singing together. It was a concert worth all the years of waiting. As I listened in ecstasy, I thought of the long succession of British poets who had paid their tribute to the midnight minstrels, and the splendid stanza by Keats came into my mind,

Thou wast not born for death, immortal Bird!

and ends

> . . . the same that oft-times hath
> Charmed magic casements, opening on the foam
> Of perilous seas, in faery lands forlorn.

Kipling, in his story, *Wireless*, referring to these lines, says: ' These are the pure Magic. These are the clear Vision. The rest is only poetry.'

How well repaid I was for my Sussex adventure! For the next morning as we walked across the fields on our way to church, we heard two other English soloists—the skylark and the cuckoo, so celebrated in British poetry. The larks rose almost vertically, as if trying for the altitude record; and after they had become invisible aloft, we could hear their voices—the poet calls it a 'sightless song.' The cuckoo I had never heard before; his song is a precise imitation of that abomination known as the cuckoo-clock, only of course you cannot train him to strike right. He is a ventriloquist; the powerful notes seemed to be directly behind my shoulder, whereas they came from a distance of about a thousand yards.

The most famous four birds in English literature are the nightingale, the blackbird, the cuckoo, and the skylark. All four are unknown in America. We have the yellow-bill and black-bill cuckoo, but they are quite unlike the English variety. As for the blackbird, I agree with Theodore Roosevelt and with Lord Grey that he is the finest singer in England. When I read many years ago Tennyson's poem to the blackbird, celebrating the beauty of his music, I could not imagine what caused the poet's enthusiasm; the word blackbird had for me a quite different connotation. Our red-winged blackbird, with the scarlet epaulets, has only a genial wheeze; while the so-called crow-blackbird sings as though he had tonsillitis, or as though his voice were adolescently changing. But the British and the continental blackbirds emit the most heavenly music. In spring dawns in Germany, they used to wake me up at four o'clock; I never thought of throwing bootjacks at them, for I was entranced. One February day, while standing in front of the University of Munich during a copious snowstorm, I saw a blackbird on the branch of a tree; he had his beak pointed toward the wind, and, while the snowflakes beat upon his little face, he poured out a stream of the loveliest music in the world.

61

DOROTHY CANFIELD

ONE day more than twenty years ago as I was at work in my library in New Haven, I was pleasantly interrupted by the advent of a distinguished-looking elderly gentleman accompanied by an extremely shy young girl. The man was the librarian of Columbia University, formerly president of Ohio State—how fortunate to be able to exchange the terrible job of college president for the agreeable position of librarian!—and the bashful girl was his daughter Dorothy. Dr. Canfield never wasted time or words on preliminaries.

' This is my daughter and she has got to write a thesis in Old French for her Ph. D. at Columbia.'

' God help her!'

' No, *you* help her!'

' But I don't know anything whatever about Old French. The only French that interests me is modern French.'

' Yes,' said he, ' but you once wrote a thesis in English and got a Ph.D.'

' That is quite true; and I made up my mind then that if the Lord would forgive me I would never write another.'

' Well, this thesis has got to be written, and we have come to New Haven to discuss the method of its production with you.'

I did my best to point out the way in which 'original work,' if it were to be valuable and important, must be done; what to include, what to emphasize, what to omit. Miss Canfield wrote her thesis with the customary bloody

sweat, successfully met all the requirements, and has whatever rights and privileges go with the title of 'Doctor.'

In the summer vacation of the year 1912, as I was sitting
in my house in Michigan after the diurnal eighteen holes,
came the diurnal parcel of new books containing a novel
by a woman unknown to fame. The novel was *The Squirrel
Cage*; the name of the author, Dorothy Canfield. I did not
connect this name in my mind with that of the former aspirant to the doctorate; but the title of the book was be-
guiling, and the first paragraph caught my attention. I
read the book from beginning to end with steadily increasing admiration. Somewhere during its perusal I *heard* the
timid, almost inaudible voice of that terror-stricken, thesis-
haunted girl in New Haven. I wrote a letter to her in care
of the publisher asking if it were really she. I received a
reply from Mrs. J.R.Fisher in Arlington, Vermont, confessing everything. What a development in four years! The
timid girl had become a Ph.D., a wife, and a novelist!

As I considered *The Squirrel Cage*, I thought how strange
it was that this author had ever supposed her 'vocation'
lay in Old French or in anything other than creative work.
For although she has since written better novels, this particular specimen has intrinsic value. It contained unmistakable evidence that its author was a genuine, realistic
writer—realistic without being sensational.

I dare say that the labour in Old French was not fruitless; the painstaking accuracy of that thesis was transferred to a wider and more interesting domain. Her education in France, where precision of language is thought to
be important, was as valuable for her as for her older contemporaries, Anne Sedgwick and Edith Wharton. All three
had a thorough knowledge of the French language and
literature.

In her next novel, *The Bent Twig*, Dorothy Canfield produced the best story of undergraduate and faculty life in

America that I have read. She described a coeducational
state institution, the kind of thing she knew as a child; for,
as I mentioned before, her father had been president of
Ohio State University.

During the war Mrs. Fisher went to France, where her
accurate knowledge of the language and of the people made
her presence of the highest value. Many women, and some
elderly men, feeling that they ought to 'do their bit,' managed to cross the water, where they were in innumerable
instances a nuisance. They could not speak or understand
the language with facility, they fell sick and had to be
taken care of; and when they were well, they had a genius
for getting in the way of those who were useful. But
Mrs. Fisher knew exactly what she could do, knew how to
do it, and did it. She took care of blind soldiers and of their
children. This would not be worth mentioning in an estimate of her literary art if it were not for the fact that it
aided in producing some of her best writing.

One of our Yale professors, now no longer living, who
was born in France, was so impatient with what he thought
was the vulgarity of America that on a sabbatical year
he went over to France thinking he would escape for a
time from a distressing environment. I discovered him in
a village in Brittany. He was desperately homesick for
America. 'Why,' said he, 'I never thought such ignorance,
stupidity, and vulgarity could exist as I have found in this
French village. And the language of the old women when
they speak angrily to each other!' He was unfortunately
able to understand everything they said.

We know what Flaubert thought of small-town life in
France. And Dostoevski said that in Russian villages the
inhabitants spent so much time poking their noses into
their neighbours' affairs that one would think they would
all be great psychologists. 'On the contrary, they are
nearly all idiots.'

Dorothy Canfield believes that a New England village contains an almost complete assortment of the various types of human nature; there one can study them better than in a large city. With her large, tolerant view of human nature, and her womanly sympathy, she gives us not a travesty, but a picture.

Of all her novels I like best *Her Son's Wife*. In the first place, her attention is concentrated on three characters; from multiplicity of characters arises a tendency to diffuseness. This book deals with a fight between two women for the possession of one man. When two men fight for a woman, the theme is not particularly interesting, both because it is so common and because there is a pact known as a gentleman's agreement—who ever heard of a lady's agreement? When two women fight for a man, the struggle is interesting because there are no rules. In this particular novel a mother, accustomed for many years to domination over her son, finds that he has married without consulting her; and has married a detestable female.

The mother is a school-teacher. On arriving home from her professional duties one afternoon she sees in the hall a woman's hat. Now just as a zoologist can from the sight of one bone reconstruct the entire animal, so a woman from the sight of one hat can visualize the form and character of its wearer. This hat is not reassuring; in fact, her worst fears are confirmed.

Some have wondered how this woman could have done her teaching when the hours before and after were filled with nerve-shattering misery. I say that it was her professional work that saved her life and her soul. For the daily round of teaching is like the work of a military captain in action. There are certain kinds of toil that can be done mechanically; the work goes on while the mind is otherwise employed. But the blessed thing about teaching is that it demands unrestricted attention. When the teacher is alone in the classroom with her pupils, no other person can help her, and she cannot think of anything else. Many teachers are doing brilliant and successful work in the classroom while suffering from ill health and financial worry. The loss of income is only one of the tragedies of unemployment.

I regard Dorothy Canfield's novels as a contribution to American literature. She has won a place in the first rank of American contemporary woman novelists, and there she stands with her compeers—Edith Wharton, Willa Cather, Pearl Buck, Anne Sedgwick, Edna Ferber, Zona Gale, Ellen Glasgow.

WAITING-ROOM
GRAND CENTRAL STATION
NEW YORK CITY
Aug. 3–1916

DEAR PROFESSOR PHELPS:

I've been trying desperately to find a moment in which I might write you, but packing and children, and getting our house ready to leave for the winter and saying good-byes have so more than filled every moment that it's only now, at five in the morning, as I arrive from Vermont on an early train, that I see a breathing-space, and feel I can write you the "report" I've been wanting so much to make to you. For, do you know, I feel that I owe you an accounting for what I do. That's one of the penalties you pay for your generous interest and sympathy! I really want you to know what I'm up to, for I'm counting on your help to make the most I can out of my life.

Sally Cleghorn—my very dear and close sister-friend—has written you that I am going to France, but she didn't tell you why, I believe. It's mainly for the very simple, elemental reason that my husband is there, and that we are the kind of husband-and-wife who find it almost intolerable to be separated. Life's too short to miss any of that perfect companionship! I'm not going into "relief work" (except what informal help I can give without interfering with my care for our children) I'm going to establish a quiet little French home in a suburb of Paris, near the American Ambulance in Neuilly where my husband will be, for the most part, in service, and just live there through the winter to come, instead of on our Vermont mountain side.

I'm not going to write, because I've written a great deal this last year, and I want to give myself time to do a lot of thinking and living before undertaking anything new. And I hope our two children will enjoy their French winter as much as a Vermont one. You must remember there is nothing new in this for me. I was half brought up in France, you know, and have established French homes and lived there at intervals all my life. It all seems quite simple and natural to me, my husband giving up a year of his life to France, and I going to live near my dear French friends in this very dark moment of their lives—like going to help out one's cousins in need. I think we'll both be happier all our lives to have done this. I hate war, I'm almost as much of a pacifist as Sally Cleghorn (though not quite!) but like nearly all of my generation I'm terribly, tragically bewildered by the complexity of the situation. And it will ease an aching heart to do the simple, obvious, human thing, even if it is not very deep or far-reaching, establish a home near my husband who is alleviating pain, and fill my house, small though it will be, with a succession of homeless Belgian and French children who can share in the mothering I give to my own. Perhaps I can think more clearly what it all means if I can stop the misery of feeling that I am doing nothing—not even the little I might do—to help out in the suffering.

I've written you all this as though you were my God-father, to whom indeed I have recently written very much such a letter. He has disapproved very much of our leaving our comfortable Vermont home, but now, I hope and believe, feels more reconciled to it. I hope you will, too. It makes a good deal of difference to me—what you think.

With every good wish

Faithfully yours,

Dorothy Canfield Fisher

114 RUE DE BRANCAS
SEVRES
SEINE ET-OISE FRANCE
All Saints Day (1923)

My Dear Professor Phelps:

Your note about "Raw Material" was the first news I had of it, and it has stayed almost the only news! The book came out in August, I imagine, and I suppose some copies were sent me as usual, but customs, or slow mails or something have delayed them. I still haven't seen a copy. We were in Switzerland well on into September, and had no word that the book was published. I felt as though I had dropped it down a well. And then came your letter, . . . can you imagine the effect? No you can't. I never had so vividly from any written communication the effect of a warm, actual handshake of encouragement. . . .

I watched some very carefully trained tennis players this summer at Evian (where we were playing this season) with a rather alarmed interest. They had had evidently the infinitely careful instruction which is given to leisure-class folks over here, their form was simply perfection, it was a delight to see them make one perfect stroke after another, like an artistic creation. But along came a middle-aged Englishman, who had evidently struggled along by himself, had any number of faulty habits, but who went right through their perfection like tissue-paper, simply because he had about forty times their motive-power. It made me think very hard about the art of writing (everything makes me think hard about that).

Ever yours,

DOROTHY CANFIELD FISHER

114 RUE BRANCAS—SEVRES
April 2, 1924

DEAR PROFESSOR PHELPS:

I'm horrified by your writing that you once addressed "a Normal School" at Sèvres! Don't you let Mlle. Amieux the Directrice, hear you! It's as if a French man of letters said that he once spoke to "a military school at West Point." We consider that this is *the* Normal School of France, and indeed, so it is! I hope you'll meet and talk to Mlle. Amieux when you're here. She's a credit to her race and sex.

Every sort of good wish to you for your year over here, and thanks for your letter.

Affectionate greetings always

DOROTHY CANFIELD FISHER

62

CONVERSATIONS WITH PAUL HEYSE

PAUL HEYSE died on the second of April 1914, at his home in Munich, having reached the age of eighty-four years. His literary career began in 1850, and he wrote steadily to his last hour; his publications covered an immense range— novels, short stories, poems, plays, with a great number of essays in philosophy and criticism. The King of Bavaria in 1854 offered him a home in Munich, with a pension of five hundred dollars a year, so that nearly the whole active life of this Berliner was identified with the intellectual centre of South Germany. In 1910 he received the Nobel Prize.

When I was young, I came across an old paper-cover translation of Heyse's long novel, *The Children of the World*. I read it with such delight that I remember my first waking thoughts every day were full of happy anticipation. I lived with that group of characters, and whenever I open the book now, I find their charm as potent as ever. My hope of sometime seeing and talking with the man who had given me so much pleasure was satisfied in 1904.

It was Sunday, the fifth of June, and a bright, warm afternoon, when I walked along the Luisenstrasse in Munich, and stopped at Number 22. Almost before I knew it, I was talking intimately with the famous novelist. He was then seventy-four, but remarkably vigorous and fresh-faced, an abundant shower of dark hair falling on his neck and shoulders, and his full beard slightly grizzled. He was immensely interested in the criticisms of his play, *Maria von Magdala*, which Mrs. Fiske had been presenting with

595

great success in America. He told me with ardent satisfaction of the large cash royalties that had steadily poured in
from across the sea. He wished to know infinite detail
about Mrs. Fiske. 'She is a most beautiful woman, is she
not?' asked the old man, eagerly. 'On the contrary,' said
I, 'she is decidedly lacking in physical charm, both in face
and figure.' This seemed a cruel disappointment to him, as
he had evidently pictured a superbly handsome creature
as the incarnation of his work. I explained to him that so
soon as Mrs. Fiske had spoken a dozen lines on the stage,
no one knew or cared whether she were beautiful or not;
her personality was so impressive, so compelling, that she
drew irresistibly the most intense sympathy; that this
seemed to me her greatest triumph, by sheer brains and
art to produce the illusion of a lovely, suffering woman.
But Heyse was not satisfied. '*Man hat mir gesagt, dass sie
sehr schön ist.*' Several other visitors entered, and Heyse,
forgetting he was a dramatist, and remembering only that
he was a doctor of philosophy, plunged into an excited
discussion about the work of Professor Justi, of the University of Bonn. Not being particularly interested, I have
forgotten everything he said about this philosopher and
art critic. I waited patiently for a change in the weather.

It came. The conversation suddenly shifted to American
literature. 'Who is your greatest living writer?' I knew
that Heyse was a grave, serious, melancholy man, but I
boldly answered, 'Mark Twain.' Heyse shook his head,
more in sorrow than in anger. 'I have always heard of
Mark Twain's humour—that he was the funniest man on
earth. I therefore read with the most conscientious attention every word of *Huckleberry Finn*. I never laughed once.
I found absolutely not a funny thing in the book.'

Before going, I asked him to write his name in my copy
of *Kinder der Welt*. He complied most graciously, though
he was surprised, and not overpleased to learn of my en-

thusiasm for this particular novel. He gave me a really affectionate farewell, and asked me to come and see him whenever I should be in Munich.

On the twenty-first of January 1912, a glorious winter day, I went to see him again, and literally sat at his feet. He was over eighty years old; he occupied a huge carved chair in the centre of his library; the winter sunlight streamed through the windows, crowning his noble head with gold. The walls of the room were entirely lined with books, and he made such an impressive picture in these surroundings, that for a time I hardly heard a word he said, so absorbed was I by the dignity and beauty of the scene.

I took a little chair, directly in front of him, looking up reverently into his face. 'I have lived in this same house nearly sixty years. When I first came here, everyone said, "Why do you live in the country, so far from the city?" But you see the city has come to me, and now I am in the very heart of Munich. I love this house and this street, for I have known no other home since I came to Bavaria.' Once more I told him of my youthful enthusiasm for *The Children of the World*. He said, 'I never read any of my own works. I have forgotten practically everything in the book you admire. But I do remember that it does not express my real attitude towards life, only a certain viewpoint. Everyone who reads that story ought also to read my *Merlin*, as it supplies exactly the proper antidote. The fact is, I read no novels at all, and have not for years. My reading is entirely confined to works on philosophy and metaphysics, which have been the real passion of my life.' He mentioned, however, a number of the young poets, novelists, and dramatists of the day, without a jealous or disparaging word. 'I have not time to read much of these young fellows, but from all appearances, I think the outlook for German literature in the next generation exceed-

ingly bright. The air is full of signs of promise. For me—
ach, ich bin alter Herr!' He said this with indescribable
charm.

I reminded him that on the coming Wednesday night a
new play of his was to have its first performance at the
Residenz Theatre. I told him how keenly I enjoyed *Urauf-
führungen* in Munich, and remarked that of course he
would be present. '*Aber nein!* I never under any circumstances attend the first performances of my plays. It is too
painful. How can I be sure, no matter how intelligent the
actors may be, that they will interpret correctly my real
meaning in my characters and dialogue? And to be in the
least misinterpreted is as distressing to me as a typographical error in one of my printed works. When I take up a
new book of mine, fresh from the press, and find a single
typographical error, I lie awake all night.'

Then the conversation turned to religion. 'Now that
I am an old man, I have changed somewhat my views
about religion. I used to think that perhaps we could get
along without it. Now I know that humanity can never
exist without religion, and that there is absolutely no substitute for it. How are the poor and the sick to live without
the hope and comfort of faith in God? Suppose a poor
seamstress has consumption, who would wish to take away
from her the only hope she has—her belief in religion?
Science and Monism can never fill any place in the human
heart. Religion alone can satisfy human longings and
human aspiration.'

When I rose to go, he accompanied me to the door. I
was deeply affected, as he knew I should not see his face
again. He seemed to read my mind, for he said affectionately, but gravely, '*Wenn Sie in Amerika wieder sind,
denken Sie an mich.*'

63

FRANCE IN 1913

THE summer of 1913 my wife and I spent mainly in France, taking with us our nieces Carolyn Hubbard, aged 19 and Annabel, aged 15. We debarked at Boulogne, spent the whole afternoon in the cathedral and the next day proceeded to Amiens. In Paris we heard *Cyrano de Bergerac* with M. Le Bargy as the hero. On the afternoon of 27 June George Santayana came to tea with us, and was most agreeable. We had not seen him since he left America in 1911. This summer, without the slightest suspicion of its being the last time when France would seem normal, we visited Reims, and made a special pilgrimage to Château-Thierry because it was the birthplace of La Fontaine. We saw Soissons, Laon, Châlons-sur-Marne, Troyes, Langres, Dijon, where the Hôtel de la Cloche looked inside exactly as it did when I stopped there in 1890. We spent a few days at Lyons, and then took the train—I tried in vain to find a boat—for Avignon. Visited the graves of J.S. Mill and his wife; the inscription on her tomb, written by her husband, is filled with superlatives. One night in Avignon we went to a motion picture, and it turned out to be a Wild West American film, with cowboys shooting; the French peasants seemed to enjoy it immensely.

On the National holiday, 14 July, we attended a bull fight in the Roman amphitheatre at Nîmes. There were 20,000 people; it had been previously announced that it would be a mild fight, with no horses or bulls killed. We visited Marseilles and the lovely little university town of

Aix-en-Provence. Carcassonne was just as good as we thought it would be, and our expectations were high. We saw Toulouse, Pau, Biarritz and San Sebastian, the only time I have ever been in Spain.

We spent that night at Rennes: My colleague at Yale, Professor Albert Feuillerat, was for some years professor at the University of Rennes; his wife is the sister of Paul Bourget.

At Vitré we found a curious church, with a fine open-air pulpit on the south side, covered with gargoyles. We visited the Château des Rochers, the home of Madame de Sévigné, only four miles away. And then we had an interesting domestic experience. Our chauffeur was eager to have us visit the home of his parents, because he wanted us to meet them, and because his duties as chauffeur in Caen had prevented his seeing them for I don't know how long. So we motored to a remote village called Bourgon, and we met these peasant parents M. et Mme Odolant. We ate a big lunch in the house of their son-in-law; the loaf of bread was longer than a baseball bat. This father and mother had never been away from the village, had never seen a railway train. They were hospitable, and could not do enough for the friends of their son. One member of our party suspected the chauffeur, and thought that he was leading us into this remoteness in order to murder us. She therefore wrote messages to America, telling where we were going when last heard from. And at table, when the old peasant got out an enormous knife to cut the bread, she felt her worst fears confirmed.

In Paris I went to a rehearsal where only music critics were admitted; when I told the man at the door I was President of the New Haven Symphony Orchestra, which happened to be true, he showed me in with courtesy. The most curious feature of the afternoon's entertainment was a dramatic version of Poe's *The Tell Tale Heart*, called *Le*

Cœur Révélateur. The curtain rose on the scene in the *Raven*, with Poe himself seated in a flood of lamplight.

In September we were in Munich and saw Richard Strauss in the Residenz Theatre conducting his new opera, *Ariadne auf Naxos*.

On 22 April 1913 Sir William Osler came to Yale and at the Elizabethan Club gave a magnificent lecture on his favourite book, *The Anatomy of Melancholy*. After he had spoken for some time, he asked me if we could endure any more; and I told him I thought the undergraduates could sit as long as he could stand. He made, as he did everywhere and on everybody, an unforgettable impression of learning, wisdom, humour and kindliness.

On 8 May J. M. Dent, the London publisher, stayed overnight at our house; he astounded me by saying he had never refused to publish a manuscript which he thought deserved publication on its merits, without any regard to financial return. I told him I thought such a policy would result in bankrupty. 'On the contrary,' said he, 'I have found it profitable.' He told me the greatest undertaking of his life and the one nearest his heart was *Everyman's Library*. One often thinks of the idealistic author and the hard-headed publisher; but I have never seen any poet or novelist more idealistic than Mr. Dent. He seemed unworldly.

64

SOME EVENTS IN 1914

On St. Patrick's Day the poet William Butler Yeats gave a reading from his poems at the Yale Elizabethan Club. At noon I had a long talk with him; he expressed hatred of George Moore, and said a great many 'events' that Moore described in his books, conversations with Yeats, etc., never happened.

Alfred Noyes and Gerald Stanley Lee were our guests on 30 March; they spoke at the annual banquet of the *Yale Literary Magazine*. Mr. Noyes regretted the current depreciation of the genius of Tennyson and made a spirited defence of his poetry.

On 19 April President Wilson gave Huerta of Mexico until six o'clock that evening to promise to salute the American flag. At six he had not saluted. War seemed imminent; a huge crowd of students gathered in front of my house, expecting a 'patriotic' speech; I ridiculed war and said the U.S.A., if it really wished to fight had better take a bigger opponent. I said a war with Mexico would be silly and criminal. Rather to my surprise, the speech was well received.

Three days later I presided at a peace meeting of the students addressed by Norman Angell.

On 23 May at Cincinnati, I spoke with President Taft at a Yale dinner. A jolly song was sung, written by Cole Porter, of the class of 1913—a foretaste of the professional success he was to enjoy in later years.

In this same month I had an unusual experience at a

girls' college in the South. The Commencement bacca-
laureate was given by the President; he read from manuscript but he had no arms and turned the pages with his
teeth. After my own address, he suggested that we go to
a ball game, three miles away; this seemed good to me, and
we hired a horse and buggy, fortunately taking along a
negro boy who crawled in behind. The horse was so enormous that I, an inexperienced driver, could hardly see over
his back. He looked like a dinosaur. On Main Street, amid
crowded traffic, the horse suddenly stood up on his hind
legs, waving his front feet in the air like an impassioned
evangelist. I had great difficulty in getting him into a
horizontal position. In about five minutes he again stood
upright and was so very perpendicular that I expected he
would fall over backwards, in which event I should not now
be describing the incident. The President, since he was defenceless, suggested that we both jump out; a large crowd
of persons had assembled, who seemed intensely amused by
our predicament. I sprang out and then caught the President in my arms. I gave the animal and buggy in charge of
the boy and we walked to the ball game.

What a driver should do when a horse insists on standing
upright and making sweeping gestures, I have not the
faintest idea. Shortly after my return home, I got a letter
from the President, saying 'I am in good health, and so, I
regret to say, is the horse. As soon as I hear of his death, I
will telegraph you.'

This was the last time I attempted to drive a horse.
Every horse I have attempted to ride or drive has endeavoured to murder me. Every horse knows instantly,
when I come near him, of my inexperience, and proceeds
to take advantage of it. I have sometimes been sitting
alongside a man driving a most conservative horse, seemingly destitute of spirit and originality. If my friend asks
me merely to hold the reins while he enters a shop for a

moment, the horse instantly begins to exhibit unsuspected depths of depravity. He will attempt to back the buggy onto the sidewalk and through the shop window. When I am asked if I am afraid of horses I say 'afraid' is too mild a term; I am in terror. When I go shooting in the South, I astonish my hosts by refusing to ride the 'most gentle' horses; I must have a wagon and a driver. I understand the man on horseback when a pedestrian asked, 'Where are you going?' and drew the reply, 'How should I know? ask the horse.'

On 3 August at our house in Michigan our friend and my former Harvard room-mate, Ralph Catterall, professor of history at Cornell, died from a stroke, after an illness of two days. With his son I accompanied the body to Ithaca; as the funeral was not to take place until late in the afternoon, Andrew D. White, who had been first President of Cornell, then Minister to Russia and later Ambassador to Germany, called and took me for a long drive over the beautiful countryside. He spoke mainly about the war which had just been declared in Europe. I remember his saying impressively, 'You will live to see the end of this war, but I shall not.' This prophecy was technically fulfilled. He was then over eighty, and he died on 4 November 1918, only a few days before the formal ending of the war; three days before his eighty-sixth birthday. His conversation in 1914, which lasted four hours, as he drove leisurely through the country roads, was most interesting. He thought that the Kaiser was personally responsible for the outbreak of the war, and hoped to gain dominion over Holland. White felt the war was a catastrophe whose evil results would be felt for a great many years. He gave interesting anecdotes of his residences in Europe. When he was in Russia, he often took walks with Tolstoy. No sooner did the great novelist appear on the street, than he was surrounded by a swarm of beggars, to whom he invariably

gave money. Mr. White remonstrated with him, but Tolstoy replied, 'Jesus said Give to him that asketh of thee,
and I have no choice in the matter.'

On 7 November we observed the Transit of Mercury,
contact coming a little after 9 a.m. We went to the old observatory, collecting Professor Beebe, and the telescope
would not work; then in desperation, I entered a room in
the Sheffield Scientific School where Professor Farnham
was giving a lecture. He consented to an immediate ad-
journment, found a surveyor's instrument and we had a
fine view of the transit.

On 18 November at a reception given in New York to
the National Institute by President Butler, we met
Eugène Brieux, the French dramatist, who had come over
to increase American sympathy for France in the war.
He was agreeable and unaffected. He said prohibition must
come after the war and it would be a good thing. It did
come and was bad. He said the Parisian critics treated him
rather condescendingly, calling him *l'honnête Brieux*. I told
him how greatly I enjoyed seeing at the Comédie Française his play *Blanchette*; but he said that had little rele-
vancy for America. 'On the contrary,' I told him, 'we
have plenty of girls who have passed through our Normal
Schools, receive the proper certificates showing they are
qualified for teaching, but cannot get any jobs.' It was a
pity that Brieux was known chiefly in America as the
author of *Damaged Goods*; that gave him the wrong kind of
reputation. I always liked particularly his comedy, *La
Française*, meant as a rejoinder to *La Parisienne*, although
there was a ridiculous American Harvard student, who
spoke French much better than English. It is seldom
that one sees English correctly given in foreign plays
and novels. Brieux felt that an international movement
should be started to make foreigners understand that
the numerous French novels and plays on adultery did

not correctly represent the standards of the French people.

On 27 November I went to Charlotte, North Carolina to address a convention of school teachers. I was asked if I should like to see the house where Mrs. Stonewall Jackson was living; I was amazed that she was living anywhere, because her distinguished husband was mortally wounded in action, in the very moment of victory, shot by mistake in the dusk by his own men, in 1863! This was 51 years later. His wife was living, but too ill to see any visitor. I stood uncovered before the house where there was a light in her room. Time seemed to go back a half-century. The death of Jackson was a fatal blow to the confederacy. When Lee heard he was wounded, he wrote him, 'I should have wished for the good of the country to be disabled in your stead.'

On 24 December we went with Henry Arthur Jones to the first night of his play *The Lie*; we shared a box with Mr. and Mrs. Joseph Choate, the dramatist Augustus Thomas, Professors Brander Matthews, George P. Baker, and the publisher George H. Doran. This was a pleasanter occasion than the first night of Jones's *The Evangelist*, for *The Lie* was a success. I had heard Mr. Choate quoted as having said in a public address, 'The happiest time of life is between seventy and eighty, and I advise everyone to hurry up and get there as soon as possible.' Knowing how happy he had been in the days of his greatest activities, I now asked him if he were correctly reported and if he definitely meant it. He replied that the report was correct and that he was sincere; after seventy he had been happier than ever before.

This autumn I contributed an article to the *North American Review*, called *War*, in which I took the ground that all wars were really civil wars and were contrary to religious teaching. This brought down on my head a good many attacks, but nothing to what I was to receive in 1917.

On 25 November Edward H. Sothern and Julia Marlowe, who were playing the entire week in New Haven, came with me to the Elizabethan Club and there Julia Marlowe read aloud to the undergraduates some of Shakespeare's sonnets from the original edition of 1609.

65

WILLIAM HOWARD TAFT

MR. TAFT was the only man in American history to hold
both the office of President and of Chief Justice of the
Supreme Court; and in private and public life he was always the same, unselfish, modest, kindly, full of mirth and
good-humour. His famous chuckle is remembered by all
who saw him. He was graduated from Yale in the class of
1878; and although he had made an enormous number of
friends in the course of his long professional and public
career, I heard him say there were no friendships so strong
as those formed in his college days. He was spiritually
healthy; he was without jealousy or malevolence or envy.
After his tragic quarrel with Theodore Roosevelt and long
before they 'made it up' he told me Roosevelt was a man
of genius, one of the greatest men he had ever known; and
that he always spoke impulsively, without any regard as to
possible consequences, as when he said to a group (I think
of newspaper men) 'Root is worth all the rest of my Cabinet put together!' Taft enjoyed this all the more because
he was included. Taft's two famous remarks about his own
nominations are well known. 'I owe both my nominations
to Theodore Roosevelt,' for he was willing to step aside in
1912 if Roosevelt would agree to do the same. The other
statement concerned Bryan, for whom Taft, like everybody else, had strong personal affection. 'Bryan announced
that I was elected President by a majority; but that I
would be defeated unanimously. Now when he said that I
thought it was one of Brother Bryan's numerous inaccu-

rate prophecies; but I believe for once in his life he was very nearly right!' (Taft got the electoral votes of only Utah and Vermont.)

Taft read aloud to me an anonymous insulting letter he had received; when he had finished, he roared with laughter, and said 'Now think how happy that fellow was when he had got that out of his system!'

After his defeat for re-election in November 1912, he was elected Kent Professor of Law at Yale *College*, as he wished to teach undergraduates. He intended to take up his residence at New Haven as soon as his presidential term expired on 4 March 1913. In common I suppose with others, I wrote him a letter expressing my delight in the honour conferred on Yale by his joining the Faculty, to which I received the following reply:

THE WHITE HOUSE
WASHINGTON
January 7, 1913

My Dear Professor Phelps:

I very much appreciate your kind letter of January 5th, and I thank you for taking the trouble to write it. The prospect of a closer association with my many friends at Yale is most attractive.

Sincerely yours,

Wm. H. Taft

He arrived in New Haven 1 April. All university lectures were cancelled and three thousand students greeted him at the railway station. When he first entered our Faculty-meeting as a new member, Dean Frederick S. Jones welcomed him as the retiring President of a young country to an old university. It appeared there was no chair in the room sufficiently large for his frame. Someone remembered that the Campus policeman, Jim Donnelley, who weighed nearly three hundred pounds, owned a colossal arm-chair. It was sent for, brought up on the elevator, and it appeared *adorned with the horns of a bull moose*! (Bull Moose was the name of the party headed by Roosevelt in opposition to Taft.) Everyone, including Mr. Taft, laughed aloud.

That Spring of 1913 I played golf very often with him; and he was the best of company, though always keen to win. One day, when he was playing in another foursome, he came into the locker-room, banged his clubs down on the floor, and gave a snort of rage. (He never swore.) I said, 'Why, you feel worse about being beaten at golf than you did on losing the Presidency!' He replied emphatically, 'Well, I do, *now*!'

Here are some letters he wrote:

POINTE-AU-PIC, P.Q., CANADA

MY DEAR BILL:

I have read your article in The Nation on "Sporting Blood" with a great deal of pleasure, and I am glad "to stand on your paper," as the Germans say. Whether what you say is true or not, it might have been true, and therefore the accuracy of history is preserved.

I hope you have been having a pleasant summer.

With affectionate regard both for yourself and your charming comrade, from Mrs. Taft and me, believe me, as always,

Faithfully yours,

WM. H. TAFT

No account of Mr. Taft's residence at Yale would approach completeness without mentioning the immense pleasure given to all Yale and New Haven by the presence of Mrs. Taft. She was so interesting, so charming, and had such a wide experience of people in Europe and America and the Far East, that the society of the University and of the city gained in every way by her residence.

I had sent him the outline of a plan by an American

poet who was deeply interested in educating children in the love and understanding of verse.

JANUARY 3RD, 1916

MY DEAR BILL:

I don't think that the proposition of Miss —— is a practical one. The objections to it are so many that I forbear to mention them. You cannot have a republic of children, because they don't know enough to run a republic, so that she will have to have somebody else run your government, and then when you have somebody else to run your government, who is to be that somebody else, and where are they to get the money, and who is going to be responsible? Bill, it is the result of poetic imagination, and has not a practical element in it. Now you send a diplomatic answer to her.

I reciprocate your good wishes, old man, and send to you and your good wife, from Mrs. Taft and me, our warmest and most affectionate New Year's greetings.

Sincerely yours,

WM. H. TAFT

SUPREME COURT OF THE UNITED STATES
WASHINGTON, D.C.

March 6, 1926

MY DEAR BILL:

I have yours of March 1st. It must have been forwarded to me at Augusta and returned here. I was only in Augusta six days. Nellie and I had a very good time. I had to avoid meetings, but I had the pleasure of seeing some dear old friends, especially Major Black, whom the President of the Hotel invited to come and spend the week at the hotel, so that I saw a good deal of him. An automobile struck him and injured his legs, so that I doubt if he ever walks again except on crutches, but in other respects he seems to be in excellent health and in very good spirits. He is a very white soul. I heard of you very much. Murray Butler was not there when we were there. Sir Robert Borden was. I had known him very pleasantly in Canada.

I have read what you have said, my dear Bill, and of course feel as grateful as I can be for your kindly words.

I hope that Annabel is well and that the old University is going on as it ought to go. It would gratify me much to have a chance to see you both and talk over matters, but I have to be very careful and stay close at home in order to do my work.

Affectionately yours,

WM. H. TAFT

SUPREME COURT OF THE UNITED STATES
WASHINGTON, D.C.

May 30, 1927

MY DEAR BILL:

It is a very great disappointment to me that I cannot be present at Commencement when Justice Van Devanter is presented for his degree. No man ever deserved a degree more, and I don't know but that you might wish a statement from me as to his standing, so that you might give more detail and more certainty as to what you have to say in presenting him. . . .

He is one of the ablest Judges in this country and one of the ablest Judges that we have ever had on the Court, but he is a very modest man and nobody knows the position he occupies on the Court but those who have to do with him in Conference. No one can appreciate his influence except through knowledge gained from the intimacy of the deliberations of the Court over opinions. He was an Indiana boy who went to Purdue University, but was obliged to give up because his father lost such money as he had, and so he did not graduate but went to the Cincinnati Law School. After that he went west and settled at Cheyenne, Wyoming, when Wyoming was a territory. He became District Attorney of the territory, and afterwards, when the Chief Justice had to be removed for something that looked very like graft, he was made Chief Justice, and when the territory came in I think he was still Chief Justice. Then he resigned and went back to the practice, and subsequently was appointed by McKinley to be Assistant Attorney General in charge of the Interior Department, which meant in charge of the land and Indian litigation of the Government. I suppose he is the most deeply versed in land and Indian litigation of all in the profession or on the Bench. He was appointed by Roosevelt to be a Circuit Judge in the 8th Circuit. The 8th Circuit is the largest Circuit in the United States geographically, and runs from the Mississippi west to the Rocky Mountains, and from Texas and Louisiana north to the Canadian border. He was there for seven or eight years, and then I made him a Supreme Court Judge, and he has been on the Supreme Court Bench now about seventeen years. He . . . does not write so many opinions, but they are all admirable when he writes them. I don't know how we could get along without him in Conference. I don't think the Bar realizes generally what a commanding figure he is on the Court. He never advertises and he never seeks publicity. He has not what some of our Judges have by reason of their relations to Law Schools—a claque who are continually sounding their praises, but when it comes to keeping the Court straight and consistent with itself, he is the man who does it, and his power of statement and his exactness and his immense memory for our cases makes him an antagonist in the Conference who generally wins against opposition. He is 68 years old, and he has two sons. One of them he sent to Yale, and he now represents the Guaranty Trust Company in Washington, and is Secretary of the Yale Association here. His wife, like yours, was born in Michigan, and like your wife a charming woman. I hope she will be able to go to the Commencement, but she is not in very good health.

In addition to all his qualities, Van is a fine fellow and a man of substance to whom you can tie. He has more familiarity with our rules than anyone on our Bench. Indeed he drafted the last set of rules himself, and he has had much to do with the legislation that has enabled the Court to reduce the arrears and to catch up with its docket. The truth is I think those who refer to the Court who are in the "know" think when they refer to the Court that they are referring to Van Devanter. Perhaps I do not need to send you a copy of the letter I wrote to the President, but I shall see if I can find it.

Affectionately yours,

WM. H. TAFT

SUPREME COURT OF THE UNITED STATES
WASHINGTON, D.C.

POINTE-AU-PIC, CANADA
July 15, 1927

MY DEAR BILL:

I have yours of July 9th and thank you for writing me. I was very much delighted to hear from Judge Van Devanter of your kindness to him and also of the high opinion that he manifested of your work as the public orator. What I wrote you about Van is entirely true, and the degree that Yale gave him was as deservedly conferred as any degree that the institution ever conferred. He is so modest that it is a real satisfaction to take part in honoring him.

You are very good to be interested in the interview that was published by the Associated Press. I did not revise the interview. Indeed I never saw it until it was published. The correspondent of the Associated Press that does the work of the Court for that institution came to me and said that they were anxious to say something about my becoming seventy. I had something that I was anxious to have them publish in respect to the work of the Court during the last year, and that was published at once. I dictated that. But this last was withheld for a month and there were some inaccuracies in it—one that I did not intend to retire in 1931 when my ten years would entitle me to a pension. If I am living in 1931, I don't know whether I shall retire or not, but certainly I did not intend to make any such announcement. While my health is better than it was last year, my heart is a defective heart, and I can only get along and discharge my duties by the exercise of the greatest care. Next year I am hoping, if I live, to attend our fifty years' anniversary. The boys are falling fast and we have to close up ranks too often.

I am very much disappointed that we did not complete the $20,000,000 fund, but hope that we shall rally to the cause and add something to our subscriptions and induce those who have been lax in the matter to make new subscriptions. No matter what we may have originally thought of the project, now is no time to have Yale fail.

I shall get "Barnum's Own Story" and read it.

Give Annabel Nellie's love and mine, keep a lot for yourself, and believe me, as always, my dear Bill,

Affectionately yours,

WM. H. TAFT

SUPREME COURT OF THE UNITED STATES
WASHINGTON, D.C.

Sept. 23rd, 1927

DEAR BILL:

Thank you for your demonstration that a man at seventy has many reasons for happiness if only he seeks and has the means of having interesting thoughts. . . .

I hope that dear wife of yours is well and is, as I know she is, contributing to your happiness as of yore.

I have been enjoying much the messages of good will that have come to me on the occasion of passing into old age. Judge Holmes denies that 70 is old age. He says that it is only the beginning of middle age. Others assure me that the decade between 70 and 80 is the best of life. Well, I do not wish to institute comparisons, but only to register my gratitude to God that I have been permitted to have had the happiness which has been mine and to be willing to accept whatever may come of sorrow still mindful of the goodness of God.

What a blessing is the affection of friends and family! How rich as compared with any other earthly boon!

With love to you both, in which Nellie joins me.

Affectionately yours,

BILL

SUPREME COURT OF THE UNITED STATES
WASHINGTON, D.C.

January 15, 1929

MY DEAR BILL:

I thank you for giving me a chance to breathe in again the atmosphere of Augusta. I miss what I used to enjoy there, but it makes me sad that Major Black has gone.

Thank you, too, for the revival of Augusta in my heart.

Nellie sends love to you both, as I do.

Affectionately yours,

WM. H. TAFT

SUPREME COURT OF THE UNITED STATES
WASHINGTON, D.C.

POINTE-AU-PIC, CANADA
August 14, 1929

MY DEAR BILL:

I am glad to hear, by your letter of August 9th, that you are in good condition, and that you are in a good work for the preservation of the good things which Nathan Straus has done for his fellowmen.

Nellie and I are delighted to hear from you and Annabel. I have been ill this summer, but I am hopeful now that I am pulling out. I have about half the vacation still to spend in regular vacation work until the first of October.

I see you write from Grindstone City, Michigan. I am delighted to see your signature and to have this evidence that you and Annabel are in good condition.

Affectionately yours,

WM. H.TAFT

Mr. Taft died 8 March 1930.

66

SOME EVENTS IN 1915–16

In New York on New Year's Day I attended the first meeting of the newly-formed American Association of University and College Professors. It was voted to exclude Presidents.

On 18 January for the first time I heard *King John*. It was played by Robert Mantell. I have never had an opportunity to hear it again, but it is effective on the stage even if it was the cause of wit in Mr. Huneker, who said Mantell played the King as if he was afraid someone else was going to play the ace.

Our niece Carolyn Hubbard stayed with us most of the winter and taught me to dance. I had never learned. It seemed strange to begin dancing at fifty, but for the next twenty years I enjoyed it.

On 6 February in Grand Rapids, Michigan, Mrs. Mary H. Gilbert gave me a copy of Anne Sedgwick's novel *The Encounter*, which I regard as one of her best. It is unfortunate that it appeared in England during the early weeks of the outbreak of the war, for in ordinary times it would certainly have attracted much attention. In this novel the character Sachs says, 'If only strength is good, yet it is still more true to say that only goodness is strong.'

Harley Granville-Barker came to New York in February to produce plays and I had many good talks with him; an amazingly interesting personality. On 26 February I saw his production of *Midsummer Night's Dream* with the 'gold heads.' I shall always remember this as the best of many productions of this play. In the next few days I saw his productions of *Androcles and the Lion* and *The Doctor's Dilemma*, both magnificent. He came to New Haven on 3 March and with Evert Wendell, Professor Jack Crawford, and a few others, we went out to the Yale Bowl (an amphitheatre holding 80,000) to test its acoustic properties. It was a bitter cold day with a howling wind; and although the Bowl had been built for spectacles and not for auditions, to our astonishment the acoustics were so perfect that spoken words were distinctly heard. As a result of this test, Granville-Barker decided to produce a Greek play here in the Spring. He and Wendell stayed overnight at our house, and I shall always remember our jolly breakfast party on 4 March. The winter sun flooded the room while our two guests kept up a flow of conversation that matched the sunlight in brilliance.

Granville-Barker gave a fine lecture at Yale and I had the pleasure of speaking at a public dinner held in his honour at New York. His visit had a definite effect on the art of American stage production.

My older colleague, Professor Thomas R. Lounsbury, died suddenly on 9 April; his funeral was held in the University Chapel on 13 April. I was one of the bearers; among the honorary bearers were Theodore Roosevelt and William H. Taft, who had not met or communicated since their unfortunate quarrel four years previously. I was standing by the coffin in the vestibule just before the obsequies, when the two men came up from opposite sides. Roosevelt gave no sign of recognition, whereupon Taft went up to him, said 'How are you, Theodore?' and extended his hand. Roosevelt shook hands silently without smiling; no further communication passed between them.

We celebrated May Day by giving a large luncheon party in honour of Mr. Adams (F.P.A.) of New York; in his Pepys's Diary column that week, he wrote, 'Up, and to New Haven, to Will Phelps's house, where was a brave luncheon; and so to the court, where C. Merz and I did play against Will Phelps and Jack Crawford, who beat us often, too. But this was chiefly Merz's fault.' This was Charles 'Doc' Merz, now the Editor of the *New York Times* and author of many books.

On 7 May (Browning's Birthday) I was Toastmaster at the dinner of the *Yale Literary Magazine*. John Kendrick Bangs was the guest of honour when, after I had reminded the assembly that this was the poet's birthday and that in his last poem he had asked all who remembered him after his death to greet him with a cheer, as he expected to be alive and happily developing, I called on the company to rise and give a cheer for Robert Browning. Mr. Bangs told me he had never been more deeply affected.

Greet the unseen with a cheer!

And on that very day Charles Frohman stood on the deck of the sinking *Lusitania* and made his famous remark that he had always considered death a great adventure.

On 15 May at the Yale Bowl in magnificent weather and before an audience of 10,000 Granville-Barker and Lillah McCarthy gave an impressive performance of Euripides' *Iphigenia in Tauris*. The appearance at the end of the play of the goddess Athene was thrilling.

An astounding solar spectacle happened on the morning of 20 May between 11.30 and noon. An undergraduate entered my classroom and excitedly urged me to come out. I immediately adjourned the class. There in a cloudless sky was the sun, a yellow ball in the midst of a huge solid black circle with a ring of fire on its circumference; from the sun (like the hub of a wheel) to the rim of fire (like a tire) all was solid black; the rest of the sky outside this circle bright blue. I have never seen anything like it before or since. On this very morning had come the news that Italy had decided to enter the war. There were 60,000 Italians living in New Haven; many of them were in terror, as they thought this spectacle was a portent. Who could blame them?

On 3 June the great surgeon Dr. William F. Verdi operated on my neck, removing something or other; I never found out what it was, but I had absolute confidence in Dr. Verdi. I was under ether three hours. Curiously enough, when I emerged, I could *hear* everything perfectly, every footstep and every word, but could see nothing. Sight came back later.

In this year I had two operations, on the outside and on the inside of my neck; the cure in both cases was permanent.

On 19 June in the open air on the Yale Campus occurred the world première of Tennyson's *Harold*, given effectively by the undergraduates. I agree with William Archer that it is Tennyson's best play, although he never saw it on the stage.

This autumn I gave the Lowell Lectures in Boston; six lectures on American literature. The audiences were so large that I was asked to repeat the course after Christmas; but I was not able to do this.

At a dinner party in connexion with these lectures, given by Dr. Sedgwick in Boston, I had the pleasure of meeting that remarkable woman, Mrs. Bell, the daughter of Rufus Choate. She was one of the best conversationalists I have ever known. She was 83, full of vigour and enthusiasm.

At the annual dinner of the Ends of the Earth Club in New York on 3 December, I had the pleasure of meeting the famous astronomer Percival Lowell. I asked, 'Aren't you the brother of President Lowell?' which was a *faux pas*. He replied with severity, 'He is my youngest brother.' I apologized with such fervour that we became the best of friends and on two subsequent occasions he sent me beautiful photographs of Saturn which he had taken at his observatory in Flagstaff, Arizona.

The American novelist Forman went down on the *Lusitania* four months after writing this letter.

CENTURY CLUB
NEW YORK
January 7/15

DEAR PROFESSOR PHELPS:

Certain good ladies of the committee of the "Lafayette" relief fund are asking university men to write a letter to their college undergraduate paper urging the mention of the fund. They have asked me to write a letter to the *Yale News* and I have said I would but it might be best, first, I think, to enquire from someone on the spot whether this would be an undesirable thing to do. So I turn, by your leave, to you. Do you know of any good reason why I, or another, should not write a brief and moderately expressed letter to the *News* suggesting that undergraduates could, through this fund, contribute about as effectively as possible to a very good and much needed work?

I am sorry to impose upon your time but in matters like this one need not apologize.

Drop me a single line, if you will, at your leisure.

With compliments and best wishes, I am

Very faithfully yours,

JUSTIN MILES FORMAN

On 6 December in New Haven we heard the first performance in America of Shaw's *Major Barbara*, with a distinguished cast. Louis Calvert, who created the role in England, was superb. Later I got to know him very well indeed. He was always agreeable, but off the stage he seemed in no way remarkable, either in appearance or in conversation; but the moment he appeared before the footlights, he was a genius. The art of impersonation is often entirely distinct from a man's personality, as perhaps it ought to be. Dr. Johnson said, 'Pritchard, in common life, was a vulgar idiot; she would talk of her *gownd*; but, when she appeared upon the stage, seemed to be inspired by gentility and understanding.'

Those who regard Johnson as elephantine should remember the graceful compliment he paid Mrs. Siddons; this was during the last year of his life, when he was ill. She came to see him and there was no chair for her. He said with a smile, 'Madam, you who so often occasion a want of seats to other people, will the more easily excuse the want of one yourself.'

On 27 December in New York we had a charming evening dining at the house of Mr. and Mrs. Otto Kahn; he was President of the Metropolitan Opera; they took us to *Martha*, which I do not remember to have heard since I heard Patti in it in 1892; Caruso was in splendid voice and high spirits, making it a great occasion.

On 14 January 1916 John Masefield gave his first American lecture at Yale. His deep cultivated voice added greatly to the charm of his reading. He told me of all his works he most enjoyed writing the play *Nan* and the poems *The Everlasting Mercy* and *The Widow in the Bye Street*. He said Dauber was a real person whom he knew and that he died in exactly the way described in the poem. After he had read for a while, he invited the audience to choose poems; whereupon *August 1914* was called for. After reciting four or five stanzas he broke down, overcome with emotion, and said he must read something else.

On 2 March in New Haven was given the first performance of Galsworthy's play *Justice* with John Barrymore. It was immensely successful and had a long run in New York. Many managers had refused it, thinking it could not possibly succeed. On the way out from the theatre a lady asked me if I did not find the play depressing. 'On the contrary, I find it exhilarating. Musical comedy I find depressing.'

As during the last few years (1930–38) we have been hearing so much about British propaganda and how the wily, wicked British lured America into the World War, I take pleasure in recording that the philosopher Lowes Dickinson of King's College, Cambridge, came to Yale on 12 April 1916 and gave an eloquent talk on peace; he was opposed to the war and to our having anything to do with it. I had a long talk with him.

On 8 and 9 December I lectured at Bowdoin College in Brunswick, Maine, on their two most famous graduates— Longfellow and Hawthorne—who were classmates but not intimate until long after graduation. On the early morning of the second day, in brilliant windless winter sunshine, I had a long walk with President Hyde in the Longfellow woods, which I shall never forget. Later in the church I entered Pew 25, where Mrs. Stowe conceived *Uncle Tom's Cabin*.

On 18 December at Yale we celebrated the two-hundredth anniversary of the birth of Gray. I read the *Elegy* in English and then Professor Robert Sanderson read his fine translation of it in French verse.

67

JOURNEY TO THE HAWAIIAN ISLANDS

In 1916 I was invited by the Yale Alumni of Honolulu to come and speak at their annual banquet, and with the invitation came a cheque covering expenses from New Haven to Honolulu and return, for us both. Before this, the longest distance I had ever travelled for one Yale dinner was in 1902, to Denver, Colorado; the Honolulu journey established a record.

In the dining-car on the morning when we were due in San Francisco, I glanced at the morning paper, just to make sure that our steamer, the *Matsonia*, would leave on time; and to my dismay, I found that on account of a strike, her sailing was postponed. This was a tragedy as the dinner was set for the night we were due at Honolulu. Looking through the shipping-list, I saw there was a steamer for Australia, the *Sierra*, due to leave the next day, which would stop at Honolulu. I hurried to the office, and found there was only one room unengaged—the Bridal Chamber! We sailed at two o'clock the next afternoon; it was bitterly cold, with fog and icy wind as we proceeded through the Golden Gate. The first five nights were overcast, so that no stars could be seen. This made the sixth and last night on board thrilling, for when I looked aloft, I saw a sky new and strange. Indeed I think the change in the constellations was the one thing that impressed me as more 'different' than any other spectacle. There was the Southern Cross, and the brilliant star Alpha Centauri (why don't they have a name for that wonderful star?), with many other stars I had never seen before; and the whole of Scorpio in all its magnificence. In the sea there was a wonderful exhibition of phosphorescent fish. At noon of that day, 18 June, for the only time in my life, I saw the Captain take the sun looking north.

When we drew up at the dock, there was a large group of Yale men, with a brass band, playing Queen Lil's national air, and we got a hearty welcome from J. R. Galt, '89, and representatives of the old Yale families of the islands—the Judds, the Cookes, the Alexanders, the Baldwins, with Chief Justice Frear and others. They gave a Yale cheer just before we landed, which brought tears to my eyes. We were taken to the beautiful home of Mr. and Mrs. Galt where we remained during our entire visit; and where the word hospitality took on new connotation; kindness, consideration, affection that never failed.

That night I spoke at the Yale Alumni Dinner; about thirty men were present. The following night I spoke at the seventy-fifth anniversary exercises of Oahu College, the oldest college in the United States west of the Mississippi.

On the following day in the open air the great historical pageant was given. In a conspicuous place sat the former Queen Lilioukuani; a most interesting, if tragic figure. Her face combined extreme intelligence with profound melancholy. As she reviewed the pageant, the procession came to a stop in front of her, and a Hawaiian made a long oration in the Hawaiian language, all of which was addressed directly and exclusively to her. I would have given much to know what he was saying. For it was a historical moment; and what were her thoughts as she saw this pageantry of her past glories, and listened to that intimate speech? After the exercises, we were presented to the Queen, and shook hands. She spoke a few words in English to us. In the procession of the pageant, the natives came first, then the missionaries, then the school-children. There were of course many floats, giving historical tableaux.

Many years before this, when King Kalakaua made his famous journey around the world, an important matter of royal etiquette in England was settled with characteristic, shrewd common sense and tact by the Prince of Wales, afterward King Edward VII. The question was as to who should go in to dinner after Queen Victoria; was this dark-skinned man from the Sandwich Islands a real king taking precedence over the Prince of Wales, or should he go in among the general nobility and diplomatic guests? The Prince said, 'Either this man is a king and must precede me, or he is a negro and should go in with a napkin over his arm.'

One day I had a grand experience riding the waves. I was not clever enough to ride a plank alone, and it was marvellous enough to see some of the natives do it. But a number of us, clad in bathing-suits, were taken out in a big outrigger three or four miles from shore. While we were waiting for the right kind of wave, I dived into the sea, which had exactly the same temperature as the air, swam around awhile, and when I climbed into the boat again, I was neither too cold nor too warm. All of a sudden one of the natives gave a sharp cry, the men paddled for shore desperately, and then, strangely enough, it was as if Neptune himself had lifted us high in the air. The thrill of that moment! Our big outrigger rose on the crest of an enormous wave; we were raised by a submarine power of irresistible, overwhelming might. Instantly the men put away their paddles and with one man to steer, we rode that one big wave two or three miles to shore,

like Arion on the dolphin's back.

It was a marvellous experience. Strange it was to look around and see other boatloads of people at various places before and behind us, and all, like the figures on Keats's urn, remaining at precisely the same relative positions.

Honolulu is the only place I have ever seen where various races and nationalities live together in absolute harmony, with no self-consciousness. I visited the Kaiulani School, where, counting the different Hawaiian strains, there were among the children 58 distinct nationalities. The American flag was brought out, the pupils saluted it in the open air, and then recited Longfellow's *The Building of the Ship*. In one of the rooms I made an address to the children of the first grade—Chinese, Japanese, Portuguese, part-Hawaiian, all Hawaiian, and American.

It was a night's voyage to Hawaii, the biggest of the islands; Mr. Galt took us there, and in an automobile on the railroad tracks, we went through miles of sugar-cane; and at various points had views of the ocean, Rainbow Falls, and other splendours.

We went to the top of the plateau later, and spent the night at the Crater Hotel. In the twilight we walked three miles across a field of dead lava, feeling as if we were in an extinct world. Looking down into the horrible boiling crater Halemauman was like looking into hell; and there was such a horrible fascination about it, that I felt an almost overpowering impulse to hurl myself into the dreadful fiery pit.

In the distance we saw the two great mountains, Mauna Loa, largest volcano in the world, with a capacity of 120 Vesuviuses, and Mauna Kea, its summit covered with snow. Both are about 14,000 feet high. At sunset the double column of smoke rising from Mauna Loa was an impressive spectacle. On Hawaii it was very hot by day and very cold by night. In Honolulu it is pleasantly warm (not too oppressive) the year round, but the frequent daily showers are a nuisance. The inhabitants refuse to call them rain; the name is *liquid sunshine*. There are so many members of the Judd family there that my wife said that the rain falls on the Judds and on the Unjudds.

We sailed for California on the *Matsonia*, so heavily loaded with sugar that the odour overcame the salty smell of the ocean. As the ship was ready to depart, our necks were swathed with the flowers called *lei*.

Those who have been around the world tell me there are only two places that can be called Paradise; one is Ceylon and the other the Hawaiian Islands. I never saw Ceylon but the Islands fully deserve the name. Mark Twain suffered from nostalgia for them all the rest of his life; and his description of them in *Roughing It* (1872) is still the best account I have seen. Now they are a part of the United States; and while there, one must never speak of returning to America or to the United States, but use only the expression 'the mainland,' for they are just as much a part of the United States as Michigan or Ohio. I had the pleasure of a long talk with Mr. Dole, the only President of the Hawaiian Republic; for after the revolution that deposed the monarchy and before the annexation, there was a period of brief independence. It took tremendous courage to assume the responsibility of the Presidency; for if the Republic had failed, and it was a narrow thing, the President would have certainly been executed. Mr. Dole was a tall, splendid man with a huge snow-white beard. He spoke so softly and with such quiet, unassuming modesty, that it seemed strange to think of the turbulent scenes when he rode the whirlwind and directed the storm.

68

VACHEL LINDSAY

THE American poet, Nicholas Vachel Lindsay, was the nearest approach to the mediaeval minstrel I ever saw. He walked from Florida to New Jersey, and later from Illinois to Arizona, carrying no luggage and no money. All that he carried was a package of his printed poems, called *Rhymes to be Traded for Bread*. He described his adventures in a charming book, *A Handy Guide for Beggars*. I regard his poetry, at its best, as original and imperishable. *General William Booth Enters into Heaven, The Congo, The Santa Fé Trail*, and many other poems, are truly great, both in their soaring imagination and in their felicity of diction. Edgar Lee Masters, who wrote the best biography of Lindsay, has said that if only Lindsay could have had an intimate friend, as Wordsworth had Coleridge, his life would have been happier and even more productive.

In 1916 I got Lindsay to lecture at Yale, the first of three or four of his appearances in New Haven.

On one evening, when he sat unrecognized in the audience, I lectured at the Brooklyn Institute on his poems and read them aloud. We returned together to Manhattan and sat up late talking. He thought I read *The Santa Fé Trail* better than he had, but I made a bad mess of the poem *1889* and we differed on the proper way to interpret *The Congo* to an audience.

Vachel Lindsay was a charming, affectionate, noble-minded idealist. He was also a man of genius.

603 SOUTH FIFTH STREET
SPRINGFIELD, ILLINOIS
October 31, 1916

MY DEAR WILLIAM LYON PHELPS:

Enclosed you will find some proof-sheets, which you need not acknowledge or return. The book will be out in a week or so, but I felt this special story might interest you.

Thank you indeed for putting my books into your courses. I hereby withdraw anything that sounded like a petition that you beat the drum on my behalf that I may have my books established among you. It seems that the drum has been beaten, the works put on the proper shelf and the war is over that I thought just begun, and I have a reasonable share of the spoils.

In your class of one hundred and twenty-five boys, twenty-five will be writing verses. I want them for my friends year by year and I am sure you can keep them for me, and that is all anyone should ask of any one institution. I am especially anxious for the five out of the twenty-five, they will be not only rhymers, but poets. I want them for nephews!

Very sincerely,

NICHOLAS VACHEL LINDSAY

603 SOUTH FIFTH STREET
SPRINGFIELD, ILLINOIS
August 8, 1917

Prof. William Lyon Phelps,
Seven Gables,
Grindstone City Michigan:

MY DEAR FRIEND: Thank you indeed for your letter. I never see your name in print, your work or an allusion in a review, but what I remember your exceedingly fraternal greeting at Yale, and am thoroughly grateful for such an ally among the wise of this generation. The war is so all-absorbing one would scarcely expect one friend to remember him, as you have remembered me in Michigan.

I make friends slowly, and am perfectly reconciled to that state of affairs, particularly when I am able to keep them. What more can a man ask in this world? To have one's writing seem a reality to even a few is a justification of one's existence. And many a worthy and painstaking writer goes through life not sure that anything he has ever done has ever been alive to anyone. I am satisfied that is the hard fate of many a good poet. And I am certainly dependent on the people who are willing to talk about my work occasionally, for more and more I see myself as a writer, and less as a public speaker. If I could get into one room the people like you who really cared, every year, I would be satisfied with about one recital, as I feel at present.

This Fall the Macmillan Company brings out *The Chinese Nightingale and Other Poems*, comprising all I have written and recited since the Congo collection. Next Spring they will bring out the book on which I have been working off and on for years: *The Golden Book of Springfield*, a prose work to which I expect to give all my time this summer and fall and all the time I am not in public in the winter. In brief it treats my home town in the same spirit in which I treat the road, in my prose books on the road. The actual Golden Book is a hypothetical book about Springfield to be written one hundred years hence. So my volume is a hypothetical review, showing what I hope that book will say, and what my intimates in this town hope it will say. Frankly the N.V. Lindsay the reviewers know came nearer existing twelve years ago, than today, my manuscripts are so far behind my notes. And a thing that has helped in this is that through changing publishers etc., my first book is my latest. If you want my ideas in order, assume the writer of the *Handy Guide for Beggars* is just out of college, of *Adventures While Preaching* beginning in the thirties, and *The Art of the Moving Picture* half way through the thirties. The Moving Picture book, in the last half embodies my main social ideas of two years ago. In mood and method, you will find *The Golden Book of Springfield* a direct descendant of the general social and religious philosophy which I crowded into the photoplay book whether it belonged there or not. I hope you will do me the favor and honor to set my work in this order in your mind, for many of my small public still think *A Handy Guide for Beggars* the keynote of my present work. But it was really my first wild dash. Well, well, it is midnight, therefore I am too silly to stop. . . .

If ever you mention my pictures, (which will of course be a favor) should you ever mount the rostrum on my behalf again, do not be too certain in an official way that they will ever come out in a book. This time next year is a long way off. But I would appreciate it if you would express toleration of such pictures as are in existence. My claim for them is that while labored and struggling in execution, they represent a study of Egyptian hieroglyphics and Japanese art, two most orthodox origins for art, and have no relation whatever to cubism,

post-impressionism, or futurism. When I was in art school none of
those movements were in existence, and frankly I have no patience
with them. I mean they give me the fidgets. Of course I do not question the taste of the man who enjoys them. But his taste is not mine.

I have been very fond of Swinburne all my life, and I should say
my drawing is nearer to his ornate mood than any of my writing has
been. But that is a matter for your judgement.

I am spending my summer absolutely alone in an empty house, and
it makes one communicative at midnight. The noise of the typewriter
becomes actual conversation in a house as empty as this one.

Very sincerely,

NICHOLAS VACHEL LINDSAY

69

AMERICA IN THE WAR

WE woke up New Year's Day 1917 in Augusta, Georgia; we had been there a few days and liked the place, the climate, and the people; and we liked them even more eight years later! On our return North, we stopped 7 January at Washington, where I called on Browning's daughter-in-law, Fanny (Mrs. Pen Browning). She told me about the poet's last days, how cheerful he was even up to the end, how he lay in bed on that last day (12 December 1889) turning over the leaves of his last book of poems, *Asolando*, an advance copy of which had been sent him. She showed me the very copy. He died at ten in the evening. He was told that the book was published in London that day; the evening papers contained complimentary reviews. 'That is very gratifying' said he; and those were his last words. She made me some presents so valuable that I was amazed; an original etching by Rembrandt and a picture of the Abbé Vogler, both of which had belonged to Browning; a lock of his hair, a book of press cuttings and other treasures.

On 22 January and succeeding five days I gave lectures at the Convocation of Bangor Theological Seminary in Maine; weather ten below zero, air crisp and inspiring. I had distinguished colleagues as speakers that week— William H. Taft, Harry Emerson Fosdick, Ritchie Smith of Princeton. Taft made a fine address on world peace, but it was clear to him and to us all that we should soon be in the war.

On 31 January in New Haven, after a magnificent recital by Josef Hofmann, I had the pleasure of meeting him at supper with a few friends. He was full of fun. He had recently played a concerto somewhere, and when asked if the orchestra had followed him well, he said, 'Yes, they followed me about two bars behind.'

On 2 March in Detroit I heard the orchestra conducted by a former Yale pupil of mine, Weston Gales; the piano soloist was Ossip Gabrilowitsch, who played the *Emperor Concerto* with genius; he was later to become conductor of the Detroit orchestra.

On 7 March the English poet W.W.Gibson gave a curiously slow public reading of his works at Yale; later, in conversation with him, I told him that I had read aloud to appreciative audiences some of his poems. 'I am sure you read them better than I could,' he said modestly and truly.

On Wednesday, 4 April, at the instigation of President Wilson, the U.S.Senate voted for war, 82 to 6; and on Good Friday, 6 April, the House followed suit, at 3.15 a.m. with fifty negative votes. The President's signature followed the same afternoon and as we emerged from hearing *Parsifal* in New York, the evening papers announced that our country was at war. No more operas were sung in German in New York for some time.

The American poet, Robert Frost, read from his works at the Elizabethan Club on 16 May; he read as if composing. He said the sound of the voice should be heard in every creative line.

On 25 October in Cambridge, Mass. I had the pleasure of dining with Miss Grace Norton; she was about eighty years old, and full of wit and intellectual energy.

In New Haven on 29 October I had the first opportunity of my life to hear *King Lear* in English (Robert Mantell).

On 17 November for the first time I heard Percy Grainger, the Australian composer, give a piano recital in

New York. He reminded me of a young tawny lion, bursting with vitality. I had good talk with him and his mother afterwards; that was the beginning of an intimate friendship.

Another memorable musical performance I heard in New York at the Punch and Judy theatre on 26 November —Bauer and Thibaud played three of Beethoven's sonatas for piano and violin; and once more I wondered at Tolstoy's impressions on hearing the *Kreutzer*; no music is more healthy and wholesome. Yet his strange novel, however falsely inspired, is a work of genius, though I wish he had never 'explained' it.

While suffering from a bad cold, I gave a lecture at Springfield, Ohio; at the conclusion a lady said to me with great earnestness, 'You have a very dangerous organic disease; I can tell it positively by looking into your eyes; my husband looked exactly that way; he died of it.' I thanked her for her warning, but told her I was sure she was mistaken. 'No,' she said, 'do not imagine it is only a cold. You have the disease.' The next day when I reached Indianapolis, I waited between trains at a club, where for five hours I read from beginning to end an early novel by Booth Tarkington, called *The Two Vanrevels*, and forgot my cold and my fatigue.

The Modern Language Association met this Christmas vacation in New Haven and I read a paper on *Robert Browning and Alfred Austin* containing entirely new material that I had discovered in the manuscripts at Balliol. Browning's Hogarthian attack on Austin does not appear in the MS. but is in the first edition of *Pacchiarotto*. I wonder what happened while he was reading the proof. And how amazed Austin would have been if he had known that year (1876) that Browning would be buried in Westminster Abbey and how even more amazed Browning would have been if he had known that Austin whom he regarded as a ridiculous mannikin would succeed Alfred Tennyson as Poet Laureate!

I do not know exactly when I began to hate war; as a boy, of course, I loved it and gloried in it. I read many histories of our Civil War and my heroes were Union generals and admirals. Early in 1898, however, the propaganda for war with Spain seemed to me silly and wicked. I could see no reason for war with Spain, and the slogan, *Remember the Maine*, left me quite cold. It seemed President McKinley did not want war, and that he was doing everything possible to prevent it. I was sad indeed when he finally yielded to the pressure of public opinion.

During that war, the leading scholar and teacher on the Yale Faculty, Professor W.G.Sumner, delivered a public lecture which he called 'The Conquest of the United States by Spain,' meaning that the results of our victory would be injurious to our peace, security, and prosperity. I admired him for his courage and independence, and as nothing happened except scattered protests from those who thought he was both mistaken and unpatriotic, I foolishly came to believe that even in war there would be freedom of speech, and that those who opposed a war in which their country was engaged would suffer nothing worse than social ostracism, which they ought to expect. This feeling of mine was strengthened by the experience of the English independent thinkers who publicly disapproved of the Boer War in 1900. If any one had told me then that free speech would be suppressed by force in a general European war, and that no country would be less free than my own, I should not have believed it.

I also remembered the public expression of hostility to the war with Mexico that had been so general and so outspoken in New England. I ardently admired Lowell's *Biglow Papers*.

Suppression of free speech is founded on fear; and I

should have remembered what happened to the Tories in the War of the Revolution and what happened to those who were called Copperheads in the Civil War. So long as a country is engaged in a small war and sure to win, those who oppose it are regarded merely as cranks, or perhaps sneered at as unpatriotic. But in an important war where the outcome is uncertain, those who oppose it are rightly or wrongly regarded as worse than the foreign enemy. I say rightly or wrongly, because it is not entirely clear to me whether a man should follow his conscience as a Christian and oppose any war, or whether he should co-operate with his fellow-countrymen after a war has actually begun. No man was ever a more complete pacifist than Benjamin Franklin; he did everything he could to prevent war with England. After America was victorious, he said there never was a good war or a bad peace. But during the war, he worked with all his genius for American victory.

'God's intimations fail in clearness rather than in energy,' said Browning; even when we feel a tremendous impulsion to do right, we are not always sure what is the right thing to do. No class of men has been more maligned by intransigent pacifists, communists, and atheists than Christian ministers who have supported their country in a war; but two things may be said in their defence.

First, ministers are naturally co-operative. They are not lazy or selfish or accustomed to isolation. They work and work hard with groups and organizations. When everyone is making sacrifices for what is believed to be the public welfare, it seems natural to them to support with zeal the common cause. They are not coldly critical of group enthusiasms; they are perhaps somewhat easily stirred by appeals to justice. And in wartime propaganda does its perfect work, and a majority of ministers in every country believe they are helping in a just and righteous cause.

Secondly, there were a great many more ministers who opposed the World War than there were men of science. All my life I had heard of the ardent love of truth displayed by scientific investigators; no matter whither the truth led, they followed. They were not swayed by sentiment, like clergymen; they did not suffer from wish-beliefs; no, they were dispassionate, uncompromising followers of the truth. Yet, when the war broke out, these men of science forgot truth and devoted all their abilities and energies to perfecting the means for a more extensive slaughter of the 'enemy.' How Haeckel used to ridicule sentimental believers in religion! Yet no old woman telling her beads was more sentimental in her faith than he was in his faith in Germany's cause; in his faith that she was fighting a noble, just war of defence.

Of all the thousands of scientific men in the world, I can think of only one who publicly opposed the war, Bertrand Russell. He went to prison for his opinions.

But many clergymen were jailed. When America entered the war in 1917, a Baptist minister in Vermont who expressed publicly his opinion that the war was wicked, was tried and condemned to a Federal prison for fifteen years. After the war was over, he was released by a presidential pardon.

Among all the 'conscientious objectors' who suffered for their love of truth, was there one distinguished scientist, except Russell? What is truth?

I mention these matters to explain the perplexity and agony of mind from which I suffered from 1914 till 1918. When the war broke out in 1914, I wrote an article for the *North American Review*, in which I took the position that all war was wrong, contrary to religion and reason and common sense; and that Christians should oppose it. This article brought down upon my head condemnation from many sources; but I had expected that, and did not mind.

I wrote other articles in behalf of peace, and made a number of public addresses. The feeling in America was so ardent that I was called pro-German; but I was not pro-German; I was pro-British. I wrote an article for the *New York Times* called *The Dance of Death*, in which I said I hoped Germany would lose the war, because I believed she was chiefly responsible for starting it; but I also said that we in America ought not to be angry with the Germans for their resentment against the United States for supplying Great Britain and the Allies with munitions. In our Civil War the American poet James Russell Lowell thus addressed Great Britain in his poem

JONATHAN TO JOHN

You wonder why we're hot, John?
Your mark was on the guns,
The *neutral* guns that shot, John,
Our brothers and our sons.

But I soon found that any appeal to reason in time of a great war was like attempting to stop a cyclone with one's breath or to check a locomotive by placing a feather in front of it.

In the months immediately preceding America's entrance into the war, David Starr Jordan, Ex-President of Stanford University in California, came to the Atlantic Seaboard to make public addresses against it. He was forcibly expelled from every college where he attempted to speak. He then wrote me from New York asking if he might speak at Yale. Although I had no authority to grant this permission officially, I thought it would be a good time to find out whether free speech was to be tolerated in our universities or not. I told him to come. Then I called on Anson Phelps Stokes, the Secretary of the University, who conferred with President Hadley, and although they both disapproved of Doctor Jordan and hoped I would not agree to his coming, they did give me permission, which I have always thought was a fine and sportsmanlike action on their part. It must be remembered that Jordan had not been allowed to speak at any other Eastern university. It was natural that some outbreak was feared if he came to Yale.

Well, I felt that the question of free speech was more important than anything else. The feeling against Jordan was terrific. He came to Yale to make his speech on 29 March, and the United States entered the war the next week. I received threatening letters and many visits from persons either begging or demanding that I refuse Jordan permission. On the morning of the fateful day, a letter appeared in the *Yale News*, signed by two undergraduates, which gave me to understand that both Jordan and I would be ridden out of town on a rail. Most fortunately for me and for the cause, my large class in American Literature, over a hundred Seniors and Juniors, had its regular meeting that noon. I told them that I had read the letter in the *News*. That I had not asked Jordan to come and thus provoke a riot. But that President Jordan, a distinguished scholar, had written me asking permission to speak at Yale. I thought the honour of Yale was involved. I could not and would not tell Doctor Jordan that Yale did not allow public expression of unpopular opinions. I considered it my duty to comply with his request. I believed in the fairness of mind of the average Yale undergraduate.

I shall be grateful to these students as long as I live. They spent the afternoon arousing sentiment in the university in favour of the meeting. I met President Jordan at the train, took him to dinner at my house, and while this was going on, a member of the Faculty called and begged me not to hold the meeting. 'There is an organized group who are going to run you out of town!'

We went to the meeting, however, and were saved by the very size of the crowd; every place taken, and the aisles so jammed with men standing that the 'organized group' whom I saw near the doors could not get at us. The front seats were taken by undergraduates in the military uniform of the United States. As we came to the platform, there was some hissing in the rear of the room which was drowned by cheers. I began by saying 'I about to die salute you!' I said I was proud that Yale permitted free speech if other colleges did not, and introduced the speaker. After the speech had gone on for fifteen minutes there was organized shouting outside 'We want Woolsey Hall!' the largest hall in the University, holding three thousand. Doctor Jordan, thinking students outside were trying to break up the meeting, made an angry remonstrance. But I sprang up and said 'Doctor Jordan, this is a great compliment. The men outside want to hear you. They cannot get in. This meeting is now adjourned and we shall all go over to Woolsey Hall.' This was a dangerous experiment because we had to walk there. But the crowd was so eager to get seats they paid no attention to us, but left the hall as if it were on fire; by the time we reached the stage of Woolsey, the huge auditorium was crowded. Some students whispered to me, 'Do you mind if we have a patriotic parade with band, *after* this meeting, to show our own sentiments?' 'On the contrary,' I replied, 'you ought to show your sentiments just as Jordan and I are trying to show ours.' The speech went on for nearly an hour; then I heard the band getting ready in the street; and I suggested to Doctor Jordan that we adjourn, as we had won our fight.

I found out afterwards that we were saved from one possible rumpus by Jim Braden, an undergraduate friend of mine, member of the football team, who later saw service in France. Guy Nickalls, the English coach of the crew, was standing in the rear of the hall, wild with rage. He announced that he was going on the platform to break my neck. Whereupon Jim Braden said, 'The first move you make, I'll smash your face in!'

Although I suffered greatly from fear—downright physical cowardice—during the days preceding this meeting, and the meeting was a terrific nervous strain, now, looking back on it, I am more proud of that affair than of any one thing in my career. For once in my life, anyhow, I really stood by my convictions in the face of peril. For, if as seemed probable, I had been tarred and feathered, and ridden out of town on a rail, could I ever have recovered from that kind of public ridicule? I honestly did not mind being killed; what I feared was the disgusting, degrading— well, I was in a cold sweat of fear. How magnificent those undergraduates were! They were all eager to enlist; the only thing they were afraid of was that the war would be over before they could get to France; yet they not only saw this double peace-meeting through, but at the end of it, gave tremendous cheers. I wrote a letter to the *Yale News*, in which I said, 'The students did not agree with President Jordan before, or during, or after his address; but a great victory has been won for free speech, a victory that left no bitterness behind it.'

Thereafter and for the next six months, I received (not once from Yale, but from many places all over the country) insulting letters, some signed, some unsigned. One prominent Yale alumnus wrote me, 'I am ashamed of you and shall be ashamed of Yale if she does not expel you.' President Hadley and the Corporation were daily besought to expel me from my professorship, being told that instead of being on the Faculty, I ought to be in prison.

I shall always be grateful to President Hadley for standing by me, especially because he did not agree with me at all. He was subjected to tremendous pressure but he insisted that I had a right to do exactly what I had done. One of my best friends was Major Danforth, of the U.S. Army, who had been detailed as professor of military tactics at Yale. I had several talks with him. He tried to convince me that the U.S. was absolutely right in entering the war and that the war itself was wholly just, but he told me he had no feeling for me personally except respect and affection.

I don't like war, but I have never known a graduate of West Point or Annapolis, or any military or naval officer, whom I did not admire.

These exciting events happened in March; it was not until August that my attitude changed, and it was certainly not then because of any special thing. I could not stand it any longer to see all my friends working for their country, while I seemed to be in opposition. This was all the harder for me, because the majority of those who attacked me said I was pro-German. I could not reconcile my religious beliefs with war.

But late that summer I came around; I took part in 'drives' for Liberty bonds, etc., I made public addresses and did what I could. I shall never know for certain whether I made this change from sincere conviction or from fear. 'Know thyself' is an old saying; but who has ever known himself? Finally I came to believe that it was necessary, now that we were in the war, to win it; and the microscopic part due from me must be contributed. If one believes fifty-one per cent in a cause, I suppose one should give it one hundred per cent support.

Cowardice certainly was a contributing motive; and yet, I am convinced that had I been *sure* it was right and just to go on publicly opposing the war, I should have done so and gone to prison. I wasn't quite sure.

The only good thing I can say of my speeches in behalf of Liberty Bonds, etc. is that I never attempted to increase the hatred for Germans; indeed, I kept my friendship with my German friends, while I lost permanently my long and intimate friendship with a French professor. I have always regretted this. In a public address, I compared Kaiser Wilhelm with Napoleon, and said they had the same selfish ambition and that the German Emperor would fail, even as Napoleon had failed. My French friend (now dead) hated the Kaiser, but could not endure any adverse criticism of Napoleon. We never spoke to each other again.

One of the innumerable casualties of the war among those who remained at home was the famous philosopher Hugo Münsterberg, who dropped dead on the floor while lecturing to his class of girls at Radcliffe College, Cambridge, Mass., on 16 December 1916. He was born in Danzig, 1 June 1863, and went to Harvard in charge of the psychological laboratory in 1892. He was a notable addition to that brilliant department of Philosophy, and when the Phillips Brooks house was in process of construction, some wag suggested that they inscribe on its façade *Ein Münsterberg ist unser Gott.*

After the European War broke out in 1914, he quite naturally expressed pro-German sympathies; but the feeling against Germany was so strong in Boston and in Harvard that he suffered acutely. In an article I wrote for the *Yale Alumni Weekly* I used his name as an illustration of how famous scientific men, who had always maintained they must follow the truth no matter what it cost, forgot the truth whenever war occurred and every man became a sentimental follower of the Religion of Nationalism. The chief illustration I used was certainly Haeckel; but I mentioned Münsterberg, because I was writing for an American university group, and he was conspicuous.

He wrote me the following letter and I wrote him an explanatory apology, I am glad to say, for it cemented a strong friendship. But he was attacked so bitterly by many other people, called a German spy and other bad names, that his health gave way. I saw him in New York, meeting him by chance in an hotel only a few weeks before his death, and we had a most agreeable conversation. It was clear to me that he was nervously overwrought, though I had no suspicion that there was anything organically wrong. Here is the letter:

CAMBRIDGE, MASSACHUSETTS,
April 24, 1916

MY DEAR PROFESSOR PHELPS:

The Boston Herald of April 19th brought out a reprint of your article in the *Yale Alumni Weekly*. I agree with essential parts of it, but just therefore you may pardon me for insisting that your remarks about me seem to me mistaken. You single me out from all the Germans in this country as a man who can see only one side in this war. I take the liberty of sending you my book "The Peace and America" which appeared in the first year of the war, and I beg you to read the chapter "The Socalled Facts" and perhaps also the chapter "The Highest Values" and finally the last one "Tomorrow." You may then be less surprised if you discover that other critics of my literary activity during the war have claimed exactly the opposite, namely that I have done more justice to opposing standpoints than anybody else.

But your attack on me interests me still more from a theoretical point of view. You say that if I had been born in France I should scoff at everything that I now proclaim to be the truth and that my scientific education and my search for facts mean nothing at all to me, because Germany faces a crisis. You even say that like religious people whom I have ridiculed I believe what I want to believe. With regard to this expression of your views, I wish you would look not into my books about the war but into my philosophical books of the last twenty years. Then you would see that according to my conviction the statement that my utterances are ultimately based on belief is not a reproach but the acknowledgment of a necessity. About ten years ago I had the great honor to be invited by Yale University as representative of Harvard to give an address before the whole academic body. I did so and published my paper under the title "Science and Idealism." An essential aim of that paper was to say what I have expressed much more fully in my book "The Eternal Values" namely that the historical world does not belong to the sphere of the psycho-physical mechanisms which are the material for the scientist who seeks facts. Historical reality is formed not by objects but by subjects whose existence is will activity, which as such can never be grouped among facts which are to be described and explained, but which must be acknowledged and interpreted and valued. To enter into this world in which alone our values and our duties lie means to affirm or to deny the attitudes and propositions of other subjects. Far from ridiculing religious people and their belief, I firmly declared that there is no reality in the historical and normative world but that which is ultimately dependent upon belief. Of course, we can, and from a scientific standpoint we must, consider every historical process also as a psychophysical happening, but that is an artificial construction, while the immediate reality in which we live our historical political life precedes such reconstructed, intellectual schemes. Reality is purposive and only the constructed world of the scientist is causal, and if the metaphysicians finally ask what is the ultimate reality, the object or the subject, the answer must be that which Fichte gave a hundred years ago, namely that it depends upon the kind of man you are, that is, it depends upon your belief.

From these philosophical views of mine, for which I have stood a lifetime, you can deduce that I am not denying my scientific education and above all that I am not neglecting the demands of truth, if I speak in political discussions a teleological language and not a causal one. I affirm certain ideals, in this particular case the ideal of an over-individual state view as against an individualistic one. In affirming them, I move in a sphere in which the category of scientific truth has no meaning whatever. The one is not true and the other is not untrue, but the one is one teleologically involved in my fundamental life assertions, and I take it for granted that an opposite affirmation is established and demanded by the fundamental life decisions of men of other nationality. I therefore feel it as very unfair if a devotion to those ideals in which I believe is denounced as a denial of my search for truth, simply because I know that others fight for other ideals.

Very sincerely yours,

HUGO MÜNSTERBERG

Tom Stix was an undergraduate at Yale when America entered the World War; he was in my class in Browning.

In 1918 he wrote the following letter to me from back of the lines at Soissons where he was brigaded with the Gordon Highlanders as a liaison officer:

I had a most extraordinary experience yesterday. Lieutenant Colonel McDonnough was taking me around and introducing me to some of the officers in the brigade. I came into a little dugout, and there sat Lieutenant Anderson, reading by the light of a candle stuck into a bottle; not an unusual picture, of course. Just after we had been introduced, Colonel McDonnough was called away, and I sat down to talk with Anderson for a little while. After we were through with the amenities he happened to remark in passing that he was a Cambridge man, and I said I was from Yale. He turned over the book that he was reading. It was a pocket edition of Browning.

"You went to Yale?" he said. "Did you by any chance know William Lyon Phelps?"

"Of course I knew Billy Phelps; everybody at Yale knows Billy Phelps." I told him that I had practically gone from one of Billy Phelps's classes and enlisted.

He looked up at me with I think a little envy. "I'd like to know that man. He can explain poetry so that anybody can understand it."

The campus didn't seem so far away.

Always,

Том

Incidentally, Tom Stix told me what I think is the most affecting incident that I have either heard or read from the World War. A few years later he included it in his book, *The Sporting Gesture*; New York, 1934. John Henderson, whom he had known at Yale, took a year at Oxford after leaving Yale, enlisted in 1914, and came out as a private in Kitchener's First Hundred Thousand; and in 1915 when he was a captain of the Highlanders, they were holding the front line in the Somme. As dawn broke, John saw a German boy hanging on the barbed wire on the ground between the British and German trenches. His foot was shot off, and he was screaming. It is said that often men who are desperately wounded in the body are silent, whereas those who are shot in the hands or feet cannot help screaming. I now quote from Mr. Stix's book:

I have seen men wounded beyond recognition who could somehow control themselves, but I have never seen a man shot in the hand or foot who could. I don't know why. Perhaps there are more nerves in the hands and feet. The boy's face was beginning to gray. It was a horrible sight. A rat walked across the parapet, went up to the wounded Boche, and began to sniff. John stood it for as long as he could, which must have been all of five minutes. Then he climbed out over the parapet and tried to shake the youngster off the wire, but he was caught too tightly. So John stood up and lifted him off. No Man's Land was only forty yards wide, and the enemy could see what he was doing. Johnny put the boy on his shoulder and started back to our lines. Then something struck him—I don't know what. He must have realized that the boy was dying. He turned around and started across No Man's Land with his burden. They were standing up in the German trenches now, applauding, and in the English trenches too. He reached the enemy's line, climbed over the wires, handed his charge over and started back for his own side. When he had gone about ten yards, a voice called, "Herr Lieutenant!" John turned, and out of the Boche trenches came the captain of the Death's Head Hussars. When he was within five or six feet of the Englishman, he stopped, saluted and put out his hand. John took it. Then the German officer took off the iron cross he was wearing and pinned it on the other man. They shook hands a second time, and each returned to his own lines. What happened? I haven't the vaguest idea of what happened to the German captain, but John almost lost his commission. "Fraternizing with the enemy" they called it.

I don't know, but I've always imagined that an incident like that had just as good a chance of stopping the War as the Sarajevo incident had of starting it.

70

ALFRED NOYES AND OTHERS

THIS winter of 1917–18 was the coldest ever known in New England and on account of the war, coal was very difficult to obtain; that, and the feeling that the war was going to last four or five more years made this a depressing time.

Sunday 30 December 1917 the thermometer outside my window was 12 below zero, the lowest registration in New Haven I have ever seen. And the cold was almost continuous from early December till March. Many city thermometers showed 18 below.

On 8 January Walter Camp in New Haven gave a luncheon in honour of the famous actor John Drew; later in the afternoon I had a long talk with Mr. Drew at the Elizabethan Club. I urged him to write his autobiography. He told me many amusing anecdotes of his career. I had seen him as Orlando in *As You Like It*, when Charles the Wrestler was impersonated by Wm. Muldoon, the champion; who made a magnificent figure on the stage. Mr. Drew said it galled the big man to have to be thrown every night by himself and one night when Muldoon fell heavily in front of the footlights, he let out a profane ejaculation that was audible in most parts of the house, adding to the gaiety of the evening.

On 26 January I saw the new painting of President Wilson by John Sargent, which was to go to the National Art Gallery in Dublin. It is reported that when a lady asked the artist what part of the portrait he thought most characteristic of his own art, he said the eye-glasses.

The general gloom in this winter war-month was light-ened for me on two occasions; on one I heard the Ninth Symphony, and on the other Sonata 111 played by Josef Hofmann. Many 'patriots' tried to prevent the playing of any German music; and many Victrola discs of Beethoven, Wagner, Bach, etc., were patriotically destroyed.

One of my students, Frederick S. Blackall, Jr., had won an ensign's commission in the Navy; while in the hospital with jaundice, he read *Pride and Prejudice* and was cured; I had myself been cured of tonsillitis by reading *Treasure Island*, so I had no difficulty in believing his story.

On 30 March clocks were pushed forward one hour in accordance with the new Federal Law. Benjamin Franklin had advocated this method of daylight saving but it took a world war over a century later to make us adopt it. He also advocated the substitution of arbitration for war; that will come, I think, in about a thousand years.

During the Autumn term at the University I taught European History to the students in the Naval reserve, and enjoyed it. My regular courses were also continued but students were few.

As the winter of 1917 was the coldest on record, the winter of 1918–19 was the mildest I have ever known. I mention this for two reasons: first, because the weather is interesting; second, as illustrating the very common de-termination of people to make themselves unhappy. After December had progressed three weeks and it was like May, I spoke of it with delight to many friends; invariably (and I mean invariably) the response was, 'Just wait; we'll catch it later' or pessimistic words in the same vein. But January was also mild, and I continued my comments, drawing always the same rejoinder; then in February I increased them, enjoying the invariable replies. It stayed mild the entire winter; and yet nine out of ten persons could not enjoy it, because they were so sure it would not last.

The English poet, Alfred Noyes, I met when he first came to lecture at Yale before the War. Of all the poets that I have heard read their own works he was the best. I heard him many times, and his work always gained by his public interpretation. He spent a year at Princeton University as visiting professor, lectured several times at Yale, was kind enough to be our guest of honour at the dinner of our undergraduate *Yale Literary Magazine*, and then, in the year 1935 in response to a cordial invitation from Mr. and Mrs. Noyes, my wife and I visited their beautiful place on the southern shore of the Isle of Wight. We stopped on the way to see the grave of Swinburne, and I deeply regret we were not able to stay over Sunday and take dinner, because Admiral and Mrs. Jellicoe, who were neighbours, were to be present. Mr. Noyes, like Chesterton, Baring, Sheila Kaye-Smith, and other distinguished British authors, became a devout member of the Roman Catholic church; his religious autobiography, *The Unknown God*, is impressive, both in its sincerity of thought and clarity of expression.

13, HANOVER TERRACE,
REGENT'S PARK, N.W.1
LONDON, ENGLAND
March 28th, '34

DEAR BILLY:

I'm asking Sheed & Ward to send you my new book (in prose) which contains several references to Browning. It's a record of my own gropings towards a few definite religious beliefs, from boyhood, through agnosticism (and the days that I fed on Dante and Darwin) to my present views. It's called *The Unknown God*, and I hope it may be of a little use to a few in this bewildered time. It has taken me some years to write, and more to think out.

If you are ever on this side, (you and yours) *do* let us know. I miss my American friends greatly; and it would be an immense joy if you could come and stay with us in our Earthly Paradise in the Isle of Wight. Our garden is now ablaze with spring flowers and great banks of primroses; and I could motor you to many haunts of the poets on the island. *Do* come, if ever you can. We are there all April, and from the end of June till Xmas. The rest of the year here in town.

With very best remembrances from my wife and myself to you and Mrs. Phelps,

Yours always,

ALFRED NOYES

Inasmuch as a few years ago the American Association for the Advancement of Atheism held a dinner in New York in honour of Voltaire, I quote from the great Frenchman:

> I tell you, without repetition, that I love quakers. Yes, if the sea did not disagree with me, it should be in thy bosom, O Pennsylvania! that I would finish the rest of my career; if there be any remaining. Thou art situated in the fortieth degree of latitude, in the softest and most favourable climate; thy houses commodiously built; thy inhabitants industrious; thy manufactures in repute. An eternal peace reigns among thy citizens; crimes are almost unknown; and there is but a single example of a man banished from the country. He deserved it very properly, being an Anglican priest who turning quaker, was unworthy of being so. This poor man was no doubt possessed of the devil, for he dared to preach intolerance; he was called George Keith, and they banished him. I know not where he went; but may all intolerants go with him.

In 1937 Alfred Noyes, the devout Catholic, wrote a biography of Voltaire, filled with glowing admiration.

On 6 January 1919 Theodore Roosevelt died and it seemed as if a sudden silence fell on the whole country. Professor Beers said it seemed as if a military band had stopped playing. Rudyard Kipling made an international impression by quoting the words of Mr. Valiant-for-Truth:

> Then said he, I am going to my Fathers, and tho' with great Difficulty I am got hither, yet now I do not repent me of all the Trouble I have been at to arrive where I am. *My Sword*, I give to him that

shall succeed me in my Pilgrimage, and my *Courage* and *Skill*, to him that can get it. . . . So he passed over, and all the Trumpets sounded for him on the other side.

In February of this year I gave the L.P. Stone lectures at the Princeton Theological Seminary, on the Bible. They were published by Macmillan in a book called *Reading the Bible*. I enjoyed this experience at the Seminary.

I was one of the speakers at a great dinner at the Lotos Club in New York on 22 February to commemorate the centenary of the birth of James Russell Lowell. The guest of honour was John Galsworthy, who charmed the audience. Other speakers were Alfred Noyes, Robert Nichols, Stephen Leacock, Sir Robert Falconer. This was the first time I had seen young Robert Nichols, the English poet, who was in his military uniform. I had a good talk with him; he was enthusiastic about the poetry of Vachel Lindsay. Nichols was amusing in describing what the professors made him do to get his degree at Oxford. 'They told me I had to read St. Paul's Epistles in Greek; why the hell should I read St. Paul's Epistles?'

On a later occasion I had the pleasure of entertaining Nichols at my house; and I placed him in the great chair that had belonged to Robert Browning. He sat down in it and composed a poem before rising.

On 28 March, at a school convention in Carbondale, Illinois, I asked Mr. Black, the Superintendent, how far away was the Mississippi River. I told him I had seen it at St. Paul, St. Louis, Memphis, and New Orleans; but I wished to see it in its glory, with no towns in the neighbourhood. It was only twenty miles away. Accordingly on that afternoon he and his daughter took me to its margin; it was in open country, but owing to the levee, it was invisible until we came within a few feet of it. The mighty river at that point was one mile wide, fifty feet deep, and running silently at seven miles an hour. It came swinging around a great bend a few miles to the North, and the trees on the Missouri side were in the living green of Spring. There were no towns in sight, not even a house; and we had the splendid river all to ourselves. In imagination I could see the raft coming along, bearing Huck and Jim.

On 9 May in Brooklyn I gave the address commemorating the centenary of the birth of Whitman. John Burroughs was on the stage but too feeble to speak to the audience. He thanked me with the tears running down his face. Never did a man have a more faithful disciple than old Walt had in John Burroughs.

Count Ilya Tolstoy, the son of the novelist, was in New Haven and I took him to the Elizabethan Club, and had a long talk with him. He shared his father's views on religion, morality, and art. He himself was a large man, very like his father in appearance. He said (with passion) '*Anna Karenina* is the worst book my father ever wrote; he wished he could destroy it and so do I.' I asked him, 'Didn't he like any of his novels?' '*War and Peace* and *Anna Karenina* he despised; but when he had finished the manuscript of *The Kreutzer Sonata* he gave it to the family to read, leaving the room as was his invariable custom, so that we could discuss it without embarrassment. After we had read it, I said "I think this is the best thing Father has done." A moment later he entered the room and said, "I have done something I never did before in all my life—I have been listening at the door. And I think Ilya is right. This is the best thing I have written." My father also was not ashamed of *Resurrection*, though as a rule he wished he had not written novels.'

Count Ilya put his hands on my rough homespun suit. 'Oh, I like these clothes! I have a suit exactly like yours in Russia, if the Bolsheviks haven't got it!'

His pocket bulged with a detective novel; he said he was never without one.

He described in detail how careful his father was in the boy's early training; when he was about twenty, his father asked him if he had had any sexual intercourse, and when Ilya replied in the negative, the great writer wept for joy and gave him his blessing.

71

MEA ORNAMENTA

THE highest ambition of every good teacher is to be excelled by his pupils. The one thing he wants more than anything else is that those whom he teaches will surpass him
in every respect—in brains, character, achievement. As
every normal father is prouder of his son's success than of
his own, is made happier by his son's accomplishments
than by his own independent work, so every normal teacher looks with happiness and pride on the success of those
who were once his students.

I cannot claim to have been a vital factor in the later
work of my pupils; all I can say is that they were exposed
to my teaching. I follow the careers of my students after
their graduation with a feeling akin to parental interest; it
is a delight to meet their wives and their children; for even
after the men have become grey or bald, they are always to
me undergraduates—my students.

There is a fundamental difference between American and
European students (not including English); American
undergraduates, as a group, are the most conservative men
in the world, and European the most radical. The majority
of our undergraduates, except in the south, where special
reasons prevail, are 'good' Republicans, believers in high
tariff, 'untainted' by radicalism; their attitude toward
anything like a popular uprising would be a burlesque, as
years ago they burlesqued Coxey's army. A large group of
Yale or Harvard undergraduates seriously leading a mob
is unthinkable, despite the fact that the radical clubs in

these institutions are more prominent than formerly. Whereas in Europe, whenever there is a political disturbance, an uprising, or a radical row, the university students are always in the forefront.

Again, when one talks with European college students, they seem at first sight to be more intellectually mature than our boys. I have talked often with German, Russian, Polish, French university youth; they discuss fluently philosophy, metaphysics, international affairs, the leading thinkers and writers of the world, in a manner that seems entirely beyond the tastes and the capacities of young Americans. I remember a time, many years ago, when I spent fifteen months on the Continent, and was daily amazed at the conversational capacity of foreign students; when I returned to America, it seemed almost as if our young men were simply boyishly healthy, well groomed and well bred.

But—after seven years I returned to these same places in Europe and met these same students—for they were still students; they were still discussing philosophy, politics, and international affairs. Yet in seven years many of those boyishly healthy Americans were holding positions of power and influence.

To a European professor travelling in America or lecturing at an American university, there is a tragic contrast in health, physical vigour, and personal charm between the aspect of his students at home and those he meets in the United States. An instructor from Belgium pointed out to me a group of Yale students, and said, 'Look at them! I did not believe there were anywhere in the world such magnificent specimens of young manhood. Our students at home are small in size, low in stature, underfed, poor, many of them unhealthy, even anaemic in appearance; your students are big, tall, clean, healthy, happy boys. I wonder if they have any idea of their good fortune. It is a delight to look at them, to teach them, to talk with them.'

There is another characteristic of American college youth. They are not unduly intellectual, but they are fired by an ambition to be of service in the world. Their aims are not selfish; and they take their places in various communities where they expect to aid in the advancement of civilization. Among my pupils I not only had boys who are now college deans, bishops, public-spirited clergymen, workers in city settlements and in foreign missions, but many who are devoting their wealth and their lives to the public welfare.

I taught university students 42 years. If you multiply forty-two by four hundred, you will get fairly near the actual number of students who have been in my classroom.

In travelling through England, France, Germany, in 1928, I found that apparently the best known of all living American writers was Sinclair Lewis. There was universal curiosity about him; any item of information had news value. I remember him well as a freshman at Yale. He came from Sauk Center, Minnesota, in 1903. His name was Harry S. Lewis. He was very tall, incredibly thin, and his head was crowned with a mass of fiery red hair. Very few of his classmates knew his Christian name; he was universally called 'Red' Lewis, both because of his hair and because of his radical opinions, which he took no pains to conceal. At that time he was a disciple of Upton Sinclair. He was not disliked in college, but was regarded with amiable tolerance as a freak. He took not the slightest interest in the idols of the place—athletics, societies, and so on; nor did he care to 'make' any of the positions in extra-curricular activities that are rewarded with social distinction. He took no interest in these things and he did not pretend to. He was a complete and consistent individualist, going his own way, and talking only about things that interested him. We at once found a common bond of friendship in our admiration for a Minnesota poet, Arthur Upson, whom Lewis brought to my house. His brief life ended tragically, but he had written some beautiful verse. On that ground of intimacy, we had long discussions on literature, the real passion of Lewis. I liked and admired him, for although our views on many subjects were and are irreconcilable, it was a pleasure to me to see a lad who thought for himself. In his senior year he became an editor of the *Yale Literary Magazine*.

After graduating from college in 1907, he worked on newspapers as a reporter, and then in the houses of various publishers. His first novel appeared in 1914, *Our Mr. Wrenn*, a book I recommend to critics who wish to understand Mr. Lewis's art. All his subsequent methods are there in embryo. He then became a successful magazine writer, but finally, although having very little money, he staked everything on one throw. He retired in absolute seclusion and spent one year writing a novel which appeared in 1920 under the name of *Main Street*.

It fired the shot heard round the world. He awoke and found himself famous, a fame immensely increased by the publication of *Babbitt*, a name that has become universal. Mr. Lewis is the same man that I knew as an undergraduate; he has developed, but he has not changed. His satires are born of a passionate desire to make the world better, for if ever there was an evangelist, it is Sinclair Lewis.

In many ways, as is natural, he has mellowed. When we remember how he used to ridicule the Rotarians and other service clubs, we should read an article about them in an English periodical in which he says that the Rotarians and their fellows are the most efficient workers for world peace now existing, and that if war ever is abolished, it will be owing to these service clubs more than to any other one thing.

Three of my undergraduate students, who were in college

at the same time, and intimate friends, have now become famous through creative literary work. The playwright, Philip Barry, 1918; the poet, Stephen Vincent Benét, 1919; the novelist, Thornton Wilder, 1920. All three showed remarkable talent in college.

Philip Barry was an editor of the *Yale Literary Magazine*, and was so much interested in play-writing that after graduating he went to Harvard and studied under Professor George P.Baker, later head of the Department of Drama at Yale. His play (written in Mr. Baker's school) received the prize, was put on later on the New York professional stage, and ran a year. It was called *You and I*, and discerning judges saw at once the dawn of a real dramatist. Curiously enough, for a time Philip Barry had thought of a diplomatic career, and was associated with the Department of State at Washington, and for one year was attached to the American Embassy in London.

The success of his first play stimulated his ambition to write something better. Two plays of his, produced in New York, *In a Garden*, and *White Wings*, were really beyond the public appreciation of that time. Edna Ferber wrote an article for the New York *World*, expressing her indignation at the financial failure of *In a Garden*.

Since then, Philip Barry has combined excellence with popular success. *Paris Bound* and *Holiday* both 'clicked,' but have not satisfied their author. He is more than a popular playwright, and will never be content with merely box-office successes, pleasant as such things must be. His play, *Hotel Universe*, produced by the Theatre Guild, puzzled both critics and audiences, but it is a beautiful and original work of pure imagination, the kind of play one enjoys better at the second hearing. I am proud of Philip Barry.

Stephen Vincent Benét is the son of an army officer. His brother, William Rose Benét, now one of the editors of the *Saturday Review of Literature*, has published several volumes of poems; and Stephen is a born, foreordained poet. At the age of seventeen, and before entering Yale, he published a volume of original poems. During his undergraduate career he took three prizes for verse. He was universally popular, having a peculiarly lovable disposition. His gift for satire and irony was exercised in such a manner that it charmed his victims. He is one of the most sparkling conversationalists I have met. He was born in Bethlehem, Pennsylvania, and has lived in Augusta, Georgia. He has a combination of northern energy with southern relaxation that makes him irresistible.

Stephen Benét wished to write nothing but poetry, but he was forced to produce novels and short stories to keep the pot boiling. Then he received the Guggenheim Fellowship, and going to Paris, he there wrote an epic poem of the American Civil War, *John Brown's Body*, which attracted universal attention, and won the Pulitzer Prize.

I have known Thornton Niven Wilder since he was a child. His father, Amos Parker Wilder, was a senior at Yale when I was a freshman, and was even then known outside of academic walls for his brilliance as an orator. Later he became a journalist. In college Thornton showed remarkable versatility. He composed and played music on the piano, he wrote plays and short stories, he wrote professional dramatic criticisms for the newspapers.

After graduation, he studied for a year at the Graduate School in Princeton, was a housemaster at Lawrenceville School in New Jersey, where he taught French, and receiving a fellowship, he lived for a year in Italy.

His first novel, *The Cabala*, displayed a literary style so full of grace and distinction that it attracted the attention of many critics; but it was too remote in matter for the popular taste. His second novel, *The Bridge of San Luis Rey*, was accepted by the publishers because they thought so fine a book ought to be printed; but they had no belief in its success with the public, and they have not yet recovered from the shock.

This novel is a masterpiece. It gave Thornton Wilder international fame (he is constantly discussed in the press of France, Italy, Spain, as well as in that of Great Britain and America), and it was to be hailed both by the critics and by some three hundred thousand readers as a notable work of art. His short novel, *The Woman of Andros*, is slighter in content but fully as distinguished in style. His next novel, *Heaven's My Destination*, is totally different from the preceding novels, being a story of contemporary American life and seeming to point toward the stage.

His first full-length play that appeared on the professional stage is *Our Town*, and the first night in February, 1938, it received enthusiastic comment from the critics and tumultuous applause from the audience. In May it was given the Pulitzer Prize, the highest honour in America, so that Thornton Wilder has twice received this Prize, for *The Bridge* in 1928 and exactly ten years later for *Our Town*. Thus he is a double winner in the field of the novel and of the drama. All three of these men—Barry, Benét, Wilder—were, in college, quiet, modest, attractive fellows, wholly free from conceit or even from pretentiousness, but all three were imbued with literary ambition.

Henry Seidel Canby, after graduating from the Sheffield Scientific School at Yale in 1899, entered the Graduate School, and I had the pleasure of being one of his teachers. He is today one of the most influential literary critics in America, and an authority on American literature. Every one of his books has added to his reputation.

Anson Phelps Stokes, former Secretary of Yale, and now Canon of Washington Cathedral, was a pupil of mine in the class of 1896. In his undergraduate days he won many prizes. Henry Sloane Coffin, the President of Union Theological Seminary, was a pupil of mine in 1897. Howard Chandler Robbins, one of the best preachers in America, was chiefly distinguished in college (1899) for his ability to write verse. Sherrill, of the class of 1911, is Bishop of Massachusetts. John Dallas (1904), is Bishop of New Hampshire. The Bishop of Southern Ohio, Henry Hobson, was one of my students in the class of 1914. Philemon Sturges was one of my pupils in the class of 1896. He is now dean of St. Paul's Cathedral in Boston. George Paull T. Sargent for some years was Dean of the Cathedral in Garden City and is now Rector of the great metropolitan church of St. Bartholomew. He was in the class of 1905.

Yale, like other New England colleges, was founded to train men for the Christian ministry; while the proportion of clergymen is not so great as it was a century ago, I submit that the quality is even higher.

Many Roman Catholics now enter Yale as undergraduates; and one of the most brilliant and learned priests in the church is Father T. Lawrason Riggs (1910), the Yale chaplain for all the Catholic students.

Eugene Meyer, a world authority on public finance, and an immense help to his country in the World War, was a pupil of mine in the class of 1895; and I could name other financiers and influential men of affairs, including Cabinet members.

One of the most promising young writers in America is Jesse Stuart. He comes from Scotch ancestry. He was brought up on a farm in Kentucky and some years ago published a collection of original sonnets called *Man with a Bulltongue Plow*. I first met him in Kentucky in 1936 where he was teaching school in the winter and working on the farm in the summer, and I told him that he would have to give up both teaching and farming for creative writing. He has since published two volumes of prose tales.

Shortly after my visit to Kentucky he wrote the following letter:

GREENUP COUNTY HIGH SCHOOL

MCKELL BUILDING
JESSE STUART, PRINCIPAL

FULLERTON, KENTUCKY

Sept. 22nd, 1936

DEAR WILLIAM LYON PHELPS:

I shall never forget the trip across Kentucky—how I left at 4 o'clock one morning to meet you at Eastern State Teacher's College, Richmond, Kentucky. I shall never forget the train you were supposed to arrive on and how I sent the porter through the coaches calling for you; about that time the train hit a truckload of pigs and we were all thrown out of our seats. Part of the pigs were killed—the better half of them took through the cornfields squealing. Several women on the train wished it had been the driver killed instead of the poor pigs since the train had whistled three times and the driver didn't pay any attention. When I got in Richmond there wasn't any Mr. Phelps and the people wondered until they got your telegram.

I shall never forget you and the talk you made, your ease of speaking, and your alert mind. I shall never forget the things you said about England. But that is a part of time past and only memory lingers, a very dear sweet memory. When I came back on the train I told a fellow my belief in immortality now was stout as an oak because I had seen a man who convinced me that man couldn't die. The fact was not in the words you said but because of you. I cannot see how any man of your type would be allowed to pass from the universe. I used to think a lot about such things and I've a story coming out in *Esquire* called "Resurrection" and I want you to read it.

May I thank you for the things you have said for me. Allow me to say that I am glad to have met you, have known you, talked to you, laughed with you, sat at the table and to have eaten with you and smoked with you. It was a pleasure and pleasant memory. I shall thank W.F.O'Donnell long as I live for inviting me over there.

Now that you are not conducting your section in *Scribner's* AS I LIKE IT, I must say that I regret it. I always read that section. . . .

My best regards to you ever William Lyon Phelps. I hope you write

your autobiography. I want a copy autographed. I'd gladly place my
order now for a first edition.

Always,

JESSE STUART

My relations with my colleagues in the Yale English
department have been more than cordial; we are devoted
friends. We have naturally differed occasionally on men
and measures, but no cloud has even momentarily obscured
the affection which has grown stronger by length of time
and intimacy of association. Most of them were my pupils,
and while I certainly do not claim credit for their achievements, it pleases me to remember the early days and our
relations in my classroom. George Nettleton, John Berdan,
John C.Adams, I have already mentioned; I am proud of
their work and of the scholarly achievements of Chauncey
Tinker, Samuel Hemingway, Robert French, Stanley
Williams, Frederick Pottle, William De Vane, all of whom
were my students.

Only two full professors of English came to Yale from
other universities; both of them have added distinction
to our department by their productions, and happiness by
their presence—Karl Young and Tucker Brooke. We are a
very happy family. The only reason I do not mention our
younger colleagues, so many of whom are brilliant scholars,
is their number. When I began teaching at Yale in 1892,
the English department consisted of Professors Lounsbury,
Beers, Albert S.Cook, E.T.McLaughlin; that was all. In
about thirty years, instead of five men teaching English,
we had fifty.

In 1894 Wilbur Cross was appointed Instructor. He rose
rapidly through the regular grades of promotion, for many
years was not only a Professor but Dean of the Graduate
School and Editor of the *Yale Review*. When he reached the
age of retirement in 1931, he was in a few days nominated

by the Democratic party for Governor of Connecticut, and has been reelected four times.

It is impossible to exaggerate the affection I have for these colleagues and for many who are teaching in other departments; I am inordinately proud to be their associate—*Meine gute Kameraden!*

72

JOHN GALSWORTHY

In the year 1906 two excellent novels appeared in England which gave their authors popularity and fame—*Joseph Vance*, by William De Morgan, and *The Man of Property*, by John Galsworthy. One of the first notable men in England to recognize the distinction of the latter book was the late Alfred Ollivant, author of the finest dog-story ever written—*Bob, Son of Battle*. He was a good friend of mine, and when I wrote to him urging him to read *Joseph Vance*, I received the following reply, written from East-bourne, 18 August 1907.

I have not read *Joseph Vance* yet. Thank you for telling me about him. He has been well reviewed here in the considerable papers but I have not heard him talked about probably because I live a very secluded life, and know no literary folk. But curiously enough, two days after getting your letter I heard from Henry Jackson, the Regius Professor of Greek at Cambridge, and perhaps our biggest scholar now Jebb is dead, and he advised me to read the book as being no-table. And I shall certainly do so.

The literary sensation here to my mind has been the publication of a book called *The Country House* by a man called Galsworthy. It is the truth to say that I had not read a page before I found myself saying, "Here is a new mind." And further reading confirmed my first impression. In the first place G. is a consummate artist—how rare for an Englishman. I have heard him compared to Flaubert. In the second place he is soaked in our great modern idea of Evolution. It is this last characteristic which puts him in a place by himself, and distinguishes him from his contemporaries, and from those who have gone before. I may say I have been waiting for his coming for years. He is the first big mind who has applied the vast resources

667

thrown open to the gaze of the men of our generation by Science to literature—perhaps it would be more accurate to say the first big Anglo-Saxon mind. Some of his effects in this kind are marvellous. He has written several books, but only two of note, I fancy—*The Country House* and *The Man of Property*. The second is very strong, almost brutal. It is a purely critical book; there is no creative beauty about it; but G's genius is essentially critical. At the same time he is on our side, the side of the angels, right enough. And if he is brutal, it is with the brutality of the surgeon. He destroys to make alive. The other book has more poetry in it. Do get them and let me know what you think of them.

Mark Twain received a tremendous ovation from the undergraduates at Oxford when taking his degree there—far greater than Kipling.

I must have written him that I preferred *The Man of Property* rather than *The Country House* (as I did and do), for on 17 October 1907, he wrote

As to *The Country House* I think one reason I like it so much is that it deals with the life I know best. Then again I think you hardly do justice to Mrs. Pendyce and her charm. There is true beauty, true romance, about her. Moreover up and down the book there are passages of poetry which say all manner of mysterious things to me— the dying rabbit bit, the bits about the race-horse, bits here and there about flowers. They whisper to me of the Oneness of things. Galsworthy is the first novelist I have come across who really understands the Doctrine of Evolution; and for that alone, apart from his critical insight, his bitter humour, his philosophy, his work is for me remarkable.

I am quite sure that some readers will snort when they see Galsworthy called brutal—but in comparison with other novels published during the early years of this century, I can understand how *The Man of Property* seemed to Mr. Ollivant 'very strong.' And after all, it is stronger than many vociferous novels of these latter days —and seems to have enough virility and vitality to out-live more sensational works.

In 1909, 'Observer,' in the London *Daily Mail*, made the following comment:

> Of all quickly made reputations, that of Mr. John Galsworthy is one of the most remarkable. A few, a very few, years ago only the really initiated ever heard of such a person; today, it may be proclaimed, both as playwright and novelist, Mr. Galsworthy occupies the central chair in the Areopagus of English letters for all-round talent and brilliancy. The case is an unusual one. Not many men succeed in fiction and the drama. . . . Now Mr. Galsworthy has succeeded in both these arts. And more. Not only does he practice them both, but he practices them both at one and the same time. . . Yet another curious thing. He has had no failures, no positive stoppage or set back, and this is the more remarkable because he has never pandered to popular taste.

I first saw Mr. John Galsworthy at the dinner in New York on 20 February 1919, in honour of the centenary of the birth of James Russell Lowell. It was a British-American dinner given by the American Academy. Among the speakers were Elihu Root, Brander Matthews, the Canadian representative, and John Galsworthy. The following evening a gala performance of *Dear Brutus* was given, a letter from Barrie read by William Gillette, with Mr. Galsworthy sitting in a box, apparently enjoying the occasion.

On 5 March Mr. Galsworthy came to New Haven, and lunched at the house of Mr. and Mrs. Henry S. Canby. He said he thought there would be in the near future only two political parties in England, Labour and Tory. He was to lecture that afternoon at Yale, and I asked him if he would give an extempore talk on his early struggles as a writer, or on his work in the theatre. The cold sweat broke out all over his face; he was in such distress that I told him such a speech would not be necessary, that it was just a suggestion. He said he could not speak one sentence *extempore*; every word had to be written and read from manuscript, as indeed he had done at the New York dinner. I asked him if he could answer questions from the students. He smiled and said 'Will you stand by me and catch me when I faint?' I relieved his mind immediately by saying no questions would be allowed.

He read a very fine address called *Talking with Oneself*. He was paid two hundred dollars which he immediately presented to the Yale (undergraduate) University Dramatic Association.

That he enjoyed the occasion is clear from the following:

THE MANOR, ALBEMARLE PARK,
ASHEVILLE, N.C.

MY DEAR PROFESSOR PHELPS

Your letter of March 11th has only this evening reached me. It gave me the greatest possible pleasure—for I loved Yale & the whole atmosphere there; and I thought the students splendid fellows. It will be a bright spot for me always, & I'm only sorry my wife wasn't there to make your acquaintance & that of many other friends. And so is she.

With very warm remembrances I am

Sincerely yours

JOHN GALSWORTHY

HOTEL CHATHAM

March 30, 1921   48TH STREET & VANDERBILT AVE.

NEW YORK

MY DEAR PHELPS:

I have been reading your Essays on myself and the rest with the greatest pleasure. Thank you very much for sending me the volume, and for the sympathetic understanding which you have extended to my work.

There's one thing in your diagnosis which puzzles me. I am unable to correlate it with so much evidence tendered me by play-goers after seeing my plays. It's your dictum "he appeals to the mind almost exclusively." Surely it is not mental appeal which moves people strongly; and yet so very many have told me of the almost unbearable emotional effect my plays have had on them. Perhaps the answer is that the emotion starts in the mind, moved by some conception of contrast. Still it *is* emotion, not mere mental interest, such as I think is the ultimate sole appeal of Shaw.

By the way, I don't think travel very responsible for my 'view' of England. It was due to three other causes, ' The Boer War'; close acquaintanceship with the vagabond of whom Ferrand is the projection; and one other (the greatest) into which I will not enter.

I am wholly with you in admiration of Barrie's " Admirable Crichton," " Dear Brutus," and " The Twelve Pound Look," and " The Will"; but in his work at large I found so many little lapses from what one can only call "taste"—austerity of sentiment—so many little scrapes at one's epidermis—that I confess to listening to him often with great discomfort, and a feeling that he cannot be acquitted of too much eye on his audience.

Perhaps I lack the blessed gift of admiration; and yet I have it for certain writers (not many) without reserve.

Your diagnosis of " Leonora" struck me as singularly clear-sighted and admirable. Where I think he went technically a little wrong was in starting with too actual a first act, or rather in not hitting that 'dramatisation of thought and impulse' nail on the head from the start; because' though you're undoubtedly right, hardly any one saw what he was after, and that surely is not what he hoped for.

Well, we shall talk anon. In the meantime ever so many thanks again.

Sincerely yours,

JOHN GALSWORTHY

By the way, please don't
expect me to speechify at
dinner. I simply can't.
  J.G.

In April 1921, he lectured again at Yale; his visit was preceded by the following letters.

Nov. 28, 1920

MY DEAR WILLIAM LYON PHELPS

It was a great delight to receive your letter, and to hear of your visit to my two plays.

We are now in California where I am writing, & both of us are revelling in sunshine.

If I do lecture at all this time which is more than doubtful, I would come to Yale with the alacrity of one who remembers with delight the welcome it gave me last time. But I think we English are over-lecturing, and I feel less fit than ever to tell anybody anything.

Please give our warm remembrances to Mrs. Phelps and all who were so good to me. We saw Mr. and Mrs. Canby in New York. I think his paper is jolly good. But am I really like that drawing? My wife says 'No,' but you never can tell, Sir, 'you never can tell.'

It is delicious here—such pepper trees!

With warm regards

I am Yours sincerely

JOHN GALSWORTHY

SAN ISIDEO RANCH
MONTECITO
SANTA BARBARA
CAL.
Dec. 30 (1920)

DEAR WILLIAM LYON PHELPS,

It is very good of you to want me to come, but I literally dare not make any hard & fast engagements; because my wife's health may necessitate our staying longer in a warm climate, and on the other hand, her health permitting, advices from England may take us back sooner than we expect. I can only tell you that I will let you know when our faces are actually set East, whether there is a possibility, and in that case, if you have a day still free I might be able to come. This would mean that you would not get more than a fortnight's notice at the outside.

With all good wishes to you in the New Year

J.G.

SAN MARCOS HOTEL
CHANDLER
ARIZONA
Feb. 7 (1921)

DEAR WILLIAM LYON PHELPS

I write this line to say that, barring accidents, we could come to Yale on Friday, April 1st., and I would discourse to the students for

50 minutes or so at some hour which would enable us to get back to New York that same night, if this were quite convenient. May I, however, beg that you will keep this arrangement, if you make it, dark for as long as ever you can, because it is breaking through my rule of not lecturing on this visit, and if known, will let me in for all sorts of invitations which it will be very difficult to refuse. In fact, it would be a boon if you didn't let the cat out of the bag till, say, a week beforehand.

We shall be here for some weeks longer; the place is very delightful, and is doing my wife good.

With very kind regards, I am

Cordially yours

JOHN GALSWORTHY

Oh! and by the way I would ask that *No Press* should be admitted.

J.G.

I was enthusiastic about Barrie's play *Mary Rose*; but Galsworthy did not like it; he told me that he thought Barrie had not dealt entirely fairly with his audience or with the theatre; although he was a great admirer of many of Barrie's plays.

It was a great pleasure to have Mrs. Galsworthy accompany him. He gave a lecture at Yale on Monday 4 April 1921, but the hall, holding eight hundred, was jammed ten minutes before the hour, and when I heard the roar of the crowd outside and saw through the windows the students climbing the fire escapes, I adjourned the lecture to the neighbouring Woolsey Hall, which holds three thousand. The transfer of the audience was a delirium, but in an astonishingly brief time the crowd flowed into the vast auditorium and filled it. At the close of the lecture, the immense stage was invaded by a throng of students, each one bringing a copy of one of his books for him to autograph. I tried to protect him; but when he heard a despairing voice on the outskirts crying 'I'll never reach him!' Mr. Galsworthy spoke up and said 'I will stay here until I have signed every book,' and he did.

My friend and former pupil, the literary scholar and bibliophile, Frank Altschul, sent me the following interesting letter he had received from his father.

C. ALTSCHUL
32 WEST 86TH ST.

NEW YORK, APRIL 9, 22

MY DEAR FRANK,

I have just read Mr. William Lyon Phelps' reviews of the *Forsyte Saga* in *The Literary Review* (*Evening Post*) of yesterday and in *The N.Y. Times Book Review* and *Magazine* of today, and have been exceedingly interested in them. As you know, I have admired the books comprising the *Saga* more than anything I have read of late years in English.

Mr. Phelps makes particular mention of the delight he experienced when Mr. Galsworthy returned to the Forsyte family in 1920. I wonder if he knows what induced Mr. Galsworthy to recall the creatures of his fancy already in 1918 when he wrote *The Indian Summer of a Forsyte*, which I am glad to notice Mr. Phelps evidently thinks as lovely as I do. If you think he might be interested, will you tell him that I have a copy of *The Man of Property* on the fly-leaf of which Mr. Galsworthy has inscribed the following:

Nov. 20, 1911

I have often been asked what became of Soames and of Irene. I have as often answered that I know no more than my questioners. In me, when the last scene of a book has been imagined and the last word written,—all is ended; and the creatures of my tale step out into darkness.

John Galsworthy

I confess I am very curious to know whether it was the repeated inquiry of correspondents, or whether anything definite is known regarding his drift of mind, in those days between 1911 and 1918, that would give a definite answer to the inquiry.

Your loving

DAD

Mr. Galsworthy told me, as he told many others, that when he finished *The Man of Property* (1906) he had no intention of ever using again any of its characters. Mr. Jesse H. Shera of New Haven on 3 January 1927 wrote to Mr. Galsworthy as follows:

The marital relations of Soames and Irene are suggestive of certain parallel elements in the somewhat similar situation of Helmer and Nora in Ibsen's *A Doll's House*, especially as presented in the final act of that play. In view of Ibsen's profound influence upon modern social thought, is it not reasonable to assume that his influence acted upon your work? If such an influence were present, to what extent were you conscious of it, and of how great importance do you consider it to be?

Secondly, at the time of the creation of *The Man of Property* did you foresee a possible future return to the theme? Does the *Salvation of a Forsyte* represent the dawning of the Forsyte conception, or was *The Man of Property* in preparation at the time, i.e. in 1900? Similarly, when was the change in Soames' character, as presented in *The Silver Spoon*, first conceived, and was this change the result of a determined plan, or was it an unconscious evolutionary growth?

Finally, from the standpoint of American jurisprudence the basis for the law suit in *The Silver Spoon*, would appear to be insufficient. How severe is the English law concerning slander and libel?

It was probably on the day he received Mr. Shera's letter than he answered it, as follows:

EN VOYAGE,
Feb. 13, 1927

DEAR SIR:

In answer to your queries of Jan. 3 which have found me out here—

(1) It might be reasonable but it is *not true* to assume that Ibsen had any influence on me. He has had none, neither in that particular matter nor in any other. I have always been a poor Ibsenite.

(2) I did not foresee any return to the theme when I wrote 'The Man of Property.'

(3) I do not see any particular change in Soames' character in 'The Silver Spoon,' as compared with his character in 'To Let'

and 'The White Monkey.' He mellows as he gets older, mainly through his love for Fleur. There has been no set plan about it.

(4) English law is pretty searching in the matter of libel and slander.

I expect this answer will come too late to be any good.

Very truly yours,

JOHN GALSWORTHY

On 18 September 1928 I spent the day with the Galsworthys at their beautiful country home at Pulborough. After eating a copious lunch, Mr. Galsworthy asked me if I would like to play some tennis doubles. I replied that I should like nothing better but that I had no clothes with me except those in which I was standing. Accordingly he lent me his shoes, socks, underclothes, trousers, shirt, and sweater, and everything from the soles of my feet to my neck fitted me exactly as if made for me. So in this humble way I am a replica of the great writer.

When the game was over, I was soaked in sweat and could not wait for tea as I had to take the train back to London. Accordingly, I took a hot bath, and Mr. Galsworthy put mustard into it, so that it was the first and last time I ever had a mustard bath. He said that it would keep me from getting cold, and apparently it did. I came down stairs and found the entire company, wrapped in sweaters and coats, having tea; I had time for one cup of the most delicious tea I ever tasted and then I was off to the train. It was the end of a perfect day.

I fell in love with their dogs, especially with a Dalmatian and an exquisite Irish setter; and as Mrs. Galsworthy said snapshots of their visit to Arizona had been taken, I begged for one. After we had returned from Europe in October that year (1928) I received the following letter from Mrs. Galsworthy:

BURY HOUSE,
BURY, NR PULBOROUGH,
SUSSEX
Oct. 6, 1928

MY DEAR FRIENDLY LYON:

Thank you for your two good letters and the clipping from your mangled article, which was natheless very interesting.

I have not been 'forgetting it'—that flattering request; but was 'laid by' (as Shakespeare says) with a baddish cold in Town, and unable to get at my snapshot negatives; but being now nearly rid of my disabilities (and I do hope your good lady is also), I have sent for some enlargements and among them that one you were pleased with, of J. G. and me squatting under a tree somewhere near the Grand Canyon. (I say *my* snapshots; but it's clear that I didn't take that one.) We returned to Bury yesterday, and it is the most glamorous weather; too lovely for words. The dogs are handsomer than ever, Rex especially. Dickie is the ghost of beauty. I'm suffering *very* slightly from embonpoint. We have a small Scottie terrier at Grove Lodge, and yesterday acquired a lovely solemn black and white spaniel. So, the dog news is all alive. Cats are very well and charming, too. Uncle and nephew had a great set-to at tennis very soon after arriving and this morning before breakfast all, with dogs and horses, have been far & wide on Mose Downs against the sky.

Hoping soon to send that humble snapshot, and with our united affectionate greetings to you both,

Always cordially yours

ADA GALSWORTHY

The two enlarged Arizona pictures delighted us and I wrote expressing appreciation.

One of the things that most gratified Mr. Galsworthy happened while I was in London. I took up the morning paper, and there in headlines which had the appearance not of literary criticism or gossip about books, but rather seemed to belong to the news of the world, was

DEATH OF SOAMES FORSYTE

It would be impossible to have a more eloquent tribute to the reality of this character. I asked his creator if he were not pleased, and he laughed and said 'Very much.'

I have often wondered if men who have lost the Christian faith in which they were brought up, would not be happier if they could also lose their conscience. If they could have no conscience at all, like Sanin, or a robust conscience such as Ibsen seemed to admire. Mr. Galsworthy lost his religious faith; but I have never known anyone anywhere who was more conscientious, more absolutely upright. His conscience often made him unhappy.

At their home in Hampstead, London, 24 July 1928, we took luncheon with them, no-one else being present. He showed us a room filled with the manuscripts of his novels, all bound in asbestos. As he could not dictate, and had never learned to play the type-writer, his books had been written in longhand. I think he intended to give them to the British Museum. I had the privilege of examining some of these manuscripts; they were filled with corrections.

We talked about the legends and myths that accumulate about every person who becomes widely known. I reminded him of a statement recently published in many English and American papers, that he had taken farewell of the stage and would never write another play. 'There is absolutely no foundation for that announcement. I never made such a remark.'

Otis Guernsey, a famous undergraduate Yale athlete in 1916, wrote to Mr. Galsworthy about *Justice* and received the following reply:

WINGSTONE
MANATON
DEVON

MY DEAR SIR:
    Your kind letter reached me yesterday. Falder killed himself because of the general over-wroughtness of his position. The knowledge that Ruth had not waited for him perhaps gave him the last squeeze;

but the idea of going back—a procession of going backs, was almost enough without. Suicide, I think, is generally an affair of an over-wrought *moment*. One may go about in a suicidal frame for weeks and not be given the last shove needful.

I'm so glad the play stirs people up.

With much appreciation of your letter, I am

Very faithfully yours

JOHN GALSWORTHY

In the Spring of 1930 I wrote him in response to an urgent request from a friend that I would ask him about the use of the 'double possessive' in one of his books. A characteristic letter came:

GROVE LODGE,
THE GROVE, HAMPSTEAD,
LONDON, N.W.3.
May 8, 1930.

MY DEAR WILLIAM LYON PHELPS

I hope you are in the most robust condition. We send you warmest greetings.

About that letter you 'respectfully refer' to me from —— Well, you see, as is very common with readers she (in the instance given) confuses the author with the character speaking. That double possessive is very common in current English speech. I should say people use about six of the single possessive to about half a dozen of the double possessive; and the example she quotes is a perfect specimen of the practice.

I'm not going to say however that I wouldn't be capable of using it myself; such is the force and attraction of corruptions, and I am, alas, the least precise of persons.

Bury is looking nice just now, and I wish I could once more place you within my integuments and defeat (ahem!) you at tennis.

Always yours

JOHN GALSWORTHY

That matron-mother of three,—with whom you played has not yet got over her delight at being told by you to 'run Child, run!'

His third and last visit to Yale was on 9 April 1931. This was preceded by the following letters.

GROVE LODGE,
THE GROVE, HAMPSTEAD,
LONDON, N.W.3.
Dec. 3, 1930

DEAR WILLIAM

Greetings! And thank you for the challenge. The onset will set us south as fast as we can leg it. The retreat will see us bobbing like peas on the knife with which, I believe, they should not be eaten. In other words—our souls will not be our own I guess, nor our bodies. If we can hop off the blade on the way to or from Boston in April 23 we will—to see you both *but not to speak*. I'm under an oath.

As to tennis. Think of my age, infirmity, & the condition I shall be in. You American youngsters of 65 have no mercy on us.

Again greetings and a Xmas blessing.

Yours,

J.G.

Address but not for dissemination
Hotel St. Moritz: 59th Street
New York

THE BELLEVUE-STRATFORD
PHILADELPHIA
April 2, 1931

MY DEAR 'BILLY'

Thank you for your note. I go to Boston on the 8th, and shall take the 9.30 a.m. back on the 9th which reaches New Haven at 1 p.m. It would be delightful if I might lunch with you and resume my journey at 4.17 p.m.—for I must be in New York for dinner that evening. But on your immortal soul you must swear that I don't have to make a speech of any kind. I don't believe I could play tennis so soon after lunch (as that would mean), so I must forego the pleasure of being beaten by you. Ada has had such a lot of travelling that I shall have to leave her behind—the train is no joke to her, poor dear. I look forward very much to seeing you both again.

Always yours,

J.G.

Ada joins me in best greetings to you both.

He arrived at one o'clock and I invited to meet him at my house a group of undergraduates called The Pundits. He was in high spirits and talked in an intimate, friendly fashion with the students. After they had left, I had an hour or two of good talk with him. The sensation of the year was Somerset Maugham's novel *Cakes and Ale* in which to everyone's amazement, the life of Thomas Hardy was apparently held up to ridicule. I have never found any explanation of this extraordinary book. A novel, written as a rejoinder, in which Somerset Maugham was made to appear in an unfavourable light, followed immediately. It was called *Gin and Bitters*, came out anonymously, and evidently Mr. Galsworthy thought the author was Hugh Walpole, for he said 'I have been reading on the train today Hugh Walpole's novel in which he attacks Maugham.' But the novel was not written by Mr. Walpole, but by Elinor Mordaunt (good name), an accomplished English novelist who has travelled all over the world.

Mr. Galsworthy could not understand why Mr. Maugham had written his story, and he would not express an opinion on the merits of *Gin and Bitters*.

It is interesting to see how one distinguished writer feels about experiments made by his contemporaries. No-one admired the genius and character of Henry James more than Barrie; yet Barrie told me he did not think that *The Turn of the Screw* should have been written. He seemed to feel it wasn't quite fair. In the same way, in this conversation with Mr. Galsworthy, although he admired Barrie immensely, he told me he thought *Mary Rose* was not quite a legitimate play; that the dramatist was not fair to his audience. However this may be, I am very glad both were written; for they are among the works of literary art that made an indelible impression.

The last time I saw Mr. Galsworthy was in 1932 in London. We lunched with them on 27 May at their house in Hampstead; he seemed in excellent health and spirits; there was no indication of sickness. He told me the Ivy Restaurant was his boothole. On first nights he could not be induced to make any appearance or speech; he would not even attend the performance, but waited doggo in the Ivy until news was brought concerning the reception of the play.

We drove with them down to the city in their car; and as I had to get out near Westminster, and was about to close the door of the car, he said 'Be sure it closes' and as I heard it latch, I said 'It clicks—just like your plays.' He laughed and seemed pleased.

He was greatly interested in a new gadget that had enabled him to smoke the pipe as often as he pleased without 'biting the tongue.' This was a system of paper cartridges filled with tobacco called 'Smoker's Circles; a Boon to Wet Smokers' each one just the size of the bowl of the pipe. You inserted it and then as the paper around the tobacco burned away, you could smoke to your heart's content. We tried it and he gave me a lot of the cartridges.

As we were leaving for America, I wrote him a note saying that the Senior class students of the Sheffield Scientific School at Yale had voted him their favourite novelist. The following is the last letter I received from him.

> BURY HOUSE,
> BURY AT PULBOROUGH,
> SUSSEX.
> June 9, 1932

DEAR WILLIAM

Thank you for that pleasing card. How strange & flattering are the tastes of the Science Students of Yale University!

I hope you will take home a suit case full of R.J.Smokers Circles.
We had hoped to see you both again, but one thing and another have
cropped up.

A good voyage to you! Our love to you both.

Always yours

J.G.

He was awarded the Nobel Prize that autumn of 1932;
and I have often wondered if it indirectly hastened his
death. Mr. and Mrs. Galsworthy often left England in the
Autumn to go to Arizona or to some warm winter climate;
this time naturally he waited, expecting to go to Stockholm
in November. It would have been a fearful ordeal for him
in any case, as his modesty and shyness would have made
a public appearance agonizing; though he was of course
gratified with the award. When the time came, he was not
well enough to attend.

He died 31 January 1933.

In 1938 appeared Mrs. Galsworthy's admirable book,
Over the Hills and Far Away. I wrote congratulating her not
only on the book but because she showed in it that the
memory of happiness was a source of happiness, and not of
unavailing regret.

LONDON, MARCH 28, 1938

MY DEAR FRIEND,

Your kind letter gave me the very greatest pleasure, as you
may easily imagine. Such generous praise from such a high authori-
tative source has seldom come my way and I thank you most
heartily.

You are so right about happiness; of course it can be in the present,
and the real. I have known times during mountain days of walking
and climbing when I've nearly swooned with joy in the beauty, the
joy, the happiness of it all. Old man Johnson had too suffering a body
ever to have experienced such hours, and he ought not to have talked
on the subject; there were so many other things that he *could* ex-
pound, explain, illuminate. But I am truly no great admirer of him,

for he was a coward about some things, and cowardice casts a horrid dinginess on a character, as I see it.

I have been wintering in England, as an experiment, and it has proved very successful. I went to Torquay in early November with no great hopes of being able to bear either climate or surroundings, and there has been hardly a day when I felt cold or disinclined to go out of doors. It is a wonderful centre for motoring, for coast and inland are both lovely, and Dartmoor, quite near, provides an entirely different landscape and climate. I came home last Thursday, leaving mid-June weather behind me.

I must again thank you for that lovely letter, which I shall give myself the pleasure of re-reading when I am feeling too down-trodden; and hoping you and your dear Lady are very well and happy,

    I am
      Affectionately yours,

           ADA GALSWORTHY

73

SECOND JOURNEY TO CALIFORNIA

IN 1919 I accepted another invitation from the University of California, this time to teach in the Summer School of the Southern Branch of the University at Los Angeles. We arrived on Sunday 29 June. That afternoon as we passed through various towns in California, the heat was so intense that I wondered how we should be able to endure it. I got off the train for a few moments at San Bernardino, and on the platform I felt as if I were walking on a hot stove; and it is not an exaggeration when I say that the soles of my shoes were hot for half an hour after. But when we arrived at the station in Los Angeles, I noticed that the men on the street were not wearing Palm Beach suits; and indeed there was a cool breeze blowing and the temperature was below seventy. Such is the difference in summer between the cool coast and even a few miles in the interior.

The sessions of the University were held in the fine building of the State Normal School at Hollywood, not nearly so famous then as in later years. We lived at Pasadena some nine miles away, in an excellent boarding-house called La Solana; and I reflected that after my death, if some curious stranger should examine my extinct cheque-books and find so many weekly stubs made out to La Solana, he would make a natural but erroneous inference. Pasadena was hot in the daytime, but it was a dry heat, not uncomfortable even at a high temperature, and in afternoon came the cool wind, so that every evening one had to wear an overcoat and then sleep under thick blankets—in other words

the perfect climate. The fine residences on Orange Grove
Avenue were closed for Pasadena is a winter resort; but I
prefer it in the summer, when the nights are always cool
and there is no possibility of rain.

We saw the great Maurice McLoughlin and his partner
Bundy play tennis, and the woman champion, Miss Mary
Browne, and one of the famous Sutton sisters. McLoughlin was kind enough to ask me to play with him one day in
doubles; I did, though my contribution to our victory was
negligible. In talking with him it was easy to see why he
was the most ardently beloved of all tennis-players; he had
an irresistible charm. We accompanied him to the train
when he left for the East to take part in the national
championships. But alas! his great days were over.

In Hollywood I had the pleasure of meeting Miss Florence Sutton. I told her I had never been beaten by a
woman, and being always on the lookout for new experiences, I asked her if she would do me the honour of playing three sets of singles. She beat me quite easily, as I could
not get more than three games in a set. Later, in one day,
with her as partner, I played eleven sets!

On one of the numerous links near Pasadena I played
golf when the temperature was 104 in the shade; and made
the best score I have ever made in my life on a full-length
course, 75.

I found in my lectures at the Los Angeles branch of the
University the same enthusiasm and devotion that impressed me so much at Berkeley in 1908; and from the
people the same inexhaustible kindness and gracious hospitality. Mr. and Mrs. John Perrin put an automobile and
a chauffeur at our disposal for the entire term of six weeks!
When we finally had to take the train East, we found our
drawing-room filled with flowers, and an immense group
of people came to the station to say farewell.

We took the Santa Fé train at Pasadena. On arriving in

New York, we went to the delightful camp of our friends Mr. and Mrs. James R. Sheffield in the Adirondacks, and there I saw Mount Whiteface for the first time since I was nine years old, when I had seen the sunset from the summit and spent the night on the mountain.

The latter part of the vacation I spent in San Antonio, Texas, where I made three addresses a day at the convention of school-teachers. I was impressed by the courage of these men and women. Every day the temperature was well over ninety, and probably over a hundred. They were packed like sardines into the vast auditorium, and compelled to listen daily to many addresses. Yet they showed enthusiasm.

One of the most interesting hours for me was speaking to the coloured school-teachers, who had a daily assembly. The grateful appreciation of these devoted men and women was deeply affecting. One of them wrote me, 'When you were speaking, I forgot I was black.'

Every morning I had breakfast before sunrise on the roof of the hotel, and every evening I had dinner outdoors after sunset. Miss Sarah King, who celebrated in 1936 her fiftieth year as teacher, gave me a genuine Spanish dinner; every dish was new to me, and they all tasted good.

I visited the Spanish church, several centuries old, and the priest showed me a strange painting of the Trinity— three young men standing close together, dressed in the height of fashion of those days.

On my way north, I stopped at Little Rock, Arkansas, simply because of childish geographical memories. I fell in love with the town, though the heat was fierce. At a railway stall I bought a copy of *Tom Brown at Oxford*, which I had not read for many years. At Memphis I crossed the Mississippi.

74

SOME POETS AND NOVELISTS

LORD DUNSANY, the Irish dramatist, gave a lecture at Yale University on a particularly appropriate day—Hallowe'en, 1919. The thing that impressed the audience more than anything else was the enormous amount of water he drank during the lecture. The huge pitcher of water stood on the table; he preferred to give his lecture sitting down. He would constantly reach over, swallow an entire glass of water, and proceed with the lecture. This went along well enough until he was reading from one of his plays in which the following incident occurred. Two filled cups were offered to a certain character. One of them was harmless; the other was poisoned. The man had to drink, and it was an even chance. As Lord Dunsany came to this dramatic point in his reading, he poured another glass of water out, held it in front of him, and read, 'Shall I drink the poisoned cup?' without observing the situation. After the lecture was over, he said to me, 'I hope the water is good; I drank an awful lot of it, didn't I?'

Sara Teasdale (Filsinger), 1884–1933, the American lyrical poet who won the Pulitzer Prize in 1917, was a good friend of mine; and we both admired the poetry of Vachel Lindsay. The Poetry Society of America offered an annual award, and in 1919 Sara Teasdale, Richard Burton, and I were the Committee. We could not agree, and finally the prize was divided between Carl Sandburg and Stephen Vincent Benét. I had an agreeable afternoon with Sara Teasdale talking about poets and poetry. Considering the excellence of her own work, she was extremely modest, painfully sensitive to adverse criticism, and appreciative of praise. I had spoken highly of her work and she alludes to that in one of the two following letters. Richard Burton has been a lifelong intimate friend; we both grew up in Hartford.

In 1937 a volume of her verse was published (no editor's name given) called *The Collected Poems of Sara Teasdale.*

1 WEST 81ST STREET
NEW YORK CITY
May 29, 1919

DEAR PROF. PHELPS:

We tried "at the hour of nine" as Romeo says, (or is it Juliet?) to reach you last night by long distance, and the combined efforts of Prof. Burton and S.T.F. were unavailing. . . .

I do wish you could have been here to argue with Burton. It would have been such fun. I liked B. ever so much. He came in all hot and excited at being half an hour late. We had a cocktail and hurried to the dining room where B. seemed to grow mightily in general good spirits.

Do you know, I've been in a state of extreme contrition ever since you were here that I didn't even offer you a glass of ginger ale? My plans for serving tea were upset at the last minute and I forgot all about three perfectly good bottles of ginger ale out in my husband's closet. Sometime when you're in town *do* come out and let me show you I'm not such a bad hostess after all. And I *did* want to dress up instead of slipping into the first thing that came to hand, all of which can be done next time, if you are so good as to make a next time.

I've been rolling the good things that you said about my poetry back and forth in my mind until I am very proud and very happy. I hope you really meant some of it. It would hearten me more than you know to be able to feel that say even three-eighths of it were truth telling. I don't know why I said three-eighths. It sounds so properly mathematical and I'm like you in mathematics, slow but not sure. Do you remember saying that in *The Advance of English Poetry*?

All good greetings, and don't forget to make a next time.

SARA TEASDALE FILSINGER

EL ENCANTO
HOTEL AND COTTAGES
SANTA BARBARA, CAL.
October 10, '19

DEAR PROF. PHELPS:

Haven't I travelled a long way since I wrote to you last? I wonder
if you were in Santa Barbara when you were out here on the coast
last summer? If you were, I know you liked it. I am way up on
Mission Ridge in the most adorable little new hotel with a real fairy-
tale garden. My husband had to go to South America and I came
out here because I didn't feel up to going with him. I haven't forgotten the promise I made myself to give you one of my most precious possessions, a drawing by Vachel from the censers and the
hearth series. I hope the whole series will be in his book of drawings
when Macs. bring it out. I'm sure you won't mind having yours used
if they ask for it.

With all good wishes for a fine autumn,

Sincerely,

SARA TEASDALE FILSINGER

JOSEPH HERGESHEIMER

Before Mr. Hergesheimer had produced anything of importance, some of his friends sent me (quite without his
knowledge) his play in manuscript called *The Zenith* and a
copy of his first published novel *The Lay Anthony*. I wrote
to my correspondents that I thought the play had no merit
and no promise. But while I did not write so disparagingly
of the novel, I said I was not impressed by it. I ought to
have perceived its latent power. Years later when Mr. Hergesheimer's position among contemporary novelists was
very high, I wondered if I had missed what I ought to have
seen in those two early works and in response to my letter
he wrote as follows:

THE DOWER HOUSE
WEST CHESTER, PENNSYLVANIA

DEAR DR. PHELPS:

You are, of course, right about the crudeness of *The Zenith*; but I am unable to accompany you so far in that opinion of *The Lay Anthony*. As a first novel it had a decided right to any support. However, looking back now on about sixteen years of total isolation, an initial book that in its year sold perhaps eight hundred, a second the proceeds of which were stolen from me; remembering an imponderable academic frown, I am almost convinced that I had the best possible experience for a remote end.

I'd like to write to you convincingly about my work; but, in addition to an innate distrust of the mere discussion of creative literature —I mean for the creator—I am very unsettled in my comprehension of the conventional phrases necessary to any such proceeding. I am glad you like *Java Head*, it was solely written for liking, is the most direct and sincerest reply I can make to your generous appreciation.

Very faithfully,

JOSEPH HERGESHEIMER

April 14, 1919

Mr. Hergesheimer's career as a novelist was so brilliant and successful that it is surprising he did not continue. *The Three Black Pennys*, *Java Head*, and *Linda Condon* are distinguished, particularly in literary style. In later years he devoted himself more to biography, writing an admirable life of General Sheridan. He came to Yale to give a lecture in which he humorously but very positively attacked American women for what he regarded their bad opinion of American authors, and he told me afterwards that this lecture not only made it impossible for him to give any more lectures but almost stopped the sale of his books. I think he admires beautiful old furniture more than anything else in the world, and when he entered my house before we went to the lecture he viewed my eighteenth century family furniture with something very near adoration.

The intense loneliness of the novelist, for most of his time is spent not in observing life but in monastic solitary seclusion, was distasteful to Mr. Hergesheimer; in later years he produced books of travel in Europe, Cuba, and other places.

He could write an interesting autobiography. He told some of us at Yale of the years of severe labour he spent at the art of English composition, after he had decided to give up painting.

ZONA GALE

When we were in Pasadena in 1919, I received a letter from the novelist Zona Gale. She was somewhat disturbed by an adverse criticism of her work. I wrote her to pay no attention to it, especially not to think of replying to it. If a critic says (for example) that a certain writer is not a literary artist, there is no good in asserting the contrary. The only effective reply is a work of literary art.

> Meet Lutwyche, I—
> And save him from my statue meeting him?

The very next year she produced a masterpiece, *Miss Lulu Bett*, which gave her an unassailable position in the front rank of living American novelists. She turned this into a play which won the Pulitzer Prize.

This correspondence in 1919 (I had not then seen her) led to an intimate friendship. Here is a characteristic letter:

DEAR WILLIAM LYON PHELPS:
How good you were to "Papa LeFleur" and how greatly I appreciate it. Thank you so much for your letter.

Michigan seems so near. I wish sometime you would ferry across! You will have received a copy of the short stories which I put together. I am going to write an article and send it to the Yale Review on what constitutes the sentimental. If in a story a girl says "I want to see my mother," that is sentimental. But if a nun says in a story, "I want to be a saint. O I hope I will get to be one. I have always thought it must be so wonderful to be a saint. That's what I want to be—a saint." Then that is an approved utterance. I suppose the point is that in any statement of aspiration or emotion in these days there must be a touch of mockery in order to make it the real and not the romantic. One wonders why. One wonders too why one need be swept into the current of these period reactions which herd and stamp all human utterance.

My love to you both,

Affectionately yours,

Zona Gale

Portage, Wisconsin
October 14, 1933

EDWIN ARLINGTON ROBINSON

One December day in the year 1896 I received through the post a thin paper-covered booklet called

THE TORRENT
AND THE NIGHT BEFORE
BY EDWIN ARLINGTON
ROBINSON, GARDINER
MAINE, 1889–1896

On the title-page was printed a disarming ironical quotation from François Coppée—

Qui pourrais-je imiter pour être original?

and at the foot of the title-page, instead of a publisher's name was the statement

PRINTED FOR THE AUTHOR
MDCCCXCVI

and across the title-page was written in ink

W.L.Phelps,
with compliments of E.A.Robinson
9 December, 1896

The printed dedication of the tiny volume was humorously modest:

> This book is dedicated to any man,
> woman, or critic who will cut the
> edges of it.—I have done the top.

I have no recollection of reading this book, and none of acknowledging it; but I must have done both, for the next year (1897) I received a bound volume of 123 pages, called

THE CHILDREN OF THE NIGHT

A Book of Poems
By
Edwin Arlington Robinson

Boston
Richard G. Badger & Company
MDCCCXCVII

A publisher's note preceding the title page said

This first edition of The Children of the Night consists of Five
Hundred Copies on Batchworth Laid Paper, and Fifty Copies on
Imperial Japanese Vellum

and on the fly-leaf was written in ink

W. L. Phelps
from E. A. Robinson
4 December, 1897

I read every word of this volume, as is proved by a note I made at the end of it, only a few days after I received it.

For more than twenty years these two precious volumes disappeared from my sight; during that interval we moved twice. One day, somewhere in the nineteen-twenties, I found the two resting quietly among a lot of old papers, uninjured by their prolonged slumber.

I mention these facts, because the first of these books is now one of the most valuable to collectors in American Literature, and the second fetches an exalted price; the fact that they are both autograph copies adds to their value.

I never saw Robinson until Yale gave him the honorary degree of Doctor of Letters in 1922. He was quiet, reticent, modest, and produced an impression of absolute sincerity.

Edwin Arlington Robinson was born at Head Tide, Maine, 22 December 1869, and died in New York, 6 April 1935. He was never married. He was three times awarded the Pulitzer Prize in Poetry. He was elected a member of the Academy on 10 November 1927.

His fiftieth birthday, 22 December 1919, was celebrated all over the United States; one of the very few occasions in the history of our country, when the birthday of a poet had a nationwide commemoration during his lifetime. It is unnecessary to say that he took no part in it, nor made any public appearance.

The year after his death, 18 October 1936, a tablet to Robinson was unveiled at Gardiner, Maine, in the presence of a large assembly. The exercises were as simple as they were dignified. Hermann Hagedorn called him a beloved figure in the American Pantheon, 'the anchorite, outside space and time, conscious of an eternal eye upon him and upon the work of his hands.'

This tablet was presented to the city by Henry Richards, husband of Laura E. Richards, author of the little book giving all the information we have of Robinson's childhood and boyhood in Maine.

It is interesting, in view of the facilities for publicity in the twentieth century, that during his entire career Robinson did everything possible to avoid attracting attention. No one could secure a photograph of him or any biographical data from himself; he refused to appear in public, he did not read or discuss his poems before audiences, he remained solitary and inaccessible. Yet he was generally acknowledged as the foremost living American poet; raised to that eminence by the sheer merit of his verse.

When in the year 1928, he was awarded by the National Institute of Arts and Letters the Gold Medal for poetry, he wrote me this characteristic letter:

> ROOM 411
> 30 IPSWICH STREET
> BOSTON, NOVEMBER 18, 1929
>
> DEAR PHELPS,
>   I am writing to you as President of the Institute of Arts and Letters to express my sincere thanks to all concerned in my receipt of the Gold Medal for Poetry this year. It is certainly a source of great pleasure and satisfaction to me. At the risk of appearing a little ungracious, may I ask if anything in the nature of a formal presentation may be omitted? As I grow older I find myself less inclined, if possible, to indulge in the luxuries of publicity. I am still human, however, and am glad to know that there are several people somewhere who like what I have done, or some of it.
>
>   Yours sincerely,
>
>   E. A. ROBINSON

His statement, 'As I grow older I find myself less inclined, if possible, to indulge in the luxuries of publicity,' has a humour all its own.

In this same year the Letters of Thomas Sergeant Perry were published, with an Introduction by Robinson. I wrote him again about the Medal and about these Letters, but I lamented the absence of an Index. He replied as follows:

> 30 IPSWICH STREET
> BOSTON, NOVEMBER 20, 1929
>
> DEAR PHELPS,
>   Thank you for your letter of the nineteenth regarding the award of the medal. Your consideration is much appreciated, and you have my gratitude.

Your approval of the Letters and the Introduction gives me great pleasure, as you know. The lack of an index has called down curses on my head, and with reason, as I have to admit.

Yours very sincerely,

E. A. ROBINSON

When Robinson began to publish his poetry in the late nineties, the times were not favourable; but the true poet should have genius for the inopportune. These two early volumes attracted very little attention; and apparently they were doomed to speedy and complete oblivion, the inescapable fate of ninety-nine books out of every hundred.

But about fifteen years later, in the revival of poetry in America, Robinson came into his own; and he deserved his fame, both for the excellence of his work and because he was one of the leaders in this renaissance. The dates are significant. *The Torrent*, 1896; *Children of the Night*, 1897; *Captain Craig*, 1902; *The Town Down the River*, 1910; *The Man Against the Sky*, 1916; and *Merlin*, 1917.

His original play *Van Zorn*, is not only very fine as drama and as literature but it exhibits a side of his talents usually unknown; it had the bad luck to appear in 1914.

I confess that I made two errors in estimating his work. I thought that when *Merlin* appeared, he was on the wrong track, that he had better let those legends alone. It seemed to me as if he were trying to dilute Tennyson; and to dilute Tennyson won't do at all. My second error was my belief that the value of Robinson's work was analytical and intellectual, rather than emotional. In 1918, I wrote,

It is of course possible that Mr. Robinson wished to try something in a romantic vein; but it is not his vein. He excels in the clear presentment of character; in pith; in sharp outline; in solid, masculine effort . . . He is an excellent draughtsman; everything that he has done has beauty of line; anything pretentious is to him abhorrent. He is more map-maker than painter.

Then, to my amazement and delight, he proved me wrong by producing in 1927 his masterpiece, *Tristram*. It not only is his best poem, it is the best poetic version of that immortal story that has ever appeared in English. It glows with passion and is radiant with beauty. And indeed, perhaps its closing lines about the other Isolde, Isolt of the White Hands, leaves on our minds the deepest impression. For here he rises from the particular to the universal.

> Isolt of the white hands,
> Isolt with her gray eyes and her white face,
> Still gazed across the water to the north
> But not now for a ship. Were ships to come,
> No fleet of them could hold a golden cargo
> That would be worth one agate that was hers—
> One toy that he had given her long ago,
> And long ago forgotten. Yet there she gazed
> Across the water, over the white waves,
> Upon a castle that she had never seen,
> And would not see, save as a phantom shape
> Against a phantom sky. He had been there,
> She thought, but not with her. He had died there,
> But not for her. He had not thought of her,
> Perhaps, and that was strange. He had been all,
> And would be always all there was for her,
> And he had not come back to her alive,
> Not even to go again. It was like that
> For women, sometimes, and might be so too often
> For women like her. She hoped there were not many
> Of them, or many of them to be, not knowing
> More about that than about waves and foam,
> And white birds everywhere, flying, and flying;
> Alone, with her white face and her gray eyes,
> She watched them there till even her thoughts were white,
> And there was nothing alive but white birds flying,
> Flying, and always flying, and still flying,
> And the white sunlight flashing on the sea.

75

A JOURNEY TO ANDOVER

(1919)

In June I went to Phillips Academy, Andover, Mass., to give the Commencement address. I took the night train from New Haven to Boston, and was eating breakfast in the Copley Plaza Hotel, when a young Yale graduate whom I had not seen since his senior year in 1913, came to my table. He asked if I were going to Andover; receiving an affirmative reply, he wished to know how I was going. 'Well, in about five minutes I shall drive to the North Station and take the train.' 'But won't you go with me? I have a taxi outside.' 'You mean you have a taxi to the North Station?' 'No, I have a taxi to Andover.' Now Andover is about forty miles from Boston. I remembered this young man very well. He had shown energy and heroism in 'working his way' through Yale only six years past; he had managed a boot-blacking and clothes-pressing establishment, had waited on table, had for four years done a vast amount of menial labour. And now he was inviting me to travel forty miles with him in a taxi. I was puzzled. 'Are you sure you have room?' 'Plenty.' So we went out, and there was a taxi, that had been steadily churning up money while we were at breakfast. We entered it and my young friend merely said to the driver, 'Andover,' and we started. He began the conversation by asking me to come to New York when I had leisure, as he would like to show me some of his pictures. I supposed he had some snapshots, and replied that I should be very glad to see them. He remarked that some of his pictures were really very good. 'I bought one last week for two hundred thousand dollars.' I looked at him. 'Yes, I have a collection of masterpieces and Italian primitives.' This seemed to me like a page out of the *Arabian Nights*. 'Look here, it's none of my business, of course, but didn't you work your way through Yale?' 'Indeed I did; but that was six years ago. My salary is now $200,000 a year, but that is the least part of my income.' We are all familiar with the millionaires who started with nothing and became fabulously rich at fifty; but here was a young man still under thirty. However, everything he told me was true; I felt as if I were in a dream, where, as Goethe says, one wonder fades into another, and the succeeding wonder takes us by surprise. I listened to one miracle after another as the taxi carried us to Andover.

It seemed to me that the record of this man was astounding, but in two hours I was to discover that he was a timid, shrinking violet in comparison with the stranger with whom I was to converse on the way back to Boston. After the Commencement exercises were over, and I was eating lunch at the Principal's house, a middle-aged man at the end of the table asked me when I was going. I told him I must take the train to Boston. 'But won't you go with me in my car?' I reflected that I had 'bummed' a ride on the way up, and I might as well repeat the act, only I thought to myself, it will be impossible to hear any such romantic tales as on the morning journey. After a polite skirmish, I agreed to go to Boston with this gentleman. He told his chauffeur to get into the back seat, as he intended to drive himself, so I sat with my host in front. He drove with ease and skill through the traffic and after we had gone two or three miles, he said casually, 'Of course if this car should break down, I can stop any

passing car and order them to take us to Boston.' Supposing
he had a mistaken sense of humour, I looked at him, and
found he was quite serious. Then he suddenly asked if I
had ever seen a man drive a car with his little finger, and
without waiting to discover whether I had or not, he
placed the little finger of his left hand on the steering-
wheel, stepped on the accelerator, and the indicator
showed we were travelling sixty miles an hour. Then,
while we were still whirling at this pace, he suddenly
threw his right arm around my neck, and forced my head
down on his shoulder. 'You see, at any moment I could
kill you. I might be driving and if my seatmate should
become offensive, I could choke him with one hand while
driving with the other. Or, I could draw a pistol with
one hand and shoot either him or any other enemy in a
pursuing car. It is really necessary for me to be able to
drive with one finger.' I saw and said nothing. What was
there to say?

I felt relieved when he took his right arm off my throat
and began to drive again in normal fashion. 'If we should
be late in reaching Boston I will telegraph and have the
train to New York stopped so that they will wait for us.'
I told him I thought that would not be wise. 'Or, I can
drive you right on to Providence and overtake the train.'
'No! whatever you do, don't do that!'

'I have three houses, one in Boston, one in Washington,
one in Maine. I keep them open with a staff of servants,
for at any moment I might have to stay in one of them.
I have a great deal to do. I went down to Washington and
talked with some of the Senators. I spoke to a few men
there who had made a profound study of a difficult subject
for years; but in talking with them only five minutes, I
understood the matter far better than any of them did,
and was able to give them valuable advice, just the
solution they needed. How do you account for my ability

to grasp a difficult subject in a moment?' I told him I thought it was genius. 'Ah, but that is nothing to my power over women. To women I am absolutely irresistible. I know five women now, who are happily married and living in contentment with their husbands. Yet, if I should go to any one of them and crook my finger, she would instantly leave her husband and come to me. How do you account for that, Professor?' and he looked at me earnestly. 'That,' I said frankly, 'is magnetism. That's what it is —just magnetism.'

He told me how he had gone to a sailing-ship lying at the port in Boston, and although he had never studied navigation, he took command of this vessel, and took it safely to the Azores. I quite agreed with him that such a thing was unusual.

But the cream was to come. After listening to a stream of talk of this kind, we entered Boston at last, and at a corner of one of the most crowded business streets, he drove our car into the middle of the cross-section, so that we held up the traffic both ways. Immediately the air resounded with the blowing of innumerable horns and curses were showered on us from every direction. The traffic policeman advanced toward us, and I knew that while some journeys end in lovers meeting, our journey's end would be the jail, where I fully expected to spend the night with my new friend.

As the policeman came alongside, my friend enquired pleasantly 'How are you, Officer?' and to my unspeakable amazement, the policeman answered smiling that he was very well. 'And Mrs. —— and your children, all quite well?' 'They are in fine shape, thank you, Mr. ——.' Around us pandemonium, horns, shrieks, curses filled the air. But the officer and my companion went on conversing with the *insouciance* of ladies at an afternoon tea. After this had lasted some time, my friend enquired, 'How long will you permit me to hold up the traffic, Officer?' 'The entire afternoon, if you wish.' And that was that.

We started at last, drove to a fine-looking house in a good residence section. He opened the door with a key, called aloud for a servant and a coloured man appeared. We had some light refreshment, my host showed me every courtesy, and I caught the three o'clock train for New Haven.

76

EVENTS IN 1920 AND 1921

ON 3 January 1920 I was one of the speakers at a dinner in New York given to Maeterlinck by the Lotos Club. I sat next to him and had much good talk. He said he understood every word of my speech because I spoke English so clearly. This dinner followed his disastrous lecture. He had come over to undertake a long lecture tour through the United States, and a tremendous crowd appeared at his first address. He knew English well but could not speak it; he had therefore hit upon the extraordinary plan of writing English words with a phonetic French pronunciation. After he had spoken some ten sentences, a woman stood up in the audience and called out, 'Mr. Maeterlinck, we cannot understand a word.' If he had spoken in French many would have understood, or he could have had an interpreter on the stage, to translate for the audience after every paragraph, as was the method adopted successfully by Senor Benavente. But Maeterlinck's language was impossible, and the coast-to-coast lecture tour was abandoned after that one attempt. In my speech I said that he had paid Americans a remarkable and unique compliment. As in the old days when toasts were given to royalty and the glasses smashed so that they could not be used a second time, M. Maeterlinck had used for our benefit a language that had never been used before and certainly would never be used again. I never heard anyone laugh more heartily than he did during my speech. His projected tour was a failure, thirty or forty dates cancelled, his nerves were on edge, but my treating the matter in this way released his pent-up nervousness. It was an Aristotelian catharsis. He laughed and laughed till the tears ran down his cheeks.

After the formal dinner was over we adjourned to another room for drinking and intimate conversation. I had the good fortune to be placed at a small table with only two men, the British Admiral Lord Jellicoe and the famous American Charles M. Schwab. I had supposed that after the terrific years of responsibility in the war when by a disaster to the Grand Fleet Jellicoe might have 'lost the war in one afternoon' the Admiral would look worn and tragic; instead of that he was the picture of robust health and jollity; a weather-beaten sea-dog, full of mirth and high spirits. And I had thought with the tremendous undertakings by Mr. Schwab, he would show signs of the strain; he looked as happy as a schoolboy and both men talked and laughed as if they had never had a care in the world.

On the afternoon of 27 February in New York I saw Ervine's fine play *Jane Clegg*; Dudley Digges and Margaret Wycherley at their best. I went back stage to congratulate them and Miss Wycherley said, 'Ah, you are from Yale; in that university the drama is always taken seriously.'

On 18 March I introduced Sir Oliver Lodge who lectured to an enormous audience at Yale. He was absolutely confident of survival after death and said he had had communications. There was nothing sensational in his manner.

CARDINAL GIBBONS (1834–1921)

As it is sometimes stated that Catholics do not emphasize the study of the Bible, the following letter from one of the greatest of them is interesting.

CARDINAL'S RESIDENCE
408 N.CHARLES ST.
BALTIMORE
January 10, 1920

Mr. Wilbur Cross,
Editor, Yale Review,
New Haven, Conn.

MY DEAR MR. CROSS:—

I read with much interest the review of Mr. Maurice Egan, based upon the work of Mr. William Lyon Phelps, "Reading the Bible," and I am happy to see an interest taken in the Scriptures. Up to seventy-five years ago, the public men of our country seemed to have been saturated with the Bible. They were familiar with its contents and quoted freely text after text. Among many others, Mr. Webster seemed to have at his fingers end the words of this inspired book. I remember to have counted in the pleading of Mr. Webster, counsel in the Girard Will Case, no less than 14 quotations from or allusions to Scripture. Apart from its inspirational character, the Bible still remains the one means of culture.

Mr. Egan is well qualified to review this work of Mr. Phelps.

With best wishes,

Faithfully yours,

J. CARD. GIBBONS

I do not know whether the following story is true or not, but if it is not true, it ought to be. After he had returned from an interview with the Pope, some Gigadibs said to him, 'Cardinal Gibbons, I don't see how you or any reasonable man can believe in the infallibility of the Pope. Do you really believe the Pope is infallible?' To which the Cardinal smilingly replied, 'He called me "Jibbons."'

A BAPTIST AND ACTRESSES

The variety of my own interests and the widely divergent moods caused by them remind me of what happened on Palm Sunday 1921. I attended the Baptist Church in New

Haven in the morning, officiating during part of the service. Then I took the train to New York, to officiate as toastmaster at the great public dinner given in honour of David Belasco. On my way to church that morning I reflected that I should be in all probability not only the one member of the congregation who was to attend a dinner celebrating the theatre on the same evening but perhaps the only person in attendance at any evangelical Protestant Church on Palm Sunday who was to spend the evening in the way I had planned.

And that night in New York as I took my place as toastmaster at this dinner given by the Society of Playwrights with five hundred guests, I could not help thinking how astonished that particular audience would be if I began my remarks by telling them how I had spent the morning!

And yet to me there is nothing 'inconsistent' in these two congregations on the same day. I love the church and I love the theatre. Religion and Drama are two of my passions; thus I myself feel absolutely at home with Baptists, Methodists, Presbyterians in church and prayer-meeting and equally at home with actors and actresses, playwrights and theatre managers.

After preliminaries, I was told that I should escort to the table in the hotel ballroom 'the most beautiful woman in America,' and Mrs. Lionel Atwill certainly was beautiful. At the table David Belasco was on my right and shaking like a leaf at the thought of speaking. He was in terror. But on my left were two of his adorers, Jane Cowl and Frances Starr, and the three of us, working together, brought him into a semblance of calm before his zero hour. They both whispered to me during the dinner of the immense kindness always shown to them by the famous director. There were many speeches—I remember an animated one by W. A. Brady. A brilliant impromptu speech by Laurette Taylor received tremendous applause. She walked out in front of the head table and made delightful remarks on the appearance of the guests of honour. It so happened that the ascetic-looking Sir Philip Gibbs was sitting next to the lovely Mrs. Atwill. 'What do that pair remind you of?' called out Miss Taylor. 'They remind me of the temptation of St. Anthony.'

The next morning the *New York World* had a good account of the banquet, but objected strenuously to a part of my introductory speech. I said that whenever I made an after-dinner address, I always made four speeches at the same time, not one of which resembled any of the other three. 'First, there is the speech that I had carefully prepared beforehand; it was very good; but not at all like the one you are hearing; the second is the one I am now speaking, and it is the worst of the four; the third is the best of them all, brilliant, witty, and full of charm; it is the one I make on the way home from the banquet; and the fourth, entirely unlike any of the others, is the report of the speech in the papers the next morning.' This pleasantry troubled the *World* reporter.

On 15 June I received the honorary degree of Doctor of Literature at Brown University, the first of my honorary degrees. It was fitting that it should be the first as my father had been a graduate and Trustee of Brown, and my oldest brother Dryden was graduated there in 1877. On 21 June I received the same degree from Colgate University, which had also given my father the honorary degree of Doctor of Divinity.

On 12 November in New Haven Marshal Foch attended the football game between Yale and Princeton. He had never seen American football and followed the plays from scrimmage with binoculars. In the middle of the second half, one of his associates asked him if he did not wish to leave. 'Why, the game isn't over, is it? I certainly shall not leave until the end,' and indeed he seemed intensely interested.

I saw an impressive performance of *The Madras House*, by Granville-Barker, given at the Neighbourhood Playhouse in New York, directed by Miss Lewisohn. I had been unable to visualize this play in reading it; and I was amazed to find that on the stage it was one of the most interesting of all modern dramas. I wish it could be revived.

Shortly after the war, Mr. Hubert Sedgwick (Yale 1893) a New Haven journalist, brought me from the Rotary Club of New Haven an invitation to become a member. I have always been glad I accepted. Rotary is a powerful force for good, locally, nationally, and internationally. A number of my colleagues on the Yale Faculty are members and the close association with men in various other occupations and professions is both agreeable and valuable. Many warm friendships have resulted, in New Haven and in far-distant places in America and in Europe.

The Rotarian, the monthly magazine published in Chicago, has contributions from men in every country; leading statesmen, economists, scientists, and others. During the last few years I have contributed a monthly article on the new books.

One of the pleasant events coming to me from Rotary is an annual excursion every August from my summer home in Michigan to Port Huron, eighty miles away. Mr. Edgar A. Guest, whose summer cottage is only seven miles distant, the Rev. Herbert Hichens, who learned golf as a child in Cornwall, England, caddying for the professionals, Mr. William Pottinger, 'Mayor' of Huron City, and I make up the expeditionary force. We drive to Port Huron, Mr. Guest and I speak at an open meeting of Rotary at lunch, and then follow exciting golf matches. For more than a dozen years Mr. Guest and I have had as our opponents two leading Rotarians of Port Huron, Mr. Louis Weil, editor of the *Times-Herald*, one of the best daily newspapers in America; and Mr. David MacTaggart, born in Scotland, and owner of a large bookshop. Our friendship with Mr. Weil and Mr. MacTaggart has added immensely to my happiness; and the gracious hospitality of Mr. and Mrs. Weil at the close of the afternoon heals the suffering caused by my misfortunes on the links.

My Father in 1860

General J.G.Harbord and I
about to go shooting in Georgia

My Father in 1888

My Mother in 1865

Mr. and Mrs. John Galsworthy
At the front porch of the Elizabethan Club
Yale University, 1921

Painting by Jere Wickwire, 1926

Mr. and Mrs. Phelps
On their front porch, 110 *Whitney Avenue, New Haven*

77

BRITISH DIALECT AND AMERICAN VOICES

DICKENS's novels are filled with talk where *w* and *v* are interchanged—*Samivel* and *wery*. I have never heard this, and most Englishmen from whom I have sought information have never heard it. But in 1927 I got a letter from an octogenarian in Toronto:

> Speaking of the English in some districts of England using W for V, I was born in a remote Essex village, and lived most of my days there until I was twenty-three. Our parish had 1,000 inhabitants and I verily believe at least 800 of them would have said a thing was "wery wexatious," "wery wexing," they would have "wisitors" and "weal and winegar" were commonly used; indeed my grandmother who was from Northampton used to say there was no letter "v" in the Essex alphabet.

The *w* and *v* are also interchanged in Bermuda.

Few books are more interesting to read than dictionaries; many years ago Henry A. Beers, Professor of English Literature at Yale, gave a regular college course in *Webster's Unabridged Dictionary*. But the most interesting dictionary I have ever seen is *A Dictionary of Modern English Usage*, by H. W. Fowler. It combines learning, wisdom, humour, common sense, and an almost infallible good taste. It appeared in the nineteen-twenties, and has become not only a popular reference work, but a classic of literature. After my review of it in *Scribners*, the following letter came from its distinguished maker.

HINTON ST. GEORGE
SOMERSET

31 December, 1926

DEAR SIR:

Your notice of *Modern English Usage* in Scribner, of which you have been good enough to send me a copy, lays me under a deep obligation. I was already aware, from some press cuttings in which a lecture of yours was referred to, that you were doing much to give the book a chance in America as well as here.

You of course praise it much more highly than it deserves; but it takes a more virtuous person than myself to resent over-praise.

Books are not a commodity that you stand in need of. Nevertheless I am tempted by your remark about personality to send you an anonymous booklet of mine in which I had occasion to talk on that subject. It is only a set of lay sermons to big public school boys and I will turn down the pages of the relevant ones.

With very many thanks for your help,

Yours very truly,

H. W. FOWLER

This letter led to a spirited correspondence; Fowler was a 'rationalist' whose lay sermons to boys are not nearly so well known as they deserve to be. In fact, the book he sent me has become a rarity.

In *Scribners* for March 1927 I expressed dissent from some pronunciations preferred by Fowler; and someone informed him that I had 'attacked' his Dictionary. Inasmuch as I had praised it publicly and privately, he was rather astonished and wrote me the following letter.

HINTON ST. GEORGE
SOMERSET

12 June, 1927

DEAR PROFESSOR PHELPS:

Many thanks for the cuttings from *Scribner*. I was rather alarmed at the news that you "attacked" *Modern English Usage* in the March *Scribner*, and, as I had not seen it, at once sent for a copy. When it came, I was equally relieved to find the "attack" confined to my

BRITISH DIALECT AND AMERICAN VOICES 713

pronunciation—a matter on which much chastisement has made me callous. In pronunciation I am neither on the side of the angels (university professors, that is) nor on the side of the devil (who is the nearest vulgarian), but take my stand with the ordinary (or lazy but civilized) human being.

Yours very truly,

H. W. FOWLER

Fowler's death, 26 December 1933, was a great loss to the world of scholarship and a sharp personal grief to me.

WASHINGTON'S ACCENT

There are questions that interest me, all the more perhaps because of the impossibility of getting an accurate answer. Why did Ben Jonson, with his tremendous size, set out to walk the 400 miles from London to Edinburgh? How much did Doctor Samuel Johnson weigh? Why did Shakespeare stop writing in the prime of life? What was the actual religious belief of the Rev. Robert Herrick and the Rev. Jonathan Swift? (I don't care about Sterne's.) What did Emily Brontë say to her dog Keeper on those long walks?

On 27 September 1907 I received the following letter from Arnold Daly, the actor-manager, written from New York.

DEAR PROFESSOR:

I am going to ask a favor of you—another favor I should say, as I am your debtor in the past.

I am rehearsing a short play concerning George Washington, just before or at the time when he was lieutenant in the Virginia Militia, and I am anxious to know if he spoke with a Virginian accent. Did the Southerners have the peculiar soft accent in those days that they use now? I can't find any authority for or against it, and I shall be greatly obliged to you, if you know of any.

Hoping you will pardon me for troubling you, I am,

Very truly yours,

ARNOLD DALY

Thirty years later I wrote to Miss Eugenia Lee of Augusta, a student in Virginia. She gave me the information that Washington spoke like an English gentleman with a voice somewhat affected by the Virginia *patois*.

I have often wished that American women would ponder carefully on Lear's description of the voice of Cordelia. I am very glad to print this verse-letter sent me by an American living in Paris.

LINES INDITED BY A GROUCHY AMERICAN LIVING IN PARIS

A pretty mid-west maiden with a smile
As lovely as a flower, called today—
Niece of an oldtime friend—smart, charming, gay,
But oh, the voice! As rasping as a file!
And when she mentioned *aunt* and called her *ant*
My impulse was to kick her in the pant.

A very little thing you say? But, man,
It's little things that cause most irritation.
Why *should* we be so careless as a nation!
Why not Ameri- (not Amurri-) can?
We're fine! Just add a modulated voice
And gods and little fishes will rejoice.

A reasonable respect for spoken English
Won't make us climb a high pedantic steeple.
Our language has a glamour which our people
All seem to do their damnedest to extinguish.
Our slang's piquant as catsup; I decry it
Not as a condiment but an entire diet.

So having spent much vitriolic juice
I add a milk-and-water: What's the Use!

PETER NITWIT

It is said that the late Andrew Lang wrote so many books that he kept unfinished manuscripts in various rooms in his house, and then continued writing a book in the room that seemed at the moment to be most comfortable. Well, it might be a good idea to have a dictionary in every room.

Shakespeare would have enjoyed reading dictionaries. He loved words as men love things of beauty and grandeur, and he loved words as men love children and pet animals. He loved to play with them, in every kind of fantastic pun, one word always suggesting another. It is interesting to read *Love's Labour's Lost* exclusively from that point of view.

78

ST. JOHN ERVINE

I FIRST had the pleasure of meeting Mr. St. John Ervine when he came to Yale to lecture in 1916. I had read a number of his novels, *Mrs. Martin's Man*, *Alice and Her Family*, and other books. He wrote one novel about the War and to please his mother said that he put no swearing into it.

It was a play by St. John Ervine that established the fame and fortune of the Theatre Guild in New York. This organization had high artistic aims and low funds, and its first performances were financial failures.

One day a gentleman walking around New York glanced at a window of Brentano's book shop, and there saw among other books *John Ferguson*. He remembered that he had met the author in England at some kind of debate, I think, and merely out of curiosity he went in and bought this printed play. There it lay for any manager in the world to use. He took it to the Theatre Guild. They decided to produce it; it was an enormous success. It ran steadily all that spring and through the hot summer and during most of the following season. They were fortunate in having Dudley Digges to act the part of Caesar, but the whole production was admirable, and I don't believe the play could have failed, even if it had been poorly produced and badly acted. It is one of the best plays of the Twentieth Century.

The Theatre Guild followed up this success by another play by Mr. Ervine, *Jane Clegg*, in which Dudley Digges and Margaret Wycherley took the leading parts. This was again both an artistic and a financial success. An amusing

716

thing happened during the rehearsal of this piece. Somewhere in the course of the play one of the characters makes
a remark to the effect that if a person has lost a leg he feels
pain in the vanished member if bad weather approaches,
and when in the rehearsal the character spoke that line, a
voice from the darkened auditorium said, 'I know now
this is not true.' For when Mr. Ervine wrote the play he
had both legs, and when the play was produced he had lost
one in the World War.

I asked him one day, 'Which would you rather have, the
ability to write plays minus a leg, or to have both legs
without that creative ability?' He replied without hesitation, 'Oh, I would much rather have one leg and be a
dramatist; yet I do miss the other leg.'

When Mr. and Mrs. Ervine came to our house in New
Haven on the occasion of the lecture he delivered at the
University, our admiration ripened immediately into af-
fection, and an unclouded, intimate friendship resulted.

We met occasionally, both in England and in America;
in 1935 Mrs. Thomas Hardy was kind enough to take my
wife and me by motor to the house of Mr. and Mrs. Ervine at Seaton in Devonshire. They had a magnificent cat
which added to the pleasure of our visit. Mr. Ervine,
greatly to my surprise, told me that he was writing a
biography of William Booth, founder of the Salvation
Army. When this book appeared, I found it one of the
most thrilling, inspiring biographies I had ever read.

For one year Mr. Ervine came to New York and was
drama critic on the *New York World*. That was the era of
prohibition, and although Mr. Ervine is not a total ab-
stainer, he announced that during his entire stay in the
United States he would not touch liquor because to do
so was against the law of the land. This was in such contrast to the habits and declarations of most visitors from
Europe that it deserves to be recorded. As a drama critic

Mr. Ervine was severe. He aroused considerable hostility, but his judgements were invariably honest and sincere and based on a thorough knowledge of the history of drama and the necessities of society. A year after this, his own play *The First Mrs. Fraser* was produced in New York, and I think a number of persons who had been angered by his very frank criticisms hoped that the play might be a failure. It was, however, a prodigious success and ran a whole year to capacity houses.

Mr. Ervine's books and plays are all good, but he is even better than his writings. His personality has an extraordinary charm. I should like to travel around the world with him.

In an article in the London *Observer*, he lamented because there was no word to describe the citizens of the U.S.A. He thought Canadians objected to our being called Americans. I heard an Englishman addressing an audience in England; he said in his speech that he 'landed in Quebec, travelled in Canada for a while and then in America.' Our Ambassador in England is called the American Ambassador. The word American is convenient and carries no assumptions.

But if we consider that many Canadians and Mexicans and South Americans really object to the term Americans as descriptive of the people of the United States, and if we also remember that the British usually speak of our country as The States, why not call all inhabitants of the U.S.A. simply Statesmen?

9, ARCADE HOUSE,
TEMPLE FORTUNE,
N.W.4
31st July, 1920

MY DEAR PHELPS:
   Your letter of the 17th of July has just this moment come to hand, and as I am going off to Scotland on Tuesday for a month and have just completed my rewriting of "The Wonderful Visit" which John

Barrymore is to do, I feel like writing to my friends . . . the kind of writing I like above all others. It is good to know that you like The Foolish Lovers. I think myself that the first 100 pages of it are better than what follows. As a whole, the book is a disappointment to me because I had hoped it would be a much bigger one. It was begun in France, interrupted by the March, 1918, offensive and by my being wounded, and was written at odd intervals, between operations, in hospital and out of it, and then abandoned for a while and finished in a great hurry before going to America. That, you will see, is hardly the best way in which to write a book. I was afraid it would smell of ether and surgery, but I hope I have kept surgeon's mess out of it.

I do not take the London Mercury, though I saw the review of my book. It was sent to me by the clippings agency. The Mercury is a curious production. Jack Squire, who edits it, is a very able man and an accomplished writer, but his judgment of other writers is remarkably bad. He was literary editor of the New Statesman until recently and for a while edited a paper called Land and Water. His own contributions to these papers invariably were well-done and nearly always of great interest. . . .

He is a man of curious antipathies and also of very strong and steadfast friendships. In appearance, he is the last word in eccentricity and decadence, but in mind he is the last word in conservatism. I have not seen him for some years, but when I last saw him, one might have imagined him as the original of the comic cartoonist's picture of a Bolshevist. Yet in mind he is almost a reactionary. He is, however, devoted to his friends and is I think an exceedingly good comrade. . . .

Squire is really a meritable person, with a genuine love and knowledge of letters, and, as I say, with an immense capacity for devoted friendship.

What you say of the reference to Hardy and the Nobel Prize appeals particularly to me. I deeply resent the attitude of many of these whippersnappers whose behaviour to America is that of immensely superior persons to totally uninformed people. Most of them are people who have never been to America and are resentful of the fact that they have not been invited there to lecture. They are generally impertinent persons, given to showing-off, and are mentally and spiritually third-rate. Most of them, when they say "America" merely mean "Ezra Pound" and it is not very easy to like Ezra Pound. I think you may discount nine-tenths of the superior attitude to America on that ground . . . anti-Poundism . . . and the remaining tenth to pure pique or ignorance!

Israel Zangwill introduced me to Heifetz when he was here lately . . . a calm, immovable lad, whose face was the nearest approach to the mask which rejoices the heart of Gordon Craig which I have seen on any human being. Why don't you write to the Mercury in the sense of your letter to me, so far as Hardy and the musical criticism are concerned. Don't trouble about me. I can bear that sort of thing with ease, but the other matters are of importance. These infants do not realize the harm they do. I consider that any man who makes mischief between England and America is a criminal. I believe and always will believe that if the Anglo-Saxon peoples can keep the peace, they can make the rest of the world keep it.

I hope you are both well. I sent a copy of my novel to Mrs. Phelps about a fortnight or three weeks ago . . . to New Haven. I hope she has received it. Thank you for sending the cuttings. It was most kind of you. I look forward to seeing you again when I return to America. My wife sends her regards to you both.

Sincerely

St. John Ervine

I first saw Sir John Squire, or 'Jack,' as he is universally called, when he, accompanied by Mr. A. P. Herbert, paid a visit to New Haven, not to lecture but to see the University. Mr. Herbert, as everyone ought to know, has long been on the staff of *Punch*, has written many novels and other books, and is a Member of Parliament for Oxford University. In talking with him he said the thing that astonished him most in American universities was the terrific competition for editorial places on the college papers; for at Yale University the competition for the editorial board of the *Yale Daily News* is so severe that it is probable that the students trying for it will never work so hard again, no matter what may be their future careers. Mr. Herbert said that at Oxford University the greatest difficulty was to induce anyone to have anything to do with the University papers. He said that he went around in the various colleges vainly attempting to find someone who would take the job. After Mr. Herbert was elected to Parliament he published an original, humorous, and scholarly little book called *What a Word*. This is one of the most valuable books on good English usage that I have ever seen; and everyone who thinks he writes or speaks correct English will, in reading it, learn something to his disadvantage. In speaking of the immense usefulness of Latin, Mr. Herbert called attention to an American newspaper heading

VETERANS' BONUS VETOED

reminding us that all three words are Latin. Everything that Mr. Herbert says and writes is original; his murder-stories are different from those written by anyone else.

I was a subscriber to the *London Mercury* during the entire administration of Squire; it pleased me to know that there was one monthly magazine in the world devoted exclusively to literature and the fine arts, without a single word on politics. Squire himself has written much good poetry, amazingly clever parodies, and one of the most diverting autobiographies I have ever read. He is, as Mr. Ervine points out, an extraordinarily interesting personality.

MARINE COTTAGE,
BEER,
EAST DEVONSHIRE
24th February, 1921

MY DEAR PHELPS:

I came down here to recover from the fatigue of very long and difficult rehearsals of "The Wonderful Visit" which has been a failure over here. I have never seen such devastating notices of any play as this one has had from the critics. However, that is all part of the fortune of war, and I hope I can take my kicks with as much fortitude as I try to bear my favours.

The Granville-Barkers live near us here—we are going there to tea to-day with Mrs. H.G. Wells and Frank Swinnerton who are staying with us. This cottage is not our own house, but we hope some day to have a home of our own in the village which is the scene of the Devon parts of " Changing Winds." The trouble is that all who live here are afflicted with what seems to be an incurable longevity, and the houses for which we hanker are slow to become vacant.

I went to see Thomas Hardy at Dorchester ten days ago, and found him very serene. It is a wonderful thing to see an old man of eighty producing poetry of such quality that young men must sometimes feel dubious about the worth of youth.

Please give my good wishes to Mrs. Phelps and be assured yourself of my gratitude and friendship,

Yours sincerely,

ST. JOHN ERVINE

HONEY DITCHES, SEATON, DEVON
29th July, 1935

MY DEAR BILLY,

I need not tell you that your praise of *God's Soldier* is gratifying to me. If ever anybody wrote a book "for no reward," as the rebel says in Lady Gregory's *The Rising of the Moon*, I'm the man. I shall be lucky if it earns me what it cost me in research alone. But although I'm not indifferent to money—I've yet to meet the author who is!—I have the natural desire of every writer to produce something in total indifference to the profit it may make; and God's Soldier satisfies me in that respect at least. I *liked* writing it, and felt lonely when it was finished. I'd do it again, if there was the need, even if I were to be told that I'd lose money heavily. The conviction that impressed itself on my mind, while I was interviewing Army officers for the book, was that efficiency by itself is not enough. There must also be spirit. Spirit, indeed, is more important than efficiency; for the spiritually-minded man will make the best of a bad job, whereas the merely efficient man won't make anything of it: he will be too disgusted with its badness. What the S.A. badly needs is a young General—not an old woman of almost seventy—whose heart is a furnace. It has hundreds of highly efficient officers, all of them good men at desks, but it needs another William Booth, a man with the saint's concentration on essentials and indifference to mere irrelevances.

Opinions of the Epilogue vary considerably. To me it is the climax of Booth's work. If he had not run so often to lawyers, that awful deposition might never have occurred. He lost virtue in legality. Bramwell was badly abused in 1929, and treated as a mere placeholder and profit-seeker, a parent ambitious for his children, but he was a man convinced that his father's system was also his Father's system: that God had inspired William Booth and that any departure from William Booth's system must bring ruin in its trail. That is the point that is still elaborately ignored by those who, though they are now uneasy about the part they played in his deposition, are bemused with nonsense about democratic organisation. How can you democratise the Almighty?

My religious views are not orthodox. Far from it. I find that when I read the Apostle's Creed, I stop at "I believe in God!" That's as far as I can get without arguing or qualifying. I share Dean Inge's belief that Christianity is a life to be lived rather than a creed to be believed, and I think that it would be enough for all of us if we reduced our creeds to the Founder's assertion that we should love God and our neighbour as ourselves. Everything that is important is in that. All else is perplexity. You will scarcely believe me when I tell you that the town of Dornoch, in Scotland, at this moment is shaken to its core because a Provost gave a children's party at Christmas and little boys and girls were allowed to dance together. The elders of the Provost's Church have solemnly suspended the Provost! . . . If I were God, I'd dump the whole lot in hell. Don't these people ever read their Bible? Are they incapable of realising the geniality of Jesus, his mateiness, his ease in any company, the pleasure his mere presence in a house gave to its occupants, how quick he was to join in the fun? I mean, Billy, that the man who turned up at a wedding feast in Cana, and, finding his host in a jamb about wine, immediately got him out of it, was not the sort of man who would have turned sulky about a children's Christmas dance. Please don't suppose from this that I'm one of those flabby people who are tolerant of everything. I'm not. But when I'm intolerant, I try to be intolerant about something that matters and not about trifles or harmless things. As a small boy in Ulster, I could not bring myself to believe that God, who had made the Universe, would fly into a rage if he saw me playing marbles on Sunday, and I suspected that my elders who said he *would*, were attributing to him their own mean natures.

But I must not inflict any more of this stuff on you who know these things better than I do. Nora and I send our love to you both.

Yours ever,

ST. JOHN ERVINE

MY DEAR BILLY,

An old play of mine, *Anthony and Anna* is in rehearsal at the moment and will be performed in London about the beginning of November. The bloody Government having heard of this, has announced its intention of holding a General Election which will do no play any good, but thank God the King has had the decency to arrange for his son's wedding to take place about the same time, so we shall have two rumpuses simultaneously instead of two separately, which would have about completed our ruin.

Yours ever,

ST. JOHN ERVINE

I had written asking him if the hymn *There are no flies on Jesus* was ever sung by the Salvation Army, as several persons said they had heard it. St. John Ervine is surely the only man not in the Army who had actually read every number of their periodical *The Warcry*.

MY DEAR BILLY,

I've never heard of that hymn, and I feel certain it exists only in somebody's imagination. The number of people who tell you that they know *positively* this, that or the other makes me wonder why Ananias was singled out for summary treatment. When a man assures me that he *knows for a fact* so-and-so, I say to myself, "Damned liar!! . . ." At the risk of being called one myself, I want to say "I know for a fact you're telling lies!"

But supposing there had been such a hymn, what's wrong with it? Isn't "There are no flies on Jesus" merely a colloquial rendering of Galatians vi, 7: "Be not deceived; God is not mocked: for whatsoever a man soweth, that shall he also reap." There was a very popular padre in the War who once said to the Tommies, "Don't you chaps run away with the idea that God's a bloody fool!" A number of refined persons were extremely shocked, but the Tommies loved the man and instantly perceived his point. Supposing a simple preacher in a village in America said to a congregation of rustics, "You can't put anything over on God!" would anybody in his senses suppose him to be blasphemous or even vulgar. He would surely be talking to them in the language they understood, the language that most vividly conveyed to their minds the thought he was trying to express. Shaw's *Blanco Posnet* puts the argument, I think, with great force. We Protestants rejected Latin from our religious services, in spite of its manifold advantages, such as its universality, because we wished to have them rendered in language "understanded of the people." Well, there are varieties of ways of understanding language, and although a hymn, with "There are no flies on Jesus" is not likely to move you or me, there must be millions of people to whom it instantly and more vividly than any other form of words expresses what Paul said to the Galatians.

There is a passage in *God's Soldier* where I describe Booth's attitude towards those who charged his soldiers with calling for three cheers for Jesus Christ. They hadn't, in fact, done so, but Booth rightly retorted to their accusers, "Why shouldn't they call for cheers for Christ!" and thereafter, I have been told, he himself often invited a meeting to give them. That's what I call turning the enemy's guns against him.

I remember, when I was new to London, hearing a very delicate-minded High Anglican expressing horror because some Nonconformists, during a General Election in this country, sang a hymn which began with the words:

> Take my vote and let it be
> Consecrated, Lord, to Thee.

Wasn't it shocking? the genteel Anglican asked, and "No, it isn't," I replied. (As you know I am a coarse-grained fellow!) He practically called me a blasphemer when I said that this hymn seemed to me entirely religious. Here was a man humble and devout enough to ask God to show him how to cast his vote at an election, so that it should result in the greatest possible good. I saw nothing irreligious or vulgar in that. Indeed, I recommended the refined Anglican to take the hymn to heart.

The fact is, Billy, this is the sort of thing Jesus himself was always doing. *God's Soldier* was reviewed in *The New Statesman* by a most refined person, one Raymond Mortimer. He thought the book a dull one and found fault with Booth for his vulgarity. Jesus was never vulgar, he said. I wonder what Mortimer would have said about Him if he had been a contemporary of Jesus. I have a feeling he would have called him a low-class ranter who went about the country railing against the authorities and filling the minds of common people with sensational thoughts about the coming kingdom. He would certainly have found fault with Him and have called him a brawling cad for kicking up a row in the Temple. If I may judge what Mortimer's actions would have been then by what they are now, he would certainly have been on the side of the exquisites of the time, and more likely to be sharing the opinions of the Sanhedrim or the Romans than those of the Galilean . . . unless, of course, he was living in Jerusalem's Bloomsbury, when he would have canted in terms of Virginia Woolf.

I have just read an extraordinarily good book, called *Jesus*, by Professor Charles Guignebert, Professor of The History of Christianity in the Sorbonne, which has been translated into English by Professor S. H. Hooke, Professor of Old Testament Studies in the University of London. If you haven't read it, and it is not available to you in America, let me send it to you. I am under so many obligations to you, chiefly for your friendship, that I'd like to give the book to you for Christmas.

I've had a very busy time since we met. I have been appointed again Shute Lecturer in the Art of the Theatre at the University of Liverpool—I held the office twelve years ago—and I have composed the five lectures I am to deliver under the general title of "Present Time Tendencies in the Theatre." Then I am to give three lectures in November, under the title of "Adventures in Drama" to the Royal Institution, and another, entitled "Propaganda and the Playwright," as part of my duty as Professor of Dramatic Literature at the Royal Society of Literature. The lot are written. In addition to these lectures, I shall be dashing up and down the country, just like you, lecturing here, there and everywhere. Somehow, I must manage to write another Ulster play I have in my mind and get rid of ideas that have been forming in my head for a long time in a book to be called "Faith at Fifty." So the winter will be fierce.

Nora's name, by the way, is a contraction of her proper name, "Leonora," so the Irish version, "Norah," has no relation to her. She sends you both her love. So do I.

Yours ever,

ST. JOHN ERVINE

I have since been informed by the leading officers of the Salvation Army that the hymn *Flies* was never sung or used anywhere by the Army.

HONEY DITCHES, SEATON, DEVON
27th January 1936

MY DEAR BILLY,

I have two causes for gratitude to you: one, your note, which arrived this morning, with its extract from one to you written by Professor Carlton Wells; the other, your extraordinarily interesting article on Mark Twain in the last *Yale Review*—a very good number, by the way. Wilbur Cross amazingly keeps up the quality of the *Review*. I like a man who *edits* his paper. Wilbur Cross seems to do that. When I was in New York, all the editors seemed to edit their papers from their bedrooms. They telephoned all day long. Dial-fiends, I called them. The damned fellows didn't know or didn't do their jobs. They lay in bed all morning and telephoned. But Cross obviously works at his job. The result is a readable review—a rare thing these days. Your contribution to the Winter Number was as good an article on a writer as I have read for a long time. How odd that Twain should have thought little of Dickens! Meredith, I remember, made what seems to me a fatuous remark when he said that *Pickwick Papers* would not live, and gave as his reason, the fact that it is the essence of Cockneydom. I should have thought that a book which contained the essence of anything had a fair prospect of immortality. It must gall Meredith in heaven to hear that Dickens is always "out" of our public libraries, while *his* works are always "in," mouldering on the shelves. Men of genius appear less able than ordinary people to recognise genius. Tolstoy thought little of Shakespeare, Ibsen thought Tolstoy was a fool, and Strindberg foamed at the mouth every time Ibsen's name was mentioned! . . .

That, I suppose, is natural: the genius is so busy seeing his own point of view, that he either cannot see any other person's or is annoyed with it when he can. It is a comic reflection that one has to be an ordinary person to recognise variety of genius or see more than one point of view. But I should have thought that Twain would have loved Dickens. I shall break my heart if anybody tells me that Dickens could see nothing in Mark.

Has anybody, besides me, pointed out that the great American authors, Emerson, Walt Whitman, Mark Twain, Edgar Allan Poe and the rest, all belong to the period of your history when your people could be called homogeneous? Lincoln belonged to that homogeneous age. There hasn't been *greatness* in American literature since its people became heterogeneous, and there won't be until they become homogeneous again. Cleverness, yes, any amount of it—glimpses even, of genius—as in Sinclair Lewis, Susan Glaspell, Willa Cather, but genius itself, no. That woman, Emily Dickinson, had a hint of it, and I suspect that Edna St. Vincent Millay belongs to the great tradition, but I'm waiting, as I am sure you are, for the authentic genius. Eugene O'Neill looked at first as if he might be the man, but alas, alas! . . . All that dreary half-highbrow stuff about masks and psycho-analysis. I'd give the whole of *Strange Interlude* and *Mourning Becomes Electra* for the poetic spirit that suffused *Beyond the Horizon*. But I've not lost hope of O'Neill. The poet in him is not dead, but snoring. Why don't you wake him up?

Do you ever see Edna St. Vincent Millay? I met her once, on my first visit to America, but I remember her very vividly: a wispy, pale girl with a thin body, but a vigorous mind and an assured manner. John Drinkwater and she and I were to speak at one of those interminable dinners in which your countrymen delight: dinners that go on and on and on, with innumerable courses and terrible bouts of oratory. There were thirteen speakers that night, and the only comfort I had was that John Drinkwater was the thirteenth. I was the twelfth. My God, how bored I was. But in the middle of the orgy of speeches, Edna Millay rose up to speak, and she sauced everybody. My heart leaped within me. Thank heaven, I said to myself, somebody's being cheeky! She was wearing a white dress, and she looked pathetically young, but she talked well, *and she's a poet*. Hardy liked her work. I once heard him say so.

Professor Carlton Wells' reference to letter-writing interests me. I like writing letters, and I think the modern habit of scribbling notes is deplorable. We're cheating posterity when we send the barest lines to our friends for we are robbing those who come after us of all hope of intimacy with us. I suppose our letters are poor because we take for granted everybody's familiarity with ordinary events, through the newspaper and the radio (We call it the wireless). We do not say what we think of current events because we assume that current events are everybody's knowledge and there is no need, therefore, to mention them. But supposing all reference to King George's death were omitted from private correspondence on the ground that everybody knows he is dead, how little posterity would glean from newspapers of the private person's feelings about him. We loved our king. I can't hope to make you realise how much we loved him, how very dear that simple, sincere, unaffected English gentleman was to his people, but you'll have seen the newspaper reports of the way in which great crowds have stood in queues five miles long to pay their tribute of respect to his dead body. Queen Victoria was a venerable being, almost a legend to us; King Edward was a likeable, human person, but we weren't sure of ourselves with him; King George, however, commanded both our respect and our affection. We liked him and we admired him. Insensibly he grew into our love, and we never saw the old man without pleasure. I think his life is a remarkable proof of the way in which upright character prevails. His early manhood was overshadowed by the fact that he was not the heir; then when the Duke of Clarence died, he was in the shadow of the Queen and of his father. Edward VII was so popular that there seemed no hope of any popularity for George, and the facts of his reign, at the beginning, were not auspicious for him. The War might have wiped him out. After it was over, his son's popularity looked as if it were going to throw him into another and deeper shade. But somehow, nobody can tell exactly how, the King came through his oppressions and troubles to our inalienable love. There isn't a taint of insincerity in the demonstrations of that love at this moment. The King's death was a bitter blow to us. We did not believe that he was going to die, and the swiftness with which the end came was profoundly shocking.

Did I ever tell you the story of the little Elizabeth and her grandfather. He was very fond of the child, and had her to play with him while he was convalescing after that bad illness. One day she was naughty and refused to be good. "Very well," the King said to her, "if you won't behave properly I'll leave the room!" She made no sign of amendment, and the King walked away. He had scarcely gone when the child cried out, in an agitated voice, "Grandpa England! Grandpa England!" and the King came running back, fearing she had hurt herself. "You forgot to shut the door after you!" she said when he had returned.

King Edward the Eighth has started well. Everything he has done, however small, seems to have been right. I think he'll be a very fine king, entirely different from his father, but no less liked. The first thing he did after his father's death was to have all the clocks at Sandringham, hitherto kept half an hour fast, put right. I shall not be cowardly enough to refuse to see something symbolic in that act.

But talking about letters, I remember in the War asking to be allowed to censor the letters of the men in my battalion. I thought I should learn from them what the private soldiers thought about the War. They never mentioned it, except to wish it were over. All their references were to small domestic events. "So glad you went to Aunt Pollie's on Sunday and had a nice tea!" Things like that, much more important and much more enduring than war. I'd give the world—wouldn't you?—for a bundle of letters, not intended for publication, written by Anne Hathaway? Or a bundle from Shakespeare to his friends, to his wife, to his daughters and his son?

I didn't intend to burden you with this effusion when I started to write you, but I felt in the mood to write—one ought not to write letters unless one is in the mood—and your letters always provoke me to say something.

Our love to you both.

Yours ever,

ST. JOHN ERVINE

P.S. A friend in Liverpool has just sent me a cutting from a newspaper published in that city. It seems that young women between 16 and 20, aspiring to be secretaries, had to sit for general knowledge examination. One of the questions asked was "Who is St. John Ervine?" Two of the answers were "one of the men who attempted to climb Mount Everest, but never returned," and "he lived a long time ago and was canonised by the Pope."

HONEY DITCHES, SEATON, DEVON
23 Septr. 1937

MY DEAR BILLY:

About six weeks ago, we both drove over to Dorchester to see Florence Hardy, and found her lying in a tent on the lawn, longing to die. She has extraordinary fortitude and is the calmest invalid I have ever seen. But she wants to die quickly, and is appalled by the thought of a long drawn death. She told me she had had a letter from you. We talked about Barrie, who had visited her in the London Nursing Home a few days before his death. She says she saw death in his face, but that he seemed to have no notion of anything much being the matter with him, and left her with promises to go to Dorchester to see her. About a week later, he was dead. The failure of *The Boy David* affected him profoundly: a bitter blow to his pride; and I feel that he fell under it and did not try to rise again.

Yes, I'd say I'm a Christian, but I doubt if many Christians would. I can enlist as a disciple of Jesus, the man, but I cannot offer any allegiance to Jesus, the god. The doctrine of his divinity withdraws him from human experience and puts him apart for ever. It was easy for a god to spend thirty years on earth, since that's no time at all in eternity, and anyhow he knew he'd rise again; but a young workman who conceived a great idea and tried to pass it on and was crucified for doing so, catches my love and enables me to believe that if I had enough will and strength I could do what he did or some of what he did. I haven't any hope of ever emulating the activities of an immortal and omnipotent deity.

I begin to feel as if I were the world's crock: one leg, one eye, lungs like bellows, and a periodical bout of lumbago. I went to Port Patrick in Scotland a fortnight ago, hoping that northern air would do me good. It did, and would probably have done more if I had not had the misfortune to travel in the same carriage with one of those female fresh air fiends whose first act on entering a train is to fling open all the windows and doors. She was a big woman, with a weatherbeaten face and excessive feet, and she spent almost the entire journey from London to Scotland in tabulating things in a sort of ledger. Obviously, a busy woman, always going to committees and conferences and reading agenda. I wished her in hell. For I landed at Port Patrick with a streaming cold which did my bronchitic-asthma no good. As I was recovering from the cold, my back decided to have its mid-term bout of lumbago. So I was in a bloody state. I have had singularly few illnesses in my life, nothing beyond infantile complaints and few of those, and I'm not accustomed to all this sickness. It looks as if the Almighty were trying to cram into one year of my life the illnesses that other people spread over a lifetime—Sorry for that bad blob!— but I can't say I like the experience much.

And now I must hop off to a rehearsal. Love to you both from us both.

Yours sincerely,

ST. JOHN ERVINE

HONEY DITCHES
31st May 1937

MY DEAR BILLY:

I've never known anybody so rebellious against old age as G.B.S. is, nor have I ever known anyone who fended it off so long and so successfully. But it is getting the better of him now. Mrs. Shaw, who is eighty, looks years younger than he is, although she is his junior only by about twelve months, and she is remarkably active and alert. So, indeed, is he, but because he has never shown any ageiness before, the few signs that are visible now surprise his friends far more than more numerous signs in other people.

I am interested to hear that you heard the Coronation service so clearly. Two things surprised me about it. One was the strength of the King's voice, a much more pleasing voice than Edward's, which was horridly Cockney. The other was how large a part the Archbishop of Canterbury played in the service. Scarcely anybody else had a word to say, the Queen, indeed, hadn't any lines at all. I think the King ought to have had "a bit of fat" as actors say, somewhere in the middle, a sort of Richard the Second declaration, "I'll be your leader," and the Queen really ought to have been allowed one line. It was Cosmo Gordon Lang's day out.

Why were you surprised at the failure of "Night Must Fall" in America? Apart from its eeriness and the skill with which it was acted, it did not stand examination. It ought to have ended in the second act. If that detective had been up to his job, he would have had the hat box opened—and then the murder would have been out. I'm working on a play at present, and I hope to finish it by the end of July. An old piece of mine, *Anthony and Anna*, has been running now for 646 performances, and seems likely to be good for at least 700. Yet I had a deuce of a job to get it produced.

The animals are all well, and Titus is flattered at being remembered by you. He sends you miaows in greeting. Our love to you both. What, by the way, is the meaning of this "emeritus" stuff? Don't tell me you, who seem to have solved the problem of perpetual motion and eternal youth, have been superannuated—for I won't believe it if you do. I can more readily believe in the old age of Bernard Shaw than I can in the old age of Billy Phelps.

Yours ever,

St. John Ervine

HONEY DITCHES,
SEATON, DEVON
July 25th, 1938

Professor W. Lyon Phelps,
Grindstone City,
Michigan, U.S.A.

My dear Billy,

What a terrible name for a town: Grindstone City. Dickens must have invented it. It certainly does not sound like the name of any city in which you could live, though heaven knows you keep your nose to it, for I have never known so hard a worker as you are. I believe that the fiction of hardworking American men is entirely based on your activities, and that you are the only person in your country who really does a long day at anything. I used to watch the American business men wearing themselves to skin and bone in New York. They sat at lunch so long that I sometimes thought they must have been having all the day's meals at once. They played draughts (or checkers as we call them in Ulster) for an hour. At the end of that time they went to their offices and pretended to be whirlwinds for the rest of the day, and finally were carried home in a semi-comatose condition to their deluded wives who let themselves be humbugged into the belief that their spouses were—what do you call it?—worn to a frazzle and capable of appreciating only one of the less exacting movies. You have a lot to answer for: the deceiving of millions of innocent American women who still believe the terrific lie that their husbands every day exhaust themselves. If one of these trusting females begins to suspect the truth, her husband immediately says, "Why, look at William Lyon Phelps! He's a typical American, and never stops working even at golf!" On the day you die, Billy, the bluff will be called, and the disillusionment of the American woman will begin. The American man will then have to start doing some honest-to-God work or admit that he is one of the world's greatest loafers. The average Englishman does more work in a morning than the average American man does in a day.

I remember when I was in America, asking a publisher to send some books to that charming old lady, Mrs. Cadwallader Jones, the sister of Edith Wharton. Mrs. Cadwallader Jones lived only a few blocks away from the publisher's office, but the delivery of those books took the best part of a week: four days to be exact. I discovered that the parcel had to pass through many departments before it could be delivered, and as far as I could make out, each department had to hold a conference on it. When I returned to London, I asked a friend who is a publisher how long it would take his office to deliver the same number of books the same distance. He said he thought they might take twenty minutes over it! . . . I then told him how deliveries are hustled in New York. That was only one instance of about a dozen dilatory deliveries or incompetently performed jobs of which I had personal experience in New York; and now, when I hear people talking of American hustle and expedition, I just lie back and laugh. You, in fact, are the only American known to me who has ever hustled in his life, and if it had not been for you, the legend could never have been spread. Why, I once worked under an editor in New York who edited his paper from his bedroom!

We get along here. Alarums and excursions are reported every fifteen minutes. War is about to be declared; war has been declared; war has been postponed; war has been cancelled. But somehow we contrive not to take much notice of the sensationalists. All our pacifists have become aggressively militaristic—those of them, that is to say, who have safely passed the military age—and they go about boiling their blood all day long. That is *all* they do with their blood. Gentlemen who were conscientious objectors in 1914–18 are now howling in hordes for the effusion of other people's blood and getting themselves into quite a state because Chamberlain won't instantly consent to general slaughter. Why don't they show the rest of us a good example by going to Spain and shedding some of *their* blood? They might at least get it off the boil! . . . My own feeling is one of horror at the cruelty that seems to prevail in the world. Here we are in an age of what is solemnly called progress . . . and yet there is as much brutality in our lives as there was in the lives of our remotest ancestors, if, indeed, there is not more.

My conviction is that the next great fight mankind will have to make if it is to save itself from extinction will be against the State. Its tyranny steadily increases. We have even reached the stage at which young men who believe themselves to be high-minded, but are in reality degenerate, advocate the extinction of the individual and his entire submersion in the community. I have lately read one of those futile clever-clever books, in which assertion is assumed to be argument, called *A Short History of the Future* by John Langdon-Davies, in which the ant, which apparently has not altered itself in the slightest degree for ages and ages, is held up to human admiration. It is what a man should desire to be. The whole object of life should be to perpetuate ourselves. That object secured, there is nothing else for us to desire. There are to be specialised breeders on whom the rest of the community will wait. The Heap is what matters. The idea may seem fantastic and farfetched as New York, but I fear that a great many people may be brutally butchered in refuting it, if, indeed, its refutal is achieved. It does not appear to matter who triumphs, the Fascist or the Communist, the result will be the same, the exaltation of the State, which will not only be permitted, but encouraged, to commit acts for which individuals would very rightly be hanged. I cannot understand why it is wrong for me to steal or commit murder, but right for the State to commit one or the other.

Hitler, at this moment, is stealing the property of the Jews in Germany and Austria. If he were to steal it for his own profit, he would be run in by the police, but because he calls himself the State, he can steal it with impunity and amid resounding cheers from the young who, as always, are the stoutest upholders of oppression and brutal tyranny. (How did this legend get about that the young are generous-minded and full of high ideals? If it were not for the middle-aged and the old, liberty would long ago have died).

The tragically farcical fact about all this State worship is that what is called the State is only a gang of political thugs who have somehow contrived to seize authority and who call themselves the State. Hitler is the State; Mussolini is the State; Stalin is the State. In other words, individualism seems to have gone mad. One person, calling himself the community or the spirit of the people, arrogates to himself the right to do what he likes, which means, of course, that the rest of us have to do what he likes. And that is called the Community Spirit! . . . I have lived in England now for thirty-seven years, and I think that Job, in comparison with the English, was positively impatient. There are times when I think they are the world's fatheads, willing to put up with anything, even their own cooking; but those times do not last long, and the conviction returns to my mind that the British people are undoubtedly chosen of God. I would rather be poor in England than rich in America. The longer I live in England, the more certain I feel that it is the only country in the world that is fit to be inhabited. After that outburst, Billy, you will probably want to hit me on the nose.

I doubt if I shall go to America again. The idea of any travelling appeals to me less and less. We all rush about far too much, and I can't see that we are any the better for it. I believe more and more that Pascal was right when he said that all our troubles come from our inability to sit still in one room. I meet people who are perpetually flinging themselves about the earth, and all they gain from the performance is a fit of the jitters. The only thing that gets me really going is any attempt to interfere with the right of the individual to the utmost freedom of action and speech and thought that is compatible with the equal freedom of other people. I'll shed oceans of gore in defence of that.

We're very happy in this house. The garden has grown very lovely, though it is still a young one, and we have continual happiness in the thought that we made it, that everything it contains was put into it by us—even the grass; for it was a ploughed field when we bought it.

Titus continues his highly individual life—no dictator will ever sub-
due cats—but my dog, Jock, who was my constant companion, is
dead. He was killed by a passing lorry. The inevitable blasted errand
boy left the gate open, and Jock thought he would cross the road to
savour the smells in a field opposite our house. Unluckily, two large
dogs were in that field and they made a rush at Jock who hurriedly
ran back to the road and collided with the lorry. That was the end of
nine years of devotion. I used to sneer at dog lovers and was fright-
fully sarcastic over John Galsworthy who was devoted to his dogs;
but I became as fond of Jock as the most infatuated dog lover could
be, and his death was a blow to me. I could not have believed that
I would feel the death of an animal so much as I felt his. He was a
dear companion, and I still miss him though he has been dead since
Easter. Isn't it extraordinary this friendship and affection between
men and dogs? It is one of the most unaccountable things in life.
Jock showed no distress when his Jill was killed. He sniffed at her
once and then turned away, apparently unperturbed. Yet when I
went to London and left him behind, he was full of resentment and
lay about the house, brooding. There must be some good in human
beings, since dogs like them so much, or is it that dogs have no sense?

Leonora sends you both her love. So do I.

Yours ever,

ST. JOHN ERVINE

Bernard Shaw has been dangerously ill, but is now much better and
seems likely to continue to improve.

79

'AS I LIKE IT'

On 10 February 1922, Dr. Will Howe, of the firm of Charles Scribner's Sons in New York, came to New Haven, with the suggestion that I write a monthly article on books for *Scribner's Magazine*. I promised to consider this, and a few days later, meeting by appointment Mr. Charles Scribner and Mr. Howe at lunch at New York, I consented. I made only two conditions. I was to write anything I pleased, and nothing I wrote should be altered or 'edited' in the office of the magazine. Although the magazine was financed by the publishing firm of Scribners, I was not to consider that, but was to treat their books with no more consideration than those from other publishers. These two conditions were immediately accepted. I was asked to suggest a title for my articles, and I chose *As I Like It*.

Some years later on a school examination in New York, in reply to a question 'Who wrote *As You Like It*?' the candidate replied, William Lyon Phelps. I wish I had.

My articles began in the number of the magazine for September 1922, and appeared regularly in every monthly number, until September 1936, when the management and policy of the magazine were changed.

In my farewell in the number for September 1936, I said:

From September, 1922 to September, 1936, inclusive, I have never once been asked to review any book published by Scribners, nor has any written opinion of mine on any subject been altered in the office of the magazine. I suggested the title AS I LIKE IT, and it has been just that and nothing else. I appreciate more than I can say the courtesy and fairness consistently shown me by my employers. I have served under two editors, Robert Bridges and his successor, Alfred Dashiell. With both of these men, and with their entire office staffs, my relations have been not only cordial, but ideal. I shall never forget the kindness with which I have been treated.

I wish to thank also those who have written me letters which have contributed so much to the value of my monthly articles; these letters have come from every part of the world; many of them have been written by distinguished authors, all have contained either valuable information or interesting suggestions. I am deeply grateful to my correspondents.

I wish also to thank the thousands of readers who have done me the honour to read my monthly discussions; no writing that I have done has ever given me more pleasure, and this is largely owing to the immediate and gratifying response from innumerable friends. *Ave atque vale.*

It is true that I never enjoyed writing more than I enjoyed writing these *causeries* during the fourteen years. They attracted the attention of readers and authors in every corner of the world; and the letters from George Santayana, St. John Ervine, Charles Morgan, Sir James Barrie, and many others added immensely to my pleasure.

I made epistolary friendships in every state in the Union and in nearly all foreign countries; so that I look back on these fourteen years with unalloyed delight.

The news of the death of Arthur Nikisch on 23 January depressed me; he was expected to come to America the next season. I have heard all the great orchestra conductors of the last fifty years, and he seemed to me the best. I never saw him with his own orchestra in Leipzig, but I heard him many times in American cities; and in 1912 in conducting at Munich *Die Meistersinger* he revealed new wonders; he raised the orchestra, the singers, and the audience into a land of enchantment.

At Dartmouth College in June I gave a series of lectures on American literature; I had the honour of being associated in this enterprise with the famous American historian, Charles A. Beard. We both lectured every day for over a week. We left on 30 June and made an excursion to Montreal and Quebec, seeing Quebec for the first time. Our room in the Hotel Château-Frontenac overlooked the mighty river. It was interesting to walk about Quebec and find many residents who could not speak English.

On 3 August Mr. E.F.Hey, a piano-tuner from the county town of Bad Axe, came to inspect our Knabe piano, which had been left in our country home in Michigan for several winters. It had been condemned by professional musicians, as half the notes refused to strike. I had endeavoured to induce Mr. Hey to rent me a piano for the summer, but he insisted that if I had a Knabe, it would be a much better instrument than any I could hire from him. In spite of my assertions that my piano was worthless and that he would have the journey for his pains, he travelled 26 miles to look at it. He took out the entrails about ten in the morning, placed them outdoors in the strong sunshine, left them there until the middle of the afternoon, then replaced them in the piano, tuned the instrument, and to our amazement, it was as good as new and has been perfect ever since. I was so astounded by this miraculous resurrection, that I printed in *Scribner's Magazine* an account of what this village piano tuner, in a remote part of Michigan, had accomplished after the instrument had been professionally pronounced dead. I had the satisfaction of finding my account of it copied in journals in every country in Europe, in South Africa, Australia, and New Zealand!

On 7 November the novelist Hugh Walpole made his first visit to Yale and gave a fine lecture on *The Psychology of the Novel*. He stayed at our house and we had much good talk. Of all the British novelists who come to

America to lecture, he is the most accomplished as a public speaker.

In December we went for the first time to Miami, Florida, for the Christmas vacation. There the weather is eternal summer; on the very rare occasions when the thermometer drops to 55 degrees, the public schools close. It is the only place I have been where the fall of night produces no change in temperature; it comes down with velvet softness and without the semblance of chill. In subsequent years we made many visits to Miami, but finally chose Georgia as a more inspiring climate. Miami has summer in January and Georgia in the same month has autumn.

EUGENE O'NEILL

The foremost living American playwright has always allowed his plays to speak for themselves and for his art; he has so far as I know written no articles about the drama and has consistently refused to lecture; his excellent reasons are given in the following letter.

> PEAKED HILL BAR
> PROVINCETOWN, MASS.
> Oct. 27, 1922

MY DEAR PROFESSOR PHELPS:

I am very grateful to you for the honor of your invitation but I have never lectured and don't believe I ever will. Frankly, there is a certain prejudice in my mind against it. It seems to me that authors should neither be seen nor heard outside of their work—(not this one, at any rate, for I'm quite certain my plays act better than I ever could—which is faint praise for them indeed!) So, both from the standpoint of personal discretion and of Christian charity toward the audience, I feel bound to decline.

But again, all gratitude to you for the honor of selecting me. I appreciate that immensely and regret that I cannot accept.

Faithfully yours,

EUGENE O'NEILL

I went with my friend, Tom Cushing, to the opening night of his play *La Gringa* 2 Feb. 1927. This play introduced to New York an actress who was in a few years to become universally known. She captivated the audience immediately. In reviewing the play for the papers I spoke in high terms of her beauty and intelligence and received the following letter.

115 WEST 73 STREET,
NEW YORK CITY

MY DEAR MR. PHELPS

A thousand thanks for your lovely note and your kindness at "Town Hall"—I can't tell you how happy I was—praise from you, is praise indeed!! In fact my head has been swelling visibly ever since!

"La Gringa"—alas—Requiescat in Pace—it is hard to please New York, isn't it? I am heartbroken for dear Tom Cushing—he is such a lamb and worked so hard over this.

I hope to have the pleasure of meeting you sometime—and please let me thank you once more. I was very very grateful.

Most sincerely,

CLAUDETTE COLBERT

Monday—the eleventh of February

80

A VISIBLE CHURCH IN AN INVISIBLE TOWN

Looking at a map of Lower Michigan, one will see it is shaped like a mitten on the left hand, with a distinctly marked Thumb. The Thumb-Nail is Huron County, the county town being Bad Axe, and the old railroad terminus being Grindstone; the nearness of the two places inspiring obvious pleasantries. Four miles east of Grindstone is Huron City, once a fairly large and prosperous lumbering village, and now so small that strangers drive through it without seeing it. Many have motored on ten miles in the vain endeavour to find it.

Seventy-five years ago pioneers from Connecticut were very busy there; as payment for making roads in the interior and building long piers into Lake Huron, they received grants of forest lands from the Federal Government. The entire Thumb was covered with superb pine trees, standing like columns in a vast cathedral. The founders of Huron City felled the tall timber, floated the logs down Willow Creek, sawed them in the Huron City sawmills, and loaded the boards on steamers at the Huron City Dock. Then came the devastating forest fire of 1871, which began on the same day as the Chicago conflagration. The prosperous town of Huron City was erased, and the lumbering business received a mortal blow. Still, the hardy men rebuilt the town and carried on as best they could. But the second forest fire of 1881 took the pine trees that were left, and everything in Huron City with them. Once more Huron City was rebuilt; but it soon became clear that the Thumb-Nail and the Thumb itself would be forced to go through the slow and difficult transition from lumbering to agriculture. Thus the people not only left Huron City, but literally took their houses with them. Today Huron City has no railroad, no postoffice, no telegraph—the only buildings are a country store, a Methodist church, a Community House, an unused skating rink, a school, and three or four dwellings. Situated directly on the shore of Lake Huron, with the finest summer climate in the world, neither sultry nor cold, it is an ideal place for a summer home. And as I have spent nearly every summer there for fifty-five years, I ought to know.

Mr. Langdon Hubbard, of Bloomfield, Conn., founded the town in the 'fifties, made roads through the forests, and built the first pier. Eighty years ago he made it possible to have regular religious services. For a long time the school-house served this purpose, but in 1885 Mr. Hubbard made provision for a church edifice, which has been open since that date. The Methodist minister assigned to this 'charge' preaches in three places; in the morning at Redman, eight miles away, in the afternoon at Huron City, and in the evening at Port Hope, where he lives. In the days of horses, this was a serious undertaking; for the roads were never good, even in the best of summer weather, and for the rest of the year they were almost incredibly bad. But with the advent of the Ford Car, all this has been changed. Now we have excellent roads, and the Huron City Church is easily accessible to those who live within a radius of a hundred miles and more.

I wish the following account of a successful experiment might induce summer visitors from city to country elsewhere not to be content with merely taking rest and recreation, but to give as well as receive—to identify themselves with the life of rural communities, and if they have any talent for usefulness, to employ that in summer service. Browning says,

> God uses us to help each other so,
> Lending our minds out.

Many religious people dream of a genuine Christian Community Church, where devout people from various denominations and sects will worship together without any self-consciousness; that is, without being aware that they are doing anything unusual. What ought to be common is extremely rare. Of course there are Community Churches which are little more than Assembly Halls and Forums; it is comparatively easy to unite people on a negative platform; they come together because there is no definite Christian teaching. Many such churches do a vast amount of good in their consecration to social service, relief of the poor, and spiritual elevation. But the more difficult problem is, how are we to get earnest and devoted Presbyterians, Methodists, Baptists, Congregationalists, High and Low Episcopalians, Christian Scientists, and Catholics, to come together in the same building and listen to the Gospel?

Naturally, you say, they won't; it can't be done. It is a pretty dream, desirable in many ways, but beyond the bounds of possibility. Yet in our Huron City Church, to use Kipling's phrase, 'the thing that couldn't has occurred.' Representatives from all the churches mentioned above, together with many others, come cheerfully to Huron City every Sunday afternoon in July, August, and September.

About fifty years ago, at the request of the Methodist minister (for the Huron City Church is a Methodist church, under the control of the Methodists), I occasionally took the pulpit and preached an informal sermon. These substitutions increased in number year after year; and finally, in 1922, with the courteous permission of the Methodist pastor, I took entire charge in summer of the Huron City Church, preaching regularly at three o'clock in the afternoon for thirteen consecutive Sundays.

The automobile had made it unnecessary to seek a good or convenient location for a church; any location will do; if the services are interesting and beneficial, people will come. Ordinarily one might think that with the extensive secularization of Sunday, the most hopeless time to have a church service would be three o'clock. But we hold our services at that hour for two reasons; we do not wish to interfere with any other church whose services are held morning or evening; we take the one time in the day that no one else wants. Furthermore, this makes it possible for clergymen of all denominations to attend our church; we often have in the audience twenty ordained ministers of the gospel. It is interesting to see an Episcopal rector in full uniform sitting with a Baptist evangelist.

I have been asked, 'What do you preach to such a collection of sects? Do you give a literary lecture or a moral talk?' My answer is that I preach only the simple gospel and nothing else; and there being so many members of so many sects in the audience, I leave out non-essentials and dogmas peculiar to individual churches (winds of doctrine) and stick close to the central theme of the New Testament.

No subject is more interesting than religion; the trouble with many ministers is that they preach everything except religion, and wonder why their audiences diminish. I never mention politics and I never mention prohibition and I never discuss either Fundamentalism or Modernism. I remember an earnest Protestant pastor (now with God) who conceived it his duty during an entire Presidential campaign to preach against one of the candidates; the trouble with any minister who has only one idea is that his flock know what he is going to say; they lose interest and stay away. And this man kept it up; after the candidate whom he had opposed was elected, and he with other men at a club was listening to the election returns, he cried out in distress of mind, 'Oh, what shall I do now?' Professor Lounsbury remarked, 'There is only one thing, Doctor, for you to do now; and that is, to preach the gospel.'

In the year 1925, it became necessary to increase the size of our church, which, through the generosity of one man, was accomplished; again, during the winter of 1929–30, with the help of this man and others, we doubled again the size of the edifice. Now we have regular pews for eight hundred people, and by means of chairs, we increase the capacity to one thousand.

During the summer of 1930, by passing around cards once or twice for people to sign, it appeared that there were in our average congregation a score of Roman Catholics, seven or eight Christian Scientists, several hundreds respectively of Methodists, Presbyterians, and Episcopalians, a number of Baptists and Congregationalists, a few Mormons, Unitarians, Jews, and members of other religious denominations. Many motored a hundred miles and more to come to the church. But we are chiefly interested in reaching the resident farmers of the Thumb and their families, who come from every direction. In addition to the people who live and work in the Thumb the year round, there are in July and August 'resorters,' some of whom have cottages seventeen miles away at Harbor Beach and others seven miles away at Pointe aux Barques.

No member of the congregation enjoys this church more than I. As I go into the pulpit and look over that audience of hard-working farmers, their wives and babies, and know that they and many others have given up their Sunday afternoon and motored many miles to be present, I feel a thrill unspeakable.

In one respect our church is like a mediaeval parish church; after the service, the people are in no hurry to leave. They gather around the doors outside in the cool summer air, and exchange news and pleasant gossip. Often a family that used to live in the Thumb and has moved to Detroit, one hundred and thirty miles away, will meet and talk with their old friends and former neighbours. There is no formality about this church and there is no one to greet visitors with a professional smile and handclasp; people enter this building as they enter their own home, knowing there will be neither coldness nor officious effusiveness. Nor are they ever urged to come again; they will come again when they feel like it.

On one occasion immediately after the service, when nearly everyone had gone outside, an over-enthusiastic gentleman came up to the pulpit and said emphatically, 'I want you to know that I'm a Unitarian! I don't care one whoop for the damn dogmas you people believe; but I like this church; it's the first time I've been here; and I want to give fifty dollars to it; so long as you understand I am a Unitarian!' Although his excitement had an alcoholic foundation, he showed his interest in a practical way; for the collections taken during the summer support this church during the barren winter months. He wrote his cheque in a firm hand; I thanked him, and saw him no more. Before adding it to our contributions, however, I made enquiries to see if he could afford it, as I did not wish him to regret his good impulse after his zeal had cooled. I found that he was abundantly able to spare the fifty dollars. Then I sat down and wrote a letter to the most ardent Unitarian in America, Chief Justice William Howard Taft. 'There was a Unitarian in our Methodist Church last Sunday; he seemed abnormally excited, but he was a thorough gentleman, for he contributed fifty dollars.' I immediately received a reply: 'I am not surprised there was a Unitarian in your Methodist Church; and I am not very much surprised that he was excited;

but I am amazed that you got fifty dollars out of him. I never knew any Unitarian who was that much ahead.'

During the summer of 1930, our church received another compliment, equally charming and equally unexpected. As we were assembling a few minutes before three on a brilliantly clear Sunday afternoon, a message was handed to me from Port Austin, a town eight and a half miles distant. It seems that on that very afternoon a professional baseball game had been advertised to begin in Port Austin at the exact hour of our service, but, said the writer of the note, 'There are so many people in our town who want to attend service in the church at Huron City, we are going to postpone the game till a late hour in the afternoon; and won't you announce the fact?' Well, although I have no objection to outdoor games on Sunday, it is not my habit to make such announcements from the pulpit; but this seemed too interesting to pass over. I informed the audience that we had received a great compliment; there were so many persons in Port Austin who wished to come to our church that they thought it best to postpone the ball game; 'and so, you who sacrificed a ball game to come hither, may know that after this service is over, you will still have time to see part of the contest.'

I chronicle this because it is *News*. Talk about the man biting the dog! When summer afternoon church services are given up because too many people want outdoor recreation, that is not news. But to postpone a professional ball game, where some of the players had been brought from Detroit to play, and to postpone it because of a church service nearly nine miles away!

New Year's day 1923 dawned hot and sultry in Miami; temperature of the air at dawn was 77, and the ocean when we went swimming was 73. On returning to New Haven, we found deep snow.

On 13 January before dawn we watched the magnificent spectacle of the occultation of Venus by the moon—the first time it had occurred for forty years.

Having discovered that no public or university library in America possessed a copy of the first edition of Browning's *Pauline* (1833) and having secured one from Mr. Sessler's bookshop in Philadelphia for $1,000, a remarkably low price (one having sold for $17,000), I determined that this should be presented to the Yale University Library formally, with pomp and ceremony. Accordingly, on Browning's birthday, 7 May, at noon I led a procession of my Browning undergraduate students, about four hundred of them marching two by two. We advanced through the Yale Campus to the doors of the Library, where the Librarian, Andrew Keogh, in cap and gown, made an address in response to mine, and received the book amid tremendous cheering from the students. Those who came to scoff remained to cheer. The New York newspapers were highly amused because the students cheered for Browning as they were accustomed to do only at great games of football; and Heywood Broun, in his column, said this explained for the first time why Yale had not been so successful in athletics as in former years. 'They are cheering poetry instead of football.'

Margot Asquith lectured in New York and held the audience spellbound by telling how Clive, in India, told his opponent in a duel to go to hell. (She did not mention that she had got the story from Browning.) Heywood Broun, in his account of the lecture, said the story was the climax of the address and that it was new. He received scores of letters from my undergraduate students which proved that they were in the habit of reading both Browning and Mr. Broun's column—as they are still.

On 20 May I gave some lectures in Aberdeen, South Dakota. When the train entered this state and made its first stop, I sprang out, hurled some of the soil in the air and shouted *South Dakota*! much to the amusement of the crowd. I had been in every one of the forty-eight states of the Union except this.

I had some golf there and was interested by the printed notice on the score-card—'Ball rolling into gopher hole may be dropped without penalty.'

On 24 May I spoke at the dinner of the Connecticut Medical Society, being the only one present who was not a physician. The toastmaster, introducing me, pretended to find fault with something I had recently published, saying my punctuation was not perfect, that I had not properly used the comma. In reply I said it was better to have a wrong comma than to have a bad colon.

81

MRS. WHARTON; CONRAD; BENAVENTE

In 1923 Mrs. Wharton came from her home in France to New Haven in America to receive the honorary degree of Doctor of Letters from Yale. She has always hated hot weather and the heat on that June Commencement day was terrific; in giving out the degrees as Public Orator, I lost four pounds. She suffered even more, but made no complaint. In presenting her for the degree, I said

DOCTOR OF LETTERS

EDITH WHARTON

American novelist of international fame. Chevalier of the Legion of Honour in France. For nearly twenty-five years she has produced novels, some of the most notable being *The House of Mirth, Ethan Frome, The Age of Innocence.* Her books are marked by sincerity in art, beauty in construction, distinction in style. She writes short stories and full-length works with equal skill. She is a master in the creation of original and living characters, and her powers of ironical description are exerted to salutary ends. She is a realist in the best sense of the word; revealing the inner nature of men and women without resource to sensationalism and keeping ever within the boundaries of true art. She holds a universally recognized place in the front rank of the world's living novelists. She has elevated the level of American literature. We are proud that she is an American and especially proud to enroll her name among the daughters of Yale.

On 13 August 1928 we were in Paris and she very kindly invited us to lunch with her at her summer home, Villa Colombe, at St. Brice sous Forêt. It is a beautiful place, a fine old eighteenth century house, with magnificent gardens.

Her only physical exercise and her chief recreation were gardening; we walked about the gardens with her. She also commented on various French and English writers, speaking with great admiration and affection of the French dramatist Edouard Bourdet, an intimate friend of hers. We had just seen his brilliant comedy *Vient de Paraître*, which we enjoyed so much we saw it three times.

I asked Mrs. Wharton if she were writing another novel, and she smiled rather sadly, and said 'I am always writing!'

When her autobiography *A Backward Glance* appeared in 1934, I could not help telling her how much I admired it.

PAVILLON COLOMBE
July 21, 34

DEAR MR. PHELPS:

How very kind of you to snatch a moment from your holiday and tell me that you liked my book. I hoped you would, for I knew there were pages in it where our thoughts wd meet.

I'm glad you liked what I said of dear Clyde Fitch. My chance meeting with him is a very pleasant memory, and I am interested in knowing the name of the play with that delicious first act in the Vatican.

If you wd cure New York of having heat waves in June I shd come out to see you all; but even our temperate wavelet here this summer has sapped my activities—a bad thing at a time when we all have to be living in Grindstone City! (I admire the irony with which you have selected your holiday home & wish I knew why it was called so).

Well, I say a hopeful aurevoir soon, in one hemisphere or the other, & send, meanwhile, my best greetings to Mrs. Phelps & to you.

Yrs ever sincerely,

EDITH WHARTON

She died at her French home 11 August 1937.

I first saw Joseph Conrad on the evening of 10 May 1923 at the house of Mr. and Mrs. Arthur Curtiss James in New York. He looked like a sea-captain, with his pointed, grizzled beard, weather-tanned skin, and a far-horizon speculation in his eyes. He read aloud from his novel *Victory* and talked interestingly about the book. It is curious, considering that perhaps his chief claim to distinction was his mastery of English literary style, that he spoke the language so badly; not only with a very strong foreign accent, but with frequent mistakes in the pronunciation of words. Strange indeed to hear a man read from his own works and not be able to pronounce correctly the words and sentences he had written with such accuracy and beauty! But when we remember that he knew no English until he was twenty-one and thereafter for many years his speaking vocabulary was largely confined to the sea, that when he became a writer he spent most of his waking hours in solitary composition, and was reserved in company, it is not so remarkable.

He made a great impression on his audience, however, by his natural dignity, courtesy, and modesty.

The next day, 11 May, Mr. and Mrs. F. N. Doubleday kindly invited us to spend the night at their beautiful home on Long Island, where Mr. Conrad was staying. At an intimate family dinner that evening, he was absolutely charming. I had supposed, from the austerity of his mind and art, that he would be difficult to approach. Quite the contrary; he was not only affable; he was affectionate.

On Tuesday of the following week, 15 May, Mr. and Mrs. Doubleday brought him to our house in New Haven by motor; and he spent the night. We took him to see the Elizabethan Club and various college buildings, and the next morning I had a long intimate conversation with him. He was not at all well, suffering from gout, in constant physical pain; he uttered no word of complaint and was the incarnation of courtesy and kindness and consideration. In the course of conversation, he said, laughing, 'This is the difference between H. G. Wells and me. Wells does not love humanity but thinks he can improve it; I love humanity but I know it is unimprovable.' I spoke to him about Galsworthy; he exclaimed 'Isn't Jack a dear fellow!'

After luncheon, the Doubledays took him away to Springfield in their motor. I helped him on with his coat. He looked at me earnestly a moment and said, 'I know you like my books because you have said so in print; but I hope you like me myself a little?' I replied, 'Why, Mr. Conrad, I love you!' Immediately he started to kiss me and almost had his arms around my neck, when his British training suddenly seemed to get the better of his Polish blood, and with a gesture of apology, he refrained. I should, of course, have been pleased had he embraced me.

It was not in the least necessary for him to write, but the following letters are characteristic.

1st June '23

My dear Professor.

Accept my warmest thanks for the more than friendly terms of your letter. I have in your house an unforgettably kind and charming reception and you gave me an impression of Yale Coll: which shall be treasured. I commend myself to Mrs. Phelps' and your memory, as your affectionate friend

J. Conrad

HOTEL KIMBALL
SPRINGFIELD, MASSACHUSETTS
16.5.23

Dear Mrs. Phelps

I do not know how to express to you my deep sense of your charming hospitality and friendly kindness. Pray take the will for the deed and believe that I am saying no more than the bare truth when I assure you I have found an unforgettable impression under your roof.

Will you kindly convey to the Professor my affectionate regards and allow me to subscribe myself your very grateful and most faithful servant

Joseph Conrad

On Saturday 17 March 1923 Señor Benavente, the famous Spanish dramatist and winner of the Nobel Prize in Literature, gave a lecture at Yale University on the Francis Bergen Memorial Foundation. Professor Underhill of Columbia stood on the platform with him. Benavente spoke in five-minute intervals in Spanish, Mr. Underhill translated aloud in English, and thus the audience had the pleasure of hearing the beautiful Spanish language and of understanding what was said. We were all impressed by Mr. Underhill's skill in his accurate and fluent rendering in English, without the use of notes.

A great Spanish dinner was given to the distinguished guest that same evening at the Hotel Taft and on the following morning I gave a breakfast at my house. Señor Benavente sat in the chair that had formerly belonged to Robert Browning, presented to me by Yale undergraduate Pundits of the Class of 1914. It was not only one of Browning's chairs—it was *the* chair, the chair at his desk, in which he composed.

Benavente was thin and slight, but hardy and wiry in appearance. He eats and sleeps very little—hardly enough to keep alive, one would think; and he smokes a large number of cigars daily. He reminds me in these ways of my dear friend Daniel Frohman, who sleeps about four hours out of the twenty-four, eats almost no breakfast and no lunch at all, never drinks, and smokes about twenty-five quotidian cigars. Both men are not only vigorous, but full of cheerfulness and high spirits.

It may have been Spanish courtesy and charm, but Benavente seemed to enjoy his visit to Yale as much as we enjoyed having him—and he could not have enjoyed it more.

On one occasion—not at Yale—Benavente, discussing the interesting fact that theatre audiences are always on the side of virtue, always sympathize with self-sacrifice, nobility of soul, and upright behaviour, said that if these people in daily life exhibited one-tenth of the virtue which they evidently believe in and admire in the theatre, the millennium would be a reality.

82

AN AMERICAN IN ENGLAND

IF, instead of being human, I belonged to a breed of cattle or to any species of herb-eating beast, and could choose my country, I should choose England. It is the paradise for grazers. The climate is so moderate that the kine live outdoors, winter and summer, day and night; there is so much rain that the grass is ever dewy and lush; there are hardly any flies or biting insects; there is water, water everywhere, and all of it to drink; there are few vast lonely places—pleasant farms, hedgerows, and diversified scenery greet the eye. Furthermore, the men and women understand quadrupeds and treat them with respect.

It is only by studying maps that we realize the unimportance of size. A map that shows Siberia makes England look insignificant; but think of the comparative contributions of these two countries to history!

England has the same area as the State of Michigan or of North Carolina; but this area holds forty-five million people, the largest city in the world, and several other towns of over a million each; it contains an amazing variety of scenery, Roman remains, splendid mediaeval Gothic cathedrals, and the loveliest countryside in the world. Looking through the windows of the English train from Dover to London, one sees tidy villages, small farms divided by hedgerows, thousands of trees with star-proof foliage; the very atmosphere seems denser and more soft. I can only vaguely imagine the heartrending homesickness that must torture Englishmen under the pitiless glare of the sun in India and in Africa, when they remember the dewy freshness of their native land.

Late September is a bad time in London, for the interiors of all buildings, theatres, and trains are much too cold for comfort, and yet the calendar is not sufficiently advanced to obtain artificial heat. Everyone seems to follow the example of the terrible father of Eugénie Grandet, and lights no fires until a certain date, regardless of the temperature. I wore my overcoat throughout every performance I attended at the theatres; but something happened at the Royalty Theatre which is so surprising it ought to be recorded. The auditorium resembled the others in being admirably adapted for cold storage; but in addition, this had an icy draught that hit the back of the neck with precision. As soon as the first act was over I hastened to the box-office, complained of the draught, and the girl on duty replied that she would immediately telephone somebody or other and have it stopped. I thanked her, but did not expect anything; in a pair of minutes the draught ceased. It was almost the first time in my life when I have known a complaint to produce a favourable result.

An amusing incident happened at this play. We took my brother-in-law and his wife; it was his first appearance after an attack of flu, apparently rather a narrow escape from pneumonia. The play was by Arnold Bennett, and when the first curtain rose, it revealed a sick man with a thermometer in his mouth; the physician removed the instrument, looked at it and said '104!' Our companion left his seat and ran down the aisle and out.

The English trains are fast and for short distances—and most distances in England are short—they are incomparably superior to our 'cars.' The fact that the compartments all have doors opening on the station platform means that every train can be emptied of passengers and baggage in a few minutes, and you step from the platform into the compartment on the same level, and do not have either to hoist your travelling-bag, or fight your way with it down a long aisle. You do not have to wait at every station till every person and his luggage has left the train before you can enter it.

Furthermore, you do not have to smoke in a lavatory, an abomination that is taken as a matter of course on many American pullmans. Outside of the worst city slums there are few more odious spectacles than the lavatory of an American sleeping-car; especially when the men are dressing, shaving, and performing other necessities in the morning.

Then, English trains, being lighter than ours, and perhaps having engine-drivers who are more considerate of the passengers than some of ours are, start as gently and as silently as a bicycle; whereas ours, often starting in the night, rend soul and body asunder, and if you are in the dining-car you have to be an expert food-dodger.

The express trains from London to Edinburgh, about four hundred miles, run the entire distance without a single stop, the longest non-stop trains in the world. One of their cars is fitted up as a lounge, equipped with large revolving easy chairs, and has extra large windows. There is a dining-car, with seats of special design. Half of this car is fitted with three small compartments, in which meals can be served; and, if there are four passengers travelling together, they can enjoy their food in peaceful isolation. The three compartments have been differently designed, and are called respectively the Jacobean, the Grey, and the Chippendale rooms. Beneath the carpet is a heavy layer of felt to deaden outside sounds. There are full-length mirrors.

Yet for a person travelling alone for eight or ten hours, an American first-class train is the best in the world. I call no train first-class unless it has both a club-car and an observation-car. The individual is sure of his own pullman chair by a window, and if he wants a table the porter will bring him one.

But in England, especially for those of advanced years, the best way to see the country is to go to a city hotel, make that the base of operations, travel by train in baggageless delight whithersoever you wish, and return to the city hotel in the afternoon or evening. While travelling, one has a perfect, uninterrupted view of the incomparable English countryside.

For example. We wished to visit Somersby in Lincolnshire, the microscopic village where Tennyson was born. We left London in the morning and travelled to the city of Lincoln in three hours, the train running smoothly at tremendous speed. At Lincoln we hired a motor-car, which took us forty miles to Somersby. We visited the church where Tennyson's father preached and where the poet was baptized. The church, when crowded, would hold about thirty-seven people. The grave of the Rev. Mr. Tennyson is in the churchyard, in a sad state, with uncut grass. The rectory, where Tennyson was born, is almost directly opposite; a family is living there, and we could not enter. The famous brook—is anything so inexplicably immortal as a river?—goes bickering along, even as the poet described it. The seven elms (see Tennyson's *Ode to Memory*) are near the front door of the rectory, and one can hear the church-bells of four other villages, as Tennyson told us in *In Memoriam*. When the poet lived there the entire population of Somersby was sixty-two. And as the Rev. Mr. and Mrs. Tennyson had twelve children, the Tennysonian proportion was considerable. When Alfred's college friend, Arthur Henry Hallam, came there on a visit in the summer vacation from Cambridge, he said that one hundred years hence pilgrims would come from all over the world to see Tennyson's birthplace. That sounded like a monstrous hyperbole, but time has made it true.

We motored back to Lincoln, had lunch at the White
Hart, spent an hour and a half looking over the giant
cathedral—my favourite English church—took the train,
and were back in London at half past five in the afternoon.
The most comfortable way to see England.

A few persons among the millions who have walked on
Fleet Street may remember that back from the street on
the north side at St. Dunstan's church stood a grimy old
statue of Queen Elizabeth. Thanks to the enterprise and
generosity of Dame Millicent Fawcett and some other
ladies, the statue has been cleaned and repainted; it was
ceremoniously unveiled. *The Times* had an interesting editorial, called 'Gloriana in Fleet-street.'

It was made in 1586, when the Queen was fifty-three (but no artist
nor courtier would dare to remember her age) and had been not far
from thirty years on the throne; and it was made for Lud Gate, which
in that year was rebuilt. Gloriana, ever fair and ever young, faced
westward; and back to back with her, looking up Ludgate-hill to
Paul's church, stood King Lud (who, as every one knows, had built
the first gate long before the Christian era began) and his two sons.
They wore Roman dress; and lucky is Fleet-street today that the
sculptor, whoever he was, did not put the Queen in Roman dress too.
When the inhabitants of the two Farringdons insisted that, Lud or
no and Gloriana or no, Lud Gate must come down, the poor King and
the princes were left in the parish bonehouse. The masterful Tudor
woman, clinging to existence as firmly as ever, came westward to old
St. Dunstan's Church, and survived yet another move to the new
St. Dunstan's Church which men see today. And, all these years
after, this statue, the only known contemporary statue of the great
Queen, the only known relic of any of the City of London's gates (for
Temple Bar was not technically a City gate), has been by generous
women cleaned, painted, restored to notice and to respect. Painted
she was originally; and very likely in colours much stronger than
those which make her look so fresh and dapper today. Elizabethans,
like men of the Middle Ages, could not think of a statue unpainted.
"The statue is but newly fix'd, the colour's not dry," cries Paulina in
alarm when Perdita is in too great a hurry to kiss the hand of her
mother. Today Gloriana is new painted, a delightful spot of purity

in a grubby region. Fleet-street will be proud of her; and the ghosts
of old Templars and courtiers with whom she danced and jested will
steal out to look upon her. Let us hope that among them will be some
profitable ghost who will make it his business to keep the statue as
clean as it is today.

On the south side of the river, near the Elephant and
Castle, stands the old York Street Chapel, where Robert
Browning was christened. Together with some adjoining
buildings it is now used as the Robert Browning Settlement; the warden was the Rev. J. W. Graves, a graduate of
the Yale Divinity School. I do not know of any more useful
and important work among the poor than is being done
here under the devoted leadership of the Warden, who is
'on the job' from seven in the morning until midnight.
The children receive instruction in books, games, and general behaviour, free legal service is provided, an Old Man's
Club has been formed—the place, in the heart of a district
crowded with very poor people, is a centre of wise, efficient charity. I wish Americans might visit this institution
on the Walworth Road and see for themselves the splendid
work and realize the desperate need of it. You cannot give
money to a better cause, though you will never be asked
to give anything. Mr. Graves seemed to be working beyond human endurance; but he said he was in perfect
health, and seemed in high spirits. I recalled the famous
sonnet by Matthew Arnold describing his conversation
with a preacher in the slums.

Not content with charitable work alone, Mr. Graves
kept an upper room as a Browning museum. It is filled
with interesting memorials of the poet, his manuscripts,
account-books, and other precious things, which are gladly
shown to visitors. Mr. Graves told me a remarkable story
of an incident that happened during his American journey,
when he was exhibiting the Browning memorials in a large
city. Someone stole the most valuable manuscript. In de-

spair he went to the chief of police. The chief asked him if he had tried every possible means to recover the treasure. 'Yes,' said Mr. Graves, and the officer asked: 'Have you prayed about it?' Mr. Graves is a devout clergyman, but he confessed that he had not yet prayed for this particular thing. 'Well,' said the American police chief, 'whenever I have a particularly perplexing problem, I go home, and my wife and I pray earnestly for help and guidance. I advise you to do the same.' Mr. Graves took this advice, and the next day the treasure was found; the thief confessed.

On the night I gave a lecture on 'The Life of Browning' at this settlement, the gentleman who presided was none other than Browning's personal friend, Mr. W.G.Kingsland, well past eighty. Mr. Kingsland was a printer who, over fifty years ago, became inspired by Browning's poetry and wrote a little book called *Browning the Chief Poet of the Age*. Browning sent him a remarkable letter; the original is on exhibition among famous letters in a public room at the British Museum.

England is full of contrasts.

Through the ineffable peace of its countryside run the fast crowded express trains; the newspapers of London, with a circulation far greater than any in New York, are, a few hours after publication, within every town and village in the country; one may sleep at night in a country village that itself always seems asleep, and go to business in the world's largest metropolis.

One of the noisiest street corners of the world is Charing Cross, where the Strand empties into Trafalgar Square; and only a few yards away is one of the quietest streets in the world, Adelphi, a narrow way between Charing Cross and the Thames Embankment.

The leading journalist in London is an American— Ralph D.Blumenfeld, born in Wisconsin in 1864, but a resident of London since 1894. He has been in newspaper work all his life. In his youth he was a Chicago reporter and editor, correspondent of the United Press, general superintendent of the New York *Herald*; and it was under his direction that the sensational one-story building of the *Herald* was erected at the junction of Broadway and Sixth Avenue at Thirty-fifth Street. Then he went to London and became the editor of the London *Daily Express* and *The Evening Standard*. He has a genius not only for newspaper work, but for designing newspaper buildings. He took me from cellar to roof of the sensational new home of the *Daily Express*, on Fleet Street. It is built with front and sides entirely of glass, from pavement to top. There are no columns in the structure.

The United States of America is not so very young, as we have celebrated our one hundred and fiftieth anniversary; but to an American travelling in England, our own country seems an infant. I took dinner in a college hall in Oxford, and after dinner we went first to one room for this and that; and then to another. I asked my table companion, 'Have you always been coming to this room after dinner?' He replied, 'Oh, dear no! we have been doing this only since the seventeenth century.' He seemed to regard it as a questionable innovation.

Oxford and Cambridge illustrate, as do so many places in England, how age can take on dignity and honour.

One meets everywhere in England heroic fathers and mothers, and wives who lost their men in the war. In London I took tea one afternoon at Mrs. Alec Tweedie's, a painter and a writer. She told me that her husband died many years ago, leaving her with two baby boys. She brought them up carefully, gave them a splendid education, and just after they had been graduated from Cambridge, the war came, they enlisted and were killed. It was only her interest in the life of the mind that made it possible for her to carry on at all.

WILLIAM ARCHER AND THE AIR

Archer was a modest man with a fine sense of humour. He never took himself too seriously, but no man ever took his work as a critic more seriously, more conscientiously than he. He represented the highest standards of journalism, and was proud to be a newspaper man.

He described his own attitude as a drama critic as follows: 'The faculty for making the best of the actual without losing sight of the ideal.'

In 1894 he made this public statement:

> I was born with an instinctive, unreasoning, unreasonable love for the theatre, the place of light and sound, of mystery and magic, where, at the stroke of the prompter's bell, a new world is revealed to the delighted sense. That unreasoning love is still strong within me. If all the germs of progress were stamped out, and the stage declined entirely upon spectacle and buffoonery, I should still, I believe, find a melancholy fascination in the glare of the footlights. But close upon the heels of this mania for the theatre came another and still more absorbing passion—the passion for high thoughts and beautiful words, for things delicately seen, and subtly felt, and marvellously imagined—in short, for that divinest emanation of the human spirit which we call literature. These two things have I loved, sometimes blindly and foolishly, sometimes, I hope, with understanding; and it has been the instinctive, inevitable effort of my life to make these two one flesh.

This happy union Archer detected immediately when he saw on the English stage in 1895 Edmond Rostand's *La Princesse Lointaine*. This was two years before Rostand produced *Cyrano*. Archer wrote a long criticism of *La Princesse Lointaine*, in which he expressed his towering admiration for the comparatively unknown author; and the letter he received from Rostand must have been re-read many times by Archer in later years. Rostand said:

> Cette défense si fine et si spirituelle de ma pièce, ce commentaire délicat de mes plus secrètes intentions, cette analyse qui est assuré-

ment la plus complète qui ait été faite de mon œuvre, je la dois à un
étranger? Comment avez vous fait, Anglais, pour comprendre des
choses que tant de Français n'ont pas comprises?

Although Archer had something of the typical Scots-
man's reserve, and was not given to superlatives, he took
no pleasure in ironical or destructive criticism.

> The worst sort of criticism is sterilizing criticism. I would rather see
> columns of fatuous gush about a foolish play than a brilliant but
> discouraging and sterilizing criticism of a play with any germs of
> good in it.

Such a remark is all the more interesting, coming from a
man who never wrote or spoke a sentence that could be
called gush.

The lifelong friendship between Shaw and Archer was
marked by extreme frankness on both sides; the numerous
letters back and forth are a commentary on the contemporary stage, and a revelation of the characters of both
men. In 1921 Archer wrote to his friend:

> I doubt if there is any case of a man so widely read, heard, seen,
> and known as yourself, who has produced so little practical effect on
> his generation. I am strongly under the impression (I may be wrong)
> that you have less of a following today than you had twenty years
> ago. . . . You have no serious competitor; but your public (small
> blame to them) declines to take you seriously.

Yet on 17 December 1924, just before he underwent the
operation from which he did not recover (he died 27 December), he wrote to Shaw:

> This episode gives me an excuse for saying, what I hope you don't
> doubt—namely, that though I may sometimes have played the part
> of the all-too-candid mentor, I have never wavered in my admiration
> and affection for you, or ceased to feel that the Fates had treated me
> kindly in making me your contemporary and friend. I thank you from
> my heart for forty years of good comradeship.

Shaw was deeply affected by this, and responded in a fore-word to Archer's *Three Plays* (1927), as warm-hearted a tribute as Shaw ever wrote.

I am glad to see also in the admirable biography by his brother Lieut.-Col. Charles Archer, a good account of William's only son, Tom, who was killed in the war. He was a fine young man. One day in New Haven, Archer and his son and I took a long walk and I got to know Tom fairly well. As a child, he must have been irresistible; some of his conversations with his father are diverting. When he was six, the following dialogue took place:

T. What did King Lear die of, father?
W. Well, you see, he was a very old man—and his daughters had been very cruel to him—and he had been out all night in a ter-rible storm—
T. That's the worst of old people—the least thing upsets them!

We should remember Archer with gratitude, for he was a lifelong, devoted friend to America.

Never have I heard any one speak the English language more correctly, more clearly, and more winningly than he.

I shall always remember the last meal we had together, because it was only a few weeks before his death, in the autumn of 1924. He invited me to dinner at a London club, and tried in vain to persuade me not to take the air-plane to Paris on the next day. He said there were many accidents. Then he told me the best play in Paris was *Knock*, and he was right. I never saw a man in better ap-parent health than Archer was on that evening.

Despite Archer's advice, the next day we *flew* from Lon-don to Paris. For the first time in my life I travelled in an airplane.

In about two weeks occurred the funeral of Anatole France. In Paris a distinguished man of letters is not merely admired; he is idolized. He is a super-hero. The populace regard him with the kind of reverential awe accorded in England and in America by schoolboys to a great football player. Anatole France died at Tours on 12 October 1924. His body was brought to Paris, and the coffin placed on exhibition in his home near the Bois de Boulogne on Friday, 17 October. At dusk I went thither to do homage. There was a dense crowd. We stood in line, entering the house and passing silently through the chamber of death. I asked a policeman if the procession of worshippers had been continuous all day, and he informed me that every moment it had been just as I saw it. Fifteen thousand people viewed the coffin that Friday, and we either left cards or signed our names in a big book. The next day, Saturday, there was a public funeral in front of the house on the *quai* where he was born; the coffin, fittingly enough, was placed in the shadow of the statue of Voltaire. There were funeral orations by men of letters and political radicals, and there were many thousands assembled to do him honour.

As a man of letters, Anatole France was an aristocrat; in politics, he was a radical. Thus his appeal was universal, and it was interesting to see all classes of people represented among the mourners.

Of the honours paid him, and they were innumerable and varied, one particularly impressed me. There was to have been a play at the *Comédie Française* on the afternoon of the funeral. Although the house had been sold out, the performance was cancelled, and the money returned to ticket-holders. For a state-theatre to give such recognition—involving a heavy financial loss—is a fact worth remembering. Men of genius are so few and so esteemed that even the usually unpardonable sin of political heresy is overlooked in the acclaim given to their literary ability.

French literature probably contains more first-rate prose

writers than the literature of any other land; Anatole
France is among them. I cannot see that he contributed
any constructive ideas to the world; he was not a thinker
or a philosopher. But style is the best preservative. As a
master of prose style, he belongs with Flaubert and the
other immortals.

The day before his death he was conscious. He asked the
physicians to tell him his exact condition, and they replied
cheeringly that he must continue to hope, because there
was no organic difficulty. Then he remarked, characteris-
tically enough: '*Donnez-moi une petite maladie, par grâce,
que j'en finisse!*'

It is affecting to recall that the last word he uttered was
a cry of appeal to his mother to come and help him, for he
was suffering; thus the dying octogenarian returned dream-
ingly to the days of his babyhood. When this last word was
reported in the press, M.Hubert Morant, in the *Journal
des Débats*, called public attention to the fact that the first
book of Anatole France, published in 1859, bore the following dedication:

À UN PÈRE ET UNE MÈRE BIEN AIMÉS

Chers parents,
    Les premiers mots que prononce l'enfant sur la terre sont: "maman,
papa!" S'il souffre, il crie: "Maman! s'il veut quelque chose, s'il a
besoin d'aide, il dit: "maman."

The French people are grateful to artists and men of
letters, and take care that their memories shall be cherished. Sunday 19 October was the seventy-fifth anniversary of the death of Chopin. Accordingly public exercises
were held at his tomb, in Père Lachaise, with commemora-
tive addresses.

This hero-worship must affect the boys and girls in the
schools. The homage paid to men and women who have

distinguished themselves in some form of art is a factor in the education of French youth. Everyone knows how much attention is given in French schools to literary composition and to every form of expression. And as the road to public success and distinction so often leads through the prize-competitions in various schools and institutions, all things work together toward one goal. The successful poet, dramatist, novelist, singer, actor, painter, architect, has a position universally envied.

That Parisians are not hostile to German art is abundantly proved by the fact that *Parsifal* and *Die Walküre* are given at the opera. Even more striking was the production in 1924 of that one hundred per cent German play, *Old Heidelberg*, which had a long run at the Porte Saint-Martin. I went to see this best of all college plays, and although it seemed strange to hear the German student songs sung in French, it was a competent and delightful performance. The house was packed, and everyone seemed to enjoy the glorification of the old German university town, and at the parting of Karl Heinz and Käthie (Charles Henri and Catherine) the good Frenchmen around me were weeping unrestrainedly. I did not see a German in the audience.

The most amusing French comedy running in Paris was *Knock* (pronounce the initial K), or, *Le Triomphe de la Médecine*, written by Jules Romains. This is a delightful satire on physicians, on patients, and on humanity. Young Doctor Knock is just the opposite of Monsieur Coué. Coué endeavoured to persuade sick people that they are well; Knock persuades well people that they are sick, an easier task. He enters a village where illness is unknown, but he soon has all the inhabitants in a sanatorium, by the simple process of beginning with free examinations.

83

EDNA FERBER

NEARLY all our distinguished American women novelists of the twentieth century were either graduates of universities or, like Edith Wharton and Anne Sedgwick, educated in Europe; Dorothy Canfield belonged to both classes. But Edna Ferber from the age of seventeen has been on her own. Born in Kalamazoo, she entered newspaper work on graduating from high school, and after writing a number of magazine stories and popular novels, she turned from the production of tales written for the market to the creation of literature. She has interpreted various sections of the United States. *So Big*, which I like best of all her novels, although she does not, deals with people and localities in and near Chicago. *Show Boat* is, I suppose, the best novel ever written of the moving theatres of our great southern rivers. *Cimarron* is an interpretation of the opening and settling of Oklahoma; *American Beauty*, of the invasion of Connecticut; *Come and Get It* deals with the lumber magnates and lumberjacks of Wisconsin. She is an accomplished and successful playwright.

The first time I persuaded her to lecture at Yale she came with Mrs. George Kaufman. After the lecture they took dinner at our house, and I, as is my custom, said grace. There was a moment's pause, and to cover what might have been a slight embarrassment, my wife said to me, 'I didn't hear a word you said,' to which I replied, 'I wasn't speaking to you.' This amused Miss Ferber so much that she told it to Alexander Woollcott, who not only printed it in his daily article in the New York *World*, but, I believe, broadcast it later. Miss Ferber some years after made a second visit, bringing her charming nieces with her.

FIFTY CENTRAL PARK WEST
September 20th
1926

DEAR MR. PHELPS:

There are, I should say, ten or twelve show boats now playing the rivers of the United States. Because of the dangers of the Mississippi they rarely play that river now. But they are well known on the Ohio, the Missouri, the smaller rivers of the middle west, and on the eastern rivers and the southern. The James Adams Floating Theatre, for example, plays Maryland and North Carolina. She's probably somewhere in Maryland now. They are much grander and larger than they used to be, of course. And they make a lot of money. You should see Mrs. Adams' diamond ear-drops, and Mr. Adams' Packard car!

I'm sorry you didn't like *Show Boat* as well as *So Big*. I like it better. But that you liked it at all is good news.

Sincerely,

EDNA FERBER

FIFTY CENTRAL PARK WEST
March 6th
1927

DEAR MR. PHELPS:—

I've had a change of heart about that 3,000 audience. For the sort of thing I do it's nonsense to shout at an audience of that size. I don't want to do it. I'd rather entertain, amuse, or interest 700 people than baffle, irritate, and fail to reach 3,000. I don't want to speak in the larger hall unless that hall is made for rather intimate speaking. Remember, I don't lecture. I have no MESSAGE. I refuse to shout.

Also, I'd like to have you believe me when I say I'm not trying to be snooty about autographing books, but I hate to do it. I don't know why. I just hate to.

I haven't any subject. I shall read 'The Gay Old Dog,' a short story, and talk informally for a few minutes before reading.

I hope none of these decisions will make you hate me.

EDNA FERBER

March 25th
1930

DEAR WILLIAM LYON PHELPS:

My thanks to you for the letter asking me to become a member of the Town Hall Club. I hope you won't think I am thoroughly mad when I say that I have a sort of horror of joining—I belong to no organization except the Authors' League of America. I don't know any reasonable explanation for this feeling, but there it is.

I'm happy to learn that you like *Cimarron*. My experience with it, after publication, has been devastating. I mean that I wrote or thought I wrote—a book about one amazing phase of American life, colored with irony. Its whole intent was, for that matter, ironic.

It has been received as a straight romantic Western. I feel as though I were living in a nightmare. I hate Sabra Cravat, and I find her considered a fine flower of American womanhood (in the reviews).

Oh, well——

EDNA FERBER

THE LOMBARDY
111 EAST FIFTY-SIXTH STREET
NEW YORK
October 23d
1931

DEAR WILLIAM LYON PHELPS:—

It's no good my trying to tell you what your letter did to me. I had been, as you may know, pretty well panned by many of the boys who write pieces for the papers. They had their Connecticut information straight from McGuffey's First Reader, which tells all about how the New Englanders loved the Serl, and how noble New England is, was, and always will be.

Then one of them . . . left me staring and open-mouthed with the statement that *American Beauty* obviously had been written for a possible motion picture sale. This quiet, tight and rather poisonous book which I had written with infinite pains, and because not writing it made me more uncomfortable than writing it.

So now and then I succumb, partially at least, to a series of these attacks. What weapon have I with which to reply to them? None that I feel justified in using. Then you come riding toward me. And if you think you don't look like a knight in shining armor—plumes, pennants, sword, white charger, velvet trappings and all—then you just don't know this romantic old girl.

EDNA FERBER

III EAST FIFTY-SIXTH STREET
November 30th
1931

My dear W.L.P. (I think I'll have to do something about shortening that. I'm sort of hoping this will turn into one of those Shaw-Terry correspondences). How about making it Wilp? No, that won't do. Anyway, dear William Lyon Phelps, your syndicate letter about AMERICAN BEAUTY is grand, and the things you know about me and my feelings are uncanny.

I am going to Washington on Thursday to dine with the Hoovers, much to my surprise. I have never met them, and I hope that Herb has long cherished a secret passion for me.

I shall be back by Friday or Saturday, but I suppose you'll take advantage of my absence from New York to sneak into town and be off before I can see you.

III EAST FIFTY-SIXTH STREET
January 5th
1932

Dear Wilp, I hope you got my wire.

I may bring with me a couple of nieces, so don't be surprised if I appear flanked by two beautiful misses with spangles in their eyes and delusion about Yale athletes being found in my audience. May I have some sort of high reading stand thing, for odds and ends of papers?

I'm sorry not to seem polite about signing books. It's a custom that I always have loathed.

Yours,

E.F.

PEBBLES
SASCO HILL
SOUTHPORT
CONNECTICUT
September 6th
1934

If you think, Deceiver of Girlish Hearts, that I don't see through your devilish machinations and that I am unaware of the fiend that lurks behind your false smile and fair words, you simply do not know the Fighting Ferbers. Because, look, when the man I love dashes off to Michigan the minute I come to Connecticut, and comes zooming back to Connecticut the instant my face is turned toward Michigan, I need no crystal-gazer to tell me that all is over. This, Mr. P., is the end.

If I ever again visit Ironwood! As soon as the book comes out (I'm plugging away, day after day, and have been at it for a solid year and more) I never again can visit Ironwood. Slowly the United States is closing in on me like Poe's prison walls. CIMARRON shut me out of Oklahoma (and a good thing, too. What a hell-hole!) AMERICAN BEAUTY made my name synonymous with poison in New England. SHOW BOAT had the whole sunny south sueing me. SO BIG and THE GIRLS got me in bad in Chicago and the middle west. After this book, which is pretty much northern Wisconsin and some Michigan, I am going up with one of those stratosphere (that isn't spelled right but you know what I mean) boys and stay up until America freezes over.

I shall be here until October first. I've had a lovely though grinding summer.

FERBER

CONTE DI SAVOIA
March 10th
1935

Your letter, dear Wilp, came to me at Gibraltar, on my way home. How dear of you—how kind! Most of the reviews had been forwarded to me and I was feeling rather low in my mind, what with one thing and another. They seemed to me, with one or two exceptions, to be pretty bad. Curiously enough, I don't so much mind those reviewers who say, of any book of mine, "This is terrible." Or, "I don't like this stuff, or the writer, or the way it's written." The thing that infuriates me is when one of these lads says, sagely, "This will not endure." As though anyone ever wrote a book with the feeling of penning deathless prose. Holy God, I'm glad if I can just get it down on paper, groaning and sweating.

I remember when so BIG was published Burton Rascoe came to interview me, and to do a review of the new book. In the review he said;

> "This book is selling, and will sell more. But in one year it will be as dead as this interview, and as forgotten."

That was in 1924. so BIG has sold, year after year, for eleven years, and this year has been brought out in a new edition. When I wrote it I wanted only to get it out of my system. Whether anyone ever would read it at all was something on which I never once reckoned. Oh, well.

I'm writing this propped up in bed at ten in the morning, and I should be out on deck looking at the Azores, which are just now going by. But I'd rather talk to you, my dear.

I've been reading Maurice Baring's SARAH BERNHARDT, and at the end the tears were streaming down my cheeks.

I'll be home March 15th. I should so love to see you. Can't we do a matinee together some time? I promise not to talk during the performance, or to tear bits of paper from my program, or rattle beads.

EDNA

791 PARK AVENUE
March 25th
1938

For once I don't agree with you, dear Wilp. I honestly don't believe that the critics are, as you say, out to get the old established writers. You named two or three books that had been badly received. Sonny, that book by Sinclair Lewis was a dud. Pearl Buck's is dull and the heroine is a prig. ACTION AT AQUILA is rejected by the human eye, and that's my story and I'll stick to it. And I suspect that if the boys didn't like my book it was because it wasn't very good, either. And there you are.

My love to you,

EDNA

84

THE CONVERSATION CLUB IN AUGUSTA

(1925–38)

SEVERAL Christmas vacations my wife and I spent in Miami, Fla., where we made many friends among the people and where I particularly admired the courage of the citizens in their united and successful efforts toward recovery after two great disasters, the cyclone-floods and the financial crash. We especially enjoyed the Christmas vacation of 1922–3 which we spent at the home of Mr. William J. Matheson in Coconut Grove. He was one of the most interesting men I have ever known.

But we have come to regard Augusta, Georgia, as our winter home. It has often been jocularly said that heaven has the climate and hell has the people, but Augusta has the best winter climate I have ever seen, and I have never found people more attractive than the permanent inhabitants. After two brief visits in 1910 and 1916 we arrived in Augusta on my sixtieth birthday, 2 January 1925, and remained nearly four months.

In those days there were at the hotel many interesting men; every morning the Conversation Club, consisting of some five and twenty, conversed for two hours. For three months there was no cessation of good talk. We had no President, but we had a King, the royal golfer Walter J. Travis. The Prime Minister was Sir Robert Borden, of Canada; Secretary of State, Nicholas Murray Butler, of New York; Treasurer, the Honourable Charles F. Brooker, of Ansonia. Then we had the four Georges: George Crocker, the Iron Man and hole-in-one specialist; George Clapp, of Boston; George M.Gray, of New York, crossword fiend, and George the Fourth was George Ade. The Manager was Daniel Frohman, who made a permanent impression not only on the Club, but on the city of Augusta, because he generously produced three plays in Augusta's Little Theatre Guild. Louis Cheney, of Connecticut, and Louis Coolidge, of Massachusetts, and Frank W.Hubbard, of Detroit, perhaps the youngest presidential elector, came in March. Baseball was represented by Judge K.M.Landis and John M.Ward and peaceful revolution by Harvey Firestone.

Cabot Morse, the son of the distinguished historian and biographer, John T.Morse, was with us three months. Ex-Governor Durbin of Indiana contributed political conversation, John V.Farwell, of the Yale Corporation, and Frank L.Babbott, president of the Brooklyn Institute; W.Orison Underwood headed all the lawyers supported by Sidney Miller and George J.Peet; bankers in James A.Blair and Jacob Farrand; railroads in Patrick Crowley; the trustees of the University of Pittsburgh were represented by David Gillespie; critics by Clayton Hamilton; McGill University, of Montreal, had a good exhibit in J.T.McCall; the courts of Ohio in Judge Henderson of Columbus; among the great athletes were Joshua Crane, of Massachusetts; Wesley Oler, Senior, of Connecticut; the Duke of Lancaster, from the Copley Plaza, and Mr. Justice Thompson, of Philadelphia. One of the most interesting members was Major Black, eighty-four years old, a Confederate veteran; and thereby hangs a tale.

One morning Major Black—the finest of Southern gentlemen—was asked if during the War he penetrated as far as Ohio. He remarked that he did get into Ohio, and became the guest of the Federal government, which escorted him to a prison on Johnson's Island, at Sandusky. This drew an exclamation from Daniel Frohman. He and his brother Charles were born in Sandusky, and when Daniel was a small boy, he used to go near Johnson's Island, and there 'cockasnook' at the Rebel prisoners. At that time he met Major Black and now met him again in the Conversation Club after an interval of sixty years!

Walter J. Travis was as interesting off the links as on the greens.

During February and March there was almost no rain and no wind. One stilly cloudless day after another. But in January we had five days' continuous rain, which brought the Savannah River to the almost unprecedented height of thirty-seven feet. Hundreds flocked to the bridge every day to see the mad flood. And had it not been for the efforts of one man, who sat at the table next to mine in the hotel, the city would have been under water, and the loss of property would have gone into millions. This gentleman was ex-Mayor Barrett, who, in the year 1912 persuaded the citizens, and only with the greatest difficulty, to erect a levee. In four years it was completed.

Naturally enough, during this river-elevation of 1925, Mr. Barrett became a hero. A statue is to be erected in his honour, though he cared for no memorial except the levee.

Among the many distinguished guests at the hotel in 1925, I became acquainted with two philanthropists, Nathan Straus and Adolph Lewisohn, both of whom were genial and full of ideas. As is well known, Mr. Straus for many years gave his wealth, his time, and himself to the pasteurization of milk, thereby saving the lives of thousands of children.

One day the all-star cast of *The Rivals* came to Augusta, and we met them at a luncheon, where speeches were made

780 THE CONVERSATION CLUB IN AUGUSTA

by Mr. Fiske, Thomas A. Wise, Chauncey Olcott, James T. Powers, Daniel Frohman, and others; all being the guests of the Little Theatre Guild of Augusta. We saw an excellent performance, which took me back to the year 1896.

	New Haven 8 May 1896	Augusta 1 April 1925
Sir Anthony Absolute	William H. Crane	Thomas A. Wise
Capt. Absolute	Robert Taber	Kenneth Thomson
Faulkland	Joseph Holland	Fred Eric
Acres	Joseph Jefferson	James T. Powers
Sir Lucius O'Trigger	Nat Goodwin	Chauncey Olcott
Fag	E. M. Holland	Gerald Rogers
David	Francis Wilson	George Tawde
Mrs. Malaprop	Mrs. John Drew	Mrs. Fiske
Lydia Languish	Julia Marlowe	Lola Fisher
Lucy	Fanny Rice	Marie Carroll
Thomas		Herbert Belmore
Julia Melville		Lotus Robb

The beautiful Lola Fisher was unable to appear at the luncheon; so I went behind the scenes after the first act, and she gave me two photographs of her wonderful cat, which had a face like a Cimabue madonna. Miss Fisher was even then suffering from tuberculosis and I think she knew the end was near.

The following correspondence needs no explanation.

To the President and Corporation of Yale University,

ESTEEMED AND RESPECTED SIRS:

We, the humble subscribers, addicted to the use of all manna that falls from Heaven, do hereby petition that Professor William Lyon Phelps be assigned to resident service as Missionary Bishop of Augusta, Ga., for the month of March of each year and given a full supply of comfortable rooms, conversation and golf balls.

And your petitioners will ever pray.

NICHOLAS MURRAY BUTLER, and others, listed above.

And the president's reply, significantly dated April first:

To Nicholas Murray Butler, Esq.,
And Twenty-five Other Petitioning Malefactors of Great Wealth.

SIRS:

The President and Fellows of Yale University are graciously pleased to take cognizance of your humble petition that one William Lyon Phelps, the same being sound in the faith of the Baptist Communion, be annually assigned during the month of March to resident service as Missionary Bishop of Georgia. Being firmly convinced of the deep spiritual need of our petitioners and of the pagan conditions among which they dwell, our hearts are moved to grant this request. But, be it well known to ye all and several that His Reverence must, at your expense, be well and fitly housed and fed, with golf balls of the newest breed liberally supplied, and that once at least upon each Sabbath Day ye are to gather and listen to his ministrations.

Given under our hand and seal this first day of April, Nineteen hundred and twenty-five.

SEAL   JAMES R. ANGELL

On the resignation of President Hadley, when the Corporation were considering various names, Otto Bannard asked me 'How would you feel if we should take a President who is not a Yale graduate?' I replied, 'I should feel exactly as a Catholic would feel if a Mohammedan were elected Pope.' But after Dr. Angell was chosen, I was loyal not only from a sense of duty, but very soon and permanently because of his ability and character. It is remarkable that he, coming from State Universities into perhaps the most traditionally conservative community in academic life, should have combined his great executive ability with such consummate tact.

In Augusta I have had the honour of playing golf with migratory champions, Glenna Collett, Maureen Orcutt and Helen Detweiler; their playing with me was an act of queenly condescension. And with Lansing Lee and other *inhabitants* I have had many a game of golf, shot innumerable quail, and had many conversations at midnight.

Augusta's foremost living citizen in 1938 is Dr. Eugene Murphey, who was born in Augusta and has never lived anywhere else although he has travelled extensively. He is a first-rate physician, in active practice; he reminds me of Sir William Osler in his love of literature, in his varied reading, and in his insatiable intellectual curiosity. Besides being very well informed, he is one of the foremost ornithologists in America. His conversation is illuminated by knowledge, wit and wisdom, and his home on Telfair Street, presided over by his charming wife ' Mis' Willie,' is a place where food, drink, and conversation are perfect.

In proportion to the population (60,000) Augusta has probably more first-class physicians than any other city in America. The University Hospital and the Medical School partly account for this; also amazingly good luck. When I was very ill, Dr. W. W. Battey, Jr., physician and surgeon, took such magnificent care of me that I owe my complete restoration to health entirely to his skill coupled with his friendship; Dr. Seidenstricker, Head of the University Hospital, Dr. Warren Coleman, heart specialist, and Dr. Peter Wright are absolutely first-class. These men, including, of course, Dr. Murphey, would be distinguished physicians in any city or in any medical school in the world, and they are not the only men of their class in Augusta.

One evening the famous and beloved American novelist, Mary Roberts Rinehart, arrived at our hotel in Augusta on a motor journey to Florida. She had the flu and a temperature of 102; but she was full of vivacity, talked about books and life with her customary vigour, and continued her travels with her son the next morning. Her autobiography, *My Story*, would be exciting reading if it were her only book. And indeed I find it more thrilling than her mystery stories, exciting as they are.

85

NOTES OF TRAVEL AND OTHER NOTES

ONE winter afternoon in 1927 I took the train from New York, expecting to reach Philadelphia about half-past five, which would give me plenty of time to change and dine and reach the Metropolitan Opera House at half-past eight. But a blizzard had been raging, the train was more than two hours late, and I had no time even to change. As soon as I reached the hotel, I entered a taxi, clad in my light tweeds and told the driver my destination. On one of those narrow streets choked with snow, the taxi came to a standstill, and all efforts to revive the engine were fruitless. 'Can't you make her go?' 'She's dead, boss.' I got out and stood in the middle of the narrow snowy thoroughfare, and when the first car came along, I raised my hands, believing it would not run over me. The driver stopped with a shrieking of brakes and some language. I explained my predicament. I was due in five minutes at the auditorium and it was a long distance. 'Get in!' He drove with terrific speed, running up on the sidewalks and around lamp-posts to avoid vehicles. We drew up on time in front of the vast building. I looked up at him out of the corner of my left eye, as I wondered whether he were a gentleman and would feel insulted or whether it would be safe to offer him money. I decided on the latter course and gave him a bill. He accepted it nonchalantly and said 'Just a moment. Let me give you my card.' 'Why?' I wondered. He handed me a card with his name and telephone number. Then he whispered, 'Any time you want any real good liquor, you call me up.' Those were the days of prohibition. The man was a bootlegger!

I walked out on the platform in my daylight clothes and told the whole story to the audience before beginning the lecture. It is my custom to call for questions at the close of my lectures. Ushers collect written questions on literature from the audience, bring them to the platform and I answer them. That night seven of the cards brought to the desk had the same question: ' What was that telephone number?'

On 9 January 1928 at the Shubert Theatre in New Haven, under the direction of Winthrop Ames, Mr. George Arliss, for the first time in his life, appeared in a Shakespearean role. The play ran smoothly, the whole cast was adequate, Peggy Wood made a brilliant and charming Portia, neglecting the statuesque for the human; but naturally the chief interest centred on Mr. Arliss's interpretation of Shylock. I had seen in this role Edwin Booth, Henry Irving, Richard Mansfield, Walter Hampden, Edward Sothern, Ernst von Possart, David Warfield. Edwin Booth was the most impressive. The poorest was Henry Irving, for it seemed to me that in representing him as a sympathetic character he reversed the dynamics. Mr. Arliss made him sinister but human; he was a patrician; he had that air toward his Christian adversaries that comes from a sense of superiority; they wanted money and he had it. He spoke his lines quietly but with a suggestion of reserved power. Next to his Disraeli, I think Shylock is Mr. Arliss's best performance. The whole production showed the impeccable taste and intelligence characteristic of Winthrop Ames, whose death (1937) was a sad loss to the theatre and an intense personal grief to thousands of individuals.

Jan. 13, 1928

DEAR DR. PHELPS

Allow me to thank you for your splendid tribute to our production and to me. It has been a disappointment to me that I have not been able to spend any time with my friends of New Haven. We have practically lived in the theatre. I hope I may come later when I am not in the throes of a new production.

With kind regards,

GEORGE ARLISS

President Coolidge's famous utterance 'I do not choose to run' made the word *choose* so famous that for several years any repetition of it drew an audible response. When Portia said 'But this reasoning is not in the fashion to choose me a husband. O me, the word choose!' a ripple of mirth flowed over the audience.

When Stephen Benét's *John Brown's Body* appeared in 1928, it scored an instant success; it seems to belong to American literature. The following letter came from the locality where it was written:

36 RUE DE LONGCHAMP, NEUILLY-SUR-
SEINE, FRANCE

DEAR PROFESSOR PHELPS:

Thank you for your letter—I am glad if you liked the book. It was a long job and I was very much surprised—still am—at the reception it has had. Now I should like to get to work on something else—but this has been a vile winter over here and I am still dry as far as writing goes. However, they say the sun will emerge sometime, though it hasn't yet been authenticated.

With all best wishes

Sincerely

STEPHEN VINCENT BENÉT

220 EAST 69TH STREET
NEW YORK

DEAR BILLY:

I am having Doubleday send you a copy of Paul Engle's "American Song" because it seems to me the sort of thing you'd be particularly interested in. He's a young Iowan, now at Merton, on a Rhodes —and he is the first voice in poetry that I know of that represents the new, young generation just out of college—and it seems to me good speech. It's authentic, American, and it has a queer new idealism that ought to surprise a good many people—though not yourself, after the years at Yale. But I think you'll like it—and if you can do anything for it, that would be simply swell. You know what a row most young poets have to hoe—and this is a real one.

With all good wishes

STEVE BENÉT

In 1928 one curious repetition which I may have been the only one to witness should be recorded. On a certain Thursday afternoon I went to see *Interference* at the Lyceum Theatre in New York. In the middle of the second act the leading man was violently threatening a certain woman, who was intelligently presented by Miss McDonnell. At exactly the proper moment she fainted. Not a person in the audience suspected the truth until her threatener requested 'Sterling' to lower the curtain. Then a man came before the curtain and announced: 'Miss McDonnell has fainted. We must ask the kind indulgence of the audience to wait five minutes in order to see if she can proceed. If she is unable to do so, we must find her understudy.' In five minutes, and to great applause, Miss McDonnell did proceed. Well, exactly two weeks after this strange interlude, I was in the neighbouring Belasco Theatre, witnessing *The Bachelor Father*. In the course of the second act the curtain was rung down; a man came before it and said: 'Miss June Walker fainted at the close of the first act; we must ask the kind indulgence of the audience to wait five minutes to see if she will be able to continue. If she cannot, we must find her understudy.' In five minutes, and to great applause, Miss Walker did continue. Now then: is there a peculiar fatality attached to Thursday matineés, or did these actresses faint because I was in the audience?

On 7 June 1927 died one of the best columnists America has ever had—Keith Preston of Chicago. I agree with Harry Hansen that the following is one of Preston's most characteristic contributions:

THE LIBERATORS

Among our literary scenes,
Saddest this sight to me,
The graves of little magazines
That died to make verse free.

Among the men I met in June in a golfing expedition to Manchester, Vermont, was a certain gentleman who spoke of his favourite mixture for the pipe with such earnestness that his face took on a holy look. 'Why,' said I, 'you ought to be Professor of Nicotine.' 'Yes,' added Professor E.B.Reed, 'and then you could preach the tobacco-laureate sermon.'

During the season of 1926–7, Helen Hayes revived with immense success Barrie's *What Every Woman Knows*. When she reached New Haven, I took to the performance two undergraduates at Yale, one from Oxford, one from Cambridge, one a Scot and the other English. They had never seen this play and enjoyed the opportunity each had to laugh at the other. I took them to Miss Hayes's dressing-room after the play; she was amused at their coming together.

Helen Hayes made her first journey abroad a few weeks later.

GRAND HOTEL, NAPLES
JUNE 18, 1927

DEAR MR. PHELPS—
    You were very kind to me in New Haven. I feel you were chiefly responsible for our splendid week there. The extent of my gratitude proven by my leaving Naples for five minutes to tell you of it. I

have never been so happy in my life as in this past week. We leave for Rome tomorrow. I hope I don't burst with the joy of that.

Many good wishes

Sincerely

HELEN HAYES

Elizabeth Haldane, sister of Lord Haldane, exhibited learning and common sense in all her books, which I read with enjoyment. I wrote how much I admired her book on George Eliot.

CLOAN, AUCHTERARDER,
PERTHSHIRE.
Aug. 6, 1927

MY DEAR SIR:

I am extremely gratified by hearing that my George Eliot meets with your approval & greatly pleased that you have noticed it in so important a journal as "Scribner's."

The study of this great woman gave me much pleasure & I only wish I could have done more justice to her. Her work seems to sur‐pass most of the fiction of the day & I have great hope that there may be a revival of George Eliot as there has been (in this country at least) a revival of Trollope.

With warm thanks for your courtesy in writing, I am

Very truly yours,

ELIZABETH HALDANE

The name of your home brings such happy recollections of the reading of Hawthorne's masterpiece. [Seven Gables, our summer home in Michigan.]

Miss Haldane died in December 1937.

TWO TRAGIC WORDS BY SWIFT

In the course of my life I have seen hundreds of rare manu‐scripts and first editions; but I have never received a greater thrill than when Mrs. Prescott showed me her copy

of a book by Jonathan Swift with his own manuscript
annotations. The reason for this particular thrill is seen in
two words. In his regular birthday poem for Stella, with
the date 1724-5, called *Stella's Birthday*, and first published in the last volume of his *Miscellanies*, 1727, the last
four lines of the poem express the hope that when Stella
grows old she will ever appear young to him provided his
hearing should be better than his *sight*. The four lines run
as follows, in the edition of 1727:

> Thus you may still be young to me,
> While I can better *hear* than *see*;
> Oh, ne'er may Fortune shew her Spight,
> To make me *deaf*, and mend my *Sight*.

In Mrs. Prescott's copy I saw that, fifteen years after he
had written the poem, Swift had underlined the word
'deaf' and then written in the margin 'now deaf—1740.'

That volume, apart from this 'tremendous trifle,' has
had a curious history. I am glad I saw it when I did in
Mrs. Prescott's house in Stamford, Conn., for it might
have been my last opportunity. Some years later she told
me she had exchanged it for something she wanted even
more. In 1938 appeared Harold Williams's admirable edition of Swift's *Poems* (3 vols. Oxford) and in response to
my enquiry, he was kind enough to write, 'I have seen the
set of the Pope and Swift *Miscellanies* to which you refer
several times, and both in Ireland and England. I never
saw it while it was in America. For a long time it was in the
library of Lord Powerscourt in Ireland. Then it passed to
Mr. W.G. Panter, who lived near Dublin. After his death
it found its way to . . . Mrs. Prescott. . . . It has now
come back to England, and is in the possession of Lord
Rothschild.'

Two New Haven women whom I knew well, in their
lives illustrated the highest possibilities of nobleness and

courage. Mrs. Virginia Curtis, who lost her husband early in life, had two sons in my class in college. Tom was the valedictorian and John the fourth in rank. Only a few years after graduation Tom died of a fever; and John, who was at a distant sanatorium after a nervous breakdown, committed suicide. She was informed of this by a newspaper reporter who woke her at two o'clock in the morning. She lost the major part of her fortune by a frost in Florida that destroyed her property. A highly educated woman, devoted to studies in various languages, she went to bed one night without any premonition of evil, and woke up in the morning incurably and totally blind. I often talked with her after these shattering disasters, and never heard her utter one word of complaint. She was always calm and always interested in contemporary books and events. Although she was a devout Christian, she never uttered a sanctimonious expression or any of the stock phrases of holiness. But once, when we were talking about religion, she remarked quietly that if religion were not true, life would be meaningless, a tragic farce.

Mrs. Henry P. Wright, the wife of the Dean of Yale College, also had two brilliant sons who were in the highest group of scholars. Alfred died of tuberculosis shortly after graduation; Henry became a Professor at Yale and exerted a widespread and inspiring influence on colleagues and students; he died suddenly in early middle age. Her only daughter, an admirable scholar and school-teacher, died of cancer in the thirties. Her husband died before the death of Henry and her daughter. Then Mrs. Wright became totally blind. Mrs. Curtis was serene and composed like a Stoic; Mrs. Wright was cheerful and *radiantly happy*. She told me once that she was so grateful for life. 'Grateful!' I exclaimed. 'Why, of course, why not? I have devoted friends, I am not ill, I have so many beautiful things to think about.' And indeed she was fortunate in the devoted care of Josephine, her son Henry's wife, who is a saint; and other more distant relations and friends were often with her. But *grateful*? These two women seemed to me like heroines of Greek tragedy; they suffered the worst disasters that can befall any one. They were living illustrations of the triumph of Christian faith.

There is no doubt that women have more courage than men. And there is a reason for it; they need it more. It takes courage just to be a woman.

> Tell me, are men unhappy, in some kind
> Of mere unhappiness at being men,
> As women suffer, being womanish?

86

GENE TUNNEY

On Thursday 22 December 1927, while we were staying at the house of Mr. William Matheson at Coconut Grove, Florida, I went over to Miami Beach and had a long talk with the champion heavy-weight boxer of the world, Joseph J.Tunney of New York, universally known as Gene Tunney. I knew he was fond of reading Shakespeare. I told him that I was teaching Shakespeare at Yale, and that during the coming Spring term I should be very glad to have him address my class. He immediately agreed.

When this was announced in the newspapers, I was called up on the telephone by a reporter and asked 'Can Tunney really talk in public on Shakespeare, or is this just part of the ballyhoo for the next fight?' I replied that if we should change places, Mr. Tunney would look much better lecturing on Shakespeare than I should in the ring with Jack Dempsey.

Mr. Matheson invited Tunney to meet the Bishop of Florida and Mrs. Mann, together with Ruth Bryan Owen, and several others, at lunch. Although Tunney is a big man and weighed two hundred pounds, his hands and feet are small. He stood beside Mrs. Owen, a tall woman, and we found her hands were longer, though not as broad as his. Tunney and the Bishop carried on a spirited conversation; and Tunney told us how he came to enjoy Shakespeare. It was when he was a private soldier in the World War. There was a comrade who was always talking about Shakespeare; and Tunney, becoming interested, made up his mind he would read him. He had the bad luck to begin with *Winter's Tale*. He read it through from beginning to end and it made no impression. I think most adventurers would have stopped there. Not so Tunney. *He read through Winter's Tale ten times.*

After the tenth reading, he felt he had mastered it. He then went on to read the other plays. In a similar manner, by concentrating his listening powers, he became a passionate lover of the best symphonic music and of the operas of Wagner.

On 23 April Tunney addressed my Shakespeare class. The large auditorium was jammed, with crowds standing up. Tunney used no notes. He spoke informally for three-quarters of an hour. He told the students they had had every educational advantage and he had had none. 'But when you are graduated and out in the world, then your case will be like mine. Your professors will not be able to help you; you will have to do it all for yourself. If you succeed, it will be because you have had the necessary will-power and perseverance.' He said perhaps his favourite play of Shakespeare was *Troilus and Cressida*. For it applied exactly to his own case. 'Why have I been invited to speak at Yale? Surely not because I have anything important to say about Shakespeare. I have been invited because I am the champion boxer of the world. I am that *now*, and there is great interest in everything I do and say. I am followed around by crowds. But how long do you suppose that will last? It will last just as long as I am heavy-weight champion. Ten years from now nobody will care what I do or what I say. It is important for me therefore to make the most of the present moment, for the present moment is all I have.'

He said Shakespeare understood that situation perfectly. Hector was the heavy-weight champion of the Trojans and the only man among the Greeks who could stand up to

him was Achilles. But Achilles would not fight. He sulked
in his tent. And yet he was very angry when Ulysses and
the other Greeks put up Ajax to fight Hector; and all their
cheers were for Ajax. 'Now Ajax,' said Mr. Tunney, 'was
a big powerful man without much brains, just like Jack
Sharkey.'

The next day a reporter called up Sharkey at his training-
camp and said 'Tunney says you are like Ajax.' It is possible that Mr. Sharkey thought Ajax was some kind of a
disease, for he responded, 'You can tell Tunney there is
nothing the matter with me at all.'

I believe every newspaper in the world contained some
kind of report of Tunney's address. Press cuttings were
sent me from India, New Zealand, Alaska, Japan—indeed
from everywhere. For the moment, Tunney found himself
more famous for having lectured at Yale than for having
defeated Dempsey; and I found myself more famous for
having invited him than for any book I had written or any
professional work I had done.

From the *Münchener Neueste Nachrichten*:

SHAKESPEARE—KOLLEG DES BOXERS

Wie Professor Phelps, der den Lehrstuhl für englische Literatur
an der amerikanischen Yale Universität innehat, mitteilt, hat er
Gene Tunney, den Schwergewichtsboxmeister der Welt, eingeladen,
an der Universität Vorlesungen über Shakespeare und seine Zeit zu
halten. Tunney hat den ehrenvollen Auftrag auch angenommen,
Professor Phelps traf den Boxmeister während seines Aufenthalts in
Florida und spricht sich begeistert über die Sachkenntnis und das
Urteil aus, das Tunney in der Unterhaltung mit ihm offenbarte.

About thirty years before this occasion, when on St.
Patrick's Day, 1897, Jim Corbett fought Fitzsimmons at
Carson City, Nevada, several prominent undergraduates
at Yale had sent a small Yale flag for Corbett to place in
his corner as a talisman during the fight. Although Corbett

did not do this, the fact that the flag had been sent got into the newspapers, and the result was a scandal. Hundreds of persons insisted that these students be expelled, and I well remember that there was a long and exciting Faculty meeting, and that they were saved only by a close vote. One of the students was Payne Whitney.

Suppose the Faculty could have known that in thirty years the champion boxer of the world would lecture at Yale on Shakespeare!

That summer of 1928 Tunney was in the island of Brioni in the Mediterranean; there he was joined by the most famous literary man in the world and by the most famous musical composer—Bernard Shaw and Richard Strauss. The three men took long walks together. Mr. Shaw told me, 'The newspaper men kept coming over from the mainland; they cared nothing whatever for anything I said or that Strauss could say; our opinions did not interest them. But the moment Tunney opened his mouth the reporters took down every word. They wished to know his opinions on every subject.'

Some literary man, I have forgotten which, said he would rather be champion boxer of the world than a great poet. 'For how wonderful it must be to go to any city in the world and know that you can lick any man in that town.'

When one considers the number of strong fellows in every city, it seems incredible that any one man can feel certain of whipping them. I asked Tunney about that, and he replied 'Well, there is room for only one champion at a time. The place is free and open to any man who can take and hold it.' Then, after some reflexion, he said, 'There are five qualities necessary if one wishes to be champion of the world, and all five are seldom found in one man.'

The candidate for the championship must possess great strength; he must have a body far stronger than that of the average healthy young man. Of course there are thousands of whom this is true; there are any number of powerful young men. The second qualification is panther-like agility, speed, and nimbleness; this quality, when it is combined with immense weight and strength, is not so common. The man must be like an elephant in solid strength and like a leopard in ease and grace of movement. Still, while the combination is not so common as either quality taken singly, there are plenty of young men who are both strong and fast. The third quality is courage, the foundation of all virtues for any ambitious man, no matter where his ambition may lie. Many men are secretly afraid, no matter how confident their bearing, or how assured their speech. The successful fighter must either be without fear or succeed in overcoming it. Tunney told me (and without a shade of conceit) that he was not afraid of anybody or anything.

The fourth quality must be the ability to take punishment without becoming disabled. This is different from courage. Just as the bravest man may be seasick, or dizzy at a great height, so the bravest man in the ring may receive a blow either so powerful or so well directed that he cannot go on, and the fight is lost. This was the case with Corbett in his memorable contest with Fitzsimmons. He had courage, confidence, and will power; but when Fitzsimmons hit him in the solar plexus, he was like a man paralysed; he was through. If he had been able to endure that blow, he could have gone on and probably won. 'Now,' said Tunney, 'if I had received that particular blow, it would have hurt, I should have felt the terrible impact, but I should not have become disabled. In Chicago, Dempsey repeatedly hit me fearful blows; they were like the shock of a pile-driver; every one of those blows hurt; yet I was able to go on. One reason was that whether I am in training or not, I keep my body, by the proper exercises every day, in such condition that it can success-fully withstand almost any human blow.'

And he explained how, on rising from bed every morn-ing, he sat down, put his feet under the radiator, and bent over backward, keeping the abdominal muscles hard as steel. Should the ordinary healthy man try that motion just once, the result would be hernia.

The fifth, last, and by no means least of the qualifica-tions is perfect control of the nerves; for strange as it may seem in the case of professional boxers, all of whom are of exceptional strength and bodily vigour, more men fail to reach the championship through bad nerves than through any other defect. Prizefighters suffer from insomnia even more than brain workers, and it is easy to see why. The ordinary prizefighter is not a man of many intellectual re-sources; he cannot divert his mind with a variety of things. Thus, when he is in training for a contest and the day of doom draws near, he becomes more and more nervous. He cannot exercise every moment, and when he is not in full bodily activity, he finds it difficult to relax and feel cheerful, because he is thinking all the time of the great day. Finally, when he steps into the ring, his nerves are in a frazzle.

I envy Gene Tunney his nerve control more than his strength or agility. On the day before his contests and on the morning thereof, he was as calm and self-possessed as if nothing unusual were going on.

He said something of value to every man and woman without regard to the nature of their work. He regarded it as fortunate that he loved good books and music, etc., quite apart from the intrinsic value of such things; be-cause, during his weeks of active training, he could at any moment divert his mind by reading a good book or listen-ing to the piano. It is not healthy for any man or woman to be obsessed by one thought; the mind becomes hag-ridden, and the nerves go to pieces. The brain needs variety; thus the more avocations a man has outside of his work, the more efficiently he will do that work, and the fresher and healthier his mind will be.

Thus all the five qualities enumerated by Gene Tunney are very seldom found in any one man. 1. Strength. 2. Supple agility and speed. 3. Courage. 4. Ability to take punishment. 5. Complete control of the nerves.

The ideal element in Tunney's nature enabled him to see the goal long before he reached it, as one sees the towers and pinnacles of a city from afar. He has all along been aided by sensitiveness to beauty, which has found expression and which has brought him refreshment and inspiration in poetry and music. Stephen Phillips's poem, *Marpessa*, is one of his favourites, and he carried it everywhere. Another of his best-loved poets is Francis Thompson, original, imaginative, and spiritual. In music, the *études* of Chopin move him more deeply than anything else. Among novelists, his most intimate friend is Thornton Wilder.

Unlike many self-made men, he has allowed neither success nor flattery to turn his head. He is not conceited; yet in his ring contests and in his preparation for them he was filled with confidence. His nature illustrates the difference between confidence and conceit.

This cheerful confidence did not make him careless, either in the ring or out of it. He made his own training rules and never departed from them. And even when he was not in training, he kept himself in condition by neither smoking nor drinking, by being careful in diet, *and by not getting excited*. On the day he fought Dempsey at Chicago, he had a good dinner at three o'clock, then read Somerset Maugham's novel *Of Human Bondage* for an hour and a half, and actually forgot he was to fight that evening!

Confidence means two things; it means that one is certain of one's ability to perform the assigned task, certain of being equal to the situation; and secondly, it means that one enjoys the work in the assurance that one can do it well. The great surgeon goes to the hospital, not with fear and trembling, but with the certainty that he will perform the operation as it should be performed; so he is happy in his work.

87

JOURNEY TO EUROPE IN 1928

WE landed at Plymouth in a dense fog. At dinner a large
and old yellow cat walked solemnly about the room. I
picked him up and caressed him. Immediately a waiter
came to me in horror. 'Do not hold the cat, sir; he is very
dangerous; he does not allow anyone to touch him; and
we have had some most unfortunate experiences.' Accordingly I put the cat down; but although he had not purred,
he submitted to my endearments with no show of resentment.

Mr. and Mrs. Harley Granville-Barker were living at a
beautiful old manor house at Netherton Hall, not far from
Plymouth; a telephone message came inviting us to visit
them. It was a magnificent place over three hundred years
old. The weather was perfect and that afternoon I had
eight sets of lawn tennis with our host and with Mrs. Dash-
wood (E. M. Delafield).

After dinner Mrs. Granville-Barker played beautifully
on the clavichord. A genuine English breakfast was served
the next morning and for the first time we became acquainted with 'back' bacon. The coffee was delicious;
Mrs. Granville-Barker is an American.

NETHERTON HALL,
COLYTON, DEVON
24.7.28

MY DEAR "BILLY"

So glad you've had a good time. And why shouldn't you have?
You bring the good time with you. We've even given you some

summer weather. That I do take credit for—but only that. I made arrangements for it with the B.B.C.

Glad in particular that you met Hawkins and know his Memoirs—you knew him before, of course. There's no book I'd rather have America read to learn what the English governing mind is like—and what the English voice is when you can hear it for the bawling of Beavermere and Rotherbrook.

Don't tell me to come back and 'produce.' One ploughs the sands lightheartedly when one is young: when the sun's past meridian one thinks of leaving some thing behind. As we've no theatre in England which lets one do that—we had a European war instead; you can't have *all* the pleasures of life—I've turned (but I always planned to) to the printed page.

Our kind thoughts to you both and a pleasant time abroad—as we call the mere continent and I hope you do, this not being 'abroad' for you. But come back to England and count always on a welcome not least from

Yrs

H.G.B.

This letter alludes to a delightful day we had spent with 'Anthony Hope' and Lady Hawkins. In the third paragraph Mr. Granville-Barker expressed an intention which during the following ten years was magnificently fulfilled.

One day we went out to Hampstead to call on my friend, the veteran dramatist Henry Arthur Jones. He was in poor health, weakened by several major operations, but his mind alert and keen as ever, deeply interested in contemporary life and letters. He lived with his daughter, Mrs. Doris Thorne, who is keeping up the family traditions. Mr. Jones showed me over his house, filled with furniture made by William Morris and tiles and pottery by William De Morgan.

One afternoon at Mrs. Clifford's house on Chilworth Street, I met my former pupil at Yale, Frederick Kaye, who became a distinguished scholar and Professor of

English literature at Northwestern University. His early death closed a brilliant career.

7 CHILWORTH STREET
LONDON, W.2

Nov., 1928

I was delighted to get your little letter, dear Billy, for your learned Professorship seems to wish me to call you that. But your word about Fred Kaye made me very sad. We have known him so well and had many happy hours with him. He is a curious and delightful combination of the real lover of work and student, and the simple hearted school boy. I think he has overworked his too subtle brain? We are haunted by the dread of hearing—it is what my husband did. *His* brain was always clear and eager, but the rest of him was not strong enough to bear the strain.

We think of you both so often—*what* a joy it was to see you two dear people and how kind you have been to me in Scribner and elsewhere—so much more than I deserve. I wish you had been here just a week earlier to meet those nice people who took themselves off too soon to the country. Still I love to think you had a good time and good weather. We have been having, so far in, a wonderful November—so mild and soft—just mitigated by one terrible gale last Friday. I lunched today with Lady Walston, the widow of Sir Charles Walston (*Waldstein* before the war). She would have so much liked to meet you. She was abroad. . . .

I wonder if you were satisfied with your Presidential Election? We all voted Hoover over here; we remember all he did (for the starving Belgians especially) in the war. Well? What next?

St. John Ervine's Theatre articles in the Observer are much read. He is alive—has fine qualities. Do you remember the play at the little "Ambassador Theatre"? You were both at the first night. It is still running and has emerged with a solid success. Is it done over there?

Now I must stop—with love to you both.

Yours as always,

LUCY C.

The play she mentions in the last paragraph was *Many Waters*, which had great success in London and not much in New York.

On 13 July I saw the grave of Hardy in Westminster Abbey; and once more verified the original inscription on the grave of Ben Jonson:

O RARE BEN JOHNSON

Yes, the *H* is in the name on the inscription, though it is often stated otherwise.

Mr. Leon M. Lion, the famous actor-manager, identified with the producing and acting of Galsworthy's plays, invited us to a matinée of *Justice*; we talked with him and with Michael Morton after the performance. During this conversation, a letter was brought from a man waiting in the street, saying he had served a term in prison, and wanted Mr. Lion to give him financial assistance. Ever since his first appearance in this play Mr. Lion said he had had requests from convicts every day; and that Mr. Galsworthy got even more.

On the next day at Hammersmith we heard a delightful performance of Bickerstaff's *Love in a Village* produced by Sir Nigel Playfair. That evening Mr. and Mrs. Charles Morgan gave us a dinner at the Garrick Club, where we met the Rev. Mr. Fry and his wife (Sheila Kaye-Smith), Mr. and Mrs. Ellis, and Mr. and Mrs. Brett Young.

I am glad Mr. Young refers in this letter to *My Brother Jonathan*, for I think it is one of his best.

CASTLE HOTEL,
HORNBY,
NEAR LANCASTER

DEAR WILLIAM LYON PHELPS,

When we dined with the Morgans at the Garrick you were so kind as to ask me if I would lecture at Yale when I came to America. We are sailing for New York on the Carmania, on October 27th, and shall be staying there with our headquarters at our old friends, the T. W. Lamonts (107 East 70th St.) until the New Year. I should love to talk to your young men, who must be one of the best audiences in the world, on THE IDEALS OF A NOVELIST. (Incidentally, I've tried to follow those ideals in my new book, MY BROTHER JONATHAN, which I asked Knopf to send you.) I also hope very much to see, for the first time in my life, the Yale-Harvard game in November. The only engagement I have booked at present—for, as you know, this is a pleasure-trip, not a lecture-tour, is a lunch in N.Y. on December 6th. Perhaps you will be good enough to let me know on my arrival at the Lamonts' if the idea of my subject appeals to you.

It will be a great delight for both of us to renew our acquaintance with Mrs. Phelps and your charming self. Our meeting at the Garrick was a delightful surprise; I had heard so much about you from Archie Marshall and other friends, including Hugh Walpole, with whom we spent last week-end at his Lakeland cottage. And I do hope you'll like MY BROTHER JONATHAN, because, if you don't, I'm afraid you'll never like anything else of mine, being positively convinced—quite apart from my natural predilection for the latest-born—that it's my very best.

Very sincerely yours,

FRANCIS BRETT YOUNG

On 16 July we lunched with Mr. and Mrs. Walter Payne and with Sir Nigel and Lady Playfair. During the conversation, both Sir Nigel and Mr. Payne said there were many good things about the censorship as practised in England. I was not quite sure whether they themselves were unreservedly in favour of it, but they said some theatre managers were; that when the Lord Chamberlain refused a licence, that ended the matter, and they were saved from expense. On the other hand, when he gave permission, that made it impossible for any crank or any organization to interfere with the play or to threaten its withdrawal. If a censorship is to be established, and on the whole I don't believe in it, the English method is the only good one. The Lord Chamberlain is a great personage. He is irresponsible, as he should be. He never has to explain or give any reason. He does or does not give permission and that's the end of the matter. In America, one judge will refuse, and after that is efficiently advertised, another judge permits the show, thus assured of a sensational success, to proceed.

Tuesday evening, 17 July, I lectured on Browning at the Browning Settlement in South London; in the audience were Thornton Wilder and his family.

Wednesday evening 18 July we went to the first performance of *Many Waters*. The leading woman's part was admirably given by Marda Vanne. Later we were so fortunate as to come to know her well, both at her house in London and at our own house in New Haven when she came over to take this same part in New York.

On 19 July I dined with the novelist Archibald Marshall and the famous journalist S.K. Ratcliffe, at Brooks's, and then I took them and my colleague Professor Karl Young to a concert at Queen's Hall given by the Yale University Glee Club.

On a brilliant day in July 1928 we saw the cricket-match between Eton and Harrow at Lord's, the English equivalent of a Yale-Harvard football game. Only as it is played in the midst of summer, the thousands of men and women, dressed in their absolute best, make a never-to-be-forgotten spectacle. As we wandered about among the throng only one element of tragedy marred the gay scene. This was the almost complete absence of men between the ages of thirty and forty. Old and middle-aged men, boys and girls, but an entire generation was missing—the war had taken them.

We were fortunate in being accompanied by the novelist Archibald Marshall and by Gerald Campbell, sports writer for the London *Times* and an old cricketer. They explained to me the mysteries of the game and the significance of the occasion.

Over a hundred years ago, when Eton beat Harrow as she did on this day also, an Eton schoolboy-poet produced the following poem.

Ye silly boys of Harrow School,
  Of cricket ye've no knowledge.
It was not cricket, but the fool,
  Ye played with Eton College.

Alas, there was a boy at Harrow named George Gordon, later Lord Byron. He instantly replied:

If as you say we played the fool,
  No wonder we were beaten;
For at that game no other School
  Could e'er compete with Eton.

One afternoon we went to Chelsea to take tea with Mr. and Mrs. Charles Morgan. Mr. Morgan was in Oxford when the war broke out. He immediately enlisted and when the war was over returned to the university, was graduated with high honours, and soon was appointed drama critic on the London *Times*, the blue ribbon of that profession. He told me that although he enjoyed writing criticisms his particular ambition was to be a novelist. A few years later he published *The Fountain*, which had enormous success in England and in America.

His next novel, *Sparkenbroke*, is a combination of philosophy and mysticism, as well as an exciting story, for although Mr. Morgan is a practical and sensible English critic, there is a deeply spiritual side to his nature which gives a poetical and elevating atmosphere to all his novels.

G. K. CHESTERTON

We went to take lunch with Mr. and Mrs. G. K. Chesterton in an old Tudor farmhouse in Beaconsfield. They had a lovely garden, and the whole place made an ideal setting for persons so thoroughly and traditionally English. And I highly enjoyed talking with Mrs. Chesterton's mother, eighty years old.

In 1890 I had bicycled by this place, on the high road

from London to Oxford. Mr. Chesterton was then sixteen years old. But a few yards from his garden I dismounted to read the inscription on the grave of the seventeenth-century poet, Edmund Waller, who, when past eighty, wrote:

> The soul's dark cottage, battered and decayed,
> Lets in new light through chinks that time has made.
> Stronger by weakness, wiser men become
> As they draw near to their eternal home.

I hope that will be true of me if I succeed in living that long.

Mr. Chesterton was one of the busiest men in the world and never seemed to be in a hurry. During the Boer War, while he was making a speech, the mob got excited and somebody stole his watch. He never carried one again. 'Why, how do you manage without one?' He laughed. 'Oh, it doesn't really make any particular difference what time it is, and if I really want to know, I ask.' He edited, in addition to his poems, novels, religious works, essays, biographies, *G. K.'s Weekly*, a worse burden than the Old Man of the Sea. But its object was to promulgate ideas in which he believed.

When he was taken to see the great White Way in New York he made a remark that ought to live forever. He looked up at the amazing illumination and said: 'What a place this would be for a man who could not read!'

I asked him what impressed him as the chief difference between the aspect of England and America. He said: 'Your wooden houses.' I had never thought there was anything unusual about wooden houses, because we take them for granted. But a wooden house in England is a rare spectacle. It seems incredible that there can be enough stone in that small island to supply the demand.

Mr. Chesterton gave me a copy of the booklet contain-

ing his famous debate with Bernard Shaw. I would I had
been present. It was not the clumsy contact of the irresistible force and the immovable object; it was a duel between
two of the best swordsmen in England, each of whom had
an affectionate admiration for his opponent's skill.

Mr. Chesterton not only gave the impression of thoroughly enjoying life; he had an extraordinary kindness, a
certain gentleness, a consideration for others, that went
well with his masculine vitality. He never lost what Browning called the 'faculty of wonder.' He never outgrew his
zest for life. In *Saint Barbara*, he wrote

> When all my days are ending
> And I have no song to sing,
> I think I shall not be too old
> To stare at everything;
> As I stared once at a nursery door
> Or a tall tree and a swing.

I found this comment in a French newspaper, (I think
Figaro) a few days after his death.

On a rapellé, ces jours, nombre de mots que G.K.Ches-
terton avait semé tout au long de sa vie et de son œuvre.
Celui-ci est, croyons-nous, inédit.

Grand et fort, Chesterton se moquait volontiers de son
obésité. Récemment, un de ses amis lui reprochait sa
rudesse.

"Peut-être suis-je rude," dit-il, "mais du moins je suis
toujours courtois. Ce matin, j'étais assis dans l'autobus,
et bien, j'ai cédé ma place à trois femmes."—*Figaro* (?)

In an essay on American morals, G.K.C. made a pertinent and significant enquiry into certain conceptions, perhaps more common in America than elsewhere, of right
and wrong. One reason for his poking fun at us on ethical
questions arises from the fact, I believe, that Americans as
a class are more *anxious to be right* than the people of any
other country. That leads us no doubt into some absur-

dities. Here is what G.K.C. said about an American attitude toward smoking.

> . . . I remember once receiving two American interviewers on the
> same afternoon; there was a box of cigars in front of me and I offered
> one to each in turn. Their reaction (as they would probably call it)
> was very curious to watch. The first journalist stiffened suddenly and
> silently, and declined in a very cold voice. He could not have con-
> veyed more plainly that I had attempted to corrupt an honourable
> man with a foul and infamous indulgence; as if I were the Old Man
> of the Mountain offering him the hashish that would turn him into
> an assassin. The second reaction was even more remarkable. The
> second journalist first looked doubtful; then looked sly; then seemed
> to glance about him nervously, as if wondering whether we were
> alone, and then said with a sort of crestfallen and covert smile: " Well,
> Mr. Chesterton, I'm afraid I have the habit."
>
> As I also have the habit, and have never been able to imagine how
> it could be connected with morality or immorality, I confess that I
> plunged with him deeply into an immoral life. In the course of our
> conversation, I found he was otherwise perfectly sane. He was quite
> intelligent about economics or architecture; but his moral sense
> seemed to have entirely disappeared. He really thought it was rather
> wicked to smoke.

Now it is just possible that these two men were misunderstood by G.K.C. They were in the presence of a great
man; they had never seen him before; they were naturally
awkward and embarrassed. I am certain that if Bernard
Shaw should offer an American reporter a cigar—which he
would not do—the stranger would be in some confusion.

But I agree with Mr. Chesterton that there is more often
in America than in any other country a misconception of
morals which has done a great deal of harm. Excessive
smoking for the very young and for certain invalids is
probably not hygienic; just as coffee is bad for people who
suffer from heart disease. But that smoking in itself and
for the average person should have a flavour of wickedness is unfortunate; it confuses standards of morals and

actually makes some people who enjoy smoking feel that they are indulging in secret vice.

There should be no flavour about smoking except the flavour of tobacco; and yet I was brought up to believe that smoking was wrong, 'inconsistent with a Christian life.'

While the daily consumption of even a moderate amount of alcohol is probably injurious to the majority of persons, and while we should probably be better off if no alcohol were obtainable, I am convinced that the idea that to taste wine or beer is a sin has wrought injury. If we could regard wine as it was regarded by the early Christians, indifferently, as we regard tea or coffee, that is, without a shade of wickedness, it would probably be better for the morals of the human race, and there would be fewer hip-pocket flasks and less swinish drinking.

I remember how shocked and bewildered I was when first reading *Tom Brown at Oxford* to find that the most serious and most spiritually minded men drank together as naturally as they ate. When the late Mr. James B. Reynolds went forty years ago to a certain town in Belgium to form a Y.M.C.A. among university students, their meeting was opened with prayer and beer.

In 1928 Thornton Wilder published his first successful book, *The Bridge of San Luis Rey*. This book attracted almost as much attention in Europe as in America; and, showing the diversity of views that it caused in the very same week, in the summer of 1928 I happened to read a French critic who said that Mr. Wilder's style reminded him of Prosper Mérimée and that he was in his attitude toward religion an ironical sceptic. Later in the week I was talking to G. K. Chesterton in England and he asked, 'Mr. Wilder is an ardent Roman Catholic, is he not?' and when I informed him that he was not, Mr. Chesterton said *The Bridge* sounded exactly as if it were written by a practising Catholic.

DAVIS HOUSE
LAWRENCEVILLE, NEW JERSEY

Dear Mr. Phelps:

I was balanced for a long while over the League's invitation, but at last I decided not to dare. I simply never will be able to speak on my feet. In the spring of 1929 I am doing some readings for Lee Keedick (to take the place of the Davis House in an empty life) but reading my three-minute plays is a different matter. Speaking is so natural and so happy with you that you can scarcely imagine my dread of it; but it's very real. I have told Mr. Ely how proud and eager, from every other point of view, I would be to do it.

When I last saw you I hadn't the faintest notion what I would write about next. Now I know that it will be a curious novelization of Terence's *Andria*; a picture of life on an Aegean island, the pagan world shot through with intimations of Christianity.

In the meantime the Davis House goes on; it keeps me in the village and is full of detail, but very satisfying.

Many letters come to me from people who were introduced to the book by you, and full of beautiful references to yourself and the place you have made in the best part of their lives. I cannot imagine you ever tired or anything less than eager; if ever so, remember all this affection and remember mine

ever so

Thornton

March 9, 1928

After reading Dickens and other novelists, I often wondered what it must be like to live in chambers in the Inns of Court. Well, I found out. I took tea with Maurice Baring in his rooms in Gray's Inn. Here we were, in the heart of London, only a few steps from Fleet Street, and we might have been in the country. Although the windows were open, it was so quiet we could have conversed in whispers. Major Baring is one of my favourite novelists. There is an original flavour in everything he writes, coming from a charming personality, enriched by years of experience in Russia and in remote parts of the earth.

I received from Percival Christopher Wren an autograph

copy of a special illustrated edition of *Beau Geste*, a novel
I admire without reservations.

WESTWOOD HOUSE,
TALBOT WOODS,
BOURNEMOUTH
13th Dec. 1928

DEAR PROFESSOR LYON-PHELPS

Very many thanks for your letter of 3rd Dec. I am very gratified
to learn that the copy of "Beau Geste" gave you so much pleasure.

I thank you for the generous compliment you pay me both in your
allusion to "The Three Musketeers" and in your recommendation
of my books in your public lectures.

I shall look forward to the pleasure of meeting you when you are
again in England.

With the compliments of the Season

Yours very sincerely,

P. WREN

88

ANTHONY HOPE

On 20 July 1928 we motored to Epsom Downs not to see the Derby, but for a purpose more exciting. It was to take lunch with Sir Anthony and Lady Hawkins. Many years before I had heard Anthony Hope give a public reading in New Haven; and ever since the publication of *The Prisoner of Zenda* and *The Dolly Dialogues* in 1894, I had been eager to meet their author. My eagerness was strengthened by two quite different facts; one was the publication of his autobiography and the other was Lady Hawkins, not only because she was Lady Hawkins, but because she was a sister of Lewis Sheldon, a Yale pupil of mine in the class of 1896.

They lived in a beautiful old house with a charming garden close to the immense heath. They made the day memorable with their delightful hospitality and with stimulating conversation. They read aloud to us important letters from Barrie, Lord Charnwood, Thomas Hardy, and many other contemporaries.

I had reviewed his autobiography, expressing my admiration for the book and its author; but I said that as a public reader of his works he was ineffective. I had heard he had said that when he was reading aloud on the stage he was usually thinking of something else; to which I mentally added 'So is the audience.'

On this visit we discussed that matter with considerable earnestness; for he believed he read aloud very well, and Lady Hawkins assured me that everyone was delighted with his readings from *The Dolly Dialogues*. It is probable the night I heard him in New Haven was not a fair test; I remember there was a tremendous blizzard and the audience was small. Certainly the brilliance and vivacity of his conversation would indicate that he would read aloud extremely well.

He was so unpretentiously modest and unaffected it was not easy to draw him out to discuss his own works; but he was certainly gratified, as he had every reason to be, with the success of his autobiography.

I told him I had enjoyed his novel *The Secret of the Tower*, which I had read in 1919; he laughed aloud, and said 'Ah, if you really like that book, I shall not have a high opinion of your critical judgement.'

Like so many authors, he did not believe his most popular book was his best. He said he had written *The Prisoner of Zenda* at tremendous speed, that he had been astonished at its popularity, and that he had written much better books on which he had spent more time and effort. I then asked him which of all his works he thought was the finest; and without hesitation he said *The King's Mirror*. He was kind enough to give me an autograph copy of it. I read it attentively and thought I saw why he regarded it so highly.

The following letter shows that he had been mis-quoted. I had sent him a proof-sheet of my review of his autobiography in *Scribners*.

28 April/28
HEATH FARM,
WALTON-ON-THE-HILL,
TADWORTH,
SURREY

DEAR PROFESSOR PHELPS,

I am very grateful for your letter and for the Scribner "Proof" which you have sent with it. I have read both with the greatest pleasure. I have little right to put forth a book of memories (even a small one!) at all and even less to have it published in America: indeed I am sure that the publishers undertook it more from kindness to me than from any chance of profit.

At any rate—so far as I am concerned—I am content with having pleased *you*,—even if I have not pleased—or reached—any other reader. But I think that, thanks to you, I shall reach some more—for your imprimatur is, I know, a powerful one.

I don't exactly "place" that melancholy reading of mine—in a blizzard and a void! Pretty bad, I daresay. But my remark to the interviewer is, as we used to say in the law, "not admitted"—which was different from being "denied." In fine—I am proud—as well as pleased—that you have written as you have about me—and send you thanks most cordial. I grow old, and shall probably do little more. And how little it all is! You know—I *am* right *once* in the little book—unless in the Arts, you are great, you are nothing!

Yours very truly

ANTHONY HOPE HAWKINS

HEATH FARM
WALTON-ON-THE-HILL
TADWORTH
SURREY
10th July/28

DEAR PROFESSOR PHELPS,

I have waited to answer your kind note of the 14th June till the time when you expect to be in London.

It would be a great pleasure to me to meet you. But I have now no house in town and come up there very seldom. My wife and I would be delighted if you and Mrs. Phelps could find time to run down here some day. We are less than 20 miles out by road. What about lunch next Saturday or Sunday, or any day next week? Or in the afternoon, if you can't manage lunch (but I hope you can!)? Our country here is really rather beautiful.

If you come by train (Tadworth Station—and look out for a possible change at Purley) we will meet you. But the road is better,—via Sutton to Welton Heath Golf Club (which very likely your driver will know). The London side of the club building is a lane, go up it to the top—where stands a horribly ugly village "hall," and I stand exactly opposite. Do let us hear that you can come. Call up my wife. I am deaf on the telephone.

As for your enclosure—I think I stand mid-way in opinion between you and the lady! I think I read the "romantic" stuff very badly, but the "Dollies" rather well.

Yours very truly

ANTHONY H. HAWKINS

Sir Anthony told me about a great public dinner he had attended in London in honour of Mark Twain, when most of those present were hearing him for the first time. There was intense curiosity when he rose to speak. He, the Master of the Pause, stood for some seconds in silence. Then, very slowly, and with pauses, he drawled 'Homer is dead— Shakespeare is dead—and I am far from well.' The typical American humour of exaggeration was given to an audience whose conception of humour was understatement. But his manner and his expression were so droll that the dinner-guests roared with laughter and Mark Twain came into his kingdom.

At another time a dinner was given in honour of Sarah Bernhardt. On the same day the indomitable actress had given a matinée followed by an evening performance and now she had to attend this banquet. She seemed the incarnation of vigour and energy.

During that summer of 1928 I had the good fortune to meet not only a large number of remarkable men and women, but also extraordinary animals. I should have liked to take home with me a beautiful Irish setter, Rex, a member of the Galsworthy household; and to annex two literary cats, one of whom belonged to Thomas Hardy while the other lived with the famous novelist, Sheila Kaye-Smith. Both of these cats were magnificent Persians. There is a well-known picture of Sheila Kaye-Smith and her cat, so that in a way I felt acquainted before the actual meeting took place. This is a Supercat. He had an expression on his austere and majestic countenance that would do credit to the President of the League of Nations. His gracious owner told me many interesting facts about him that displayed his intelligence. It is more than possible that he inspired the second noun in her novel *Iron and Smoke*.

We had the pleasure of hearing an excellent sermon preached by her husband in his London church on Gloucester Road. The Reverend T.P. Fry is a remarkably interesting personality, and was then an Anglo-Catholic. I had supposed that *The End of the House of Alard*, my favourite among the works of Sheila Kaye-Smith, was written after she had become engaged to Mr. Fry; was perhaps a tribute to his influence. She said that it was written before, and that it represented her own independent view; though she is too fine an artist to make this book or any other a medium of opinion.

Both of them subsequently became Roman Catholics.

89

GEORGE MOORE

In July and again in September of 1928 I had good talk
with George Moore at his house in Ebury Street. His published conversations with the late Edmund Gosse and
others have made this 'long, unlovely street' distinguished,
for Mr. Moore was one of the very few who could write
profound and penetrating literary criticism in the manner
of informal talk. Being a genuine literary aristocrat, he
had the unaffected affability of his class, a combination of
ease and elegance. He wasted not a moment on the weather,
but immediately began to say things worth remembering.
I am unfortunately no Boswell, but I can give the substance of what he said, though not altogether as he said it.
He was in the serene seventies, physically weak from a
recent operation, and a major one drawing nearer; but
there was no sign of illness in his face or in his voice. Unlike many sufferers, he showed no inclination to talk of his
ailments, of his medicines or physicians, or of his operations; the main interest of his life was art, and he was as
keenly interested in it as he had been fifty years before.

Two other subjects seemed to arouse his excitement; the
only two I did not care to hear him discuss. One was the
utter worthlessness of the writing of Thomas Hardy,
worthless in thought ('The man never could think—he had
no mind') worthless in style ('he never wrote well') worthless in construction ('he knew nothing of the art of fiction').

The other was sex. He would repeatedly draw the conversation around to that. He was kind enough to give me a

copy of his *Daphnis and Chloe* and he read aloud a certain passage with immense gusto. He said 'Adultery? adultery? everybody commits adultery.' I said with a laugh, 'Not everybody; I know someone who has never committed adultery.' *'What?'* he shouted in amazement. If I had told him of some miracle, he could not have been more astounded.

'I am writing a novel of Greek life in the time of Pericles, and I need in my mind's eye a picture of the coast of the island of Euboea. To write a good novel of men and women, one should go far back in time. Human nature has never changed and the intellectual capacity of the human mind has increased not at all. Our age is so fuddled with machinery, physical luxuries, conveniences of every kind, that personality is being swamped. Men and women as they really are interest me; it is necessary for me to isolate individuals for purposes of study and analysis; hence I must go back in time, when people lived as men and women, not as standardized machines.

'The fact that the majority of persons in ancient times had no formal education does not mean they lacked intelligence or determination or passion. Today we have an immense diffusion of culture, which is far from being a universal blessing, for true culture is an individual affair, and can be acquired only by persistent individual effort. The difficulty nowadays is that thousands of young men and women who go to colleges and universities have culture spread over them; they are buttered with it. But that does not mean they are truly educated, for they have mastered nothing for themselves. They live social, communal lives, like cogs in some vast machine, but they do not live personally and individually, as men and women used to do.'

He wished to know what had first occasioned my interest in his work, and I told him of a course in literature I had given as a young teacher at Yale in 1895. I had included a book recently published, *Esther Waters*. 'Oh, I have since written many books better than that,' he said with emphasis. 'Yes,' I replied, 'that may be true, but *Esther Waters* is the novel that made your name known all over the world. One of the best things in it is the description of Derby Day, an amazingly vivid picture. I have never seen the Derby, and I shall not have to see it, because your account of it is absolutely real.' He smiled and said, 'Ah, you are right. That is really good. I made a success of that chapter. The Derby I did very well, very well indeed.'

Then I spoke of *Evelyn Innes* and of its sequel, *Sister Teresa*. He shuddered with horror. 'Oh, that is a bad novel, very bad. I rewrote it and rewrote it in the vain endeavour to improve it. But it was hopeless. I could make nothing of it. Just as I believe the worst of all sins is bad writing, so I believe the highest virtue is found in corrections, in an author's revisions. If you wish to estimate the true value of an author's art, study his revisions. But no amount of correction could save that book.' I reminded him of two striking passages, the one where it is written 'You never see poplar trees except at evening,' which he had quite forgotten, and the other where Evelyn plays the *Lohengrin Vorspiel* to the nun, who had never heard such music. She asked the nun for her impressions, and the nun gave a picture of mountains before dawn, exactly what she saw and felt while the music was being played. Mr. Moore was aroused. 'Why, you have hit upon the only good thing in the entire novel. That *is* good, and it may have been what Wagner himself had in mind while composing that passage.' I then turned the conversation to his recent book *Avowals*, and told him I thought the best thing in it was the criticism of Rudyard Kipling. 'Look here, how is it that you pick out the best pages in every one of my books?

The remarks on Kipling are certainly the best I wrote in that volume.' Perhaps it was a good time to stop; I made no further selections.

In the room where we sat there were some admirable oil paintings, including some excellent likenesses of himself, and on the table were some French translations of his works, and, as might be expected, a copy of *Mademoiselle de Maupin*. I looked around for the cat, because George Moore is a cat lover, and once wrote a famous description of a cat, and of its quiet dignity in the hour of death. The absence of his contemporary cat was explained by the presence of a canary which someone had recently given him, and the cat was banished to the kitchen. 'This is a very stupid cat,' said he, 'and you would not care to make his acquaintance. But I had a cat who used to spring from the floor to my shoulder, and often when I was writing he would leap on the desk and take the pen from my fingers, urging me to stop work and play with him. Cats wish to be entertained as much as dogs.' I reminded him of the passage in Montaigne where it is suggested that the cat is perhaps as much amused by us as we are by the cat. 'Ah, Montaigne is an inexplicable writer. I cannot understand him at all. I can make nothing of him.'

Mr. Moore read aloud to me from the manuscript a short story he had recently composed. He read it extremely well. When he finished he said, ' Turgenev would take off his hat to this.' The conversations in the story harmonized perfectly with the descriptions of nature. I told him it was like a solo violin accompanied by the orchestra. 'But that is exactly the effect I wished to produce. You are a musician.' 'No, I am not a musician, but I love music, and have cultivated the art of listening.' While he was reading, the canary began singing, furnishing an exquisite *obbligato*. The pale September sunlight filtered into the room, no sound from the windless street was heard, and the memory of

George Moore in his armchair reading aloud beautiful English prose, while the canary was singing, abides with me.

On another occasion, I asked him about his early life. The early years in Paris nearly made a Frenchman out of him. 'Had I stayed in Paris another year I should have become quite French, and should have written all my books in French, which would have been a pity, because one cannot write satisfactorily in any language but one's own.' He by no means shared the general admiration for Conrad's style. 'The man could not write good English to save his life. He did not know good English, and those who praise him do not know what they are talking about.' I made some reservations here, but did not care to start a controversy, because I wanted him to go on talking about his early years.

'I left France for England with only one purpose, to write the aesthetic novel. The artistic novel in Victorian days did not exist in England. Thackeray, Dickens, and George Eliot wrote novels about various classes of people, but they were all afflicted with a conscience; they had a moral bias, fatal to art. Nearly all Englishmen are cursed with a conscience—it is a bad thing to have. In the ordinary sense of those words, I have no religion and no morality. The Victorians never wrote exclusively from the standpoint of pure art, to tell the truth about men and women as they really are, with no regard to conventions. I did this. I founded the artistic novel in England, and after a long struggle, won my battle. It has been my whole life's work. When I published *A Mummer's Wife*, I accomplished something original and new. *Esther Waters* had an immense success, but it is far from being my best book.' I asked him about his earlier attempts, *Mike Fletcher*, for example. 'Oh, that is no good at all. I was trying myself out, taking the first steps. In later years I accomplished

what I was aiming at in *The Lake*, but you have not seen
the genuine version of *The Lake* any more than you have
seen the correct edition of *Memoirs of My Dead Life*.' I
told him I was sure I had, because nothing could possibly
have been expurgated from the copies I read.

I reminded him of one of his novels which seems to have
escaped public attention—*Spring Days*. I was impressed
by his description there of the greenery of early spring,
which he called a 'shrill' green. 'Ah, but you know that
early green is really not green at all. It is yellow.' That is
what I have always thought and never dared to say, thinking it must be some form of colour-blindness. But if
George Moore, he who said an accurate sense of colour
was more important than a sense of right and wrong, can
say it. . . .

Alas, the conversation turned on Thomas Hardy.
Mr. Moore was a great critic, but like all great critics, he
had his perversities. His contempt for the novels of Hardy
was an obsession. 'Hardy could not write English. *Tess*
is a ridiculous book,' and he began to point out what he
regarded as absurdities, Angel Clare carrying Tess, a heavy
woman, and so on. I asked him how he accounted for the
almost unanimous praise by critics. 'Oh, they were personal friends of Hardy.' I regard Hardy as one of the
greatest writers of modern times, a great artist and a great
man. I ventured to say something about the artistic structure of his books, but he would not listen. It was impossible to discuss this question. I cannot make out why he
was so strenuous about it, unless he felt that public opinion
was so mistaken about Hardy that it was his duty to take
the opposite view.

There is no reason why a sharp difference of opinion
should interfere with friendship or with mutual respect.
But Mr. Moore's attacks on Hardy, inopportune as they
were, cost him the friendship and esteem of some of his

GEORGE MOORE

contemporaries. And this was only one of many controversies in which he was engaged. No writer took less pains to preserve the affection of his friends. I wondered at this, and I asked him if the things he said so publicly of prominent persons never caused him worry. I could not see how he could involve himself in so many quarrels and indiscretions and preserve peace of mind. 'Is it because you are an Irishman?' 'Irish?' he replied, 'Irish? I am no more Irish than you are. My people have been in Ireland only three hundred years. That does not make me an Irishman.' Yet I ventured to remark that just for his own contentment and tranquillity he might have found it better not to involve himself in so many controversies. 'It does not worry me in the least. I say exactly what I think. The only thing that worries me is when I have not written well.'

If I could not applaud his discretion or his amenity, I certainly admired his courage. Here he was, alone in the world, an old man, with a terrible operation facing him, without a grain of religion, but apparently also without a grain of remorse. His Credo, like that of Dudebat in *The Doctor's Dilemma*, was Art. This is the only thing he ever believed in, and old age, solitude, and illness changed his mind not one iota.

On another occasion, we talked of American literature, and I rejoiced greatly when he said Nathaniel Hawthorne was by all odds the foremost of American writers. He especially admired the first half of *The House of the Seven Gables*. He dwelt on the incidents of this story with the keenest admiration. 'Hawthorne was an artist of the first rank. I have never read *The Scarlet Letter* because I know I should find it too painful. I should not be able to endure it.' He was undoubtedly right in his surmise. *The Scarlet Letter* is Hawthorne's masterpiece, but the tragedy is founded on a conception of sin so alien to the pagan mind of George Moore that it would not only have been distressing, it would have been incomprehensible.

He went on to speak of some of his visitors. 'One day an American novelist called on me. His name is Drooser, Dowzer, what is it?' I suggested Theodore Dreiser. 'That's the man. And a good fellow he is. We had an interesting talk. I never have read anything by him, but I enjoyed talking with him. We have the same American publisher, Horace Liveright. Dreiser gave me a really wonderful description of Liveright, as he appears in the morning, afternoon, and night, and he did it so vividly that I felt I was present in Liveright's room.'

We talked of Victor Hugo, whom he does not admire. 'Hugo had great facility in writing platitudes.' I asked him wonderingly if he did not admire Hugo as a lyrical poet. I called attention to the songs in *Les Burgraves*. Mr. Moore was deeply interested in the art of translation, as in every fine art, or in anything relating to excellence in composition. I thought Rossetti had made wonderful verse-translations of the songs in *Les Burgraves*, and as Mr. Moore did not remember them, I recited them. He was excited. 'They are splendid! recite them again.'

Those who imagine that conversation is a lost art ought to have talked with George Moore. Though everything he said was worth listening to, he did not deliver himself of solemn pronouncements, declamation, or long monologues. He treated his visitor with natural and unaffected courtesy, and made him feel that he was sharing in the conversation on a plane of equality, which is the secret of the art of conversation.

Although Mr. Moore was entirely without fear in his attacks on his contemporaries, there are incidents that incontrovertibly prove that Mr. Moore did have some regard for the feelings of the men of genius whom he admired. I learn from a bookseller's catalogue that in October 1930 Moore wrote to Shaw saying that in a newspaper interview he was quoted as speaking contemptuously of Shaw; and that he assured Shaw he had said nothing of the kind.

Shaw wrote back to Moore on the blank space in Moore's letter to show Moore that he would not even preserve anything that looked like an apology. He wrote, addressing him as 'My dear George,' said there could not be any cause for offence and that the difficulty was that the journalists had every prominent man classified. The journalist evidently believed Moore was contemptuous, Shaw satirical, Oliver Lodge superstitious, the Archbishop of Canterbury pious, etc. Shaw said he knew the game only too well, having frequently suffered from it himself. Then he went on to say he was delighted that Moore had escaped with his life from the surgeons, for he had been horrified to learn that Moore had fallen into their hands. He signed the letter 'Ever the best of friends, G.B.S.'

At the same time Moore wrote to Barrie, whom he had also been represented as attacking. Barrie replied that he had retained and increased his admiration for the work of Moore. He followed this the next month with a second letter beginning 'My dear Moore' in which he says he is glad the newspaper did publish such an interview because it gave him an opportunity to renew his friendship. He said he was living like a hermit, but asked Moore to dinner; no one else would be present. He added that when he had previously observed that Moore was turning playwright, he had come near writing him and offering him suggestions from his own experience that might be useful.

Extracts from those letters were printed in the catalogue of Bertram Rota, which offered for sale all four manuscripts. Moore told his correspondents he had written to the newspaper correcting the statements ascribed to him.

121 EBURY STREET
THURSDAY NIGHT

DEAR MR. PHELPS,

I know of no day or time more agreeable for aesthetic talk than Sunday morning and shall expect you about eleven o'clock if I do not hear that after consideration one of the other days you mention will suit you better.

Very sincerely yours,

GEORGE MOORE

Even as Æ. was beloved and respected both by Irish Republicans and Irish Unionists, so was he by Yeats the poet and George Moore the novelist, who certainly had no liking for each other. It may be that in those three remarkable volumes *Ave, Salve, Vale,* which purport to be accurate narrations of events, Moore was more of a novelist than in the books he called novels. Certainly as literature they are far greater than *The Brook Kerith,* which I was never able to finish.

Although Æ. was full of humour and his comments awakened irresistible mirth, I never heard him laugh; I cannot even imagine Yeats laughing; but Moore laughed loud and often, usually *at* somebody or something, especially when he was pointing out what he thought were the absurdities in the novels of Thomas Hardy. Despite Moore's anti-Hardy obsession, where I could not follow him at all, he was, like Henry James, a truly great literary critic.

90

Æ.

On 9 February 1928 Æ. (George W. Russell) spent the day in New Haven. He attended my undergraduate class in Browning at eleven, stayed with me at my house until five, when he lectured at the University and then came back with me for dinner and the evening. He said 'I am and always have been a pacifist; but what am I to believe now? Although I have always condemned violence, we got nothing in Ireland by peaceful means. Yes, all the freedom the Irish have attained has been won by fighting, violence and bloodshed.'

I have been fortunate enough to know some of the leading writers that Ireland has given to the world in the twentieth century—Bernard Shaw, W.B.Yeats, St. John Ervine, George Moore, Lady Gregory, Lennox Robinson, Padraic and Mary Colum, Æ., and others; but while Shaw and Ervine are greater dramatists, Moore a greater novelist, Mary Colum a more accomplished literary critic, Yeats a greater poet, the greatest personality in Ireland was Æ. He was a poet, a novelist, a painter, an agriculturist, a journalist, a statesman, a farmer, and many other things; but his chief distinction was as a conversationalist. Toward the end of his life, he was successful as a public speaker.

Johnson said if one wished to find out whether or not a man had a first-rate mind, one must come close to him in intimate conversation. Well, everyone who knew Æ. recognized his unique powers; never have I heard talk that combined so much learning, intelligence, and charm. 'The air seems bright with his past presence yet.'

Bernard Shaw says Americans have an athletic pronunciation. It is well said. Our voices are often too penetrating to be agreeable; perhaps what they lack in melody they make up for in audibility. Æ.'s voice was of a triple softness. It was an Irish voice, that seemed to come through the fogs and mists of his native land. This softness was further softened by his copious beard; the voice came sifting through the whiskers. It was further softened by clouds of tobacco smoke, for he was a chronic pipe-smoker; hour after hour this soft dreamy Irish voice came through the whiskers and through the smoke, so that I felt as if I were listening to the Delphic oracle, which I am sure never uttered such continuous wisdom.

On this ninth day of February 1928 he talked to me for ten hours; and I could have heard him till his voice gave out. Now nothing is more exhausting than to listen to a steady stream of gabble; and it happens that the specific gravity of talk is often in inverse proportion to its volume. The astonishing thing is that every sentence he spoke with such fluent ease was worth hearing. Every word was interesting. In one respect Oscar Wilde (another genius in conversation) would not have approved of Æ., for Wilde said he disliked people who were not serious about their meals. Well, Æ. was not serious about his meals; but in some way he contrived to eat plentifully without even checking the flow of talk. After he had been talking from twelve till one, I suggested lunch; we went into the dining-room and he ate everything set before him without looking at it; he was braver in this respect than Benjamin Franklin, who invented bi-focal glasses so that he could look at his food and at beautiful women.

After lunch he went on talking till five, when I reminded him of the hall filled with people at the University awaiting his appearance. We went there, he spoke easily and magnificently for an hour on the platform; then we returned home, conversing on the way. At seven we again entered the dining-room where he performed in an even more impressive manner the miracle of lunch. Then I listened with enchantment to his talk until ten o'clock.

He said that narrative poetry no matter how good was always second-rate, because it was on one plane. The highest form of poetry was always the poetry of transfiguration. I immediately asked him to read one of his poems, which he did, chanting it with a rhythm that will be remembered by thousands of people; for whether on platform or in an armchair, he had only one way of repeating verse; it would have been monotonous from any other man. This is the poem he chanted:

DUST

I heard them in their sadness say
" The earth rebukes the thought of God;
We are but embers wrapped in clay,
A little nobler than the sod."

But I have touched the lips of clay;
Mother, thy rudest sod to me
Is thrilled with fire of hidden day
And haunted by all mystery.

It is amazing that he remembered every line of verse he had written. John Eglinton says that Æ. remarked of Yeats, that if he had written a poem in the morning and you asked him to repeat it in the evening, he would have to read it from the manuscript. Æ. could have dictated without hesitation every page from memory in every volume of poems he had ever published!

He did not give any illustrations of transfiguration in poetry except the one that I asked him to repeat; he went on to talk of something else. But I believe a perfect illustration of what he meant is the short piece *Overtones* by the American poet, William Alexander Percy.

> I heard a bird at break of day
>   Sing in the autumn trees
> A song so mystical, so calm,
>   So full of certainties,
> No man, I think, could listen long
>   Except upon his knees:
> Yet this was but a simple bird,
>   Alone, among dead trees.

Even if Æ. had never published anything, he would not be forgotten; he had a rich personality. Everyone reads *Robinson Crusoe*, but only a minority remember even the name of the author; very few indeed read the works of Sir Philip Sidney, but his personality is not forgotten.

The universal respect and affection given to Æ. are an imperishable tribute to his mind and character; George Moore, who treated his enemies and his friends so often with insults, gave the world an artistic portrait of Æ., for whom he had affection, and what was unique with Moore, reverence. That great Pagan, who said his 'only recreation was Religion,' was awestruck by Æ., and his reverence was not diminished by a long friendship.

After I had printed in *Scribner's Magazine* an account of his ten hours' talk, he wrote to me

84 MERRION SQUARE,
DUBLIN
6–12–28

DEAR PHELPS,

I have read with consternation the paragraph about me in Scribners. Did I go on talking like that? I always supposed I was a silent man! I think I am, but my shyness must have burst when I was in your country and without my being aware of it. The desperately shy man goes on talking desperately. Please put it down to that. I am accustomed to sit silently when really good talkers like Yeats,

James Stephens, Stephen MacKenna, Oliver Gogarty or George
Moore start talking. They were prodigally endowed by nature with
eloquence or wit. I would never break in on any of these once they
got started. If I could induce Oliver Gogarty to go to America it
would hear really good talk flashing out in every sentence. When
George Moore wondered whether our round towers were Christian
or unchristian, Oliver settled the question in ten words: "Pre Christian, of course! no parish priest could get through the doorway."
Perhaps this sounds irreverant to you. I hesitate to repeat his philo-
sophic reflection after he said that. "You know when the Word
incarnates in Ireland it suffers from fatty degeneration of the heart."
I am afraid his conversation would be censored in your country.
Most such conversation would be. Our Government is making a
beginning not with the spoken but with censoring of the written
word. Any literature "calculated to excite sexual passion" is prohibited as "indecent." Romeo and Juliet would go out and Shelley's
"I arise from dreams of thee." I see our literature getting more and
more Puritan and our conversation getting more and more Restoration. Come here five years after the censorship and you will find
the country publicly pure and privately abandoned. And the conversation will probably make your hair stand up. But I must not
ramble on or you will say once I begin writing I never stop with the
pen any more than I do with the tongue. Forgive its ten hours of
wagging.

Yours sincerely,

A.E.

84 MERRION SQUARE,
DUBLIN
10.6.29

MY DEAR PHELPS.

I forgive you but I doubt whether Oliver will forgive you or myself
for raking up the irreverent wit of his boyhood. He could not go to
the United States now. Your countrymen would have been better
pleased if they had known the precautions he took to avoid the danger
of knighthood. He wrote to Lloyds the insurance brokers to get a
quotation on the premium he must pay to insure himself against
the risk. He told them it was customary in his city when a doctor
had attained a certain degree of eminence in his profession that he
should be offered a knighthood. "This," said Oliver, "is a very

serious matter for me. Half my clients are nationalists; the other
half imperialists. If I accept this knighthood which shall be offered
to me I shall lose my nationalist clients. If I refuse it I shall lose my
imperialist clients." Dublin in pre-treaty days was locally known as
"the City of Dreadful Knights" and you can understand why a
poet should try to insure himself against the risk. Oliver's surname
was —— I will not tell you the right name as he may desire sometime to go to the States and the story cannot be brought up against
him.

Yours ever,

A.E.

152 EAST FORTIETH STREET
May 5, 1931

DEAR BILLY:

I find everybody refers to you by this familiar title so I am adopt-
ing it as I am going back to Ireland and you cannot cast on me a
frown of professorial dignity in rebuke of my familiarity.

I would come with pleasure to talk to your class only I am fixed
up on my last day here with many engagements and I start off on
the 7th to Montreal.

I would have been very glad to see you—you are a most compan-
ionable person—and to have initiated you further into the mystery
of commingled tobacco and coltsfoot. I am so afraid you will not
get the proper blend.

Sincerely yours,

"A.E."

20
—
9
31

17 Rathgan Avenue
Dublin
Ireland

DEAR BILLY. May I trespass on your good nature. A Mrs. —— wrote
to me saying she was writing something about me in the Yale Review
and asked some questions. I answered her and mislaid her letter
afterwards. Now she writes again and I cannot make out her address

except that it is in "Conn" and she has some strange hieroglyph
before that of which below is a faithful copy

"Westville"

This is unintelligible. As you are at Yale I surmise a relation of some
sort or knowledge of the Yale Review—that the Yale Review has
probably some knowledge of Mrs. — —. Therefore on all these sup-
positions I am daring to send you a letter addressed by name to her
in the hope that from the Yale Review it might get to her. I have no
U.S.A. stamps but I let you into the secret of increasing the enjoyment from your life by telling you about Coltsfoot. That is worth
the two cents you must pay on the letter. If you boggle at this send
it unstamped to her c/o Yale Review. She deserves the punishment
for writing so badly.

With best wishes and apologies,

A.E.

P.S. I enclose her last note. You knowing all geography of the land
about might be able to interpret the hieroglyphics.

A.E.

Mrs. George Russell was a self-effacing, unselfish woman. When she was slowly dying of cancer, a friend called
upon her. She said 'Do go into the next room and tell my
husband how much you like his new book. It will cheer
him immensely and take his mind off, for a time from his
grief about my illness.'

If there were such a thing as an epidemic of cancer (and
my friend the great specialist Doctor Francis Wood says
there is not), one might believe that these three persons,
so closely united, were sufferers from a common cause; for
Susan Mitchell the Secretary, Mrs. Russell, and Æ. himself, all died from cancer within a few years. When I mentioned this to Dr. Wood, he said 'No, there is no common
cause and no pathological significance because three persons closely associated every day for years died of cancer;
it was just a shake of the dice; it just happened.'

In 1928 Æ. had just returned from his lecturing tour in America, when he was offered an honorary degree of Doctor of Literature from Yale. He immediately returned to receive this academic honour. As I was the Public Orator, I had the pleasure of presenting him for the degree which I did with the following words:

GEORGE WILLIAM RUSSELL, LITT.D.

The foremost citizen of Ireland. He is the very genius of the unexpected, an Irishman who loves peace. He is a patriotic internationalist who loves all nations including his own. His versatility is remarkable; he has attained distinction in widely different fields of human effort. He is a mystic and a farmer; a poet and a practical statesman; a journalist and a painter; with a character of such nobility and unselfishness that even George Moore treats him with respect. Absolutely independent, with a courage that abhors compromise, he is admired and trusted by all political parties in Ireland, including Ulster and Cork, Protestants and Catholics, Republicans and Tories. The best thing that could happen to that country would be to make him Dictator for Life. He is an authority on poetry and public finance; he is both spiritual and shrewd, this combination giving to his imaginative work the element of transfiguration, for in his own words, it takes two currents to make the electric light. Perhaps of all the arts which he has mastered, he is greatest in the fine art of conversation; he should have a Boswell. He is in a double sense a man of letters, for he has given special and lasting significance to the two letters A.E.

91

CAPTAIN LIDDELL HART AND GENERAL J.G.HARBORD

CAPTAIN LIDDELL HART, the military historian of the London *Times* and author of many books ranging from war to contemporary masters of the game of lawn tennis, began his career at an early age. He was born 31 October 1895, so that when the War broke out he was only 19. He was at that time a student at Corpus Christi, Cambridge. He served in the European War and was wounded. His publications began when he was 22 years old with *New Methods of Infantry Training*, and his career since then is well known. When he published in 1928 his *Ten Years After*, I wrote to my friend, Major General J.G.Harbord, and asked his opinion about it. And considering the great reputation of both experts, the following letters should be of interest.

General Harbord is one of the finest men I have ever known. He is as modest as he is able, and there is no better companion anywhere. I have been shooting with him; I have played innumerable games of golf with him, and my respect for his ability is equalled only by my affection for him.

233 BROADWAY, NEW YORK
ROOM 1856
March 17, 1928

DEAR BILLIE:
    Your letter of March 14th, about Liddell-Hart's book on the Generals, has been received and would have been answered sooner but

836

that I wanted to take another look at the two articles on the Americans,—Pershing and Liggett. I read the Pershing article in the Atlantic when it came out early in the winter, but wanted to take another look at it. I found last night, which was the evening I had reserved for this purpose, that Emma had sent the book over to her Father, in Washington, to read and it has not yet been returned, so I am unable to freshen my memory.

My impression is that the book is fair and unprejudiced, and is a very correct estimate of what I believe the place in history of those several gentlemen will be. I had a personal acquaintance with Lord Haig, with Joffre, Foch and Petain. My actual acquaintance was perhaps closer with Marshal Petain and Lord Haig than with the others named. I think the estimate of General Haig was a very fair one, so too with the estimate of Petain whom I, myself, have always rated higher as a General than I rate Foch. The choice of the latter as Commander-in-Chief of the Allies seemed to me to be more or less of a political accident. He had, of course, an excellent reputation after the first Battle of the Marne, but in the spring of 1917, after the Nivelle Offensive, the French Government evidently rated Petain higher than Foch because they selected him for the Command of the French Armies when the two Generals were equally available for selection. Foch then drifted on for another year as Chief of Staff at the War Office but exercising authority as such only in theatres of war other than the Western Front. As I have understood it, he exercised no control over Petain and the French Armies in France during that period. When the disaster at Caporetto occurred there was a strong feeling, probably groping toward unity of command, which crystallized in the form of the Supreme War Council at Versailles where each Prime Minister of the Allied countries was to be a member, each with a Military Adviser. Our General Bliss, who had been retired for age from the position of Chief of Staff of our Army, was made the American member. There was a quarrel among the British which resulted in the relief of Sir William Robertson as Chief of the Imperial General Staff and the substitution of Sir Henry Wilson, in my judgment a less able man; and Foch, and Clemenceau, were the French representation. This Supreme War Council, naturally, began to aggrandize itself and seek power. The first apparent move in this direction was to attempt to form an Allied Reserve by contributions of troops from each of the Allied Armies on the Western Front. This determined upon, it was evident, even to a bunch of Prime Ministers, that such a formed Reserve could not be commanded by a committee which was really what the Supreme War Council was, so the natural act was to take the most experienced and Senior Officer connected with the Supreme War Council and give him the job,— that meant Foch. Due to the inability of Haig and Petain, however, to spare their quota of troops for this Allied Reserve, it had not been formed when the German Offensive of March 21st was undertaken which resulted in the practical destruction of the British Fifth Army and created a situation which forced the unity of command, and Foch again, naturally, was agreed upon for Commander-in-Chief. That, itself, was accomplished in two bites. He was first, still acting apparently for the Supreme War Council, appointed to coordinate the action of the Allied Armies. Coordination, without authority to command, is an unworkable situation, and the next step was to make him Commander-in-Chief. Petain who, as I said above I regard as a better General, had by his contempt for politicians made himself persona non grata with the high civil authorities in France while, in the meantime, Foch had been more and more in contact with them and had won their esteem.

As I said above, I have not read the article on Pershing since November or December, when it came out in the Atlantic, but there were two things, which I seem to recall as having attracted my attention at that time, which were wrong. One was that in General Pershing's pressure for open warfare, or war of movement as they sometimes call it, instead of the continuation of trench warfare, he was not fully aware of the effect of machine guns which, of course, had been developed in the War to an extent never before known. That is not the case. General Pershing was fully aware of the potentialities of all the weapons that were being used in the War but he found in France the opposing forces glaring at each other from trenches, in some cases only a few yards apart and some of which had been occupied for four years. He realized that in order to win the War somebody on one side or the other must crawl out of his trenches and move forward, taking all the risks that pertain to such a movement. The professional training of American Officers, as was of course true of our Allies before the outbreak of the War, had been in open warfare and had never contemplated a stalemate in permanent trenches. These considerations led General Pershing to insist on a different character of warfare than that which he found on arrival. It seems to me, too, that the article on Pershing criticized the great loss of Officers, particularly of Company rank, as compared to the enlisted casualties, which the Allies were accustomed to attribute to our inexperience in warfare. The truth is that there are certain things in war which every nation has to learn for itself. The losses of Officers in the American Expeditionary Forces corresponded very closely with the losses of the Allies and of the enemy in the first year and a half of the War. We could not profit by their experience in that particular case. Those losses did not result principally from inexperience. At the beginning of a war Officers, indeed the officer class generally, have to demonstrate their mettle and their capacity for leadership before their men including the willingness to take risks. The less trained the men are and the less unprepared the nation, the more certain it is that the officer class are obliged to demonstrate their capacity for personal leadership. It always results in an undue proportion of losses among the class which the nation can least afford to lose. This is exactly why the Allies lost heavily of Officers in 1914 and 1915 and why we lost heavily in 1918, and it also explains why we could not benefit by their experience and thus avoid such losses ourselves. It is particularly true of a democracy, where officers are selected from the same level as the enlisted men, that they get no more than scant official respect from their men until they demonstrate physical courage.

This has grown to be a very long letter and sounds a little diffuse. I thought, however, from your inquiry as to my opinion, that perhaps it was not out of order to mention these matters. Liddell-Hart appears to me to be a very able writer on military subjects. I understand he fills the place on the London Times which was so ably filled for many years by the late Colonel Repington. I have an idea that, ten years after the War, he has pretty correctly stated what will be the ultimate verdict of history on the men of whom he writes.

FROM CAPTAIN LIDDELL HART

I always read with keen interest as well as most appreciatively your comments on my writings. And in this case I am the more interested because of the quotation of the letter from General Harbord, a man for whom no student of the war can help feeling great admiration. Indeed it was because of my impression of Gen. Harbord in the light of what I heard of him from all quarters that in "appreciating" Pershing I attached special weight to Gen. Harbord's own comments. For in writing upon Pershing I was more handicapped than in other cases, having less intimate evidence and knowledge than when dealing with the leaders of the European armies. As regards Gen. Harbord's two points of criticism of my essay I would say that my suggestion was that he underestimated the paralysing power of machine-guns rather than "he was not fully aware of the effect." My opinion was based not merely on the results in the Meuse-Argonne but on the frequent reiteration of the view among his associates and himself that grenade and trench-warfare had paralysed the offensive spirit of the French and British, without qualifying reference to or suggestion of the part that machine-guns had played as the primary cause.

I feel that the method adopted in the U.S. Army to counteract this paralysis would have failed against the Germans of 1916, and I see Gen. Liggett rather endorses such a view, and even against the Germany of early 1918. If . . . November 1918 partially justified this training doctrine it was, at the least, tending to extreme optimism to base a training doctrine on the hypothesis that the fighting morale of the Germans—half-starved, stricken by sickness, and bombarded by wailing letters from home,—would sink so rapidly as it did between July and September 1918. As regards the second criticism, this is evidently based on a lapse of memory—as Gen. Harbord suggests may have occurred owing to a lapse of time since he read the *Atlantic* article. I nowhere criticised the excessive loss of officers compared with enlisted casualties. Indeed, I specially refrained from doing so. For I agree most emphatically with the penetrating comments which Gen. Harbord makes in this connection. An excessive toll of officers is an inevitable price which must be paid for unpreparedness and for democracy.

I hope that these observations may interest and not bore you. Once more with warm thanks, and cordial regards, I remain

Yours very truly,

B.H. LIDDELL HART

In 1929 appeared Captain Liddell Hart's biography of General Sherman; an admirable book.

92

EVENTS IN 1929–30

AMONG living American novelists none has a higher standing than Willa Cather. Her art like her nature has mellowed with maturity; there is a spiritual advance from irony to sympathy; with this growth in grace there is an added literary distinction. The rather venomous acidity of *A Lost Lady*, *My Mortal Enemy*, and *The Professor's House* changed into the profound insight (born of love) into the characters of obscure people shown in *Death Comes for the Archbishop*, *Shadows on the Rock*, *Obscure Destinies*, *Lucy Gayheart*. When I read *My Mortal Enemy*, I could not tell which was the enemy, the husband or the wife. One day my friend the novelist Lee Dodd told me he had asked her and she had told him; whereupon he told me and I have forgotten.

In June 1929 at the Yale Commencement it was with unusual pleasure that, as Public Orator, I had the honour of presenting her for the degree of Doctor of Letters:

> Born in Virginia, a graduate of the University of Nebraska, for some years a Pittsburgh journalist, Willa Cather is today one of the leading English-writing novelists of the world. Her worst novel *One of Ours* received the Pulitzer Prize because in that year her worst novel was better than everybody else's masterpiece. It is impossible to classify her work; she has attained eminence in such different fields of literary art. *The Professor's House* is a dynamic and terrifying story; *Death Comes for the Archbishop* is a static and tranquil book, written without emphasis, and full of beauty. It is impossible to say what the nature of her next book will be, but we know that it will make an impression on competent critics. Miss Cather has

given honour to American literature, and we are proud today to include her among the daughters of Yale.

On 25 October 1929 appeared in New Haven the British actor Leslie Howard, for the première of that magnificent play *Berkeley Square*. At about five o'clock I went over to the theatre and found Leslie and the whole company in a state of feverish excitement. I invited him to take dinner with me and the undergraduate Pundits at six o'clock. One of the actresses exclaimed, 'Oh, Mr. Phelps, do take him! It will do him good. He is not needed here any more and it will refresh him before he goes on the stage.' In the presence of the undergraduates he seemed to forget the imminent ordeal. He was a delightful dinner companion and so captivated the students that they elected him an honorary Pundit.

We went from the dinner to the theatre; the play had an enormous success and ran for a year in New York. I particularly enjoy fourth dimension plays like this and *Outward Bound* and *Hotel Universe* and *Lost Horizons*.

In 1930 the famous American actress Minnie Maddern Fiske came to play in New Haven, and I asked her to address my class in Contemporary Drama. She did so, but on that day she was so excited by the news that there was to be a bull-fight in New Jersey, that she devoted her remarks exclusively to denouncing the wickedness of such barbarism and asked the students to promise that they would write letters of protest. 'Those who will promise to write a letter today, please raise your hands!'

DEAR PROFESSOR PHELPS:

I shall be delighted to speak a few words to the students tomorrow before the matinee. And now comes the great favor! I am going to ask you if I may speak to the boys upon the subject that is occupying me today? It has nothing to do with the theatre but it is a critical

moment in another department of life and I want and need the help
of the students. *I shall be grateful beyond words for their help.*

With warmest good wishes,

M.M.FISKE

The fiery speech she made to the students was as dramatic and as effective as many of her professional imper-
sonations in the theatre.

On 10 June, as the guest of Mrs. Benjamin Stern of New
York, a charming and cultivated woman, we had the honour of meeting the great *prima donna* Lucrezia Bori. She
was as attractive personally as she was on the stage. She
told me she was born one Christmas Eve in Spain, in a
carriage.

Lucrezia Bori was not only a great singer and actress,
she showed executive ability of a high order, with energy
as powerful as it was productive, when the campaigns were
made for the continued support of the Metropolitan Opera
House in the years of depression.

On 16 October at my house in New Haven, I gave a
dinner in honour of Sir Edmund Chambers, the famous
Elizabethan scholar. That evening he spoke on Shakespeare at the Elizabethan Club. Thinking he might be impressed by the things we had there, I showed him the oil
painting of Elizabeth, for which she sat to Zucchero. His
only comment was, 'Zucchero was always painting her,
wasn't he?' I still think the picture is valuable.

I was amazed at the appearance of Chambers; as he
has been all his life a research scholar, I expected to see a
frail, pale, bookish-looking man. But he looked more like
an Elizabethan soldier of fortune, big, aggressive, and although he was 64 years old, his abundant hair was coal-
black.

If there is any man alive who is absolutely satisfied with
his career, that man should be Chambers. He never wanted

to teach. He wanted to be a research scholar, devoting himself to the early religious drama, and the Elizabethan, and to writing the most complete biography of Shakespeare. He has done and done magnificently everything that in his youth he wanted to do. *Finis coronat opus.*

And was there ever a more typically British scholar? If one judged him only by his preface to *The Mediaeval Stage,* one would almost think he had carelessly written the book whilst resting his body between important sets of tennis. It is in reality a work of monumental research and of permanent value.

In this year of 1929 for the first time in my life I acquired asthma. On the advice of Lafayette Mendel, my distinguished Yale colleague (physiological chemistry) whose death was such a loss to science, and of Dr. Henry Swain, who knew my throat and nose as Mark Twain knew the Mississippi Channel, I consulted Dr. Bret Ratner in New York and was greatly impressed by his ability and personality. Following his instructions I gave away my four cats and a parrot and sent the dog into the country. In a few months the asthma vanished.

On 1 November at the house of Professor and Mrs. Ross Harrison of Yale, I had the pleasure of meeting Julian Huxley, tall, black-haired, spectacled, charming, unaffected. He told me his brother Aldous's bitter, ironical way of looking at life was largely caused by the fact that when the war broke out in 1914 and he was anxious to serve in the army, his eyes were so bad that he feared he was going blind and had to spend many months in a dark room. Julian showed intense pride and affection in Aldous, and seemed to think Americans might get a false impression of his character. However, he is greatly admired and highly valued by Americans. I dislike his books, but I am in a hopeless minority.

On 5 November it was announced that Sinclair Lewis had received the Nobel Prize, the first American to be so honoured. When his wife Dorothy Thompson informed him over the telephone he laughed, not dreaming that she meant it.

In order to attend the farewell dinner given to him in New York by various writers, I had to take the train from New Haven at 6.20, reach New York at 8.15, hurry to the dinner, make my speech, leave the dinner, and take the ten o'clock train home; for that morning I had had three lectures at the University, a public address at a luncheon, and a public lecture at four o'clock. At the dinner I sat with Mrs. Corinne Roosevelt Robinson, Fannie Hurst, and Mrs. Alice Duer Miller.

Corinne Robinson, the sister of Theodore Roosevelt, adored her brother and was very like him; filled with gusto and the joy of living, and with invincible courage. I liked her immensely; and our acquaintance began with her forgiveness. She wrote asking me to come to some gathering in New York, where her brother would be present. It was early in the War. I wrote thanking her but declining to come, saying that if Mr. Roosevelt knew my views about the War, he would refuse to shake hands with me. To my surprise and pleasure, she wrote me a charming letter in reply, and after that, I met her often. Fannie Hurst is always the best of company; and so is Alice Duer Miller.

In this year 1930 I received from the University of Syracuse the honorary degree of Doctor of Sacred Theology, D.S.T., which some of my friends thought was *Daylight Saving Time*, of which I have always been an advocate.

93

EDISON

THURSDAY 20 February 1930 was the hottest 20 February in the records of the New York weather bureau. Nearly seventy degrees. That night I attended a dinner at the Harvard Club given by Thomas B. Wells in honour of H. M. Tomlinson of England. Hugh Walpole, Harry Hansen, William Bolitho, Professor Samuel Morison, Sava Botzaris, Cass Canfield, Eugene Saxton, Leo Hartman were present. Wells told me that Tomlinson was more like Jesus Christ than any man he had ever known. Tomlinson impressed us by his modesty, sincerity, and unaffected *goodness*.

When I came out at midnight, it was difficult to believe it was February; the air was balmy.

Next morning my wife and I entrained for Winter Park, Florida; it was fearfully hot on the train and during the few days we spent at Winter Park, the temperature reached 96 every day.

I was to receive the Honorary degree of Doctor of Laws from Rollins College; but the great event was the appearance of Thomas Edison, who broke his almost invariable custom of refusing degrees, and was made Doctor of Science. He was 83 years old, and I was amazed to see him reading without glasses the fine print of the programme. After the ceremonies were over, I asked him if he always read without glasses. He laughed and took from his pocket a pair of spectacles. 'I can read well enough without them, but I use them when I feel like it.'

We all had lunch at the house of President and Mrs. Hamilton Holt with Mr. and Mrs. Edison. Edison sat at the head of the table and seemed to me the happiest man I had ever met. He was smiling, cheerful, with an expression of extraordinary kindness and benevolence. He allowed us to write questions which he read and answered; he was stone deaf. For nearly an hour we passed questions up to him, and he read them aloud and answered them.

The scientific matter that most interested him at the moment was the question of making rubber in his laboratory, so that the United States would not have to import it for the next war. I do not know whether he succeeded in this or not; but he was certain that there would be another big war in which our country would be engaged, and that the most patriotic thing he could do would be to supply rubber.

I then asked him if the story of his first opportunity in life, as a newsboy on a train in Michigan was true; I heard it first from his friend Irving Bacheller; he said it was, and repeated it substantially as follows:

When he was a small boy, he sold papers every day on the train running between Port Huron and Detroit, a two-hour journey. He wanted to devote his time to mastering telegraphy; but he had no resources, and the daily earnings from the sale of papers were small. One day, as he entered one of the cars, there sat a gentleman who was gorgeously drunk. Alcohol had made him generous, so that he wanted to give away the whole world. He was accompanied by a manservant, whose name I cannot remember, but it was Biblical, so suppose I call him Obadiah.

The affluent gentleman looked at young Edison and asked, 'How many papers have you got there, boy?' and on being told, he said, 'Obadiah, take all these newspapers and throw them out of the window.' This was done and paid for. Then the boy went back to the baggage car and brought out his entire supply of magazines. 'How many magazines you got there, boy?' They were carefully counted and their current value computed. 'Obadiah, take all those magazines and throw them out of the window.' Done and paid for. Young Edison went back to the baggage car, and soon returned staggering under the load of his complete stock of books. The gentleman was even more interested. It took some time to count them and appraise the value of each. It was a large sum of money. 'Obadiah, take all those volumes and throw them out of the window.' The railway tracks must have looked as if a circulating library had been visited by a cyclone. This time the boy became a capitalist, and determined on the spot to leave the newspaper business and devote himself to telegraphy and electricity.

He remembered his now empty iron trunk. He returned to the baggage car, and came back dragging the metallic receptacle. 'Boy, what do you charge for that trunk?' Edison named his price. 'Obadiah, take that trunk to the platform and push it off.'

This was Edison's first start in life. It was fortunate for him that this gentleman happened to be on the train that particular morning, and that his fancy took that quixotic turn.

I attended some of the classes at Rollins College where the usual system of instruction is reversed. The teacher asks no questions. He sits in a room with the boy and girl undergraduates who are studying; then any one who so desires asks the teacher questions. I do not know whether this system would work in other colleges or not. But it is only fair to say that in response to many questions I put to individual students and members of the Faculty, I invariably received enthusiastic affirmations of its success.

NATHAN STRAUS AND THE GRAND DUCHESS

On Sunday morning 11 January 1931 the family of the great philanthropist Nathan Straus called me by telephone from New York, saying that Mr. Straus had died at four o'clock that morning, and it was the unanimous request of the family that I make the address at his public funeral, to take place on Tuesday.

Early Tuesday morning I took the train to New York and at the station entered a taxi to be taken to the beautiful Temple Emanu-El for the funeral exercises. When I gave that address to the taxi driver, he said 'Then you are going to the funeral of one of the best men who ever lived.'

The magnificent auditorium was filled; the bearers were prominent citizens of New York, headed by Mayor Walker. Three Rabbis read Psalms and offered prayer, and I was the only non-Jewish person in the pulpit and the only speaker. Mr. Straus had told his sons that no long oration must be made and that he must not be praised; that they should ask me to make the address, and that I must confine myself to a brief account of the facts in his life. Accordingly I did so; but I quoted the remark made to me by the taxi driver.

The most conspicuous object in the temple was the coffin, a plain, unpainted pine box. Here he set an example which ought to be followed, but which will not. Mr. Straus thought it was contrary to ethics to spend a great sum on a coffin when the money could be put to so much better use in charity.

666666666666666666

Not many days before his death I had a remarkable conversation with Nathan Straus. He was on his deathbed and he knew it; yet as I bent close to his face, he whispered 'I am one of the happiest men in the world, for although I am weak and hopelessly ill, I know that I have done the right thing with my wealth, in giving so much of it away while I was alive and well. I know many rich men who are laying up for themselves a miserably unhappy old age. They will not give away large sums of money, which they ought to do, if they wish to be at peace when they come to be where I am now. John D. Rockefeller has been so wise in this respect. He is a man of the noblest and finest character. He has shown us all what to do with our wealth.'

I took pains to speak very clearly as he seemed so desperately ill. He said, 'Don't try to raise your voice; I can't make a sound above a whisper but I hear perfectly.'

He then once more repeated to me his favourite quotation 'Money given in health is gold; money given in sickness is silver; money given at death is lead.'

I first saw Mr. and Mrs. Nathan Straus at the Bon Air Vanderbilt Hotel in Augusta, Georgia, in January 1925. We became close friends; after that time, I saw them often at their home in New York City, and at Mamaroneck.

Both of them were devout and deeply religious Jews; their charity and love for mankind knew no racial or theological boundaries.

On 24 March 1931 the Grand Duchess Marie of Russia was to give a lecture at Derby, Conn., about twelve miles from New Haven. I was asked to introduce her, and had a little talk with her beforehand. She was gracious and charming. I told her I had to leave before her lecture would be over, because I was due to give a lecture on her book in New Haven, later that same afternoon!

I took out my pen to write something for her, and she exclaimed, 'Oh, you use a stylographic pen! It is the only

kind I can write with, and I cannot find one in America.'
I begged her to accept mine.

She spoke English with absolute accuracy, only it was
almost too precise; it was faultily faultless. I asked her how
she learned various European languages at the same time
in her infancy; how it was possible to learn English, for
example, and not lose what she had learned of German. She
said she was not taught Russian until she had learned English, French, and German. That she was given a governess
in each of those languages. That they were forbidden to
speak to her in any language other than their own; that she
was forbidden to speak to them in any other. That if she
asked for anything in a language not their own, they were
forbidden to give it her.

A few days later I gave a public lecture at the Town Hall
in New York; the Grand Duchess was in the audience and
I had lunch with her afterwards. She complimented me on
my pronunciation of Russian proper names, saying I pronounced them like a native. English-speaking people usually pronounce erroneously the vowel *u* in Rasputin.

On Monday 13 April the Grand Duchess, accompanied
by her Secretary, Miss Tobias, came to Yale and delivered
a lecture on the Francis Bergen Memorial Foundation.
We gave a dinner at our house that evening and she spent
the night with us. At this dinner-party she amused everyone by her descriptions of her lecture tour in the West.

She then began to talk about the author of *San Michele*,
the book which at the moment was running neck and neck
with her own, in the list of best-sellers. There was nothing
bad enough she could say about him.

We told her when she went to bed that night that we
would send up breakfast to her room the next morning at
any hour she preferred; as it was the first time we had ever
entertained a Grand Duchess, we wondered what she
would like to eat. 'Ham and eggs,' she said.

When she came downstairs, she insisted on attending my regular undergraduate class in Browning. 'I want you to teach the class exactly as if I were not in the room.' I told her no women were ever allowed in undergraduate courses at Yale, but that I was sure an exception could be made. A curious thing about this visit of the Grand Duchess's was that it gave my wife an opportunity to hear me teach, something that had never happened before. We had been married nearly forty years and I had been teaching the same length of time; but on account of the rule forbidding women, she had never seen me in action. Accordingly, as the Duchess was to be admitted, my wife accompanied her and Miss Tobias. They took seats in a row of undergraduates; and I went ahead with the Browning lesson, calling on the students to recite. Then, about fifteen minutes before the close of the hour, I said, 'Gentlemen, we are honoured by the presence of the Grand Duchess Marie of Russia; and I am sure you would enjoy hearing her say a few words.' All the students rose, and the Grand Duchess sat down at the teacher's desk, an unusual spectacle in a Yale classroom. She said 'May I smoke?' I replied, 'Smoking is forbidden in classrooms, but as we have broken one rule already, we shall be glad to break another,' and I gave her a light.

She spoke informally and easily about her life in Russia, showing no bitterness against the Bolsheviks. Then the students asked questions, to which she made frank and definite answers.

After the class, she wished to see the Yale Library, and accompanied by a bodyguard of students, we walked across to the great building. In a half-hour she had to take the train to New York; she said she had enjoyed every moment of her Yale visit, and kissed my wife affectionately.

On her next return from Europe, she was obliged by an immigration law to have a certificate of character, and asked me to furnish her with it, which I was very glad to do.

She made a most agreeable impression, both on the lecture audience and on the students, and indeed on every one she met at Yale. There was not a trace either of shyness or of condescension. Perfect ease of manner.

On May 18 the twenty millionth Ford car arrived in New Haven on its festal journey through the cities of the United States. I was asked to appear in it with the Mayor in the procession. We did this, and Mayor Tully and I signed the book in front of the City Hall.

On 23 May in New Haven, on the front wall of the house at 40 Trumbull Street, where the famous composer Ethelbert Nevin had lived, a tablet was unveiled in his memory. Mrs. Nevin was present and I made the address. My wife and I had lived in the same block, at 44 Trumbull Street, from 1894 to 1898.

On 3 June 1931 I received a most valuable gift. Michael Phipps of the Senior Class, who had just finished his course with me in Tennyson and Browning, brought me as a present from his father the copy of Tennyson's Poems that *belonged to Browning*, with Robert Browning's signature on the title-page.

On Saturday afternoon 24 October 1931, I saw for the first time at a matinée in the Lyceum Theatre, New York, the (now) famous English actor, Charles Laughton. He had not been known in America at all before this autumn. He appeared in a play called *Payment Deferred*, and made a tremendous impression. Not long after that, I went to hear it again, also at a matinée, and went back to speak to him; he was walking up and down gesticulating wildly and cursing. 'The ——! the damned ——!' He explained, as soon as he became coherent, that during the whole performance, some ladies in the second row were conversing with apparent indifference both to the actors and to their neighbours in the audience. I do not blame him.

Since that time, Mr. Laughton has become universally

known both on the legitimate stage and on the screen. I admire his art in everything except in the film of *The Barrets of Wimpole Street*, where I think he was miscast.

On 12 November I was formally admitted to the American Academy of Arts and Letters, my new colleague being the sculptor Adolph Alexander Weinman.

On 22 December in California, my brother Dryden William died. He was 77 years old and was never married. He was buried in Grove Street cemetery, New Haven, on 29 December.

In 1920 Mr. Cox was the Democratic candidate for the Presidency against Mr. Warren Harding, the Republican. Although I knew Mr. Cox would be defeated, I voted for him for two reasons. First, I believed in the League of Nations. Second, I could not digest Harding. There were three respects in which Harding and I were exactly alike. We were born in the same year; we were brought up as Baptists; and we were both unfitted to be President of the United States.

MIAMI, FLORIDA, MAY 16, 1931

MY DEAR DR. PHELPS:

It has been a long time since Easter when your greetings came and well wishes in my sickness. However, this is the first opportunity I have had to make acknowledgment.

The affair of the appendix didn't amount to much, but I picked up a couple of annoying things which have kept me on my back and I am just getting a peep over the trenches. Life looks very interesting again. It does a crusty old cuss good to be thrown on his back and discover that there is a great deal more sweetness in the world than he knew anything about.

This is the first sickness I have ever had. My average of good health is still high and if I were anything but thankful in making the final appraisal, somehow I feel I would be irreverent.

It was gracious and thoughtful of you to think of me. Please be assured of my appreciation.

Sincerely,

JAMES M. COX

One of the things I regret most in the age of mass production is the obsolescence of the skilled artisan. From childhood to middle age I was intimately acquainted with shoemakers in New Haven, Providence, and Hartford—every one of them was an interesting personality. When I was a boy I never had more than one pair of shoes at a time; so when repairs became necessary I went to the tiny shop of the shoemaker and sat there for two hours in my stockinged feet, whilst he soled and heeled the shoes. He was always glad to talk and I was glad to listen; so whilst he worked the shoemaker talked of politics, theology and life in general. When I was grown up and there were still individual shoemakers in business for themselves and none other, such men as Otto Heinz and Millspaugh in New Haven made my athletic shoes to order and I loved to talk with them on many themes. I have not seen an individual shoemaker for thirty years.

Mass production has not yet extinguished barbers. The barber during the last forty thousand years is an individualist and invariably a conversationalist. I have never known a silent barber and almost invariably their remarks are interesting.

On 16 July 1931 I had the pleasure of conducting a merry celebration in the town of Harbor Beach in Michigan, seventeen miles from my summer home. A few years previously I had discovered that two barbers in that village, James Lytle and Abner Lee had been nearly forty years in partnership in the same business in the same place. I asked them if they had ever had a quarrel. Never. 'Have your wives ever quarrelled?' The same number of times.

Accordingly I told them something should be done to commemorate them and their work. On 16 July 1931 we held a public celebration in their honour. All shops and banks in the town were closed from twelve to two. Frank Murphy, then Mayor of Detroit (later Governor of Michigan), who was born in Harbor Beach, arrived by airplane from Detroit. Edgar A. Guest read an original poem. About three hundred men, the capacity of the hall, were present; the only women allowed were the wives of the two heroes.

One of the most interesting characters in New Haven is George Miller, the professional barber at the Graduates Club. When I discovered in 1936 that he had practised his profession for exactly fifty years in the same town, New Haven, and with no pause, I decided that the occasion called for a public celebration. Accordingly, we organized a dinner at the Graduates Club in his honour. This dinner was attended by the Governor of the State of Connecticut, Wilbur L. Cross, by Dr. Harvey Cushing, and by a number of other distinguished members of the Yale faculty. Hundreds of letters were sent in to Mr. Miller from his present and former clients. Mr. Miller is not only a philosopher, as many barbers are, but is also a wit. He said, 'It's curious that people go to fortune-tellers for knowledge of the future when they should come to me, for in my profession I can always see a head.'

95

HENRY FORD

Now that Edison has gone into the world of light, there is only one American left who is known in every corner of the world. The name Henry Ford is a label of the man; he might just as well have been called John Doe or Richard Doe, John Smith or Henry Ford; and yet this name expresses his character and habits more accurately than a spectacular appellation. For, apart from his genius and the wealth it created, he is an average American; sensible, practical, honest and honourable, faithful to his ideals.

In 1931 Henry Ford made my family and me a magnificent present. *He gave us one entire day.* It often happens, especially in America, that the richer a man is in money, the poorer he is in time. I know prominent men who literally have not one hour to spare; they cannot afford it. Well, Mr. and Mrs. Henry Ford sent word to us that they would set aside for our pleasure one whole day; and it happened to be perfect autumn weather.

About nine o'clock we all met in a suburb of Detroit at the house where Henry Ford was born. This modest structure of wood he has preserved and kept in perfect condition. Outside a dazzling white, inside spotless order. Kitchen, bedrooms, parlour, and workroom are exactly in the condition that they were in 1863. Stoves, lamps, candles, wallpaper, pictures, all correct. We saw the room where he was born; and the first lathe he used, the first watches which he had taken apart and repaired. From earliest childhood he loved to see the 'wheels go round.'

The difference between him and other boys who like to take machines to pieces is that he never destroyed or wasted anything. When he took a sick watch apart, and performed a major operation on its entrails, he restored it to perfect health.

His wife was born in an almost similar house in the vicinity, but they did not meet until they were in their 'teens. They became acquainted at a church social, were married, and lived happily forever after—a perfect union.

From the birthplace we motored to Dearborn, one of the most interesting small towns in the world. The change from the unpretentious farmhouse to the magnificent estate where Mr. Ford lives today, represents the change in fortune; although there has never been any change in his simplicity and unassuming manners. The great house is filled with treasures brought from Europe.

In the commodious garage, among the Lincolns, is the first car invented and driven by Henry Ford. In the second story of the building is an immense workshop, with scores of watches in various states of repair.

Then we went to the model village, where one lives in the past. As Mephistopheles, by a wave of magic, restored the aged Faust to his vigorous youth, so our American magician has enabled us to live and move and have our being in the environment of a hundred years ago.

We travelled in an old-fashioned high carriage, drawn by a pair of horses, driven by a coachman in appropriate costume, with two coach-dogs running close to the horses' hoofs. These dogs, who look as if they had swallowed huckleberry pies which were showing through, are as devoted to the horses as the horses are to them.

As we drove about the village, we saw a yoke of oxen drawing a load. A bell sounded in the old-fashioned schoolhouse; the children came out on the village green to play football; and Henry Ford and I played with them. We entered the beautiful Colonial church, with its severely lovely interior. The organist was playing, and we listened to the music, as he played Mr. Ford's favourite pieces. We visited the old-fashioned inn, which might have stood anywhere on the English countryside, with its quaint rooms and cheerful bar-parlour. The handbills and advertisements on the walls made us believe we were living in history.

The country store and post office are combined in one humble building. I love the smell of a general store; a combination of chewing tobacco, leather, spices, coffee, gingersnaps, sugar, candy, whips, hardware, and everything else.

In a small shanty, heated by an old-fashioned stove, we had our tintypes taken; and no one seemed to enjoy this more than the Ford family.

But the most remarkable feature of this remarkable village is the complete stone house, brought from England. Mr. Ford went to Gloucestershire to a little town called Chedworth, not far from the attractive town of Broadway, and selected an ancient Cotswold cottage. This he bought. The house was taken down, every stone numbered, brought across the ocean, transported to Dearborn, and erected exactly as it had stood for centuries in England, with original furniture of the period.

Here we were joined by the son, Edsel Ford, and his wife Eleanor; they have four children. Edsel and his wife are as natural and simple in appearance, manner, and conversation as if they were average members of a village community.

The food was cooked in a vast open fireplace in the kitchen (hanging of the crane, spit, and everything complete) and was served to us on a narrow refectory table centuries old.

If one enters the enormous museum at the great centre portal, the first thing to attract the eye is a memorial to

Henry Ford's most intimate friend, Thomas Edison. In an enclosure there is a large square of cement which, before it hardened, was autographed in huge written letters by Edison; so that his gigantic signature will remain there forever. Not only the signature of his hand, but the mark of his foot is preserved.

Just as the personality of a creative artist in literature or architecture is sometimes as interesting as his productive work, so the personality of Henry Ford appeals to me with more force than any of his numerous inventions.

I had had the pleasure of meeting and talking with him on many occasions. I had always been impressed by his placid demeanour; I had never seen him look worried or anxious, had never heard him raise his voice. He possessed the secret of equanimity.

But not until this day had I enjoyed the pleasure of spending a whole day with him and his family amid the things he had created and collected; so I had not realized the delightful boyish side of his disposition. All day long he was exuberant, ebullient, laughing and joking. His wife, his son, his daughter-in-law had the same infectious high spirits; so our whole party was in a gay and carefree mood.

It may be that Mr. Ford's habit of life contributes something to his cheerfulness. He is almost an ascetic in eating; he eats what he likes but he does not like to eat much. He never drinks or smokes. He is so thin that he seems almost transparent. No wonder he loves the old dances; he is as light on his feet as an adolescent.

In some manner, which I wish I understood (excellent digestion may have something to do with it), he can change the gear of his mind as easily as that of his car. At any moment, when he wishes to rest, he can turn off responsibilities or cares, shift the gear, and relax.

In the summer-time, he gets up at six o'clock or even earlier, goes out of doors and runs about a mile at a dogtrot. Then he is ready for work. I queried him: 'How about breakfast?' for, with me, breakfast is important. I am happy before breakfast because I am going to have it; I am happy during breakfast, because I enjoy it; I am happy after breakfast, because I feel its inspiration.

But Mr. Ford eats nothing till one o'clock. Having important things to consider, his mind is clearer and works with more precision if his stomach is empty.

His interests are in the future and in the past. As an inventor and as an executive, no one is ahead of him. He is always looking forward to see what is going to happen and is ready to meet coming conditions. Then of late years he has taken an increasing interest in the reconstruction of the past. His Wayside Inn at Sudbury, his village at Dearborn, his collections of antiques, his passion for old music and old-fashioned dancing illustrate this.

And indeed he himself is a combination of past and future; more so than any other person I know. He practises the old-fashioned virtues of purity, abstinence, regularity, honesty, industry, self-reliance; in business his methods are always a little ahead of everybody else.

He is an amazing combination of shrewd practical common sense with extreme idealism. I wish he might live five hundred years on this planet, for his life is a multitudinous blessing.

There is one more characteristic which not every one realizes—humour. In the famous days of the Peace Ship, one of its passengers returned to America and announced that he was through with the project because the company was made up of cranks and fools. A reporter called up Mr. Ford and said that the Reverend Doctor Blank had quit, because he said the company was made up of cranks and fools. 'Have you anything to say?'

Mr. Ford replied 'Apparently the situation is being improved by resignation.'

96

JOURNEY TO ATHENS

THE year 1932 was one of the happiest years in my happy life and made especially memorable because I saw for the first time two things I had always longed to see—Athens and a total eclipse of the sun.

On 19 February we sailed for Greece on the *Saturnia*. We had two reasons for taking this ship: one, that it sailed to Greece; the other, that we were informed it would stop at the Azores, Lisbon, Gibraltar, Cannes, Naples and give the passengers a fine opportunity to see these historic places.

Our first stop was Boston, which I had never before approached from the sea; I had had no idea of the picturesque beauty of the harbour. We were late in arriving, and very late in leaving.

On 25 February we reached the Azores, after dark, so we could see nothing. Some passengers who lived there left the ship, and a few got on board; we supposed we should wait till daylight and then have an opportunity to land. But the Captain said that was impossible; we thus moved on in the night. On 27 February we entered the Tagus and saw Lisbon after dark. The best scenery was in the sky. Over the city hung the three brightest stars in the universe, Venus and Jupiter and Sirius.

I had always wanted to see Lisbon, both for its own sake and because Henry Fielding is buried there, and I wished to do homage at his tomb. With his usual bad luck, he died there in 1754; if he could have hung on for one more year, he might have enjoyed a more exciting death in the earth-quake. In Lisbon they still call it an earthquake—one does not have to remember to say 'fire.' The harbour is superb; an entire fleet of battleships could perform manoeuvres in the enclosure.

Many passengers were reading Lawton Mackall's witty and charming book, *Portugal for Two*. And we were all ex-pecting to see the great city, and the little town of Belem, and beautiful Sintry by the light of day. It was not to be. We came like a thief in the night, with a cargo of two million dollars in gold, taken off the ship by Portuguese soldiers. We drove around the old city in the dark and saw the magnificent fifteenth century cathedral by *match-light*.

The February night was clear and mild, and we walked about the streets; the cafés at midnight were crowded by men engaged in eager conversation, who apparently had no thought of sleep. Not a woman was to be seen in any of these spacious halls, and our ladies aroused considerable in-terest. The broad boulevards were also densely populated.

We finally went into a small shop with tables, something like an American drug store, and there we had some port wine and I smoked a Brazilian cigar, cheap and excellent. At the top of a steep, precipitous hill, which rose out of the midst of the town, we had a splendid view of the city with its illuminated streets. Lisbon seemed to me so beau-tiful and so interesting, that I wish we had been allowed to see it by day.

Our ship left sometime after midnight, and we were eager to see the straits of Gibraltar and the massive cliffs. But we arrived at Gibraltar after dark, and no one was al-lowed to land except those who were not to return. It was dark, it was foggy, it was rainy; but for about six seconds I saw a great hill or mountain on the African side, the only time I have seen Africa.

I had hoped to compare the Gibraltar cliff with its likeness in the Prudential Insurance Company's advertisement, but we saw nothing; a few days later, we had equally
bad luck with Aetna's; so the only insurance advertisement
we verified was the Travelers'.

At Cannes, our next stop, which we reached in the night,
no one was allowed to land except those who intended to
stay, and no visitors were permitted to come on board.
Thus, an old friend of mine the scholar Robinson Smith,
who had travelled from Nice to meet me there for a half-
hour's conversation, had his journey for his pains. It was
just as cold at Cannes as it had been in Boston. A lady who
embarked there told me she had sat on a stove for six
weeks in a vain endeavour to be warm.

Our next stop was at Naples. I have seen many pictures
of the beautiful bay of Naples, but in my visits to Italy, I
had never been south of Rome. We reached Naples about
ten o'clock in the evening, and drove around the city in
the night; our ship proceeded on its way about two in the
morning.

At about eleven o'clock that morning, I was standing
on deck looking at Stromboli and saying to myself that
anyhow here was one object we had seen by daylight,
when the deck steward came up, and said, 'You know, sir,
Stromboli is much more beautiful if seen in the night.' I
lay down in a deckchair and laughed helplessly; he does
not yet know why.

On the early morning of Friday 4 March we looked out
of our cabin window and there was Greece! Wild and sombre, romantic and mysterious, the austere mountains covered with snow. We landed at Patras, and the moment I
stepped on shore, I knelt and kissed the ground.

Greek railways need a publicity agent. No one speaks
well of them. When we were told it would take eight hours
for our train to cover the 135 miles between Patras and

Athens, we were not exhilarated. But once started on that journey, I should not have cared if it had taken twenty hours. We came to Greece solely because of its literary associations; but if no book had ever been written there, it would be well worth a visit because of the splendour of the scenery.

From the windows of the train, the waters of the Corinthian Gulf, the grey-green olive trees, the dark green pines and cypresses, with the mighty barrier of snow-clad mountains, make an indelible impression. And the journey began and ended with Byron, the most potent foreign name in the country; he is adored by the Greeks. Close to Patras is Missolonghi, where he died; and near Athens is Sunium, with the pillar of the temple whereon he carved his name.

We went to the Acropolis with no teacher and no guide. The March air was suave; the intense blue of the sky was stainless. We *lived* in the Parthenon, in the Erechtheum, in the Wingless Victory. These buildings were not erected for architects, any more than Euripides wrote for professors; they were for us; common people who love beauty. They were as perfect in grace as in sublimity. Their massivities were as free from vulgarity as their tenuities. The Parthenon is overwhelming in its solid and severe austerity, in its colossal grandeur; while the tiny Niké and the Caryatides on the Erechtheum are as lovely as a perfect miniature. Those Greek architects played with stone as Beethoven played with an orchestra; they could make stone look as immovable as the eternal cliffs and as fluid as running water. The only thing they could not do was to be pretentious or insincere or ugly.

It is well to look at the buildings on the Acropolis without any verbal accompaniment; as it is well to listen to music without trying to explain what it means. Let Beauty have her chance—there is a whole education in that. As the poet Flecker said, 'The business of poetry (or art) is not to save men's souls, but to make them worth saving.'

We arrived in Athens on a Friday. On the next day, thanks to my friend Professor Samuel Bassett of the American school, I had the privilege of seeing and hearing the foremost Greek citizen of the twentieth century, Veniselos. And it was a great occasion, one of the most important in many years. Parliament convened at half-past four. The Royalists, few in number, sat at the extreme right, the Socialists and Communists at the left, and the Liberal majority in the centre. In front of the front row, the only persons to have desks, sat the Cabinet with Veniselos the Prime Minister, and the President of the Council. The Presiding Officer rang a bell; the minutes of the last meeting were read; a few speeches were made by various members during which reading, writing, and general conversation went on freely. But the moment Veniselos was called to the Tribune, and began his address, there was silence.

For many days it had been understood that the Premier would on this occasion make a general statement of the financial policy of the Government, and deliver an ultimatum. I could feel the tense interest, the suppressed excitement, as he began to speak. He had a natural, unaffected dignity and sincerity that should and did impress every one. The whiteness of his beard was accentuated by a black skullcap, which, when the heat of the room became almost unbearable, he would remove to wipe his brow, head, and neck. As Casca remarked, his speech was all Greek to me; but I was filled with admiration for his manner. Rhetorical flourishes, declamatory gestures, shoutings, tricks of oratory, were absent. He made this highly important address to a crowded Parliament and galleries as if he were speaking to a board of bank directors. His tones were quiet, matter-of-fact, the essence of plain, practical common sense. I did not wonder at his commanding influence.

That there is a yellow press in Greece and that many were afraid of it would appear from a speech made by Veniselos in the Senate.

> Everybody here is in terror of the press; for the immunity of the press, which we are trying to remedy by a law recently voted, makes everybody shudder at the thought that a newspaper may penetrate into private and family affairs, and display in publicity not dirty linen but clean linen made dirty. From the most obscure citizen up to a member of Parliament, up to a minister, up to a party leader, everybody is afraid of the newspaper. For my part, I do not pretend to be better than others. I certainly have my faults, but they are compensated for by one characteristic; I am one of those rare Greek politicians who have never been afraid of the press.

In addition to the American, British, and other schools of classical studies at Athens, there is the admirable institution known as Athens College, not far outside the city limits, where several hundred Greek youths have a liberal education under the direction of Homer W. Davis, assisted by an able American faculty. With the exception of one course given in Greek, the curriculum is in English and I have the best of reasons for believing that our language is efficiently taught. The students have tremendous enthusiasm for the study of the English language and literature. I gave a lecture there to three or four hundred Greek boys. They seemed to understand everything I said and were quick in seizing every point. Before the lecture they sang the school song in English, written by Mr. Darbishire, one of the teachers; after the lecture they sang *My Country, 'tis of Thee* followed by the Greek national anthem in their native tongue. Then came a graceful compliment to Yale, with an episode in Yale's history new to me. One of the teachers had discovered it. President Davis, in a felicitous speech gave the facts; then one of the Greek students, in excellent English, handed me a large volume, *Modern Greek-English Dictionary*, by A. Kyriakides, inscribed

> The students of Athens College present this Dictionary to the students of Yale University in grateful recognition of the aid given to the cause of Greek independence by students of Yale in 1823.

And here are the accompanying documents:

(FROM THE *National Gazette* [PHILADELPHIA] 18 DECEMBER 1823)

I

YALE COLLEGE
DEC. 13, 1823

SIR:

We enclose the sum of $800 collected in the College for the use of the Greeks. We request you to receive it, and forward it, with other collections for this purpose, or appropriate it, in such other way as will most benefit the cause. We subjoin the Resolutions adopted at our meeting, and with the most ardent wishes for your success in this work of national benevolence, have the honor to be, Sir, your most obed't servants.

In behalf of the Committee
To Wm. Bayard,
Chairman of the Greek Com. H.Y.

II

NEW HAVEN COMMITTEE
18 DEC. 1823

A meeting of the citizens of N.H. was held on the 17 inst. to concert measures to aid the Greeks. Noah Webster was called to the Chair, and Charles H. Pond, appointed Secretary. A committee consisting of the following gentlemen was appointed to prepare resolutions to be presented at a future meeting:

Noah Webster
David Daggett
David C. DeForest
Charles Dennison
Chauncey A. Goodrich
Charles H. Pond
Roger S. Baldwin.

III

(FROM THE *American Daily Advertiser* [PHILADELPHIA], 26 DEC. 1823)
The editor of the *Connecticut Mirror*, speaking of the patriotic donation to the Greeks from the students at Yale College, says: ' We hope that when the Greeks obtain their freedom, and have a chance to reward their benefactors, they will send out, to show their gratitude, an explanation of certain hard words and dubious expressions, which are now and then to be found in Lucian's Dialogues and Demosthenes' Orations, with a glossary of expletives, heteroclites, etc. which if they should arrive in middle college, of a hot afternoon, just before the bell rings for recitation, would to many be peculiarly acceptable.'

And here they are, in this Dictionary, which I took back to Yale. No gift could have pleased me more than this tribute to the University which I had the honour to represent.

It is interesting to watch the excavations in Athens. At the Agora, under the direction of Mr. and Mrs. Shear, we saw an amphora in perfect condition taken out of the ground where it had lain since 1000 B.C. They have made many valuable and exciting discoveries.

On the Acropolis we had the good fortune to meet the veteran savant Professor Belanos, who is in charge of the restoration of the Parthenon. He took us over the vast structure, explaining the new work.

Most fortunately for us, among our travelling companions on the ship were Professor and Mrs. Edward Capps of Princeton. More than forty years ago Mr. Capps and I were graduate students at Yale. For many years he has been one of the foremost classical scholars in America; and his services in connexion with the Loeb Classical Library—an undertaking of immense and permanent value, so dear to the heart of that great London publisher, William Heinemann—have been important. But it was not until we entered Athens together that I realized how great was

his reputation among native Athenians and the resident
foreign scholars. Their respect for his learning is equalled
by their affection for the man.

We were invited to a state dinner by Mr. and Mrs. Veniselos for Wednesday evening, 15 March. My wife was sick
in bed. I woke up Monday morning with a high fever and a
bad case of tonsillitis. I sent for Doctor Dorando, an admirable Greek physician who speaks English. I told him
he must cure us both in 48 hours, because we were going
to the dinner on Wednesday night. He shook his head
gravely and said he would do his best. He gave me sixteen
grains of quinine and on Tuesday the following day, sixteen more. On Wednesday night, though rather shaky,
we went to the state dinner in the Veniselos mansion at
nine o'clock. The guests of honour were Professor and
Mrs. Capps, and others were Professor and Mrs. Carpenter, Mr. and Mrs. Adossides, Professor and Mrs. Davis,
the Police Commissioner, and some foreign diplomats.

Although Mr. Veniselos had had an exhausting day with
constant committee meetings and a full dress debate in
Parliament, he gave no sign of it; he was full of gaiety and
made every one feel at ease. My wife sat on his left and
as he spoke English only with difficulty, they conversed in
French. She asked him about the political situation in
Greece, which relieved her from the necessity of saying
anything at all. I sat on the left of Mrs. Veniselos, who
speaks English fluently. She was in gay spirits and we had
a good time discussing American and English detective
stories, her favourite reading. A few years later, when she
was recovering from several gunshot wounds meant for her
husband, we sent her many of these thrillers, which she
devoured with delight.

Suddenly there was a pause in the dinner-talk, one of
those pauses supposed to occur every twenty minutes on
such occasions. I took advantage of it and addressed the

Prime Minister. I told him that Yale University was the only American university that had, and had had for fifty years, a Greek *yell*. I had to explain what was meant by a yell; even then he did not see why we yelled, and I told him I could not explain it myself, but we yelled. This yell, I told him, was shouted in unison at all football games; and as it came from the *Frogs* of Aristophanes, one of the classics of his native land, I thought he ought to hear it, if only from patriotic motives. I therefore gave the Greek yell of Yale:

> Brekekekex! koax! koax!
> Brekekekex! koax! koax!
> O, wop! O, wop!
> Parabolou!
> YALE!

He and the others were so pleased that I suggested we all shout it together. This was done several times by the entire company and with great enthusiasm.

41 AVENUE DE KIFISSIA
ATHENES
July 2nd 33

MY DEAR PROFESSOR PHELPS,

Thank you for your kind sympathetic cable & for the books you are so kind as to send me. I hope I will receive them before my departure on July 8th. We sail for Paris (22 rue Beaujon).

I am happy to say that I have entirely recovered from my bullet wounds & am feeling very well & fit. Fortunately these were not in any vital part.

Mr. Veniselos is today contesting the election of Salonika & writes to say that never in his whole political life has such a wonderful reception been awarded him.

Thank God his "charmed" life has been saved. Please remember me to Mrs. Phelps & with kindest regards, Believe me,

> Yours v sincerely,
>
> HELENA VENISELOS

Several attempts had been made during his long career to assassinate Veniselos; on this latest occasion, he and his wife were in an automobile, when a number of shots were fired at him. None hit him, but three or four wounded his wife.

HALEPA, CANEA, CRETE

8th January 35

MY DEAR PROFESSOR PHELPS,

With the advent of the New Year let me wish you & Mrs. Phelps every possible happiness & above all health. I have received a few days ago the two books you were so kind as to send me & for which please accept my thanks. It is indeed kind of you to remember me & I am deeply touched by your kind thought.

Mr. Veniselos is, I am happy to say, in the best of health & spirits, and joins me in sending you & Mrs. Phelps our warmest greetings.

Yours v sincerely,

HELENA VENISELOS

The books alluded to in these letters were English and American detective novels.

On Friday 18 March I attended the regular weekly luncheon of the Rotary Club. The meetings of Rotary are unlike those to which I am accustomed in America. At home luncheon is usually served promptly at quarter past twelve; the speaker of the day talks from one to half-past one, when the meeting is over.

There are about forty-five members of the Athenian Rotary Club; they meet every Friday at the Petit Palais; the only other American present on this occasion was Professor Alexis of the University of Nebraska. He and I arrived about noon; the members dropped in casually, as if time were of no importance, and finally we sat down about half-past one, and the meeting lasted until half-past four. It was necessary to converse in French, for Greece is one of the few countries in the world where French, and not English, is the second language. If one enters Athenian society or wishes to meet Athenians in business, French is necessary. A daily paper is printed in French; and there are French movies.

But the thing that impressed me about this Rotary Club was that nearly every resident member was a distinguished scholar. I was presented to ten or eleven men in succession, and every one was a Professor. Finally, when I met a rotund, jolly-looking individual, I asked 'Are you also a Professor?' 'No, thank God, I am a wholesale wine merchant.'

Finally, it was time for the address of the day, delivered by a Rotary member. He was the Head of the School of Architecture, and the designer of the magnificent tomb of the Unknown Soldier, unveiled while we were in Athens. His address was in Greek, and appeared to be extremely technical. But the moment he had finished, at least a dozen members asked him questions in turn, and some of them seemed to be heckling him. The discussion was animated.

That was the most highbrow Rotary Club meeting I have ever attended.

Some weeks later I attended the Rotary Club in Florence, which was much like an American meeting. The address was by Sig. Salvini, a charming gentleman, son of the great Tommaso Salvini. I told him I had heard his father play Othello, on his last tour of the United States in 1889. Also that several times I had heard his brother as Romeo in the company headed by Margaret Mather. 'Ah, my brother! I so seldom hear about him now. He died many years ago, when he was still very young.'

Looking out of our hotel window in Athens one morning, I saw theatre advertisements on various posts.

AGAMEMNON BY AESCHYLUS

Inasmuch as that play was written and played at Athens in the fifth century before Christ, it was exciting to see such a playbill.

On Sunday, 20 March, the National Theatre opened with *Agamemnon*; it was played of course in modern Greek, but to hear it in the city of its birth was thrilling. The acting was very fine; especially that of the two women, who played Clytemnestra and Cassandra.

It is not merely in age that Athens is venerable; it is because in the fifth century before Christ, about the year 450, the citizens of Athens—that is to say, the voting population—reached a higher level of intellectual excellence than those of any other city before or since. Those citizens more than two thousand years ago breathed a purer and a nobler air; they knew a spiritual exaltation compared to which our finest American cities of the twentieth century are as a primary school to a university.

As Goethe has said, we should praise individuals who have illuminated the world and also praise the communities that produced such men and gave to them not only the necessary stimulation, but the indispensable appreciative audience. In that far-away century in Athens there was an intellectual ferment, a passion for the finest works of art; so that the average Athenian citizen was as competent a critic of drama, architecture, sculpture, as the average American citizen is of professional baseball.

Athens *today* is not superior in culture to New York; quite the contrary. New Yorkers have many theatres of high excellence, one of the finest opera companies in the world (even if it must rely mainly on foreign singers), innumerable opportunities to hear symphony orchestras, and great museums of art. It is the Athens of 438 B.C., rather than the Athens of 1938 A.D., which can teach us. But it is worth remembering that Athens today, in the throes of a financial crisis and with the country facing bankruptcy, saw fit, after a complete renovation, to reopen the National Theatre, subsidized by the government, and reopened with the *Agamemnon* of Aeschylus.

As I looked around on gatherings of modern Athenians, I was impressed by the triumph of the British face. Among priests, old men, and country farmers, the full beard is still in evidence; but nearly all the Athenians under fifty are smooth-shaven, and many wear the single eye-glass. The ancient Greek profile so familiar in pictures and copies of statues and coins, with the straight line from the tip of the forehead to the tip of the nose, has almost disappeared; there are more such profiles among American undergraduates than will be seen in Athens.

Thirty years ago, in our boarding-house in Munich, was a young Greek who was studying law; his name was Pericles Karapanos. I remembered him and his name perfectly; and I gave him a tremendous surprise by entering his busy law office one day. He is a very prominent man now, one of the leading lawyers in Greece, a Senator and public speaker, universally loved.

I wondered whether my digestion would last, during our stay. Owing to the fact that most of the year it is warm, Athenians have the habit of dining very late, and having two short sleeps like the old-fashioned deep-water sailor. Many go to bed at two or three in the morning, get up at seven, and go to bed again at two in the afternoon. Even in the cooler season, it is impossible to get dinner at the hotel before half-past eight, and the dining room is not fully occupied until after nine. Hundreds of men sit up nearly all night and talk.

Street life is even more animated than in Paris. When we remember that in most cities in America the sidewalks are being pared down to give more space for the parking of automobiles, it is interesting to see what an enormous place in social life here is filled by the sidewalk. Whether on the big boulevards or in the mean and narrow streets of the old town, tables and chairs are set out on the sidewalk, with many men conversing.

The New Testament, when it described the Athenians as being ever eager to see or discuss something new, might have been describing the Athenians of today. Many newspapers are hawked on the streets morning and afternoon; these are eagerly bought and read for the Greeks are a nation of newspaper readers. One of my friends asked the soldiers why, in their hours of liberty, they did not play football and other games.

'Oh,' was the reply, 'there is no time for that. Our soldiers would much rather spend their free hours in conversation. There is so much to talk about.'

And indeed they need no other athletic exercise; for their conversation is gymnastic; every part of the body is employed.

On 21 March we motored to Marathon, coming out from the olive trees toward the plain and the sea. I climbed to the top of the mound and shouted the two words spoken by the first Marathon runner, Pheidippides.

Χαίρετε, νικῶμεν!
Rejoice, we conquer!

On 24 March, in company with Professor Bassett, we took an early morning train on our way to Delphi. In Athens it was like a heavenly day in summer; when we reached Delphi, in the afternoon, it was like mid-winter, deep snow everywhere and bitter cold. The train went near the lake at Marathon, and we had a glorious view in the distance of a marvellous snowy mountain in Euboea. We saw Aulis and Thebes, and the battlefields of Epaminondas. Then the country became hilly, with thousands of sheep and millions of olive trees. The olive trees seemed to flow into every valley and every depression among hills. At Bralo, the last railway station, we engaged a motor-car and drove up the mountain through snow and along the edge of mighty precipices. We reached Delphi at half-past four; it was snowing hard. The inn was primitive; but we were glad of its shelter, and made no attempt to see Delphi until the next morning.

We rose early; the ground was covered with snow and the sky overcast. The scenery is sublime; and I do not wonder that the Greeks went there to receive messages from the Gods. We saw the Shining Rocks, the Castalian Spring (with a large cigarette advertisement), and the lovely little Doric Temple put up by the Athenians after the Battle of Marathon. And we saw the theatre.

Then I consulted the Oracle and was informed that it was safe to return by the automobile. It was fortunate that I had taken the trouble to do this; for our chauffeur flatly refused to make the return journey, saying we must wait for the snow to melt. But when I told him that I had consulted the Oracle, and got not only permission but a definite command to set off as soon as possible, he made no further objection.

After we had started, I did not wonder at his reluctance. The road along the edge of the terrible precipice was hub-deep in snow; and the wild, desolate grandeur of the scene added to our feeling of loneliness and helplessness. But even in the snow, we met flocks of sheep conducted by fierce-looking dogs; and I saw one big brilliant woodpecker, something like the American pileated woodpecker.

It was a relief to reach level ground, where we caught the Orient express from Paris; and long before our arrival, the snow changed into rain and we saw green fields.

That day in Athens had been a four-fold holiday—Lady Day, Good Friday, Independence Day, and the unveiling of the tomb of the Unknown Soldier. The streets were filled with parades.

Two days later, Easter Day, we sailed from Athens on the cruise of the Hellenic Society from London. There were about 250 people on board, all English except about

ten Americans. The ship sailed from Piraeus at eight in the
evening, and we saw the Acropolis illumined by floodlight.

Lord and Lady Conway were on the boat and made us
feel as if we were intimate friends; and indeed we became
so. Lady Conway was an American and after we had
reached England, we spent a day at their house—Allington
Castle in Kent, an interesting place, part Roman, with
magnificent gardens. Lord Conway was a great mountain-
climber. He had written many books on mountain climbing in Asia, Europe, and South America; and having seen
the most remote wonders of the earth, in 1936 he published
his book describing his adventures in the spiritual world—
A Pilgrim's Quest for the Divine, a beautiful mystical work.

Another passenger was the distinguished historian,
H.A.L.Fisher, Warden of New College, Oxford. There were
many dons from Oxford and Cambridge, with their families. The whole expedition was composed of members of
the Hellenic Society, under the direction of Sir Henry
Lunn. Four voyages are made in the Mediterranean every
year. I do not see how any expedition could be more admirably managed than this. It was cheap, yet the passengers had every comfort. At our frequent landings, motor-
cars or special trains were invariably ready and never
crowded; everything was provided, including tips. Lectures were given on board the ship twice a day and
Canon Wigram was the scholarly guide on shore.

We sailed to Constantinople, spending two days there,
sleeping on the ship. The American Ambassador,
Mr. Grew, had just left for his new post at Paris, but hearing that we were coming, had placed the Embassy motor-
car at our disposal. General Charles H.Sherrill, the new
Ambassador, and an old Yale college-mate, had not arrived.

On Thursday 31 March, a lifelong dream was realized.
We stood on the ringing plains of windy Troy. When I was

a boy at the Hartford High School, our teacher Dr. Martin, said 'Dr. Schliemann has been digging there,' which led me to read the book *Troja*.

This was the first time we had ever been in Asia. The ship stopped at Chanak. It was bitterly cold, with an icy wind. Drawn up close to the dock were many battered old Ford cars; their drivers had been told they must not race. But their Oriental passion for competition was soon aroused, and each driver had the fierce light of battle in his eyes. It was about twenty-five miles to Troy, and the road was horrible, which made the race more exciting. Only three of our cars were upset, and miraculously there were no injuries.

The thing that impressed me most at Troy was the *wind*—windy Troy. It blew as steadily as the trades, never in gusts, but just the steady rushing of a mighty wind, as it no doubt blew in the sweaty face of Hector, as he ran from Achilles. Next to the impression made by the wind, was the topography of the Trojan plain. Troy itself was simply a mound; and I suppose the city, even in the days of Priam, was not so large as the Grand Central Station in New York. But there lay the unchanged plain, with the rivers Scamander and Simois. The sea was near by, with snowy mountains in the distance.

The excavations showed nine different cities, from the bronze age to the Roman, but not very clearly. Remains of walls and mounds and loose stones.

On the way down the Hellespont, we passed Gallipoli; all the passengers stood at attention with uncovered heads; yet the terrible losses at that place have never affected me as deeply as the death of Hector, or as the Athenian expedition to Syracuse.

In the Trojan War I am pro-Troy; in the Peloponnesian War I am pro-Athens; both times on the losing side.

The weather changed with the calendar; that last day of

March at Troy was like mid-winter. The next day, the first of April, we landed on Delos. It was clear, windless, mid-summer. Then we sailed to Crete, where they had a civilization before Homer. With the exception of Egypt and Mesopotamia, I suppose it was the oldest civilization in the world. The houses had conveniences not always found elsewhere today; hot and cold water laid on, bathrooms, and water-closets.

One of the high spots of the trip was Mycenae, and the house of Agamemnon, made even more vivid for me by the play I had seen in Athens. At Olympia it was intensely hot, and so dusty that I wondered if the contestants in the games could have been clearly discerned by the spectators.

Up along the Dalmatian coast we sailed, stopping at Ragusa, now called Dubrovnik. Sending a telegram in the post office there, I found I was one cent short; when a voice behind me said with a laugh, 'I'll lend you the cent.' It was Philip Guedalla, and when I met him again at a luncheon in London in 1935 I reminded him I had borrowed a cent from him three years before, and he said I was to remember the accumulated interest.

We reached Venice on a heavenly morning in April. At Asolo, which we had last visited 28 years before, we saw the street now named Via Roberto Browning and the grave of Eleonora Duse. She was buried close to the grave of Browning's son, but his coffin had been removed— nothing but the cavity remained. At that moment a funeral came to the place, the catafalque followed by many men on foot. After the ceremony was over, I asked Monsignor what had become of the body of Browning's son; and he said it had been moved to Florence. But I think it was really taken to Rome.

97

THE POPE

On 16 April 1932 we had an audience with the Pope. The audience was for one o'clock, and a large crowd, half of whom were Americans, assembled at the appointed hour, but the Pope kept us waiting until half-past two. I didn't understand this at the time, but when I read in William Teeling's *Life of Pope Pius XI* that he always finished what he was doing, no matter who might be waiting for him, I understood. At last the Pope appeared, clad in white, looking at us benevolently through his spectacles, and it was interesting to think that this same man, years before, had made first ascents in the Alps and several times had spent an entire night on their summits. He blessed us and walked around the room, offering us his ring finger to kiss as we knelt. He looked stoutish, healthy, and rugged. But the ceremony was one which was so often enforced upon him that both his actions and voice were mechanical.

98

MUNICH IN 1932

EARLIER in this book I have spoken of my love for Munich and its people, where we spent seven months in 1904, four months in 1911-12, and which always seems like home. In Paris I say with the Psalmist, 'By the rivers of Babylon I sit down and weep when I remember Zion.' But I am never homesick in Munich.

In the Spring of 1932 I met there my old University friends, Professor Schick (now Emeritus), Jules Simon, Hanns Oertel, formerly my colleague at Yale, and Professor Max Förster, my colleague to be; in addition to these and other friends and our beloved 'Eltern' at the Pension Nordland, there were two of my younger Yale colleagues in the English Department, Professors Robert D. French and Rudolph Willard. The University formally began its semester on a May morning; but as Professor Max Förster informed me, 'the informal opening of the university will take place at the Hofbräu this evening.'

He and Willard and I went down a narrow, dark street, left our hats and coats in a cloak-room, opened a door; we were in a vast room where about eight hundred men and women were seated at long tables, drinking the fresh beer of spring. In the gallery a band was playing, and the huge crowd were singing student songs. There was good fellowship—but no drunkenness, no disorder. Peasants, workers, students, servants, scholars, professors, business men, political magnates, officials, musicians mingled together with freedom. Such a thing as an 'introduction' to a neighbour would have been absurd. Although we had never seen our tablemates before, in three minutes we were old friends.

A strange thing happened. Four university students came up to the German professor with me, and he gave them three marks—seventy-five cents. They overwhelmed him with grateful appreciation. They were young gentlemen, well-dressed, with excellent manners.

I asked: 'Is it possible that you can tip students? In America a professor will sometimes help a poor student, but it has to be done secretly.'

'Ah,' the professor replied, 'most of these boys are desperately poor. They have no spending money whatever. They cannot even buy a glass of beer.'

'Well,' I asked, 'is it all right for me to contribute a little?' For at that moment four or five other students came up.

He said, 'Call it a donation to their society, and it is all right.' So I handed out three marks to the newcomers.

They immediately cheered lustily for America and for the 'American professor.' I meditated on the strange fact that only a few years ago we were at war with these people, for wherever I had gone in Munich I had found the most popular of all visitors were the Americans. When it was time to go, a group of students formed a bodyguard, and we walked clear through the hall to the exit, the students singing and cheering, while the crowds through which we passed raised their beer mugs.

While we were sitting there, I thought how impossible such a scene would be in England; there no one would speak to anyone else unless he knew him, and then hardly above a whisper. But my German professor said it would be equally impossible in North Germany. It was only in Munich that such informality reigned, that it was perfectly understood, and taken for granted.

I thought too how fortunate it was that such friendliness could exist. Several thousand students come to a great university for the first time, many of them lonely and homesick; an evening like this starts off the semester, and they have friends.

And in spite of the tremendous noise made by the band, the singing, the shouting, cheering, and laughing, there was not a single unpleasant sight.

I remarked to a student on the general good-fellowship of the assemblage. He replied, 'Munich is simply one whole family.'

It seemed to me (and this is my contributory thought to disarmament and world peace) that it would be a good idea to abandon Geneva as a meeting-place and have all sessions of international delegates in the Hofbräu Haus at Munich. (Munich was chosen in 1938.) Frenchmen, Germans, Italians, British, Russians, Japanese, Chinese, Americans all would lose their animosities after associating two or three evenings in this genial atmosphere.

The English department of the university asked me to give a lecture there on English Romanticism of the eighteenth century. There is such keen interest in English literature and the English language among the students that the regular lecture-room proved inadequate and we had to move to the largest hall in the building. I spoke slowly, and as distinctly as possible, and most of the students seemed to understand.

In spite of the general financial distress, the Germans in Munich are *theatre-minded*; they know that operas and plays are not luxuries, but necessities; thus at every performance I attended—and during two weeks I went to twelve—the house appeared to be sold out. But the Germans do not waste money on taxicabs; when the big audiences flowed out of the theatres at the close, there would be only three taxis waiting, and I never had any trouble in getting one.

The foremost living writer in Germany, Gerhart Hauptmann, began his career with a naturalistic play *Before Sunrise (Vor Sonnenaufgang)* which attracted the attention of the police. In 1932 he wrote *Before Sunset (Vor Sonnenuntergang)*, a play dealing with a love affair between a widower of seventy and a young girl, with a naturally tragic conclusion. This was well given at the Playhouse. I also saw there a translation of St. John Ervine's clever comedy, *The First Mrs. Fraser*, which is called *Die Erste Mrs. Selby*. It was greeted with tremendous enthusiasm. I talked with the leading young actress of the company and she said to appear in several different plays every week while rehearsing others was exhausting; but when I told her that in New York every new play was expected to run for months with the actors learning nothing else, she said, 'But how destructive that must be for their art!'

99

AN AMERICAN IN PARIS

An American woman in Paris is like a duck in water; it is her natural element. It takes about two seconds for the city by the Seine to hypnotize her. She loves it in her youth, she revisits it in maturity, she is homesick for it in her old age.

American women, who are as expert in shopping as Oriental rug-dealers, and whose audacity in entering expensive shops makes men breathless, are often called extravagant. But it should be remembered that they can make a few dollars last out a whole afternoon of visits to various shops; and that, unlike men, they never buy anything of which they do not approve. Any mediocre clerk can persuade a man that shoes fit him when he knows they do not; he buys in haste and repents at leisure.

If men were not so uncomfortable in shops, it would pay them to see the expression on the face of a Parisian salesman when he begins to show goods to some American woman whom he recognizes as a foe worthy of his steel. He is an expert seller and she is an expert buyer; it is a duel worth watching; and the amount eventually paid by the American husband or father should be regarded as the price he has paid for a ringside seat.

No man can feel toward Paris as a woman does; for Paris is itself a woman. Many men love it, but only women understand it. Paris is the most beautiful city I have ever seen; but I never feel at home there, though I have spent many months within its fair domain. I never fully analysed my sensations until an American scholar expressed them for me—'In Paris I feel as if I were surrounded by polite foes.' The French have a terrific family instinct; every housewife and mother seems to be on guard. If you speak to a woman on some proposition that may concern her purse, her home, or her offspring, her face assumes the expression of an American business man when asked for a loan.

Paris is the most beautiful city in the world; but it should not be forgotten that Paris is northern. The epithet 'sunny France' does not apply to Paris, where the climate is about the same as that of London; very, very bad. The clouds return after the rain. Anatole France in his entertaining novel, *The Crime of Sylvestre Bonnard*, describing his heroine's eyes, says, 'her eyes were grey; the grey of the Paris sky.' A typical day in Paris has a low-hung, impenetrable sky, slimy pavements, and a thin drizzle in the air.

Yet, while I do not think that in heaven I shall ever be homesick for Paris, it is, in addition to being beautiful, somewhat like the New Jerusalem:

> And the nations of them which are saved shall walk in the light of it; and the kings of the earth do bring their glory and honour into it.
>
> And the gates of it shall not be shut at all by day; for there shall be no night there.
>
> And they shall bring the glory and honour of the nations into it.

Paris draws distinguished men from every corner of France; and writers and painters from every country.

Furthermore, these poets and dramatists and novelists and sculptors and painters are national heroes; even small boys look upon them with awe. Streets and avenues and squares bear the names of great writers; and statues—not to warriors, but to novelists and sculptors—form a large portion of the stationary population.

Although France is in its feelings more self-sufficient than any other nation (one meets few Frenchmen outside of France), she is becoming more and more hospitable to foreign works of art.

If the national genius of England is represented by the English Bible and by Shakespeare, the national genius of France is represented by Racine and Voltaire. Religious ideals and romantic poetry for one; classic severity and a mocking smile for the other. Until Voltaire, French critics regarded Shakespeare as a barbarian; while the early performances of Wagner and of their own Victor Hugo turned into free fights.

Well, Shakespeare is coming into his own, even in Paris. In 1932 he was the most popular playwright in the French capital. One of the national theatres, the *Odéon*, had to give a vast number of performances of *King Lear* to satisfy the demand; and the other, the *Comédie Française*, repeated *Hamlet* over and over again, selling out the house every time. When I remember that an excellent performance of *Hamlet* had failed in New York the previous season, it did me good to sit in a French theatre and hear Shakespeare's masterpiece in French played to a house jammed to the last inch of space, and greeted with enthusiasm.

Some French writers think the passion for outdoor sport has been destructive to the French intellect; that it has killed the theatre, injured the book trade, and turned French boys and girls into healthy animals. However this may be, there is no doubt the British idea of sport has conquered young France; and a good thing it is for their health and presumably for their morals. The boys are playing football, tennis, golf; the expert boxer is a god; the girls have gone in or 'all out,' as the English say, for tennis. Sport has become a national passion, and the most acceptable present you can give to a French boy or girl is a tennis racket. The effect of sport is so far-reaching and for the most part so excellent that we should rejoice. It means health, vigour, courage, respect for an opponent, self-reliance, ability to take victory without conceit and defeat without excuse, good fellowship, and many other fine qualities.

One of the most spectacular sights in Paris is a funeral. Two hundred years ago Jonathan Swift said with his accustomed acidity, that the happiest looking people in the world are those who are attending a funeral. After one has recovered from the shock of this statement, and given it due reflexion, one will find in it some truth. The 'guests' are going to the cemetery, but they are coming back. I suppose it is for the same reason that people at funerals eat so tremendously; subconsciously they wish to stay alive. The Americans, most luxurious people in the world, make even a funeral comfortable; going and coming in motor cars. But the French, however they may actually feel, look at a funeral as they ought to look—solemn; because they follow the hearse *through the streets on foot*. I happened to be on a walk one day on the Boulevard Montparnasse when I heard funeral band music. I waited. The procession came along and I walked with it. It was the funeral of a general; the catafalque was spectacular and was followed by a long line of men and women. A military band in front of the hearse played in succession the three great funeral marches—Chopin's, Beethoven's, and Wagner's.

There is another custom in French funerals that might well be imitated elsewhere. Whenever a funeral procession passes, no matter how meagre or humble, every passer-by takes off his hat. I asked a Frenchman if this custom had a religious origin. 'Oh, no,' he replied, 'we are simply saying goodbye.'

One of the advantages of being in Paris is that we are near the finest works of architecture—the Gothic cathedrals of northern France. No buildings in the world are so beautiful as the cathedrals of Chartres, Mont Saint Michel, Rouen, Amiens, Reims, Laon, Bourges, Le Mans, Notre Dame of Paris. It is impossible to enter the cathedral of Chartres and be just the same person afterwards. The population of the world may be divided into two classes—those who have seen Chartres and those who have not.

The most characteristic quality of Parisian art and of Parisian people is grace. They hate ugliness and they hate awkwardness. French gardens, French meals, French people are graceful. They serve food in a dainty and attractive way. They wear their clothes as if they were a part of their personality. Books that are immoral are not vulgar; their plays have the same characteristic.

It is amusing to see how the Parisian will not admit that anything he manages is ugly. A woman in Paris who kept a boarding-house was showing me rooms. We came to one so small that I would not use it for a dog-kennel. I said it was impossibly small. She said, 'It is *mignonne, très mignonne*!'

PIRANDELLO, BERNSTEIN, DAUDET

IN 1932 the famous Italian dramatist Luigi Pirandello was living in Paris in a pleasant flat on the top floor of a building near the Arch of Triumph. But as revealing either the narrow limits of fame or the suspicious nature of French females, when I reached the penultimate height, rang and asked the trim housemaid if M.Pirandello lived there, I received an emphatic negative '*Mais non.*' Nobody can say 'no' quite so negatively as a French woman. It means not only 'no,' it means 'get out of here as soon as possible, I don't know who you are and don't want to know, there is nothing in this house that concerns you, you mind your business and I'll mind mine;' all that is expressed in the word *non* and yet it was not spoken rudely or vulgarly; merely decisively. Such an attitude, instead of making me angry or embarrassed, amuses me. I asked if M.Pirandello lived on another floor of the same building; she did not know; she had never heard of him. I walked a few steps up to the next floor, rang, and M.Pirandello himself came to the door.

A short, solid, healthy-looking man, with grey hair and goatee. Very kind he was and cordial. Although he had on his desk the English translation of one of his books (American edition), he apparently did not speak English; we carried on in the language of the country where we were. Frenchmen say he speaks French with a decided accent; he certainly spoke it well enough for me. I understand French more easily when it is spoken by a foreigner than by a native.

I expressed my delight in the performance of *As You Desire Me* on the New York stage; and of my good fortune in seeing *Henry IV* at the Little Theatre in New Haven, directed by Jack Crawford. I asked him if it were not true that the key to the 'mistaken identity' in so many of his plays lies in what we *believe* rather than in what may be called fact. If the husband in *As You Desire Me* had gladly and confidently embraced his returning wife, instead of seeking proofs of her identity, she then *would have been* his wife. 'Most certainly! all my plays deal with spiritual realities; the reality in the mind is more real than reality in fact.'

I asked him which he preferred—the writing of novels or plays. He had no doubt about this; plays were nearer his heart.

His personality revealed quiet dignity, simplicity, sincerity.

The next afternoon I had a delightful conversation with Henry Bernstein, the most successful of living French playwrights. His house, filled with magnificent paintings and other works of art, was temporarily closed; and he was staying in a hotel. Mr. Bernstein is a tall and powerful man, built like a good Number Five in a University crew; his height seemed accentuated by a long dressing-gown. He has vitality, is cordial, and speaks with vivacity. He apologized for his English; unnecessarily, for he spoke it with fluency. He loves America and the Americans, and believed that our financial depression was only temporary. 'The Americans are too great and resourceful a people to stay down.' He had an original theory to account for part of our troubles. 'You make things altogether too well; your machines are made with such skill and such excellent material they don't wear out; one never has to buy anything new. My automobile is American, and it will last for many years.'

He thought our greatest writer was Ernest Hemingway. I remonstrated. 'Ah, of course he has faults, but what vigour, what power, what originality!' Like so many Parisians, he does not admire Rostand; 'our really great French mind was Ernest Renan.' He naturally prefers irony, the keen, sceptical, pure intelligence, to romance. I was not surprised. But when I asked him what he thought of the lyrical genius of Victor Hugo, he laughed and quoted André Gide, who on being asked who was the greatest of all French poets, said 'Victor Hugo—hélas!'

On my saying that only a Frenchman could really appreciate Racine and *enjoy* the golden age of the seventeenth century, he said, 'Oh, the seventeenth century is overrated.'

Late on the same afternoon, accompanied by my friend and former pupil, Hudson (Boz) Hawley, of the Associated Press in Paris, I went to see Léon Daudet in his office as Editor-in-Chief of the daily Royalist paper, *L'Action Française*.

Léon Daudet, son of the great Alphonse Daudet, although a Parisian born and bred, has the warm-hearted, passionate, expansive, temperament of the South, whence his father came. He is roly-poly in shape, keenly intelligent, with a remarkable flow of conversation. Everything he says is interesting. Although he must know English well, no English was spoken during the hour we spent together. Remembering how busy the writer of a daily paper is, I rose, after we had been there some twenty minutes, and he asked '*Comment? vous êtes pressé?*' and I gladly sat down again.

He is a good enthusiast and a good hater. His book *Reminiscences* (translated by Arthur K. Griggs) is vitriolic; but he has a genius for friendship, and absolute reverence for the memory of his father. He belongs to the Goncourt Academy and told us with much pleasure that the ten

members, on a secret ballot to determine the greatest
French novel of the nineteenth century, put Flaubert's
l'Education Sentimentale first and Alphonse Daudet's
Le Nabab second. In the history of French literature, he
regarded the sixteenth as greater than the seventeenth
century, because it contained Rabelais and Montaigne.

M. Daudet had the previous week attended the performance of *Hamlet* in French at the *Comédie*, and I quote from
his interesting review.

> La première, c'est que Shakespeare peignait, sous forme de dra-
> matisation de chroniques anciennes et le folklore, des événements et
> allusions à des événements tragiques de la Cour de la reine Elisabeth,
> comme Racine peignait, sous des masques antiques, des figures pas-
> sionnées de la Cour du Grand Roi. . . .
> Ma seconde remarque est d'une portée plus générale. Ce qui donne
> au drame shakespearien en général, et à Hamlet en particulier, cette
> envolée extraordinaire, c'est qu'il est baigné de surnaturel, mieux,
> de divin; mieux encore, de divin chrétien. . . . Il est à la chrétienté
> ce que les grands tragiques grecs sont au paganisme; et toutes ses
> finales, après tant de crimes et d'épouvantes, sont baignées de pardon,
> de sérénité, d'espérance, de sacrifice consenti, en somme: de libéra-
> tion. . . .
> Notre temps, si tragique, emporté par plusieurs tempêtes vers des
> récifs inconnus ou barbares, convient au déploiement en nous de
> Shakespeare. Sa gloire rencontre nos horreurs, nos pitiés, nos amours,
> nos remords, jusqu'à nos songes. Les vibrations de son tocsin s'ac-
> cordent aux vibrations du nôtre. Ses gouffres, nous les avons sous nos
> yeux. Toutes les larmes incluses en ses tragédies ont été versées pen-
> dant quatre ans. Tous les cris de ses héros mourants ont été poussés
> pendant quatre ans. Mais le chemin qui monte de ses profondeurs est
> manifestement—pour qui s'est imprégné de lui et a vécu de lui,
> Shakespeare—celui de la Croix.

Conversation with M. Daudet is enlivening because he
possesses such strong convictions in art, politics, and religion; he has none of the indifference, polite scepticism, and
irony characteristic of many writers.

He told us stories and anecdotes of his father; and as I

took leave, he kissed me affectionately on both cheeks. During this embrace, Hawley, who had never seen his professor thus saluted, stood petrified like Lot's wife—and the story by this time has lost nothing in his telling of it.

Léon Daudet is an illustration of one of my favourite theories, that one cannot be unhappy so long as one remains profoundly interested in life. The world has not gone as M. Daudet would like to have it; in religion and in politics, he is in a minority. But he gave the impression not only of being genial, but of being happy. It is difficult to say how many Christians today would go to the stake rather than renounce their faith. I feel certain, that if such an emergency arose, Léon Daudet would stand singing in the flames.

I had stimulating conversations in Paris with my friends Padraic and Mary Colum. Wonderful talkers are they both! Mr. and Mrs. Colum have a charm all their own; they are not like anybody else. He has an imaginative quality as shown in his poems and fairy tales; and she is a profound and penetrating literary critic. They look out on the world without prejudice. In some strange fashion they combine the mellowing of experience with the candour of a child.

101

HELEN WILLS MOODY

WHOEVER reaches the top in any department of intellectual, artistic, or athletic competition has some interesting personal qualities. It is impossible for one to reach lonely eminence without them.

Of course the world loves a champion, and crowds follow him about; there is intense curiosity to see him. But I mean something quite different from the adoration of success. Also something quite different from the excitement over athletic sports.

The father of Helen Wills brought her up to be a tennis champion. She did not take to the game naturally as a child; she preferred to play Indians and what not. But she has left it on record that her father aroused both her interest and her ambition.

At the age of fifteen, she won the national junior championship for girls. The next year she was ranked third among the women players of the United States, and the year following she was Champion. The rest is history. At her first appearance in Wimbledon in 1926 for the British championships, she was beaten by Kitty McKane, after having the match apparently safe in her hands. Never again was she to come so close to winning, and lose.

The question that will always be discussed by those interested in tennis is this: Granted that Suzanne Lenglen was the greatest of all European women players and Helen Wills the greatest of all American women players, which of these two was better than the other at her prime? It is impossible to answer this accurately. Suzanne won her first British championship in 1919 and, with the exception of one match with Mrs. Mallory in America, was never defeated. She met Helen only once, on the Riviera in 1926. Suzanne won, 6–3, 8–6. After the match, Helen was asked to comment on her opponent, and she said, 'Suzanne is just as good as I thought she was.'

Now, this one match—the only time the two girls ever met in singles—does not answer the question given in the preceding paragraph. On that day, and in her own country, Suzanne won. But she was in the plenitude of her powers and Helen had not reached her own pinnacle. Furthermore, it must be remembered that in order to be a world champion, *one should be successful not only at home, but abroad, and under varying conditions*. Although the majority of experts say that Suzanne was a greater player at her best than Helen became, I venture to disagree. And for the following reason.

Suzanne won all her matches either in France or in neighbouring countries. Helen had to travel six thousand miles to play in Europe. Even if one granted that Suzanne at her best was better than Helen's best *in France*, it does not follow that she could have beaten Helen in a home-and-home match.

I am certain, if the two girls had been contemporary, and had reached their peaks, say, in 1930, that in seven matches, three to be played in France, three in America, and one whose locality should be chosen by lot, Helen would have won.

Perhaps she never was quite so brilliant as Suzanne. Certainly not so spectacular, so theatrical, so sensational. But she was stronger physically, had more endurance, and better match temperament. And in 1938, by winning for the eighth time at Wimbledon, she made a record no man or woman has ever equalled.

When she began to appear in tournaments, she was called

on both sides of the Atlantic 'Little Poker Face.' No matter whether she were playing well or badly, whether she lost or won, whether the linesmen gave favourable or abominable decisions, no one could read her thoughts. She never said a word, she never made a gesture, she never tried to wilt a linesman by giving him the evil eye. From beginning to end of a match, her expression was without expression. And this did not mean she was grim, or tense; it meant she was calm. I was certain, merely by what I had read about her, that this magnificent calm on the field of battle, did not come from stolidity, but from self-control. No one is stolid who is ambitious; she was afire with ambition.

This opinion of mine was confirmed by the article she wrote for a book *On the Meaning of Life*, compiled by Will Durant, and published in 1932. Some chapters are taken up by contributions from writers, H.L. Mencken, Sinclair Lewis, Theodore Dreiser, Charles A. Beard, Will Rogers, et cetera. Her contribution not only reveals a clear intelligence: but in describing herself she repeated several times the phrase 'My restless heart.' Her chief characteristic is restlessness. She *must* be active. She is driven by a demon of ambition that will not let her rest.

Her greatest conquests are those over her own temperament. She is naturally excitable, hungry for fame; yet in action, her face never betrays emotion. She achieves self-domination.

Some years ago, Stanley Doust, a member of the Australian Davis Cup team in 1913, writing about Helen Wills Moody in the London press said she was a model not only in her playing but in her behaviour on the courts; and suggested that every aspirant should imitate her.

The glacial calm of Mrs. Moody in action is as impressive as the dynamic romantic exuberance of Borotra or Suzanne Lenglen. Bunny Austin in the London *Evening News* after the tournament in 1938 expressed it perfectly. 'Mrs. Moody

is a tennis goddess. .... I cannot believe that she is made of
the common clay of ordinary mortals, but of a substance
more rarefied, more goddess-like, a substance such as Jupiter might have donned when, seeking to fulfill his desires,
he descended from his Olympian heights. .... that goddess-
like quality is still hers; spectators and players alike are
still enmeshed in the web of her beauty; the hall mark of
the champion is still upon her; win or lose, we are grateful
to her for her reappearance.'

In addition to the adverse criticism that came from certain
persons on the occasion of her default to Helen Jacobs in the
American championship, Mrs. Moody had to suffer again in
1938. She had fought her way to the finals in the Wimbledon
tournament and the stage was set for a tense drama—once
more the two Americans faced each other across the net. Toward the end of the first set, Helen Jacobs had an accident
which palpably made her continuance in the contest hopeless. However she went on. Many of the spectators felt
that Helen Wills should have gone up affectionately to her
rival, and shown sympathetic concern or have suggested
a pause or anyhow suggested something. Mrs. Moody
went ahead and finished the match as soon as possible.

Now whilst the two girls are not enemies, the newspapers
have played up their rivalry to such a pitch as to make
every contest between them full of tension. It seems to me
that Mrs. Moody did exactly the right thing; not merely
technically, but in harmony with the best traditions of
sport. If the two girls had had the same intimate friendship like that existing between Budge and Mako, then
Mrs. Moody would of course have stopped playing and run
over to her friend. But with the conditions as they were,
the final insult to Miss Jacobs would have been sympathy
and pity (publicly exhibited) by her rival.

I remember a match at golf where there was great tension. The players were in general equally able; but one of

them missed three short putts in successive holes. When he missed the third one, his opponent said, 'That's too bad!' to which came the immediate response, 'Damn you, don't you pity me!'

Mrs. Moody is a painter, an etcher, a writer. Her own books, *Tennis* and *Fifteen-Thirty*, are not only well written; they are illustrated by portraits from her own hand. She has given exhibitions of her paintings and drawings in Paris, London, and New York. During the French championship tournament in 1932, she gave a public exhibition of her work with the pencil.

The best tennis I ever saw her play was at Paris in May 1932; and not in the tournament, which she won. While I was watching the progress of this tournament, I happened to see her and Sidney Wood slip out of the stand. I followed them, and saw them play two long deuce sets. I had not realized it was possible for any woman to reach such excellence. As it was only a practice match, she did not care whether she won or lost; hence she made miraculous drives and returns. Of course the best man will beat the best woman. I have been told that Suzanne never forgave Tilden for beating her two love sets.

In a long and interesting conversation I had with Helen Wills Moody in New York, she was kind enough to speak freely of her work. Tennis was not her life ambition; she wants to achieve success in some field of effort where she can steadily develop.

She told me one thing which answered a question I have always put to myself. Why is it, when our players travel so much in foreign countries that so few of them become proficient in foreign languages? I had thought they were not only neglecting a great opportunity, but that they would actually play better if they could divert their minds by hard study. She told me that study, even reading, could not accompany tournament play. If she is to play in the afternoon, she never reads in the morning. Reading takes a little off the keenness of perception. The eyes must be clear.

As to whether tournament players enjoy the game more than duffers, that is open to doubt. But it is certain that Helen enjoys her competitive matches, partly because of her ambition. Off the courts she is an admirable conversationalist, and it would be a pleasure to talk with her even if she had never seen a tennis ball.

March 9, 1936

DEAR MR. PHELPS,

I have just finished *The Last Puritan*, which was given me by Maxwell Perkins in Scribners—he said it was going to be another "best-seller." This isn't what I wanted to tell you.

It is this, and for no special reason—I mean I have no right really, because the subject is so far removed and does not concern me— except because of the fact that the name, Santayana, has been in my mind for such a long time.

It was you, as I remember, who gave me a letter some years ago to him, which I never delivered because I was so busy with the tennis. Even had I been able I should have so hesitated that I don't think ever I could have presented it.

Do you remember that the reason we met was because in 1931 you read a little thing I had written for Will Durant which was called "On the Meaning of Life"? I always have thought that this was a very happy stroke of fortune for me that you did happen to see it. In this little article which was sincerely written then, but not an expression for me now of what I think "of life," I was surprised the other day, when going over some papers, to find something which I think is true—and I wonder how I recognized it then. I said of Santayana: "He is seeking something, something which will explain beauty and perfection. He derives his joy from the ceaseless activity that goes with the quest."

It is poorly expressed, but is it not true of him?

I had no idea that Santayana liked sport either. But having instinctively admired him, and having never forgotten him after college days, even though I was hardly prepared to understand what he wrote, I am in quite an inexpressible way touched by the book, *The Last Puritan.* It does not seem the least strange to me that the people in the book speak in such an unlifelike way. They seem the more real because of it. Is it true that it is a quite extraordinary way of achieving realness? And at the end where he says or rather questions (which is unnecessary, since he has proved it to be a fact) "what realities might the spirit call its own unhurt illusion save . . . those very illusions which have made up our story." He would not need to point out that this truth belonged to this particular story, rather it belongs to "life," which is what he really means.

It is obviously the business of books to awaken our interest, and one that does not can't be worth much. On the other hand, do books often do what *The Last Puritan* does? Santayana has always fascinated me—even his name, before I read anything by him—because it made me think of yellow butterflies on a crimson background.

If I could only once see him—to speak to him would not be necessary. But he is quite old, and I shall travel less, so that it is probably not possible.

I am really painting, and have finished four canvases of a requested twenty—so have sixteen to go! Like practically every person who considers himself an artist I believe I have just discovered a "way" of painting, a plan or formula—so that now all I have to do is "practise" every day, because I know my direction. Youthful confidence is pathetic in a way because it is so sure of itself—but if we could borrow from Santayana some joy in the activity of the doing, there is perhaps recompense enough.

I must not bore you.

I adored seeing New Haven, as I told you, but couldn't have been more stupid in choosing a week end when you were away. The X's were very kind, and the Carpenter boy delighted, as was I, about the tennis in the gymnasium. What a marvellous place it is!

I feel I should ask you to forgive my long letter, since it is only based upon an idea, which came as a surprise to me upon reading a book, but which I felt in some way was related to you, because of the little circle of the Will Durant article, your letter to Santayana that you gave me, and what I found in *The Last Puritan*. He should have taught philosophy in only this way—but perhaps it has taken this many years to know that. Every conclusion takes a certain amount of time, and in this particular field, it may be that the best conclusions follow a lifetime. I wonder if they do.

With love,

HELEN

This letter appeared in her book, *Fifteen-Thirty* (1938, Scribners).

102

LITERARY AND CELESTIAL EVENTS

In 1932 I saw for the first time a total eclipse of the sun. On 3 August I took a night train from Michigan to Montreal; it was ninety-four in the shade, and the weather predictions for the next day were *cloudy*. Early the next morning, eating breakfast at the Ritz-Carlton in Montreal on the terrace underneath a gun-metal sky, I pondered whether I should go to Magog, eighty-seven miles away, or to Sorel, about sixty. Both towns were in the centre of the line of totality, and in both the sun was to be eclipsed for the longest period on this occasion, one hundred seconds. I had made up my mind to go to Magog, because the Canadian astronomers had gone thither, accompanied by astronomers from Great Britain and South Africa; whereas apparently no scientific gentry had considered Sorel.

After breakfast I telephoned Mr. J.G.McConnell, an undergraduate of Corpus Christi, Cambridge, whom I had met on the voyage of the Hellenic Society in the spring; as he and I had both seen Troy together, why not the eclipse? His father is the owner of *The Montreal Star*, and lives on a magnificent estate ten miles out of the city. Young Mr. McConnell came immediately to the hotel and we planned an expedition to the eclipse. As he was not able to leave Montreal until one o'clock, and as the totality began at the mystic moment of 3.22, we reluctantly abandoned the attack on Magog, and decided to advance on Sorel. On the way out, the sky, which had been cloudy all the morning, became even more so; no sign of shine, no streak of blue. But before our arrival the sun suddenly appeared, a small corner of it already bit off. By the time we reached Sorel, the sky around the sun was stainless; but a sinister cloudbank was rapidly approaching and it was a question whether the eclipse would take place before the clouds reached their mark, or whether we should see a total eclipse of both sun and moon at the same moment, which, although an unusual spectacle, is nothing to write home about. I have watched many exciting races; but never one more thrilling than this. The sun won; we had a perfect view of the eclipse; and a few minutes after totality, the clouds covered the thin melon-slice, and the sky remained overcast until nightfall.

After our return to Montreal we found that none of the million inhabitants had seen anything; at Magog the sky was cloudy so the astronomers saw nothing; and indeed Sorel was one of the very few spots where the eclipse had been visible.

It is impossible to describe a total eclipse of the sun or to convey anything of the impression it makes on the beholder. Talking one day with the famous engineer Charles Augustus Stone, who had been all over the world, I asked him if the Grand Canyon of the Colorado were not the most sublime spectacle he had ever seen; 'Yes, with one exception—a total eclipse.' He had, I believe, seen seven total eclipses. At this eclipse in 1932 the beginning of totality was a supreme moment in my life. I saw the prominences, the corona, Bailey's beads; and the sudden darkness was made even more impressive by the planet Jupiter.

Through illness I had missed the eclipse of 1925; it was a terrible disappointment; and yet there are educated people who care nothing for eclipses. Some otherwise intelligent friends of mine left New York the day before that eclipse, when they could easily have waited. And another friend told me that as he and his brother (a Harvard graduate) were in exactly the right position to see it, his brother, one minute before the eclipse, said 'Well, this is my regular time for going to the bathroom,' and went indoors. Hundreds of busy men travel six thousand miles on the mere chance of seeing what this university graduate thought quite unimportant.

On 7 November 1932 Richard Harrison, the Negro actor who became famous in every part of the United States for his amazing impersonation of God in the play *The Green Pastures*, was kind enough to speak to my Yale class in Contemporary Drama. He gave a fine address, and I had a long talk with him afterwards. He told me he had been a waiter in the Hotel Pontchartrain in Detroit and that in his spare time he had learned many passages from Shakespeare by heart. At social meetings with other waiters, he was often called upon to declaim passages from Shakespeare or from other authors, so that although he had no professional experience when he came to take the leading part in the play, he felt at home on the stage. He was very modest and natural and altogether a charming person.

On the evening of 14 December in New Haven I saw a moon-rainbow for the first time in my life. Browning's striking description of a moon-rainbow in *Christmas Eve* had made me hope that some day I might see one for myself. They are in most latitudes extremely rare. In New Haven there had not been one in twenty-two years, when I saw this in 1932. It was not a particularly good moon-rainbow at that.

ANZIA YEZIERSKA

A good friend of mine is Anzia Yezierska, who, born in Russia, came to America as an immigrant in 1901, knowing no English. She worked in sweatshops, in factories, as domestic servant, and stole time from sleep to learn our language. At one time in the course of these terrible struggles for bread, she applied at one of the New York hotels for a job as scrubwoman; but her clothes were so poor and her appearance so devastated by hunger, that she was rejected. Five or six years later she returned to that same hotel as a famous American novelist, the guest of honour at a fashionable luncheon. She wrote novels and short stories about the poor in New York; in 1932, when her book *All I Could Never Be* appeared, I received from her the following letter.

ARLINGTON, VT.
Oct. 20, '32

MY DEAR PROF. PHELPS,

It was so kind of you to send me your encouraging few words about *All I Could Never Be*.

I thought it might interest you to know how the book came to be written. During the war, when rich and poor, educated and ignorant, native-born and newly-naturalized citizens were thrown together into a common cause, I happened to come in contact with a group of educators who were making a research study of the Poles. A wealthy American who lived in one of the large eastern cities, thickly settled with Poles wanted to know what kept those Poles isolated islands of foreignness, untouched by the American life about them. The men chosen to carry on the study were Ph.D. professors in sociology and education. I, working for them as their Polish interpreter was the only unschooled person among them.

The "scientific approach" of these sociology professors seemed to me so unreal, so lacking in heart and feeling. But I was too inarticulate to formulate a better way. At the end of the study, it seemed to me they knew less about the Poles than when they began. When they started out, they knew they didn't know, but after a few months investigation they had cut up the Poles into little sections, which they pigeon-holed and tabulated into sociological terms. They began turning out reports that seemed to bring out to me the deep, unutterable gulf between the professors who were analyzing the Poles and the Poles who were being analyzed.

At the end of the study, everyone was asked to write a report. I was the only one who could not write it. And this failure to write the report preyed upon me and tormented. I was a prisoner of an experience from which I could not escape till I saw Browning's lines: "All I could never be, All men ignored in me, That I was worth to God. . . ."

This novel ends the cycle of my experiences as an immigrant. I have started something entirely new. A play. And I know about as much of the technique of play writing as I knew about the writing of novels. I feel like a person who has set out in an air-ship across unknown seas—how—where will I come out in this new venture? God only knows. But Ah—the thrill of wrestling with dreams forever beyond us.

ANZIA YEZIERSKA

103

EMERITUS

THE rules of Yale University governing the Faculty require that on the Commencement following one's sixty-eighth birthday one must retire from active teaching. This is just and beneficent; even if a professor at that age shows no diminution in vigour, there are younger men in his department who have a right to look forward to promotion. Accordingly at the close of lectures in the Spring term of 1933, my forty-one years of active teaching at Yale came to an end. I do not like farewells; when I met my class in Browning for the last time, I conducted it exactly as if I were going to meet them the next day. But the students would not have it so, and made a demonstration I shall always remember.

My last Academic Year, October 1932–June 1933, began and ended with two magnificent gifts, both in their intrinsic value and in the spirit of the givers.

I received from my brilliant colleague Chauncey Brewster Tinker a testimonial of affection in the form of a gift of such extraordinary value that when I found it on my desk I was completely overcome. It was the *original manuscript* of Walter Savage Landor's poem on Browning which gave Browning and his fiancée such delight in November 1845. The gift was accompanied by the following letter:

1293 DAVENPORT COLLEGE
NEW HAVEN
October 1st, 1932

DEAR BILLY:

I was a member of your first class in Browning—only, in those first days, it was 'Chaucer and Browning.' By way of explaining this somewhat unusual conjunction, you expatiated on points in which the two poets resembled each other, and you recited Landor's Sonnet on Browning with its fine reference to Chaucer. I heard of that Sonnet for the first time in your class, and therefore, as you begin your last course in Browning, I am asking you to accept the manuscript of the poem as a slight expression of my indebtedness to you during my student days and for thirty long years of cloudless association as members of one department.

Yours affectionately,

C.B.TINKER

On 18 June 1933 I received another stunning surprise. I was asked to take dinner with some friends at the New Haven Lawn Club. Expecting to meet a little group, I found over eighty members of the Yale Pundits, graduates and undergraduates. The Reverend Father T.L.Riggs, 1910, presided, and I was presented with a large collection of manuscript letters by Browning which had never been printed. They were enclosed in a beautiful case suitably inscribed.

104

OTHER EVENTS IN 1933

A Literary Feast

THE dinner at the Hotel Plaza in New York, on 4 May 1933 of the Friends of the Princeton Library, was a notable gathering of literary folk. Five hundred and fifty people were present; at the head table sat Burton Hendrick, Michael Pupin, Emory Holloway, T.S.Stribling, Margaret Ayer Barnes, Hamlin Garland, Leonora Speyer, Ernest Poole, J.Harlin O'Connell, Owen Davis, Marquis James, Frank D.Fackenthal, Elmer Rice, Robert Frost, Pearl S. Buck, James Truslow Adams, Nicholas Murray Butler, General Pershing, Philip Ashton Rollins, Edward D.Duffield, Willa Cather, Governor Wilbur Cross, Henry James, Charles Edward Russell, Morrie Ryskind, Oliver La Farge II, Bernadotte E.Schmitt, Hatcher Hughes, Herbert Putnam, Charles Warren, William Cabell Bruce, Henry F.Pringle, Maud Howe Elliott, Charles Howard McIlwain, Allan Nevins, Ira Gershwin. Mr. Rollins, as Chairman of the Friends of the Princeton Library, proposed a silent toast to John Galsworthy, and then introduced President Duffield, J.Harlin O'Connell, and finally me, the new toastmaster. At that moment we went on the air, and I felt like a traffic policeman at a king's garden party; never have I had to hustle along so many distinguished people, in order that they might all be heard over the radio within one hour.

Mr. Henry James spoke on biography, Willa Cather on

the novel, Mr. Adams on history, Elmer Rice on the theatre, Robert Frost on poetry, Mr. Putnam on libraries, and General Pershing, who had come all the way from Arizona to attend the dinner, gave a delightful talk and said it was a pleasure to meet so many distinguished persons whose books he had not read. He also remarked that when he was an instructor in mathematics at the University of Nebraska, one of his pupils was Willa Cather, and she gave no promise of distinction. When, years later, he heard her name, he said, 'That can't be the same Willa Cather; the girl I taught didn't seem to know anything.' Then Mr. Fackenthal, Provost of Columbia University, announced the new winners of the Pulitzer Prizes in letters. T.S.Stribling in fiction for his novel *The Store*, Allan Nevins in biography for *Grover Cleveland*, Archibald MacLeish in poetry for *Conquistador*, Maxwell Anderson in drama for *Both Your Houses*, the late Frederick J.Turner in history for *The Significance of Sections in American History*.

Mr. Stribling and Mr. Nevins spoke for the prize-winners, and the exercises closed with a graceful address by President Butler.

On 11 January 1933 Miss Sackville-West, the British novelist, came to New Haven to give a lecture and spent part of the afternoon at our house. She is a tall, healthy, black-haired woman, natural, talking easily and freely on contemporary affairs.

On 16 January the poet-laureate of England, John Masefield, lectured at Yale, and I had the honour of introducing him. I could not help thinking how much more at home he appeared to be on the platform than in 1916; now speaking informally and reading from his poems in his deep-sea voice. He was much interested in the beauty of Harkness Tower, and he insisted on getting out of the automobile and walking over in the darkness of the Quadrangle where he could see it outlined against the night sky.

On 17 March 1933 I met Pearl Buck, who was travelling in America for the first time in many years. Her novel, *The Good Earth*, was such a success that there was widespread curiosity in America to meet the author. There was nothing exotic about her appearance or accent. She was an American woman of fashion, very attractive, and wholly unaffected. She told me, however, that whenever she had to prepare any formal address, which she did not like to do, if it were in English she read it from manuscript. If it were in Chinese, she delivered it *extempore*. I told her that when I read *The Good Earth*, if I had not known the author was a woman, I should not have been able to tell whether it was a man or a woman, a Presbyterian or an atheist, a conservative or a communist; that I had never read an American novel so wholly objective. She told me she would rather have me say that than make any other comment.

I felt certain, although she was soon returning to China, that she would not stay there. After making such a success and meeting the men and women of letters in New York, I did not believe she could ever permanently separate herself from American life, and in a few years my belief was confirmed.

3 PING TSANG HSIANG, NANKING, CHINA
November 13, 1933

DEAR DR. PHELPS:

Here I sit by my own fireside in Nanking, remembering last year in America, and one of the pleasantest memories is you. I am so glad I had the pleasure of meeting you, of being in your delightful home and of meeting Mrs. Phelps. It was an honor to receive the citation from you in June, an honor to walk with you in the procession. I forget none of it, nor shall I. I hope I can see you again next summer.

I discover, now that I am back in this country, that I am more American than I knew I was. I felt myself growing American last year, loving the country more and more, and loving its people. I wasn't sure, however, until I came back here, whether or not I could live there. Now, having come back to this well known and very well loved environment, I find my feeling toward America does not change. I could live there quite happily.

These days here, nevertheless, are crowded with beauty. In my garden are chrysanthemums and roses, each doing their last best before the frosts come. And the hills are most beautifully ruddy in the sunshine. They are not wooded as so many American hills are, but are bare against the sky. Now upon their long slopes the peasants are cutting their supply of winter fuel. The dull blue of their garments is lovely against the reddened grass. China is so variable a country for beauty. At such times as these I think it the most beautiful country I have ever seen. But at other times it can be ugly and sordid and evil looking. One never feels the land is free of men, as American countryside is—Here the land seems man-possessed, utilized by both living and dead until the very contours of the landscape have a strangely human look. I cannot explain what I mean; perhaps it is as any very old country looks.

Meanwhile, *Shui Hu* is being lived once again. A few weeks ago a large bandit horde ravaged villages only twenty miles from here. But within this great city wall, built before Columbus discovered America, we live, snug and secure. I wish you might visit me. And yet, you are so American, I think of you as so essentially American, I wonder if you'd like us here? At any rate, we would like you!

Always gratefully yours,

PEARL S. BUCK

On 23 February I gave lunch to T. S. Eliot in New Haven, when he came to lecture at Yale. We talked a good deal about Paul Elmer More, whom we both admired. Mr. Eliot gives one the same impression in conversation that one receives in reading him—intense sincerity. We met again a few months later when we both received the honorary degree of Doctor of Letters from Columbia University in New York.

On 2 April I had the pleasure in New York of hearing Toscanini conduct two symphonies of Beethoven; and of dining with him afterwards at the home of Mr. and Mrs. Muschenheim. Toscanini was most kind and gracious, but was evidently greatly disturbed over the newspaper discussion concerning his invitation to conduct the following summer at Bayreuth. He finally decided not to go.

On 29 April I saw Lillian Gish at her very best in a play called *Nine Pine Street* dealing with the murder supposedly committed by Lizzie Borden. Lillian always had a *succès de beauté* but in this melodrama she displayed great histrionic ability. I talked with her afterwards in her dressing-room; and we both regretted the play had been put on so late in the season.

On 11 May the Royal Scot train, brought over from Scotland to be exhibited at the Fair at Chicago, appeared in New Haven. I received an invitation from the management of the New Haven Railroad. Accordingly I took a train to Providence, and after five minutes returned to New Haven on the Royal Scot. Outside of the British and American officials, there were only two or three invited guests. It was a fine train, but I was surprised there were no screens in the windows.

On 15 May I gave a lecture in Richmond, Virginia, and was invited to lunch by the famous novelist Ellen Glasgow, where I also met Mr. and Mrs. James Branch Cabell and the American Ambassador to the Argentine. It was a happy occasion. A month later I wrote to Miss Glasgow, and received the following letter from Baltimore.

June 18th, 1933

DEAR DOCTOR PHELPS,

What a friend you are! I feel as if I had known you always, and well.

For four weeks, in all this intolerable weather, I have been held here by an illness that required, it appears, Baltimore doctors. Your letter came like a ray of Maine sunshine.

Richmond is lovely in October or November—why not make your next visit, the one with Mrs. Phelps, in the autumn?

Sincerely yours—and Affectionately,

ELLEN GLASGOW

The weather that May day in Richmond had been fearfully hot; yet with that discomfort and with the journey to the Baltimore physicians imminent, Miss Glasgow had exhibited true Southern hospitality—warm-hearted, gracious and sincere.

I was astonished that Mr. Cabell attended my lecture; for I am sure that most men of letters never attend any lectures except their own, and who can blame them?

105

VARIOUS NOTES IN 1934-5

On 11 January 1934 I had luncheon with Emma Eames and took her to see Eugene O'Neill's religious play, *Days Without End*; its failure was partly attributable to poor casting but Robert Lorraine was magnificent. When the leading actors were recalled, Emma Eames shouted his name with immense enthusiasm. He was evidently astonished and looked in our direction appreciatively. But he was even more pleased when, a few days later, at the Coffee House, I told him who it was who had saluted him.

On 4 May at a dinner of the Round Table in New York, President Nicholas Murray Butler presiding, I met for the first time H.G.Wells. He was in high spirits, in spite of the fact that he predicted a world war in 1940. I reminded him that the Chancellor of the Exchequer had recently said in Parliament, 'We have gone from Bleak House to Great Expectations.' 'Yes,' said Wells, 'but in Great Expectations they didn't get the money.' He laughed when I told him the story of the undergraduate's question in zoology. The Professor had mentioned some bug and remarked 'A single bug of this kind will produce in one year eighty thousand offspring.' He then asked if there were any questions, and a youth asked, 'If a single bug can produce eighty thousand, how many will a married bug produce?'

In the Autumn of 1934 the D'Oyly Carte Gilbert and Sullivan Opera Company came to New York and took the city by storm; they were equally triumphant in other cities in America and on visits in subsequent years. These artists

916

have done more to increase and to cement good-fellowship between the British and American people than almost any other agency. They did not know when they planned their first invasion whether it would be successful or not; they knew our country was the home of jazz and its relations; they could not be certain that light operas more than fifty years old, given without changes or concessions, would be received with enthusiasm. But their productions were the most successful theatrical events of the season. The result is that these British singers love Americans as never before; and Americans are so enchanted by the presentation of these operatic masterpieces that we have an affection for these singers and musicians that cannot be diminished by time.

It is an error also to suppose because this music is 'light' that it is unimportant; Arthur Sullivan is the greatest musical composer in the history of the British Isles.

On 22 November at a New York luncheon I met the world-famous Mary Pickford and had a long talk. She was unaffected but intensely serious, interested over the reception to her first book, *Why not try God?*

On 7 December at a New York dinner I had the pleasure of meeting John Buchan, subsequently Lord Tweedsmuir and Governor General of Canada. He said the horsemanship displayed in coach-driving in his latest novel *The Free Fishers* was absolutely accurate. I wondered at the variety of important work he seemed to accomplish with ease.

On 20 June 1934, as Public Orator of Yale University, at the Commencement Exercises, I had given out all the degrees except the two for the President of Harvard and the President of the United States. Suddenly the Governor of Connecticut, from his place among the members of the Corporation, rose, and addressed the President of Yale. I was taken aback for the moment, but naturally believing that the Corporation had decided it would be more fitting for Roosevelt to receive his degree from the Governor, I hurried to my place and sat down. Professor Nettleton whispered to me 'Get up! get up!' I whispered back, 'He's going to give the degree to the President!' 'No, no! he's giving it to you!' I was flabbergasted—fortunately I could turn my back on the audience to receive the degree; fortunately also there was so much applause when I received it that I had time to recover myself before proceeding, for I think it was the most stunning surprise of my life.

It was the only instance where an honorary degree was given without preliminary notice to the recipient; the reason is as follows. One year before this Commencement, I called on the Secretary, Carl Lohmann, and told him that while in all probability I should not be considered for a degree, I wished to save Corporation time by saying flatly and positively that I should not under any circumstances accept it. I felt that Yale had many scholars on her Faculty of the highest merit, whose work could not attract public attention; that I had received degrees from other universities and some other professor must be chosen instead of me. I left no doubt in the mind of the Secretary that I should refuse it if offered, and then I dismissed the subject from my thoughts.

What happened was this. Several months before Commencement the Secretary called on my wife when I was away. She kept this secret from me for four months, so that I had no suspicion whatever. We had gone to our summer home in Michigan, and when the time came for me to prepare to go to New Haven, she expressed a desire to accompany me. I was surprised, but had no suspicion of the reason; she said she wished to be present when the President of the United States received his degree, for it had happened only twice before, the instances being George Washington and Rutherford B. Hayes. This seemed a satisfactory reason for making the journey.

After Commencement was over, a friend asked me if I had had any intimation; and on my negative reply, he said that after he had witnessed the affair, he made up his mind either that it had come as a complete surprise or that I was the best actor that had ever appeared on any stage.

I shall not forget the expression on the face of Dr. Conant, the President of Harvard, when I was pronouncing the citation for his degree. After appropriate praise, I said 'In his whole career he has made only one serious mistake' and paused; his face suddenly darkened and as suddenly lightened when I added 'and that is now about to be rectified.'

I have always taken delight in the performances of magicians; and after the late Howard Thurston's amazing miracles at the Paramount Theatre in New Haven, I went back and had a long talk with him.

THURSTON THE MAGICIAN
7 OAK ST.
WEEHAWKEN, N.J.
January 10, 1935

DEAR DOCTOR PHELPS:

Thanks for your nice letter. From the sixty million people I have entertained and the countless thousands I have met, you are one of the few outstanding individuals that will cling to my memory.

With sincere esteem,

HOWARD THURSTON

SUNDAE

Crossing the ocean in the steamer *Bremen* in 1935, the German head steward asked me for the origin of the word 'sundae.' I could not give him any accurate information but when I made a comment on this in *Scribner's Magazine*, I got letters from every section of America. One of the most interesting is from the distinguished owner, publisher and editor of the *Tulsa Tribune* in Tulsa, Oklahoma, Mr. Richard Lloyd Jones.

DEAR DR. PHELPS:

Words are full of romance. I too enjoy the history of words, so was I attracted to your references in October Scribner's to the delectable 'sundae.' Perhaps the dictionary makers did not know what I think I know about the origin of that term. And perhaps I do not know the truth.

I grew up as a Chicago kid who did the things that most city boys do. I chased the fire engines all over Chicago and early was as much a patron of the soda fountains as my purse would permit. I remember when the sundae first appeared over the marble fountain counter and I remember the soda jerkers of that time relating the story of the origin which was something like this:

Evanston, Chicago's Godly neighbor, "Heavenston" as the good Frances E. Willard used to call it, was in those days at least rather Methodist minded. The piety of the town resented the dissipating influences of the soda fountain on Sunday and the good town fathers, yielding to this churchly influence, passed an ordinance prohibiting the retailing of ice cream sodas on Sunday.

Some ingenious confectioners and drug store operators, in 'Heavenston,' obeying the law, served ice cream with the syrup of your choice without the soda. Thereby complying with the law. They did not serve ice cream sodas. They served sodas without soda on Sunday. This sodaless soda was the Sunday soda. It proved palatable and popular and orders for Sundays began to cross the counters on Mondays.

Objection then was made to christening a dish after the Sabbath. So the spelling of 'sunday' was changed. It became an established dish and an established word and finally the Heavenston 'sundae' appeared even in Congregational Connecticut.

I do not vouch for this as being totally accurate history, but it is the history of the word which was common gossip in my boyhood at the time the 'sunday' appeared at the soda counters which I patronised.

If this story may not be known to you, I just thought it might interest you. So with my warmest personal greetings, as always, I drop it in the mail shute for you.

Always cordially yours,

RICHARD LLOYD JONES

Miss Rachel Crothers, the foremost woman American playwright, and in 1937 particularly distinguished by her play *Susan and God*, consented some years ago to give a lecture at Yale, which delighted the huge audience.

125 EAST 57TH STREET

MY DEAR PROFESSOR PHELPS—

I accept all your charming invitations with great pleasure—with the exception of staying till the next day—which will not be possible.

As to the lecture—which will be nothing after all but a most informal talk—I think I had better stick to what I know most about—and that is the actual production of a play from the minute the idea comes to the fatal raising of the curtain.

So will you call it that please—The Production of a Play?

You know the audience and I do not—but I find in my brief experience at this thing that all sorts of audiences enjoy hearing an act of a play read—so I suggest that I talk for about half an hour and finish with the first act of Expressing Willie.

Looking forward with great pleasure to being with you and Mrs. Phelps—

Most cordially—

RACHEL CROTHERS

106

EMMA EAMES AND MUSIC

In *The Ring and the Book* Browning unconsciously described this great prima donna in the phrase 'the good girl with the velvet in her voice.' In my chapter describing my bicycle trip in Europe in 1890 I have mentioned the first time I saw Emma Eames singing 'Marguerite' in Paris. The next time I heard her was in Boston in 1892 when she sang with Jean and Edouard deReszké. She was the best Marguerite and the best Elsa I have ever heard or seen. I heard her many times in the Metropolitan Opera House until her retirement which took place in the plenitude of her powers. Born in Maine, she was a Yankee with an inflexible will; and when she made up her mind to retire, she retired. In those days I worshipped from afar, but in 1924 when my wife and I were in Paris, we called upon her at her hotel in the Place Vendôme. In the course of general conversation I happened to remark that inopportune intruders and jovial back-slappers were as well-known and as unwelcome in Bible days as they are now. When she asked me to illustrate, I quoted from the Book of Proverbs: 'He that blesseth his friend with a loud voice, rising early in the morning, it shall be counted a curse to him.' She laughed and asked me if I could prove that was in the Bible. I said there would be no difficulty if she would provide a copy, which she immediately did, and I wondered then how many great prima donnas carry a Bible with them. This meeting in Paris led to many meetings later both in Paris and in New York, and I had the honour of writing a preface to her autobiography called *Memories and Reflections*.

A matter that has always troubled me is this: How do singers ever learn to sing the most ravishingly affecting passages with *emotional* control? It is essential that they sing not only on the pitch and with perfect emission of tone, but that they sing with passion. Yet the singer must himself never be overcome by the beauty of the song. Nothing is more distressing than to see an orator or a singer more excited than his audience.

Now we know that Dr. Johnson never could repeat aloud the stanza from *Dies Irae* beginning

Jesu, me sedisti lassus,

because he always burst out crying. And the austere Housman has left it on record that there are passages that he was never able to read aloud. When Hawthorne read aloud to his wife the manuscript of *The Scarlet Letter*, during the last scene on the scaffold, his voice rose and fell as uncontrollably as the waves of the sea. (She fainted.)

This question is entirely different from the controversial question of the feelings of an actor on the stage, which used to be discussed with such acrimony during the career of the great Coquelin. He insisted that the actor should himself never be moved in the slightest; that he should be cold as ice; that it would be as fatal for him to *feel* the words as it would be for a surgeon to be overcome by sympathy during an operation. There were many actors who disagreed with Coquelin; who said that if they did not themselves feel as deeply as if they were indeed those whom they were impersonating, they could not act effectively.

No, what I am discussing is quite different from that. When we in the audience are so moved—as I always am by Elsa's dream and Lohengrin's farewell to the swan—how can the singers have such control that they sing with

absolute accuracy? Some have told me that the answer to
this question is *Double Personality*. If they were alone
practising, they would indeed often be overcome by emotion; but on the stage and before the public, their own
personality disappears—they are not themselves but are
the persons they are representing.

Of course if the danger of emotional breakdown were
overcome by anxiety not to wander from the pitch or not
to produce clear tones, that would result in extreme self-
consciousness; this would be worse than emotional surrender, as if the singer were more interested in himself and
his performance than in the part.

In response to my request, Madame Emma Eames was
kind enough to write to me:

30 SUTTON PLACE
March 23, 1938

DEAR BILLY

What a difficult letter to answer is yours just received! To make
"very clear" to the average mind what you ask me is very different
from making it clear to you.

I begin by saying how entirely I agree with Robert Louis Stevenson
when he says "Until the excitable amateur is dead the artist is not
born." To convince the hearer, however, one must conceive a role in
passion but until the human passion has been mastered and the expression of it translated into a higher sphere, one cannot convince
one's audience. The generation of artists to which I belonged sought
calm—the calm of *self possession* which with a sure technique, animated by the invocation of the original emotion enabled one to carry
and compel the audience to one's own emotion and vision. Emotion
like fire and water is a good servant but a bad master. Though the
public is often moved by one who has animal magnetism and simply
"blows off steam" it is *obliged* to come under the spell of the real and
sincere artist with elevated standards of art and convictions.

I quite understand why you are overcome by emotion when reading
aloud for you have not been able to take the time to analyse your
emotion and possess it. When I studied Sieglinde in Die Walküre I
had to wait 2 years before I could trust myself to master my emotion

and not to choke over certain phrases and even then I had to adjust my mind to the shock in order to avoid choking.

There are certain things which I read aloud that I always shall choke over—it does not matter and even in your case it does not for being in personal and intimate contact with your hearers they share even more your emotion. My "job" asked for something quite different. As I was completely possessed and obsessed by my own work I do not know much about the approach of many other singers to theirs. Calm was preached to me from the first by all teachers Gounod and Jean de Reszké included and glad am I of it as otherwise my emotions would have run away with me. Which, even in an argument gets the better of it? The one, who keeps calm and coolheaded! I feel as though I had not half answered, or answered well, your letter but I hope this may *do*.

Ever your truly affectionate friend

EMMA

CLARA CLEMENS

Although I first saw Clara when she was hardly more than a baby, my acquaintance with her began in April 1904, when she made her début as a concert singer in Florence, and a few days later I met her in her parents' villa outside the town. This led later to an intimate friendship not only with her but with her husband, Ossip Gabrilowitsch. We first met him with his wife in Munich when he was preparing for his American career. Mr. Gabrilowitsch became not only one of the best concert pianists in the world but one of the most distinguished of orchestra conductors. I have never known a man of higher integrity, or of greater sincerity. I had great respect for him and profound affection. He was kind enough to *give* a piano recital at Yale and for a few hours preceding it we had a long talk. He asked me then, 'What was the name of the Hartford physician who was responsible for the first use of anesthetic?' And I said, 'I can't remember.' Then he burst out laughing and said, 'Neither can I,' to which he added,

'How strange it is! We both know the names of most of
the famous military men of the world, and we can't remember the name of one of the greatest benefactors of mankind.' Mr. Gabrilowitsch hated vulgarity in every form,
and he could not bear any display of it in connexion with
religion. I told him that a certain American editor asked a
clergyman to write a Life of Christ that would be adapted
to the ordinary reader. When the editor received the manuscript, he wrote to the clergyman, 'This won't do at all.
What I want is a snappy Life of Christ.'

Clara Clemens's life of her father which followed her admirable public lecture about him is one of the best books
on Mark Twain ever written, for she herself has inherited
a good deal of her father's literary skill, his humour, and
his sincerity. I have always thought that if she had cared
to do so, she could have become a remarkable actress, as
she had great skill in impersonation.

The death of Vladimir de Pachmann on 6 January 1933
brought back to me a host of recollections. I heard him a
good many times when he was in his prime and also when
he was so old, feeble and shaken that he went through his
concert performance like a somnambulist. And even when
I spoke to him after a concert he didn't seem to be fully
conscious. But I first heard him at Chickering Hall, Boston,
in 1892. He played, as was his custom, an all-Chopin programme including the B-flat Minor Sonata containing the
Funeral March. In those days he wore a full black beard
and continually talked to the audience in his broken
English, saying, 'Wasn't dat nice?' and similar remarks.
Often he would pretend to play fortissimo, bringing down
both his hands with a tremendous crash and then just brush-
ing the keys and playing pianissimo. Yet these monkey tricks
(Huneker called him a Chopinzee) really didn't interfere
with the beauty of his interpretation and his miraculous
finger technique. The day after that concert, Philip Hale

wrote a column in which he said that the effect of such
playing was like an old woman looking at her bridal dress
through eyes filled with tears. I have heard all the great
pianists of the world, but I have not heard anything quite
like De Pachmann playing Chopin.

On 10 March 1923 the Russian singer Chaliapin gave
a concert in Woolsey Hall, Yale University, and Mr. Rudolph Steinert, whose guest he was, kindly invited me to
join a small party of four of five persons at supper after
the recital. Chaliapin (I greatly prefer the correct English
spelling Shaliapin instead of this French form, but only
Rosa Newmarch and I have ever dared to do it) was in the
highest spirits, laughing aloud constantly and pretending
to boast of his various wickednesses. He seemed like a
great, healthy, overgrown boy. The only bad thing about
him that evening was his English, which was as bad as his
French was good.

At my request, Mr. Steinert was kind enough to write
out his own recollections.

We invited a few guests to meet him at Ceriani's, a small Italian
restaurant in New Haven where Rosa Ponselle had been entertainer
before her days of glory.

During the early part of the evening he spoke hardly a word, giving
all his attention to a large sirloin steak which he devoured. He next
concentrated on mixing a salad in a huge bowl with much deliberation and ceremony. After steak and salad had been washed down
by a bottle of Chianti and the inner man was at last satisfied he
pushed back his chair, at peace with the world. His spirits rising,
he crossed the room to a small upright piano, sat down and sang one
song after another, accompanying himself and keeping us in roars of
laughter as he brought out the humor of the songs by acting and
grimacing.

This mood passed. He came back to the table and talked seriously
of bygone days. He was saddened by conditions in Russia and by the
loss of his personal properties through confiscation.

Among his anecdotes that evening was the tale of a concert in a
small Russian community where people had gathered from far and

near to hear him. While he was singing a pianissimo passage and the house was hushed to listen, he noticed a disturbance in one corner of the hall. Later he learned, to his amazement, that a child had been born. He always felt that this was a tribute to his art. He loved especially to sing to these Russian peasants, having been one of them himself. With the new regime all this was changed.

In a more confidential vein, he turned to me and told me a tale of another evening. This time he was to give a concert in a great city. In the lobby of his hotel he was introduced to a very charming woman. Conversation with her made him forget time and place. Suddenly he pulled out his watch, saw that it was nine o'clock and realized that he was already half an hour late for his concert. He rushed to the theatre to find the auditorium completely dark and the audience dispersed. Next day the newspapers flaunted headlines, "Chaliapin Drunk. Did not appear at Concert." "All this," said he, "made me feel very badly. But," he ended, "She was a BEAUTIFUL lady."

Chaliapin returned again and again to the little broken down piano and he sang with such gusto that it seemed the roof must surely fly off that small shabby room. It was three or four in the morning before the party broke up.

Chaliapin died in April 1938.

It is interesting that the three greatest bassos I have ever heard were all giants—Edouard de Reszké, Pol Plançon, and Chaliapin. All three I heard as Mephistopheles in *Faust*; and Plançon and Chaliapin I heard singing (many years between the recitals) *The Two Grenadiers*. The first time I heard Plançon was in 1890; and the last time I heard Chaliapin was about forty years later.

Our beloved Walter Damrosch used to play and conduct before cheering thousands; now over the radio he has audiences of many millions.

September 29, 1930

MY DEAR FRIEND:

What a charming little book on music you have been kind enough to send me! It is just what one would expect from your pen, for it expresses what seems to be the very keynote of your character—a power to feel and to enjoy intensely the beautiful things in life. Goethe says, " Wenn ihr's nicht fühlt, so könnt ihr's nicht verstehen." I read with so much interest how the "feeling" for music came to you only gradually and then the understanding followed as a matter of course.

With cordial greetings to you and your wife,

Always sincerely yours,

WALTER DAMROSCH

107

ENGLAND IN 1935

If James Russell Lowell had been living in England in 1935, as he was in the eighties, he would probably amend one of his most famous verses so that it would read

What is so rare as a fine day in June?

We arrived in London 29 May and sailed for home from Southampton on 22 June. Beginning with the first of these dates, it rained every day with the exception of the last. I don't mean that every day it rained all day; but it rained a good deal every day, and there were only two mornings when, on rising, we saw any bit of blue sky.

The majority of intelligent persons would probably say that no matter what we profess, we do in truth always seek our own happiness. I have never subscribed to this creed; and my recent two months in Europe have strengthened my convictions. So far as happiness is concerned, I believe the average intelligent Englishman is happier in England than he is in America or in Germany, France, or Italy. I believe the average person of any country is happier in his native land than anywhere else. Why, then, does anyone travel?

The British novelist, J.B.Priestley, once remarked that he would rather live in his suburb of London than in Florence; I understand that remark and I approve of it.

I am certainly happier in the United States than I am in any foreign land; I know, when I deliberately plan a journey to Europe, that I should be happier if I remained at home.

The poet Bryant made seven journeys to Europe, was always homesick there, and yet always went back. I have no difficulty in understanding that. There are two reasons: first, the best part of any journey is after it is over; second, we go abroad, not to seek happiness, but to acquire a few ideas.

I used to wonder why the poet and novelist Oliver Wendell Holmes, after making one journey to Europe, did not go again for fifty years; the answer is that he preferred his personal comfort and happiness. Furthermore, what with the Harvard Medical School, and literary work, he was a busy man. Incidentally, living in Boston, he wrote a poem called *Homesick in Heaven.*

I do not think what I am saying is inconsistent with the definition of happiness that I am always quoting—the happiest person is the person who thinks the most interesting thoughts. One should travel abroad to add to one's stock of interesting thoughts. One is aware of this increase after one's return.

I remember reading in Mark Twain, of the meeting of two Americans in Europe. 'Are you homesick?' 'Hell, yes!'

London in the rain is not enchantingly beautiful; but it is more interesting than America in the sunshine. Sitting in the window of our hotel in London, I could see Westminster Abbey, the Houses of Parliament, nine bridges, and the ever-exciting river itself, with its twice-a-day tide, and its eternal activity. Two thousand years of history are on the surface of that river. The Connecticut River cannot in such matters compare with it; *but how I love Connecticut*! The south shore of England has a more varied view of the sea than my home in Michigan has of Lake Huron; *but how I love Michigan*!

My beloved colleague, the late Professor Perrin, who

spent his life teaching Greek, went to Athens for a sabbatical year; after he had been there three days, he wrote me from the Acropolis, saying, 'If you can get me any job at Yale, say being janitor of one of the dormitories, cable me at once!'

I go abroad and hope to go again, because my mind needs the stimulation of Europe; because it is well for one's mental and spiritual development to live for a time in other countries; and because I have friends in Germany, France, England, and everywhere else; and it does me good to see them.

Certainly our stay in London was never more interesting, never more mentally profitable than in this June of 1935; we renewed old friendships, made many new ones, and stored up memories that will enliven our minds and warm our hearts for the rest of our lives.

We spent a glorious day with Alfred Noyes and his family at their beautiful home on the south shore of the Isle of Wight. There the sun shone bravely. At Oxford, Arthur Goodhart gave a luncheon to me and some of my former Yale students. He has had an extraordinary career; a graduate of Yale in the class of 1912, he became Fellow of Corpus Christi, Cambridge, then Fellow of University College, Oxford, and Professor of Law. At Cambridge I saw for the first time the bumping races on the Cam, after lunch with Robert Lassiter (Yale 1934) in his rooms in Clare College. Then, with some other Yale men, we walked out to Grantchester, immortalized by Rupert Brooke; we saw the river, the old church, and the vicarage; I had the pleasure of seeing Mary Ellen Chase, who was spending a sabbatical year in a beautiful English cottage, writing a novel.

The English novelist, Mrs. Belloc-Lowndes, sister of Hilaire Belloc, was kind enough to let me read remarkable manuscript letters by Dante Gabriel Rossetti, by the father of Charles Dickens (recommending his son for a position), by members of Shelley's family, and others. At her house we had the delight of meeting the painter Sir William Rothenstein and Lady Rothenstein; his autobiography is one of the best. And no wonder; he was an intimate friend of Whistler, Sargent, Oscar Wilde; all the painters, poets, novelists, dramatists, and wits of the nineties. He told me Oscar Wilde was the best talker, the best conversationalist he had ever known; that his flashes of wit and humour were absolutely spontaneous. Like everyone else who knows Rothenstein, he has immense admiration for the genius and for the character of Max Beerbohm. I asked Sir William a good many questions about the late George Calderon, who was killed in the war. His translation of two plays by Chekhov was accompanied by an introduction, the most penetrating piece of literary criticism I have ever read on the Russian dramatist.

I spent a memorable afternoon with Sir James Barrie in his lofty flat overlooking the river. Since the property roundabout once belonged to the Duke of Buckingham, there are five streets in that district named separately after these five words: *George Villiers Duke of Buckingham.* I found George Street, Villiers Street, Duke Street, and Buckingham Street; Sir James told me they were a little puzzled what to do with the word *of*; finally they named a little passage there, a tiny by-street *Of Alley.*

All Americans everywhere should be proud of R.D. Blumenfeld. I call him the Uncrowned King of Fleet Street. But he has been crowned as well; for he was chosen Master of the Ancient and Worshipful Company of Stationers and Newspaper Makers, the highest honour any newspaper man can receive. This company goes back long before the invention of printing. In his book *R.D.B.'s Procession,* you see Mr. Blumenfeld in the insignia of office, along with the Prince of Wales, the titular Master. As he looks back to his boyhood in Wisconsin, and the long march upward, he should be satisfied.

On the Thursday in June before we sailed, he gave me a luncheon at the *new* Stationers Hall in the City, built shortly after the fire of 1666; and a beautiful hall it is. About twenty men were present, all writers and publishers, with the one exception of Mr. Selfridge, who, like his host, came from Wisconsin, and became the merchant prince of London; we three Americans sat at the head of the table. Then on my right was Bernard Shaw, on his right Philip Guedalla, across the table Bruce Lockhart, Ralph Straus, Gilbert Frankau, Christopher Stone, Ivor Nicholson, Sir Denison Ross, and Lord Strabolgi. Mr. Shaw seemed the personification of health and vigour and high spirits.

I wonder how many persons would have enjoyed taking my place. I was suddenly called on to make a speech! While it is probable that making a speech causes me less distress than most men seem to feel (a friend said of me, 'it rests him to open his mouth'), imagine having to make an original address, with Bernard Shaw at a distance of three feet!

The London *Evening News* asked me to write an article on *The Paradox of the English*, which I did with alacrity. Fleet Street is exciting; and I was glad officially to belong to it, if only for one day. Accordingly I wrote an article on the difference between the English temperament and English poetry, and in a few hours I received from Rottingdean in Sussex the following telegram, which gave me great pleasure.

> AN ENGLISH POET SENDS YOU HIS WARM THANKS FOR YOUR SPLENDIDLY GENEROUS ARTICLE TODAY
>
>   SIR WILLIAM WATSON

Watson is surely 'among the English poets,' though I had mentioned no names in my article.

One day we went out to a distant suburb of London to take tea with the author of *Goodbye, Mr. Chips*. Mr. and Mrs. James Hilton lived by choice in a quiet corner, in order to have peace and leisure wherein to work. He was just what you would expect from reading his novels; what more can I say? The success of *Lost Horizon* and of *Mr. Chips* did not turn his head. I was glad to have a chance to talk with him, for I am interested in the career of a man who produced thirteen novels, reaching success only with the thirteenth.

At a luncheon given by Lady Harcourt, we met the Spanish Ambassador to Great Britain, and Madame Perez de Ayala. They are charming. Sir William Max Müller, the former Minister to Warsaw, was present. His father was the famous Max Müller, the Oxford philologist, whose translation of Kant's *Critique of Pure Reason* gave me two years of hard study under the late Professor Ladd at Yale. I was particularly interested in meeting at this luncheon Lord and Lady Gainford. Lord Gainford was formerly the Right Honourable Joseph Pease, and held various high offices in the cabinets of the Liberal Governments of 1905–16. He is a Quaker, as were all the Pease family in the old days, and at one time he was Chief Whip of the Liberal Party. I had an interesting conversation with him about British politics. I asked him many questions about John Morley; when he was a young man, he was Morley's secretary.

On this visit to England I had the pleasure of doing what I had wanted to do for forty years—I took tea on the terrace of the Houses of Parliament. I had read of this in many novels, and the terrace had looked so attractive from the river that I had hoped some day I might have this privilege. Well, on an afternoon between showers, having been invited by Lord Iddesleigh, this wish was realized. Lord Iddesleigh is the son-in-law of Mrs. Belloc-Lowndes, and is a member of the famous publishing firm of Eyre and Spottiswoode.

Early in the afternoon I was invited by Sir Arnold Wilson, member of the House of Commons, and Editor of *The Nineteenth Century*, to attend the session of the House; Sir Arnold, by the way, in addition to other accomplishments, speaks Latin fluently. At this session I heard the Prime Minister, Mr. Baldwin, and the Chancellor of the Exchequer, Mr. Chamberlain, make a few remarks; but most of the time was taken up by a Socialist who wished the taxes on the rich to be increased. At about half-past four, I went with Lord Iddesleigh to the terrace, where we were joined by my friend Lord Conway. About half-past five, I attended the session of the House of Lords, where an important debate was going on, the subject being India.

English people are rather surprised and often, I think, quietly amused by my zeal in visiting places in England of literary interest. Well, here is something I *dreamed*, and I think for a dream my answer was rather good. In my dream I was conversing with an English man of letters, and told him I was about to visit the place where a great writer had lived centuries ago; he said 'You will waste your time. There is nothing left there for you to see.' And in my dream I replied, 'His spirit is still there!'

ANNE SEDGWICK

The death of Anne Sedgwick (Mrs. Basil de Selincourt) in 1935 was a severe loss to American literature. I was often asked in public lectures why I called her an American; the majority of people believed she was English. I always replied that I called her an American because her father and mother were Americans and she was born in Englewood N.J. She was taken to France when hardly more than a child, educated in Europe, and married to an English gentleman. I had the pleasure of seeing her several times, both in London and in her beautiful home near Oxford. Her work was not only distinguished, there was a spiritual quality in it unusual in contemporary fiction. I have always believed that if her novel, *The Encounter*, had not been published in August 1914, it would have produced a profound impression. After her death her letters were collected by her husband. Everyone who read her books and everyone who met her personally had the highest intellectual respect for her art and for her character.

Although several of her novels had deservedly an immense circulation, notably *Tante* and *The Little French Girl*, I regard *The Encounter* as her masterpiece. Its appearance just after war was declared prevented its merits from being generally known. And yet there was something prophetic in her contrasting the powerful man who worshipped Force with the cripple Conrad who believed only in Goodness. In reply to my letter about this, she wrote me that I was entirely right in believing that Conrad represented the inner philosophy of the book. I had written to her that in the general wreckage of the world he seemed to me the rescuing sail on the horizon. 'I am so glad that you felt he *was* the rescuing sail; I did, of course.'

The most memorable event in my life in 1937 was the fiftieth reunion of my class at Yale. When I was an undergraduate, men who had been out ten years seemed rather elderly; those who had been graduated twenty-five years seemed venerable; those of the vintage of fifty years were curiosities.

But when our class met in June 1937, and marched around the baseball field, we felt like undergraduates. Our Class Secretary, Professor Robert Nelson Corwin, is wonderfully efficient and his annual reports at our meetings are literary masterpieces. He holds the class together. Some men returned who had never been back; the most conspicuous being John Calhoun Simonds of South Carolina, a grandson of Yale's greatest statesman John C. Calhoun, valedictorian of the class of 1804. We were delighted to have Simonds with us and he was interested in seeing our Calhoun College and meeting the Master, Arnold Whitridge, a grandson of Matthew Arnold. Our class presented Secretary and Mrs. Corwin with a fine gift. Our classmate Ira Copley, former Congressman and now owner of a chain of newspapers, took us to the boat race at New London in his yacht.

In 1912 and again in 1932 '87 presented me with the *long distance cup*, for although I live in New Haven, on both these occasions I returned from Europe simply to be with my beloved classmates.

One of the greatest events in 1938 happened on the last Sunday in March. I arrived at St. Louis early in the morning, and was met at the station by Edward Hidden, '85 and Bill Haverstick, '34, representing old and young Yale and both intimate friends. This was the last time I saw Ned as he died some months later. They asked me what I should like to do, as my lecture was not to take place till the afternoon. I said 'All my life I have wanted to see the junction of the two mighty rivers, the Mississippi and the Missouri.' They had lived in St. Louis all their lives and had never seen it. Bill Haverstick drove the car; the junction was seventeen miles north of St. Louis; and it was at a desolate plain so that we walked the last mile. This utter desolation added immensely to the unspeakable grandeur of the scene. The wide blue Mississippi came down from the north and the wide brown Missouri came out of the west; and at their union I descended to the shore, dropped some of the water solemnly on my head, and then stretched out my arms in a salutation. Bill took a fine photograph of the scene. I have always been awestruck by great rivers and these two historic waterways uniting gave me one of the supreme moments of my life.

108

RADIO

I BECAME a radio speaker late in life; at first I did not enjoy it, because having been accustomed to look into the faces of an audience while addressing them, I felt when speaking into the microphone as if I were soliloquizing in the dark. But as soon as letters began to arrive from several thousand miles away, saying my voice had come into their houses as clearly as if I had been there, the experience became exciting and has remained so. Even if there is an audience in the studio where I am talking on the air, I do not really see or feel them as I do the invisible audience sitting under vine and fig tree. Every radio speaker receives what is known as 'fan mail'; some of these letters are especially appealing. A former student of mine at Yale, who had not been back at the University for thirty years, and was living on the top of a mountain in Utah, turned on the radio not knowing what was on the air, and he said it was as if he were back in the classroom. Another, living in Paris, returned home with his wife at one o'clock in the morning, thought they would turn on the radio for a half-hour before going to bed, and were greeted by my familiar voice. Captain Alan Villiers, commanding the sailing-ship *Joseph Conrad* was somewhere south of the Azores, turned on his radio, with a similar result. After I had spoken between the acts of the opera at the Metropolitan Opera House, New York, I received letters from friends in Honolulu and then from Egypt, saying it was exactly as if I had been talking with them!

Tom Stix, who was an undergraduate at Yale when the war broke out, was the first to persuade me to speak over the microphone; I gave an address on good reading, and then a Commencement address to the youth of America on Courage. This was followed by a regular engagement lasting thirteen weeks. The year after that, another former student, Herschel Williams, got me an engagement for twenty-eight weeks on the 'Swift Hour' (1934–5), with Sigmund Romberg conducting the orchestra and playing original and classical music. I enjoyed this experience as much as any I have had. Even now, after three years, I am constantly spoken to by strangers, who hear my voice on the train or on the golf course, and ask me if I am not, etc. Not only are these experiences agreeable because of the number of invisible friends one collects, but I have always intensely enjoyed the radio hour in the studio with my singing or playing or performing colleagues. It has always been like a happy family engaged in a fascinating game.

Another kind of work I took up late in life was writing for newspaper syndicates; first once a week and later every day. My employer was George Matthew Adams; I enjoyed the work and I enjoyed working for him and for those in his office.

town; his inability to take care of himself makes him not only ridiculous, but pitiable.

We often think that business men in the city indulge in more exciting, that is to say, more speculative enterprises, than men in the country have ever heard of; brokers, investors and theatre managers play for high stakes. Success means a fortune, and failure means not only no gain, but the loss of the investment. Yet in a certain sense there is no enterprise more speculative than farming; for its success depends on an element beyond human control—the weather.

Even the most capable farmers stand the chance of losing the hard work of a whole year by an evil change in the weather. I have known many who have suffered in this way, and I am amazed at their courage and patience. No poker-face gambler takes his losses with more outward serenity than the average farmer. I know a great many farmers intimately. I have seen them lose an entire crop by too much heat or too much rain, or by one catastrophic storm. I have never heard one whine about this, nor have I seen any of them completely cast down.

For many years I have lived during the winter in a sizable city, and very near the city of New York. For many years I have spent a quarter of my life—July, August, September—in the country; that is to say, in a place in Michigan on the shore of Lake Huron, where there is no town, no railway station, no post office. In this agricultural county, I know the resident farmers and their families; and I know their parents and their grandparents. Thus, although I was born and brought up in the city, I have actually lived what, in total, amounts to fifteen years in the country; have lived, not as a migratory summer visitor, but as one of the folks.

I like people as individuals, not as representatives. I do not like Americans because they are Americans or dislike foreigners because they are foreigners. I do not like people because they live in New York or like them less because they don't.

I have perhaps been unusually fortunate in meeting charming and attractive men and women all over the world, and among all races and classes. I mean simply that I have met so many young and old people who are so much better than I am, that I have never been able to attain to the state of mental and moral superiority that is necessary to the denouncer, the fault-finder. It is impossible for me to say whether the people who live in the cities or the people who live in the country are superior; I have known men and women of beautiful character who live in New York and London, and I have known men and women equally admirable who live in country places.

The most obvious differences between city people and country folks are, I think, superficial. Emerson said: 'Cities force growth, and make men talkative and entertaining, but they make them artificial.' Another writer said: 'Men, by associating in large masses, as in camps and cities, improve their talents, but impair their virtues; and strengthen their minds, but weaken their morals.'

These two statements mean that in every city there are more opportunities both for intellectual development and for demoralization than in the country; but character may shine out as brightly in one as in the other.

So far as the financial advantages of living in city and country are concerned, the law of compensation seems to arrange that. In times of prosperity, people in the city are perhaps better off. There is plenty of work and the pay is good. But in times of depression, the farmer is relatively better off. He has his home, with all that it implies, he has his food. Then the streets of every American city (and America is better off than Europe, and Europe better off than Asia) contain men who are looking not only for work, but for food and shelter.

When the famous scholar and foreign ambassador, Andrew D. White, was over eighty, he said to me, 'I wish you could do something to induce Americans to live in the country. The moment an Englishman makes a little money, he secures a place in the country; but the moment an American makes money, he goes to the city.'

It is true that the average Englishman loves to have a home in the country; but the conditions of life are different in England.

Henry Ford has done more than any other individual to make it possible for Americans to live in the country the year round. Every one remembers how those who could afford it used to have a country home ten or twenty miles from the city, where the wife and children spent the summer, and where the man came for the week-end. Now in innumerable instances this is the only home they have. More than ever before the countryside is becoming the dormitory for the city. But these people who live in the country in the night and on Sundays are not the genuine country folks.

It is possible that in the future we shall see more, and not less, of these men and women. I have lived long enough to observe, even in fairly prosperous times, many—especially of the younger generation—leaving the farms and going to the city 'for good;' and after a few months or a few years, I have seen them gladly returning to the farm. To their dismay, they found that in the city they had to pay money for food that they had always obtained for themselves; with every other thing proportionally expensive.

The chief thing about an American farmer is his independence. At work there is nothing over him but the sky; he acknowledges no superior but God. He has his home and his land. Furthermore, he is nothing like so lonely or isolated as he used to be. Civilization depends on communication. I can well remember, in this very country where I am now writing, the times when folks in remote farmhouses saw no one outside of their family for weeks. The roads were bad in summer, terrible in spring, and impassable in winter. Now there are good roads throughout this country, and every farmer's family has an automobile. In his house is a phonograph, a telephone, and a radio. The whole world is becoming one community. Just as there is now really one city along the Atlantic coast from Portland, Maine, to Norfolk, Virginia, so the time will come when the distinction between city and country will be slight.

But even if I live to see the time when country and town are one geographically, I shall never forget the splendid men and women I have known, who, in the lonely days of isolation, cleared the land, tilled the soil, and brought up their children. Heroes and heroines are like wild flowers; you find them in remote places.

INFORMALITY

In a lecture at Harvard in the early nineties by Professor R.G. Moulton, comparing modern times with the Elizabethan, he called our age *The Age of Anti-Conspicuousness*. In reading Dekker's *Gull's Hornbook* it was clear that the Elizabethan swells tried in clothes, manner, and appearance to attract as much attention as possible; whereas Englishmen and Americans three hundred years later dressed in the fashion not to attract attention but to avoid it. With this endeavour at protective colouring naturally came a growth in informality; one wonders now in 1938 whether it is possible to become more informal than the majority of men and women are at present.

Many people today, especially those of the older generation, observing everywhere the lack of formality in dress, social relations, and speech, believe that good manners have vanished—that young men and women are rude to their elders, rude to those in authority, and rude to each other.

We must be careful not to confuse the absence of elaborate formalities with bad manners. In comparing our age with that of fifty years ago, the most apparent social change is the decrease of formality. In those days American college undergraduates wore whiskers, tall silk hats, and frock coats; yet they were young, and probably more generally given to dissipation than college undergraduates are now. College professors in those days wore broadcloth coats with tails, and exposed a vast expanse of gleaming shirt-bosom. But a large proportion of their time was given neither to teaching nor to research in scholarship, but to the enforcement of discipline. Every college instructor was a policeman.

Today in many college enclosures the students are by no means formally arrayed, and it is not an unusual sight to see a professor in sport clothes. But the relations between students and members of the faculty are very often on the basis of intimate friendship. The absence of formality on the surface is accompanied with real respect on both sides, and with sincere affection. This is certainly an improvement.

Whether it is the growth of athletics, with its natural release for the superabundant vitality of youth, or whether it is a general advance in civilization, I cannot say; but it is certain that the decrease of formality in dress and speech has been accompanied with an improvement in academic manners. Seventy-five and even fifty years ago, the classrooms in American colleges were frequently scenes of turbulent disorder.

The social life of American colleges to a large extent runs parallel to that of the world outside; and I believe that what is true of academic manners is largely true of city and village life in general. The lack of formality is balanced by an increase of considerateness.

This whole question of formality is interesting. It is not at all surprising today, when we meet a gentleman who seems to have plenty of time for courtesy, that we call him a 'gentleman of the old school.' Quite so; but fifty years ago, when one met that kind of a man, one *then* called him a 'gentleman of the old school.' And I suspect that one hundred and perhaps two hundred years ago, the same object inspired the same description.

What does this mean? Except in clothes, is there after all such a tremendous difference? We are certainly informal in 1938; but in 1838 were they always as formal as we think? When we attempt to reconstruct in our minds the image of a long-past time, it is difficult to imagine the people in their more intimate aspects. It is easier to imagine Demosthenes delivering a public oration than it is to imagine him in his house after supper, roaring with laughter at a funny story. Yet the Greeks and the Romans spent more of their time in natural, intimate relations than they did in any official capacity. In the reconstruction of history, we must not make the mistake that children make, of being unable to realize a human being when he is enveloped in a uniform.

Or, on the other hand, has the whole world been steadily growing more informal from the very beginning to this moment? Even though Adam and Eve wore only their skin, did she address him something like this: 'The evening meal is prepared, and it merely awaits your lordship's convenience?' And did he reply: 'Ah, my queen, one moment, while I regard the last rays of the dying sunlight on the broad bosom of the Euphrates, and then I shall be ready to allay the pangs of hunger?'

And if they did talk in that elaborate fashion, they did not love each other any more than if she had said, 'Come along, Charley—everything will get cold.'

Among the best detective stories are those by the late Earl Derr Biggers, dealing with the Chinese sleuth, Chan. He speaks to all and sundry with the prolonged and involved phraseology of self-abasement characteristic of oriental politeness. 'Will you deign to make use of my contemptible intellect, or perhaps first condescend to enter my wretched hovel and partake of abominable food?' But this elaborate formality deceived the guest no more than the speaker. Chan is satisfied with his house, better satisfied with his food, and most of all satisfied with himself.

It may be that the decrease in formality through the ages is owing partly to the increasing preciousness of time. In the eighteenth century, before they had any time-saving devices, everybody apparently had leisure—leisure to write letters, leisure for conversation, leisure for prolonged politeness. Now everybody who amounts to anything is busy. We are impatient with superfluous preliminaries and embroideries, and wish, as the saying is, to get down to brass tacks. For the modern American is shockingly poor in time. He never seems to have any.

To support the proposition that the lack of superficial courtesy is a sign of the growth of civilization rather than the reverse, several things can be said. I heard an elderly pessimist, shaking his silver head sadly, make the following contribution to modern thought:

'The young people of today have no manners at all: if this goes on, we shall relapse into barbarism.'

But was not elaborate and formal courtesy one of the chief characteristics of barbarism? Read what Benjamin Franklin said about the courtesy of the Indian savages of North America; and what did Sam Houston think of their manners in comparison with those of white men? When the Indians discussed anything, they had infinite time. They sat in solemn conclave, passed the meditative pipe slowly around, and when one spoke, nobody any more thought of interrupting him than we think of interrupting the preacher in church. And even the silliest propositions were listened to with grave courtesy. Compare a modern meeting of bank directors with a committee of Indian braves.

Turning from savages to so-called civilized persons—the elaborate courtesy of the age of chivalry was only a thin veneer, barely concealing a cynical contempt. We know the rules of that game. The knight must professedly adore fair ladies, and be ready at any moment to risk his life for a damosel in distress. Her slightest whim is his law; he must be prepared to go upon a difficult, distant, and dangerous quest to satisfy her caprice. But although knights greeted ladies with formal respect, as if the ladies were of some superior race, we know today that if the Knights of the Round Table were functioning, nearly every one of them would be in jail. Underneath that studied devotion, there was little respect for women and little reason for it.

The formal courtesy of man to woman has been replaced in the twentieth century by comradeship.

Perhaps the most striking proof that extremes in elaborate courtesy bear no real relation to warmth of heart is seen in the old-fashioned custom of the duel. When one man sent a challenge to another with the intention of murdering him, nothing could exceed the courtesy with which the whole matter was arranged.

And now that the duel has disappeared from many places, the extreme courtesy which characterized it has been transferred to the duels between nations, to the apparatus of murder on a gigantic scale. When the ambassador of one nation takes his leave because the two countries are about to engage in wholesale slaughter, the formalities on both sides are without spot or blemish.

On the other hand, the surest sign of intimacy is the absence of formality. If a man is walking on the street, overtakes a woman, and they walk along together, it is (almost) certain they have met before. Intimate friends never have to make conversation unless they feel like it. William Dean Howells left it on record that on one occasion he and Mark Twain travelled side by side in the train from Hartford to New York, three hours; neither read anything, neither said a word.

And the most intimate of all relations, that of marriage, is characterized by the annihilation of formality, the obliteration of reserve.

The growth of real courtesy, as distinguished from the

enamel of formality, is shown, I think, in the increasing good nature and tolerance of crowds—with two notable exceptions: an infuriated mob, which is less intelligent and more cruel than any collection of wild beasts; and the crowded conditions of modern transportation. A visitor from Mars who should obtain his first impression of ladies and gentlemen in the New York subway at the rush hour would hardly believe that the human race had ever produced anyone like Jane Addams or Nathan Straus.

But in general, the crowds on their way to a football game, at a circus, listening in the night to election returns, or merely the crowds of human beings in densely populated thoroughfares, seem to me on the whole to be good-humoured, tolerant, and even kind.

The growth in genuine courtesy and good manners characteristic of this present time is born not only of increased consideration for others, but of increased sincerity. The relations between boys and girls, between men and women, between children and parents, between pupils and teachers, between the younger and the older generation, may seem to some easily shockable persons to be lacking in good manners; but in many ways there is an improvement, and the improvement comes from increased sincerity.

The chief difference between the manners of today and those of fifty years ago is that then Age and Authority and Females received as a matter of course a certain lip service which had nothing to do with the individual. Today there is an increasing impatience with rendering homage except when the individual by his own mind or character deserves it; and when he does deserve it, he receives it in its most gratifying form.

Some years ago, when a member of a congregation argued (outside the church) very candidly with the minister, the latter's wife said to me, 'Do you believe that is the way anybody should address a clergyman?'

CITY OR COUNTRY

By birth I belong to the city. I was born in New Haven in the centre of the town. My first recollection of the country —as distinguished from nearby Connecticut villages—was a summer outing in the Adirondacks.

In the Adirondacks, I was a citified boy in a strange land. Everything was different—the splendid mountains, the wide open places (so unlike the wide open places in the city), the keen, cold air of August evenings, and the absolute silence of the nights—broken only by the musical sound of 'streams inaudible by day.' The native folks seemed different from city people. They were just naturally friendly. Accustomed as I was to pass strangers on city streets without a word or a look of greeting or recognition, it seemed pleasant and sociable to salute everybody with a 'good morning' or a remark about the weather. These people also seemed more self-reliant. In the city every man had only one job, which is one more than many of them have now. Every woman went through a weekly round of familiar duties or social affairs. Every boy went to school and played games the rest of the time.

In the country every man seemed to be able to take care of himself in a dozen different ways; one felt that if he were cast ashore on a desert island, he could get along somehow. Every woman was 'capable.' Each one did every kind of housework, indoors and out, incidentally preparing the next meal and the next baby. The small boys were useful, whether they wished to be or not; their multitudinous tasks

But today we believe that depends on the individual clergyman, rather than on the office.

But perhaps the most striking and genuine improvement in good manners shown by this generation in comparison with former times is concerned with business—buying and selling, everything pertaining to commercial life. Surely there has never been any period in history where courtesy was so universally regarded as an asset. You might raise the objection that this form of courtesy is no more sincere than the traditional politeness of chivalry. But if, in every department of commercial affairs, courtesy today is regarded as part of the essential equipment of a successful man, it is a tribute to its value.

For courtesy is now the rule rather than the exception, a very different state of affairs from that which I can remember. Many years ago railway ticket-sellers, tellers in banks, clerks in shops, were often studiously disagreeable except to the very rich. That method of behaviour has gone forever.

III

REFLEXIONS IN THE NINETEEN-THIRTIES

WHEN Andrew D.White published his famous book, *A History of the Warfare of Science with Theology in Christendom*, he quite naturally supposed there was no doubt as to the victor. He was a good man and loved truth, and freedom in searching it. He thought theology had waged a steadily losing battle all along the line; and its defeat, if not so immediate, was as certain as that of King Canute. Religion had lost one position after another; Science, always opposed and hindered and delayed by the struggle with theology, had nevertheless advanced, because the Truth was on its side. Furthermore, this conquest of religion by science was something that all reasonable men should greet with joy; it meant the removing of shackles of superstition, a free field for independent individual investigators. This was to be at last a brave new world, where men and women, released from all theological or governmental restraint, were to live in the clear and bracing atmosphere of truth.

Very good: very good indeed: we are now living in this Paradise which the former men of science saw afar off. Except in certain localities, there is no restraint on scientific investigation and scientific experiment; the modern hero is the man of science, regarded with universal respect and admiration; and perhaps with some mystical wonder, like the mysterious priests of old. For just as ignorant people believed that the priests had access to sources of knowledge beyond the range of the crowd and that they lived in a world of their own—so today, the vast majority of mankind, being ignorant of science, have almost a superstitious reverence for those who live in laboratories and commune there with occult forces.

Why then is our modern world so full of despair? Why have not mental 'enlightenment' and mechanical resources brought more happiness? Why this bankruptcy of hope? For if hope deferred maketh the heart sick, hope destroyed maketh the heart dead.

My own ignorance of science is so abysmal that any remark of mine on any particular science would be an impertinence. But I am sensitive to mental temperatures; I can tell the direction in which certain scientific pronouncements would lead us.

I heard a justly famous scientific man make an elaborate statement by which we were asked to believe that man had not only no soul, but no mind; that is to say, man was exclusively a physical creature. This seemed to me a vicious circle. Here was a man using the splendid powers of a splendid mind to prove that he had no mind.

After the lecture, I asked another scientific man who was apparently in agreement with the speaker's opinions, 'Are you ever dubious about the value of your researches? Does it ever occur to you that the results of all your efforts to reduce man to a collection of particles of matter might have a tragic aspect?' I asked the question because the lecturer seemed to be in such high spirits; he believed not only that everything he said was true, but that it was a truth in which we should rejoice. 'If we do really amount to nothing, aren't you ever in the least disturbed by the results of your investigations?' And he replied, 'Ah, but we have such a good time in making the investigations!'

In the realm of applied science, its experts have been of incalculable benefit to mankind. The enormous decrease in infant mortality, and annihilation of many diseases like yellow fever, the saving of physical agony in modern surgery, the all but incredible aids to the preservation of human life and the prolongation of its activities; the over-coming of difficulties in transportation, the resources now furnished to the crippled, the deaf, and the blind, one could go on for hundreds of pages, and not even begin to exhaust the blessings given to humanity by scientific men; and it would take still more pages for me adequately to express my grateful appreciation.

But just as many men are sceptical as to the value of re-ligion, so I am sceptical as to the indiscriminate attitude of reverence to all applied science. An individual poisoner is regarded with detestation, and if caught, is in some dan-ger of execution. Is it a cause of rejoicing that all over the world there are distinguished men of science who employ their intelligence and their knowledge and their energy to the invention and improvement of poisons that in the next war will destroy thousands of innocent women and chil-dren? Should our attitude to such inventions be one of un-alloyed reverence? Was it beneficial to mankind that the revolver and the automatic and the 'silencer' were in-vented? When the next war comes, its wholesale methods of torture and destruction will have had their origin in laboratories.

And it is interesting to observe that, although individuals are restrained now in the production of food and other useful and valuable articles, there is no restraint whatever placed on the amount or the efficiency of production of the means of torture and death. Here the accepted principle is still *laissez-faire*.

I hope that these queries will not make any reader imagine that I am 'opposed to science.' I might just as well be opposed to gravitation. I am inordinately proud of being a member of the American Philosophical Society, one of whose objects, in the language of its founder, Benjamin Franklin, is to 'promote useful knowledge.' I am merely asking one general question, which can be compressed into one word, WHITHER?

Modern novelists are as a rule more cheerful than the books they write; on the other hand, I wonder if modern scientists are always in their hearts as cheerful as they look. I wonder if they ever have secret misgivings as to the ultimate value to humanity of their contributions. Browning's Pope asked himself this serious question:

> The sum up of what gain or loss to God
> Came of His one more Vicar in the world.

And as all the culture, knowledge, philosophy of the ancient world resulted in a general mental and moral bankruptcy, and were not only powerless to save the world, but left it hopeless, would it be strange if the net results of the prodigious advance of modern science should bring about another collapse? My own attitude toward science is one of respectful agnosticism; I am not sure that its services to the world are wholly beneficial. And I refuse to regard either the mental attitude that it so often encourages, or the engines of destruction that it invents and improves, with enthusiasm. Before accepting every statement sent out by 'science' I want to be certain that it has been definitely and permanently proved to be true.

In the meanwhile there is a possibility that science, after taking away the last hope of mankind, will supply the only possible remedy by inventions so powerful that mankind will be destroyed. A possibility only, not a probability. Hope in the end always triumphs over despair; and religious truth is indestructible.

I shall certainly not commit intellectual suicide by refusing to accept anything proved; having spent a large part of my time on earth searching for truth, I am not going to resist it whenever or wherever I find it. But I cannot help wondering as to ultimate values.

AUTUMNAL REFLEXIONS

It is Saturday the twenty-second of October 1938, and the hour is eight in the morning. I shall see Yale play the University of Michigan at football this afternoon; then I shall be in a state of excitement unfavourable to thought. But this morning alone in my study under the roof of my house at 110 Whitney Avenue, New Haven, with the sunlight flooding the room, surrounded by my books, I am looking backward over my life. As soon as this book is finished and indeed it will be soon, I hope never to look back again. *Prospice!*

Well, as this is the last time, I should like to recall some of my experiences of sheer delight. I shall mention only a few, for there are hundreds of days when I have been filled with happiness. Omitting religion and family life, the two greatest sources of happiness I know, which need no explanation to those familiar with them, and which no language could explain to others, I must honestly say I have found life good. I would not have missed it for anything. There have of course been misfortunes, illnesses, periods of mental depression, failures, loss of friends, and the general sense of frustration that afflicts every candid mind. But these are shadows, and my life has mainly been passed in sunshine.

Of course I should like to be an immortal poet or an immortal something-or-other; to feel the steadfast assurance that one had left on earth some enduring work that would remain as a permanent memorial. But although one knows, as I do, that everything one has done will be speedily forgotten, I do not see why that should make one miserable. Why spend one's life or even one's last moments in crying for the moon? Why not make the best of the good old world?

My life has been divided into four parts—Work, Play, Development, Social Pleasures. Work is man's greatest blessing. Whenever it is in any way possible, every boy and girl should choose as his life work some congenial occupation. It has always been necessary for me to work, but if at any time during the last twenty years some eccentric person had left me a million dollars, I should have gone right on working at my chosen profession, teaching, writing, and public speaking. I enjoy all three. I enjoy them so much that I have no hesitation in saying that I enjoy them more than vacations.

I have also had an enormous amount of fun out of play. I like all kinds of games, except alley-bowling, just as I like all famous music except that by Meyerbeer. In every game I have never succeeded in rising above mediocrity; but here again I doubt if the great players (whom I nevertheless envy) have enjoyed playing football, baseball, hockey, tennis, golf, billiards, pool, duplicate whist more than I. If I were now given the opportunity to spend every day for the next five hundred years in an invariable programme of work all the morning, golf all the afternoon, and social enjoyment all the evening, I should accept with alacrity, making only one stipulation—that at the end of the five hundred years I should have the privilege of renewal. And that's that.

In cultural development, by which I mean the enrichment of the mind by Nature and Art, I have had unspeakable delight. Yet I am neither a naturalist nor an artist. I don't know anything about flowers, and very little about animals. I cannot draw or paint, or make anything with my hands.

But no one loves the scenes of nature more than I. The first sunset that I remember with enjoyment occurred when I was ten years old; and how many I have seen since then! I have seen the Matterhorn from the Gorner Grat, Mont Blanc from Chamonix, and the divine flush on the summit of the Jungfrau.

Fifty years ago I heard for the first time the Ninth Symphony; and while I have heard it often since then, the most memorable occasion was in May 1912 when I heard it at Paris, played by a magnificent orchestra, conducted by Felix Weingartner; I have heard *Die Meistersinger* in Munich, conducted by Arthur Nikisch, my favourite among all orchestra conductors. I have heard the *Emperor Concerto*, with Ossip Gabrilowitsch at the piano; I have heard *Tod und Verklärung* with Stokowski and the Philadelphia Orchestra, I have heard Toscanini conducting the Seventh Symphony; I have heard De Pachmann (in his prime) play Chopin's B flat minor sonata, Paderewski play Liszt's Hungarian Rhapsody No. 2, Josef Hofmann play Beethoven's Sonata 111. I have heard *Carmen* sung by Emma Calvé, Emma Eames, Jean de Reszké and Lasalle; *Tristan und Isolde* sung by Jean de Reszké and Lilli Lehmann; *Faust* sung by Jean and Edouard de Reszké, Emma Eames, Maurel, and Scalchi; *Mignon* sung by Mme Lucrezia Bori; I have repeatedly heard the three greatest bassos of modern time, Edouard de Reszké, Pol Plançon, and Chaliapin.

In the theatre I have seen Edwin Booth as Shylock, Mansfield as Richard III, Irving in *The Lyons Mail*, Possart as Mephistopheles, Sarah Bernhardt as La Tosca, Duse as Francesca, Salvini as Othello, Maurice Evans in the unabridged *Hamlet*, and twice have I seen the Passion Play at Oberammergau. All these are memorable experiences. But if I should attempt to recall all the glorious things I have seen in nature and in art, I should have no time for fresh experiences that await me.

As for social pleasures, one of the highest enjoyments is

agreeable company for good conversation; and I especially like men, women, and children.

One of the chief sources of happiness in my life has been my family associations. My cousins who have always lived in New Haven are descended from that same Colonel William Lyon, my great-grandfather. Judge William Lyon Bennett is now ninety years old; his mind is clear and vigorous and his conversation always interesting. His brother the late Thomas Bennet was a member of the Yale Corporation; he married Jennie Winchester, the daughter of the famous arms inventor, O. F. Winchester. Their son, Winchester Bennett, now living in New Haven, married Susan Silliman Wright, a daughter of Professor Wright of Yale; and their daughter Mollie married Mr. Trevelyan, a son of the famous historian, Sir George M. Trevelyan, O. M., professor at Cambridge. Harriet Bennett, now living in New Haven, has published many poems, and Ethel, daughter of William Lyon, is an artist. My Bennett cousins and their parents and grandparents have always been associated with Yale.

My wife's brother and my most intimate friend, Frank Hubbard, was married a few months after my own marriage, to Miss Elizabeth Lockwood daughter of St. John Lockwood, a graduate of Yale; their two daughters married Yale graduates. My brother Arthur's boy is a Yale graduate and his son is named William Lyon Phelps. My personal associations with all of my own relations and of those of my wife have been and are ideal in affectionate intimacy. I mention these things because they have added to my happiness; and because they are uncommon.

I know of no greater fallacy or one more widely believed than the statement that youth is the happiest time of life.

The foundation of this statement—the assumption on which it rests—is false. The assumption is that men and women are merely animals; but the differences between human beings and animals are greater and more important than the resemblances. The mind is more important than the body.

We are like animals in our physical sensations; we have hunger, thirst, lust, love of warmth and shelter; we suffer from physical injuries. But we have something they have not, something that literally makes all the difference in the world. We have the *power of development.*

We have the marvellous, boundless, incomparable gifts of observation, thought, and imagination.

Walt Whitman expressed it both concretely and poetically in his poem *To the Man-of-War Bird,* where, after showing the enormous superiority of the bird's flight over land and sea in comparison with the slow and limited motion of man, he concluded

> In them, in thy experiences, hadst thou my soul,
> What joys! what joys were thine!

And now the airplane gives man the experiences.

I am considering only this present life, this life on earth; and if this is all we have, we are still more fortunate than the animals, because ideas are more interesting than food. But I think our capacity for development supplies an intelligent reason for believing in a future life. If my clever and attractive dog should live to be one hundred or one thousand, he would be no further along than he is now. Whereas every child has potentialities for which eternity is not too long. This is what makes teaching so exciting—it is more exciting to teach boys and girls than it is to train horses and dogs.

To see the first awakening of intellectual interest in a young man gives a thrill; for it is a sign of life, of growth, an awakening of dormant powers.

Education means drawing forth from the mind latent powers and developing them, so that in mature years one may apply these powers not merely to success in one's occupation, but to success in the greatest of all arts—the art of living.

If one is fortunate enough to have attended a good school and a high-grade college, that is well. But it is better to have really educated oneself without these advantages than to have had the advantages and missed the opportunities.

It is with some misgiving that I see today evidences of a desire to get-rich-quick in ideas, even as so many have found disaster in the attempt to get-rich-quick in money; and the latter is certainly easier than the former. There is no short cut to the riches of thought. Acceleration is not upward, but downward. Merely because an ambitious and industrious student might learn of assigned lessons in two years at college what an average undergraduate would learn in four, does not mean that the former has got out of college life the enrichment of the latter. Oxford and Cambridge mean more than the mere curriculum.

I have no doubt the average person enjoys excitement more than comfort; although comfort means the absence of difficulties, and excitement means an increase of them. Now it is well to remember that many comfortable persons are unhappy, whereas nobody in a state of excitement is wholly unhappy. Melancholy visits the empty mind and settles there; the mind full of interesting or exciting ideas cannot be invaded by depression.

As we advance in years from childhood to youth, from youth to middle age, from middle age to old age, we really grow happier, if we live intelligently. The universe is spectacular, and it is a free show. Increase of difficulties and responsibilities strengthens and enriches the mind, and adds to the variety of life.

> The noble soul by age grows lustier:
> Her appetite and her digestion mend.

To live abundantly is like climbing a mountain or a tower. Why is it that men every year pay money for the privilege of leaving the comfortable plains and highways, in order to climb through appalling difficulties and obstacles to the top of a mountain? Someone asked one of the adventurous heroes who tried to climb Mount Everest, 'Why do you want to climb it?' He answered, 'Because it is *there*.' (And now he is there.)

It was not the mere love of fame, though possibly that had something to do with it; it was because, in his quiet and safe lodgings in London, surrounded with comforts and luxuries, the mountain was *calling him*!

> Hark to it calling, calling clear
> Calling until you cannot stay
> From dearer things than your own most dear
> Over the hills and far away.

To climb the highest mountains is not for the average man; it is only for those especially gifted in body and mind, and for few of those.

I have myself climbed more towers than mountains; for although the works of nature exceed the works of man in beauty and grandeur, I have found the works of man more interesting. To me nature is not so interesting as human nature.

It is a pity that the great humorist, Mark Twain, was such a pessimist; yet it is true that excess of humour is often accompanied with excess of melancholy. The most terrible and consistent pessimist in English literature was Jonathan Swift, who was also one of the greatest humorists of all time. I suppose there is some balance, some compensation, in such a temperament. Then it is true that mere laughter and demonstrative gaiety are not the highest forms of happiness. The love of a man for a maid, though it may reach ecstatic happiness, is without humour. One touch of humour might be fatal to it. In other deepest enjoyments there is no humour. The delight we take in music and in painting and in sunsets is humourless. In *The Merchant of Venice* Jessica said to her lover,

> I am never merry when I hear sweet music.

Mark Twain said life would be infinitely happier if we could only be born at the age of eighty, and gradually approach eighteen. This would mean we should gradually lose our intelligence, our experience, our ideas, our work, our personality, even our manhood. We should exchange profound happiness for animal spirits.

To say that youth is happier than maturity is like saying that the view from the bottom of a tower is better than the view from the top. As we ascend the spiral staircase, and glance from time to time through the narrow slits in the stone, the range of our view widens immensely; the horizon is pushed farther away. Finally as we reach the summit it is as if we had the world at our feet.

St. Simeon Stylites, who spent sixty years on top of a tower, was better off than a hermit in a cell.

The pursuit of knowledge, the advance of thought, the gain in experience, the growth of a man or a woman from youth upwards, are like the struggle up a height. Lessing said he would choose the pursuit of truth rather than the knowledge of truth, if he had to choose between the two. The very problems of life, the meaning of life itself, become more interesting as we grow older. John Donne wrote

> On a huge hill
> Cragged and steep, Truth stands, and he that will
> Reach her, about must, and about must go;
> And what the hill's suddenness resists, win so.

Unhappiness comes from thinking about oneself, rather than of something outside of oneself. The reason we are so unhappy when we have a toothache is because we cannot think of anything except the ache. A toothache is importunate; it will not be denied. Shakespeare said that not even a philosopher could endure a toothache patiently. Children are made unhappy by physical aches and pains or by their inability to get what they want; and they are without resources, as helpless as a disappointed dog. Young people suffer from self-consciousness, the curse of adolescence. But as we grow older, we have more things to do and more things to think about. There is no comparison at all between the vague happiness of an irresponsible youth, and the real happiness of a busy man or woman, with a home and an occupation, whose work, ideas, and opinions count for something.

The ideas that come from one's work, from reading, from thought, from music, from art, and from mere observation of the world of men and women, are, curiously enough, both a refuge and an inspiration. They refresh and they stimulate. The best insurance against old age and disability is an interesting mind; and such a mind gives a stimulus to more enjoyment.

> This world's no blot for us,
> Nor blank; it means intensely, and means good;
> To find its meaning is my meat and drink.

I have seen persons in absolute agony; it seems incredible then, that the time will ever come when they will find a newspaper interesting, or that they will enjoy unconsciously simple pleasures like eating or drinking, or the air of an October morning. But the moment when that dull look of grief in the eyes is replaced by even a flicker of interest, they are on the way to recovery.

The art of living can be cultivated; the more we stock our minds with interesting thoughts, the richer we are. And these riches remain; they cannot be lost. They add

Perhaps nothing nowadays is a more common target for ridicule than the hustler and booster, whether he boosts as an individual or as a member of a service organization. The man whose motto is 'bigger and better business,' a bigger town, with a bigger population and bigger buildings, is laughed at for his enthusiasm and for his perspiring efforts. Much of this laughter is merely the cynical adverse criticism of men who have never done anything themselves, never will do anything, and so pretend to be faintly and superciliously amused by the optimistic exertions of others. We may dismiss these unproductive and complacent occupiers of the seats of the scornful, for they are comparatively few in number and their opinions are of no moment. But the rational basis for laughter at the booster is that the hustler and the booster often have a false standard of excellence.

When a noisy man roars in your face that the population of his particular town has doubled in ten years we have a right to enquire, what of it? Is it a cause for rejoicing? When you climb into a trolley car on a rainy day you do not rejoice because the population of the trolley car doubles in three minutes. A mere increase in the number of persons at a given spot does not necessarily mean that collectively or individually they are any better off. What we wish to know is something quite different from the word 'more.' Is the community growing in intelligence? Are there better schools, better theatres, better art museums, better churches, better orchestras—are the individual inhabitants growing?

Strangely enough, some of the professional men of science, who are often the first to laugh at the booster because he applies the quantitative rather than the qualitative standard of measurement, are themselves guilty of the same fault on a larger scale. They do not apply standards of size to a growing business or a growing village; they apply these standards to the universe.

to the happiness and to the excitement of d

In my life of professional teaching, I have
deavoured to make young men more efficient; I
to make them more interesting. If one is inte
is usually interesting. The business of the teac
to supply information, it is to raise a thirst. I li
pictures on the walls of the mind, I like to make
for a man to live with himself, so that he will no
with himself. For my own part, *I live every day
were the first day I had ever seen and the last I were go*

The Book of Proverbs, speaking of the ideal wor
she can laugh at her approaching old age. It
well if all women (and men) would remember
cultivation of the mind is the best insurance, not
death, but against life. Those marvellous old peop
French aristocracy of the eighteenth century, were a
after in society as if they had been fair to see. T
indeed defied both life and death. King Stanislas,
received from his daughter, the Queen of France, a
dressing-gown, got his death from it, when one
caught fire. An old woman, endeavouring to help hi
severely burned, and in the midst of his agony,
'How strange that at our ages you and I should
burn with the same flame!' He was eighty-eight.
two weeks of suffering, he died, and in his last hou
tated a letter to his daughter about the gown. 'You
it me to keep me warm; it has kept me too warm.'

Wit is a great preservative. Age acted on the old
of the *salons* like a whetstone. They feared not the l
grace and youth; they had the happy assurance that c
from the knowledge of being *wanted*. They had fa
but they never bored any one. They were beloved by
temporaries and envied by the young. There is never m
trouble in any family where the children hope some
to resemble their parents.

Some astronomers have recently been fond of reminding us that our sun itself is only a tiny star—one out of many billions—and that our earth is but the tiniest speck. They are fond of drawing diagrams showing the comparative size of our sun and that of other globes in the starry skies, and the earth dwindles to a mere point. 'Therefore,' say these scientists, 'how unimportant is man and how ridiculous that he should consider either himself or his earthly abode a matter of any importance to God or to space or time or gravitation;' the conclusion following that religion and morals are matters of small consequence and we need not bother our heads about them.

Now it seems to me that expressions of this kind are as fallacious and as injurious as any booster's standard of mere quantity; for what are these gentlemen trying to say except that as the earth is so tiny in comparison with other stars it must necessarily follow that man himself is a very unimportant factor in the universe? I believe the earth to be the most important spot in the entire creation and that the most precious thing on the earth is man—men, women, and children.

When I was a graduate student at Yale, I studied the complete works of the German philosopher Lotze, with not so much success as the late Lord Haldane, but with assiduity and enthusiasm. Lotze gave the best definition of existence. 'To be is to be in relations.' It is an accurate definition of life. A dead body, no matter where the soul or mind or spirit may be, has no relations with anything. It doesn't know its latitude or longitude, it doesn't know whether it is winter or summer, it doesn't know whether it is raining or the sun is shining, it doesn't know what is going on in the world of politics. Guy de Maupassant described a cemetery: 'The people in there are not reading the newspapers.'

Well, if a dead body is dead because it has no relations

with anything, it would seem to follow that the more relations we have the more life we have. If a man is interested only in his business, then so far as the worlds of music and art and science and foreign politics are concerned, he is dead. They do not exist for him any more than if he were in the grave. But if in addition to his business he is also interested in music or in playing games or in foreign politics he is just that much more alive. People of tremendous mental vitality are intensely interested in a variety of things. The late Theodore Roosevelt was interested in everything from a bumble-bee to a battleship, and I have never known a man more bursting with vitality.

I am interested in everything in the world except the higher mathematics; and I should be interested in that branch of study if I had sufficient intelligence. A very simple test that one can apply to oneself to discover a range of interest is to take up the daily newspaper and see if there is something on every page of interest: foreign news, national news, local news, athletics, the theatre, music, books, stock exchange, etc., and if there is something on every page that interests a man, he is very much alive.

Not only does this mean richness and abundance of life and a continually enlarging curiosity, but it is the best form of insurance against 'grey ultimate decrepitude' and against all troubles, disasters, sorrows, and heartbreak that everyone must pass through. For when one is despondent, one cannot recover by will power. One cannot say, 'I am feeling miserable, but I will be cheerful,' for the more will power he uses, the worse he feels. It is like sinking in a quicksand where every effort sends one deeper. But if one is alert and has an active mind continually interested in a variety of subjects, sooner or later his mind will be diverted from himself and from his sorrows to something quite different; and at that moment convalescence and recovery set in. Even if one is unhappy, one may find life interesting.

The world itself in this year of grace 1938 is in a much worse condition than it was thirty years ago, but it is more interesting.

I am filled with wonder and admiration whenever I think of the poem *Remembrance*, written by Emily Brontë when she was about twenty-five. It is one of the greatest love poems in literature; but we can account for that by the miracle of genius as we can account for great pieces of music being written by people with little experience. But where did Emily learn the secret that even great philosophers have sought in vain? Where did she learn not only in the midst of unhappiness but without the slightest hope of ever having any happiness, that life could not only be endurable but exciting? This is the stanza of her poem that gives me such respect not only for her courage but for the quality of her mind.

> But when the days of golden dreams had perished,
> And even Despair was powerless to destroy,
> Then did I learn how existence could be cherished,
> Strengthened and fed, without the aid of joy.

Her mind was so rich in thought, so alert and vigorous in intelligence, that looking forward to a future barren of happiness she still found life supremely worth living. And this was not the defiant, stoical courage of despair; there was no resignation in it.

The whole question of optimism and pessimism is interesting. There are many more consistent Christians than there are consistent pessimists. People who call themselves optimists are usually thought to be rather shallow, whereas people who call themselves pessimists are thought to be profound. Yet we nearly all of us congratulate others on their birthdays, and if we do that sincerely we are optimists. That does not mean that we think this the best of all possible worlds or that we think life a succession of beautiful experiences. But it does mean that we consider life as an asset and that we consider it good fortune to have been born. For a shallow optimism I have no respect whatever. But if optimism means one believes that in the long run truth will survive error and good will triumph over evil and that life is an experience for which one is grateful, then I am most certainly an optimist. There are few genuine pessimists, and although I do not share their beliefs, I respect them. The great Jonathan Swift was an absolute pessimist. He invariably celebrated his birthday by wearing black and by fasting, because he was so sorry he had been born. To the average man such an attitude is comic. In one of Strindberg's plays a question is asked, 'How is your wife?' 'She is almost blind.' And after an exclamation of sorrow, 'No, she says there is nothing worth seeing and she hopes she will soon be deaf because there is nothing worth hearing, and she says the best thing about being old is that you are almost through.' Such pessimism is genuine but seems almost absurd, so contrary is it to the deepest instincts of humanity. Like the remark of the gentleman from North Carolina—'The moment you're born, you're done for.'

INDEX

ABBOTT, Prof. Frank, 142
Abbott, Dr. Lawrence, 186
Adams (F.P.A.), 618
Adams, George B., 425
Adams, George Matthew, 940
Adams, James Truslow, 910, 911
Adams, John Chester, 285, 359, 360, 664
Adams, Maude, 112
Ade, George, 536, 778
Advance of the English Novel, the, 326
Advance of English Poetry in the Twentieth Century, the, 326
Æ. (See George W.Russell)
Aikins, H.Austin, 225, 244
Airplanes, 510
Aitken, Robert Grant, 77
Allen, Hervey, 172
Ames, Winthrop, 507, 784
Amsberg, Prof., 226
Anderson, Mary, 117
Angell, James R., 781
Angell, Norman, 602
Archer, William, 479, 568, 620, 765–767
Arliss, George, 479, 784
Armstrong, Prof.A.J., 512, 545
Armstrong, Paul, 482
Arnold, Matthew, 140, 762, 938
'As I Like It,' 737–741
Ashford, Daisy, 575
Asquith, Margot, 749
Astronomy, 73–79
Atherton, Gertrude, 443
Atwill, Mrs. Lionel, 707
Austen, Jane, 385, 408, 467, 535
Austin, Alfred, 635

BABCOCK, Harmon S., 23
Bacon, 187, 293
Bacon, Prof. Thomas R., 495
Baker, George Pierce, 247, 480, 606, 660
Bakewell, Charles M., 248
Bangs, John Kendrick, 619
Baptism, 17, 23
Barbers, the, 855–856
Barbour, Clarence A., 109
Baring, Maurice, 109, 651, 811
Barnum, 183
Barrett, Lawrence, 208, 269, 270
Barrett, Wilson, 113, 242
Barrie, Sir James M., 90, 117, 205, 310, 330, 397, 398, 400, 401, 553, 565–583, 669, 673, 730, 738, 787, 813, 826, 933
Barry, Philip, 660
Barrymore, John, 622
Barrymore, Lionel, 479
Baseball, 214, 354–356
Bassett, Prof. Samuel, 866, 876
Battey, W.W.,Jr., 782
Battle, William J., 249, 512
Bayne-Jones, Stanhope, 510
Beach, Judge John K., 515
Beard, Charles A., 738
Beebe, William, 78, 605
Beecher, Henry Ward, 21, 369
Beers, Prof. Henry A., 188, 190, 221, 259, 289–291, 297, 316, 323, 425, 502, 652, 664, 711
Beethoven, 226, 238, 865, 889, 913
Beginnings of the English Romantic Movement, the, 217, 296, 316

Belasco, David, 707
Beljame, Prof., 428, 436
Belloc-Lowndes, Mrs., 932, 935
Benavente, Señor, 755–756
Benét, Stephen Vincent, 660, 688, 785–786
Benét, William Rose, 660
Bennett, Arnold, 167, 558–559, 570, 576, 758
Bennett, Harriet, 961
Bennett, Thomas, 961
Bennett, Judge William Lyon, 961
Bennett, Winchester, 961
Berdan, John Milton, 279, 285, 360, 506, 664
Beresford, John, 176
Bergner, Elisabeth, 577
Bernhardt, Sarah, 112, 115, 116, 435, 464, 465, 816, 960
Bernstein, Henry, 892–893
Berryman, 48, 52
Bible, the, 181, 207, 922
Bicentennial (at Yale), 405
Bicycling (in Europe), 211, 217, 225, 227, 320, 384, 390, 392–393, 806, 922
Bigelow, Poultney, 443
Biglow, Ray, 371, 372
Billiards, 68, 70, 71, 376
Billings, Josh, 67, 186
Birds, famous, 586
Bishop, William Henry, 181, 446
Bixby, Rev. Dr., 17
Björnson, 520
Black, Major, 778
Blake, Mrs. Kingsley, 550
Blumenfeld, Ralph D., 763, 933
Boer War, 380, 387, 466, 636, 807
Booth, Edwin, 111, 112, 114, 269, 271, 784, 960
Borden, Sir Robert, 777

Bori, Lucrezia, 843, 960
Borrow, George, 181
Bourne, E.G., 425
Boyesen, Prof.H.H., 223
Braden, Jim, 641
Breakfast, 861
Brett, George P., 321
Bridge, 360, 361
Bridgeport Tennis Tournament, 287
Bridges, Robert, 738
Brieux, Eugene, 605
Briggs, L.B.R., 247, 252, 253, 254, 255, 273, 376
Bronson, Lewis, 358
Brontë, Emily, 205, 713, 971
Brooke, Tucker, 665
Brooker, Hon. Charles F., 777
Brooks, Phillips, 234
Broun, Heywood, 170, 749
Brown, Dr. William Adams, 241
Brownell, W.C., 317
Browning, Elizabeth Barrett, 367, 447, 452, 453, 454, 476, 565
Browning, Oscar, 340
Browning, Mrs. Pen, 633
Browning, Robert, 18, 44, 59, 65, 66, 133, 157, 175, 205, 207-210, 215, 229, 236, 311, 323, 326, 336, 338, 364, 367, 375, 379, 388, 415, 424, 433, 434, 446-447, 452-456, 474, 494, 501, 512, 525, 539, 540, 542-549, 552, 560-562, 565, 584, 619, 633, 635, 637, 646, 653, 744, 749, 762, 805, 828, 852, 880, 905, 908-909, 922, 957
Browning, Robert Wiedemann Barrett, 447, 453, 454-456
Brush, Katharine, 480
Bryan, W.J., 412, 608
Bryce, Hon. James, 380, 381
Buck, Pearl, 592, 912
Bull, Billy, 369
Bull Moose, 610
Bull-fight, 599, 842
Bullitt, William C., 508

Bundy, 686
Burroughs, John, 509, 654
Burton, Prof., 275
Butler, Nicholas Murray, 413, 605, 777, 780, 911, 916
Byers, Eb, 378
Byron, 222, 806, 865

CABELL, Mr. and Mrs. James Branch, 914
Cable, George W., 68
Caffey, Francis, 249, 257
Calderon, George, 933
Caldwell, Ernest, 191
Caldwell, Erskine, 68
Calvé, Emma, 960
Calvert, Louis, 112, 117, 621
Camp, Walter, 649
Campbell, Gerald, 805
Campbell, Mrs. Patrick, 112, 116, 379
Campbell-Bannerman, Sir Henry, 381
Canby, Dr. Henry S., 426, 662, 669
Canfield, Dorothy, 588-594, 771
Canfield, Dr., 495, 588
Capps, Prof. and Mrs. Edward, 869
Cardwell, Edward, 183
Carlyle, 42, 43, 138, 181, 206, 207, 454
Caruso, 622
Case, Austin, 129
'Casey at the Bat,' 170
Cat v. Dog, 31, 821
Cathedrals, 890
Cather, Willa, 592, 841, 910-911
Catholic Church, 17, 228, 706
Catterall, Ralph Charles Henry, 266-267, 379, 380, 427, 604
Centennial, the (Philadelphia), 24-25
Chace, Malcolm, 357
Chaliapin, 927-928
Chamberlain, Joseph, 381
Chambers, Sir Edmund, 843
Chaplin, Charlie, 190, 194
Chapman, Plays of, 304

Chase, Frederick L., 76, 357
Chase, Mary Ellen, 932
Chatfield-Taylor, Mr., 509
Chaucer, 209, 305, 383, 909
'Chaucer and Browning,' 209
Chautauqua, 222, 410, 505
Chekhov, 350, 351, 933
Cheney, Tim, 378
Cherbuliez, Victor, 174
Chesterton, G.K., 39, 63, 172, 205, 241, 349, 450, 651, 806-810
Child, Prof. Francis J., 208, 246, 252, 257, 274
Chinese Schoolmates, 84
Chittenden, Prof. and Mrs. Russell, 515, 524
Choate, Joseph H., 379, 606
Chopin, 214, 769, 889, 926
Christianity, 200-201, 338
Christian Science, 220
Christmas at School, 15
Church, Howard, 359
Churchman, Dr. Philip, 427, 436
Classics, the, 147, 148
Class of 1896, 78, 279-280, 285-287, 291, 302, 361, 481, 662, 813
Class Reunion, fiftieth, 937
Clemens, Clara, 65, 456, 925-926
Clemens, S.L., 66
Cleveland, Grover, 314
Clifford, Mrs.W.K., 551, 555-558, 801
Clutton-Brock, Prof., 179
Cobb, Collier, 249
Cochran, Alexander Smith, 292-293
Coffin, Henry Sloane, 663
Colbert, Claudette, 741
Cole, Belle, 236
Coleman, Prof. Christopher, 286
Coleridge, Lord Chief Justice, 140, 549
Collett, Glenna, 781
Collins, J.Churton, 179
Colum, Mary, 828, 895
Colum, Padraic, 828, 895
Compulsory English compositions, 273

Conant, Pres., 330, 919
Conrad, Joseph, 38, 430, 494, 570, 752–754, 822
Conscientious objectors, 638, 733
Contemporary prose fiction (or drama), 297–302, 325, 477, 493, 566, 905
Conversation Club, 777–778
Conversion, 145
Conway, Lord and Lady, 878, 936
Coogan, Jackie, 189
Cook, Prof. Albert S., 462, 664
Cook, Bob, 435
Cook, Mr. and Mrs. Gustavus Wynne, 76
Coolidge, Calvin, 66, 785
Coquelin, 117, 431, 923
Corbett, James J., 510, 794, 796
Corbin, Arthur, 359
Corbin, D.P., 24
Corbin, John, 482
Corbin, 'Pa,' 369
Corliss Engine, 24
Corneille, 437, 476
Cornell, Katharine, 112
Corwin, Prof. Robert Nelson, 937
Coué, Monsieur, 220, 770
Courtney, 381
Cow, the American, 174
Cowan, Henry, 202
Cowl, Jane, 707
Cox, James M., 854
Cox, Rowland, 286
Coy, Prof. (of Andover), 252
Coy, Ted, 371, 372
Crawford, Jack, 168, 358, 618, 619, 892
Croker, Richard, 77
Cross, Wilbur, 666, 856
Cross-country championship, 354
Cross-eyed cat, 36
Crothers, Rachel, 921
Cummings, Constance, 11
Cunninghame-Graham, R.B., 119, 120
Curtis, George William, 104

Curtis, Mrs. Virginia, 790
Cushing, Dr. Harvey, 856
Cushing, Tom, 213, 741
Cushing, William Lee (and Mrs.), 211, 212, 214–216

DALLAS, Bishop John, 663
Daly, Arnold, 461, 713
Damon, Lindsay Todd, 275
Damrosch, Walter, 214, 928–929
Dancing, 617
Daniels, Winthrop M., 202
Dante, 205, 448
Dashiell, Alfred, 738
Daudet, Léon, 893–895
Davenport, Charles, 248, 267
Day, Clarence, 300, 480, 481
Day, Mr. and Mrs. Harry, 550
Day, Thomas Mills, 73, 74
Daylight Saving, 650, 845
Delabarre, Edmund, 363
Delafield, Miss E.M., 559, 800
De Mar, Clarence, 375
De Morgan, William, 145, 322, 468–472, 487, 494, 667, 801
Dent, J.M., 601
De Pachmann, Vladimir, 926, 960
De Reszké, Edouard, 291, 292, 922, 928, 960
De Reszké, Jean, 268, 922, 960
Detweiler, Helen, 781
De Vane, William, 665
De Vigny, Alfred, 177
De Wolfe, Elsie, 123
Dickerman, Sherwood O., 286
Dickens, 577, 711, 822, 933
Dickinson, Lowes, 623
Dillingham, Charlie, 53
Dodd, Lee, 841
Dog v. Cat, 31
Dole, Mr. (Pres. of Hawaii), 628
Dole, Nathan Haskell, 189
Doran, George H., 606

Doubleday, Mr. and Mrs. F.N., 753
Dowden, Edward, 466
Drake, Sir Francis, 230
Drew, John, 649
Drinking, 810
Drinkwater, John, 420
Drummond, Prof. Henry, 105, 199–203, 217
Dumas, Alexandre, 169, 205
Duncan, G.M., 425
Dunsany, Lord, 688
Durfee, Edward L., 286
Duse, Eleanora, 115, 116, 421, 880, 960
Dwight, Timothy, 161, 221, 276, 288, 297, 301, 505, 512

EAMES, Emma, 235, 916, 922–924, 960
Eaton, Theophilus, 3
Eaton, Walter Prichard, 480
Edgett, Edwin F., 275
Edison, Thomas, 507, 846–848, 857, 860
Editorial work, 44, 150, 319, 320
Egan, Maurice Francis, 515
Einstein, Lewis, 434
Eldridge, Jay G., 286
Elgar, Sir Edward, 461
Eliot, George, 67, 223, 242, 788
Eliot, Pres. (of Harvard), 249, 263, 267, 303, 376, 413, 495
Eliot, T.S., 913
Elizabethan Club, 293, 753
Elizabethan Drama, 291–292
Elman, Mischa, 506
Emerson, 67, 206, 343, 351, 352, 376, 391, 944
Emery, Henry C., 425, 440
Emery, Winifred, 380
Erlanger, Abraham L., 482
Ervine, St. John, 113, 397, 705, 716–736, 738, 828, 885
Essays on Books, 326
Essays on Modern Dramatists, 580

Essays on Modern Novelists, 321, 557
Essays on Russian Novelists, 325, 562
Etiquette, 164, 534, 947
Europe, first journey in, 113
Evans, Prof. Alexander, 545, 547
Evans, Maurice, 112, 960
Evarts, William M., 149
Everard, Lewis C., 510
Ewart, Charlie, 373
'Experience Meeting,' 332

FAGUET, Emile, 435
Falconer, Sir Robert, 653
Fano Club, founding of, 545
Farewells, 192, 908
Farnam, Prof. Henry W., 462, 605
Farr, Hollon A., 286
Farrington, Edward, 212, 215
Faulkner, William, 68
Fell, E.Nelson, 309
Féraudy, 112, 438
Ferber, Edna, 592, 660, 771–776
First airplane trip, 767
First book, 217, 316–326
First book-review, 42
First diary, 48–57
First honorary degree, 708
First meeting with a king, 519
First public lecture, 304
First radio speech, 939–940
First Sabbatical, 427
First theatre, 111
Fischer, Kuno, 229, 289
Fisher, H.A.L., 878
Fisher, Irving, 141, 425 479
Fisher, Mrs.J.R. (See Dorothy Canfield)
Fisher, Lola, 780
Fiske, Arthur Irving, 340
Fiske, Mrs. Minnie Maddern, 595, 842
Fitch, Clyde (William C.), 122–125
Flaubert, 437, 590, 769, 894
Fletcher, Horace, 480
Foch, Marshal, 708

Football, 84, 122, 214, 369–374, 858, 876, 888
Foote, Arthur, 357
Footguards, Governor's, 4
Forbes-Robertson, 507
Ford car, 853
Ford, Edsel, 859
Ford, Henry, 857–861, 945
Forman, Justin Miles, 621
Förster, Max, 882
Foster, Dr.J.P.C., 412–413
Fowler, Clarence V., 286
Fowler, H.W., 711–713
France, Anatole, 67, 767–769, 887
Frank, Clint, 373
Franklin, Benjamin, 44, 76, 166, 196, 637, 650, 829, 950, 957
Free speech, 640–642
Freer, Charles Lang, 483
French, Robert, 665, 882
'Fresh-air crank,' 173
Friends of the Princeton Library, 910–911
'Frisco,' 496
Frogs, 107–108
Frohman, Charles, 619, 779
Frohman, Daniel, 482, 755, 778, 779, 780
Frost, Robert, 634, 911
Fry, Rev.T.P., 803, 817
Funeral, a, 889
Fünfstück, Bernhard, 357
Furness, Horace Howard, 514

GABRILOWITSCH, Ossip, 634, 925, 960
Gainford, Lord and Lady, 935
Gale, Zona, 60, 592, 692
Gales, Weston, 634
Galsworthy, Ada (Mrs. John), 677, 683
Galsworthy, John, 38, 112, 117, 185, 398, 507, 529, 570, 622, 653, 667–684, 754, 803, 816, 910
Galt, J.R., 625
Gardiner, the great historian, 380
Garnett, Dr. Richard, 317
Gates, Andrew F., 150
Gates, Lewis, 268, 275

Gay, Frank, 45–47
Gaylord, Mr. and Mrs. Franklin, 526
George, Lloyd, 381
Germans and Jews, 490, 734
Gibbons, Cardinal, 705
Gibbs, Josiah Willard, 425
Gibbs, Sir Philip, 708
Gibson, W.W., 634
Gilbert and Sullivan Opera Co., 916
Gill, Charley, 369
Gillette, William, 34, 36, 63, 112, 482, 574, 669
Ginn and Co., 318
Gish, Lillian, 914
Gissing, George, 437
Gladstone, 181, 243, 505
Glasgow, Ellen, 592, 914
Gleason, Arthur, 377
Goethe, 43, 44, 97, 146, 151, 205, 207, 289, 322, 343, 422, 431, 458, 700, 874
Goldman, Emma, 189
Golf, 175, 354, 358, 363–366, 378, 412, 441, 476, 490, 493, 515, 610, 686, 709, 750, 781, 787, 836, 888, 899, 959
Gooch, F.A., 425
Goodell, Thomas D., 425
Goodhart, Arthur, 582, 932
Gordon, Dr.A.J., 245
Gordon, Dr. Arthur, 245
Gosse, Sir Edmund, 320, 398, 494, 818
Grainger, Percy, 634
Grand Duchess Marie (of Russia), 850–853
Granville-Barker, Harley, 112, 617, 619, 709, 800
Graves, famous, 520, 527, 539, 599, 651, 803, 807, 880
Graves, Rev.J.W., 762
Gray, Thomas, 319, 320, 622
'Greatest hymn,' 238
Gregory, Herbert E., 286
Gregory, Lady, 828
Grenfell, Sir Wilfred, 80
Grew, Joseph C., 350
Grey, Sir Edward, 381
Gruener, Gustav, 425

Guedalla, Philip, 880
Guernsey, Otis, 359, 678
Guest, Edgar A., 709, 856
Guitry, Lucien, 435
Guitry, Sacha, 96, 98, 348, 438
Gummere, Francis B., 487

HACKETT, Francis, 323
Hadley, Arthur Twining, 161, 195, 405, 421–423, 425, 559, 639, 642, 781
Haldane, Elizabeth, 788
Haldane, Lord, 203, 335, 969
Hale, Prof. Edward Everett, 318
Hale, George Ellery, 77
Hall, Joseph, 49, 100
Hallam, Arthur Henry, 204, 760
Hamilton, Cosmo, 35
Hamlin, Judge Elbert, 78, 287
Hampden, Walter, 431, 784
Happiness, 895, 930–931, 958, 961, 965–966
Harbord, Major-General J.G., 836–840
Harcourt, Lady, 935
Harding, Warren, 854
Hardy, Thomas, 204, 205, 322, 389–404, 426, 551, 570, 571, 573, 576, 681, 803, 813, 816, 818, 823, 827
Hardy, Mrs. Thomas, 394–398, 400–404, 717, 730
Harper, William R., 25, 142, 222, 267, 275–278, 413
Harris, Henry, 482
Harris, Samuel, 482
Harrison, Richard, 905
Harrison, Prof. and Mrs. Ross, 844
Hart, Horace, 105, 225, 236, 237, 244
Hart, Capt. Liddell, 836–840
Harte, Bret, 491
Hartford Public High School, 49, 100
Hates, 193

Hauptmann, Gerhart, 529–532, 885
Haverstick, Bill, 938
Haweis, Rev.H.R., 380
Hawkes, Herbert E., 285
Hawkins, Lady (See Anthony Hope)
Hawley, General, 24
Hawley, Hudson, 893, 895
Hawthorne, Nathaniel, 67, 448, 824, 923
Hayes, Helen, 112, 574, 787
Hayes, Rutherford B., 24, 149
Hearst, William R., 494
Heavy books, 180
Heifetz, Jascha, 506
Hemingway, Samuel, 665
Henderson, John, 647
Henderson, W.J., 238
Henries, Ella, 17
Herd, Alex, 366
Hergesheimer, Joseph, 690–692
Herrick, Robert, 288, 495, 713
Hess, William M., 286
Hey, E.F., 739
Heyse, Paul, 595–598
Hiccoughs, 433
Hichens, Rev. Herbert, 709
Hidden, Edward, 938
Hildreth, Richard, 539
Hill, A.S., 251, 252, 275
Hill, G.Birkbeck, 386
Hill School (Penn.), 211
Hilton, James, 935
Hobson, Bishop Henry, 663
Hockey, 376, 412
Hocking, Mrs.W.E., 550
Hodder, Prof., 249
Hodge Brothers, the, 370
Hofmann, Josef, 634, 650, 960
Hog Latin, 53
Holden, E.S., 77, 485, 495
Hold-up, the, 129–131
Holt, Hamilton, 847
Home-run, 355–356
Homer, 158, 205, 241
Hope, Sir Anthony, 813–816
Hoppe, Willie, 71

Horton, Rev. Jacob, 284
Housman, Alfred E., 110, 204, 398, 923
Houston, David, 249
Howard, Leslie, 842
Howe, De Lancey, 275
Howe, Dr. Will, 737
Howells, John Mead, 482
Howells, William Dean, 254, 322, 351, 502–504, 951
Hubbard, Annabel, 61, 68, 149, 284
Hubbard, Frank, 54, 61, 62, 68, 71, 104, 129, 149, 359, 778, 961
Hubbard, Langdon, 743
Hubbard, Nellie, 426
Hubbard, Richard, 56, 61
Hudson, W.H., 356
Hughes, Charles Evans, 507
Hugo, Victor, 238, 825, 888, 893
Human duplicity, 163
Human Nature in the Bible, 326
Huneker, James, 416, 419
Huron City Church, 744–748
Hurst, Fannie, 845
Hutchins, Pres. (University of Chicago), 331
Huxley, Julian, 844

IBSEN, 158, 181, 188, 195, 205, 208, 324, 458, 477, 479, 516, 520, 572, 573, 678
Informality, 158, 284, 947–953
Inge, Dean, 361, 557, 558
Introductions, 304
Ireland, Archbishop, 405
Irish Rebellion, 506
Irving, Henry, 112, 116, 117, 119, 571, 575, 784, 960

JACKSON, Mrs. Stonewall, 606
Jacobs, Helen, 899
James, Mr. and Mrs. Arthur Curtiss, 753
James, Henry, 205, 550–557, 576, 681, 827, 910

James, William, 248, 332
Jameson, J.F., 314
Jellicoe, Lord, 705
Jenks, Prof. Jeremiah,
378
Jewell, Marshall, 107
Jewell, Pliny, 107
Johnson, Dr., 205, 923
Johnson, Frederic B., 286
Jones, Frederick S., 609
Jones, Henry Arthur, 466,
480, 482, 514, 606, 801
Jones, Richard Lloyd,
919
Jones, Tad, 371, 372
Jordan, David Starr, 639
Judd Family, the, 628
Jusserand, J.J., 476

KAHN, Mr. and Mrs.
Otto, 622
Kant, 204
Karapanos, Pericles, 875
Kaufman, George, 445
Kaye, Frederick, 801
Kaye-Smith, Sheila, 651,
803, 816
Keats, George, 294, 477,
585
Keller, Prof. Albert G.,
195, 285, 359
Kellogg, Charles A., 44,
51
Kennedy, Leonard, 364
Kent, Charles F., 425
Kent, William, 145, 150,
494
Keogh, Andrew, 293, 326,
749
Keyes, Prof. and Mrs.
Homer Eaton, 443
King, Edward, 204
King, Miss Sarah, 687
Kingsley, Charles, 238
Kipling Club, 312, 313
Kipling, Rudyard, 312–
313, 322, 398, 652, 744,
820
Kittredge, Prof. George
Lyman, 247, 252, 255,
274, 275, 318, 376
Klein, Charles, 482
Knipper, Madame, 351
Knock, 770
Komisarzhevsky, Ma-
dame, 485

'LAD' and three doctors,
484
Ladd, Prof. George T., 203,
935
Lamar, 370
Lampson, William, 302
Lang, Henry, 425
Lassiter, Robert, 932
Laughton, Charles, 853
Leacock, Stephen, 653
Le Bargy, M., 431, 599
Lectures, Courses of, 21,
485, 491, 497, 620, 633,
653, 686, 738, 749, 908
Lee, Abner, 855
Lee, Gerald Stanley, 602
Lee, Lansing, 781
Lee, Sir Sidney, 165, 423,
424
Lee, Yan Phou, 86, 145
Le Gallienne, Eva, 574
Lenglen, Suzanne, 896–897
Lewes, George Henry, 223
Lewis, Charlton M., 146,
425, 502
Lewis, John, 16
Lewis, Joseph, 146
Lewis, Sinclair, 568, 658,
845, 898
Lewisohn, Adolph, 779
Libbie, Aunt, 3, 10, 28, 54,
82, 87–90, 127
Liberty of expression, 310
Lindsay, Nicholas Vachel,
629–632, 653, 688
Linsley, Elizabeth, 54, 87
Linsley, Rev. James H., 5,
87
Linsley, Sophia Emilia
Lyon, 3
Lion, Leon M., 803
Literature, 308
Living, the art of, 963, 966,
969
Lloyd, Prof.C.A., 37
Lockwood, Fred, 427
Lodge, Sir Oliver, 705
Lomax, John A., 512
Long, Augustus, 249
'Long vacation,' 326
Lorraine, Robert, 916
Lounsbury, Prof. Thomas
R., 323, 324, 423, 502,
618, 664, 746
Love affairs, 109
Lovett, Robert, 288

Lowell, Amy, 294
Lowell, James Russell, 285,
351, 637, 639, 653, 669,
930
Lowell, Percival, 620
Ludington, Charles H.,
150
Lunn, Sir Henry, 878
Luquiens, Fred B., 359,
360
Lynd, Robert, 326
Lyon, Dr. Emory, 17, 18,
23
Lyon, Sir John, 3
Lyon, William, 4, 5, 961
Lytle, James, 855

MACAULAY, 181, 185
Macaulay, Rose, 178
MacInnes, Charles, 382
Mackaye, Percy, 494
Macmillan Co., 321
MacTaggart, David, 710
Maeterlinck, Maurice,
112, 415–418, 438, 507,
704
Mahaffy, Prof.J.P., 143,
223, 466, 505–506
Manly, John Matthews,
248, 288, 363
Mansfield, Frank, 4
Mansfield, Richard, 112,
115, 124, 160, 431, 460,
784, 960
Mantell, Robert, 617, 634
Marcou, Philippe, 226
Marlowe, Julia, 507, 607
Marquis, Don, 168
Marriage, 217, 284
Marshall, Archibald, 574,
805
Martin, Winfred R., 102–
103, 235
Masefield, John, 39, 622,
911
Mason, Julian S., 313
Mass production, 855
Mathematics, 19, 56, 91,
93, 96, 126, 141, 147–
148, 211, 340, 970
Mather, Mary, 101
Matheson, William J., 777,
792
Matthews, Prof. Brander,
606, 669
Maude, Cyril, 380

Maugham, Somerset, 182, 429, 681, 798
McCarthy, Lillah, 619
McClenahan, Robert S., 286
McConnell, J.G., 903
McCormick, Chauncey, 464
McCune, Dr. William Pitt, 547
McGiffert, Prof. and Mrs., 427
McKenzie, Prof. Kenneth, 446, 465
McKinley, Pres., 636
McLaughlin, Mr., 144, 665
McLoughlin, Maurice, 686
Medlar novelists, 194
Meigs, Dr. John, 211, 424
Mercer, Beryl, 580
Mercury, Transit of, 605
Merritt, Alfred K., 359, 475
Merry, Dr.W.W., 241
Merz, Charles, 619
Meyer, Eugene, 663
Mezes, Sidney, 512
Mill, John Stuart, 206, 207, 599
Miller, Alice Duer, 307, 310, 847
Miller, Dickinson Sargent, 249
Miller, George, 856
Miln, George C., 111
Milton, 205, 240
Mims, Stewart, 359
Ministers, 637–638, 745
Mirbeau, Octave, 438
Missionary Bishop of Georgia, 780–781
Modern Novels, course in, 297–302, 321
Modjeska, 116
Moody, D.L., 80, 105, 201
Moody, William Vaughn, 288
Moon, eclipse of, 74
Moon-rainbow, 905
Moore, George, 206, 367, 458, 602, 818–827, 828, 831
Moore, Herbert, 222
More, Paul Elmer, 326, 913
Morgan, Charles, 738, 803, 806

Morgan, J.Pierpont, 507
Morgan, William C., 286
Morley, Lord, 181, 341, 381, 935
Morris, E.P., 425
Morris, Gouverneur, 312
Morris, Ray, 32
Morse, John T.,Jr., 42, 327
Mounet-Sully, 435
Muldoon, William, 649
Müller, Max, 935
Mumford, C.E., 164
Münsterberg, Hugo, 248, 332, 644–645
Murphey, Dr. Eugene, 782
Murphy, Frank, 855
Murray, Joe, 167
Murray, Thomas E.,Jr., 167

NAZIMOVA, Madame, 112, 188, 195, 477
Nettleton, George, 285, 359, 664, 918
Nevin, Ethelbert, 853
New Haven Lawn Club, 357
Newman, John Henry, 238
Newton, Prof. Alfred, 382
Ney, Paul, 426
Nichols, Robert, 653
Nikisch, Arthur, 738, 960
Niven, Isabel, 213
Nordica, Madame, 458
Norris, W.E., 477–478
Northrop, Prof. Cyrus, 137, 138, 142, 144, 185
Norton, Charles Eliot, 248, 267
Norwood, Dr. Cyril, 156
Noyes, Alfred, 304, 602, 651–653, 932

OERTEL, Hanns, 425, 462, 882
Ollivant, Alfred, 322, 585, 667, 668
O'Neill, Eugene, 740, 916
Operas, 441, 443, 634, 917, 939
Optic, Oliver, 46
Optimists and Pessimists, 971–972
Orator, Public, 506, 583, 751, 835, 841, 917
Orientals, 182

Orcutt, Maureen, 781
Osbourne, Lloyd, 496
Osgood, William Fogg, 4, 339
Osler, Sir William, 293, 601, 782
Oviatt, Edwin, 360

PADEREWSKI, 377, 960
Page, Thomas Nelson, 249
Palmer, George Herbert, 248, 272, 332
Parker, Prof. Horatio, 458
Passion Play at Oberammergau, 112, 113, 231, 383, 960
Patterson, Andrew, 249
Payne, Mr. and Mrs. Walter, 804
Peace Ship, 861
Peace, world, 659
Pearson, H.G., 275
Peck, Prof. Tracy, 425, 478
Penn, William, 240
Penney, Tom, 105
Penniman, Dr. James Hosmer, 36
Penrose, Morris, 99
Pentecost, Rev. George F., 81
People, City and Country, 942–946
Pepys, 382, 383
Perkins, Arthur, 73
Perkins, Henry A., 286
Perrin, Mr. and Mrs. John, 686, 931
Perry, Thomas Sergeant, 186, 267, 350–353, 696
Perry, Mrs. Thomas Sergeant, 350, 351
Pershing, General, 911
Peters, Frank, 369, 370
Peters, George, 52, 54, 62, 74
Petrarch, 446
Pettee, George, 105, 225, 229, 368
Phelps, Dr. Arthur Stevens, 4, 8, 10, 17, 23, 53, 54, 91, 99, 126, 127, 134, 367, 368, 490, 961
Phelps, Céleste, 4
Phelps, Dr. Dryden Linsley, 4

Phelps, Rev. Dryden William, 4, 17, 50, 54, 126, 284, 367, 368, 409, 426, 490, 708, 854
Phelps, James, 4
Phelps, Sophia, 4, 8
Phelps, Rev. Sylvanus Dryden, 3, 26–27
Phelps, William Lyon, 961
Philbin, Stephen, 501
Phillips, A.W., 425
Phipps, Michael, 853
Pickard, Samuel T., 419
Pickford, Mary, 917
'Pied Piper of the East Side,' 175
Pierpont, James, 425
Pinchot, Gifford, 494
Pirandello, Luigi, 891–892
Plançon, Pol, 236, 928
Playfair, Sir Nigel, 803, 804
Poe, Edgar Allan, 214, 601
Poets, four greatest, 205
Poker, 496
Pomeroy, John Norton, 105, 144, 145, 150
Pope, the, 881
Porter, Cole, 602
Porter, Prof. and Mrs. Frank, 168
Porter, Noah, 145, 161
Possart (See von Possart)
Pottinger, William, 709
Pottle, Frederick, 665
Poynton, A.B., 582
Pratt, Francis R., 70
Preaching license, 199
Preston, Keith, 787
Professors, 328–331
Prohibition, 605, 717, 784
Pronunciation (British and American), 572, 711–715
Pullman, George M., 209
Pundits, the, 124, 681, 909
Purdy, Prof. Richard, 400, 403
Puritans, 6

QUEEN Lilioukuani, 625
Queen Victoria, 379

RACINE, 888, 893
Raleigh, Sir Walter, 181, 182
Ratcliffe, S.K., 805

Reading the Bible, 653
Reed, Rev. Edward, 172
Reed, Prof. Edward B., 172, 787
Reeves, Sims, 236
Religion, 142, 159, 201, 271–272, 337, 598, 706, 745, 954–957, 958, 969
Retirement, 908
Reynolds, Horatio, 137, 425
Rice, Elmer, 911
Richards, Alfred Ernest, 442
Richards, E.L.,Jr., 369
Richards, Eugene, 369
Riel, Hervé, 434
Riggs, Father T.Lawrason, 663, 909
Riley, James Whitcomb, 405–411
Rinehart, Mary Roberts, 782
Ritchie, Lady (Annie Thackeray), 553, 559–561
Ritter, William E., 249
Robbins, Fred O., 286
Robbins, Howard Chandler, 663
Roberts, Lord, 35
Robinson, Mrs. Corinne Roosevelt, 845
Robinson, Edward Arlington, 351, 353, 693–698
Robinson, Rev. Ezekiel, 162
Robinson, Lennox, 828
Robson, Eleanor, 388
Rogoff, John, 175
Romberg, Sigmund, 940
Röntgen, Prof., 444, 531
Roosevelt, Kermit, 501
Roosevelt, Theodore, 405, 501, 608, 618, 652, 845, 970
Root, Elihu, 507, 669
Roots, Logan H., 249, 257
Rose, Lincoln, 105, 106
Rossetti, 205, 238, 448, 824, 932
Rostand, 205, 431
Rotary Club, 709, 872–873
Rothenstein, Sir William, 933

Rowell, Charles, 374
Rowell, Henry T., 547
Royal Scot train, 914
Royce, Josiah, 248, 272, 332, 333
Rufus, 38–40, 427
Running, long-distance, 354
Russ, Charles C., 419
Russell, Bertrand, 638
Russell, George W. (Æ.), 827–835
Russo-Japanese War, 456

SACKVILLE–WEST, Miss, 911
Salvini, 231, 873, 960
Samaroff, Madame, 238
San Francisco Fire, 476, 491
Sandburg, Carl, 688
Sanders, Frank K., 289
Sanford, Prof. Sam, 421, 461
Sankey, Ira, 80
Santayana, George, 199, 203, 248, 332–349, 376, 378, 599, 738, 901
Sargent, George Paull T., 663, 933
Scarborough, L.R., 286
Schaefer, Jake, 71
Schevill, Rudolph, 286
Schiller, 458, 461
Schopenhauer, 203–206, 207, 217, 266, 335, 341
Schwab, Charles M., 705
Schwab, John C., 425
Science and Religion, 955–957
Scott, Walter, 316
Scribner, Charles, 317, 737
Scribner's, 317, 346, 581, 711, 712, 737, 919
Sedgwick, Anne, 589, 592, 617, 771, 936–937
Sedgwick, Hubert, 709
Seguin, Dr. Edward Constant, 260
Setchell, William A., 246
Seymour, Pres. Charles, 330
Seymour, George, 550
Seymour, Thomas D., 425

Shakespeare, William, 44, 46, 89, 111, 112, 144, 170, 179, 204, 205, 207, 209, 237, 247, 257, 293, 338, 421, 443, 458, 477, 507, 514, 534, 565, 577, 607, 713, 715, 784, 792–793, 843, 888, 905, 966
Shaler, Prof. Nathan, 248
Shapley, Harlow, 76
Shaw, Bernard, 38, 117, 119, 181, 356, 367, 397, 398, 463, 479, 554, 557, 568, 570, 571, 572, 574, 576, 581, 621, 731, 766, 795, 808, 826, 828, 829, 934
Sheffield, Mr. and Mrs. James R., 687
Sheldon, Lewis, 813
Sherman, Charles P., 286
Sherman, Stuart P., 426
Sherrill, Bishop, 663
Sherrill, Gen. Charles H., 878
Schick, Prof., 882
Shipman, Arthur, 57, 150
Shooting, 59–60, 61–62, 130, 359, 836
Sieper, Ernst, 444
Simon, Dr. Jules, 444, 882
Simonds, John Calhoun, 937
Sinclair, May, 551, 557, 558
Sinclair, Upton, 658
Skeat, W.W., 383
Skinner, Otis, 388
Smith, C.H., 425
Smith, Chard, 362
Smith, Floyd R., 103
Smith, Hopkinson, 249
Smith, Logan Pearsall, 335
Smith, Robinson, 864
Smoking, 172, 809
Sneath, E.H., 289, 425
Sorel, Madame, 438
Sothern, Edward H., 421, 507, 607, 784
Sousa, John Philip, 482
Speer, Robert M., 202
Spencer, Herbert, 72, 181, 224
Spinello, M.J., 286
Spurgeon, Rev. Charles, 237

Stagg, Amos Alonzo, 222
Standish, Dr. Myles, 219
Starr, Frances, 707
Stebbins, George C., 81
Steinert, Rudolph, 927
Stern, Mrs. Benjamin, 843
Stevenson, 205, 322, 494, 496
Stevenson Club, 312
Stewart, Douglas, 286
Stix, Tom, 647–648, 940
Stoker, Bram, 119
Stokes, Canon Anson Phelps, 286, 538, 639, 662
Stone, Charles Augustus, 904
Stowe, Harriet Beecher, 63, 623
Stokowski, 960
Strathmore, the Earl of, 3
Straus, Nathan, 779, 849–850
Strauss, Richard, 601, 795
Strindberg, 205, 972
Stroud, Blanche, 4
Stuart, Jesse, 663
Sturges, Philemon, 663
Sumner, William Graham, 195–198, 286, 287, 425, 507, 540, 636
Sun, total eclipse, 862, 903–904
Sundae, 919–920
Sutton Sisters, the, 686
Swift, Jonathan, 186, 204, 206, 251, 385, 713, 789, 889, 964, 972
Sylva, Carmen, 244
Syndicates, newspaper, 940

TAFT, William Howard, 478, 506, 602, 608–616, 618, 633, 747
Taft, Mrs. William Howard, 610
Tarbell, Prof. Frank B., 140–143, 267, 288, 420
Teaching and writing, 305–307
Teasdale, Sara, 688
Tennis, 214, 287, 351, 354, 357–359, 363, 412, 432, 441, 443, 493, 619, 676, 680, 686, 800, 888, 896

Tennyson, Alfred, 144, 159, 204, 205, 207, 366, 385–386, 448, 451, 465, 498, 538, 549, 560, 586, 602, 620, 635, 697, 760
'Tennyson and Browning,' 209, 294, 491, 853
Terry, Ellen, 116
Terry, Wyllys, 369
Thackeray, 181, 183, 553, 560, 822
Thomas, Augustus, 606
Thomas, Miss M.Carey, 295–297
Thompson, Dorothy, 845
Thompson, Francis, 205, 798
Thompson, Frederic, 482
Thurston, Howard, 919
Tighe, Ambrose, 137, 287, 288
Tinker, Chauncey Brewster, 360, 547, 664, 908–909
Tolstoy, 189, 324, 502, 565, 604, 635
Tolstoy, Count Ilya, 654
Tomlinson, H.M., 846
Toothpicks, 534–535
Torrey, Prof. Charles C., 360, 425
Toscanini, 913, 960
Tovey, Rev.D.C., 319, 320
Tovey, Sir Donald Francis, 319
Towne, Charles, 180
Toy, Professor, 249, 271, 272
Trains, English, 758
Travis, Walter J., 364, 365, 777, 779
Trevelyan, Sir George M., 961
Trevelyan, Sir George Otto, 185
Tunney, Gene, 792–799
Tunnicliff, Helen Honor, 267
Turgenev, 132, 223, 325, 350, 437, 559, 562–563, 821
Twain, Mark, 62–72, 166, 171, 322, 326, 405, 456, 477, 483, 492, 596, 628, 816, 926, 931, 951, 964
Tweedie, Mrs. Alec, 764

Tweedsmuir, Lord, 917
Twichell, Rev. Joseph, 49, 64
Typographical errors, 180–181, 304

UNDERHILL, Professor, 755
University Grammar School, 17, 23, 41, 91
University of Chicago, founding of, 142, 267, 275, 278
University of Christiania, Centenary, 516–521
University students, comparison of, 656–658

VAN NAME, Addison, 425
Vanne, Marda, 805
Vardon, Harry, 377, 378
Veniselos (the Prime Minister), 866, 870
Venus, occultation of, 749
Venus, transit of, 74–75
Verdi, Dr. William F., 620
Verne, Jules, 437
Vignaux, 71
Villard, Oswald Garrison, 275
Villiers, Capt. Alan, 939
Vincent, George E., 222
Voltaire, 35, 44, 652, 768, 888
Von Bülow, Hans, 214
Von Possart, Ernst, 112, 117, 443, 784, 960
Von Schrader, Dana, 160

WAGNER, 208, 362, 793, 889
Wagner, Siegfried, 457
Walking, 104–105, 136, 366–367, 369
Walpole, Sir Hugh, 39, 681, 739, 846
War, 636–646

Ward, Dr. Henshaw, 37
Ward, Mrs. Humphrey, 322, 486, 552
Warfield, David, 784
Warren, Charles, 359
Watson, Sir William, 934
Webster, Daniel, 42, 196
Weil, Louis, 710
Weingartner, Felix, 960
Weinman, Adolph Alexander, 854
Welch, Dr. William, 262
Wells, Chauncey W., 286
Wells, H.G., 251, 753, 916
Wells, Thomas B., 846
Wendell, Evert, 618
Wendell, Prof. Barrett, 172, 182, 247, 249, 250, 252, 254, 264, 268, 273, 274, 317, 376, 478
West, Rebecca, 305
West Middle District School, 24, 45, 61, 92, 98
Westminster School (N.Y.), 211–216, 218
Wharton, Mrs. Edith, 554, 589, 592, 751–752, 771
Wheeler, Hon. Everett, 314
Whist, 360, 376, 459
Whistler, 437, 483, 933
White, Andrew D., 604, 945, 954
Whitman, Walt, 654, 962
Whitney, Emily, 479
Whitney, William Dwight, 102, 140, 361
Whitridge, Arnold, 938
Whittier, 419, 480
Wilcox, Ella Wheeler, 180
Wilde, Oscar, 122, 124, 140, 176, 459, 506, 829, 933
Wilder, Thornton Niven, 213, 575, 660–662, 798, 805, 810
Willard, Rudolph, 882
Williams, H.S., 425

Williams, Stanley, 358, 359, 664
Wills (Moody), Helen, 896–902
Wilson, Al, 373
Wilson, Sir Arnold, 936
Wilson, Prof.E.B., 525
Wilson, William L., 314
Wilson, Woodrow, 314, 478, 602, 634, 649
Winchester, O.F., 961
Winsor, Frederick, 275
Wister, Owen, 414
Witherspoon, Herbert, 292
'Women are more like cats,' 33
Wooden houses, 807
Woolsey, T.S.,Jr., 363, 502
Wordsworth, 98, 170, 237, 466, 629
Work, 959
World's Fair, 25
World War, 185, 202, 289, 356, 434, 623, 634, 646–647, 717, 792, 837–840
Wren, Percival Christopher, 811–812
Wright, Dr.F.T., 166
Wright, Henry P., 301, 409, 425, 790
Wright, Mrs. Henry P., 790

YALE Bowl, 618
'Yale Consolidated,' the, 355
Yeats, William Butler, 39, 602, 827, 828, 830
'Yell,' 871
Yezierska, Anzia, 905–907
Y.M.C.A., founding of (in Russia), 526
Young, Francis Brett, 803–804
Young, Karl, 359, 665, 805
Younger generation, the, 154–162

ZEPPELIN raids, 570